University of Northumbria at Newcastle
LIBRARY

THE AFRICAN HUMAN RIGHTS SYSTEM

International Studies in Human Rights

VOLUME 69

The titles published in this series are listed at the end of this volume.

The African Human Rights System

Its Laws, Practice, and Institutions

by

VINCENT O. ORLU NMEHIELLE
Lecturer, Faculty of Law,
Rivers State University of Science and Technology,
Port Harcourt, Nigeria

MARTINUS NIJHOFF PUBLISHERS
THE HAGUE / LONDON / NEW YORK

A C.I.P. Catalogue record for this book is available from the Library of Congress.

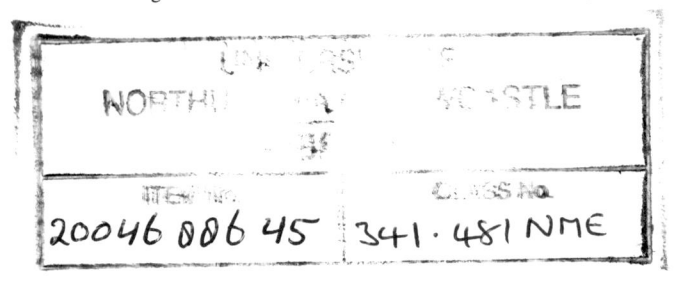

ISBN 90-411-1731-8

Published by Kluwer Law International,
P.O. Box 85889, 2508 CN The Hague, The Netherlands

Sold and distributed in North, Central and South America
by Kluwer Law International,
101 Philip Drive, Norwell, MA 02061, U.S.A.
kluwerlaw@wkap.com

In all other countries, sold and distributed
by Kluwer Law International, Distribution Centre
P.O. Box 322, 3300 AH Dordrecht, The Netherlands

Layout and camera-ready copy:
Anne-Marie Krens – Tekstbeeld – Oegstgeest – The Netherlands

Printed on acid-free paper

All Rights Reserved
© 2001 Kluwer Law International
Kluwer Law International incorporates the publishing programmes of
Graham & Trotman Ltd, Kluwer Law and Taxation Publishers,
and Martinus Nijhoff Publishers.

No part of the material protected by this copyright notice may be reproduced or
utilized in any form or by any means, electronic or mechanical,
including photocopying, recording or by any information storage and
retrieval system, without written permission from the copyright owner.

Printed in the Netherlands.

DEDICATION

To my dear and loving family: my dear wife, Nkechi (N'kay),
who is expecting our last baby; son, Vincent Jr.;
and daughters, Sharon, Shalom, and Immanuela, my doctoral baby,
for their patience, sacrifice, encouragement and inspiration.

FOREWORD

by
Louis B. Sohn
Distinguished Research Professor of Law
The George Washington University Law School

The newspapers of Europe and North America are full of reports about the various bloody revolutions in Africa, in which even children are being employed as soldiers. Very seldom there is an article about the positive things happening in Africa. In particular, the lawyers of Europe and America have not the faintest idea how much the lawyers and governments of a majority of African countries have been able to do in order to develop a legal system for the protection of human rights, by one instrument after another.

This book by Vincent O. Orlu Nmehielle, S.J.D., shows how, step by step, the lawyers of Africa were able to persuade most of their governments to develop a system of human rights for the peoples of Africa. Starting with various African States adhering to several United Nations human rights documents, and with a reference to the UN's Universal Declaration of Human Rights in the Charter of Organization of African Unity, agreement was reached in 1981 on adopting Africa's own African Charter on Human and Peoples Rights, including provisions on topics not covered by the United Nations instruments. The African Commission on Human and Peoples' Rights has slowly increased its activities and jurisdiction. The author provides a detailed analysis of its accomplishments, and notes the areas in which its jurisdiction should be increased. He also points out that an agreement was adopted for the establishment of an African Court with a broad jurisdiction. When enough African States accept its jurisdiction, the African Court would have a chance to provide better protection to the peoples of Africa against violations. The Court itself, and those that apply to it, and their lawyers, will find in this book important assistance. Any foreign lawyers doing business in Africa will find this book helpful in their work.

It can also be hoped that this book would encourage the lawyers of Asia to persuade their governments to establish a human rights tribunal for Asia, thus completing the circle of institutions needed to protect all the peoples of the world.

SUMMARY OF CONTENTS

FOREWORD	vii
SUMMARY OF CONTENTS	ix
TABLE OF CONTENTS	xi
ACKNOWLEDGMENTS	xvii
ABBREVIATIONS	xxi
LEGAL INSTRUMENTS AND DOCUMENTS	xxiii
LIST OF CASES	xxvii
INTRODUCTION	1
1 BACKGROUND TO HUMAN RIGHTS IN AFRICA	7
2 NORMATIVE INSTRUMENTS OF THE AFRICAN HUMAN RIGHTS SYSTEM	75
3 INSTITUTIONAL STRUCTURE OF THE AFRICAN HUMAN RIGHTS SYSTEM	169
4 PROCEDURES OF THE AFRICAN COMMISSION	187
5 REFORMING THE AFRICAN HUMAN RIGHTS SYSTEM	243
6 THE PROTOCOL ON THE ESTABLISHMENT OF AN AFRICAN COURT ON HUMAN AND PEOPLES' RIGHTS	259
7 NON-GOVERNMENTAL HUMAN RIGHTS ORGANIZATIONS AND THE AFRICAN HUMAN RIGHTS SYSTEM	309
CONCLUSIONS	325
SELECT BIBLIOGRAPHY	333
APPENDICES	353
INDEX	437

TABLE OF CONTENTS

Foreword	vii
Summary of Contents	ix
Table of Contents	xi
Acknowledgments	xvii
Abbreviations	xxi
Legal Instruments and Documents	xxiii
List of Cases	xxvii
Introduction	1

CHAPTER 1 BACKGROUND TO HUMAN RIGHTS IN AFRICA — 7

I Human Rights in Pre-Colonial Africa — 7

II Human Rights in Colonial Africa — 17
   A. French Colonialism — 20
   B. Belgian Colonialism — 22
   C. British Colonialism — 23

III The United Nations and Human Rights — 30
   A. The Charter of the United Nations — 30
   B. The Universal Declaration of Human Rights — 34
   C. Other Human Rights Instruments and Organs — 38

IV Other Regional Human Rights Systems — 43
   A. The European System — 43
   B. Institutional Machinery of the European System — 47
   C. The Inter-American System — 54
   1. The Inter-American Convention on Human Rights — 58
   2. Institutional Organs of the Inter-American System — 60

		a. The Inter-American Commission on Human Rights	60
		b. The Inter-American Court of Human Rights	62
V	THE ORGANIZATION OF AFRICAN UNITY (OAU) AND HUMAN RIGHTS		67

CHAPTER 2 NORMATIVE INSTRUMENTS OF THE AFRICAN HUMAN RIGHTS SYSTEM — 75

I	THE CHARTER OF THE OAU		75
II	THE AFRICAN CHARTER ON HUMAN AND PEOPLES' RIGHTS		82
III	RIGHTS GUARANTEED UNDER THE CHARTER		84
	A.	*Civil and Political Rights*	85
	1.	Right to Life and Integrity of the Person	85
	2.	Right Against all Forms of Slavery, Slave Trade, Torture and Cruel, Inhuman or Degrading Treatment	88
		a. Slavery and Slave Trade	88
		b. Torture, Cruel, Inhuman or Degrading Punishment	90
	3.	Right to Liberty and Security of the Person	92
	4.	Right to Fair Trial	94
	5.	Freedom of Conscience, the Profession and Practice of Religion	104
		a. Freedom of Conscience	104
		b. Freedom to Profess and Practice Religion	105
	6.	Freedom of Expression	106
	7.	Freedom of Association and Assembly	109
		a. Freedom of Association	110
		b. Freedom of Assembly	112
	8.	Freedom of Movement and Allied Rights	113
		a. Freedom of Movement Within a State, to Leave, and Freedom to Return	114
		b. The Right to Seek and Obtain Asylum	115
		c. Right Against Extra-Judicial Expulsion or Mass Expulsion	116
	9.	The Right to Participate in the Government of One's Country	118
	10.	The Right to Property	119
	B.	*Economic, Social and Cultural Rights*	121
	1.	The Right to Equitable and Satisfactory Conditions of Work	124
	2.	The Right to Health	126
	3.	The Right to Education	128
	4.	Protection of the Family and Other Rights	131
		a. Protection of the Family	131
		b. Rights of the Child	132

	c. Women's Rights	133
	d. Protection of the Aged and the Disabled	136
C.	Group or Collective Rights	138
1.	Right of Self-Determination	142
2.	Right Over Wealth and Natural Resources	146
3.	Right to Economic, Social and Cultural Development	149
4.	Right to Peace	151
5.	Right to Environment	154

III OTHER HUMAN RIGHTS INSTRUMENTS   158

IV THE CONCEPT OF DUTY VERSUS RIGHTS UNDER THE AFRICAN CHARTER   161

V CLAW-BACK CLAUSES UNDER THE CHARTER   165

CHAPTER 3 INSTITUTIONAL STRUCTURE OF THE AFRICAN HUMAN SYSTEM   169

I THE ORGANIZATION OF AFRICAN UNITY   169

II THE AFRICAN COMMISSION ON HUMAN AND PEOPLES' RIGHTS   170
    A. Composition of the Commission   171
    B. The Commission's Mandate   175
    1. Promotional Mandate   176
    2. Protective Mandate   180
    3. Interpretative Mandate   181
    4. Other Tasks   183

III THE SECRETARIAT OF THE AFRICAN COMMISSION   183

CHAPTER 4 PROCEDURES OF THE AFRICAN COMMISSION   187

I STATE REPORTING   187
    A. Procedure on State Reporting Before the Commission   191
    1. Receipt of Reports   191
    2. Actual Session   192
    3. Follow-up Procedure   193
    4. Non-Submission of Reports   193
    B. Assessment of the State Reporting Mechanism   194

II	THE COMMUNICATIONS PROCEDURE	198
	A. Communications from States	198
	B. Bringing an Inter-State Complaint before the Commission	199
	C. Other Communications (Non-State or Individual Complaints)	203
	1. Jurisdiction	203
	2. Bringing Individual Communications Before the Commission	207
	a. Objective	207
	b. Admissibility Requirements	211
	3. Inclusion of Author's Name	214
	4. Compatibility with the Provisions of the OAU Charter or the African Charter	215
	5. Communication not to Contain Disparaging and Insulting Language	216
	6. Communication not Exclusively Based on Mass Media News	218
	7. Exhaustion of Local Remedies	219
	8 Burden of Proving Exhaustion of Local Remedies	225
	9. Submission of Communications Within a Reasonable Time	226
	10. Communications Settled Through Other International Mechanisms	227
	D. Post Admissibility Procedure	230
	1. Consideration of Communications on the Merits	230
	2. Legal Representation	231
	3. Interim or Provisional Measures	232
III	REMEDY UNDER THE CHARTER	236

CHAPTER 5	REFORMING THE AFRICAN HUMAN RIGHTS SYSTEM	243
I	BASES FOR REFORM	243
II	THE DEBATE ON AN AFRICAN COURT OF HUMAN RIGHTS	249
III	THE MAKING OF THE AFRICAN COURT ON HUMAN AND PEOPLES RIGHTS	255

CHAPTER 6	THE PROTOCOL ON THE ESTABLISHMENT OF THE AFRICAN COURT ON HUMAN AND PEOPLES' RIGHTS	259
I	ESTABLISHING THE COURT	260
II	RELATIONSHIP BETWEEN THE COURT AND THE COMMISSION	261

III	JURISDICTION AND ACCESS TO THE COURT	263
	A. Adjudicatory or Contentious Jurisdiction	263
	B. Jurisdictional Access to the Court in Contentious Cases	265
	C. Advisory Jurisdiction	272
	D. Subject Matter Jurisdiction	275
IV	APPLICABLE LAW AND CONSIDERATION OF CASES	276
	A. Sources of Law	276
	B. Consideration of Cases	277
V	ORGANIZATION OF THE COURT	282
	A. Structure	282
	B. Composition	283
	C. Functioning of the Court	288
VI	JUDICIAL AND SUNDRY EMPOWERMENT OF THE COURT	291
	A. Independence	291
	B. Evidence and Rules of Procedure	295
	C. Remedial Powers of the Court	298
	1. Findings	298
	2. Provisional Measures	299
	3. Judgement and Enforcement	301
VII	RATIFICATION, ENTRY INTO FORCE AND AMENDMENT OF THE PROTOCOL	305

7 NON-GOVERNMENTAL HUMAN RIGHTS ORGANIZATIONS AND THE AFRICAN HUMAN RIGHTS SYSTEM — 309

I	STATUS OF NGOS UNDER THE AFRICAN CHARTER	311
II	NGOS AND THE AFRICAN COMMISSION	312
	A. Promotion-Based Cooperation	313
	B. Protective Cooperation	314
III	THE PLACE OF NGOS UNDER THE PROTOCOL ON THE AFRICAN COURT	317
IV	NGOS AND THE FUTURE OF HUMAN RIGHTS IN AFRICA	319
	CONCLUSIONS	325
	SELECT BIBLIOGRAPHY	333

APPENDICES	353
I The Charter of the OAU	355
II The Constitutive Act of the African Union	363
III The African Charter on Human and Peoples' Rights	379
IV The Rules of Procedure of the African Commission	397
V The Protocol on the Establishment of an African Court for Human and Peoples' Rights	427
INDEX	437

ACKNOWLEDGMENTS

Accomplishing the enormous tasks required in writing this book is not one that can be ascribed to me alone. This work was submitted for a Doctor of Juridical Science (SJD) Degree, and many individuals were responsible in making it a reality, and to them I owe a lot of gratitude. I must express my heart-felt thanks to my supervisors and members of my Dissertation Committee at the George Washington University Law School (National Law Center), Washington, DC, USA, for their faith in me and the direction they gave to me.

I must thank Professor Thomas Buergenthal, Lobingier Emeritus Professor of Comparative Law and Jurisprudence, my first academic advisor and supervisor, who initiated this challenge before answering the higher calls of international judicial service, first as Vice Chairman at the Dormant Account Claims Resolution Tribunal, Zurich, and later, as Judge of the International Court of Justice, The Hague. On my first meeting with Professor Burgenthal after I enrolled in the SJD program, he said to me: "give me a book on the African system that I can rely on." As the former Director of the International & Comparative Law Program and Presiding Director of the International Rule of Law Center, Professor Buergenthal not only presided over my admission to the SJD program, but also over the International Rule of Law Fellowship that was awarded to me to cover my tuition costs for the first year of the program. Without this fellowship it would not have been possible for me to begin the program.

In the same vein, I am eternally indebted to Professor Louis B. Sohn, Harvard Bemis Emeritus Professor of International Law, and Distinguished Research Professor of International Law at the George Washington University Law School, who was not only a member of my committee, but my co-supervisor, and later became my substantive supervisor at short notice, after Professor Buergenthal left. Professor Sohn was responsible for the day to day direction of my dissertation, despite his advancement in age and potentially fragile state of health. He not only refined my ability in the art of international legal research, he counseled me, pointed me to relevant authorities and literature, corrected and criticized me, and suggested new things, as he read chapter by chapter, the work that inspired this book. In all, he gave himself wholly to this work even when he was not in the best state of health. I am highly privileged to have had the opportunity to be one of Professor Sohn's academic grandchildren, knowing that he produced Professor Buergenthal at Harvard many decades ago, with whom he co-produced me a year ago.

Similarly, I am sincerely grateful to Professor Ralph G. Steinhardt, Arthur Selwyn Miller Research Professor of Law and Associate Dean of the International and Comparative Legal Studies Program, the third member of my committee, for his role not only as a committee member, but also as the succeeding academic and administrative head of the international and comparative law program. As Director of the program, he approved the extension of my International Rule of Law Fellowship for the remaining duration of my studies at the law school. This enabled me to wade through the ever-increasing tuition costs of American law schools.

I would like to thank Mr. Desire Ahanhanzo, the document specialist at the African Commission on Human and Peoples' Rights, Banjul, The Gambia, and Ms. Agnes Mabotja, who was an intern at the Commission, for their assistance in the collection of the necessary documents of the Commission and the African system. Many thanks also to my Christian brethren, especially the African Christian Fellowship (ACF), Washington, D.C. Chapter and the churches where I worshiped in the United States, my friends and well-wishers for their support and encouragement. Of these, I will like to single out Pastor Ephraim Ike and family of South Bend Indiana, for standing as guarantor for me, Pastor Aniete Ikene and family, Dr. and Dr. Mrs. Luc and Gretchen Reydams, also of South Bend, Indiana for their support, and Dr. & Dr. Mrs Babajide and Nike Oguntimein of Springdale, Maryland, for their support and sacrifices in the course of my program at the George Washington University Law School. The Lord will surely reward them.

I must specially mention my dear friend and colleague, Professor Jo Marie Pasqualucci of the University of South Dakota Law School for all her encouragement, support, and sincere concern for my welfare in the United States. She also made meaningful suggestions on the recent changes in the Inter-American system. In the same vein, I must express my gratitude to my friends and colleagues at the Law firm of Amorow & Kum, Hyattsville, Maryland, where I worked: Professor Joseph M. Kum, principal partner, and professor of political science and international relations at Bowie State University, Maryland; Oscar L. Amorow, Esq, partner; Fatai A. Suleman, Esq; and others, for all their encouragements and support. I must thank Ms. Ziona A. Daramola, a former television and broadcast journalist for reading and editing the final manuscript of this book. She worked day and night to clean up what my tired eyes failed to see. I am very grateful to my publishers for committing to publish this book, especially to Ms. Lindy Melman for coordinating all the aspects of the publication. Finally, I am eternally grateful to the management of the Rivers State University of Science and Technology, Port Harcourt, Nigeria and its Faculty of Law where I teach, for granting me a study leave for the duration of my academic pursuits in the United States, and extended leave thereafter, to make my eventual return a little smoother.

Vincent Obisienunwo Orlu Nmehielle, Esq,
Washington, D.C.

ABBREVIATIONS

ACHPR/LR	Law Report of the African Commission on Human and Peoples Rights
ACHPR	African Charter on Human and Peoples' Rights
AHSG	Assembly of Heads of State and Government
CEDAW	Convention [Committee] on the Elimination of all forms of Discrimination Against Women
CLO	Civil Liberties Organization
DOC.	Document
ECA	Economic Commission for Africa
ECOSOC	Economic and Social Council
Ed.	Editor
Eds.	Editors
FAO	Food and Agricultural Organization
G.A. Res	General Assembly Resolution
I.C.J. Rep.	International Court of Justice Report
ICCPR	International Covenant for Civil and Political Rights
ICESCR	International Covenant for Economic, Social and Cultural Rights
ICJ	International Court of Justice/International Commission of Jurists
Id.	Ibidem
IL.M.	International Legal Materials
ILO	International Labor Organization
IMF	International Monetary Fund
NGOs	Non Governmental Organizations
OAS	Organization of American States
OAU	Organization of African Unity
RES.	Resolution
U.N. Doc.	United Nations Document
UNTS	United Nations Treaty Series
UN	United Nations
UNESCO	United Nations Scientific and Cultural Organization
UNHCHR	United Nations High Commissioner for Human Rights
UNHCR	United Nations High Commissioner for Refugees
WHO	World Health Organization

LEGAL INSTRUMENTS AND DOCUMENTS

Abolition of Forced Labor Convention, 1957 (Convention No. 105).

Additional Protocol to the American Convention on Human Rights in the Area of Economic, Social and Cultural Rights (Protocol of San Salvador), adopted November 17, 1988.

African Charter on Human and Peoples Rights, adopted 27 June 1981 in Nairobi, Kenya, OAU.Doc. CAB/LEG/67/3, Rev. 5, reprinted in 21 I.L.M. 59 (1981).

African Commission on Human and Peoples' Rights, The Mauritius Plan of Action, 1996-2001.

African Charter on the rights and welfare of the Child, adopted by the OAU in 1990. See Africa Legal Materials, 3 African Journal of International and Comparative Law 173-190 (1991)

African Commission on Human and Peoples Rights, Geographical Distribution of Countries Among Commissioners for Promotional Activities. Doc/OS/36e(XXIII).

Amendments of the General Guidelines for the Preparation of Periodic Reports by States Parties, DOC./OS/27(XXIII)

American Convention on Human Rights, adopted on November 22, 1969, 9 I.L.M. 673 (1970).

Bamako Convention on the Ban of Importation into Africa and the Control of Transboundary Movement and Management of Hazardous Wastes Within Africa, 30 I.L.M. 775 (1991).

Charter of the United Nations, 59 Stat. 1031, T.S. No. 993, 3 Bevans 1153.

Comments and observations received from Member States on the Draft Protocol on the Establishment of an African Court on Human and Peoples" Rights, OAU/LEG/EXP/AFCHPR/Comm.(3).

Constitutive act of the african union, Done at Lome on 11th July, 2000.

Convention on the Rights of the Child, 28 I.L.M. 1448 (1989).

Convention on the Elimination of all Forms of Discrimination Against Women,19 I.L.M. 33 (1980).

Convention on the Prevention and Punishment of the Crime of Genocide, 78 U.N.T.S. 277.

Convention Against Torture and Other Cruel, Inhuman or Degrading Treatment or Punishment, 24 I.L.M. 1027(1984), as modified, 24 I.L.M. 535 (1985).

Convention on the rights of the Child, 28 I.L.M 1448 (1989). Adopted by the U.N. General Assembly on November 28, 1989. Entered into force on September 2, 1990.

Declaration on the Granting of Independence to Colonial Countries and Territories, 1960, UN G.A. Res. 1514(XV), December 14, 1960; 15 U.N. GAOR Supp. (No. 16) at 66, U.N. Doc. A/4684 (1961).

Declaration of Principles on International Law Concerning Friendly Relations and Co-operation Among States in Accordance with the Charter of the United Nations. Adopted by the UN General Assembly, 24 October 1970. G.A.Res. 2625, U.N. GAOR, 25th Sess., Supp., No. 28, at 121, U.N.Doc.. A/8028 (1971); 9 I.L.M. 1292 (1970)

Declaration on the Preparation of Societies for Life in Peace, G.A. Res. 33/73, 33 U.N. GAOR Supp. (No. 45) at 55-56, U.N. Doc. A/33/45 (1979).

Declaration of Tehran, 23 U.N. GAOR Supp. (No. 41) at 1, U.N. Doc. A/Conf.32/41 (1968).

Declaration and Decisions adopted by the Thirty-Fourth Ordinary Session of the Assembly of Heads of State and Government, AHG/Dec. 126 (XXXIV) (1998).

Declaration on the Preparation of Societies for Life in Peace, U.N. GAOR Supp. (No. 45) at 55-56, U.N. Doc. A/33/45 (1979); U.N. Res. 39/11 (1984).

Draft Protocol to the African Charter on Human and Peoples' Rights on the Establishment of the African Court on Human and Peoples' Rights, OAU/LEG/EXP/AFCHPR/PROT(2)

Draft Protocol to the African Charter on Human and Peoples' Rights on the Establishment of the African Court on Human and Peoples' Rights, OAU/LEG/EXP/AFCHPR/PROT.(I)Rev.1

Draft Protocol to the African Charter on Human and Peoples' Rights on the Establishment of the African Charter on Human and Peoples' Rights, OAU/LEG/AFCHPR/PROT.(III)Rev.1

Eight Annual Activity Reports of the African Commission on Human and Peoples' Rights, adopted in 1995.

Eleventh Annual Activity Report of the African Commission on Human and Peoples' Rights, Doc/OS/43(XXIII).

Fifth Annual Activity Report of the African Commission on Human and Peoples' Rights (1992-1993).

Forced Labor Convention, 1930 (Convention No. 29).

International Covenant on Economic, Social and Cultural Rights, 993 U.N.T.S. 3. Annex to G.A. Res. 2200.

International Convention on the Elimination of All Forms of Racial Discrimination, 5 I.L.M.352 (1966).

International Covenant for Civil and Political Rights, 999 U.N.T.S. 171. G.A.Res. 2200.

List of Countries Which Have Ratified the African Charter on Human and Peoples' Rights, DOC/OS/INF.5(XXIV).

List of Countries Which have Signed, Ratified/Adhered to the Protocol to the African Charter on Human and Peoples' Rights on the Establishment of the African Court on Human and Peoples Rights, Doc/OS/INF.5(XXIV).

Ninth Annual Activity Report of the African Commission on Human and Peoples' Rights, AHG/210(XXXIII).

OAU Council of Ministers Resolution on Dumping of Nuclear and Industrial Waste in Africa, adopted at Addis Ababa, 23 May 1998. CM/Res. 1153 (XLVIII); 28 I.L.M. 567 (1989).

Plan of Action of the African Commission 1988, Doc. AHG/155(XXIV) ANNEX VIII.
Proceedings of the International Labor Conference, 48th Session, 1964
Protocol No. 11 to the Convention for the Protection of Human Rights and Fundamental Freedoms, Restructuring the Control Machinery Established Thereby, E.T.S. No. 155.
Protocol to the African Charter on Human and Peoples' Rights on the Establishment of an African Court on Human and Peoples' Rights, OAU DOC.CAB/LEG/66.5 (1998)

Recommendations and Resolutions Published by the Secretariat of the African Commission on Human and Peoples' Rights (ACHPR, Banjul: The Gambia, December 1998).
Regulations of the Inter-American Commission on Human Rights, modified in 1996.
Report of the Fifth Session of the UN Economic, Social and Cultural Rights Committee, U.N. Doc. E/1991/23/Annex VI).
Report of the Second Government Legal Experts Meeting on the Establishment of An African Court on Human and Peoples' Rights, OAU/LEG/EXP/AFCHPR/RPT(2).
Report of the First Meeting of the Working Group on the Additional Protocol to the African Charter on Women's Rights, DOC/OS/58(xxiv)
Report of the Secretary-General on the Conference of Ministers of Justice/Attorneys-General on the Draft Protocol on the Establishment of the African Court on Human and Peoples' Rights, DOC.CM/2051(LXVII).
Report of the Third Government Legal Experts Meeting, Addis Ababa, Ethiopia, OAU/LEG/EXP/AFCHPR/RPT(III) Rev.1.
Rio Declaration on Environment and Development. Adopted by the U.N. Conference on Environment and Development (UNCED), U.N. Doc. A/CONF.151/26 (vol.1) (1992), 31 I.L.M. 874 (1992).
Rules of Procedure of the Inter-American Court of Human Rights, 1996.
Rules of Procedure of the African Commission on Human and Peoples' Rights, adopted on 6 October 1995.

Seventh Annual Activity Reports of the African Commission on Human and Peoples' Rights, adopted in 1994.

Sixth Annual Activity Report of the African Commission on Human and Peoples' Rights (1991-1992).
Statute of the Inter-American Commission on Human Rights, OAS Res. 44 (1979).
Statute of the Inter-American Court of Human Rights, OAS Res. 448 (1979).
Statute of the proposed International Criminal Court adopted in Rome on July 17, 1998
Stockholm Declaration of the United Nations Conference on the Human Environment. U.N. Doc. A/CONF.48/14/Rev.(1972)

Tenth Annual Activity Report of the African Commission on Human and Peoples' Rights, AHG/210(XXXIII) Annex II.
The Implementation of Resolution AHG/230(XXX) of the Heads of State and Government of the OAU on the Establishment of an African Court on Human and Peoples' Rights, DOC/OS/34b(XXIII).
The Final Communique of the 23rd Ordinary Session of the African Commission on Human and Peoples' Rights, 20-29 April 1998, DOC/OS/45(XXIII).
The American Declaration on the Rights and Duties of Man, O.A.S. Res. XXX, 9th Conf. (1948), O.A.S. Doc. OEA/Ser. L/V/1.4, Rev. XX (1965).
The European Convention of Human Rights and Fundamental Freedoms, as amended by Protocol 11.
The African Commission on Human and Peoples' Rights, Examination of State Reports: 13th Annual Session- Nigeria- Togo (April 1993).
The European Convention of Human Rights and Fundamental Freedoms, 312 U.N.T.S. 221, E.T.S. 5.
Treaty of Versailles, 1919.

U.N. Commission on Human Rights Res. 5(XXXII), 60 U.N. ESCOR Supp. (No. 3) at 62, U.N. Doc. E/5768 [E/CN.4/1213] (1976)
U.N. Commission on Human Rights Res. 4(XXXIII), 62 U.N. ESCOR Supp. (No. 6) at 75, U.N. Doc. E/5927 [E/CN4/1257] (1977); 1979 U.N. ESCOR Supp. (No. 6) at 27, U.N. Doc. E/CN4/1347]
Unesco, Symposium on New Human Rights: The Rights of Solidarity, Mexico City, 1980 at 3 UNESCO Doc. 55.81/conf.806/4.
UNESCO Recommendations of November 19, 1974 (UN Human Rights Compilation) Vol. I(2).
Universal Declaration of Human Rights, G.A. Res. 217A (III), U.N. Doc A/810 at 71 (1948).
UN Resolution on Permanent Sovereignty Over Natural Resources, G.A. res. 1803 (XVII), 17 U.N. GAOR Supp. (No.17) at 15, U.N. Doc. A/5217.

LIST OF CASES

A et al v. S, U.N. Hum. Rts. Comm., Selected Decisions Under the Optional Protocol at 17, U.N. Doc. CCPR/C/OP/1, U.N. Sales No. E.84.XIV.2(1985).
Advisory Opinion OC-2/82, Ser.A, No.2, 29 (1982).
Alhasan v. Ghana, Communication No.103/93.
Aloeboete et al v. Suriname, (Reparations) Judgment of 10 September, 1993, 15 Inter-Am. Ct. H.R. (Ser. C); 14 Hum. Rts. L. J. 425 (1993)
Amnesty International v. Tunisia, Communication No. 69/92.
Amnesty International v. Sudan, Communication No. 48/90
Amuh Joseph Vitine v. Cameroon, Communication No. 106/93.
Angelini v. Sweden No. 10491/83, 51 DR. 41 at 48 (1986).
Annette Pagnoule (Abdoullaye Mazou) v. Cameroon, Communication No.39/90.
Association of Member Episcopal Conferences v. Sudan, Communication No. 89/93.

Bamidele Arturu v. Nigeria, Communication No. 72/92.
Bistíos-Rojas v. Peru (1990-1991), 11 Hum. Rts. L.J. 275.
Blake v. Guatemala(1995), 3 IHRR 539 (1996).
Burkina Faso v. Republic of Mali, I. C. J. Report, 554, at 566-567 (1986).

Caballero Delgado and Santana v. Colombia, Preliminary Objections, Judgment of 21 January, 1994. Series C No. 17.
Carpio Nicolle v. Guatemala (1995-1996), 3 IHRR 529 (1996).
Case 10.548, Inter-Am. Court 25, OEA/ser.G/CP, doc.2146 (1991).
Case 9748 v. Peru, Res. No. 30/88 of September 14, 1988, Inter-American Commission on Human Rights, Annual Report 1988-89, 30-33.
Case 9786 v. Peru, Res. No. 33/88 of September 14, 1988, Inter-American Commission on Human Rights, Annual Report 1988-89, 30-33.
Chunimá v. Guatemala (1991-1992), 2 IHRR 411 (1995)
Civil Liberties Organization v. Nigeria, Communication No. 45/90.
Civil Liberties Organization v. Nigeria, Communication 67/91.
Civil Liberties Organization (Nigerian Bar Association) v. Nigeria, Communication No. 101/93.
Colotenago v. Guatamala (1994-1996), 2 IHRR 414, 421 (1995).

Committee for the Defense of Human Rights (Jennifer Madike) v. Nigeria, Communication No. 62/91.
Congress for the Second Republic of Malawi v. Malawi, Communication No. 63/92.
Constitutional Rights Project (Wahab Akamu et al.) v. Nigeria, Communication No. 60/91.
Constitutional Rights Project (Zamani Lekwot & 6 Others) v.Nigeria, Communication No. 87/93.
Constitutional Rights Project v. Nigeria, Communication No. 139/94.

El Amparo v. Venezuela (Case No. 10.602). Annual Report of the Inter-American Court of Human Rights, 1995, OAS/Ser.L/V/III.33, Doc. 4, 23-29 (January 22, 1996).
El Hadji Boubacare Diaware v. Benin, Communication No. 18/88.
Eshugbai Eleko v. Nigerian Government (1931) A.C. 662 at 673.
Exceptions to the Exhaustion of Domestic Remedies Case, Advisory Opinion OC-11/90 of August10, 1990. Series A No. 11. Inter-American Court of Human Rights, OEA/Ser.L/V/III.23/Doc.12 (1990).

Fairben Gabi & Solis Corales v. Honduras, (*Preliminary Objections*) Judgement of June 26, 1987, OEA/Ser.L/VIII.17, Doc. 13 (1987).
Frederick Korvah v. Liberia, Communication No. 1/88.

H v. France, A 162-A Para 58 (1989).
Hadjali Mohaand v. Algeria, Communication No. 13/88.
Henry Kalenga v. Zambia, Communication 11/88.
Hilarie Badjogume v. Benin, Communication No.17/88

Interhandel Case (Preliminary Objections), ICJ Rep. 7 (1959).
International PEN (Senn & Sangare) v. Cote d'Ivoire, Communication 138/94.
International Pen v. Nigeria, Communication No. 137/94.
International Pen v. Burkina Faso, Communication No. 22/88
International Commission of Jurists (ICJ) v. Rwanda, Communication No. 46/90.
Ireland v. UK A 25 para. 167 (1978).

John Modise v. Botswana, Communication 97/93.

Katangese Peoples' Congress v. Zaire, Communication No. 75/92.
Kenya Human Rights Commission v. Kenya, Communication No. 135/94.

Lawyers Committee for Human Rights (Sheif Sharif Hamad) v. Tanzania, Communication No. 66/92,
Lawyers Committee for Human Rights v. Zaire, Communication No. 56/91.
Les Témoins de Jéhovah (Jehovah's Witnesses), et al. v. Zaire, Communication No. 56/91.
Ligue Camerounaise des Droits de l'Homme v. Cameroon, Communication No. 65/92.
Louis Emgba Mekongo v. Cameroon, Communication No. 59/91.

Monja Joana v. Madagascar; Communication No. 108/93.
Mpaka-Nsusu Andre Alphonse v. Zaire, communication No. 18/88.

Nicaragua v. United States of America) (1986) I.C.J. Rep. 14.
Njoka v. Kenya, Communication No.142/94.
Norwegian Loans Case, ICJ Reports, 9 at 34 (1957).
Nziwa Buyingo v. Uganda, Communication No. 8/88.

O, H, W, B and R v. United Kingdom, 1987, Series A, Vols. 120 and 121.
Oke Lanipekun and Others v. Amao Ojetunde (1944) A.C.170.
Organization Contre la Torture v. Rwanda, Communication No. 49/91.
Orton & Vera Chirwa v. Malawi, (and group of cases) Communications Nos. 64/92, 68/92 and 72/92.
"Other Treaties" Subject to the Consultative Jurisdiction of the Court (Art. 64, American Convention on Human Rights), Advisory Opinion No. OC-1/82 (Inter-Am. Ct. of Human Rights, Sept. 24, 1982).

Paul Haye v. The Gambia, Communication No. 90/93.

Recontre Africaine pour la Defense des Droits de l'Homme (RADDHO) v. Zambia, Communication No. 71/92.
Recontre Africaine pour la Defense Droits de l'Homme v. Mauritania, Communication No. 96/93.
Reggiardo Tolosa v. Argentina (1993-1994), 2 IHRR 411 (1995)

Seyoun Ayele v. Togo, Communication No. 35/89.
Stran Greek Refineries and Stratis Andreadis v. Greece, Judgment of 9 December 1994, Series A, No. 301-B, 19 EHRR 293 (1995)

Tanko Bariga v. Nigeria, Communication No. 57/91.
The Registered Trustees of Constitutional Rights Project v. The President of the Federal Republic of Nigeria and 2 others, (Unreported), Suit No. M/102/93 of May 5, 1993, reprinted in 1,2 & 3, Journal of Human Rights Law and Practice 219 (1993).

Union des Scolaires Nigeriens-Union Generale des Etudients Nigeriens au Benin v. Niger, Communication No. 43/90.
Union Inter-africaines des Droits de l'Homme v. Zaire, Communication No. 100/93.
Union International des Droits de l'Homme v. Rwanda, Communication No. 99/93.

Velasquez Rodriguez v. Honduras (Preliminary Objections), Case 7920, Ser. C, No. 4 Inter-American Court of Human Rights Report 35, OAS Doc. OEA/Ser.L/V/III.17/Doc. 13 (1987).
Viviana Gallardo et al, v. Costa, No. G. 101/81, judgment of November 13, 1981, 20 I.L.M. 1424 (1981); 9 Hum. Rts. L.J. 328 (1981).

World Organization Against Tourture v. Zaire, Communication No. 25/89.

INTRODUCTION

At a time, slavery and colonialism were the worst human rights violations that ravaged the African continent. Under these evil dispensations Africa groaned for her children who were subjected to sub-human standards by foreign entities and cried for their emancipation from the overbearing powers of these entities. Respite in this regard came with the end of colonialism and Africa began to shape its own development, though along the lines impacted by colonial governance. Whatever the case was, "independent" African States began to be in charge of their own affairs, with many of them adhering to the United Nations Charter (UN Charter) and other international human rights instruments.[1] The expectation was that the atrocities of slavery and colonialism would "never again" rear their heads in independent African States. This was, however, not to be the case as African leaders generally failed to live up to the promises born out of independence.

According to Eze, "in spite of adherence to and apparent commitment to the protection of human rights, experience in most African countries ranges from anarchy, as in the case of Uganda under Amin, to modest progress in the field of human rights promotion and protection. For the most part a gap exists between declaration and actual practice."[2] This remained the position, and in most part, continues to be the position in many African countries. The tendency may have been to explain away the contradiction between declarations espoused by African States and their actual practice, as resulting from the absence of an autochthonous African human rights mechanism that would bring the message nearer home, rather than adopting principles imposed on Africa by "neo-colonialists." African human rights discourse thus assumed a new dimension with the adoption of the African

---

[1] See OSITA C. EZE, HUMAN RIGHTS IN AFRICA: SOME SELECTED PROBLEMS 23 (The Nigerian Institute of International Affairs/Macmillan Nigeria Publishers Ltd, 1984).

[2] *Id.* Other examples of oppressive African regimes of the past include those of Bokasa's Central African Empire, Nguema's Equatorial Guinea, Babangida and Abacha's Nigeria, Mobutu's Zaire, and current Biya's Cameroon, among others. The atrocities and carnage that went on in Rwanda is another recent disregard of the virtues espoused at independence.

Charter on Human and Peoples' Rights (African Charter or the Charter)[3] in 1981 by the Assembly of Heads of State and Government (AHSG or OAU Assembly) of the Organization of African Unity (OAU).[4] African States were convinced of the need to have a home grown regional human rights commitment in the light of international standards laid down by the Universal Declaration of Human Rights (Universal Declaration) and other subsequent norm creating international human rights instruments, as well as the experiences of other regions. Similarly, African States, which all the time were preoccupied with struggles against colonial domination, realized that with more than two decades of the end of *de jure* colonialism, there was the need to organize for the protection of the rights of African people against violations by their home governments.[5]

Thus, at their summit meeting in 1979, the AHSG of the OAU called for the establishment of a group of expert to prepare an African Charter on Human Rights.[6] It has been suggested, that this call had part of its roots in the United Nations, as the UN had for several years been promoting the establishment of an African machinery at seminars on human rights held in different African capitals.[7] Similarly, the UN had various African situations under investigation at that time, especially that of Uganda; and African representatives on the UN Commission on Human Rights were torn between evidence of serious violations and sentiments of African political solidarity.[8] Important African personalities in the UN who were always accused of defending African countries that were condemned for violations in the UN, felt some pressure to do something within the OAU context.[9] With the coming into force of the African Charter in 1986, many commentators saw the document as impressive and unique in its elaborate provisions, and as

---

3   AFRICAN CHARTER ON HUMAN AND PEOPLES RIGHTS, adopted 27 June 1981 in Nairobi, Kenya, OAU. Doc. CAB/LEG/67/3, Rev. 5, reprinted in 21 I.L.M. 59 (1981). The Charter entered into force on October 21, 1986. The Charter was drafted pursuant to Decision 115 (XVI) Rev.1 by which the Assembly of Heads of State and Government requested the Secretary-General of the OAU at is Sixteenth Ordinary Session held in Monrovia, Liberia, from July 12-20, 1979, to organize as soon as possible, in an African capital, a restricted meeting of highly qualified experts to prepare a preliminary draft of an African Charter of Human and Peoples Rights.
4   See Vincent O. Orlu Nmehielle, *Towards an African Court of Human Rights: Structuring and Empowering the Court*, VI ANNUAL SURVEY OF INTERNATIONAL & COMPARATIVE LAW 27 (2000).
5   *Id.*
6   B.G. Ramcharan, *The Travaux Préparatoires of the African Commission on Human Rights* 13 HUM. RTS. J. 307 (1992).
7   *Id.*
8   *Id.* One must admit that the state of human rights in many African Countries at that time (though the situation currently is still not fantastic) was unremarkable. There was the air of totalitarianism, either in the form of military governments or one-party dominated autocracy, which attracted much of regional and international outcry and the need for action.
9   Ramcharan, *supra* note 6, at 307.

breaking new grounds in the area of "peoples rights" and the incorporation of economic, social and cultural rights, as well as other such progressive provisions. Critical analyses of the Charter have, however, revealed that the mechanism created under the Charter is bereft of adequate authority to effectively realize the mandates enshrined in the Charter. Similarly, the lack of provision for a judicial organ under the Charter, in this case a court, compounds the ability of the African human rights mechanism to effectively achieve its mandate under the Charter.

Accordingly, this book attempts to evaluate the mechanism created by the African Charter in terms of the laws, practice and institutions of the African human rights system, emphasizing a comparative approach. A central theme of the book is the effectiveness of the mechanism in the resolution of human rights disputes in Africa in the over ten years of its existence. Having in mind the wide scope of this inquiry, the book is divided into seven chapters, each of which addresses specific issues of the study. Chapter one examines some background issues to human rights in Africa. Specifically, the chapter, *inter alia*, looks at human rights in pre-colonial Africa. The issue here is whether pre-colonial African societies had the notion of law, and by extension, the concept of human rights. This is against the view that human rights as a concept was alien to pre-capitalist societies. Similarly, the chapter examines human rights in colonial Africa as it relates to the practice of the major colonial powers such as France, Belgium and Britain. Further, the Chapter looks at the United Nations and human rights in terms of the contribution of the UN: the adoption of the UN Charter, the Universal Declaration and other international human rights instruments and organs that have advanced human rights and influenced human rights discourse in Africa. Also, the chapter briefly examines other regional human rights mechanisms, such as the European and Inter-American systems of human rights, which preceded the African system. The chapter concludes with an examination of the human rights agenda of African States under the auspices of the OAU, following the end of colonialism.

Chapter two deals with normative instruments of the African system. Here, while there is some investigation of the normative value of the OAU Charter to the African human rights system, the chapter is devoted primarily to an analysis of the various rights guaranteed in the African Charter, as the main normative instrument of the African system. These rights are discussed individually under broad categories of civil and political rights; economic, social and cultural rights; and group rights. Under each of these categories, the chapter analyzes and evaluates the practice of the African Commission, the implementing organ of the Charter, through the cases and its procedures. The practice and procedures of other international and regional systems are comparatively analyzed where applicable. The chapter also inquires into the normative effect of "other human rights instruments", which the Charter recognizes as possible inspiration to the African Commission in striving to achieve the mandates enshrined in the Charter. In addition, the concept of duties versus rights under the Charter is examined. The chapter ends with a discussion of the "claw-back" clauses in the Charter.

Chapter three considers the institutional structure of the African system. The chapter examines the place of the Assembly of Heads of State of the OAU and other offices within the OAU in the African human rights mechanism in relation to the African Commission as the institution principally charged with implementing the African Charter. In the same vein, the African Commission itself is also examined with regard to its composition and mandate. The question of how the composition of the Commission has impacted its effective functioning is discussed. Similarly, the chapter investigates whether the African Commission has adequately achieved the elaborate mandate of human rights promotion, protection and other tasks enshrined in the Charter over the period of its existence. Finally, the chapter briefly examines the part played by the secretariat of the Commission in assisting the Commission to achieving its mandate.

Chapter four deals with the procedures of the African Commission. Particularly, the State reporting and communication procedures are examined. Under the State reporting procedure, the manner in which States Parties have complied with their obligation under the Charter to regularly submit reports every two years on their domestic application of the requirements of the Charter, is looked at. More significantly, the communications procedure under which cases or complaints are brought to the African Commission is elaborately considered. Here the working of the inter-state complaint procedure, as well as individual or "other communications" procedure is analyzed. The chapter pays particular attention to the individual complaint mechanism, which is the one area where the African Commission has exercised ample quasi-judicial powers, especially in interpreting substantive provisions of the Charter and the admissibility requirements for complaints under the Charter. The chapter concludes with examining what remedies are available under the Charter in the light of the procedures of the African Commission.

Chapter five examines the arguments on reforming the African human rights system. The chapter elaborates on the bases for these arguments. In addition, the chapter reviews the debate on the establishment of a human rights court, as part of the African human rights mechanism. This culminates in a discussion of the drafting history of the recent Protocol on the establishment of an African Court on Human and Peoples' Rights pursuant to Resolution AHG/230(XXX) of the Assembly of Heads of State and Government at its 30th ordinary session in Tunis in June 1994.

Chapter six focuses on the African Court on Human and Peoples Rights. The primary concern here is an evaluative analysis of provisions of the Protocol establishing the Court. Each article of the protocol is analyzed in the light of the Court's potential in effectively dealing with human rights dispute resolution in Africa, in relation to the provisions of the African Charter. The chapter also examines the relationship between the African Commission and the Court in the exercise of their various mandates under the Charter and Protocol, respectively. The question whether the Commission would not fare better as a promotion organ, and the Court as a protective organ, is addressed. Where appropriate, provisions of the Protocol are compared with similar provisions in other regional and international human rights instruments with the aim of ensuring that the Court achieves the objectives of the African Charter in reinforcing the protection of human rights in the continent.

Chapter seven is devoted to considering the impact of human rights non-governmental organizations (NGOs) on the African human rights system. Here the focus is on the role NGOs have played and their impact on the work of the African Commission. Similarly, the impact that NGOs will have in the era of the African Court and on the future of human rights in Africa is discussed. Thus, the chapter examines the status of NGOs under the African Charter, the relationship between the African Commission and NGOs, the place of NGOs in the Protocol on the establishment of the Court, and NGOs and the future of human rights in Africa.

Finally the book ends with conclusions based on the findings from the enquiry that it makes. These findings are expected to be a basis for further improvement of the African human rights system to enable it to serve as an effective human rights dispute resolution mechanism in the continent in the 21st Century and beyond.

1

BACKGROUND TO HUMAN RIGHTS IN AFRICA

I   HUMAN RIGHTS IN PRE-COLONIAL AFRICA

The debate on the existence of human rights as a concept in pre-colonial African legal thought is a very controversial one, and is hinged on another controversial subject: whether law existed in pre-colonial Africa. We will dedicate this segment of this background chapter to inquire into this conundrum. There will be two levels of this inquiry. We will first of all look into the existence of law in pre-colonial or traditional African society. This will be followed by the human rights debate.

Some Western scholars have questioned the notion of law in pre-colonial Africa. This stems from the historical obscurity given to Africa by early Western historians. Hegel in his Philosophy of History positioned Africa outside history and civilization.[10] The reason for this lack of recognition of the existence of law in early African societies has been attributed to the fact that African societies in the pre-colonial era were very traditional in nature, governed by custom rather than law. Thus, nineteenth century scholars tried to distinguish between custom and law. To them custom was absolutely rigid, and obedience was ensured by the overwhelming power of group sentiment which was amply fortified by magic.[11] According to the argument, under the circumstances, "it was impossible to make any distinctions between legal, moral or religious rules, which were all interwoven into the single rules of customary behavior".[12]

According to Eze, this argument that traditional societies did not possess a legal system was based either on inadequate information or lack of appreciation of the true nature of pre-colonial African societies on the one hand; and on the

---

10   *See* ALTERNATIVE HISTORIES AND NON-WRITTEN SOURCES: NEW PERSPECTIVE FROM THE SOUTH 4 (Proposal for an International Seminar organized by the South-South Exchange Programme for Research on History of Development (SEPHIS), Amsterdam, at La Paz, 12-15 May 1999).
11   *See* EZE, *supra*, note 1, at10.
12   *Id. citing* LLOYD, INTRODUCTION TO JURISPRUDENCE 566 (Stephen and Sons, 1972).

Western scholars' concept of law as emanating from the State.[13] One would agree with Professor Eze that defining law to be that which emanates from a State, as a particular form of societal organization, ignores that law did exist outside the framework of a State in the modern sense. One would also agree with the reasoning that this argument has the implication that African societies operated in total legal vacuum before the Arabs and the colonialists overran the continent.

The existence of law in pre-colonial Africa was a result of the stage of development of its societies in that era. Thus, in Africa, while one may agree that the predominant socio-economic formations before colonial penetration were communalism, slave owning societies and feudalism; laws had to, and did exist to govern these societies and the relations within them.[14] Sociological, economic, historical and anthropological studies in the last three decades of the twentieth century have resulted in works that have thrown more light and provided useful information for a reasonably accurate appreciation and assessment of Africa's past political, social and economic formations.[15] While there may not have been legal studies focusing directly on the existence of law as a concept in pre-colonial Africa, these studies fairly incorporate the existence of law in the political, social and economic settings of pre-colonial Africa. Scholars of African political, social and economic history agree that African societies in pre-colonial era achieved a reasonable degree of political, social and economic organization that had the characteristics of modern States.[16] It is well known that kingdoms flourished in Africa as far back as the Fourth Century. In West Africa, there were the Ghana, Songhai, Mali and Walata empires.[17] In the South-East, there was the Zulu empire, in Central Africa the kingdom of the Monomotapa, and in East Africa the ancient Bunyoro Empire and the Buganda Kingdoms.[18] According to Eze, Walter Rodney argues that "up to the fifteenth century when the colonialists arrived

---

13 *Id., EZE, supra,* note 1, at 9.
14 *Id.*
15 *See* generally, T.O. ELIAS, THE NATURE OF AFRICAN CUSTOMARY LAW (Manchester University Press, 2nd Impression, 1962);WALTER RODNEY, HOW EUROPE UNDERDEVELOPED AFRICA (London, Bogle-L'Ouverture, 1972), and BASIL DAVIDSON, OLD AFRICA REDISCOVERED (London, Longman Group Ltd., 1970), *reprinted* in EZE, *supra* note, 1 at 257. *See* also *Edward Kofi Quashigah, Legitimate Governance: The Pre-Colonial African Perspective* in LEGITIMATE GOVERNANCE IN AFRICA: INTERNATIONAL AND DOMESTIC LEGAL PERSPECTIVES 43 (EDWARD K. QUASHIGA and OBIORA C. OKAFOR, eds., The Hague: Kluwer Law International, 1999).
16 According to Elias, "in African law although theories about social contract have not been formulated in this way, yet the indigenous ideas of government are not essentially dissimilar, at least in its presuppositions, to that of Grotius as well." *See* T. O. ELIAS, AFRICA AND DEVELOPMENT OF INTERNATIONAL LAW 36 (Martinus Nijhoff, 1988) also *reprinted* in *Edward Kofi Quashigah, supra* note 15 at, 43.
17 *See* EZE, *supra*, note 1, at 10.
18 *Id. See* also ELIAS, THE NATURE OF AFRICAN CUSTOMARY LAW, *supra,* note 15, at 9.

in Africa, State formation was in an embryonic stage. The Western Sudanese techniques of political organization and administration reached many neighboring regions and influenced the emergence of innumerable small states scattered throughout the coastal region from Senegal river to the Cameroon mountains."[19] Rodney argues that the levels of development between Europe and Africa were comparable, based on the confirmation of the first Europeans to reach East and West Africa by sea. He, however, cautioned that it would be self delusion to think that all things were at par, because the Europeans did have an edge.[20]

Another scholar who agrees with the progressive development of pre-colonial African societies is Basil Davidson. He observes that "behind the obscurities of early West African History ... one may reasonably detect iron smelting and international trade as underlying factors which had decisive influence in the hands of men who practiced them. Political and military concentration became possible and, at least for those who could rule, desirable alliances of interests emerged, became fused into centers of power, acquired geographical identity, reappeared as territorial states: even when, as was surely the case, the people of the riverside villages and the nomads following their herds would continue to live much the same way as they lived before".[21] Accordingly, not only did pre-colonial Africa witness the emergence of States, but there were also some levels of technological development and capacity, based among other things, on accepted separate territorial identity, to enter into international relations.[22] In addition to the level of development, the structures of various African societies also had some effect on the level of development of the legal systems. Elias, the late Nigerian international jurist argues that "African societies with strong centralized political systems tended to have a more advanced body of legal principles and judicial techniques than had those with more or less rudimentary political organization. In the former, there were usually hierarchically graded courts ranging from the smallest chiefs to kings' courts, with well defined machinery for due enforcement of judicial decisions. In the latter, rules rather than rulers, functions rather than institutions, characterized the judicial organization of these societies."[23] He opines that the fact that in the latter, the legal arrangements were informal in nature, should not be interpreted as an actual situation of chaos, "since the mechanism of choosing the adjudicating elders for the settlement of disputes, as well as that of enforcing their decisions,

---

19 See EZE, *supra*, note 1, at 10, citing RODNEY, *supra*, note 15 at 70. *See* also, generally, F. AJAYI and I. ESPIE, (eds.), A THOUSAND YEARS OF WEST AFRICAN HISTORY (Ibadan: Ibadan University Press, 1965) also *reprinted* in EZE, *supra* note, 1, at 257.
20 RODNEY, *supra*, note 15 at, 82.
21 DAVIDSON, *supra*, note 15, at 84.
22 *Id.*, at 83.
23 See ELIAS, *supra*, note 15, at 30.

followed clearly recognized pattern, even if the means adopted appeared casual to the unwary observer."[24]

In his study of southern African societies, Gluckman[25] saw a traditional African society with a fairly advanced legal system. He observed that the body of law in Loziland consisted of rules of varying types and origin. These in their own right are the various sources of law as commonly defined in Western jurisprudence. He found that in Lozi, as in Western jurisprudence, these sources consisted of customs, judicial precedents, legislation, laws of natural morality and of nations, good morals and equity.[26] The bottom line of his argument is that the judicial process in Loziland on the whole corresponded to, rather than differed from, the judicial process known in Western societies.

Meek, as far back as 1937, also argued along the same line as did Gluckman, regarding traditional legal systems in Zululand, East Africa and West Africa. He was of the opinion that the mentality of "Primitive" peoples did not differ from that of Europeans, as was known by any European who had lived at close quarters with natives.[27] It was therefore not to be expected that the norms governing conduct in these African societies should diverge very profoundly from that of early European societies. What were crimes or torts to Europeans were for the most parts crimes or torts to the African societies.[28]

The point being made here is not to get even with Western societies in selling the notion that the concept of law in pre-colonial Africa existed in much the same fashion as in the west. It is rather that those scholars who deny the existence of law in pre-colonial Africa tend to give the impression that African legal systems must be comparable to those in the more advanced societies of Western Europe in order to be valid. This notion would be misleading in the sense that no two societies could actually be the same in terms of development of legal norms and socio-political principles. One would agree totally with Eze that in looking at socio-economic formations, at each stage of the evolution of human society, a legal system and indeed laws corresponding to a given state of socio-economic development existed to regulate it.[29]

---

24 *Id.*
25 M. GLUCKMAN, THE JUDICIAL PROCESS AMONG THE BARTOSE OF NORTHERN RHODESIA 231 (Manchester: Manchester University Press, 2nd edition, 1967) *reprinted* in EZE, *supra* note, 1 at 11.
26 EZE *Id.* at 231.
27 C.K. MEEK, LAW AND AUTHORITY IN A NIGERIAN TRIBE xiii (London: Oxford University Press, 1937) *reprinted* in EZE, *supra* note1, at 11.
28 *Id.* at xiii
29 EZE, *supra*, note 1, at 12.

This author will argue that the whole colonial agenda of Europe was responsible for attempts to discredit the legal formation and development of pre-colonial African societies. It is unimaginable that societies would have gone along without an established legal order of things. The fact that religion or metaphysics is said to overwhelmingly influence African customs does not in any way discredit the attributes of the norms existing in these societies from being law. In Africa as in other modern societies, certain mores deriving originally from religion or general morality have not only influenced the development of positive legal rules, but have in fact come to form part of them. The natural law argument that law derives from God or a Supreme being has long been a substantial element of African legal philosophy, even though it may not have been couched into a thesis by any ancient African legal philosopher. It is nothing but a belief in religion as a source of law, which in turn was applied and enforced in modern European States.

The other segment of the argument is whether human rights as a concept existed in pre-colonial Africa. Many African scholars defend the existence of human rights concept in pre- colonial Africa.[30] Rhoda Howard and Jack Donnelly are the Western scholars in the forefront of the argument that human rights did not exist as a concept in pre-colonial Africa.[31] To Howard, African proponents of the concept confuse human dignity with human rights. According to her, "the African concept of human rights is actually a concept of human dignity, of what defines "the inner" (moral) nature and worth of the human person and his or her proper (political) relations with society. Despite the twinning of human rights and human dignity in the preamble to the Universal Declaration of Human Rights and elsewhere, dignity can be protected in a society not based on rights. The notion of African communalism, which stresses the dignity of membership in, and fulfillment of one's prescribed social role in a group (family, kinship group, tribe),

---

30　See generally, Kwasi Wiredu, *An Arkan Perspective on Human Rights*, in HUMAN RIGHTS IN AFRICA: CROSS- CULTURAL PERSPECTIVES 243 (ABDULAHI AN-NA'IM and FRANCIS DENG, eds., 1990); Francis Deng, *Cultural Approach to Human Rights among the Dinka*, in *id* at 261; Makau Wa Mutua, *The Banjul Charter and the African Cultural Fingerprint: An Evaluation of Language of Duties*, 35 VA. J. INT'L L. 339 (1995).

31　See Rhoda Howard, *Group Versus Individual Identity in the African Debate on Human Rights*, in HUMAN RIGHTS IN AFRICA: CROSS- CULTURAL PERSPECTIVES, *supra*, note 30, at 159; *Rhoda Howard, Evaluating Human Rights in Africa: Some Problems of Implicit Comparisons,* 6 HUM. RTS. Q. 160 (1984); *Jack Donnelly, Human Rights and Western Liberalism*, in HUMAN RIGHTS IN AFRICA: CROSS- CULTURAL PERSPECTIVES *supra* note 30 at 159; JACK DONNELLY, UNIVERSAL HUMAN RIGHTS IN THEORY AND PRACTICE (1989). *See also* R. J. VINCENT, HUMAN RIGHTS AND INTERNATIONAL RELATIONS 13- 18 (Cambridge: Cambridge University Press, 1986), who is considered to be of the same view with Howard and Donnelly.

still represents accurately how many Africans appear to view their personal relationship to society."[32]

It appears that Howard has a problem with the idea that African communal characteristic could harbor the concept of human rights within it. The fact that an African's sense of well-being and due regard finds distinct expression in a group makes it impossible for the learned author to equate human dignity with human rights. Thus, the concept of justice unlike human rights, is rooted not in individual claims against the State, but in the physical and psychic security of group membership as argued by the same author.[33] Rather than agree that pre-colonial Africa had embedded in its notion of human dignity, the concept of human rights, Howard strongly insists that "although relatively homogenous, undifferentiated simple societies of pre-colonial Africa had effective means of guaranteeing what is now known as human rights, there was nothing specifically African about them."[34] Instead she refers to the situation as the communitarian ideal which represented typical agrarian, precapitalist social relations in non-state societies.[35]

Jack Donnelly, as an ally of Rhoda Howard in this debate, also dismisses the notion that pre-colonial African societies knew the concept of human rights. Like Howard, he opines that that argument is now lame since the communitarian ideal had been destroyed and corrupted by the "teeming slums" of non-Western States, the money economy, Western values and products;[36] even if it could be agreed that societies based on communitarian ideals existed at a point in time in Africa.

A number of African scholars have risen in defense that the concept of human rights was in existence in the pre-colonial era in Africa, thereby sharply disagreeing with the views held by Howard and Donnelly. A notable critic of their views is Mutua. He dismisses the notion held by the duo that human rights are only possible in a post-feudal state, and that the concept of human rights was alien to specific pre-capitalist traditions and ideals such as Buddhism, Islam, or pre-colonial African societies.[37] His interpretation of this view is that it is a suggestion that these

---

32 *Rhoda Howard, Group Versus Identity in the African Debate on Human Rights, supra,* note 31, at 165-166.
33 *Id.* at 166.
34 *Rhoda Howard, Evaluating Human Rights in Africa: Some Problems of Implicit Comparisons, supra,* note 31, at 176.
35 *Id.*
36 JACK DONNELLY, UNIVERSAL HUMAN RIGHTS IN THEORY AND PRACTICE, *supra,* note 31 at 119.
37 *Mutua, supra,* note 30, at 355. *See also A. Legesse, Human Rights in African Political Culture,* in THE MORAL IMPERATIVES OF HUMAN RIGHTS: A WORLD SURVEY 123-138 (K.W. THOMPSON ed.; Washington, D.C.: University Press of America, 1980); J. NYERERE, UJAMA: ESSAYS IN SOCIALISM 106 -108 (London: Oxford University Press, 1968); I.G. SIVJI, THE CONCEPT OF HUMAN RIGHTS IN AFRICA 12 (CORDESIA, 1989) and *C. C. Mojekwu, International Human Rights: The African Perspective* in INTERNATIONAL HUMAN RIGHTS: CONTEMPORARY ISSUES 85-95 (J. L.

traditions can make no normative contribution to the human rights corpus; and that societies governed under a centralized modern State necessarily westernize through industrialization and urbanization, and thus become fertile ground for human rights to germinate.[38] Mutua, as well as this author, agrees that pre-colonial values have been undermined by change as a result of interaction between different cultures brought about by colonization of African peoples, but that it will be difficult to believe that the change process arising from this interaction will totally or completely invalidate or eradicate them, just like it will be difficult to imagine that the modernization of Asia and the Arab world will completely destroy the cultural norms and forms of consciousness evolved through Buddhism and Islam.[39]

Foremost in Mutua's criticism of the views of Howard and Donnelly is the implication in their works, that only European liberalism can be the foundation for the concept of human rights. He argues that this view destroys the claim that human rights are universal[40]. We should be able to note that the universality of human rights does not derive from Western imposition of the concept on colonized societies. It rather means that the concept of what is articulated today as human rights is prevalent universally; that is, in every culture, since the concept derives directly from a person's humanity. That does not mean that what constitutes the contents of the concept is static, devoid of any progressive development. Human rights as a concept is dynamic, with new additions to the contents as societies evolve and develop.

African writers in their attempt to counter the view on human rights in pre-colonial Africa have tried to trace historical practices in some pre-colonial African societies that accord with present day notions of human rights. The Akamba of East Africa and the Akan of West Africa are cited as examples. According to Wiredu, within Akan society, the individual had both descriptive and normative characteristics which endowed the person with individual rights as well.[41] The

---

NELSON & V.M. GREEN, eds., New York: Human Rights Publishing Group, 1980).

38 *Mutua, supra,* note 30, at 356.
39 *Id.* It needs to be stressed that culture is dynamic, and the whole point of cultural interaction is the possibility of the interacting cultures to affect each other. The fact that the modern State is becoming a feature of African societal organization does not eliminate the ability of pre-colonial norms to influence the lives of Africans. The view that the old ways have been eroded by modernization is just a fact of the nature of culture, not that the old ways were not in existence or that they depended on the Western ideals to be legitimated. In fact, not all the old ways have been eroded. Every culture has the tendency of phasing out some of its mores as time progresses, especially those that cannot be said to be generally accepted by those within that culture.
40 Mutua, *supra,* note 30, at 356.
41 Wiredu, *supra,* note 30, at 243.

Akamba it is said, believed that all members of the society were born equal and were supposed to be treated as such regardless of sex and age.[42] Thus, the Akan and Akamba pre-colonial societies are credited to have had the belief that the individual as an inherently valuable being, was naturally endowed with certain basic rights.[43] The existence of political right in these societies is based on their practice of choosing their rulers. The Akan political society was organized according to the principle of kinship made in such a way that a lineage of those who were descended from the same ancestry formed the basic political unit. Adults in each lineage elected an elder, while linage heads in turn , formed the Town Council which was chaired by a chief, who though chosen according to descent, was in part elected.[44] The chief of the Town Council did not exercise his power unilaterally, as decisions of the Council were taken by consensus. The decisions of the Council were subject to criticism by those who found them objectionable. It is even claimed that there existed the "the right of the people, including elders, to dismiss a chief who tried to be oppressive.[45] In their judicial process the two societies in reference demonstrated an individual-conscious justice system. The Akamba justice system involved a trial with each party to a dispute appearing

---

42 *See Mutua, supra,* note 30, at 349, citing JOSEPH MUTHIANI, AKAMBA FROM WITHIN 84 (1973).
43 *Id. Mutua.*
44 *See Wiredu, supra,* note 30, at 248-249.
45 *Id.* at 251. The chieftaincy institution in Africa, where it existed was regulated by customary rules that evolved over the years to ensure the efficacy of the institution and to protect the rights of the subjects. In effect, it is argued that the philosophical notions of social contracts between rulers and citizens also existed in pre-colonial Africa. *See* H. GLUCKMAN, THE IDEA IN BARTOSE JURISPRUDENCE 30 (New Haven: Yale University Press, 1962) *reprinted* in *Quashiga, Legitimate Governance: The Pre-Colonial African Perspective, supra* note 15, at 50. It is suggested that the manner in which the installation ceremonies of such rulers were conducted depicted the relationship between the rulers and the citizens. One example of this, which Selassie points out, is the installation ceremony of an *Asantehene* (King of the Asanti Confederation now in present Ghana) in which the king was admonished against tyranny as follows:

Tell him that
We do not wish for greediness
We do not wish that he should curse us
We do not wish that his ears should be hard of hearing
We do not wish that he should call people fools
We do not wish that he should act in his own initiative
We do not wish things done as in Kumasi
We do not wish that it should ever be said, " I have no time, I have no time"
We do not wish personal abuse
We do not wish personal violence

See B. H. SELASSIE, THE EXECUTIVE IN AFRICAN GOVERNMENTS 123 (London Heinemann, 1974), *reprinted* in *Quashiga, Id.*

before the Council of Elders with his or her own jurors who rather than preside over the case advised the party on how to win the case. The case progressed to a finding with the appropriate punishment for the guilty or liable party, depending on the infringement or crime committed.[46] Protection was also given to the individual right to cultivate land.[47] Akan society similarly upheld the principle of innocence until proven guilty in it's socio-legal consciousness. Wiredu explains that it was a fundamental principle of Akan justice system that no human being could be punished without being availed the opportunity of a trial.[48]

Timothy Fernyhough is one of the few non-African scholars who has objectively shared the view of the existence of human rights in pre-colonial Africa in reaction to the views expressed by Donnelly and Howard, noting how politicized the debate has become.[49] According to him,

> ... fairly similar views have led to very different conclusions. From one perspective the human rights tradition was quite foreign to Africa until Western, "modernizing" intrusions dislocated community and denied newly isolated individuals access to customary ways of protecting their lives and human dignity. Human rights were alien to Africa precisely because it was a precapitalist society, social organization. From the opposing viewpoint there is a fundamental rejection of this as a new, if rather subtle, imperialism, an explicit denial that human rights evolved only in Western political theory and practice, especially during the American and French revolutions, and not in Africa. Behind this protest is the very plausible claim that human rights are not founded in Western values alone but may also have emerged from very different and distinctive African cultural milieus.[50]

The arguments on human rights in pre-colonial Africa could go on for a very long time with recurring opposing views and those that are geared toward defending its existence and vice versa. The point remains that the whole debate is riddled with sentiments. The Western scholars who deny the existence of human rights in pre-colonial Africa run the risk of being accused of advancing some imperialist scholarly views which do no more than bring back pictures of colonialism, while African scholars who defend its existence and, especially as to its African uniqueness, could be tagged overzealous. Fernyhough does a nice job by reminding Howard and Donnelly who could be called ethnocentric universalists, to stick to

---

46 See MUTHIANI, in *Mutua, supra,* note 42, at 350.
47 *Id.*
48 See *Wiredu, supra,* note 30, at 252.
49 *See* generally, *Timothy Fernyhough, Human Rights and Precolonial Africa,* in HUMAN RIGHTS AND GOVERNANCE IN AFRICA 39 (RONALD COHEN *et al,* eds., Florida: University Press of Florida, 1993).
50 *Id.* at 40-41.

a consistent theory of human rights in the sense that if they believe that human rights derive directly from a person's humanity and embody human dignity, which makes them inalienable and universal, it would be contradictory for them not to apply their own definitions and philosophical concepts of human rights to pre-colonial Africa.[51]

On the other hand, some African scholars have overplayed the issue of the uniqueness of African concept of human rights in order to advance the cultural relativism theory, which at best is an exaggeration, in the face of the acceptance that human rights as a concept is universal. We must accept the fact that even though the notion of human rights was prevalent in pre-colonial Africa, it existed more as a concept rather than a defined set of rights as later enumerated in the international Bill of Rights. Accordingly, the lack of a thorough definition by content of what constituted human rights in pre-colonial Africa does not defeat the assertion of the existence of human rights in that African era. Human rights are dynamic. Not all that are considered today as human rights were a part of the concept at the time of formal articulation of the concept. This author has argued elsewhere[52] that the history of African pre-colonial development showed advanced state structures which recognized some notions of human rights; but that the formal articulation of human rights had its origin in Western legal and political philosophical thought, especially after the atrocities of the world wars and the ravages of colonialism.

In the debate, this author will agree with Mutua[53] that the view of the ethnocentric universalist is at best counter productive, as it leads to proposing that Western culture is superior to African culture. This he adds, serves only to alienate African State authorities who would purposefully manipulate concepts in order to continue their repressive practices.[54] The realization of respect for human rights in Africa depends a lot on how African leaders perceive the origin of the concept. African leaders since colonialism have resisted, albeit arrogantly to prove the point of national sovereignty, all suggestions that they must follow Western concepts of governance. We are in an era in Africa where there is the need to emphasize that the accountability that existed in governance in the pre-colonial era should be observed by the present African leadership. The writing off of African pre-colonial societies as primitive, precapitalist societies without any notion of the concept of human rights will only go to defeat the present

---

51 *Id.* at 47.
52 Vincent O. Orlu Nmehielle, THE AFRICAN CHARTER ON HUMAN AND PEOPLES' RIGHTS AND THE HUMAN RIGHTS QUESTION IN NIGERIA 23 (LL.M. Thesis, University of Notre Dame Law School, Notre Dame, Indiana, 1996).
53 *Mutua, supra,* note 30 at 358.
54 *Id.*

African struggle to achieve a greater degree of respect for human rights and good governance.

II   HUMAN RIGHTS IN COLONIAL AFRICA

The relative dignity and human value enjoyed by Africans in the pre-colonial era became negatively impacted by colonialism as an aspect of foreign intervention in Africa. Also, the Atlantic trade in African slaves, which foreran colonialism, and begun in 1510, reached its height in the 18th century and was complemented by the Arab operators in East and Central Africa.[55] Slave trade and colonialism responded to the economic changes in Europe. The industrial revolution in Europe required cheap sources of raw materials produced by cheap labor; it also required a market for surplus goods.[56] With the end of slave trade in sight, due to humanitarian sentiments against it, colonial subjugation of Africa was the desired alternative in the quest for the expansion of commercial activities.

With the abolition of the slave trade in the 1840s it became clear that European presence in Africa must be translated into other commercial activities as each European power competed against the other. According to Professor George Ayittey, throughout the second half of the nineteenth century the British, French, Dutch, Portuguese, and other Europeans brutishly jostled one another for influence and control over trade of certain valued commodities.[57] They built forts and castles, especially along West African coasts, not only to defend commercial interests against foreign interlopers, but to expand trade. In order to secure commercial advantages, they signed friendship treaties with African kings. So intense was the competition for commercial hegemony that in 1884 Chancellor Bismarck of Germany convened a conference of European nations with the avowed purpose of reducing tensions among them. The effect of the conference was to establish rules for recognizing spheres of commercial suzerainty. A frenetic scramble ensued to establish such spheres of dominance where none existed before.[58]

The outcome of that conference was the Treaty of Berlin of 1885. The treaty was specifically directed towards the prevention of war among the European

---

55   See Umozurike U.O, *The Significance of the African Charter on Human and Peoples' Rights* in PERSPECTIVE ON HUMAN RIGHTS 45 (AWA U. KALU & YEMI OSINBAJO, eds., Nigeria: Federal Ministry of Justice, 1992).
56   *Id.*
57   *See* GEORGE AYITTEY, AFRICA BETRAYED 81 (New York: Transnational Publishers Inc., 1992).
58   *Id.*

scramblers for African peoples and territories. While the treaty laid the ground rules for colonialism it also intensified it.[59] According to Professor Umozurike, the slave trade and colonialism had such devastating effect on human rights that it required decades of redemptive work to revive the tradition of respect for human rights in Africa.[60] The colonial period witnessed a systematic subjugation and exploitation of the African people for the benefit of the European metropolitan powers. Tendentious treaties were extorted from African rulers, in some cases by sheer military force. De facto protectorates became colonies.[61]

The effects of the occupation of Africa by the colonialists were varied and depended on the practice of the particular European power.[62] Generally, however, there was an attempt at total annihilation of the African customary legal order. Customary law existed long before European colonization, but with the institution of colonialism, it had a direct and decisive impact on African customary law. According to professor Eze,[63] with colonialism, African law ceased to be endogenously developed, as its development was no longer by Africans, neither did it continue to evolve according to African needs. Also, the power to make laws, or apply sanctions in accordance with the laws that existed before, passed to the colonialists. African societies became subject to political, economic and social domination. The deculturalization that ensued made those Africans who were in contact with colonial administration dissatisfied with their own traditional value systems and education.[64]

Also, colonialism presented an enormous potential for the plunder, abuse, misrule and mistreatment of African natives without much check. Ayittey captured the situation with the example of a Frenchman in his 20s, who had just finished school and was entrusted with enormous colonial power. He would be posted to a colony as *commandant de cercle* with complete authority over some 200,000 African natives. He could literally do as he pleased since his personal powers were guaranteed by the *Statut de l'indigent*, the most hated feature of the colonial system in French West Africa.[65] The *indigenat* consisted of regulations that allowed colonial administrators to inflict punishment on African subjects without obtaining a court judgment or approval from the metropolis. It allowed the colonial officers

---

59 See Umozurike, *supra*, note 55 at 44.
60 *Id.*, citing UMOZURIKE, U.O, INTERNATIONAL LAW AND COLONIALISM IN AFRICA, (Nwamaife, 1979). See also Umozurike, U.O., *International Law and the African Slave Trade*, 16(2) HOWARD L.J. 334-349 (1971).
61 See AYITTEY, *supra*, note 57, at 81.
62 See the discussion on the various systems of colonial Administration in Africa *infra* at pages 28-29.
63 See EZE, *supra*, note 1, at 14.
64 *Id.*
65 See AYITTEY, *supra*, note 47 at 83.

to jail any African for up to two years without trial, to impose heavy taxes and punitive fines, or to burn the villages of those who refused to pay.[66] This is a phenomenon that is presently displayed in different forms. The highhandedness of the colonialists continues to be the mode of operation of many African regimes.

The exploitation and subjugation witnessed during the colonial era were done with impunity in deliberate violation of international standards. One of such examples, is the noble International Labor Organization's (ILO) minimum standards for dealing with labor under the ILO Conventions. According to Mbaye, the application of these standards in the colonial territories appeared to be practically outside the purview of the Conventions, or the colonialists chose on their own not to apply them without any consequences.[67] While it is true that there was selective application of ILO standards in the colonies and territories by the colonial powers, it must be noted, however, that the ILO as an institution made enormous efforts to make sure that its principles of social policy for non-metropolitan territories were enforced in colonial territories. Examples of such efforts include the Forced Labor Convention[68] and the Abolition of Forced Labor Convention.[69] These Conventions were reactions to labor practices and standards that persisted in dependent territories or colonies as "modern" forms of slavery even after the abolition of slavery.[70] These were geared toward making Member States of the ILO responsible for non-metropolitan territories, such as colonies under their control. This effort culminated in the 1964 amendment of the ILO constitution under which Article 35 was to be repealed and replaced by new paragraph 9 of Article 19. Under this provision, "Members ratifying Conventions shall accept their provisions so far as practicable in respect of all territories for whose international relations they are responsible."[71] These efforts met with serious difficulties for the lack of sufficient number of ratifications. However, with increasing decolonization, the system which had permitted the application of ILO Conventions

---

66 *Id.*
67 See Keba M'Baye, *Human Rights in Africa* in THE INTERNATIONAL DIMENSIONS OF HUMAN RIGHTS 583 (KAREL VASAK and PHILIP ALSTON, eds; Greenwood Press, 1982).
68 Forced Labor Convention, 1930 (Convention No. 29).
69 Abolition of Forced Labor Convention, 1957 (Convention No. 105).
70 HÉCTOR BARTOLOMEI DE LA CRUZ, GERALDO VON POTOBSKY & LEE SWEPSTON, (hereafter DE LA CRUZ, *et al.*), THE INTERNATIONAL LABOR ORGANIZATION: THE INTERNATIONAL SYSTEM AND BASIC HUMAN RIGHTS 130 (West View Press, 1996). Convention No. 29 was to be applied principally to non-metropolitan territories, but its broad approach allowed its expansion beyond the notions of slavery and colonies. Convention No. 105 did not replace Convention No. 29, but supplemented it, requiring the abolition of forced labor in situations relating to political repression. *Id.* at 132.
71 See *Id.* at 54, *citing* PROCEEDINGS OF THE INTERNATIONAL LABOR CONFERENCE, 48TH SESSION, 1964, Appendix, p. 830.

with or without modifications to many non-metropolitan territories, lost their effects. As many States became independent and joined the ILO, they ratified obligations which had previously been undertaken on their behalf.[72]

A broader discussion of the nature of human rights in colonial Africa would require us to examine, albeit briefly, specific systems of colonialism as adopted by the various European powers. The major colonial powers were France, Britain and Belgium. Portugal and Spain exacted some measure of colonial authority as well.

A.   *French colonialism*

The philosophy underlying French colonialism was that of political and cultural assimilation. Under this system the colony became an integral part of the mother country rather than a separate but protected state. The colonized people were expected to assimilate the French culture. The rationale for assimilation was based on the belief that French culture was superior.[73] The French colonialists, it is said, felt that they had a *mission civilisatrice*, therefore, French law and jurisprudence prevailed.[74] The policy was aimed at entirely turning the African to a French in all aspects of his or her thinking.

Theoretically, the possibility of acquiring French citizenship was open to Africans, and some even became members of the French Parliament, but by the nature of things only few could take advantage of the offer. An African had to satisfy certain conditions to be able to acquire French citizenship under the assimilation policy. He must have attained a certain level of education, including knowledge of the French language, and done military service, as well as not having contracted a polygamous marriage. In all, he must renounce customary law.[75]

---

72 *Id.* For further details on the ILO's social policy in non-metropolitan territories and efforts during colonialism, *see* INTERNATIONAL LABOUR OFFICE, THE INTERNATIONAL LABOR CODE VOLUME I, 1951 (Book X) 927-1100 (Geneva, 1952) . On the ILO generally, *see*, NICOLAS VALITICOS & G. VON POTOBSKY, INTERNATIONAL LABOR LAW (2nd edition, Boston: Kluwer Law & Taxation Publishers, 1994); *Virginia Leary, Lessons from the Experience of the International Labor Organization* in THE UNITED NATIONS AND HUMAN RIGHTS: A CRITICAL appraisal 580 (PHILIP ALSTON, ed., Oxford: Clarendon Press, 1992); *Virginia Leary, Human Rights at the ILO: Reflections on Making the ILO User Friendly* in THE MODERN WORLD OF HUMAN RIGHTS; ESSAYS IN HONOR OF THOMAS BURGENTHAL 375 (ANTONIO A. CANÇADO TRINDADE, ed., San José: Inter-American Institute of Human Rights, 1996); VICTOR-YVES GHEBALI, THE INTERNATIONAL LABOUR ORGANISATION :A CASE STUDY ON THE EVOLUTION OF U.N. SPECIALIZED AGENCIES (The Hague: Martinus Nijhoff Publishers, 1989).
73 AYITTEY, *supra*, note 47 at 87.
74 *Id.*
75 *See* EZE, *supra,* note 1, at 15.

The glaring situation of things under the assimilation policy made it impossible to have a general application of the policy. The policy in many cases had to be modified to what had been termed the second strand of French colonial policy: the policy of association.[76] The concept of association is said to have been developed and applied by Savorgnan de Brazza in Central Africa.[77] Under this concept, its advocates believed that, though assimilation was desirable, it was impracticable because non-Western people were racially inferior and would never be accepted, even if fully assimilated. Thus, association would on the other hand, permit the colonized people to develop within their own cultures.[78] The policy was similar to the British system of indirect rule. Association differed in some fundamental respects. The French colony was part of France rather than a separate political entity. The French also had no intention of using traditional rulers as intermediaries. They allied themselves with African rulers in order to neutralize them until they could be eliminated or deposed at convenience. Those who remained were put in the position of serving as agents of the colonial State rather than rulers in their own right. One such example was the conquering of Dahomey by the French in 1894 under General Dodds, who dismembered the kingdom. Only the central province, the area around Abomey, remained intact; the other provinces were put under direct French rule or made into new kingdoms.[79] Where there were no central authorities, as in stateless African societies such as the Fulani and Somali, the French created new chiefs.[80]

Despite the system of colonial policy adopted by the French, at the political level, French colonialism meant that the traditional rights of African societies to participate in their own government were often postponed and were initially nonexistent. Ayittey is of the view that the French colonial policies posed the gravest danger to indigenous African institutions, especially the great paramount chieftaincies, which were deliberately destroyed.[81]

---

76 The French soon realized that French laws could not be imposed hocus-pocus on peoples with different cultural and political backgrounds who had not attained a comparable level of economic development. Thus, customary laws and Islamic laws were recognized and applied by different institutions created for the purpose, subject to the qualification that they were not contrary to the principles of French civilization.
77 *See* AYITTEY, *supra*, note 47, at 87.
78 *Id.*
79 *Id.*
80 *Id.*
81 *Id.* at 86.

B. Belgian colonialism

Belgian colonial expedition in Africa centered around the Congo and embraced also the Rwanda-Burundi regions. The personal influence of King Leopold II of Belgium prevailed in this region. Later, Congo graduated from the personal rule of the king to the status of a Belgian colony.[82] Colonial rule in the Congo was a tripartite arrangement: rule by corporation, which consisted of the crown, the Catholic Church and large companies in which the crown held substantial stock. The colonial administration of the Congo under these arrangements was brutal, portraying a picture of almost total human degradation. Because of the preoccupation of King Leopold with reaping benefits from the Congo, the king indeed regarded the territory as his private property. The king's assertion of ownership over the territory in his own words, run thus: "the Congo has been and would have been but a personal undertaking. There is no more legitimate or respectable right than that of an author over his own work, the fruit of his labour... My rights over Congo are to be shared with no one, they are the fruit of my own struggles and expenditure".[83] That spirit governed the administration of the Congo, which was managed with utmost brutality and exploitation of the Congo People. In addition to the exploitation of Congo's ivory and rubber, was cheap African labor that was secured by force, taking the form of labor tax that was imposed to compel Africans to work.

The brutality and exploitation of the Congo by King Leopold II attracted widespread protests. This forced the Belgian Parliament to annex the Congo Independent State as it was called under Leopold's sole "ownership", and brought it under Belgian State rule, after the adoption of the Colonial Charter of 1908, as the Belgian Congo.[84] The takeover by the Belgian Parliament achieved little by way of reform after that date. From the period of the takeover, Belgian colonial policy was one of paternalism or tutelage. Under that policy, Africans were considered to be incapable of guiding their own destinies. Thus, the colonialists controlled every aspect of African life and welfare. The Belgian Congo was administered directly from Brussels to the effect that all edicts and directives came from Brussels. The Congolese were not consulted in the administration of their own affairs. Belgian overlords felt free to interfere in the selection of African leaders in their protected States. Professor Ayittey considers that, of all Europe, the Belgians were the most contemptuous of their colonial subjects. They imposed

---

82   See EZE, *supra*, note 1, at 18.
83   See P. DAYE, LE CONGO BELGE 33 (Bruges-Paris, 1927), cited in EZE, *supra*, note 1, at 18.
84   EZE, *supra*, note 1 at 19. *See also* AYITTEY, *supra*, note 47 at 87.

the most stringent conditions on them.[85] "The African could not travel in the Congo without a permit, possess arms or drink anything stronger than beer. He could be a bishop, a journalist, an accountant, a medical assistant, a teacher, a civil servant or a druggist, but not an architect or an attorney. By the 1930s there were several lawyers in British and French West Africa, but not a single one in the Congo."[86] The reason for restricting Africans in the Congo from the study of law was because of colonial politics. Lawyers meant politics, and politics would instigate demands for political rights outlawed for the Africans.

Despite the total control that Belgium had over their African colonial subjects, the subjects were never considered citizens nor given the opportunity to become one as was done by the French. Unlike the British and the French, the Belgians did their utmost to keep their Africans subjects out of Europe, particularly out of Belgium itself. Africans in other European colonies could attend universities in Europe, but not the Congolese. Although the Belgians did not normally contemplate citizenship for Africans, if, however, it was unavoidable, citizenship was to be granted under very strict conditions. Africans had to be fully educated and acculturated before they could become Belgian citizens. In addition, Africans had to have permanent employment with Europeans before they could become *immatricules* (registered) and live under Belgian law.[87] These requirements were so rigid that only few Africans became *immatricules* under Belgian colonial policy.

C. British colonialism

The British colonial administration in Africa adopted the policy of indirect rule by which they made use of the administrative machinery that the "natives" had created. Under this system, each colony was divided into regions under regional or chief administrators, each region into provinces under provincial commissioners, and each province into districts under district commissioners. Each district consisted of one or more of the traditional states, and the day to day affairs and local ordinances were left in the hands of traditional rulers and their council of elders.[88]

---

85 AYITTEY, *supra*, note 47 at 88.
86 *Id.*
87 *Id.* at 89. The same situation prevailed in Portuguese colonies in Africa. To secure citizenship in the Portuguese colonies, the African had to be well educated, Christian and monogamous. Once the person's application was accepted and he became a Portuguese citizen, he was saved from the indignity of having to carry a passbook and was exempt from compulsory labor. Only few Africans became citizens under this policy. For example, in the Portuguese colony of Guinea, only 1,418 out of a total African population of 550,457 had become *asimilados* by 1950.
88 AYITTEY, *supra*, note 47 at 86.

According to Boahen and Webster,[89] the African chief was the instrument of local government. He appointed all local officials who were responsible to him. He or his official presided over the law courts, which, as far as possible, applied African law. His agents levied taxes for the local treasury. Part of the revenue was sent to the central government and the remainder kept for local improvements such as roads, sanitation, markets, and schools and to pay salaries of local officials.

Observers contend that two factors account for the adoption of the indirect rule policy by the British. First, in the 1860s Britain was generally reluctant to extend direct rule over territories thousands of miles away, as that would entail considerable expense. Thus, the British colonizers were apparently interested in preserving African institutions to use them as intermediaries and to minimize the cost of administering the territories that would have resulted from direct utilization of British labor.[90] Secondly, Britain was more preoccupied with its Asian Empire, particularly India, than with its African possessions, which were to be prepared for eventual self rule.[91]

While the reasons above may have accounted for the adoption of the indirect rule system, it is equally true that the practice was facilitated by the reluctance of the British to turn Africans into Britons. It was rather race related than the usual reasons given. Lord Lugard[92] alluded to the above reasoning as the essential nature of British indirect rule policy in Africa when he stated:

> Here, then, is the true conception of the interrelation of colour: complete uniformity of ideals, absolute equality in the paths of knowledge and culture, equal opportunity for those who strive, equal administration for those who achieve; in matters social and racial a separate path, each pursuing his interested traditions, preserving his own race purity and race pride; equality in things spiritual, agreed divergence in the physical and material.

For proponents of colonialism, the above statement would entail nothing but an endorsement of diversity. In the opinion of this author, there is nothing diverse about the statement. One would agree with Professor Eze in his criticism of that statement as reminiscent of the apartheid philosophy of separate but equal development in reasoning. It was founded on racist arrogance and in practice, it resulted

---

89 A. A. BOAHEN & J.B. WEBSTER, HISTORY OF WEST AFRICA 742 (New York: Praeger, 1970).
90 *See* EZE, *supra* note 2, at 18. *See* also AYITTEY, *supra* note 47, at 86.
91 *Id.*
92 Lord Lugard was the British Governor General who championed the amalgamation of Northern and Southern Protectorates of Nigeria in 1914 to form the present single entity known as Nigeria. *See* LORD LUGARD, THE DUAL MANDATE IN BRITISH TROPICAL AFRICA 5 (Hamden, Conn.: Archon Books, (1965).

in a very vertical relation between the colonizers and the colonized. It is at best antithetical to the notion of equal opportunity, and the notion of racial pride can be no other than a ruse to camouflage the basic inequality inherent in colonial imposition.[93]

In construing the British colonial policy of using African institutions, one must look at it in the light of the above argument. The African traditional chief, where this institution flourished, became a tool in the hands of the British colonizers for the main purpose of maximizing exploitation, and where it did not exist it was invented and imposed on societies that were generally not hierarchically structured. This gave the traditional chiefs a recognized status as British officials, as well as well defined tasks. There were basic negative consequences of this approach, two of which can be identified. First, despite the addition of tax collection duty on behalf of the administration to the traditional functions of the traditional chiefs, indirect rule (or any system of colonial rule for that matter) tended to conserve and reinforce the authoritarian aspect of the powers of the chiefs who frequently abused them. Their authority went beyond the limits that would have been tolerated in traditional African societies. Secondly, the imposition of colonialism derailed the dynamic evolution of African institutions that would have increasingly developed and become more democratic as a result of inevitable intercourses between various groups, notably, the emergence of the elite who would be opposed to absolute traditionalism.

As far as customary law was concerned, the British, like the French and the Belgians recognized, and provided for the application, of customary law. Essentially, the policy of the British government in respect of customary law as well as Islamic law was to use both for the purposes of local administration in so far as possible, except when they had been varied or superseded by statutes and ordinances. The courts established by the British government had the duty of enforcing the native laws and customs as part of the laws of the land, in so far as they were not barbarous.[94] Most colonial Supreme Court statutes contained provisions which prescribed two situations in which native law and custom would apply: (1) where the parties to an action were natives; (2) where neither party to a dispute had agreed to, or must be taken to have agreed, that its obligations should be regulated exclusively by some law or laws other than native customary law. It was further provided that where there was no express rule to regulate a matter

---

93 See EZE, *supra*, note 1, at 19.
94 Most of the cases decided in Nigeria in the colonial era in the context of the suitability of customary law as the law of the land applied this test. *See Oke Lanipekun and Others v. Amao Ojetunde* (1944) A.C.170. *See also Eshugbai Eleko v. Nigerian Government* (1931) A.C. 662 at 673. *See generally*, M.B. HOOKER, LEGAL PLURALISM: AN INTRODUCTION TO COLONIAL AND NEO-COLONIAL LAWS 129 (Oxford: Clarendon Press, (1975) *cited* in EZE, *supra* note 1, at 20.

in dispute, the court was to be guided by the principle of justice, equity and good conscience.[95] In addition to making a distinction between Africans and Europeans, British colonial laws also contained the so-called repugnancy clause, which was generally formulated as follows:

> Nothing in this Ordinance shall deprive the courts of the right to observe and enforce the observance, or shall deprive any person of the benefit, of any native law and custom not being repugnant to natural justice, equity or good conscience , or incompatible, either in terms or by necessary implication, with any Ordinance or any rule, regulation, order, proclamation or by-law made under any Ordinance for the time being in force in the territory.[96]

On the basis of the repugnancy doctrine, the British abolished certain customary practices considered objectionable, such as trial by ordeal, the custom of killing twins, caste systems and witchcraft.[97] In the field of family law, British colonial law accepted continuation of polygamy provided it could not be combined with other forms of marriage, such as civil marriage.

In evaluating British colonial laws, one must look at the laws in their totality in terms of their effect on the rights of the colonized people, while not dismissing their positive impact on objectionable traditional practices. The very exploitative nature of colonialism itself required a certain measure of suppression of the rights of the Africans, despite the importation of British laws into Africa. Colonial rule was essentially authoritarian and even the introduction of English law as the basis for the local legal systems did not result in the colonial subjects enjoying the full rights of liberty, due process, free speech and other rights, which the common law is said to guarantee to the English themselves. The convenient although ill-defined doctrine of indirect rule, buttressing the powers of the traditional rulers, the creation of special native courts to apply unwritten customary laws and administrative orders, the exercise of powers of political detention or deportation and use of laws of sedition and censorship framed more widely than in England, were all significant intrusions upon the rule of law which preserved English liberties.

In addition, in British colonies with white settler regimes, the denial of fundamental human rights was accentuated. The colonial administration established and maintained by means of law a governmental and social system characterized by authoritarianism and racial discrimination in such fields as the administration of

---

95 *Id.* at 102.
96 *See* Chapter 3 of Laws of Northern Rhodesia, section 17 (1954); Chapter 4 of Laws of the Gold Coast, section 74(1) (1936); Chapter 211 of Laws of Nigeria, section 19 (1948).
97 *See* C.A. Oputa, *Crime and the Nigerian Society* in T .O ELIAS, S.N. NWABARA & C.O. AKPAMGBO, AFRICAN INDIGENOUS LAWS 12 (Enugu, Nigeria: Government Printer, 1975).

justice, the development of representative institutions and agrarian administration.[98] The essentially repressive and discriminatory nature of the colonial system and its hostility to human rights is borne out by such powers as preventive detention and the restriction of the freedom of movement, conferred on the Commissioner of the East African Protectorate. Neither did the colonial legislature create adequate appeal machinery, nor were fundamental and justiciable limitations of power placed on either the legislature or executive. The legislature had a wide measure of freedom in the areas in which it could legislate and the emergency powers granted to it could only have exacerbated the denial of fundamental rights and freedoms.[99]

In comparing the different colonial policies of the different colonial powers that plundered Africa, there is the tendency to inquire into which policy was better than the other. To some scholars, the British system of indirect rule was better than the direct administration of the colonies adopted by the French and Belgians.[100] The reason for this opinion is that in the manner the various policies were carried out, indirect rule offered the dependent peoples the greatest possibilities of acquiring self-determination by constitutional means.[101]

It is not in doubt that one system of colonization would be better than the other, especially with the predicaments that the colonized peoples faced. But in the totality of things, a closer look at these policies will reveal that they had the same objectives and produced more or less similar consequences for the colonized peoples, despite whatever name they bore or philosophies under which they were formulated. With the passage of time, the various colonial powers amended their policies in manners that made the various policies similar based on the success or lack thereof in terms of particular policies that were executed in different parts of the colonies.

Colonialism had never been a good thing to any people. All colonialists were interested in exploiting the colonies. The concern was more in siphoning off their resources, and this was facilitated by various policies, irrespective of which colonial power adopted them. Differences in method of achieving this objective were based on the philosophical and historical experiences of the colonizers. The French and Belgian practice of attempting to transform Africans into Frenchmen and Belgians was only partially successful, since very few Africans became

---

98 *See* Y. GHAI & J.P.W.B. MCAUSLAN, PUBLIC LAW AND POLITICAL CHANGE IN KENYA 407-408 (Nairobi: Oxford University Press, (1970).
99 *Id.*
100 G. Padmore, *Pan-Africanism or Communism*, PRESENCE AFRICAINE,197 (1960), cited in EZE, *supra*, note 1, at 21.
101 EZE, *supra*, note 1, at 21. *See also* M. CROWTHER, WEST AFRICA UNDER COLONIAL RULE 198-199, 233-235 (London: Hutchinson, 1968).

actually assimilated into either the French or Belgian way of life.[102] The British indirect rule system on the other hand created a body of "elite" with Anglo-Saxon values, which became restless, demanding self-rule.

The argument could be made that the French and Belgians, by admitting Africans into certain levels of administration, made them less inclined to demand independence as early as did the elites in British colonies, which were excluded from direct involvement in colonial administration in favor of subdued reactionary traditional chiefs.[103] This is merely a "positive" difference between two evils. The colonial policies of the imperialists were not for the betterment of Africans. In spite of many assertions to the contrary, they were racist, and degraded Africans in many respects. All colonizers practiced forced labor, the French, and particularly the Belgians, more than the British. Freedom of movement was restricted so as to ensure the provision of cheap labor both for the administration and colonial corporations. From African perspective, attempts to extend the relevant provisions of the Treaty of Versailles,[104] which created the International Labor Organization (ILO), under which members agreed to apply to their possessions; conventions they had adopted, did not really materialize.[105] The reason for this feeling is that the colonialists, in any event, had the power to modify these objectives in accordance with local circumstances and even to decide on the issue of applicability on the basis of whether local conditions permitted it or not.[106] This feeling, however, does not undermine the effort of the ILO in adopting such conventions that were geared toward colonies for purposes of diminishing forced labor in the colonies, such as the Forced Labor Convention and the Abolition of Forced Labor Convention already mentioned, among others. The argument is that these conventions were observed in breach rather than in compliance by the colonial powers.

---

102 Nevertheless, it should be observed that the French were able to increase the number of Francophone nations, a very important issue in the competition with the Anglophones.
103 It needs to be noted however, that this was not the root cause of the independence movement. The whole humanitarian movement in opposition to colonialism as such, the emergence of socialism in opposition to capitalism, the weakening of the power base of the imperialist countries, especially after the Second World War had left them with ailing economies that required, for their revival massive external aid. Also, their failure to reassert their imperial designs in South-East Asia, coupled with the sharpening of consciousness of the colonized peoples, were the fundamental forces that led to the demise of colonialism at least in its traditional form.
104 Treaty of Versailles of 1919.
105 Article 421 of the Treaty provided that:
The members engage to apply the conventions which they have adopted in accordance with the provisions of this part of the present treaty to their colonies, protectorates and possessions which are not fully self-governing: except where owing to the local conditions the convention is inapplicable, orsubject to such modifications as may be necessary to adopt the convention to local conditions.
106 Article 421(2) of the Treaty of Versailles, *supra*, note 89.

The history of French colonialism, for example, demonstrated the futility of such expectations, as the exploitative nature of colonialism was antithetic to the objectives set forth in ILO Conventions. Other conventions adopted by the ILO and aimed at assuaging the burden of the colonies met with more or less the same fate in French colonies[107]

Furthermore, the colonies were excluded from deriving benefit from the whole movement towards the protection of human rights that had been galvanized by the League of Nations (the League) and further developed under the United Nations (UN). The Universal Declaration of Human Rights,[108] for example, while theoretically intended for the benefit of the colonized peoples and nations, was not in fact applied to check discrimination and other injustices resulting from colonialism. This was in spite of the provision of paragraph 1 of the Declaration to the effect that: "the subjection of peoples to alien domination and exploitation constitutes a denial of fundamental human rights, is contrary to the Charter of the a United Nations and is an impediment to the promotion of world peace and cooperation." As a result, some African commentators feel that it was not until the Declaration on the Granting of Independence to Colonial Countries and Territories by the UN in 1960,[109] that serious consideration was given to conditions of peoples and nations under alien domination.

The point remains that colonialism was disrespectful of African traditions and values. It relegated Africans to subservience in all fields. It arrested and destroyed the internal dynamics of the evolution of African societies. There is no doubt, that by abolishing certain objectionable traditional practices that were prevalent in pre-colonial Africa, such as human sacrifice, slavery, etc., which were carried over to colonial Africa, the colonialists did contribute to selective progressive development of human rights. But on the balance, there is no arguing the fundamental negative effects of colonialism on colonial and independent Africa. It was not only founded on racism and naked exploitation, it also denied and inhibited fundamental human rights, and was essentially against the promotion and protection of human rights in Africa. The consequences of colonialism can be seen in the high handedness and authoritarian nature of many African regimes, which have adopted the oppressive mechanisms of the colonial masters against their own people.

---

107 EZE, *supra*, note 1, at 17.
108 G.A. Res. 217A (III), U.N. Doc A/810 at 71 (1948).
109 UN G.A. Res. 1514(XV), December 14, 1960; 15 U.N. GAOR Supp. (No. 16) at 66, U.N. Doc. A/4684 (1961). *See* EZE, *supra*, note 1, at 17.

III THE UNITED NATIONS AND HUMAN RIGHTS

A. *The Charter of the United Nations*

As rightly suggested by Thomas Buergenthal and Dinah Shelton, "attention to human rights is a bright thread woven through the United Nations Charter..."[110] This attention arose as a result of the lessons drawn from the appalling atrocities of the Second World War. Thus, the peoples of the UN, determined to "reaffirm faith in fundamental human rights, in the dignity and worth of the human person, in the equal rights of men and women... have resolved to combine [their] efforts to accomplish these aims..."[111] In an effort to accomplish the aims contained in the preamble to the UN Charter, the Charter contains seven articles devoted to bringing human rights within the UN agenda.[112]

In addition to maintaining international peace and security, the UN Charter in Article 1(3) makes provision for international cooperation in solving international problems of an economic, social, cultural, or humanitarian character, and *in promoting and encouraging respect for human rights and for fundamental freedoms for all without distinction as to race, sex, language, or religion,* as one of the objectives of the United Nations.[113] (Emphasis is this author's.) Article 55 of the UN Charter complements the above purpose of the United Nations by placing obligations on both the UN and Member States which would ensure the promotion of universal respect for, and observance of, human rights and fundamental freedoms for all, without distinction as to race, sex, language, or religion.[114] Under Article 13, the General Assembly of the United Nations would initiate studies and make recommendation for the purpose of promoting as well

---

110 BUERGENTHAL THOMAS & DINAH SHELTON, PROTECTING HUMAN RIGHTS IN THE AMERICAS: CASES AND MATERIALS 17 (International Institute of Human Rights, Strasbourg/N.P. Engel, Fourth Revised Edition, 1995). In context, *See* generally THE UNITED NATIONS AND HUMAN RIGHTS: A CRITICAL APPRAISAL (PHILIP ALSTON, ed., Oxford: Clarendon Press, 1992); AN INTRODUCTION TO THE INTERNATIONAL PROTECTION OF HUMAN RIGHTS: A TEXT BOOK (RAIJA HANSKI & MARKU SUKSI, eds., Tarku/Abo, Finland: Institute for Human Rights, Abo Akademi University, 1997); UNITED NATIONS, UNITED NATIONS IN THE FIELD OF HUMAN RIGHTS (New York: United Nations, 1994); THE UNIVERSAL DECLARATION OF HUMAN RIGHTS: A COMMENTARY (ASBJORN EIDE, *et al* eds., Oslo: Scandinavian University Press, 1992).
111 Second Paragraph of the Preamble to the United Nations Charter.
112 *See* Articles 1, 13, 55, 56, 62, 68 and 76 of the United Nations Charter.
113 On the objectives or purposes of the United Nations, *see* generally LELAND GOODRICH & EDWARD HAMBRO, CHARTER OF THE UNITED NATIONS: COMMENTARY AND DOCUMENTS 22-23, 85-121 (Boston: World Peace Foundation, 1949); LELAND GOODRICH, THE UNITED NATIONS (New York: Thomas Crowell Company, 1959).
114 Article 55(c) of the United Nations Charter.

as realizing, *inter alia*, human rights and fundamental freedoms.[115] The obligations assumed by State Parties to the UN Charter under Article 55 would in turn be realized by those States under Article 56, pledging themselves to take joint and separate action with the United Nations for the achievement of the purposes set forth in the said Article 55.

Apart from direct provisions affecting the UN and States Parties to the Charter, the Charter also makes provisions directed at institutions of the UN along the same line of promotion of human rights and fundamental freedoms. In this vein, Article 62 of the Charter gives the Economic and Social Council (ECOSOC) the discretion to make recommendations for the purpose of promoting respect for, and observance of, human rights and fundamental freedom for all.[116] Also, in instituting the trusteeship system under the UN, Article 76 makes provision for the basic objectives of the system, one of which is to encourage respect for human rights and for fundamental freedoms for all without distinction as to race, sex, language, or religion.[117]

From the provisions of the UN Charter on human rights it has become accepted in international law that States which engage in a consistent pattern of gross violations of human rights are in violation of the obligations enshrined in the Charter.[118] This interpretation would not have been possible under the predecessor of the Charter, the Covenant of the League of Nations, which was entirely

---

115 Article 13(b) of the United Nations Charter.
116 Article 62(2) of the United Nations Charter.
117 Article 76(c) of the United Nations Charter. According to Drzewicki, it is debatable, however, whether the trusteeship system really advanced the human rights of the subjects of the trust, especially in Africa where the system culminated in systematic colonialism. *See*, Kryzysztof Drzewicki, *The United Nations Charter and the Universal Declaration of Human Rights* in AN INTRODUCTION TO THE INTERNATIONAL PROTECTION OF HUMAN RIGHTS: A TEXT BOOK 65, at 68 (RAIJA HANSKI & MARKU SUKSI, eds., Tarku/Abo, Finland: Institute for Human Rights, Abo Akademi University, 1997). African scholars, including this author, also hold the above sentiment. This position, it may be argued, does not to take into consideration, the efforts made by the Trusteeship Council and the General Assembly of the UN.(GA) to the effect, that the Trusteeship Council and to some extent, the General Assembly considered the annual reports of each administering authority and the petitions by the inhabitants of the trust territories; and the fact that in addition, missions were sent to examine the situation when some problems required it. In the same vein, these bodies are credited to have continuously insisted that the administrative authority in the territories should promote the political, economic, social and educational advancement of the inhabitants, as well as their progressive development towards self-government or independence, the result of which was that the trust territories in Africa were the first African countries to become independent and to establish a more democratic system of government before the others. While the said efforts were made by the Trusteeship Council and the General Assembly, and as such, should be recognized, the issue is whether the trusteeship system was not an acceptance of colonialism in another form.
118 *See* BUERGENTHAL & SHELTON, *supra*, note 110, at 18.

silent on human rights issues.[119] The Charter thus set human rights in the forefront of international law despite the perception of some that it was a compromise document of the San Francisco Conference of 1945 with human rights clauses that show signs of ambivalence and vagueness.[120]

Considering the period of time in question it is significant that the Charter conferred on human rights the rank of a long-term and constant objective of the UN, rather than an *ad hoc* arrangement. The Charter assumes in essence a permanent and dynamic attitude on the part of the UN and its members towards respect for human rights. It creates innovative approaches in its human rights provisions. The human rights provisions are formulated in an independent context as one of the prerequisites for ensuring international peace and security, friendly relations among nations, welfare of peoples and other socioeconomic objectives.[121] Human rights were thus placed against a background of political, economic and social aspects as envisaged under Articles 55 and 56 of the Charter. It has been observed that while the relationship between peace, development and human rights may not be an entirely new concept, it lifts the interdependence between the concepts to the level of the primary purposes of the UN.[122] That is, obligations of international cooperation for the achievement of the values of international peace and security, friendly relations among nations, welfare of peoples, human rights etc., created a normative framework and potentials for further joint and separate actions by the United Nation and member States.

It is not in doubt that the UN Charter set the stage for the internationalization of human rights, with its lofty statements on human rights. The Charter has, however, been criticized in its upholding of double standards in dealing with colonialism. For some commentators, the provision for the trusteeship arrangement was nothing but a reflection of that double standard by the colonial powers, which designed the arrangement.[123] It was nothing but colonialism in disguise. Despite

---

119 *See, Drzewicki, supra*, note 117, at 67.
120 *Id.* It must however, be observed that the compromise at San Francisco was not to include weak provisions on human rights in the UN Charter. It is evident that the Charter conferred on human rights the rank not of an *ad hoc*, but of a long-term and constant objective of the U.N. The compromise at San Francisco was rather that there was no time to prepare an International Bill of Rights, but that a special commission for the promotion of human rights would be promptly established by the Economic and Social Council (ECOSOC) under Article 68 of the Charter. This arrangement was followed by ECOSOC, which as its first act, established the Commission on Human Rights to start the drafting of the human rights instruments. It went to work, drafting the Bill of Rights, and finished the Universal Declaration in two years, a feat for that kind of record.
121 *See, Drzewicki, supra*, note 117, at 68.
122 *Id.*, citing NORMAN BENTWICH & ANDREW MARTIN, A COMMENTARY ON THE CHARTER OF THE UNITED NATIONS 116-117 (London: Routledge and Kegan Paul Ltd., 1950).
123 *See, Drzewicki, supra*, note 117, at 68.

the seeming success of the arrangement in "helping African" countries under it to gain independence and democratic governance, as already alluded to,[124] from the African perspective, the trusteeship arrangement in Africa proved disastrous in terms of promotion and respect for human rights as another form of colonialism, contrary to the injunction under Article 76 of the UN Charter.[125]

Other areas of the human rights provisions of the Charter, in which some international law scholars have noticed several deficiencies, include the lack of definition for the terms "human rights" and "fundamental freedoms", and the lack of specific provisions under the Charter for any machinery to be used to secure their observance. According to an early statement credited to Brierly[126] the absence of a definition of human rights and freedoms greatly weakened the legal content of the Charter clauses dealing with human rights. While it would have helped had the Charter contained appropriate definitions, the lack of it does not in itself weaken the Charter as today's evidence in terms of the content of subject has shown.[127] The seeming lack of definition in the Charter may have turned out to be a blessing in disguise in the face of the elaborate definition as to content contained in the Universal Declaration of Human Rights,[128] the International Covenants and other instruments, including the establishment of conventional and extra-conventional monitoring procedures. Thus, it was good that the compromise at San Francisco was arrived at. It may be that the elaborate content of rights that we have today would not have been easily agreed upon, had the UN Charter contained definition of rights from the beginning.

The Charter has also been criticized as containing human rights clauses, which though are part of a binding treaty, are somewhat general, cautious and open ended in the manner they were drafted.[129] This was attributed to the prohibition of

---

124 *See supra*, note 117.
125 It is worth noting that only two African countries were at the San Francisco conference for the signing of the UN Charter on June 24, 1945 as de facto independent states, namely Ethiopia and Liberia. They remained the only African member states of the UN when the Charter entered into force in October the same year. Africa was thus, still heavily under colonial rule and could not have done anything regarding the trusteeship arrangement in addition to colonialism.
126 *See* J. L. BRIERLY, THE LAW OF NATIONS: AN INTRODUCTION TO THE INTERNATIONAL LAW OF PEACE 293-295 (Sixth Edition, Oxford: Clarendon Press, 1963), *reprinted in Drzewicki, supra*, note 117, at 68, foot note 8.
127 As already indicated, it must be pointed out that the UN Charter was not intended to deal with the specific contents of human rights. That was to be done later as part of the compromise at San Francisco. *See supra*, note 120.
128 G.A. Res. 217A (III), U.N. Doc A/810 at 71 (1948).
129 *See Drzewicki, supra*, note 117, at 69. The learned author argues that it is no coincidence that the Charter contains such terms as "promoting", "encouraging" and "assisting in the realization of", instead of tougher terms like "protecting", "maintaining", "safeguarding" or "guaranteeing" human rights and fundamental freedoms.

intervention by the UN in matters which are essentially within domestic jurisdiction of Member States contained in Article 2(7).[130] The tendency was to interpret this provision as precluding inquiry into a State's human rights practice, since that would fall into matters within the domestic jurisdiction of States. South Africa used this interpretation in challenging criticisms of its obnoxious apartheid policy. The UN, however, decided early that the very discussion, study, inquiry, making recommendations on human rights problems, or outright rejection of a State's human rights practice does not constitute an intervention in the sense of Article 2.[131] This early decision of the UN was based on the premise that the very fact that human rights are listed so many times in the Charter, is a proof that a violation of human rights is a matter with which the UN can deal.

While there may be apparent deficiencies in the human rights clauses of the UN Charter, they remain the center piece and foundation of international human rights debate from which all other instruments would draw inspiration. More importantly, looking at the practice of the UN in the last fifty years, one can legitimately conclude that human rights have gained a permanent place among players in the international community. The concept continues to be dynamic requiring unavoidable and profound adjustments and reforms.

B. The Universal Declaration of Human Rights

The lack of a definition of the human rights concept in the United Nations Charter was largely remedied and satisfied with the adoption of the Universal Declaration of Human Rights. The adoption of the Declaration is said to have been envisaged as the first item on the United Nations agenda in its program of constituting an International Bill of Human Rights.[132] The UN Human Rights Commission was mandated to organize and prepare the Declaration. The Commission began its work in 1947 with its drafting committee chaired by Mrs. Eleanor Roosevelt. The Declaration was adopted by the UN General Assembly on December 10, 1948.[133]

---

130 *Id.*
131 LELAND GOODRICH AND EDVARD HAMBRO, CHARTER OF THE UNITED NATIONS: COMMENTARY AND DOCUMENTS 110-121 (Boston: World Peace Foundation, 1949), *cited* in Drzewicki, *supra*, note 117, at 69.
132 *See* LELAND GOODRICH, THE UNITED NATIONS 247-250 (New York: Thomas Crowell Company, 1959).
133 U. N. G.A. Res. 217 (III 1948). The Declaration was adopted by forty-eight votes in favor, eight absentions, comprising Byelorussia, the former Czechoslovakia, Poland, Saudi Arabia, South Africa, Ukraine, the former USSR and former Yugoslavia, and no vote against. For more on the legislative history of the Declaration, *see Jakob Moller, The Universal Declaration of Human Rights: How the Process Started* in THE UNIVERSAL DECLARATION OF HUMAN RIGHTS: A COMMENTARY

Apart from the preamble which reaffirms the commitment to the promotion of human rights at national and international levels, the Declaration contains an affirmation of the philosophical foundations of human rights and the general principles that play a crucial role in the whole of human rights law.[134] The Declaration makes provision for substantial rights from Article 3 to 21. These rights include civil and political rights, as well as social, economic and cultural rights. Under civil and political rights are the right to life, liberty and security, freedom from slavery and servitude, freedom from torture and inhuman treatment or punishment, the right to recognition as a person before the law, freedom from arbitrary arrest, detention or exile. Included also are the right to equal protection of the law, the right to an effective remedy, the right to a fair trial, the right to freedom of movement and residence, the right to nationality, freedom of thought and conscience and religion, freedom of opinion and expression, freedom of assembly and association, the right to own property, the right to participate in the government of one's country, etc.

As regards economic, social and cultural rights, the Declaration contains the right to education, social security, right to work, right to protection against unemployment, right to equal pay, right to reasonable hours of work, right to adequate standard of living, right to rest and leisure and right to participate in cultural life. It is argued that this modest list of socio-economic rights was a consequence of the controversies about their legal character.[135] On the other hand, their incorporation, however, constitutes a substantial innovation in modern international law of human rights.[136]

The Declaration under Article 29(2) recognizes the possibility of States limiting its provisions by law, but "solely for the purpose of securing due recognition and respect for the rights and freedom of others and of meeting the just requirements of morality, public order and the general welfare in a democratic society." This

---

(ASBJORN EIDE, *et al* eds., Oslo: Scandinavian University Press, 1992). *See also* ARTHUR ROBERTSON & JOHN MERRILS, HUMAN RIGHTS IN THE WORLD: AN INTRODUCTION TO THE STUDY OF THE INTERNATIONAL PROTECTION OF HUMAN RIGHTS 25-26 (Third Edition, Manchester: Manchester University Press, 1992).

134 *See* Articles 1-3 of the Declaration. *See also* Articles 28-29.
135 *See* Drzewicki, *supra*, note 117, at 73.
136 *Id.* The controversy as to the legal character of economic, social and cultural rights is a continuing one. Some international legal scholars are of the view that they are not realizable in the same way that civil and political rights are. The flow of the argument recognizes the different legal and political orientations of the commentators. Scholars from developed countries with market economy lay more emphasis on civil and political rights, while those from developing countries, with some form of controlled economies stress the need for the realization of economic, social and cultural rights. The bottom line of the argument should be that both forms of rights complement each other in terms of their tangible nature. The argument should not be oversimplified to the extent of discountenancing one form of rights in its entirety.

provision is aimed at keeping a balance in society, which every democratic society should be allowed to do for good reasons. It should not be a basis for States to engage in flagrant limitation of the rights contained in the Declaration. Article 29(3) adequately addresses this point as "nothing in the Declaration may be interpreted as implying for any States, group or persons any right to engage in any activity or to perform any act aimed at the destruction of any of the rights and freedoms set forth" in the Declaration.

The question may be asked as to the legal status and character of the Universal Declaration of Human Rights. The Declaration was adopted as a resolution of the UN General Assembly; so it is not a treaty, which is subject to ratification or adherence, and thus was originally considered not legally binding by virtue of being a "mere declaration." Many scholars, however, believe that the Declaration has over the years acquired a binding character. Proponents of this view, argue for its status as customary international law, if not in its entirety, at least some of its provisions.[137] They attribute this character of the Declaration to its repeated invocation over more than fifty years by the UN and other international organizations, its use in diplomatic exchanges between governments, its incorporation into treaties and national constitutions, and its application by national and international tribunals.[138]

Opponents of the above view on the other hand, submit that the establishment of a customary international legal rule requires the existence of general, uniform and consistent practice by States followed by the emergence of an *opinio juris* (conviction of belief by States in the obligatory character of such practice).[139] To these scholars, the practice of world-wide violations of human rights before and after 1948 contradicts the above requirements of general, uniform and consistent practice by States. In other words, for a formation of custom the decisive factor is the actual practice and not lofty statements by governments, often colored with hypocrisy. Thus, what is important are the deeds not the words of government.

While there may be some merit in the opposing view point on the level of the normative value of the Universal Declaration, the whole argument is reduced to unnecessary academic exercise in the face of how important the Declaration has proved to be over the years. By the adoption of the Declaration, Member States

---

137 THOMAS BUERGENTHAL & DINAH SHELTON, *supra*, note 110, at 19. *See also, Kiss Alexandre, The Role of the Universal Declaration of Human Rights in the Development of International Law* in UNITED NATIONS, BULLETIN OF HUMAN RIGHTS: SPECIAL ISSUE: FORTIETH ANNIVERSARY OF THE UNIVERSAL DECLARATION OF HUMAN RIGHTS 47-52 (New York: United Nations, 1988). Kiss argues that the principles proclaimed in the Universal Declaration have a rank of higher rules.
138 THOMAS BUERGENTHAL & DINAH SHELTON, *supra* note 110, at 19.
139 MARTIN DIXON, TEXT BOOK ON INTERNATIONAL LAW 24-33 (Second Edition, London: Blackstone Press Limited, 1993).

CHAPTER 1 37

of the United Nations have made a political commitment to implement the rights contained in it. The importance of the Declaration in terms of its legal and political significance may be illustrated by several developments and tangible achievements. This author would agree with Dixon[140] that the precise effect of the Declaration was to urge States to establish procedures for future protection of human rights. The Declaration achieved this feature as a universally accepted normative reference system which permeated the domestic legal systems of numerous States by the incorporation of its provisions into national constitutions and other legislative instruments.[141]

The Declaration constitutes the first internationally adopted catalogue of human rights which sets a common standard of achievement for all peoples and all nations.[142] In the form the rights are catalogued, the Declaration became the defining instrument of human rights, making up for the definition which was lacking in the UN Charter. It therefore set the stage for further international law making in the field of human rights.[143] A good evidence of this is the influence it had on the International Covenant on Civil and Political Rights which was adopted in 1966, and the impact it exerted on other human rights instruments adopted within the United Nations and by regional organizations. This impact may be identified not only in explicit references to the Declaration, usually contained in preambles, but in the formulation of specific rights and freedoms. All in all, the Declaration opened the way for what may be regarded as the codification and progressive development of international human rights law.[144] The inspirational role of the Universal Declaration has not been exhausted. In fact, it cannot be exhausted. In the opinion of this author, the Declaration has acquired the status of custom as far as international human rights law goes.

---

140 *Id.* at 279.
141 For example, several African States which later became independent adopted the rights enshrined in the Declarations into their constitutions. So also was the case regarding some of the new European democracies.
142 *See Drzewicki, supra,* note 117, at 75.
143 *Id.*
144 *Id.*

C. *Other un Human Rights Instruments and Organs*[145]

The pioneering effort of the United Nations in global recognition of human rights culminated in a series of international instruments aimed at continuing definition of the contents of the human rights concept in addition to the Universal Declaration of Human Rights. Notable among these instruments are the International Covenant for Civil and Political Rights (ICCPR)[146] and the International Covenant on Economic, Social and Cultural Rights (ICESCR).[147] These two Covenants together with the Universal Declaration for Human Rights make up the International Bill of Human Rights. While the rights contained in these covenants cannot be said to be exactly the same as those contained in the Universal Declaration, it is true that the two covenants mirror the Universal Declaration, making necessary adjustments in terms of what Member States were ready to bind themselves with.[148] This is because the Covenants are treaties, and as such establish binding obligations on their States Parties. The Universal Declaration on the other hand, was a statement of global aspiration on the progressive development of international human rights. While only States Parties are bound by the Covenants, the Declaration by now binds all States, many of which have incorporated it into their constitutions. Similarly, the rights contained in the ICESCR are longer and more elaborate than those contained in the Universal Declaration. The Covenant is thus more comprehensive in defining economic, social and cultural rights, and makes provision for the progressive realization of those rights.

The ICCPR did not only make detailed provisions as to what constitutes civil and political rights, it also established the Human Rights Committee as a super-

---

145 *See* Generally, THE UNITED NATIONS AND HUMAN RIGHTS: A CRITICAL APPRAISAL, *supra*, note 110.; J. HUMPHREY, HUMAN RIGHTS AND THE UNITED NATIONS: A GREAT ADVENTURE (1984); D. MCGOLDRICK, THE HUMAN RIGHTS COMMITTEE: ITS ROLE IN THE DEVELOPMENT OF THE INTERNATIONAL COVENANT ON CIVIL AND POLITICAL RIGHTS (1991).
146 999 U.N.T.S. 171. Adopted by the UN General Assembly at New York on December 16, 1966. G.A.Res. 2200. The Covenant entered into force on March 23, 1976. The Covenant is supplemented by the two Optional Protocols: The First Optional Protocol entered into force in 1976. This Protocol creates an individual petition procedure under the mechanism established by the Covenant. The Second Optional Protocol which aims at abolishing the death penalty was adopted on December 15, 1989. It entered into force on July 11, 1991.
147 993 U.N.T.S. 3. Adopted by the U.N. General Assembly at New York on December 16, 1966. Annex to G.A. Res. 2200. Entered into force on January 3, 1976.
148 The Covenant on Civil and Political Rights, for example, contains guarantees of freedom from imprisonment for debt, the right to humane treatment of detainees, and certain rights of the child not contained in the Universal Declaration. The right to own property, the right to seek and enjoy asylum, as well as the right to a nationality are not mentioned in the Covenant on Civil and Political Rights. There is an introduction of a derogation clause in the Civil and Political Rights Covenant, which would permit state parties to suspend many of the rights during "public emergency that threatens the life of a nation" as contained in Article 4 of the ICCPR.

visory mechanism to monitor compliance of Member States with obligations under the Covenant.[149] The Committee comprises eighteen members, who are independent experts nominated and elected by the States Parties to the Covenant. The Committee supervises State compliance with the Covenant by reviewing and commenting on periodic reports which must be filed by States Parties, by administering an optional inter-State complaint mechanism provided for in the Covenant, and by considering individual petitions submitted pursuant to the First Optional Protocol to the ICCPR.[150] In the exercise of its functions, the Committee has evolved practices, such as interim measures, which make the individual petition system work, and the issuance of General Comments, which provide a commentary, as well as serve as authoritative interpretations of the ICCPR provisions.[151]

The supervisory mechanism for the ICESCR is the Committee on Economic, Social and Cultural Rights. Although both the ICCPR and the ICESCR came into force in 1976, and the Human Rights Committee came into existence the following year, it was not until 1986 that the Economic and Social Council (ECOSOC) of the UN created the Committee on Economic, Social and Cultural Rights.[152] The reasons for the delay in establishing the Committee on Economic, Social and Cultural rights are obvious. First, unlike the Human Rights Committee, which was directly provided for under the ICCPR, the ICESCR did not provide for any supervisory mechanism on the level of the Human Rights Committee. Second, the debate as to the tangibility, and doubts whether economic, social and cultural

---

149 *See* generally Articles 28 to 45 of the ICCPR on the establishment, composition, functions, etc. of the Human Rights Committee.
150 *See* BUERGENTHAL & SHELTON, *supra*, note 110, at 19. *See* also *Torkel Opsahl, The Human Rights Committee* in THE UNITED NATIONS AND HUMAN RIGHTS: A CRITICAL APPRAISAL 369-443 (PHILIP ALSTON ed. Oxford: Clarendon Press, 1992). For a specific and more comprehensive work on the Committee, *see* D. MCGOLDRICK, THE HUMAN RIGHTS COMMITTEE: ITS ROLE IN THE DEVELOPMENT OF THE INTERNATIONAL COVENANT ON CIVIL AND POLITICAL RIGHTS, *supra*, note 145; MANFRED NOVAK, UN COVENANT ON CIVIL AND POLITICAL RIGHTS: COMMENTARY (N. P. ENGEL, 1993); P. R. GHANDHI, THE HUMAN RIGHTS COMMITTEE AND THE RIGHT OF INDIVIDUAL COMMUNICATION: LAW AND PRACTICE, (Aldershot: Ashgate Publishing, Ltd., 1998).
151 *Id.* BUERGENTHAL & SHELTON, *supra*, note 110, at 20.
152 *Philip Alston, The Committee on Economic, Social and Cultural Rights* in THE UNITED NATIONS AND HUMAN RIGHTS: A CRITICAL APPRAISAL 473-508, at 473 (PHILIP ALSTON ed. Oxford: Clarendon Press, 1992). The Committee was established by virtue of ESC Res. 1985/17. The Committee held its first session in 1987. *See* also generally, ASBJORN EIDE, CATARINA KRAUSE AND ALLAN ROSAS (eds.), ECONOMIC, SOCIAL AND CULTURAL RIGHTS: A TEXT BOOK (Dordrecht: Martinus Nijhoff Publishers, 1995); MATHEW C. R. CRAVEN, THE INTERNATIONAL COVENANT ON ECONOMIC, SOCIAL, AND CULTURAL RIGHTS: A PERSPECTIVE ON ITS DEVELOPMENT (Oxford: Clarendon Press, 1995); THE RIGHT TO COMPLAIN ABOUT ECONOMIC, SOCIAL AND CULTURAL RIGHTS (FONS COOMANS AND VAN HOOF, eds., Utrecht: The Netherlands Institute of Human Rights, 1995).

rights were realizable, affected Member States' willingness to establish such a supervisory body. The supervision of compliance with the provisions of the ICESCR was thus left at the level of ECOSOC.[153] ECOSOC's attempt at carrying on this function culminated in a series of thoroughly ineffectual monitoring by a succession of working groups nominally set up, as part of the Council's own machinery.[154] Despite the late coming of the Committee on Economic, Social and Cultural Rights, it has succeeded in evolving a set of procedures which goes beyond copying the Human Rights Committee or a replication of the procedures followed by other UN treaty bodies. Just like the Human Rights Committee, the Economic, Social and Cultural Rights Committee examines States Parties' reports and issues General Comments, which among other things, are aimed at laying down some solid foundations for future development of jurisprudence in the area of economic, social and cultural rights.[155]

Apart from the Universal Declaration, the ICCPR, and the ICESCR, there are other numerous global human rights and humanitarian treaties and instruments under the auspices of the UN. Among these treaties are: Convention on the Prevention and Punishment of the Crime of Genocide,[156] International Convention on the Elimination of All Forms of Racial Discrimination,[157] Convention on the Elimination of all Forms of Discrimination Against Women,[158] Convention Against Torture and Other Cruel, Inhuman or Degrading Treatment or Punishment,[159] Convention on the Rights of the Child,[160] etc. Some of these instru-

---

153 *See* Articles 16 – 22 of the ICESCR.
154 *Philip Alston, The Committee on Economic, Social and Cultural Rights, supra,* note 152, at 473.
155 *Id.* at 494. For example, the third General Comments contained in the Report of the Fifth Session (U.N. DOC. E/1991/23/ANNEX VI) provides an explicit clarification by the Committee on the nature of States Parties' obligations, with particular reference to Article 2(1) of the ICESCR. The Comments note that the Covenant imposes various obligations which are of immediate effect, contrary to the assertions of those who argue that the Covenant is wholly aspirational. The committee singles out two such obligations: the non-discrimination provisions and the undertaking to "take steps". The Committee is of the view regarding the latter that appropriate steps "must be taken within a reasonably short time after the Covenant's entry into force for States concerned" and that they should be "deliberate, concrete and targeted as clearly as possible towards meeting the obligations recognized in the Covenant.
156 78 U.N.T.S. 277. Adopted by the UN General Assembly on December 9, 1948. G.A.RES. 260 A (III). The Convention entered into force on January 12, 1951.
157 5 I.L.M.352 (1966) Done at New York on January 7, 1966, and entered into force on January 4, 1969.
158 19 I.L.M. 33 (1980). Adopted by the UN General Assembly on December 18, 1979. G.A. RES.280. The Convention entered into force on September 3, 1981.
159 24 I.L.M. 1027(1984), as modified, 24 I.L.M. 535 (1985). The Convention was adopted without a vote by the General Assembly of the United Nations on December 10, 1984. The Convention entered into force on June 26, 1987.

ments, apart from the Genocide Convention,[161] have supervisory and implementation mechanisms to ensure compliance with Member States obligations under them.

Human rights under the auspices of the UN also permeated the activities of its specialized agencies, which though operate under their own instruments and constitutions have objectives that take human rights issues into account. Such agencies include, the International Labour Organization, (ILO), the World Health Organization (WHO), the United Nations Educational, Scientific and Cultural Organization (UNESCO), The United Nations High Commissioner for Refugees (UNHCR), The Food and Agricultural Organizations (FAO), and to some practical extent, the World Bank and the International Monetary Fund (IMF).[162] Of these agencies the ILO and UNESCO are known to have developed enforcement procedures that extend to their human rights objectives.[163] From the inception of the ILO in 1919 through 1946 when its constitution was revised to the present, its primary purpose included improving working conditions, living standards and equitable

---

160 28 I.L.M. 1448 (1989). Adopted by the UN General Assembly on November 28, 1989, and entered into force on September 2, 19990. All the above UN instruments have been published by the United Nations Human Rights Center in HUMAN RIGHTS: A COMPILATION OF DOCUMENTS, UN Doc.ST/HR 1/HR Rev. 5, parts 1 & 2 (1994).

161 Punishment under the Convention is left with national courts. It is worth noting that with the creation of the *ad hoc* tribunals for the former Yugoslavia and Rwanda by the UN Security Council in 1993, genocide was extended as part of the jurisdiction of the Rwanda tribunal in 1994. Under Article 5 of the Statute of the proposed International Criminal Court adopted in Rome on July 17, 1998, the jurisdiction of the court would include the crime of genocide; crimes against humanity; war crimes and the crime of aggression. Articles 6, 7 and 8 define genocide, crimes against humanity and war crimes, respectively.

162 The Articles of Agreement of the World Bank and the IMF do not per se have human rights as an objective of the agencies. Practically speaking, the agencies now take human rights issues into consideration in their dealings with member countries. They now emphasize legal and judicial reforms that will enhance the rule of law as an incident of good governance. They also encourage the promotion of "economic and social human rights" which play a catalytic role in creating conditions in which all basic rights can develop and flourish. For more discussions on the role of the World Bank in human rights, *see* IBRAHIM SHIHATA, THE WORLD BANK IN A CHANGING WORLD 133 (Dordrecht: Martinus Nijhoff Publishers, 1991). *See* also *Sigrun I. Skogly, The Position of the World Bank and the International Monetary Fund in the Human Rights Field* in AN INTRODUCTION TO THE INTERNATIONAL PROTECTION OF HUMAN RIGHTS: A TEXT BOOK 193-205 at 195; KATRINA TOMASEVSKI, DEVELOPMENT AID AND HUMAN RIGHTS REVISITED (London: Pinter Publishers, 1993); *Katrina Tomasevski, The World Bank and Human Rights* in HUMAN RIGHTS IN DEVELOPING COUNTRIES: YEARBOOK 75-102 (MANFRED NOVAK & THERESA SWINEHART, eds., Kehl: N.P. Engel Publishers, 1989).

163 *See* BUERGENTHAL & SHELTON, *supra*, note 110 at 24, *citing* N. Valticos, *The International Labour Organization* in THE EFFECTIVENESS OF INTERNATIONAL DECISIONS 134 (S. SCHWEBEL ed., 1971); V.Y.GHEBALI, THE INTERNATIONAL LABOUR ORGANIZATION: A CASE STUDY ON THE EVOLUTION OF U.N. SPECIALIZED AGENCIES, *supra*, note 72.; E.A. LANDY, THE EFFECTIVENESS OF INTERNATIONAL SUPERVISION: THIRTY YEARS OF ILO EXPERIENCE (1966).

treatment of workers.[164] In its effort to pursue the realization of these objectives, the ILO has developed a considerable body of law, with more than 160 labor conventions, and effective international supervisory machinery to monitor compliance with its standards.[165] Similarly, the UNESCO has made significant strides in its effort to promote human rights within its mandate of science, culture and education. This it did by establishing a procedure in the 1970s aimed at considering communications that allege human rights violations affecting its mandate.[166]

The importance of human rights in the UN system became more emphasized when the office of the High Commissioner for Human Rights was established in 1994.[167] This development was due to the major impetus this much needed office received at the 1993 Vienna World Conference on Human Rights, having been in the works since the 1950s. The occupant of the position is designated the UN official with principal responsibility for UN human rights activities under the office of the Secretary General of the UN,[168] with a broad mandate to prevent the violation of human rights and to ensure their protection. With less than seven years of existence, it may be too early to evaluate the success of that office. The creation of the office no doubt puts human rights close to the center stage of the UN agenda, and at par with humanitarian issues as well as international peace and security.

---

164 The scope of the ILO was greatly enlarged in 1944 by the Philadelphia Declaration. The Declaration was annexed to the revised ILO Constitution of 1946. This revision culminated in the substitution of the "general principles" of 1919 with the principles contained in the Declaration. The Declaration now constitutes the charter of ILO's aims and objectives. *See* M. HUDSON, INTERNATIONAL LEGISLATION, 124, 743 at 770 (New York: Oceana Publications, 1970); GHEBALI, *supra*, note 72, at 61.

165 BUERGENTHAL & SHELTON, *supra*, note 110 at 24. *See also Klaus Samson, The Standard-Setting and Supervisory System of the International Labour Organization* in AN INTRODUCTION TO THE INTERNATIONAL PROTECTION OF HUMAN RIGHTS: A TEXT BOOK, *supra* note 149 (RAIJA HANSKI & MARKU SUKSI, eds., Tarku/Abo, Finland: Institute for Human Rights, Abo Akademi University, 1997); N. VALTICOS & G. VON POTOBSKY, *supra*, note 72.

166 BUERGENTHAL & SHELTON, *supra*, note 110, at 24, also *citing Philip Alston, UNESCO Procedure For Dealing With Human Rights Violations* 20 SANTA CLARA L. REV. 665 (1980), and *S. Marks, The Complaint Procedure of the United Nations Educational, Scientific and Cultural Organization* in H. HANUM, GUIDE TO INTERNATIONAL HUMAN RIGHTS PRACTICE 86 (2nd ed., 1992). *See also Fons Coomans, UNESCO and Human Rights* in AN INTRODUCTION TO THE INTERNATIONAL PROTECTION OF HUMAN RIGHTS: A TEXT BOOK 181 ((RAIJA HANSKI & MARKU SUKSI, eds., Tarku/Abo, Finland: Institute for Human Rights, Abo Akademi University, 1997); David *Weissbrodt and Rose Farley, The UNESCO Human Rights Procedure: An Evaluation*, 16 HUM. RTS. Q. 391-415 (1994).

167 UN G.A. RES. 48/141 of January 14, 1994.

168 UN G.A. RES. 48/148(94). For a detailed history of the office of the UN High Commissioner for Human Rights (UNHCHR), *see generally, Janet E. Lord, The United Nations High Commissioner for Human Rights: Challenges and Opportunities*, 17 LOY. L.A. INT. & COMP. L. J.329 at 330.

The UN human rights initiatives are relevant to Africa in many ways. The Organization of African Unity in the preamble to its Charter reaffirmed the adherence of African Nations to the UN Charter and the Universal Declaration of Human Rights with the conviction that the principles contained in those instruments "provide a solid foundation for peaceful and positive cooperation among States."[169] Additionally, not only are all African nations now members of the UN compared to only two African states, Ethiopia and Liberia in 1948 and 41 in 1969;[170] many African countries, apart from ratifying the UN Charter, have either signed or ratified various UN human rights instruments. Their ratification of the UN Charter has been often followed by inserting the Universal Declaration in their constitutions, and ratifying the Covenants.

IV. OTHER REGIONAL HUMAN RIGHTS SYSTEMS

Notwithstanding that this book focuses on the African human rights mechanism, it is quite instructive to introduce, albeit in summary, the two regional human rights regimes that preceded the African system in regional protection of human rights. These regimes are relevant to the African system. While the African system may not mimic them, it could be inspired by the jurisprudence they have developed over a longer period of time, and the legal framework they have put in place. These regimes are also of comparative importance in the study of regional protection of human rights in light of the fact that regional human rights jurisprudence derives from general international human rights principles.

A. *The European System*

The European human rights system has come a long way. This system produced the first regional human rights mechanism,[171] and it is the latest to be sub-

---

[169] *See* ZDENEK CERVENKA, THE ORGANIZATION OF AFRICAN UNITY AND ITS CHARTER 102 (New York: Frederick A. Praeger, Publishers, 1968).

[170] *Id.*

[171] The European Convention for the Protection of Human Rights and Fundamental Freedoms, 1950, commonly known and hereinafter referred to as the European Convention on Human Rights (the European Convention). The original text of the Convention is published in 312 U.N.T.S. 221. It has been variously amended by subsequent Protocols. The latest of these protocols is Protocol 11, which abolished the two-tier control mechanism: the European Commission on Human Rights and the European Court of Human Rights, and replaced it with a single European Court of human rights. Under Protocol 11, provisions of Articles 1-18 of the original text of the European Convention, which cover substantive rights remain unchanged. The Protocol, however, replaced the text of

stantially reformed with regard to its control mechanism.[172] After the founding of the Council of Europe in 1949, Member States of the Council took a major step in realizing one of the principal objectives[173] of the organization by drafting, and adopting the Convention for the Protection of Human Rights and Fundamental Freedoms on November 4, 1950. The Convention came into force on September 3, 1953 and has virtually been ratified by all members of the Council.

Building on the aspirations contained in the Universal Declaration of Human Rights, the Convention represents a collective guarantee in European context of a number of principles set out in the Declaration. This guarantee is accordingly supported by an international judicial machinery making decisions that must be accepted by Contracting States.[174] It has been observed that the most important and original feature of the European Convention is the system it established for the protection of the human rights guaranteed under it.[175] Two main reasons

---

Sections II to IV (Articles 19 to 56) of the Convention and Protocol No. 2. The text off other provisions of the Convention and Protocols have been amended as appropriately necessary. For a text of the European Convention on Human Rights and Fundamental Freedoms as amended by Protocol 11, and the Protocol itself, *see* JACOBS and WHITE, THE EUROPEAN CONVENTION ON HUMAN RIGHTS 422, Appendix 2 (Oxford: Clarendon Press, 1995).

172 For detailed discussions on the old European Human Rights System, *see* generally, THE EUROPEAN SYSTEM FOR THE PROTECTION OF HUMAN RIGHTS (R. ST. J. MACDONALD, F. MATSCHER & H. PETZOLD, eds., (hereafter MACDONALD *et al,* eds.) Dordrecht: Martinus Nijhoff Publishers, 1993); D.J. HARRIS, M O'BOYLE & C WARBRICK, LAW OF THE EUROPEAN CONVENTION ON HUMAN RIGHTS (London: Butterworths, 1995) (Hereinafter, HARRIS *et al*); P. VAN DIKE & G.J.H VAN HOOF, THEORY AND PRACTICE OF THE EUROPEAN CONVENTION ON HUMAN RIGHTS (2nd Edition, Deventer: Kluwer, 1990); J.G. MERILLS, THE DEVELOPMENT OF INTERNATIONAL LAW BY THE EUROPEAN COURT OF HUMAN RIGHTS (2nd Edition, Manchester: Manchester University Press, 1993); FRANCIS G. JACOBS AND ROBIN C. A WHITE, THE EUROPEAN CONVENTION ON HUMAN RIGHTS *supra,* note 171; A. H. Robertson, *The European Convention for the Protection of Human Rights* 27 BRITISH YR. BOOK INT'L L 145 (1950); A. H. ROBERTSON, THE COUNCIL OF EUROPE (2nd Edition, Manchester:Manchester University Press, 1961); A. H. ROBERTSON, HUMAN RIGHTS IN EUROPE (3rd Edition, Manchester:Manchester University Press, 1993); Colin Warbrick, *Coherence and the European Court of Human Rights: The Adjudicative Background of the Soering Case* 11 MICH. J. INT'L L. 1073 (1990); J.A. Andrews, *The European Jurisprudence of Human Rights* 43 MD. L. REV. 463 (1984).

173 Article 3 of the Statute of the Council of Europe requires that every member of the Council 'must' accept the principles of the rule of law and the enjoyment by all persons within its jurisdiction of human rights and fundamental freedoms. Article 8 of the Statute emphasizes the importance of Article 3 to the effect that a member that seriously violates its provisions may be requested by the Committee of Ministers to withdraw from the Council. If the Member State does not comply, the member may be expelled. *C/f.* The *Greek* case leading to the withdrawal of Greece from the Council of Europe between 1967 and 1968 ,11 YEARBOOK OF THE EUROPEAN CONVENTION ON HUMAN RIGHTS, 690-780 (1968).

174 *See Juan Antonio Carrillo Salcedo, The Place of the European Convention in International Law* in THE EUROPEAN SYSTEM FOR THE PROTECTION OF HUMAN RIGHTS (MACDONALD *et al,* eds.), *supra,* note 172, at 16.

175 *Id.*

are given for the Council of Europe taking up the issue of human rights soon after it was founded. The first was the grim experience through which Europe passed during the years immediately preceding the Council. Many European statesmen of the immediate post-war epoch had been in resistance movements or in prison during the Second World War and were acutely conscious of the need to prevent any reoccurrence of dictatorship in Western Europe.[176] They knew that as long as human rights were respected, democracy would be secure and the danger of dictatorship and war would be remote.[177] Also, they were aware that the first step towards dictatorship was usually, the gradual suspension of individual rights, which if it went on unchecked, would become increasingly difficult to stop. It was therefore, vital to lay down in advance the rights and freedoms that must be respected in a democratic society and to create institutions to see that they were observed.[178]

Secondly, there was the problem of ideological conflict between Eastern and Western Europe. Thus, the post-war movement for the unification of Europe was not only the result of a conviction that this was a desirable goal in the abstract; it was also a strong reaction to the threats posed by the former Soviet Union, which was very real at that time.[179]

In its original formulation, the European Convention that was adopted guaranteed a limited number of civil and political rights as contained in its part I, which include, the right to life,[180] freedom from torture and inhuman or degrading punishment,[181] freedom from slavery and servitude,[182] the right to liberty and security of the person,[183] the right to a fair trial,[184] protection against retroactivity of the criminal law,[185] the right to respect for private and family life, the home and correspondence,[186] freedom of thought, conscience and religion,[187] freedom of expression,[188] freedom of assembly and association,[189]

---

176 J. G. Merrils *The Council of Europe (I): The European Convention on Human Rights* in AN INTRODUCTION TO THE INTERNATIONAL PROTECTION OF HUMAN RIGHTS: A TEXT BOOK (RAIJA HANSKI & MARKU SUKSI eds.), *supra*, note 110, at 221; referring to the address given by Mr. Ryssdal, President of the European Court of Human Rights in Rome on the occasion of the Fortieth anniversary of the European Convention, on November 5, 1990.
177 *Id.*
178 *Id.*
179 *Id.*
180 Article 2 of the Convention.
181 Article 3.
182 Article 4.
183 Article 5.
184 Article 6.
185 Article 7.
186 Article 8.
187 Article 9.

the right to marry and found a family,[190] the right to an effective remedy if one's rights are violated.[191]

As noted earlier, the Convention has been variously amended by Protocols, which *inter alia,* have added other rights not originally contained in the Convention. Protocol No. 1 added three further rights: the right to property,[192] the right of parents to ensure the education of their children in conformity with their own religious and philosophical convictions,[193] and the right to free elections.[194] Protocol No. 4 introduced four more rights: freedom from imprisonment for debt, liberty of movement and freedom to choose one's residence, freedom from exile and the right to enter the country of which one is a national, and prohibition of the collective expulsion of aliens.[195] Protocol No. 6 brought in the prohibition of the death penalty in time of peace.[196] Protocol No. 7 incorporated five additional rights:[197] the right of an alien not to be expelled from a State without due process of law, the right to appeal in criminal cases, the right to compensation for a miscarriage of justice, immunity from being prosecuted twice for the same offence, and equality of rights and responsibilities of spouses as regards matters of private law character between them and in their relations with their children. Protocol 11 brought about a more drastic reformulation of the European system by eliminating the dual control mechanism and replacing it with a single supervisory organ, among other reforms. (The reform brought about by Protocol 11 will be discussed, albeit, briefly below).

Apart from setting out the rights listed above, the Convention in Articles 14 to 18 makes provisions relating to the exercise of the rights guaranteed. Article 14 contains a wide-drawn prohibition against discrimination in the enjoyment of the rights. Article 15 permits the suspension of some of the rights in time of war or other emergency threatening the life of the nation, but only to the extent strictly required by the exigencies of the situation and after a notice of derogation has been filed with the Secretary-General of the Council of Europe. Article 16 allows the imposition of restrictions on the political activity of aliens. Article 17 prohibits the interpretation of the Convention in a way that implies any right to engage in

---

188 Article 10.
189 Article 11.
190 Article 12.
191 Article 13.
192 Protocol No. 1, Article 1.
193 *Id.* Article 2.
194 *Id.* Article 3.
195 *See* Protocol No. 4, Articles 1- 4.
196 *See* Protocol No. 6, Articles 1-2.
197 *See* Protocol No. 7, Articles 1-5.

any activity or performance of any act that is aimed at the destruction of any of the rights set forth in the Convention. Article 18 emphasizes that the restrictions which are permitted under the Convention may not be applied for any other purpose, other than those for which they have been prescribed.

B. *Institutional Machinery of the European System*

For the implementation of the rights enumerated above, the original Convention established an institutional machinery which consisted of the European Commission of Human Rights (the European Commission) and the European Court of Human Rights (the European Court).[198] These institutions were to ensure the observance of the obligation of States Parties. In addition, the Committee of Ministers, as the governing body of the Council of Europe is charged with supervising the enforcement of the decisions of the Court and deciding what measures are to be taken when it determines that there has been a violation of rights guaranteed in the Convention.[199]

As already indicated, of all amendments to the European Convention, Protocol 11 reorganized the European system in terms of its institutional control mechanism.[200] Pursuant to this Protocol the two-tier machinery consisting of the Euro-

---

198 Article 19 of the original Convention before the reforms introduced by Protocol 11.
199 *See* old Article 32, now Article 46(2).
200 Protocol No. 11 to the Convention for the Protection of Human Rights and Fundamental Freedoms, Restructuring the Control Machinery Established Thereby, E.T.S. No. 155. The Protocol was opened for signature on May 11, 1994 and entered into force on November 1, 1998, after all Members States of the Council of Europe, that is, parties to the European Convention had ratified, accepted or approved it. For detailed discussions on the new control mechanism of the European system established by Protocol 11, *see* Andrew Drzemczewski, *The European Human Rights Convention: A New Court of Human Rights in Strasbourg as of November 1, 1998,* 55 WASH. & LEE. L. REV. 697 (1998); *Nicolas Bratza & Michael O'Boyle, The Legacy of the Commission to the New Court Under The Eleventh Protocol* in THE BIRTH OF THE EUROPEAN HUMAN RIGHTS LAW: STUDIES IN HONOR OF CARL AAGE NØRGAARD 377.(MICHELLE DE SALVIA & MARK VILLIGER, eds., 1998); LOUIS HENKIN, GERALD L. NEUMAN, DIANE F. ORENTLICHER & DAVID W. LEEBRON (Hereafter HENKIN, *et al.*), HUMAN RIGHTS 551, at 552-553 (New York: Foundation Press, 1999); HENRY J. STEINER & PHILIP ALSTON, INTERNATIONAL HUMAN RIGHTS IN CONTEXT: LAW, POLITICS AND MORALS 590 (Oxford: Clarendon Press, 1996); *Yvonne Klerk, Protocol No. 11 to the European Convention for Human Rights: A Drastic Revision of the Supervisory Mechanism under the ECHR,* NETHERLANDS Q. HUM. RTS. 35 (1996); *R. Bernhardt, Reform of the Control Machinery Under The European Convention on Human Rights: Protocol No. 11,* 89 AM. J. INT'L L. 145 (1995); *Henry G. Schermers, Adaptation of the 11 the Protocol to the European Convention on Human Rights,* 20 EUROPEAN LAW REV. 559 (1995); *Andrew Drzemczewski, A Major Overhaul of the European Human Rights Convention Control Mechanism: Protocol No. 11* in COLLECTED COURSES OF THE ACADEMY OF EUROPEAN LAW 121 (Academy of European Law, ed., 1995); *Andrew Drzemczewski & Jens Meyer-Ladewig, Principal Characteristics of The New EHCR Control*

pean Commission and the Court was replaced with a single full-time Court in 1998. Various reasons are given for the drastic measure that came with the adoption of Protocol No. 11 in 1994. According to Brazta and O'byle, the steadily increasing workload of the European Commission and Court of Human Rights over the years and the resulting problem of the length of convention proceedings gave rise to reflection towards the end of the 1980s on how the Convention's enforcement machinery could be streamlined as a means of preserving and building upon its achievements.[201] It was, however, not until 1993 that the proposal for a single Court was endorsed by a meeting of the Council of Europe's Heads of State and Government in the Vienna Declaration of 9 October 1993, leading to the adoption of Protocol 11 on May 11, 1994.[202] In addition to the increasing workload of the old Commission and the old Court (which in turn resulted in enormous backlogs of complaints and cases), Drzemczewski adds that the growing complexities and the widening of the Council of Europe's membership to include countries of Cental Europe and Eastern Europe, necessitated the revision of the European Convention." The prior Convention was originally designed for ten or twelve Member States, and it became quite impossible for it to work effectively with the expected forty or more States Parties. It was agreed that a revision of the Convention control mechanism was therefor essential to strengthen its efficiency. The new system should, in particular, make the machinery more accessible to individuals, speed up the procedure, and make for greater efficiency."[203] There was yet, the desire to modernize the system, by providing for an unfettered right of individual access to the Court, despite the effect of Protocol 9; to improve the transparency of the system, as well as the need to check the influence of the Committee of Minsters, a political body, on the judicial process.[204] To Brazta and O'byle, however, the fundamental purpose of Protocol 11:

Mechanism As Established By Protocol No. 11 Signed on May 11, 1994, 15 HUM RTS. L. J. 81(1994); *Karel de Vey Mestdagh, Reform of the European Convention on Human Rights in a Changing Europe* in THE DYNAMICS OF THE PROTECTION OF HUMAN RIGHTS IN EUROPE 337 (RICK LAWSON & MATTHIJS DE BLOIS eds., 1994); *Henry G. Schermers, The Eleventh Protocol to the European Convention on Human Rights*, 19 EUROPEAN LAW REV. 367 (1994).

201 *Nicolas Brazta & Michael O'byle, The Legacy of the Commission to the New Court under the Eleventh Protocol* in THE BIRTH OF EUROPEAN HUMAN RIGHTS LAW: STUDIES IN HONOR OF CARL AAGE NØRGAARD, *supra*, note 200, at, 377 also *reprinted* in HENKIN, *et al.*, *supra*, note 200, at 554-558.

202 *Nicolas Brazta & Michael O'byle, Id.*

203 *Drzemczewski, The European Human Rights Convention: A New Court of Human Rights in Strasbourg as of November 1, 1998, supra*, note 200, at 715.

204 *See Klerk, supra*, note 200, at 35-36; STEINER & ALSTON , *supra*, note 200, at 590; *Mestdagh, supra*, note 200, at 339-346; *Schermers, The Eleventh Protocol to the European Convention on Human Rights, supra*, note 200, at 369-372, and HENKIN, *et al.*, *supra*, note 200, at 554-556.

is to bring about an improvement in the Convention's enforcement machinery which will lead to the examination of human rights complaints by a single [Court] within a reasonable time. With the removal of the duplication of procedures that characterises the existing machinery, encompassing both the Commission and Court, there ought to be a significant reduction in the amount of time it takes to process the large volume of complaints registered by the single Court.[205]

In addition to the reasons given above, one would agree that the complexity in the old system was exacerbated by the adoption of the various protocols. It became clear that the changes brought by Protocols 1 to 10 created chaos, making a single text of the European Convention necessary. Accordingly, Protocol No. 11 abolished the European Commission and Court of Human Rights under the two-tier system and replaced it with a permanent European Court of Human Rights. The Court has full-time functions, taking over the functions of the former organs. As already indicated, the Protocol replaced the provisions of Articles 19 to 56 of the original Convention, with the new Articles now governing the composition and powers of the new court.[206]

The new Court is composed of a number of judges equal to that of the Contracting Parties.[207] This provision is slightly different from Article 38 of the old Convention, which required the number of judges equal to that of the Member States of the Council of Europe. As rightly suggested by one commentator, the difference is small, because new members of the Council of Europe are expected to become parties to the Convention within a short time.[208] The qualifications of the judges of the new Court remain the same as those of the judges of the former Court: "The judges shall be of high moral character and must either possess the qualifications required for appointment to high judicial office or be juriconsults of recognized competence."[209] The judges are required to act in their individual capacity and not engage in activities that will be incompatible with their independence.[210] The judges, however, are now elected by the Parliamentary Assembly with respect to each High Contracting Party by a majority of votes cast

---

205 *Brazta & O'byle, supra,* note 200, at 379, also *reprinted* in HENKEIN, *et al., supra,* note 200, at 555.
206 Article 19 of the European Convention, as amended by Protocol 11 and Protocol 11, Article1. *See also, Merrils, supra,* note 176, at 237-238; *Drzemczewski & Meyer-Ladewig, Principal Characteristics of The New EHCR Control Mechanism As Established By Protocol No. 11 Signed on May 11, 1994, supra,* note 200, at 81-86; *Bernhardt, supra,* note 200, at 145-154; *Klerk, supra,* note 200, at 35, and *Schermers, The Eleventh Protocol to the European Convention on Human Rights,* supra, note 200 at 372-373.
207 European Convention, Article 20.
208 *See Klerk, supra,* note 200, at 37.
209 European Convention, Article 21(1).
210 *Id.* Article 21(2) & (3). The provisions of Article 21 correspond with old Articles 39(3) and 40(7).

from a list of three candidates nominated by the High Contracting Parties, both in composing the Court and in filling of vacancies, or in the event of the accession of a new party to the Convention.[211] The term of office for the judges is six years with the possibility of re-election rather than 9 years under the old Convention.[212]

Apart from the various specific amendments of the European Convention, the main aspects of the reform introduced by Protocol 11, include the mandatory nature of individual petitions as against the former optional nature.[213] Similarly, under Article 33 of the new Convention, the Court will have jurisdiction over inter-state cases. In the same vein, the Court's supervisory function has been streamlined. The Court under Article 27 sits in Committees, Chambers and Grand Chamber, and occasionally in plenary. The Committees comprise of three judges to decide on admissibility based on unanimity. If the committee is not unanimous, the issue will be decided by a Chamber of seven judges. The Chamber will also decide cases on their merits, unless the Chamber decides to relinquish jurisdiction in favor of a Grand Chamber of seventeen judges. Under the new provisions, a Grand Chamber can also review decisions made by a Chamber if a case raises an important issue, and a panel of five judges of the Grand Chamber decides that it is appropriate to do so. In addition, the Grand Chamber has exclusive jurisdiction on inter-state complaints and requests for advisory opinions. The plenary Court will only deal with organizational matters, such as appointing Presidents of Chambers, constituting Chambers, adopting Rules of Procedure and the election of Presidents and Vice Presidents of the Court.[214]

For each case that is registered, a Judge Rapporteur will be appointed to prepare the case and will have also the duty to sit on the committee of three judges, which will examine its admissibility. The Committee may by unanimous decision declare the case inadmissible or strike the case off the list. If no admissibility decision is reached by a Committee, the application will be referred to

---

211 *Id.* Article 22(1) & (2). Under the basic criteria laid down for the election of the judges, States had to provide a list of three candidates accompanied by a detailed biographical note on each of them in English or French, structured in accordance with a model curriculum vitae established by the Parliamentary Assembly. *See* Drzemczewski, *The European Human Rights Convention: A New Court of Human Rights in Strasbourg as of November 1, 1998, supra,* note 200, at 702.
212 European Convention, Article 23(1). Under Article 23, a retirement age of 70 has been introduced, and there is no longer a prohibition on two judges having the same nationality.
213 *Id.* Article 34.
214 *See* European Convention, Articles 28-31. *See also, Brazta & O'byle, supra,* note 200, at 378; Drzemczewski, *The European Human Rights Convention: A New Court of Human Rights in Strasbourg as of November 1, 1998, supra,* note 200, at 698-699; Drzemczewski & Meyer-Ladewig, supra, note 200, at 81-86 *and Klerk, supra,* note 200, at 39.

a Chamber which will decide on the admissibility and the merits of the case.[215] As under the old system, once a case has been declared admissible, the Court will have the dual function of establishing the facts and placing itself at the disposal of the parties with the view to securing friendly settlement.[216] The life span of committees established for particular cases is one year, while Chambers will last for three years. The President of the Court, the Vice-Presidents, the Presidents of the Chambers, and the judges, who have been elected originally to represent in the Court the State against which a complaint has been lodged, will be *ex officio* members of the Grand Chamber.[217]

One other important feature of Protocol No. 11 is the abolition of the decision-making role of the Committee of Ministers whereby the Committee determined whether there had been a violation of the European Convention, especially if the former Commission chose not to refer the case to the then Court. Accordingly, the role of the Committee of Ministers is limited to supervising the execution of the Court's judgment.[218] All allegations of a violation of a Convention right will thus be adjudicated on by the Court only.[219]

To ensure effective transition between the old system and the new one, Protocol 11 made provisions for transitional arrangements. Article 4 of the Protocol specifies that the Protocol enters into force on the first day of the month one year after the last State Party to the Convention has ratified the Protocol.[220] This provision as already indicated, was fulfilled on November 1, 1998, when the Protocol entered into force. In the same vein, Article 5 of the Protocol contains necessary transitional provisions for the application that had been lodged before the old Commission at Strasbourg before the entry into force of the Protocol. If at the time the Protocol entered into force, there are pending applications, which the old Commission had not declared admissible, such applications would be examined by the new Court.[221] Where on the other hand, applications have been

---

215 *Id.* European Convention, Articles 28-29. *See* also COUNCIL OF EUROPE, EXPLANATORY REPORT TO PROTOCOL NO.11 TO THE EUROPEAN CONVENTIONON HUMAN RIGHTS, Doc. H (94) 5 (1994), pp. 38-50, also *cited in Brazta & O'byle, supra*, note 200, at 378 for detailed explanation of the procedure under the new system.
216 European Convention, Articles 38-39
217 *Drzemczewski & Meyer-Ladewig, supra*, note 200, at 81.
218 European Convention, Articles 46(2).
219 *Brazta & O'byle, supra*, note 200, at 378
220 This is to enable the system make arrangement for the setting up of the new Court, such as election of new judges, the appointment of other officials of the Court, and such other appropriate measures that are steps in establishing the new Court. *See Drzemczewski, The European Human Rights Convention: A New Court of Human Rights in Strasbourg as of November 1, 1998, supra*, note 200, at 700.
221 Protocol 11, Article 5(2).

declared admissible, the Commission would have one year thereafter to continue with such applications under the old system, but applications that are not completed within the one year period would be transmitted to the new Court to deal with them as admissible cases in accordance with the new system.[222] Similarly, cases pending before the old Court, which had not been decided at the Protocol's entry into force would be transmitted to the Grand Chamber of the new Court.[223] The Protocol also allowed the Committee of Ministers the power to complete cases pending before it at the entry into force of the Protocol, and thus to continue to deal with cases not transmitted to the Court under old Article 48 of the European Convention.[224] According to Drzemczewski, although, this would, in all probability, prolong consideration of cases before the Committee of Ministers for potentially several years after the entry into force of the Protocol, the drafters of the Protocol were concerned not to make the Committee of Ministers redundant. They thought it inappropriate, by the means of the Protocol, "to try to tie the hands of an organ whose existence predated the European human rights mechanism, and especially as the Council of Europe's executive works independently of the Convention mechanism."[225]

Some commentators have questioned the very premise on which the reform of the European system is based. They argue that the old system was, with an increase in resources and streamlining of procedures, capable of reforming itself and managing the constantly growing number of applications linked to membership of the Convention community by Central and Eastern European States.[226] Brazta & O'byle, seeing the above view as having merit, opine that a basic paradox inherent in Protocol 11 and the single Court is namely:

> the real risk that in seeking to bring about a much needed improvement in the Strasbourg system a new institution will be brought into being in conditions which will make it extremely difficult, if not impossible to achieve the goals of reform. The scenario reads as follows.(sic) Ensnared at its inception by the accumulated backlog of both the Com-

---

222 *Id.* Article 5(3). However, for applications for which the Commission had adopted a report under old Article 31 of the European Convention as to whether there had been a violation of the European Convention, the procedure for bringing cases under the old Article 48 of the Convention and Protocol 9, where applicable, will apply. In other words, the Commission or a State Party, as well as an individual applicant under Protocol 9, will have the right to refer the case to new Court. *See* Protocol 11, Article 5(4). *See* also, Drzemczewski, *The European Human Rights Convention: A New Court of Human Rights in Strasbourg as of November 1, 1998, supra*, note 200, at 701.
223 Protocol 11, Article 5(5).
224 Protocol 11, Article 5(6).
225 Drzemczewski, *The European Human Rights Convention: A New Court of Human Rights in Strasbourg as of November 1, 1998, supra*, note 200, at 702.
226 *See Brazta & O'byle, supra*, note 200, at 379-380.

mission and the Court and called upon at the same time to develop its own operational identity and integrate a further six or more new States from Central and Eastern Europe- including Russia and the Ukraine- and perhaps the European Union- the new enterprise will be immediately confronted with serious teething problems. The Commission will bequeath several registered cases, which it has not yet had the opportunity to examine, to the new body. In addition it must be remembered that many of the admissible cases which the Commission will continue to examine in the course of the year following the entry into force of the single Court, will ultimately be referred to it and that those cases which the existing Court has not had an opportunity to examine will be automatically referred to a Grand Chamber of the new Court.[227]

While the above quote may represent the potential situation with the new European human rights system, the authors of the quote are right in suggesting that, for the new system to function effectively, there must be a large degree of continuity from the old Commission and Court in terms of not only of membership and staffing, but also of working methods and case-law.[228]

If one should assess the European system, the conclusion would be that the achievement of the mechanism has been quite staggering. The case law of the system, which will still be relevant despite the reform, has exerted and continues to exert an even deeper influence on the laws and social realities of not only State Parties to the European Convention, but on Europe as a whole. Any assessment must, however, recognize the crucial importance of the cooperation by governments of the Member States in providing the necessary political will, which has been instrumental in enabling the system to work. The credibility that the old system enjoyed as the most effective international system for the protection of human rights introduced anywhere in the world, and hopefully, which the new system will enjoy, would not have been possible without this will. In other words, States must determine to make regional human rights organs work.

Accordingly, Africa can draw inspiration from the long history of the European system, especially the present reform. It is not just a coincidence that the African system is also undergoing reform: the establishment of an African Court on Human and Peoples' Rights. While the African reform has adopted much of the structure

---

[227] *Id.* at 380.
[228] *Id.* It is reasonable to expect that despite the reform, the New European Court will be impacted by the experience, procedures and jurisprudence of the old system in achieving continuity. It must be observed, however, that while there is no guarantee that the new system will be more efficient than the one it replaced, the suggestion that is that the expansion of the Council of Europe "without reforms would mean a great many part-time or full-time commissioners or judges. The task of coordinating 80 or more commissioners and judges is probably perceived as too unwieldy, no matter what other reforms might be instituted." *See* MARK W. JANIS, RICHARD S. KAY & ANTHONY W. BRADLEY, EUROPEAN HUMAN RIGHTS LAW: TEXT AND MATERIALS 88, at 117 (Oxford: Clarendon Press, 1995).

of the old European system, this author is of the view that a reform that borrows more from the new European system in terms of supervisory functions and a little blending of its structure with the old European system, will advance the resolution of human rights dispute in Africa. In other words, while it is good to maintain the African Commission in addition to the new African Court, the Commission should be a promotional body without any judicial or quasi-judicial functions. Judicial functions should be the sole responsibility of the Court. (This issue will be elaborated in Chapters three and seven when we consider the African Commission and the African Court on Human Rights, respectively in the light of the African reform).

C.   The Inter-American System[229]

The Inter-American human rights system has a unique character in terms of the evolution of its dual supervisory machineries. One is said to have evolved from the Charter of the Organization of American States (OAS), and the other was created with the entry into force of the American Convention on Human Rights

---

229 For detailed discussions on the Inter-American Human Rights system *see* the following: THE INTER-AMERICAN SYSTEM OF HUMAN RIGHTS (DAVID J. HARRIS & STEPHEN LIVINGSTONE, eds., Oxford: Clarendon Press, 1998); *David Harris, Regional Protection of Human Rights: The Inter-American Achievement* in *id.*; 1-30; *Tom Farer, The Rise of the Inter-American Human Rights Regime: No Longer a Unicorn, not yet an Ox,* in id., 31-64; *Christina Cerna, The Inter-American Commission on Human Rights: Its Organization and Examination of Petitions,* in *id.* 65; SCOTT DAVIDSON, THE INTER-AMERICAN HUMAN RIGHTS SYSTEM (England: Dartmouth Publishing Company Limited, 1997); *Harmen vander Wilt, The OAS System for the Protection of Human Rights* in AN INTRODUCTION TO THE INTERNATIONAL PROTECTION OF HUMAN RIGHTS: A TEXT BOOK 305 (RAIJA HANSKI & MARKU SUKSI eds., Tarku/Abo, Finland: Institute for Human Rights, Abo Akademi University, 1997); THE MODERN WORLD OF HUMAN RIGHTS: ESSAYS IN HONOR OF THOMAS BUERGENTHAL 375 (ANTONIO A. CANÇADO TRINDADE, ed., San José: Inter-American Institute of Human Rights, 1996); THOMAS BUERGENTHAL & DINAH SHELTON, PROTECTING HUMAN RIGHTS IN THE AMERICAS: CASES AND MATERIALS, *supra*, note 110; THOMAS BUERGENTHAL, HUMMAN RIGHTS IN A NUTSHELL 174 (2nd Edition, St. Paul, Minnesota: West Publishing Company, 1995); *Thomas Buergenthal, The Advisory Practice of the Inter-American Human Rights Court* 79 AM. J. INT'L L. 1 (1985); *Dinah Shelton, The Jurisprudence of the Inter-American Court of Human Rights* 10 AM. U.J. INT'L L. & POL'Y 333 (1994); F. V. GARCIA-AMADOR, THE INTER-AMERICAN SYSTEM: TREATIES, CONVENTIONS AND OTHER DOCUMENTS, VOLUME 1: PARTS I & II (New York: Oceana Publications, Inc, 1983); SCOTT DAVIDSON, THE INTER-AMERICAN COURT OF HUMAN RIGHTS SYSTEM (England: Dartmouth Publishing Company Limited, 1992); L. Leblanc, THE OAS AND THE PROMOTION AND PROTECTION OF HUMAN RIGHTS (The Hague: Martinus Nijhoff Publishers, 1977); *L. Leblanc, The Economic, Social and Cultural Rights Protocol to the American Convention and its Background* 10 NETHERLANDS Q. HUM.RTS. 130 (1992); *Cecilia Medina, The Inter-American Commission on Human Rights and the Inter-American Court of Human Rights: Reflections on a Joint Venture* 12 No. 4 HUM. RTS. Q. 439-464 (1990); MEDINA CECILIA QUIROGA,

(Inter-American Convention).[230] This feature became important in holding states responsible for human rights violations as long as they continue to be members of the OAS, even though they have not ratified the Inter-American Convention.

Apart from historical initiatives aimed at bringing American States together,[231] the Inter-American system of human rights had its formal origin at the Ninth Conference of American States held in Bogota in 1948, at which the OAS Charter constituting the legal basis for the Organization of American States was adopted.[232] It was also at that conference that the American Declaration on the Rights and Duties of Man[233] was adopted, several months before the Universal Declaration was adopted by the UN, and two and a half years before the European Convention was adopted.[234] There is often the critical view that the OAS Charter made only few references to human rights. Reference is often made to the provision which states that the American States reaffirm and proclaim as a principle of the organization, "the fundamental rights of the individual without distinction as to race, nationality, creed or sex," as the notable provision on human rights[235] It must, however, be observed that there are indeed several references to human rights in the Charter of the OAS, which are not in one place, but are scattered throughout the Charter. Thus, in addition to the notable principle men-

---

THE BATTLE OF HUMAN RIGHTS: GROSS SYSTEMATIC VIOLATIONS AND THE INTER-AMERICAN SYSTEM (Dordrecht: Martinus Nijhoff Publishers, 1988); *Mary Parker, Other Treaties: The Inter-American Court of Human Rights Defines Its Advisory Jurisdiction* 33 AM. U.L. REV. 211 (1983)); Jo M. Pasqualucci, *Provisional Measures in the Inter-American Human Rights System: An Innovative Development in International Law* 36 VAND. J. TRANSNAT'L L. 803 (1993); Jo M. Pasqualucci, *The Inter-American Human Rights System: Establishing Precedents and Procedure in Human Rights Law* 26 U. MIAMI INTER-AM. L. REV. 297 (1995).

230 BUERGENTHAL & SHELTON, *supra*, note 110, at 37.
231 The first International Conference of American States, as the inter-American conference was called, took place in the city of Washington from October 2, 1889 to April 19, 1890. The second conference was held at Mexico City (1901-1902). *See* F. V. GARCIA-AMADOR, THE INTER-AMERICAN SYSTEM: TREATIES, CONVENTIONS AND OTHER DOCUMENTS VOLUME 1 PART 1, *supra*, note 229, at 66. *See also Louis B. Sohn, The Contribution of Latin American Lawyers to the Development of the United Nations Concept of Human Rights and Economic Social Justice* in THE MODERN WORLD OF HUMAN RIGHTS: ESSAYS IN HONOR OF THOMAS BUERGENTHAL, *supra* note 229, at 33- 34.
232 Charter of the Organization of American States, April 30, 1948, 2 U.S.T. 2394, T.I.A.S. No. 2361. The Charter entered into force in December 1951 and has since been amended by the Protocol of Buenos Aires of 1967, the Protocol of Cartagena de indias of 1985, the Protocol of Washington of 1992, and the Protocol of Managua of 1993. The latter two Protocols are yet to enter into force.
233 Resolution XXX, Final Act of the Ninth International Conference of American States, Bogota, Columbia, March 30- May 2, 1948, at 48 (PAU 1948). *See* GARCIA-AMADOR, PART II, *supra*, note 229, at 1-16.
234 STEINER & ALSTON, *supra*, note 200, at 641.
235 Original Article 5(j) now Article 3(j) of the Inter-American Convention. *See also* BUERGENTHAL & SHELTON, supra, note 110, at 40; BUERGENTHAL, INTERNATIONAL HUMAN RIGHTS IN A NUTSHELL, *supra*, note 229, at 178.

tioned above, the Charter enshrines other principles, such as, the principle that "the solidarity of the American States and the high aims which are sought through it require the political organization of those States on the basis of the effective exercise of representative democracy; the principle that "social justice and social security are bases of lasting peace"; the principle that "economic co-operation is essential to the common welfare and prosperity of the peoples of the continent", and the principle that "the education of the peoples should be directed toward justice, freedom and peace."[236]

It is true, however, that the Charter of the OAS did not define the "fundamental rights of the individual" referred to in Article 3, or other notions of human rights contained in the Charter. Similarly, the Charter did not create any individual institution to promote their observance.[237] On the other hand, the American Declaration on the Rights and Duties of Man, like the Universal Declaration under the UN system, specifically sets out what constituted the rights mentioned in the Charter. While the binding character of the American Declaration may be arguable, just like that of the Universal Declaration, one could argue that it states rules of customary international law for American States, in the same way that the Universal Declaration does at the universal level.[238]

In 1959 however, the OAS tried to revamp the weak image of the Inter-American system by establishing the Inter-American Commission on Human Rights.[239] The Commission was established as an autonomous entity of the OAS having the function to promote respect for human rights.[240] Human rights were defined in the Statute of the Commission as those set out in the American Declaration of the Rights and Duties of Man.[241] It became interesting that the supposedly non-binding American Declaration turned out to be the principal normative instru-

---

[236] See Articles 3 (d), (h) & (l) of the OAS Charter. *See* also Articles 16, 31 and 43, 45, 49 and Article 45, as amended. An introductory clause of the preamble of the Charter is noted to be closely related to the provisions of Article 3(d), which in turn is believed to be related to the inter-American system for the promotion and protection of human rights. This clause of the preamble reads: "Confident that the true significance of American solidarity and good neighborliness can only mean the consolidation on this continent, within the framework of democratic institutions, of a system of individual liberty and social justice based on respect for the essential rights of man." See GARCIA-AMADOR, PART I, *supra,* note 229, at 77.

[237] BUERGENTHAL, HUMMAN RIGHTS IN A NUTSHELL, *supra*, note 229, at 178.

[238] *Harris, Regional Protection of Human Rights: The Inter-American Experience*, *supra*, note 229, at 4.

[239] The Commission was established by a resolution of the Fifth Meeting of Ministers of Foreign Affairs in Santiago Chile. (Fifth Meeting of Consultation). OAS Doc./Ser.C/II. 5, P.10. For details on the establishment of the Commission, *see* GARCIA-AMADOR, PART II, *supra*, note 229, at 19 – 47.

[240] Article 1 of the Statute of the Inter-American Commission on Human Rights promulgated in 1960. *See Id.* at 23.

[241] Article 2 of the Statute. *See Id.*

ment of the Inter-American Commission.[242] The Commission was, however, vested with general and limited powers of research and making recommendations on human rights situations.[243] The innovation in interpreting its power notwithstanding, one would agree with Buergenthal and Shelton that the Commission was operating under a faulty and weak legal foundation. Its Statute was not a treaty as such, and its existence was "derived from OAS conference resolutions of uncertain legal force."[244]

A major step towards improving the Inter-American system was the revision of the OAS Charter through the Protocol of Buenos Aires which entered into force in 1970. The revision had the effect of changing the legal status of the Inter-American Commission from an autonomous entity of the OAS into one of the principal organs of the OAS.[245] This provided the Commission with a firmer constitutional basis. Furthermore, Article 112 of the Charter alluded to the creation of an Inter-American Convention for Human Rights, which should determine the structure, competence and procedure of the Commission. The impact of this provision is the unique feature of the Inter-American Commission earlier alluded to. It implied that all OAS member states, whether or not they ratified the American Convention, would be subjected to the Commission's competence and procedures as described in the Convention once it came into force.[246] Thus, in two respects, the regime governing States Parties to the Convention differed from the one governing OAS member States which had not ratified the Convention. First, the states which had not ratified the Convention were to be judged on the basis of the American Declaration on the Rights and Duties of Man, while States Parties should abide also by the standards of the Convention. Secondly, states which had not ratified the Convention could never be subjected to the contentious jurisdiction of the Inter-American Court of Human Rights.[247]

---

242 *See* THOMAS BUERGENTHAL & DINAH SHELTON, *supra*, note 110, at 40. *See* also SCOTT DAVIDSON, THE INTER-AMERICAN HUMAN RIGHTS SYSTEM, *supra*, note 229, at 16.
243 *See* Article 9 of the Statute of the Commission. The Commission however became innovative in the interpretation of its general powers. It acquired the power to engage in country studies and to issue country reports, as well as to make observations on human rights situations in particular countries.
244 *See* BUERGENTHAL & SHELTON, *supra*, note 110, at 40. *See* also DAVIDSON, THE INTER-AMERICAN HUMAN RIGHTS SYSTEM, *supra*, note 229 at 16. The improvement via the Protocol of Buenos Aires was preceded by the amendment of the Commission's Statute, which led to an expansion of the powers of the Commission at the Second Special Inter-American Conference held in Rio de Janeiro, Brazil in 1965. The conference adopted a resolution to this effect, entitled "Expanded Functions of the Inter-American Commission on Human Rights," OAS Doc. OEA/Ser.E/XIII. 1p., *reprinted* in GARCIA-AMADOR, PART II, *supra*, note 229, at 27-29.
245 Article 51(e) of the OAS Charter.
246 *Wilt, supra*, note 229 at 305.
247 *Id.*

The combined effect of the Protocol of Buenos Aires and the American Convention on Human Rights, adopted in 1969 was enormous. The Inter-American Commission was recognized as treaty-based, and the normative character of the American Declaration of the Rights and Duties of Man was recognized as a standard by which to judge the human rights activities of all OAS Member States.[248] Thus, the two instruments would lay the foundation for a more elaborate individual petition system, which, contrary to the general assessment of human rights violations in particular countries, would also deal with cases occurring in States Parties which usually complied with the rule of law, and were thus susceptible to correction.

1. The Inter-American Convention on human rights

The Inter-American Convention on Human Rights is similar to preceding human treaties such as the old European Convention on Human Rights and the International Covenant on Civil and Political Rights.[249] This similarity is both in substance and in their institutional framework. There are however, some distinctive features.[250] The catalogue of rights comprises such rights as the right to life, the right to humane treatment, the right to personal liberty, the right to fair hearing, the freedom of conscience and of religion, thought and expression. The distinct features of the Convention include, the right to a name,[251] the right to nationality,[252] the right to property,[253] the right to seek and be granted asylum,[254] and the right to participate in government.[255] Like the European Convention, the American Convention deals with only civil and political rights. The Convention dedicates only Articles 26 and 42 to the progressive development of economic, social and cultural rights.[256]

---

248 *See* BUERGENTHAL & DINAH, *supra*, note 110, at 41.
249 *See Wilt, supra,* note 229, at 305. On the preparatory work and history of the American Convention on Human Rights, *see* GARCIA-AMADOR, PART II, *supra,* note 229, at 47-90.
250 It must be recalled that the European human rights system now has a single Court as the supervisory organ responsible for the implementation of the European Convention, as amended.
251 Article 18 of the Inter-American Convention on Human Rights.
252 Article 20.
253 Article 21.
254 Article 22(7).
255 Article 23.
256 The Protocol of San Salvador of 1988, however, recognizes a catalogue of economic, social and cultural rights. Under the Protocol, the Inter-American Commission will have jurisdiction to receive complaints regarding only three rights: the right to form trade unions, the right to strike and the right to free education. Other rights will be governed by the reporting procedure under which Member States are to make reports of measures they have taken, necessary for the progressive achievement of those rights to the Inter-American Council for Education Science and Culture. The

According to Article 1 of the American Convention, States are under a duty to respect and ensure the rights enumerated in the Convention. The duty to ensure these right entails a positive obligation, which implies that a State may be held responsible for conduct of private individuals where the State has failed to take appropriate measures to avoid the violation of human rights.[257] The Convention on the other hand, contains a derogation clause in its Article 27, which is rather loosely drafted when compared with other human rights instrument. Unlike the European Convention on Human and the International Covenant on Civil and Political Rights, which permit the suspension of rights only in cases of emergency threatening the life of a nation, Article 27 permits derogation if the independence or security of a State Party is threatened. It has been observed that this clause could be subjected to abuse, and misinterpretation, especially, in a continent which has been notorious for cherishing the doctrine of national security.[258] Article 30, however, stipulates that the restrictions that may be placed on the enjoyment or exercise of the rights contained in the Convention may not be applied except in accordance with the purpose for which such restrictions have been established. Accordingly, the Convention provides for an extensive list of non-derogable rights in Article 27(2). This has been interpreted as a possible compensation for the acceptance of the wide discretionary powers to derogate from the rights established in the Convention.[259]

The Inter-American system has been strengthened by the recent adoption of new instruments aimed at emphasizing human rights protection in the region. These, apart from earlier Protocols to the American Convention, include, the Inter-American Convention for the Prevention of and Punishment of Torture, which entered into force on January 29, 1987, and the Protocol of Washington adopted by the OAS on December 14, 1992 in the District of Columbia. The Protocol of Washington in a new Article 9 provides for the suspension of any member whose democratically constituted government has been overthrown by force, after diplomatic initiatives have failed, and if two thirds of members agree.[260] Under the Protocol, suspended members remain bound by Charter obligations, but lose rights under the treaty.[261] While the suspension provision of the Protocol may be difficult to realize, it goes to show the importance that the OAS has begun to attach to human rights as an element of democratic governance. The threat of regional

---

Protocol recently entered into force.
257 *El Amparo v. Venezuela* (Case No. 10.602). ANNUAL REPORT OF THE INTER-AMERICAN COURT OF HUMAN RIGHTS, 1995, OAS/Ser.L/V/III.33, Doc. 4, 23-29 (January 22, 1996).
258 *See Wilt, supra*, note 229, at 307.
259 *Id.*
260 *See* BUERGENTHAL & SHELTON, *supra*, note 110, at 44.
261 *Id.*

political isolation of breaching Member States would arguably provide enough check.

2. Institutional organs of the Inter-American system

a. The Inter-American Commission on human rights

As earlier indicated the Inter-American Commission on Human Rights derives its powers from two sources: the OAS Charter and the American Convention. Article 111 of the OAS Charter calls upon the Commission to fulfil promotional, protective and consultative functions.[262] These functions are further elaborated in the second source of the Commission's powers.[263] Under Article 34 of the American Convention, the Inter-American Commission is composed of seven members, persons of high moral character and recognized competence in the field of human rights. Members of the Commission are elected in their personal capacities by the OAS General Assembly from the list of members proposed by the governments of Member States.[264]

In the exercise of its supervisory power under the American Convention, the Commission can receive inter-state and individual complaints. The inter-state complaint procedure can only be used if the complainant State and the defendant State have made a declaration in which they recognize the competence of the Commission to deal with inter-state complaints.[265] The individual petition procedure on the other hand, is compulsory[266] to the effect that each State, by ratifying the Convention automatically accepts the competence of the Commission to initiate proceedings against it on the basis of individual petitions.[267] Even though it is called individual petition, the petition need not be initiated by the particular victim in question. Under Article 44 of the Convention, any person or group of

---

262 *See* paragraph one of Article 111 of the OAS Charter.
263 For the functions of the Inter-American Commission under the American Convention for Human Rights, *see* Article 41 of the Convention. *See* also Article 18 of the Commission's Statute, which virtually reproduces the provisions of Article 41 of the Convention and adds the power of the Commission to conduct on-site observations in a State with the consent of that State, and to prepare the Commission's budget for presentation to the OAS General Assembly.
264 *See* Article 36(1) of the American Convention. On the procedures for constituting the Commission *see* Articles 36 to 38 of the Convention, and Articles 3 to 11 of the Commission's Statute.
265 *See* Article 45 of the Convention.
266 Compare the position under the European Convention, where inter-state complaints before the former European Commission for Human Rights were mandatory based on membership of the system, while individual petition power was optional via a declaration to that effect. The Inter-American system thus pioneered the compulsory power of individual complaint.
267 This is the general reading and interpretation of Article 44 of the Convention under which individual petitions are recognized. *See* DAVIDSON, THE INTER-AMERICAN HUMAN RIGHTS SYSTEM, *supra*, note 229, at 156. *See* also *Wilt*, *supra*, note 229, at 307.

persons or any non-governmental entity, regardless of whether the person(s), or entity is a victim, may lodge petitions with the Commissions.[268]

Like other human rights systems, the Commission's competence to embark on any inquiry as to whether there is a violation of human rights, whether based on an inter-state complaint or individual petition, begins with the determining the admissibility of the complaint or petition by the Secretariat of the Commission.[269] Apart from formal requirements, domestic remedies must have been exhausted, and the subject of the complaint or petition must not be pending before another international body. This requirement notwithstanding, the American Convention recognizes situations in which the requirement for exhaustion of domestic remedies would not apply. These include, where the domestic legislation of the State concerned do not afford due process of law; the party alleging violation of his or her rights had been denied access to the remedies available under domestic law, or has been prevented from exhausting them, or there has been an unwarranted delay in rendering a final judgment under the remedies indicated above.[270]

Even where petitions are admissible, the Commission is enjoined throughout the investigatory stage to place itself at the disposal of the parties concerned with a view to reaching a friendly settlement of the matter on the basis of respect for human rights recognized in the Convention.[271] Where a friendly settlement is reached , the Commission must draw up a report containing a brief statement of the facts of the case and the solution reached.[272] The report is then transmitted to the parties and the Secretary of the OAS for publication. However, there could be cases involving serious violations of human rights which may not qualify for friendly settlements.[273] In cases of this nature, as well as all others where a friendly settlement is not reached, the Commission must within a period of one hundred and eighty days draw up a report under Article 50 of the Convention. This report is usually transmitted to the States concerned. This report becomes the basis of

---

268 The Commission's competence and procedure are regulated in Articles 44 to 51 of the American Convention and further elaborated in detail in its Rules of Procedure and Regulations.
269 Article 46 of the American Convention specifies the conditions to be met for admissibility.
270 *See* Article 46(2) of the American Convention.
271 Article 48(1)(f) of the American Convention.
272 Article 49 of the Convention; New Rules of Procedure of the Inter-American Commission on Human Rights (Rules of Procedure), Article 41(5).

273 Such cases include summary executions and disappearances. *See* the Judgment of the Inter-American Court of Human Rights in the *Honduran Disappearance cases* (*Velasquez Rodriguez, Fairen Garbi and Solis Corrales, and Godinez Cruz*), preliminary objections of June 26, 1987, paragraphs 46, 51 and 49 respectively.

submitting the case to the Court under the provisions of the Convention, depending on whether the State in question has accepted the jurisdiction of the court.

In exercising its functions, the Commission possesses some serious powers to deal with adamant governments. The Commission is allowed to consider measures of preventive nature. In serious or urgent cases the Commission may request that the State should take some provisional measures to avoid irreparable damage,[274] or if the case is particularly of a serious or urgent character, the Commission may request the Inter-American Court to adopt any provisional measures it deems pertinent to avoid irreparable damage.[275] This power of ordering or requesting provisional measures has been one area of successful innovation by the Inter-American system.[276]

Furthermore, if a State refuses to cooperate in the Commission's investigatory function, the Rules of Procedure provide for a presumption of the veracity of the facts. Thus, the facts hold true as long as other evidence in the case does not lead to a contrary conclusion.[277] Similarly, in cases that have been dealt with by the Commission, if the State concerned after several exhortations, fails to comply with the measures and recommendations proposed by the Commission, the Commission may decide to submit the case to the Court if the State in question has accepted the jurisdiction of the Inter-American Court, unless there is a reasoned decision by an absolute majority of the members of the Commission to the contrary.[278]

b. The Inter-American Court of Human Rights

The Inter-American Court of Human Rights is composed of seven judges, who must be nationals of the Member States of the OAS. It is not surprising that just as in other international judicial tribunals, the persons chosen as judges of the Court must possess the qualifications of jurists of the highest moral authority and of recognized competence in the field of human rights. In addition, like the other judges, they must possess the qualifications which would enable them to exercise the highest judicial functions in conformity with the law of their States.[279] Similarly as in other international tribunals, the judges must also serve in their individual capacities, requiring them upon appointment, to take an oath or make a solemn

---

274 Rules of Procedure, Article 25(1).
275 *Id.* Article 74.
276 *See* generally, Jo. M. Pasqualucci, *Provisional Measures in the Inter-American Human Rights System: An Innovative Development in International Law* 36 VAND. J. TRANSNAT'L L. 803 (1993).
277 Rules of Procedure, Article 39.
278 Article 51 of the Convention; Rules of Procedure, Article 44(1).
279 For the composition, qualifications and other internal organization of the Inter-American Court of Human Rights, *see* Articles 52 to 60 of the American Convention on Human Rights. Compare Article 21(1) of the European Convention as amended by Protocol 11.

declaration that they would exercise their functions honorably, independently, and would keep secret, all the deliberations of the Court.[280] The jurisdiction of the Court is divided into a contentious and an advisory aspect. The Court's contentious jurisdiction is said to be an extension of the Commission's handling of individual petitions, while its advisory jurisdiction mainly entails the clarification of the conformity of national law and practice with the legal standards of the OAS human rights instruments and adjudication.[281]

In the exercise of its contentious jurisdiction, the Court may only examine individual communications if the State Party involved has recognized the Court's contentious jurisdiction either generally or in a specific case.[282] Accordingly, if the Commission is unable to achieve a friendly settlement between a respondent State and an individual who alleges that his or her right or rights under the Convention have been violated, either the Commission or the respondent State may submit the case, under Article 51 to the contentious jurisdiction of the Court. Aggrieved individuals are conferred no standing before the Court by the American Convention. Only States Parties and the Commission are vested with the power to submit a case to the Court.[283] On the part of the respondent State, it is doubtful whether the State would be wiling to submit itself voluntarily to the Court's contentious jurisdiction given the implications that the action might hold for it, namely, a possible finding of violation, a binding ruling and an award of com-

---

280 *See* Article 20 of the Statute of the International Court of Justice for similar provision on solemn declaration by the judges of the International Court of Justice before taking up their duties after election. It must, however, be observed that neither the old European Convention nor the amended version via Protocol 11 require the administering of oath on the judges of the European Court of Human Rights after their election.

281 *See Wilt, supra*, note 229, at 309. While the act of endowing international human rights tribunals with contentious and advisory jurisdictions is common to these tribunals, that of the Inter-American Court appears to be more extensive than others. For example, both under the old European Convention and the amended text, the advisory jurisdiction of the European Court of Human Rights is limited both in terms of who may request advisory opinions and the extent of their application. The advisory practice of the Inter-American Court can be said to be innovative, looking at the extent of the practice. *See Antonio Augusto Cançcado Trindade, The Operation of the Inter-American Court of Human Rights* in THE INTER-AMERICAN SYSTEM OF HUMAN RIGHTS 133, at 141-145 (DAVID J. HARRIS & STEPHEN LIVINGSTONE, eds., Oxford: Clarendon Press, 1998).

282 Article 62 of the Inter American Convention. It should be recalled that this differs from the situation under the Commission where individual access to the Commission is mandatory.

283 Article 61 of the American Convention. This provision differs from the practice under the European Convention. With the amendment of the European convention, individuals have direct access to the European Court.

pensatory damages.[284] The suggestion therefore is that it will be the Commission which would normally decide the cases to submit to the Court.[285]

The issue of access to the Court has raised the question as to how the equality of arms is guaranteed under the American Convention. It has been argued that apart from delay, which is a possible draw back of this procedure, the rights of the victims of human rights violation may be compromised as the Commission may choose not to refer some cases even though violations have been found.[286] The Court tried to close this equality gap by assigning to the Commission the duty of representing the victim in *Velasquez Rodriguez v. the State of Honduras*,[287] the first contentious case that came before the Court. The Inter-American system is, however, getting closer to the European system in conferring standing to individuals and victims, as well as their representatives in cases that are brought to the Court. Article 23 of the new Rules of Procedure of the Inter-American Court now recognizes a more direct participation of victims in the Court's proceedings. Under the Rule, after the Commission refers a case to the Court and the case is admitted, the alleged victim, their family, or their duly accredited representatives can present their requests, arguments and evidence autonomously during all the stages of the proceedings. The new Rule will go into effect on June 1, 2001. While this is a good attempt at recognizing individual access to the Court, it still falls short of direct individual access that the European system pioneered.

The Court, like other international Courts, allows both oral and written proceedings, with a standard of proof that is less formal, compared to domestic proceedings.[288] After the Court hears the necessary submissions of the parties,

---

284 See DAVIDSON, THE INTER-AMERICAN HUMAN RIGHTS SYSTEM, *supra,* note 229, at 186.

285 *Id.* It should be observed that Article 43(3) of the Rules of Procedure now gives a petitioner a say in whether the Commission should refer a case to the Inter-American Court in the case of States that have accepted the contentious jurisdiction of the Court. Under the Rule, the Commission "shall notify the petitioner of the adoption of the report and its transmittal to the State. In the case of States parties to the American Convention that have accepted the contentious jurisdiction of the Inter-American Court, upon notifying the petitioner, the Commission shall give him or her one month to present his or her position as to whether the case should be submitted to the court..."

286 Jo. M. Pasqualucci, *The Inter-American Human Rights System: Establishing Precedents and Procedures in Human Rights Law* 26 MIAMI INTER-AM. L. REV. 297 (1995). *See* also *José Miguel & Lisa L. Bhansali, Procedural Shortcomings in the Defense of Human Rights: An Inequality of Arms in the Inter-American System of Human Rights* in THE INTER-AMERICAN HUMAN RIGHTS SYSTEM, *supra,* note 229, 421, at 435.

287 Judgement of July 29, 1988, Series C No. 4.

288 In the *Velasquez case,* the Court required Honduras to produce evidence to refute the petitioners' claim of a Honduran policy of forced disappearances even though it would ordinarily have been the burden on the Commission, which alleged that such policy was in existence. The Court noted that the standards of proof were "less formal" in international proceedings than in domestic proceedings. There may be the tendency to question the Court's ruling on burden of proof in this

it passes a judgment. If the Court decides that a violation of any of the rights contained in the Convention took place, the Court would normally order that the victim be ensured the enjoyment of the rights denied, and where appropriate, that compensation be paid to the injured party.[289] States Parties are under obligation to comply with the judgment. The parts of the judgement that stipulate compensatory damages have executory force in the country concerned.[290]

The Convention leaves the enforcement of the judgment of the Court with the General Assembly of the OAS. Under Article 65 of the Convention, the Court is required to submit an annual report to the General Assembly, indicating, in particular, the cases in which a State has not complied with its judgment. It has been suggested that although Article 65 refers to regular sessions of the OAS, it does not mean that an issue of non-compliance may not be raised at a special session of the General Assembly at the request of either a Member State or the permanent Council.[291] It has further been observed that the fact that the non-compliance issue is essentially one to be resolved by the General Assembly, the question apparently becomes a political matter to be determined through the political process of the OAS.[292] That process of political determination may involve political exclusion from the activities of the OAS, despite the fact that there is no provision in the American Convention that provides for expulsion of a non-complying Member State.[293]

The Competence of the Inter-American Court to operate in its advisory capacity is based on Article 64 of the Convention. Under the Article, Member States of

---

case. It should be observed that the Commission had shown that disappearance was a policy and practice of the government of Honduras. By its nature, disappearance is designed to conceal and destroy evidence of disappearances. The Court was right therefore in allowing proof by circumstantial, indirect or presumptive evidence which leads to conclusions consistent with the facts.

289 Article 63(1) of the Convention. There is no similar provision under the European Convention.
290 Article 68 of the Convention.
291 *See Thomas Buergenthal, The Inter-American Court of Human Rights* 76 AJIL 1 at 240-241(1982).
292 *See* DAVIDSON, THE INTER-AMERICAN HUMAN RIGHTS SYSTEM, *supra*, note 229, at 226. In other systems, the issue of enforcement is usually a political one, which is left to a political body. In the European system, the Committee of Ministers of the Council of Europe is endowed with supervisory powers that ensure compliance with the decisions of the European Court.
293 *Id.*, drawing attention to the OAS practice with regard to Cuba, which suggests that there is a *de facto* power to exclude a government which fails to comply with its obligations under the Charter of the OAS. One may also suggest that the Protocol of Washington adopted by the OAS in 1992, which makes provision for the suspension of any member whose democratically constituted government has been overthrown by force, after diplomatic initiatives have failed, is a new trend on the possibility of the OAS to force Member States to the American Convention to comply with the judgment of the Inter-American Court. In Europe, Greece was faced with a situation in which it was censured by the Committee of Minsters of the Council of Europe for failing to comply with the just satisfaction awarded against it in the case of *Stran Greek Refineries and Anreadis v. Greece*, Judgement of 9 December 1994, Series A, No. 301-B, EHRR 19, 1995 p.293.

the OAS and the Organs listed in Chapter X of the Charter, acting within their competence, are allowed to seek advisory opinion on the interpretation of the Convention or other treaties concerning the protection of human rights in the Americas. The power of the Court to render advisory opinion is quite broad when compared with the power on the European Court of Human Rights to render advisory opinion under Protocol No. 2 to the European Convention.

It is not in doubt that the entities that could request advisory opinion under Article 64 are quite clear. The problem, however, seems to be the fact that these entities must seek such opinions within their area of competence, as well as the construction of "other treaties concerning the protection of human rights in American States." The Inter-American Court endeavored to answer the first question in its second advisory opinion[294] dealing with the competence of the Commission to request advisory opinion as an organ of the OAS. Here, the Commission sought a ruling as to the date on which a State ratifying or adhering to the Convention with a reservation would be regarded as a party to it. The Court, alluding to the fact that the Commission had a broad competence on the field of human rights, declared that unlike some OAS organs, the Commission enjoyed, as a practical matter, an absolute right to request advisory opinions within the framework of Article 64(1) of the Convention. Similarly, the Court declared in another opinion[295] that the competence of the Commission cannot be impeded by the mere fact that a Member State of the OAS had not ratified the Convention, irrespective of the fact that the request for such an opinion could be said to be a disguised contentious case. There the Court declared that "if the Commission were barred from seeking advisory opinion merely because one or more governments are involved in a controversy with the Commission..., the Commission would seldom, if ever be able to avail itself of the Court's advisory opinion."

The issue of "other treaties" was resolved in the *Other Treaties* opinion[296] in which the Court gave a broad interpretation of the phrase "other treaties" to the effect that "any international treaty applicable in the American States, regardless of whether it be bilateral or multilateral, whatever be the principal purpose of such a treaty, and whether or not Member States of the Inter-American system are or have the right to become parties thereto".[297]

---

294 *Effect of Reservations* (Advisory Opinion OC-2/82 of September 24, 1992, Series A, No.2.
295 *Restrictions to the Death Penalty* (Advisory Opinion OC-33/38 of September 8, 183, Series A, No. 3
296 Advisory Opinion OC-1/82 of September 24, 1982, Series A, No1.
297 *Id.* For detailed analysis of the interpretation of "other treaties" *see* also, Mary Caroline Parker, *'Other Treaties: The Inter-American Court of Human Rights Defines Its Advisory Jurisdiction* 33 AM. U. L REV. 211 (1983).

While the advisory opinions of the Court are merely declaratory and not binding, it does not mean that the opinions are negligible in their effect. They have considerable persuasive effect not only for States Parties to such proceedings, but for the entire inter-American system.[298] There is evidence to show that a number of the Court's advisory opinions have provided guidance to the Commission on various important procedural issues such as exhaustion of domestic remedies, and have begun to contribute to the Court's development of a jurisprudence in the field of the system's substantive rights.[299]

The inter-American Human Rights system has come a long way from a period of lacking normative authority to a period of effective regional articulation of the principles of human rights law and jurisprudence. Its evolution to the present stage is persuasive and should impact other regional arrangements, particularly Africa. It shows a mechanism that is willing to be dynamic in the ever increasing global demand for democratic ideals.

V   THE ORGANIZATION OF AFRICAN UNITY (OAU) AND HUMAN RIGHTS

The road that Africa has traveled with regard to emphasizing principles of international human rights has been a very slow and a somewhat selfish one. Despite the reiteration of the principles contained in the UN Charter and references to human rights in its Charter,[300] the OAU's agenda for human rights implementation in Africa at the inception of the organization was very limited. The agenda in this light traditionally gave priority to self determination (struggle against colonialism) and the struggle against racism, both generally and particularly, as exemplified in the obnoxious apartheid policy of old South Africa. Some African scholars have attributed this lack of interest in international promotion and protection of human rights to the effect of colonialism. According to Professor Eze[301] the fact that colonialism denied Africans the right to rule themselves and consequently the right to organize their economic, cultural, political and social affairs, coupled with the inherent racism of colonialism, drove African governments to emphasize certain human rights as worthy of primary concern at the international level. This author sees some point in the learned scholar's line of reasoning, but wonders whether the impact of colonialism should not have been the serious reason why African governments should emphasize elaborate principles of human rights. Furthermore,

---

298 *See* DAVIDSON, THE INTER-AMERICAN HUMAN RIGHTS SYSTEM, *supra,* note 229, at 232.
299 *Id.*
300 Paragraph 8 of the OAU Charter signed in Addis Ababa on May 1963.
301 EZE, HUMAN RIGHTS IN AFRICA: SOME SELECTED PROBLEMS, *supra,* note 1, at 193.

imbibing notions of human rights would not benefit the colonial powers, but Africans, who should enjoy every right denied during the colonial period in a dispensation of African self rule.[302] The end of the evil of colonialism should have created an urgent need to accord Africans human rights protection. It however, appeared that attempts were geared towards consolidating the struggle against colonialism and all its appendages, while no time could be taken to deal with other areas of human rights promotion and protection.

Before the formation of the OAU, advocates of Pan Africanism had shown concern for human rights among the colonized peoples.[303] It was at the Fifth Pan African Congress held in Manchester in 1945, that the first conscious effort was made to establish a link between human rights and the fight against colonialism and human rights on the one hand, and between Pan Africanism and human rights on the other. They called among other things, for the abolition of all racial discrimination, freedom of expression, assembly and of the press, and free compulsory education up to age sixteen,[304] the same rights that are still demanded today in all African states.

With the establishment of the OAU, some two decades afer the formation of the United Nations and the adoption of the Universal Declaration on Human Rights, one would have thought that the ideals that drove Pan Africanism would have also concretized the promotion of human rights went. This is more so because the founding fathers of OAU were persuaded that "the Charter of the United Nations and the Universal Declaration of Human Rights, [to] the principles of which [they] affirm [their] adherence, provide a solid foundation for peaceful and positive cooperation among States."[305] Particularly, the activities which preceded the formation of the OAU would have given one the reason to reach the above conclusion.

Before the adoption of the OAU Charter in 1963, the Congress of African Jurists, which took place in Lagos in 1961,[306] at a time when more African colonies had joined the ranks of independent states, adopted a resolution on human rights that was to lay down the basis for future efforts for the establishment of rules and mechanisms for African regional promotion and protection of human

---

302 The situation has rather been the reverse. Africa has witnessed orchestrated violations of human rights almost on the scale experienced during the colonial era. In almost all the cases, the only difference is that Africans are the perpetrators.
303 *Eze, supra,* note 1, at 195.
304 *Id.*
305 Paragraph 8, preamble of the OAU Charter, *supra,* note 300.
306 The Congress took place from January 3 to 7, 1961. It was at this meeting that the Famous Law of Lagos was drafted. *See* INTERNATIONAL COMMISSION OF JURISTS, THE AFRICAN CONFERENCE ON THE RULE OF LAW (LAW OF LAGOS, Geneva, 1961).

rights.[307] The Congress stated that in order to give full effect to the Universal Declaration of Human Rights, a suitable tribunal should be set up, to which all persons within the jurisdiction of Africa should have recourse. And that to that end, an African Convention on Human Rights was needed, since that alone would permit the realization of the dual aspirations of independent Africa, namely liberty and unity.[308] With the adoption of the Charter of OAU, however, the place given to human rights became very limited to African unity, decolonization, and the elimination of racism, all of which have been referred to as the spirit of Addis Ababa.[309] Thus, Article II (1) of the OAU Charter enumerates the purposes of the organization as:

(a) to promote the unity and solidarity of the African States,
(b) to coordinate and intensify their cooperation and efforts to achieve a better life for the peoples of Africa.
(c) to defend their sovereignty, their territorial integrity and independence,
(d) to eradicate all forms of colonialism from Africa; and
(e) to promote international cooperation, having due regard to the Charter of the United Nations and the Universal Declaration of Human Rights.

Article III makes provision for principles that would govern Member States in achieving the purposes stated in Article II, one of which is the non-intervention in the internal affairs of Member States.[310] It has been observed that this provision was drafted into the Charter to assuage the basic concern of the founding fathers of the OAU to the effect that no outside body should deal with matters within the domestic jurisdiction of Member States.[311] Human rights questions accordingly, were thus regarded as matters within the internal affairs of Member States, and therefore, must not be interfered with, as has been emphasized by African States over the years.

One must observe that the realities of post colonial Africa, necessarily required that attention should be given to the issue of human rights in a more elaborate fashion before it became too late. Colonialism was not going to last forever, neither

---

307 EZE, *supra*, note 1, at 195.
308 *Id. citing* INTERNATIONAL COMMISSION OF JURISTS, THE RULE OF LAW AND HUMAN RIGHTS: PRINCIPLES AND DEFINITIONS (Geneva, 1966 Appendix D).
309 *See* CERVENKA, THE ORGANIZATION OF AFRICAN UNITY AND ITS CHARTER, *supra*, note 169, at 13, referring to the speech of the then president of Algeria, Ahmed Ben Bella against colonial rule at the Addis Ababa Summit Conference of Heads of State and Government of Independent African States in May 1968. *See also* T. O. ELIAS, AFRICA AND DEVELOPMENT OF INTERNATIONAL LAW 121-127 (Martinus Nijhoff Publishers, 1988).
310 Article III(2) of the African Charter.
311 EZE, *supra*, note 1, at 199.

was apartheid as events have shown. Other areas of human rights needed to be given attention in the light of the evolution of society and events in other regions of the globe. The OAU could not, for example, afford to ignore African refugee problems. That is why the assistance and protection of refugees is seen as one of the positive activities of the OAU at the regional level in the field of human rights. Efforts in that direction culminated in the adoption of the OAU Convention on Refugees by the Assembly of Heads of State and Governments in September 1969.[312]

Along the same line, regarding other areas of human rights, there was the need to search for an African regional human rights mechanism after the attempt of African jurists in 1961 failed in Lagos. Such calls were made at several seminars on human rights organized by the UN[313] and some African institutions, like the Dakar Colloquium organized by the International Commission of Jurists (ICJ) and the Senegalese Bar Association. The Colloquium recommended the establishment of a Human Rights Commission as one of the means of tackling the fundamental and urgent problems of human rights in Africa.[314]

Many of the decisions and recommendations reached at the various conferences and seminars, as good as they were, were not implemented because of perceived threat to the guarded sovereignty of African states.[315] Despite the challenges posed by the developments in this area, it was not until 1979 that the Conference of OAU Heads of State held in Monrovia passed a resolution that called on the Secretary-General of the OAU to organize a meeting of qualified experts to prepare a preliminary draft of an African Charter on human rights.[316] This OAU directive was preempted by the 1979 UN Seminar on the establishment of regional commissions on human rights with special reference to Africa, which also came out with

---

312 *See* Convention Covering Specific Aspects of Refugee Problems in Africa, 1001 U.N.T.S. 45; 8 I.L.M. 1288 (1969). The Convention entered into force on November 26, 1973 upon the deposit of instruments of ratification by one-third of Member States of the OAU.
313 EZE. *supra*, note 1, at 201-202. For example, the Seminar on Human Rights in Developing Countries held in Dakar, Senegal in February 1966; the Cairo Conference of 1969, which was devoted to the establishment of regional human rights commissions with special reference to Africa based on a proposal to the UN Human Rights Commission for the establishment of regional commissions on human rights in those parts of the world where they did not exist; the ECA Conference on Legal Process and the Individual held at Addis Ababa in 1971; the Seminar on the Study of New Ways and Means for Promoting Human Rights with Special reference to the Problems and Needs of Africa, held in Dar-es Salaam from October 23 to November 5, 1973; and the UN Seminar on the Establishment of Regional Commissions on Human Rights with Special Reference to Africa, held in Monrovia from September 10 to 21, 1979. *See also, Ramcharan, The Travaux Préparatoires of the African Commission on Human Rights, supra,* note 6, at 307.
314 *See* EZE, *supra*, note 1, at 203.
315 *Id.* at 202. *See* Dec. 115(XVI)Rev.1(1979), *supra* note 3.
316 *Id.* at 203.

a proposal for the establishment of a commission which should have the function of promoting and protecting human rights.[317] The result of the OAU initiative was the African Charter on Human and Peoples Rights (African Charter),[318] which entered into force on October 1986 as the principal normative instrument of the African human rights system. The African Charter established the African Commission on Human and Peoples' Rights (The African Commission) as the implementing institution of the rights enshrined in the Charter.[319]

The adoption of the African Charter was indeed a turning point in Africa's march towards regional recognition of the principles of international human rights.[320] The question, however, remains as to the impact of the Charter and the Commission as well as the commitment of the OAU on the effective implementation of the African Mechanism as a means of resolving human rights questions in the region. That is the larger inquiry that this book is set to make in subsequent chapters. That is more so in the light of current steps the OAU is taking towards establishing an African Court of Human and Peoples' Rights to complement and reinforce the functions of the African Commission on Human and Peoples' Rights, with the conviction that the attainment of the objectives of the African Charter requires the establishment of a court.[321]

One can say that there is hope of more effective realization of human rights in Africa if the recent initiatives coming out of the Continent are any thing to go by. Member States of the OAU now appear determined to place human rights in the forefront of its regional agenda in their recent efforts to reform the OAU. At its Fourth Extraordinary Summit between 8-9 September, 1999 in Sirte, Libya, the Assembly of Heads of State and Government (AHSG) adopted the *Sirte Declaration*.[322] The essence of the meeting was to discuss ways and means of strengthen-

---

317 See Ramcharan, *The Travaux Préparatoires of the African Commission on Human Rights*, supra, note 6, at 307.
318 The African Charter on Human and Peoples' Rights, *supra*, note 3.
319 *Id.* Article 30.
320 See Claude Welch, *The O.A.U. and Human Rights: Towards a New Definition*, 19 JOURNAL OF MODERN AFRICAN STUDIES 401 (1981), and Claude Welch, *The Organization of African Unity and the Promotion of Human Rights*, 29 JOURNAL OF MODERN AFRICAN STUDIES 535 (1991).
321 The OAU, by virtue of Res. AHG/230(XXX) at its Tunis summit in June 1994 invited the Secretary-General of the OAU to summon a meeting of experts on the establishment of an African Court on Human Rights. The first of such meeting was held in Cape Town, South Africa from September 6 to 12, 1995 under the auspices of the OAU and the International Commission of Jurists in collaboration with the South African Ministry of Justice. The meeting produced a Draft Protocol OAU/LEG/EXP/AFCHPR(I))(hereafter, CAPE TOWN DRAFT PROTOCOL) to the African Charter. There were subsequent meetings in Nouakchott, Mali and Addis Ababa, Ethiopia, which revised the initial drafts, resulting in a Protocol which has been adopted by the OAU. Further details on these instruments will be discussed in chapters 5 and 6.
322 EAHG/DECL.(IV) Rev. 1.

ing the OAU to make it more effective so as to keep pace with the social, political and economic development taking place within the context of globalization.[323] In addition, the AHSG reaffirmed its determination to continue to encourage and support the on-going democratization process in the Continent. It declared that the process of democratization in Africa was critical in sustaining the Continent's efforts towards the promotion and protection of human and peoples' rights, as well as respect for the rule of law.[324] The Assembly also noted that despite contributions to universalization of human rights, violations still continued, which posed a serious impediment to the freedom and socio-economic development of the African peoples, and that the OAU thus recommitted itself to take up the challenge of promoting and protecting human rights as a matter of priority, and to ensure the early establishment of African Court on Human and Peoples Rights.[325]

Thus, the major initiative of the *Sirte Declaration* is a total reform of the OAU, by replacing it with an African Union, in conformity with the ultimate objectives of the Charter of the OAU and the treaty establishing the African Economic Community (AEC). The First OAU Ministerial Meeting to implement the *Sirte Declaration* was held in Tripoli, Libya from 31 May – 2 June 2000 to consider the proposed African Union by examining reports adopted by meetings of legal experts and parliamentarians.[326] The meeting affirmed that the process of creating the Union should involve all peoples of Africa and also discussed the establishment of a Pan-African Parliament as a consultative forum whose members would be voted by the general population of African States.[327]

The AHSG adopted the Constitutive Act of the African Union (Constitutive Act)[328] at its Thirty-Sixth Ordinary Session in Lome, Togo.[329] The African

---

323 *Id.*
324 *Id.* ¶ 13.
325 *Id.* ¶ 14.
326 REPORT OF THE MINISTERIAL CONFERENCE ON THE ESTABLISHMENT OF THE AFRICAN UNION AND THE PAN AFRICAN PARLIAMENT, CM/2162 (LXXII).
327 REPORT OF THE MINISTERIAL CONFERENCE ON THE ESTABLISHMENT OF THE AFRICAN UNION AND THE PAN-AFRICAN PARLIAMENT, CM/2162 (LXXII).
328 CONSTITUTIVE ACT OF THE AFRICAN UNION, adopted by the Thirty-sixth Ordinary Session of the Assembly of Heads of State and Government of the OAU 11 July 2000 at Lome, Togo. Promulgation of the Act is a realization of the dreams of generations of Pan-Africanists in their quest to have an umbrella African organization to promote unity, solidarity, cohesion and cooperation among the peoples of Africa and African States. *See* Preamble 1 of the Act. The African Union is modeled after the European Union. The Act provides for some new organs that were not provided for in the Charter of the OAU, namely, the Pan-African Parliament, the Court of Justice, which was initially provided for in the AEC treaty, financial institutions such as, the African Central Bank, the African Monetary Fund, and the African Investment Bank. There are also Specialized technical Committees and Commissions along the lines of the OAU Charter. *See* Articles, 5, 14, and 19 of

Union was formally established at the Fifth Extraordinary Session of the AHSG between 1-2 March 2001.[330] As already indicated, the Constitutive Act unifies the objectives of the Charter of the OAU and the treaty establishing the AEC, and transforms the OAU into the new Union.[331] Particular provisions of the Constitutive Act, affecting the question of human rights in Africa will be discussed in chapter two when the Charter of the OAU is evaluated in terms of its effect as a normative instrument of the African human rights system.

---

the Act.
[329] *See* DECISION ON THE ESTABLISHMENT OF THE AFRICAN UNION AND THE PAN-AFRICAN PARLIAMENT, AHG/Dec.143 (XXXVI). *See* also DECISIONS ADOPTED BY THE FIFTH EXTRAORDINARY SESSION OF THE ASSEMBLY OF HEADS OF STATE AND GOVERNMENT, EAHG/Dec.1-4(V), 1-2 March, 2001, Sirte Libya; DECISION OF THE ASSEMBLY OF HEADS OF STATE AND GOVERNMENT ON THE AFRICAN UNION, EAHG/Dec.1(V).
[330] *See* DECISION OF THE ASSEMBLY OF HEADS OF STATE AND GOVERNMENT ON THE AFRICAN UNION, EAHG/Dec.1(V), ¶ 1. All African States have signed the Constitutive Act of the African Union. With the deposit of the 36th instrument of ratification with the Secretary-General of the OAU by Nigeria on April 26, 2001, the Act has attained the legal requirement for entry into force. Thus, ratification by the two-thirds of the Member States of the OAU required by Article 28 of the Act has been achieved. It is expected that the Act will enter into force on May 26, 2001, thirty days after the deposit of the required number of ratifications as provided by Article 28.*See* ORGANIZATION OF AFRICAN UNITY, PRESS RELEASE NO. 52/200, April 27, 2001.
[331] Even though the Constitutive Act will replace the Charter of the OAU when it enters into force on May 26, 2001, pursuant to Article 33 of the Act, the Charter of the OAU will remain operative for a transitional period of one year or such further period as may be determined by the AHSG for the purpose of enabling the OAU/AEC to undertake the necessary measures regarding the devolution of its assets and liabilities to the African Union and all matters relating thereto.

2

NORMATIVE INSTRUMENTS OF THE AFRICAN HUMAN RIGHTS SYSTEM

I   THE CHARTER OF THE OAU

The question that echoes in the minds of scholars with African human rights interest is the normative value of the OAU Charter to the African human rights system in the interpretation of the rights guaranteed under the African Charter. From the discussions in the last segment of the previous chapter, it is clear that the OAU Charter does not appear to attach a particular significance to human rights in a more comprehensive light, with the particular aim of focusing on making African governments accountable for the fundamental rights of their subjects. Birame Ndiaye thinks that the lack of significant allusion to human rights protection by the OAU Charter should not be readily criticized.[332] His main reason for this suggestion is that the "constitutional instruments of the other regional organizations and the United Nations also contain relatively few references to human rights." He however, agrees that these other organizations go a step further in constructing a system for the promotion and protection of human rights, backed by legal binding instruments, which was not the case for the OAU.[333] The OAU Charter's emphasis is on the rights of peoples to self determination and struggle against racial discrimination in response to the ravages of colonialism.

    The attempt has been to infer a general normative value of the OAU Charter on matters of human rights by looking at the preamble of the Charter and the purposes and objectives of the OAU itself to show that the OAU Charter contains some provisions on human rights.[334] It was pointed out that the OAU Charter refers not only to the constitutional text of the UN Charter, but also mentions that the Universal Declaration of Human Rights contains principles to which OAU States

---

332 *Birame Ndiaye, The Place of Human Rights in the Charter of the Organization of African Unity* in THE INTERNATIONAL DIMENSIONS OF HUMAN RIGHTS 601 (KAREL VASAK/ PHILIP ALSTON, eds., Greenwood Press, 1982).
333 *Id.*
334 *Id.* at 603-606. *See* also EZE, *supra*, note 1, at 196.

Parties reaffirm their adherence, as they provide a solid foundation for peaceful and positive cooperation among states.[335]

The argument regarding the normative value to be inferred from the preamble of the OAU Charter on the protection of human rights could be examined on two fronts. On the one hand, it could be said that such normative value would at best be a very weak one. The basis for this position is that despite the fact that preambles of both domestic and international instruments often have the hidden function of allowing for the reconciliation of divergent and even seemingly irreconcilable conceptions, often they are not legally binding. This is especially so because their wording lacks enough specificity to allow for juridical interpretation. Similarly, preambles generally set the tone for positive provisions that might subsequently be embodied in the relevant instruments. For example, the existence of the preambles to the UN Charter notwithstanding, the organization did not fail to seek more operative instruments by proceeding to draft the Universal Declaration and subsequent instruments.

On the other hand, current trends in the interpretation of international instruments attach considerable importance to the preamble of these instruments. The preamble to the Charter of the UN is often involved in interpreting that instrument. For instance, its reference to "equal rights of men and women and of nations large and small,"[336] has helped to justify the adoption of many documents guaranteeing an equal treatment of persons and States. In particular, the phrase in paragraph 8 of the preamble to the OAU Charter makes reference to the Universal Declaration which is to be observed as much as the UN Charter. It makes clear that these two instruments need to be observed together, and that the preamble to the OAU Charter should be equally observed.

The point is that even though the OAU, like the UN itself, has the duty to implement its basic document by other documents, the obligatory character of which finds its origin in the parent instrument, that in itself does not detract from the value of the preamble. Practically, every article of an important document requires similar implementation. In turn, each implementing document may require further enactment of regulations. Similarly, each provision of a constitution requires supplementary legislation domestically, which in turn is followed by regulations adopted by appropriate department of State, and all three steps need to be considered by courts when they have to interpret one of them.

One thing that is common in the views stated above is that, making provisions in preambles of basic instruments and subsequent adoption of implementing

---

335 See Paragraph 8 of the Preamble to the Charter of the Organization of African Unity, *supra*, note 300.
336 Paragraph 1 of the preamble to the UN Charter.

instruments, are all steps which form part of a growing legal system. It follows therefore, that in the case of the OAU, by adopting the preambular provisions of the Charter, its Member States have given indication of a desire to take steps in creating normative rules for the protection of human rights even if rights may not be effectively established if they remain only as preambular provisions.

The other area where attempts have been made to bring out the human rights content of the OAU Charter is the statement of the purposes set forth in the Charter under Article II. The Article provides *inter alia*, as a purpose of the OAU, the promotion of international cooperation, having due regard to the Charter of the United Nations and the Universal Declaration of Human Rights.[337] Could the fact that the Charter expressly makes provision for international cooperation, taking into consideration the UN Charter and the Universal Declaration, without more, establish the basis for obligation on the part of Member States of the OAU to respect human rights? On the face of it, it might be read to be a clear intention of the OAU to create an obligation on their members to ensure the protection of human rights as guaranteed by the UN Charter and the Universal Declaration, since that would be a basis for their cooperation. This author's opinion on first thought would ordinarily be that, if that was the intention, it was not carried far enough. The wording of the Charter was not strong enough for one to conclude that the provision *per se* amounts to an outright incorporation of the UN Charter and the Universal Declaration into the Charter of the OAU.

On the other hand, it could be said that reference to the UN Charter and the Universal Declaration in Article II of the Charter of the OAU is an indication of the important source of the growing regional legal system. The incorporation of the UN instruments can be said to be an unequivocal creation of the legal principle emphasizing the importance of human rights in the African region along the lines of the UN Charter and the Universal Declaration, and the need for taking steps to interpret it and explain how it applies in a variety of circumstances in the region. A good example in this regard, is the interpretation of the principles in Article 2 of the UN Charter. An elaborate interpretation of these principles had to wait for the General Assembly approval by consensus, after many years of preparatory negotiations, of the Declaration on Principles of International Law Concerning Friendly Relations and Cooperation among States.[338] The International Court

---

337 Article II(1)(e) of the OAU Charter. *See also* ELIAS, *supra*, note 309, at 124-129.
338 Declaration of Principles on International Law Concerning Friendly Relations and Cooperation Among States in Accordance with the Charter of the United Nations. Adopted by the UN General Assembly, 24 October 1970. G.A.Res. 2625, U.N. GAOR, 25th Sess., Supp., No. 28, at 121, U.N.Doc.. A/8028 (1971); 9 I.L.M. 1292 (1970). For the text of the Declaration, *see* LAKSHMAN D. GURUSWAMY, SIR GEOFFREY W.R. PALMER & BURNS H. WESTON (hereafter, GURUSWAMY, *et al.*), SUPPLEMENT OF BASIC DOCUMENTS TO INTERNATIONAL ENVIRONMENTAL LAW AND WORLD

of Justice found this interpretative document helpful in the *Nicaragua v. United States* case,[339] and declared it to be a crystallization of rules of customary international law, applicable to all States, whether or not they were members of the United Nations.

Ndiaye,[340] however, suggests that the fact that framers of the OAU Charter did not require from Member States a commitment to ensure the protection of human rights as a condition for membership of the organization is an evidence that will defeat an interpretation that Article II (1)(e) possesses a normative human rights value. Furthermore, he opines that it is difficult to see how the implementation of human rights can be the basis for international cooperation without first of all making it a condition for admission, a sort of entrance fee.[341] This position appears to recommend the practice of the Council of Europe regarding its membership. Under this practice, countries that were part of the former Soviet Union when they applied for membership, had to ratify the European Convention and present proof that they really observe human rights. In addition, their delegates would not be permitted to participate in the Parliamentary Assembly of the Council if they were not elected by proper democratic processes. There is no doubt that a requirement to the above effect in the Charter of the OAU would have underscored the normative human rights value of the Charter without much arguments. The practice of the UN, however, has shown that Member States became members of the UN and various regional organizations regardless of whether they observed human rights or not.

The purposes set out in Article II of the OAU Charter, which defines the powers of the organization, have been described as restrictively formulated, thus proving that the dogma of State sovereignty was not in any way called to question in Addis Ababa.[342] In this regard, the analysis is that in the formulation of the purposes of the organization, the OAU is given the power to deal with all activities of a modern State, except those that concern the fundamental functions of a State, such as the matters of constitution, administration, justice and police, these being matters that deal directly with human rights promotion and protection.[343] While these views hold some validity, it must be emphasized that sovereignty was clearly

---

ORDER 76 (St. Paul, Minnesota: West Publishing Company, 1994).
339 Case Concerning Military and Paramilitary Activities in and against Nicaragua (*Nicaragua v. United States of America*) (1986) I.C.J. Rep. 14.
340 *Ndiaye, supra,* note 332, at 605.
341 *Id.*
342 François Borella, *Organizations Internationales Regionales: Le Regionalisme Africain, cited* in *Ndiaye, supra,* note 332, at 605.
343 *Id. See also* EZE, *supra,* note 1, at 198.

limited by the OAU preambular "adherence" to the Universal Declaration, and by the obligation to have "due regard" to that Declaration. Several African States have observed this by copying the provisions of the Declaration into their Constitutions. In addition, African States have reaffirmed their adherence to the "principles of human and peoples' rights and freedoms contained ... in the declaration adopted by... the United Nations." This was only a reaffirmation of their obligation accepted already in the UN Charter. This reminder strengthens merely a previous obligation, recognizing that African States decided from the very beginning to observe these rules that have by now become generally binding rules of customary international law.

It should also be pointed out that the second paragraph of the preamble to the Charter of the OAU accentuated the fact that "freedom, equality, justice and dignity are essential objectives for the achievement of the legitimate aspirations of the African Peoples." It is further relevant that this paragraph was involved later in the second preamble of the African Charter on Human and Peoples' Rights, and that it was in the name of these human rights principles that the African Peoples fought their battle for independence, and that it was due to non-observance of human rights by the colonial powers that other States came to their assistance. This was the reason why their main weapon at that time, the Universal Declaration, was mentioned twice in the Charter of the OAU. At that time, it was the African States' most cherished document, and at the first International Conference on Human Rights, held at Tehran in 1968, all the new African States supported the statement that the Universal Declaration constituted "a common understanding of the peoples of the world concerning the inalienable and inviolable rights of all members of the human family" and constituted "an obligation for the members of the international community."[344] The General Assembly promptly concurred with this statement.[345]

All in all, the notion that the OAU Charter excluded human rights promotion and protection from the purview of its purposes and objective principles is not totally valid. Similarly, the view that the allusions made to human rights in the Charter were only reduced to a simple reference to the Universal Declaration, and thus cannot be regarded as entailing an obligation for the Member States, misses the point. This is because every State must observe the basic human rights if it wants to be a part of the world community. The obligation is therefore clear, even if international enforcement is limited to gross violations. While it may be true that OAU's stance on human rights practice in Africa has not been remarkable,

---

344 *See Louis B. Sohn, The New International Law: Protection of the Rights of Individuals Rather than States*, 32 AM. U. L. REV. 2 at 16 (1982).
345 The Declaration of Tehran, 23 U.N. GAOR Supp. (No. 41) at 1, U.N. Doc. A/Conf.32/41 (1968).

that does not erase the obligations acquired by African States under the UN Charter and the Universal Declaration. It took the world fifty years to agree on an International Criminal Court, that might be able to enforce the law on individuals guilty of gross violations of rights. It must be pointed out that States are not in themselves guilty; only the individuals who usurped control of State are guilty, and the international community finally got a means to punish them. Thus, old theories protecting governments are no longer acceptable, as human rights in the next millennium have received an important reenforcement.

The fact that the framers of the OAU Charter did not include human rights among the principles which Article III of the Charter provides for, and which OAU Member States undertook to implement in Article VI of the Charter,[346] does not diminish the obligations mentioned above. It is true that the pledge and undertaking to scrupulously observe the provisions of Article III are central to whatever the OAU wanted to achieve via its Charter. It is also true that the notable principle that has always stood in the way of the human rights agenda in Africa is the principle of non intervention in internal affairs of states enshrined in Article III(2). It must, however, be pointed out that the effect of this principle continues to diminish as events unfold.[347]

The above arguments on the obligations of African States not withstanding, one would agree that the failure of the OAU Charter to provide for a human rights commission among the organs and specialized commissions of the OAU under Articles VII and XX, appears to give credence to the view that the Charter does not *per se* possess a normative value, as far human rights protection in Africa is concerned. This is especially so because these organs and specialized commissions are the vehicles through which the OAU would realize its objectives. Thus, creating one of those organs within the OAU Charter to address post colonial human rights questions would have been an unequivocal demonstration of the Charter's upholding of human rights promotion and protection. As Eze suggests, at the time the Charter was adopted, African States were not prepared to allow any organ other than their domestic institutions to deal with matters that touched on the

---

346 Article VI of the Charter provides that "the Member States pledge themselves to observe scrupulously the principles enumerated in Article III of the present Charter."
347 For example, the OAU supported the Nigeria led ECOWAS intervention force (ECOMOG) that reinstated Tejan Kabba, the president of Sierra Leone into power after an overthrow by the military. Similarly, at its 35th summit at Algiers in 1999, the OAU stressed the importance of regional respect for human rights and called for the amendment to its Charter to this effect. The Summit agreed that military coups in Africa would no longer be tolerated.

protection of human rights. Their preoccupation was to stamp out colonialism in all its forms in Africa.[348]

African States might have objected to imposition on them of a global human rights commission, but as soon as they had a chance to concentrate on that issue, they established a regional one in furtherance of their existing obligations. It must be stressed that human rights protection was the main weapon against the colonial powers in Africa, and by accepting them wholeheartedly the peoples of Africa got the support of other States against the violations of their human rights by those powers. The OAU, no doubt, originally failed to provide for early ways of dealing with home-grown violations that would accompany African self rule. The organization rather sacrificed that on the altar of the national sovereignty of independent African States despite the fact that its Charter's reference to the Charter of the United Nations and the Universal Declaration, while to a great extent, is an agreement with the international distaste for colonialism and all its attributes, is also an extension of obligation to Member States of the OAU to respect human rights.

Some of the shortcomings of the OAU Charter as a true normative human rights instrument in Africa, highlighted in this section, are now addressed by the Constitutive Act of the new African Union. The Act has placed the promotion and protection of human rights in the agenda of the regional body. Member States of the OAU have now pledged their determination "to promote and protect human and peoples' rights, consolidate democratic institutions and culture and to ensure good governance and the rule of law."[349] In the same vein, a new objective of the regional organization is to "promote and protect human rights in accordance with the African Charter on Human and Peoples"Rights and other relevant human rights instruments."[350] There is yet another radical provision, which initiates the "condemnation and rejection of unconstitutional changes of governments" in Africa as a principle of African States.[351] In this regard, Article 30 of the Act, which provides for suspension of Member States of the Union, emphatically states that "governments which shall come to power through unconstitutional means shall not be allowed to participate in the activities of the Union." Most importantly, the cherished policy of non-intervention in the internal affairs of Member States, which was the creed of the OAU Charter ceases to be a principle of African States. It has rather become a principle of Member States of the African Union to have

---

348 EZE, *supra*, note1 at, 198-199.
349 *See* Preamble 9 of the Constitutive Act of the African Union.
350 Constitutive Act of the African Union, art. 3(h). Similarly, Article 4(m) of the Act makes respect for democratic principles, human rights, the rule of law and good governance as one of the principles of the Union.
351 *See* Constitutive Act of the African Union, art. 3(p).

the "right ... to intervene in a Member State pursuant to a decision of the Assembly in respect of grave circumstances, namely: war crimes, genocide and crimes against humanity.[352] Promotion of gender equality has also become a principle of the regional body.[353]

By reforming the OAU, there is no doubt that Africa has started responding to global reorganization and is making every effort to reposition itself in global politics and relations. The Constitutive Act of the African Union shows a departure from traditional Africa's fear of "freedom for the peoples" from their own home rule. While the practical application of the Constitutive Act is yet to be seen, it is a bold step, which will equip the peoples of Africa in pressing for good governance and accountability. It is also an instrument that gives additional legitimacy to African human rights institutional organs in their quest to apply international norms in the resolution of human rights disputes.

II THE AFRICAN CHARTER ON HUMAN AND PEOPLES' RIGHTS

Without revisiting much of its history, the promulgation and subsequent adoption of the African Charter in June 1981 at the eighteenth Conference of the Heads of State and Government of the OAU[354] was a way of filling up the glaring lacuna in the Charter of the OAU on regional promotion and protection of human rights in post colonial Africa. Scholars proffer different reasons for the creation of an African human rights mechanism. According to Professor Umozurike, a one time Chairman of the African Commission, developments on the international plane at that time favored an idea of an African human rights mechanism. These developments included the Helsinki Final Act of 1975, signed by the United States, Canada and thirty three Western and Eastern European countries, that emphasized respect for human rights, and the emphasis placed thereafter by the next United States President, Jimmy Carter, on human rights in the international relations of the United States.[355]

Okoth-Ogendo, on the other hand, contends that the decision to establish the mechanism was taken not because there was a juridical void with respect to the promotion and protection of human rights at the continental or domestic level.[356]

---

352 *See Id.* art. 4(h).
353 *Id.* art. 4(l).
354 The African Charter on Human and Peoples' Rights, *supra*, note 3.
355 U.O. Umozurike, *The African Charter on Human and Peoples' Rights*, 77 AM. J. INT'L L. 902(1983).
356 H. W. O. Okoth-Ogendo, *Human and Peoples' Rights: What Point is Africa Trying to Make?* in HUMAN RIGHTS AND GOVERNANCE IN AFRICA 74 -77 (RONALD COHEN *et al*, eds., Florida: University Press of Florida, 1993).

He listed three reasons for the establishment of the mechanism. First, because the Charter of OAU affirms commitment to the UN Charter and the Universal Declaration, the ratification by African States of those instruments in addition to other human rights instruments, imposed an obligation for the promotion and protection of human rights. Thereby they accepted the responsibility for fulfilling the commitment to the promotion and protection of human rights. It became a part of the OAU mandate even if very little of it appeared to have been exercised in its history. Second, there was no existing machinery at the regional level for institutional coordination, supervision, or implementation of efforts towards the promotion and protection of human rights, despite international commitment to that effect. Thirdly, the need to develop a scheme of human rights, norms and principles founded on the historical traditions and values of African civilizations rather than simply reproducing and trying to administer the norms and principles derived from the historical experiences of Europe and the Americas.[357]

One is inclined to agree with the reasons given by Mr. Okoth-Ogendo, which confirm rather than disagree that there was indeed a juridical void in African regional human rights promotion and protection. To deny the existence of this lacuna is an attempt to run away from the realities of the early post-independence African human rights experience. It is quite true that the African initiative needed not mimic either the European or the more recent Latin American experience, it must, however, be emphasized that the experiences of these regions were very relevant to the construction of the African mechanism, even though the mandate of the drafters of the African Charter was to draw up an instrument based on African legal philosophy, which is responsive to African needs- African needs in the sense of incorporating African traditional values and civilization, which should inspire and characterize the reflection and conception of African human rights.[358]

The notion of African needs should not be interpreted to mean removing some rights from the contents of basic human rights, which are universal. It should rather be an addition, albeit an African contribution, to the general human rights concept. This is necessary because, there may be the tendency to interpret African needs to be in direct opposition to the fundamental principles and precepts underlying the International Bill of Rights, which are regarded as peculiarly Western, and not wholly reflective of the broad spectrum of political values to which Africa's

---

[357] *Id.* at 76.
[358] Particularly, the framers of the African Mechanism were encouraged by the American Convention, approved by Latin American States in 1969, which subsequently came into effect in 1978. It is known that the African Commission as soon as it was organized, went to Inter-American mechanism for advice. They also visited promptly the Inter-American Court of Human Rights, but the main concern was how much a commission could do, and what its efforts should concentrate on.

civilization subscribes. While there may be values that are peculiar to Africa, it needs to be stressed that these values should reinforce the human rights of the African rather than remove some of these rights by aiding their derogation.

Whatever the argument, one thing that is clear is that the African Charter is the primary normative instrument of the African human rights system. In content, language and organization, the Charter owes much to the prior international human rights documents, notably the Universal Declaration of Human Rights and the two Covenants on Civil and Political Rights and on Economic, Social and Cultural Rights. It also embodies some unique African social values, norms, and power management processes that are the bedrock of African social organizations, as well as those reflecting the political economic orientations of African States.

III RIGHTS GUARANTEED UNDER THE CHARTER

The African Charter guarantees a number of rights, which must be interpreted if they would ever mean anything to anybody. The interpretation of these rights would normally be geared towards translating them into practical realities that would serve the purpose they were meant to serve. Earlier writers on the African system were not able to provide much analysis on the interpretation of these rights by the African Commission, making it almost impossible for readers to have a grasp on the jurisprudence of the African mechanism.[359] This was not entirely the fault of the writers as the mechanism was shrouded in utter secrecy regarding the cases that went before the Commission. Also, it should be observed that there is comparatively little in the form of detailed jurisprudence from the African Commission, unlike the situation in Europe and the Americas. In recent years, the Commission has begun to show some signs of making public its decisions. It should be noted, however, that an examination of the work of the Commission reveals that there has been little juridical analysis of the rights protected by the African Charter. The analysis in this segment will focus on how the Commission has interpreted these rights in the cases that were made public. Where appropriate, reference will be made to the practice of other international and regional systems for comparative purposes only, aimed at improving the jurisprudence of the African mechanism.

For convenience, the analysis will be made under different headings representing the different clusters of rights guaranteed in the Charter. Thus, we will consider

---

359 It should be observed that the book by Evelyn Ankuma on the practice and procedures of the African Commission is the first of its kind on the African System in terms of providing some analysis on the Commission's practice as it relates to the rights guaranteed in the African Charter.

civil and political rights; economic, social and cultural rights; and group or collective rights.[360] Other ancillary provisions that impact on the construction and effectiveness of the Charter will be discussed where appropriate.

A. *Civil and Political Rights*

1. Right to life and integrity of the person

This is the first substantive right guaranteed in the African Charter. Article 4 provides that "human beings are inviolable. Every human being shall be entitled to respect for his life and the integrity of his person. No one may be arbitrarily deprived of this right." All international human rights instruments emphasize the fundamental nature of the right to life, and its preeminence among other rights. The right to life has been observed to be characterized not only by the fact of being the legal basis of all other rights, but also by forming an integral part of all human rights that are essential for guaranteeing access for all human beings to all goods, including legal possession of those necessary for the development of their physical, moral and spiritual existence.[361] Furthermore, it has been said that the right to life was only to be recognized and was not a new creation of the post-Second War human rights instruments.[362]

The importance of the right to life in Africa cannot be overemphasized. This is more so, because it is a right that has been violated with impunity by successive brutal regimes that have surfaced in the region, which have engaged in arbitrary deprivation of life. According to one report, in the period between 1992 to 1993, the UN Special Rapporteur on Extra- Judicial, Summary or Arbitrary Executions documented evidence of arbitrary execution in twenty-seven African countries.[363]

---

360 It should be stressed that the categorization of these rights is not intended to suggest the superiority of one set of rights over the other. According to the provisions of Article 1(5) of the VIENNA DECLARATION AND PROGRAM OF ACTION of 1993, all human rights are universal, indivisible, interdependent and interrelated, and therefore must be treated by the international community globally in a fair and equal manner, on the same footing, and with the same emphasis. It is not in doubt that political and economic orientation may make different segments of the international community to lay more emphasis on one set of rights than the other.

361 UNITED NATIONS COMMISSION ON HUMAN RIGHTS, REPORT OF INDEPENDENT EXPERT, LUIS VALENCIA RODRIGUEZ 26-27, E/CN/1993/15,18.12.92, *cited* in SCOTT DAVIDSON, THE INTER AMERICAN HUMAN RIGHTS SYSTEM, *supra*, note 229, at 261-262.

362 Torkel Opsahl, *The Right to Life* in THE EUROPEAN SYSTEM FOR THE PROTECTION OF Human Rights, *supra*, note 172, at 207.

363 EVELYN A. ANKUMA, THE AFRICAN COMMISSION ON HUMAN AND PEOPLES RIGHTS: PRACTICE AND PROCEDURES 112 (Martinus Nijhoff Publishers, 1996).

The exact content of the right to life has not been analyzed by the African Commission. The Commission has rather considered the violation of the right to life under Article 4 of the African Charter by looking at facts that would constitute same. In *Orton and Vera Chirwa v. Malawi*,[364] the communication alleged a violation of the right to fair trial, right to liberty and freedom from torture. The Commission, however, found also a violation of the right to life among others. Orton Chirwa, who was a prominent political figure in Malawi before independence, had been living in exile in Zambia since 1964 because of differences with then Malawi's President, Kamuzu Banda. In 1981, Malawi security officials abducted him and his wife, and took them into custody. They were subsequently sentenced to death for treason at a trial in the Southern Regional Traditional Court, having been denied legal representation. The sentences were upheld by the national Traditional Appeals Court, despite its criticism of many aspects of the trial. After much international protests, the sentences were commuted to life imprisonments. The Chirwas were held in almost complete solitary confinement, given extremely poor food, inadequate medical care, shackled for long periods of time within their cells and prevented from seeing each other for years.

After the Commission had declared the case admissible, Commissioner Mokama, who was also the Chief Justice of Botswana was entrusted to visit Malawi to discuss this case with the government, in addition to investigating the general human rights conditions in the country. The Commissioner's visit was thought to be best arranged through the government of Bostwana. The request for a visit by the Commissioner was sent through the Ministry of Justice of Botswana to the effect that the Justice Minister, who also was in charge of Malawi at the African Commission would be visiting his counterpart in Malawi and to pay homage to the life president, Kamuzu Banda. On two occasions the Malawi government rejected the visit. Mr. Chirwa later died in prison while the case was pending before the Commission. The Commission had no alternative but to find that Malawi had violated not only the right to fair trial, liberty and freedom from torture but also, the right to life, which was violated circumstantially.[365]

Article 4 of the Charter provides that no one may be arbitrarily deprived of his right to life. The Charter does not define what constitutes arbitrary taking of

---

[364] Communications 64/92, 68/92 and 72/92 filed by Amnesty International on behalf of the victims. Opinion of 3 November, 1994 (16th Ordinary Session)/28 June, 1995 (AHG/Res. 240(XXXI).(Hereafter, the *Chirwa* group of cases). See DECISIONS OF THE AFRICAN COMMISSION ON HUMAN AND PEOPLES' RIGHTS: 1986 – 1997, 63, also cited as, LAW REPORTS OF THE AFRICAN COMMISSION, SERIES A, VOLUME 1(hereafter, ACHPR\LR\A\1) (1997)

[365] Articles 4, 5, 6 and 7(1) (a) (c) and (4) of the African Charter. See THE 8TH ANNUAL ACTIVITY REPORT OF THE AFRICAN COMMISSION ON HUMAN AND PEOPLES' RIGHTS in REPORT ON THE 16TH SESSION OF THE AFRICAN COMMISSION ON HUMAN RIGHTS 68 (25th October – 3 November, 1994).

life, neither has the Commission given such a definition. It appears that the general understanding of arbitrary deprivation of life is extra-judicial killing, which meaning, the Commission agrees is well established in international law.[366] The general consensus in the interpretation of the right to life in human rights instruments is that it is not derogable, except in certain circumstances judicially recognized or resulting from lawful acts of war or self-defense.[367]

The African Commission sees extra-judicial execution as one of the areas of special emphasis in its protective mandate, especially after the Rwanda crisis of early 1990s. At its 15th Annual Session in 1994, the Commission appointed a Special Rapporteur on Summary and Extra-Judicial Executions.[368] Accordingly, the Commission has considered a number of communications alleging extra-judicial executions some of which were very poorly addressed. In *International Commission of Jurists (ICJ) v. Rwanda*[369] the massive and gross violations of the right to life that went on in Rwanda were brought to the attention of the Commission in 1990. On the receipt of the communication, the Commission requested permission from the government of Rwanda to conduct an on-site investigation of the allegations. According to Ankuma,[370] despite the quick response from Rwanda that it would welcome an objective observer, the Commission did not immediately send a mission to Rwanda, until March 1994, at its 17th Session, when the Commission decided to send a two-person mission with the assistance of the United Nations.

The situation in Rwanda was an opportunity for the Commission to make its impact felt. That was the worst human rights challenge that the African Mechanism had faced, and hopefully will ever face. Visiting Rwanda four years after a communication had been lodged was at best undesirable. While this author is not insensitive to the difficulties that the Commission may have encountered within the period, the point remains that as an organ of the OAU entrusted with the responsibility of overseeing human rights protection, it should have done more

---

366 *See* Rachel Murray, *Report on the 1996 Sessions of the African Commission on Human and Peoples Rights- 19th and 20th Sessions: 26 March-4 April, and 21-23 October 1996*, 18 HUM. RTS L . J. no. 1-4 16, at 19 (1997).
367 *See* SCOTT DAVIDSON, THE INTER AMERICAN HUMAN RIGHTS SYSTEM, *supra* note 229, at 262-263 for the interpretation under the Inter-American Mechanism. For the interpretation under the European system, *see* D. J. HARRIS, *et al, supra*, note 172, at 37, and *Torkel Opsahl, The Right to Life* in THE EUROPEAN SYSTEM FOR THE PROTECTION OF Human Rights, *supra,* note 172, at 214.
368 At the 20th Session of the Commission from October 21-31, 1997, Commissioner Dr. Ben Salem of Tunisia was still the Special Rapporteur. *See Rachel Murray, supra,* note 366, at 18.
369 Communication No. 46/90. Other communications against Rwanda were *Organization Contre la Torture v. Rwanda*, Communication No. 49/91 and *Union International des Droits de l'Homme v. Rwanda*, Communication No. 99/93
370 ANKUMA, *supra,* note 363, at 113.

to attract the attention of the regional body. The Commission no doubt adopted resolutions condemning the carnage that went on in Rwanda, but resolutions do not implement themselves. Arguably, however, the Commission could be said to have done its duty having communicated the situation to the OAU.

As earlier observed, the jurisprudence of the African Commission is still at its embryonic stage. In its interpretation of the right to life, the Commission has almost in all the cases been faced with arbitrary killings, which clearly show a violation of the provisions of Article 4 of the African Charter.[371] The Commission has not yet been tested on such issues as the appropriateness or otherwise of capital punishment, the right to life of a foetus, and other such controversial issues, that have come before other UN and regional mechanisms.

2. Right against all forms of slavery, slave trade, torture and cruel, inhuman or degrading treatment

Under Article 5 of the African Charter, there is a prohibition of all forms of slavery, slave trade, torture and cruel, inhuman or degrading treatment. The prohibition of these conducts is preceded by an emphasis on the right of every person to the respect of the dignity inherent in human beings. The philosophy underlying this provision aims at restating the value and integrity of the human person, with a view of eliminating every treatment that makes light of the dignity that inheres in every human being.

a. Slavery and Slave Trade

The question may be asked as to the reason for the prohibition of slavery and slave trade by the African Charter in the face of the fact that slavery in the actual sense, ended many years ago. Could it be that the Charter aims to prevent in the new African societies, the atrocities of the slave trade era, which have become a part of African history? Could the Charter be envisaging new forms of slavery that African societies should not tolerate? It is reasonable to interpret the prohibition of slavery to include the above reasons. The role that the slave trade played in dehumanizing Africans cannot be overemphasized, and should be guarded against in every way possible. There is, however, the possibility of contemporary slavery, which though may not be on the scale of the slave trade era, could involve some servitude of unconscionable nature.

---

371 Other such Communications include ones against Mauritania, Zaire, Sudan and Togo. The Commission has undertaken on-site missions to some of these countries, where permitted. Where it does not get the permission to visit, as in the case against Zaire, it brings the matter to the attention of the Assembly of Heads of State and Government. *See* ANKUMA, *supra,* note 363, at 113-114.

Ankuma[372] opines that the provision on slavery in the African Charter may probably be used to address some forms of contemporary slavery noticeable today in some African societies. She draws attention to some dehumanizing practices, some of which are customary. She primarily identifies the Trokosi and Almadu practices. Trokosi is said to be practiced in Ghana and Togo, and involves the pledging of young girls, sometimes from infant ages; as payment for crimes committed by male members of their families. The girls serve traditional priests, work on their farms and bear their children in a slavelike manner. Almadu, on the other hand, is an Islamic religious practice, which involves the giving out of children to the Marabou, a religious leader, with whom the children live and learn the Koran. The only way of upkeep for the children is for them to beg for alms, which they in turn surrender to the Marabou. The Marabou determines the future of the children and moves with them at will.[373] Other areas of concern are forced marriages in exchange for dowry, marital servitude as noticeable in many traditional and customary practices, domestic servitude, as well as child labor and forced labor.

The problem presented by the Charter provisions on slavery is that of enforcement, as it is a violation that cannot easily be traced to States. They are primarily violated by individuals and most times are rooted in traditional and religious cultures, which governments pledge to protect. This has accounted for the lack of complaints in this area[374] of the Charter despite the concern it has attracted among African human rights NGOs. NGOs at the 16th Annual Session of the African Commission called on the Commission to organize a seminar on the contemporary forms of slavery and to appoint a Special Rapporteur on slavery.[375]

This author is of the opinion, that on the other hand, States may not easily be absolved from liability in terms of the slavery provisions of the African Charter. Member States in Article 1 of the Charter undertook to adopt and secure the

---

372 *Id.*, at 119.
373 *Id. See* also *Edward K. Quashiga, Religious Freedom and Vestal Virgins: Trokosi Practice in Ghana*, 10 AFR. J. INT'L. & COMP. L. 193 (1998).
374 There has been no complaint to the African Commission from its inception addressing the violation of Article 5 provision on slavery and slave trade. NGOs have however given various reports to the African Commission on the prevalence of some forms of contemporary slavery as already highlighted.
375 The Commission responded to the calls made by the NGOs by considering and adopting a resolution on Contemporary Forms of Slavery in Africa at its 16th and 17th Ordinary Sessions in 1994/1995. The resolution called on all OAU Member States to ratify and effectively implement international legal instruments relating to slavery, slave trade, sale and trafficking in human beings and other practices similar to slavery. The resolution also urges African countries to adopt legislation and other measures to eliminate slavery. While the Commission agreed to organize a seminar on contemporary forms of slavery, it failed to appoint a Special Rapporteur.

provisions of the Charter within their jurisdiction by legislation or other measures. Failure to adopt legislation prohibiting slavery, or the non-enforcement of legislation in this area where it exists, is a condonation of private practice of slavery and, thus, a violation of the slavery provision of Article 5 of the Charter. NGOs need only to articulate their complaints on this rationale, for the Commission to come up with an interpretation of what rights are guaranteed under the Article.

b. Torture, Cruel, Inhuman or Degrading Punishment

Freedom from torture, cruel, inhuman and degrading punishment is one of the foremost rights in international human rights law. It is one of those rights that have been declared non-derogable even in times of war or other public emergencies threatening the existence of a State.[376] The right against torture, cruel, inhuman and degrading punishment is treated here as a block of rights. This is especially so because the difference between these concepts is a very thin one, and is not the object of this segment. The African Charter does not offer any definition of these concepts. The general reading is an assumption of certain facts as amounting to torture, cruel, inhuman or degrading punishment, provided they are intentionally done to inflict physical or mental suffering or orchestrated as a violation of human rights.[377]

Despite the provisions in the African Charter, this block of rights has seen more violations than respect in Africa where torture, cruel, inhuman and degrading punishment are constant tools in the hands of many dictators to smother their opponents. This is one area where the African Commission is said to have received numerous communications.[378] The Commission is, however, criticized, as not treating complaints alleging violations of torture, cruel, inhuman and degrading punishment with urgent attention, thereby increasing the possibility of irreparable damage.[379] The insistence by the Commission on the exhaustion of domestic

---

[376] Article 15(2) of the European Convention on Human Rights.

[377] In *Ireland v. UK* A 25 para. 167 (1978), the European Court of Human Rights defined torture as deliberate inhuman treatment causing very serious suffering. Other elements of this block of rights, especially inhuman treatment need not be intended to cause suffering for it to amount to a violation of the right. Article 5(2) of the Inter-American Convention against Torture defines torture as any act intentionally performed whereby physical or mental pain or suffering is inflicted on a person for purposes of criminal investigation, as a means of intimidation, as personal punishment, as a preventive measure, as a penalty or for any other purpose. Torture shall also be understood to be the use of methods upon a person intended to obliterate the personality of the victim or to diminish a person's physical or mental capacities, even if they do not cause pain or mental anguish.

[378] ANKUMA, *supra,* note 363, at 116.

[379] *Id.*

remedies in such cases has often resulted in such complaints being declared inadmissible.[380]

We will deal with the procedure of the African Commission in chapter four as it relates to exhaustion of domestic remedies. However, this author agrees with Ankuma that the perpetration of torture can result in irreparable damage, which should convince the Commission to treat such cases with urgency rather than dismiss them on the basis of inadmissibility. It is true, at least in African settings, that a victim of torture in government detention cannot be expected to bring a case in domestic courts without fear of repercussions. It is even in doubt if such a person would have access to a local court. It is a different scenario when the individual is allowed some access to personal freedom, in which case it could be safely argued that such a person ought to seek other domestic remedies before going to the Commission. Most of the cases alleging torture in which the Commission found the complaints inadmissible clearly show that the victims were in government detention.

It is agreed that the Commission may not physically prevent a State from choosing to violate a right enshrined in the Charter, but the thoroughness that the Commission brings to a case can affect how a State treats its decisions. The Commission can determine from the complaints, and sometimes from press publicity of the cases, the seriousness or otherwise of the allegations of violation in order to decide whether the case in question merits urgent action, even though the complaint may not have been brought under Article 58(1) of the Charter. The handling of the *Ken Saro Wiwa* complaints[381] has attracted one commentary to the above effect.[382] In that case two complaints were submitted by the International Pen and the Constitutional Rights Project on behalf of Kenule Saro Wiwa, the president of the Movement for the Survival of Ogoni People (MOSOP), alleging torture in detention; that he was chained hands and feet and detained in a solitary cell, and that his health deteriorated without medical attention, as well as not being allowed access to his lawyer. The Commission ruled that the complaint required interim measures and accordingly requested the Nigerian government to refrain from conduct that might cause irreparable prejudice to Mr. Wiwa. The Commission did not directly address the issue of torture raised in the complaints or other forms of cruel, inhuman and degrading punishment. It is internationally known that before the Commission could have any opportunity to address that case, Mr. Wiwa and

---

380 *See Nziwa Buyingo v. Uganda*, Communication No. 8/88; *Hilarie Badjogume v. Benin*, Communication No.17/88; and *El Hadji Boubacare Diaware v. Benin*, Communication No. 18/88, ACHPR\LR\A1 (1997), *supra*, note 364, at 11.
381 *International Pen v. Nigeria*, Communication No. 137/94 and *Constitutional Rights Project v. Nigeria*, Communication No. 139/94.
382 ANKUMA, *supra*, note 363, at 117.

eight other members of his organization were executed by the Nigerian government on November 10, 1995.

The jurisprudence of the Commission, it has been noted is yet scanty. There is yet to exist an articulation of what amounts to torture, cruel, inhuman and degrading punishment as has been done in the European and Inter-American systems. Apart from the general obligation to desist from torture, cruel, inhuman and degrading punishment, the Commission has not come up with any interpretation that advocates can use in the African context. Advocates are earnestly looking for direction from the Commission in this regard. There is nothing wrong in the Commission adopting the formulations of the European and Inter-American systems in the least.

3. Right to liberty and security of the person

Under Article 6 of the African Charter "every person shall have the right to liberty and to the security of his person. No one may be deprived of his freedom, except for reasons and conditions previously laid down by law. In particular, no one may be arbitrarily arrested or detained." The right to liberty and security of the person implies physical liberty of the individual in the society in terms of prohibiting unnecessary arrests and detention. In other words, no one should be dispossessed of his or her liberty in an arbitrary fashion. The provision represents an expression of the importance of this right in a democratic society. The appendage of security of the person to liberty should not be misleading. It must be read as a whole and understood in the context of physical liberty so as not to be misinterpreted to mean other aspects of social benefits. The second part of Article 6, which provides an exception to the right of liberty and the security of the person where there are reasons and provisions previously laid down by law, has been looked at as constituting a "clawback" clause and thus, dangerous. This is to the effect that what amounts to law may well be an oppressive law that facilitates the violation of the provisions of the Charter. For clarity of purpose, this author is of the view that the exception is only an indication that the right to liberty and security of the person is not an absolute right, and thus is subject to some checks. These checks must, however, be on the basis of law. The law relied upon in derogating from the provisions of the Charter must be consistent with standards recognized in true democratic societies and international law.

The situation of things regarding this right in Africa is contradictory to the provisions of the Charter. We have observed that it is an important right that ought to exist in a democratic society. Unfortunately, majority of African States are not democratic, and as such, the provision is violated with impunity. Draconian decrees are regularly churned out, giving military and civilian dictators the right to arrest and detain any person who in their pleasure they determine to merit such arrests and detention.[383] To achieve this aim, in some countries a state of emergency is often declared or perceived. The judiciary, fearing the consequences from dictatorial executives, often abdicates jurisdiction under the doctrine of non-justiciability or on the ground of an ouster of the courts' jurisdiction.[384]

The African Commission has received many communications alleging the violation of the right to liberty and the security of the person. This is particularly so in all of the cases alleging violations of the right to life and torture, cruel, inhuman or degrading punishment. The Commission's approach to the violation of this right, especially in earlier communications was not satisfactory. The Commission had regularly been very hasty in dismissing or closing the files of cases pending before them, whenever it got information that the person had been released, rather than inquire into the legality of the detention. In *Henry Kalenga v. Zambia*,[385] the Commission declared the petition amicably resolved. The victim had been held in detention without trial since February 12, 1986, and petitioned the Commission demanding his release. On March 5, 1991, the Ministry of Legal Affairs of Zambia informed the Commission that the victim had been released in 1989. On the basis of this information, without consulting the victim, the Commission adopted the view that the release of the victim from detention remedied the prejudice complained of and constituted amicable settlement. Similarly in *International Pen v. Burkina Faso*,[386] the petition alleged unlawful detention. A notification to the Commission of the release of the victim was enough for the Commission to close the file in respect of that petition.[387]

Recently, however, in response to sharp criticisms of its past decisions on many of the cases alleging the violation of the right to liberty and the security of the person, the Commission has adopted a new approach of contacting the

---

383 Examples of such decrees include the famous State Security (Detention of Persons) Decree No.2, 1984 in the case of Nigeria under which successive military governments, especially those of General Ibrahim Babangida and the late General Sani Abacha, used to put away many opponents of military rule in Nigeria.
384 N.S. REMBE, THE SYSTEM OF PROTECTION OF HUMAN RIGHTS UNDER THE AFRICAN CHARTER ON HUMAN AND PEOPLES' RIGHTS: PROBLEMS AND PROSPECTS 9 (Lesotho: Institute of African Studies, National University of Lesotho, 1991).
385 Communication No. 11/88, ACHPR\LR\A1 (1997), *supra*, note 364, at 7.
386 Communication No. 22/88, *Id.* at16.
387 Similar cases of such nature include *Comité Culturel Pour la Democratic au Benin v. Benin*, Communication No. 16/88; *Hilaire Badjogounme v. Benin*, Communication No.17/88; *El Hadji Boubacare Diawara v, Benin*, Communication No.18/88 *supra*, note 350; and *Lawyers Committee for Human Rights (Sheif Sharif Hamad) v. Tanzania*, Communication No. 66/92, ACHPR\LR\A1 (1997), *supra*, note 364, at 69..

petitioner on receipt of information of release from detention to inquire whether other reliefs are sought beyond the release from detention.[388] While this is a welcome step in the right direction, the Commission must go ahead to determine the award of compensation in cases that it finds a violation of the provisions of Article 6. The fact that Article 6 of the Charter does not make specific provisions regarding compensation should not in any way deter the Commission from applying the standard known in international law, especially as authorized in Article 60 of the Charter.

4.   The right to fair trial

Article 7 of the Charter provides:

> 1. Every person shall have the right to have his cause heard. This right shall embrace:
>
> (a) the inalienable right to an effective appeal to competent national organs against acts violating his fundamental rights as recognized and guaranteed by conventions, laws, regulations and customs in force;
> (b) the right to be presumed innocent until proved guilty by a competent court or tribunal;
> (c) the right to defence, including the right to choose a counsel of his choice;
> (d) the right to be tried within a reasonable time by an impartial court or tribunal.
>
> 3. No one may be condemned for an act or omission which does not constitute a legally punishable offence at the time it was committed. No penalty may be inflicted for an offence for which no provisions was made at the time it was committed. Punishment is personal and can be imposed only on the offender.

The right to fair trial under the African Charter, as in all other international human rights instruments, is fundamental in judicial protection of all persons in a democratic society. It embodies the concept of due process of law, which is a necessary prerequisite to ensure the adequate protection of those persons whose rights or obligations are pending determination before a court or tribunal. This concept ought to be applicable to all judicial guarantees in the Charter and domestic legislation

---

388 *See* ANKUMA, *supra*, note 363, at 123, discussing *Annette Pagnoule (Abdoullaye Mazou) v. Cameroon*, Communication No.39/90. *See* also *Committee for the Defense of Human Rights (Jennifer Madike) v. Nigeria*, Communication No. 62/91, ACHPR\LR\A1 (1997), *supra*, note 364, at 60, where despite receiving information that the detainee had been released, the Commission inquired of the petitioner if it wished to pursue the case further. The Commission closed the file after two reminders without hearing from the complainant.

of African countries, even where there have been derogations from certain of the rights protected in these instruments. The provisions of Article 7 of the Charter are attempts to represent the importance of this concept, though in somewhat limited form.

Article 7 (1)(a) guarantees an inalienable right of all persons to an effective appeal to competent national organs against acts violating their fundamental rights as recognized and guaranteed by conventions, laws, regulations and customs in force. How should this provision be construed? There are two aspects of the argument. First, the nature of the conventions, laws, regulations and customs in force. Ankuma argues that there is a problem of clarity with these provisions stressing that these conventions, laws, regulations and customs in force must, if relating to member States to the Charter, be in conformity with the provisions of the Charter.[389] By all necessary implications, it is clear that the conventions, laws, regulations and customs must relate to Member States to the Charter, to whom the Charter applies. It follows that these bodies of laws must not derogate from the provisions of the Charter, which ordinarily are minimum guarantees.

The second prong of the argument is the actual meaning of the word "appeal" in the sub-section; whether the sub-section can be construed as guaranteeing a right of appeal to a superior court from the decisions of lower courts or tribunals, or merely the right to simply seek a judicial remedy at first instance, as suggested by Ankuma.[390] Though the Commission has not specifically ruled on the meaning and construction of the sub-section, its decisions on the right to fair hearing suggest a guarantee of the right to appeal to a higher court, where one exists, as inherent in the right to fair hearing. In *The Constitutional Rights Project (Zamani Lekwot & 6 others) v. Nigeria*,[391] the victims were convicted and sentenced to death under the Nigerian Civil Disturbances (Special Tribunal) Act, which *inter alia*, provides that "the validity of any decision, sentence, judgment... or order given or made... or any other thing whatsoever done under this Act shall not be inquired into in any court of law."[392] the contention of the petitioners, among others, was that there was a violation of the right of appeal under Article 7(1)(a) of the African Charter. The Commission held that while punishments decreed as the culmination of a carefully conducted criminal procedure do not necessarily constitute violations of the rights guaranteed in Article 7, to foreclose any avenue of appeal to "competent national organs" (emphasis, the Commission's) in criminal cases bearing such penalties clearly violates Article 7(1)(a) of the African Charter

---

389 ANKUMA, *supra*, note 363, at 124.
390 *Id.*
391 Communication No.87/93, ACHPR\LR\A1 (1997), *supra*, note 364, 101 at 104, ¶ 28.
392 Part IV, Section 8(1) of the Act.

and increases the risk that even severe violations may go unaddressed. Similarly, in *The Constitutional Rights Project (Wahab Akamu, G. Adega & Others) v. Nigeria*,[393] the Commission had earlier held section 11(4) of the Nigerian Armed Robbery and Firearms (Special Provisions) Act to be a violation of the right to appeal guaranteed under Article 7(1)(a) of the African Charter. The sub-section provides that "no appeal shall lie from a decision of a tribunal under this Act or from any confirmation or dismissal of such decision by the governor."[394]

A close reading of the above-stated decisions shows that the Commission's construction of Article 7(1)(a) is inclusive of both the right to seek judicial remedy at the first instance and the right to appeal to a higher court if a person is not satisfied with the decisions of a lower court. One would agree that the framers of the African Charter did not elegantly convey this meaning at the first glance of this sub-section. That notwithstanding, it could be argued that appealing to appropriate national organs in the context of the sub-article presupposes judicial or quasi-judicial organs normally in a position to hear cases.

Article 7(1)(b) deals with the right to be presumed innocent until proved guilty by a competent court or tribunal. Presumption of innocence as an aspect of the right to fair trial is a concept applicable only in criminal proceedings. It guarantees a right that is fundamental to both common law and civil law systems of criminal justice. It means that the general burden of proof must lie with the prosecution, or in terms more appropriate for civil law systems, that the court, in its inquiry into the facts, must find for the accused in case of a doubt. African countries have both traditions or systems of law and various constitutions, which guarantee the right to the presumption of innocence. The practice in most of these countries contradicts the concept, culminating in the reverse principle whereby it becomes the burden of the accused persons to prove their innocence. In most of the military dictatorships that overran these countries, it is a right that is violated on a daily basis in reality, despite the window dressing of formal prosecutions that are put up to make it appear as though the right is being complied with.

---

393 Communication No. 60/91, ACHPR\LR\A1 (1997), *supra*, note 364, 55 at 58, ¶ 30.
394 *See* also *Civil Liberties Organization (CLO) (Nigerian Bar Association) v. Nigeria*, Communication No. 101/93, ACHPR\LR\A1 (1997), *supra*, note 349, at 112, where the Commission held that the prohibition of litigation against the Nigerian Body of Benchers by the Legal Practitioners (Amendment) Decree, 1993 constitutes an infringement on the right to appeal to national organs, and thus, a violation of Article 7(1) of the African Charter. Section 23(a)(1) decree provided that "no person shall commence or maintain an action or any legal proceeding whatsoever relating to, connected with or arising from:-
(a) the management of the affairs of the association, or
(b) the exercise or preparation by the Body of Benchers for the exercise of the powers conferred upon it by this Act."

The Charter requires that the guilt of the accused must be determined by a competent court or tribunal. The African Commission has not determined what a competent court is in its jurisprudence. It therefore, becomes difficult to place the various military and other tribunals, which many African governments have used to violate the right to fair hearing. Apart from decisions that have addressed the ouster of the right to appeal from the decisions of these courts, the Commission has not been bold to say that these courts are out of place in a democratic constitutional arrangement. The view among some African scholars is that the term "competent court" means one in which the judges must be duly qualified, meeting all the natural and legal qualifications; and one, which is adequate, suitable and capable of administering the law.[395] The reasoning is that the court must be independent and impartial, as well as separate from the other branches of government.[396] This would mean that a competent court must necessarily enjoy the independence guaranteed under Article 26 of the African Charter.[397]

While the African Charter has done well by enshrining the independence of the judiciary, it is regrettable that the judiciary in most African states is nothing but an appendage to the executive arms of government. Judges are appointed and dismissed at the whims and caprices of the executive, especially in military and one-party dictatorships. It follows that in such circumstances judges will always kowtow to the executive for their personal safety, and in order to keep their jobs, rather than be interested in developing the legal system.[398] For there to exist a functional democracy in African States, the judiciary must be independent from other arms of government. The appointment of judicial officers could be left to the citizenry either directly by election, or where the executive must make the appointment, such appointment should be subject to the ratification of the representatives of the people in the legislature.[399]

Article 7(1)(c) of the Charter provides that every person shall have "the right to defence, including the right to choose a counsel of his choice." The right to

---

395 ANKUMA, *supra*, note 363, at 125.
396 *Id.*
397 Article 26 provides that States Parties to the present Charter shall guarantee the independence of the Tribunals and allow the establishment and improvement of appropriate national institutions entrusted with the promotion and protection of the rights and freedoms guaranteed by the present Charter.
398 The few judges and other judicial officers who assert their independence are usually sentenced to early retirement, in circumstances making it impossible for some of them to practice law in the future. Nigeria is an example of one of such countries where retired judges, under any circumstances, are not allowed to practice as barristers or advocates.
399 While the mode of appointment may not answer all the issues relating to the independence of the judiciary, it is a viable way of ensuring accountability of judicial officers. They need to be answerable to the citizenry rather than to an individual who seizes political power by force.

counsel under the African Charter raises the question of legal representation in terms of what choice is available to a person needing representation. It has been suggested that the purpose of the guarantee of the right to legal representation is to ensure that proceedings against an accused person will not take place without adequate representation of the case for the defense.[400] In addition, it ensures the equality of arms, so as to place the accused in a position to put his case in such a way that he is not at a disadvantage *vis-à-vis* the prosecution.[401] More so, the accused's lawyer may serve as the watchdog of procedural irregularity in the interest of his client and for public interest.[402]

The individual has the right to be defended by the counsel of his choice, but the Charter does not make any provision in terms of State-provided legal assistance. There is thus a strong indication that the Charter does not guarantee State-sponsored legal assistance, which is one of the avenues through which indigent persons can have access to legal representation. One would not assume that the drafters of the Charter contemplated that only persons with the ability to make legal representation choice on their own need legal representation. This is one area of fair hearing where other regional mechanisms have established minimum guarantees. Article 8(2)(e) of the American Convention guarantees the "inalienable right to be assisted by counsel provided by the State, paid or not as the domestic law provides, if the accused does not defend himself or herself personally, or engage his or her own counsel within the time period established by law".[403]

The importance of legal representation, especially in criminal cases cannot be overemphasized. It is a time-honored duty of the State to legally assist indigent persons to ensure fair trial. The omission by the Charter cannot easily be reconciled with the realities faced by African masses, who are generally poor and therefore lack the means to adequately choose legal representation.[404] Legal aid is usually the avenue through which the needed legal services can be rendered to indigent persons. Some African countries have legal aid programs, but these programs are poorly funded. There ought to be minimal commitments by States and Non-Governmental Organizations in this area, if the right to fair hearing can reasonably be said to be minimally guaranteed.

---

400 HARRIS, *et al*, THE EUROPEAN CONVENTION ON HUMAN RIGHTS, *supra*, note 172, at 256.
401 *Id*.
402 *Id*.
403 The corresponding provision under the European Convention is Article 6(3)(c) of the European Convention, which guarantees the right of a person charged with a criminal offense to: "defend himself in person or through legal assistance of his own choosing or, if he has not sufficient means to pay for legal assistance, to be given it free when the interest of justice so requires."
404 *See* J. Reed, *The Advantage of Counsel*, 7 4 EAST AFRICAN LAW JOURNAL 292 (1971).

The African Commission was tested on this issue in *John Modise v. Botswana*.[405] Here the Commission was faced with a complaint in which the complainant could not exhaust domestic remedies because he lacked funds to seek judicial representation in local courts. The Commission ruled that the lack of funds to seek legal representation cannot be an exception to the exhaustion of domestic remedies requirement. The main reason that gave rise to this ruling, it has been observed, was the concern for expediency and efficiency in order to prevent frivolous claims of lack of ability to seek legal representation.[406] Efficiency and expediency ought to be the watch word of the Commission, but not at the expense of ensuring adequate protection of the right to fair hearing in the aspect of access to legal representation. That case was an opportunity for the Commission to lay down principles on legal aid as an important aspect of achieving the right to fair trial, even though exhaustion of domestic remedies was central to the Commission's ruling. It was unfortunate that the Commission was reluctant to take this bold step. This reluctance, it is suggested, may be due to the fact that the Commission did not want to alarm Member States, so that it could still enjoy the co-operation of the States Parties.[407] While it is desirable that the Commission gets the maximum cooperation of States Parties to the African Charter, a deliberate refusal to apply a principle of law for this reason, strongly undermines the independence of the Commission as required by Article 31 of the Charter.

Article 7(1)(d) guarantees the right of a person to be tried within a reasonable time by an impartial court or tribunal. Here the Charter makes a "reasonable time" guarantee, and specifies that the trial under this guarantee must be by an impartial court or tribunal. Under the reasonable time concept, which applies to criminal and civil cases, the purpose is to protect all parties to court proceedings against excessive delays. Even though the Charter does not define what constitutes reasonable time, experience in other regions has shown that the guarantee underlines the importance of rendering justice without delays, which might jeopardize its effectiveness and credibility.[408] In criminal cases, the concept is particularly designed to prevent a person charged from remaining too long in a state of uncertainty about his or her fate. The reasonableness of the length of time of the proceedings both in criminal and civil cases depends on the particular circumstances of the case. There is no absolute time limit. Factors that are always taken into account are the complexities of the case, conduct of the applicant and the conduct of the competent administrative and judicial authorities. No particular

---

405 Communication No.97/93.
406 *See* ANKUMA, *supra,* note363, at 69.
407 *Id.* at 128.
408 *See* the European Court of Human Rights decision in *H v. France*, A 162-A Para 58 (1989).

factor is conclusive; the approach must be to examine them separately and then assess their cumulative effect.[409]

The African Commission has not yet interpreted in any of its decision, the "reasonable time" guarantee under Article 7(1)(d) of the Charter. One would expect that when it does, its interpretation would not depart from the interpretation of similar provisions in other regional mechanisms. The Commission has however, decided cases bordering on the second aspect of the guarantees under Article 7(1)(d): that the trial must be by an impartial court or tribunal. In *Constitutional Rights Project (Wahab Akamu, G. Adega & Others) v. Nigeria*,[410] the Commission was called upon to determine whether the Nigerian Robbery and Firearms Tribunal established under the Robbery and Firearms (Special Provisions) Decree, was an impartial tribunal as required by Article 7(1)(d) of the African Charter. Section 8(1) of the Decree dealing with the constitution of the tribunal provided that it shall consist of three persons: one judge, one officer of the Army, Navy or Air Force and one officer of the Police Force. The petitioners contended that the Decree had transferred jurisdiction from the normal courts to a tribunal chiefly composed of persons belonging to the executive branch of government, the same branch that passed the Decree, and whose members did not necessarily possess any legal expertise; that regardless of the character of the individual members of the tribunal, its composition alone created the appearance of, if not actual lack of, impartiality, contrary to Article 7(1)(d) of the Charter. The Commission agreed with the contention of the petitioners and found a violation of Article 7(1)(d) among other provisions of Article 7 of the Charter.[411] The Commission then recommended that the Government of Nigeria should free the complainants, who were sentenced to death by the tribunal.

From the decision of the Commission, one could say that impartiality under Article 7(1)(d) is in close relationship with independence. Thus, the court or tribunal must be independent of the executive and also of the parties to the case. A tribunal that is not independent of the executive will not comply with the requirements of impartiality either, in cases to which the executive is a party. Likewise, a tribunal member will be neither independent nor impartial if he has links with a private party to the case. There was no way in which it could be said that members of the Nigerian tribunal, especially the military and police members, were independent or impartial.

---

409 HARRIS, *et al, supra,* note 172, at 222, commenting on the interpretation of the reasonable time guarantee under the European system.
410 Communication No. 60/91, ACHPR\LR\A1, *supra,* note 364.
411 *See* also the *Chirwa* line of cases, Communications Nos.68/92 and 78/92, *supra,* note 364; and *Krishna Achutan (Aleke Banda) v. Malawi,* Communication No. 64/92.

Finally, Article 7(2) prohibits ex post facto laws, and also makes provision against retroactive punishment.[412] It further outlaws transferred punishment to any other person, who is not the offender. Like many aspects of the African Charter, even though the African Commission has not interpreted the Charter provision against ex post facto laws, the prohibition of retroactive legislation and punishment is important in ensuring due process in criminal proceedings. An act or omission, on the basis of which a person is convicted must constitute an offense at the time it is committed in order not to constitute a violation of the above provision. The prohibition under Article 7(2) covers situations where a new offense is introduced with retroactive effect by legislation or case law after the accused's act or omission. It also includes situations in which the existing law is interpreted or applied with the result that an act or omission not reasonably foreseeable as being criminal at the time of its occurrence becomes such later.[413]

The second arm of Article 7(2) dealing with the personal nature of punishment is very relevant to the situation in Africa. Members of an accused person's immediate and extended families are not unknown to face arrest, detention and prosecution for offenses they did not commit under the notion that if the accused person cannot be reached, a relative of his or her's must bear the consequences of the alleged offender's acts or omission. A number of cases have come before the Commission where facts alleging transfer of punishment on such family members or relatives have emerged.[414] The notion of the personal nature of punishment under the African Charter is a principle that will go a long way to address the victimization of relatives of alleged offenders. The victims, however, need to be bold enough to seek relief under the Charter, irrespective of the fact that they may be termed "incidental or secondary victims," whose need for relief would seem to be satisfied if the complainants, as primary victims, are granted relief as suggested by one African scholar.[415]

---

412 *See* similar provisions in Article 7(1) of the European Convention on Human Rights and Article 9 of the American Convention on Human Rights. The European Convention goes further than the African Charter to expressly include a further provision to the effect that a heavier penalty should not be imposed than the one that was applicable at the time the criminal offense was committed. In the same vein, the American Convention, while similarly providing against such heavier penalty, goes further to extend the benefit of a lighter punishment to a guilty person if subsequent to the commission of the offense, the law provided for the imposition of such a lighter punishment.
413 HARRIS, *et al*, *supra*, note 172, at 277.
414 *See Alhasan v. Ghana*, Communication No.103/93, ACHPR\LR\A1 (1997), *supra*, note 364, at 116; *Monja Joana v. Madagascar*, Communication No. 108/93, *id* at 125, and *Njoka v. Kenya*, Communication No.142/94, *id* at 141. It needs to be observed that in all these cases the family members did not themselves seek relief before the Commission. The punishments meted out to them were included in the evidence submitted in proof of the principal complainants' communications.
415 ANKUMA, *supra*, note 363, at 130.

While the drafters of the African Charter should be commended for attaching great importance to the right to fair trial, there are other pertinent aspects of that right that the Charter fails to guarantee. The Charter does not make any provision regarding the right to public hearing unlike other human rights treaties and conventions.[416] These instruments, in emphasizing the importance of the right to fair trial, stress that the trial must be public, except in few exceptional circumstances where the interest of justice will be served, or for the protection of public order or national security, or when the interest of the private lives of the parties so requires it. Not including this aspect of the right to fair trial in the face of African realities is quite regrettable. Dictatorial African governments are not unknown to establish secret courts or tribunals, which conduct secret proceedings and pass secret judgements, the outcomes of which are usually predetermined.[417]

In addition, the Charter does not make any provision on the right of an accused person to be assisted by an interpreter. The right to be assisted by an interpreter is very relevant in the African context, where majority of the people are indigenous, with languages different from the official language of many African States. English, French, Arabic, Portugese and Spanish are generally the official languages of many African States, and are therefore the languages used by the courts. The fact that these languages are official does not mean that everyone within a particular State understands them. It takes education in these languages for one to be able to acquire expertise in them. Many of the indigenous people are not formally educated to possess this expertise, and therefore, cannot communicate in them. This limitation in language, coupled with complicated court procedures, makes it inevitable that accused persons should be assisted with interpreters, free of charge, in the same fashion as having a right to counsel.[418]

If indigenous African languages cannot be made official languages, as seems apparent, those not learned in the official languages should not feel any sense of less worth on an account of lack of education in those languages. African human rights scholars have begun to argue that "languages are repositories of social, cultural and ideological values and failure to recognize and use African languages on a par with received languages leads not only to miscarriage of justice but also expresses cultural domination."[419] This author agrees with this view to the extent

---

416 *See* Articles 14(1) of the International Covenant on Civil and Political Rights, 8(5) of the American Convention on Human Rights and 6(1) of the European Convention on Human Rights and Fundamental Freedoms.
417 *See* E. Bello, *The African Charter on Human and Peoples' Rights: A Legal Analysis*, RECUEIL DES COURS 156 (1985).
418 *See* ANKUMA, supra, note 363, at 131.
419 *Id.*, citing S.B.O. Gutto, *Plain Language and the Law in the Context of Cultural Legal Pluralism*, 11 SOUTH AFRICAN JOURNAL OF HUMAN RIGHTS, 311-317.

that access to justice and all human entitlements should in no way be denied to indigenous people because of their inability to communicate in the official languages. That will give rise to language discrimination, which, being another aspect of discrimination, is totally in contradiction to the African Charter. African States must accept the reality of the need to render all necessary services to all persons, irrespective of the language spoken by these persons. What may not be feasible is the replacement of the received languages with African languages, which are multifarious and ethnically-based, and thus, would lack general acceptance.

Furthermore, the African Charter does not guarantee the right against self-incrimination, or freedom from double jeopardy, nor the right to compensation in violation of the right of fair trial. The lack of a provision as to compensation raises a question regarding the overall remedy provided by the African Charter. (The question of the available remedy under the Charter will be discussed in section III of chapter four). However, the African Commission, realizing the inadequacies of the Charter provisions on the right to fair trial is taking steps, albeit installmentally to address some of these areas. At its 11th ordinary session in 1992, the Commission adopted a resolution on the right to fair trial.[420] The resolution goes beyond Article 7 of the Charter to provide for the guarantee of the right to legal aid for indigent persons, the right to the assistance of a free interpreter, and the right to appeal to a higher court. The resolution did not include the right to compensation for miscarriage of justice, freedom from double jeopardy and the right against self-incrimination.[421] This action taken by the Commission has been interpreted as "little steps forward,"giving the impression that Commission is cautious in taking major initiatives, which could undermine cooperation between it and member States to the Charter.[422]

It is desirable that the Commission gets the necessary cooperation of member States of the African Charter. That should, however, not stand in the way of effective functioning of the Commission. It is the Commission's responsibility to develop its jurisprudence through an ingenious application of the Charter. The Commission should be guided by the principle that whatever is enshrined in the Charter ought to be the minimum guarantees, and if some of the minimum guarantees are not provided for in the Charter, it is its responsibility to apply the international law standard. Articles 60 and 61 of the Charter endow the Commission with adequate power to apply international standards in its deliberations. (The

---

420 *See* Resolution on Recourse and Fair Trial, *reprinted* in RECOMMENDATIONS AND RESOLUTIONS PUBLISHED BY THE AFRICAN COMMISSION ON HUMAN AND PEOPLES' RIGHTS 16 (ACHPR, Banjul: The Gambia, December 1998). (Hereafter, RECOMMENDATIONS AND RESOLUTIONS OF THE AFRICAN COMMISSION). *See* also ANKUMA, *supra*, note 363, at 127.
421 *Id.* ANKUMA, at 128.
422 *Id.*

content of Articles 60 and 61 will be separately discussed in this chapter in connection with the question of their normative influence on the African system).

5. Freedom of conscience, the profession and practice of religion

Article 8 of the African Charter provides that "freedom of conscience, the profession and free practice of religion shall be guaranteed. No one may, subject to law and order, be submitted to measures restricting the exercise of these freedoms." A close reading of Article 8 reveals the guarantee of two forms of rights, albeit with marginal distinctions: the freedom of conscience and the freedom to profess and practice one's religion.

a. Freedom of Conscience

The right of freedom of conscience includes freedom of thought. It generally means the right to hold a belief. This belief may be religious or otherwise. Freedom of conscience would therefore, embody the right of freedom of religion, without necessarily setting out the contents of that right. The essence of the freedom of conscience is to enable an individual to hold a thought or belief that is independent of a State's' or other entity's control per se. One aspect of this control as interpreted by the European Commission on Human Rights, is indoctrination,[423] when it is aimed at preventing an individual from purely holding his or her own beliefs. On the other hand, the former European Commission was of the view that, as long as an individual's action is totally based on free exercise of his or her belief, the fact that the action may have arisen out of perceived "indoctrination or brainwashing" will not violate that individual's right of freedom of conscience under the Charter.[424] It, however, remains to be seen how an action that may have arisen out of perceived indoctrination and brainwashing could still be based on the individual's free exercise of his or her will. It may be argued though, that the perception here is not that of the particular individual involved but that of third parties.

The right of freedom of conscience would appear dormant if there is no human activity to which it could be attached. On the other hand, there may be a plethora of other rights and freedoms through which it could be manifested.

---

423 *See Angelini v. Sweden* No. 10491/83, 51 DR. 41 at 48 (1986).
424 *See* generally, HARRIS *et al.*, LAW OF THE EUROPEAN CONVENTION ON HUMAN RIGHTS, *supra*, note 172, at 361 for details on the interpretation of freedom of conscience by the European Commission.

b.   Freedom to Profess and Practice Religion

Although the African Charter does not give any indication of what amounts to the exercise or manifestation of the freedom of conscience; it might be argued that that freedom of conscience includes the right to profess and practice a particular religion. In the same vein, the exercise of the right of freedom of religion will naturally include the freedom of conscience. Freedom to profess and practice a religion under the Article 8 of the African Charter would thus entail the freedom to manifest one's religion or belief in public or in private, alone or with others, without State persecutive intervention. This manifestation could be in the form of worship, teaching, practice and observance, a catalogue of not wholly distinct activities.[425] Though not expressly provided in the Charter, freedom to profess and practice one's religion could include freedom to maintain or change one's religion or beliefs. The idea of freedom to maintain or change one's religion flows from the angle of freedom of conscience. An individual cannot be expected to stick to a specific belief in a sea of ever-changing social convictions and surroundings.

The second part of Article 8 however, makes the freedom of conscience and freedom to profess and practice one's religion subject to law and order. Though this segment of the provisions of Article 8 forms part of the "claw back clauses" found in the Charter, it seems to be concerned with the balance which must be maintained between freedom of conscience and freedom to profess and practice one's religion, on the one hand, and, on the other hand, the protection of individuals or society from religious or psuedo-religious practices, which may be deemed to affect other person's rights. Thus, while Article 8 states that no person be may be subjected to measures of constraint restricting the exercise of the freedom of conscience and the freedom to profess and practice the person's religion, nonetheless, freedom to exercise and manifest these rights may be subject to limitations prescribed by law, which are necessary to protect public safety, order, health, morals or the rights and freedom of others.[426]

One will agree with Davidson[427] that States Parties clearly have a margin of discretion in whether they consider a particular religion, or other assemblies of belief to be an appropriate matter of regulation. That margin of discretion is, in turn, subject to oversight by the appropriate organ of a human rights control mechanism, in this case, the African Commission on Human Rights. In this regard, the African Commission has been faced with complaints alleging the violation

---

425   *Id.* at 363.
426   *See* DAVIDSON, THE INTER-AMERICAN HUMAN RIGHTS SYSTEM, *supra*, note 229, at 309, commenting on a similar article (Article12) of the American Convention on Human Rights.
427   *Id.*

of Article 8 of the Charter.[428] In *Les Témoins de Jéhovah (Jehovah's Witnesses), et al. v. Zaire*,[429] the complainants alleged persecution of the Jehovah's Witnesses, including arbitrary arrests, appropriation of church property, and exclusion from access to education. After admitting the petition, and upon the failure of the Zairean Government to submit any substantive response, the Commission ruled that the harassment of the Jehovah's Witnesses, as alleged, constituted a violation of Article 8 among others, since the government had presented no evidence that the practice of their religion in any way threatened law and order. Similarly the Commission received complaints against Sudan. In one of such complaints,[430] it was alleged that persons of the Christian faith and their leaders were persecuted in Sudan. Particularly, it was alleged that missionaries were expelled from the town of Juba, priests were arrested and detained, and churches were destroyed. The Commission, in addressing the issues raised in this petition, preferred to undertake an on the spot investigation, and had been preoccupied with obtaining permission to visit Sudan.[431] The outcome of the visit if any, is yet to be made public.

In virtually all the cases actually decided, the Commission failed to define what constitutes violation of conscience, or of the right to freely profess and practice one's religion. As has been observed about the Commission, the decisions are based on actual facts as presented without a reasoned analysis on the legal implications of the facts in terms of international law. A fact may be a violation of a provision of the Charter, but that provision needs to be interpreted in line with the facts for a proper determination that the fact constitutes an action prohibited by the Charter. The African mechanism is still growing, and thus it is hoped that the desire to elevate the jurisprudence of the system will be persuasive enough for the adjudicative officers of the system to actually engage in reasoned legal analysis.

6.   Freedom of expression

The right of freedom of expression is governed by Article 9 of the African Charter, which provides that: "1. Every person shall have the right to receive information.

---

428   See *Amnesty International v. Sudan*, Communication No. 48/90, alleging a violation of freedom of conscience. The complainants alleged that hundreds of prisoners of conscience had been detained without trial.
429   Communication No. 56/91, ACHPR\LR\A1 (1997), *supra*, note 364, at 17; consolidated with *World Organization Against Tourture v. Zaire, id.*, and *Lawyers Committee for Human Rights v. Zaire, id.* (hereafter group of cases against Zaire).
430   *Association of Member Episcopal Conferences v. Sudan*, Communication No. 89/93.
431   ANKUMA, *supra*, 363, at 134.

2. Every person shall have the right to express and disseminate his opinions within the law." Under Article 9, a person not only possesses the right to express himself or herself, but also the right to receive information. The right of freedom of expression, while not above any other right by degree, has been identified as forming an essential basis for the existence and functioning of a healthy democracy in any society. The statement of the Inter-American Court of Human Rights in the *Compulsory Membership* case on this right is persuasive. According to the Court:

> Freedom of expression is a cornerstone upon which the very existence of a democratic society rests. It is indispensable for the formation of public opinion... It represents, in short, the means that enable the community, when exercising its options, to be sufficiently informed. Consequently, it can be said that a society that is not well informed is not a society that is truly free.[432]

The importance of the right of freedom of expression cannot be over-stressed. One would agree that the absence of the freedom of expression is a factor which contributes to a country's failure to respect other human rights. Additionally, it is a right which has a universal character, which contains within it the idea of the juridical right, which pertains to persons, individually or collectively considered, to express, transmit, and diffuse their thoughts. In a parallel and correlative way, the universality of the right embodies the collective rights of everyone to receive information without interference or distortion.[433]

Freedom of expression as a right in Africa does not seem to possess any of the attributes enumerated above. It is rather taken for granted in view of the fact that the State must own the press, which in turn, must speak in accordance with its bidding. However, where individual ownership is allowed, the situation reveals a strict control that eliminates any trace of freedom of expression. Apart from the formal press, individuals cannot express opinions, nor seek to receive information, which are at variance with State views and practices. Evidence of this is the number of African journalists and academics living in exile because of views they have expressed against African governments. Many others not in exile are scattered all over various prisons and detention centers in these countries.

Article 9 of the African Charter is intended to emphasize the importance of the right of freedom of expression in Africa in the same way as other regional and international legal instruments. The situation does not indicate that this em-

---

[432] *See* SCOT DAVIDSON, THE INTER-AMERICAN HUMAN RIGHTS SYSTEM, *supra*, note 229, at 310, commenting on the *Compulsory Membership* case.
[433] *Id.*

phasis has received any notable attention even by the African Commission, despite the fact that the Commission has had a number of important occasions to consider complaints alleging the violation of the Article. In *International Pen (Senn and Sangare) v. Côte d' Ivoire*,[434] rather than decide on the illegality or otherwise of the detention of the complainant journalists under Article 9, the Commission closed the case based on admissibility, on the information that the complainants had been released by the government. In that case, two journalists of a daily newspaper, *La Voie*, republished an article from *Juene Afrique*, a French-based magazine, which indicated in its headline that *Côte d'Ivore* had requested funds from France for the funeral of President Houphouet-Boigny through its President. The journalists were charged with insulting the President and spreading false information. A sentence of one year was imposed on the journalists and a fine, against which they appealed. During the pendency of the appeal, the journalists also published an article titled, "The Balance of Terror." They were later charged again and convicted for inciting violence and disturbing public order, receiving a sentence of three years each for this offence. After spending several months in jail, the complainants were granted amnesty and subsequently released. The release was communicated to the African Commission, which closed the case for that reason, among others. The Commission was of the view that if the victims required any remedies, they should first resort to the legal system of *Côte d'Ivoire*, to exhaust all domestic remedies since the complaint did not provide any "information as to whether national procedures have been pursued to seek reparations."[435] This was despite the Commission's observation that: "although the alleged victims have been released, this does not extinguish the responsibility of the government for the violations that may have been committed in respect of their imprisonment. A cause of action may still stand for reparations for the prejudice suffered by the imprisonment."[436]

The position of the Commission in this case is a little disturbing. The Commission is seen here to be making the argument that the state would have made if it were to defend itself in a petition filed by the victims. There is no doubt that the legal effect of an amnesty is to extinguish a legal conviction. It does not, however, prevent the consideration of Article 9 of the African Charter in terms of the legality or otherwise of the government's conduct. On the other hand, the journalists need to know whether their publication was consistent with their freedom of expression as guaranteed in the Charter.

---

[434] Communication138/94, ACHPR\LR\A1 (1997), *supra*, note 364, at 139-140.
[435] *Id.* at 140, ¶¶ 9-10.
[436] *Id.* at 139, ¶ 8.

Another case brought under Article 9 was the line of petitions against Nigeria.[437] Here it was alleged that over 50,000 copies of TELL Magazine, a popular magazine in Nigeria, which strives to promote human rights and democracy, were seized from the premises of its printers by heavily armed policemen. The Editor in Chief of the magazine was ordered to report to the headquarters of the State Security Service. These incidents, it was alleged, were as a result of a story carried by the magazine entitled, "The Return of Tyranny- -Abacha Bares His Fangs," in which the decrees enacted by the military government of Nigeria under General Abacha ousting the jurisdiction of the courts were analyzed. It is reported that the Commission found the petition admissible, without making a decision supported by persuasive reasoning, probably due to the fact that it had previously decided to undertake a mission to Nigeria to investigate the various complaints, which alleged widespread breaches of the rights guaranteed by the Charter.[438] The result of that mission if at all undertaken is yet to be made public.

From all indications, the African system still has a long way to go in appreciating the importance of the right of freedom of expression and the receipt of information under Article 9 of the Charter. The African Commission, which is the body presently charged with the responsibility of enforcing the Charter, therefore has a lot of work on its hands, as it strives to develop the jurisprudence of the system. The Commission must bear in mind that freedom of expression plays a crucial and central role in public debate. In addition, it possesses special scope and character in that there is a simultaneous guarantee of both the right to express and the right to receive such expressions, which in turn facilitates the free interchange of ideas needed for effective public debate within the political arena. The Commission must face the challenge of determining the scope of the right under the Charter and the kind of limitations envisaged in the "within the law" qualification of the right.

7. Freedom of association and assembly

Freedom of association and freedom of assembly are twin rights that are separately guaranteed by the African Charter in Articles 10 and 11 respectively. This book will look at these rights together because of the close characteristics of the two rights. According to the provisions of Article 10(1), every person shall have the

---

437 Communication No. 130/93, consisting of consolidated petitions from Media Rights Agenda, Constitutional Rights Project (CRP) and Civil Liberties Organization (CLO).*See* also *Media Rights v. Nigeria*, Communication No.105/93.
438 *See* ANKUMA, *supra*, note 363, at 135-136.

right to freely form associations with others; provided that he abides by the law. According to Article 10(2), no one may be compelled to join an association, subject to an obligation of solidarity provided for in paragraph 4 of Article 29.[439] Similarly, Article 11 states that "every person shall have the right to assemble freely with others. The exercise of this right shall be subject only to necessary restrictions provided for by law, in particular those enacted in the interest of national security, the safety, health and ethics, rights and freedom of others." The nature of these rights makes them interrelated. Though they are sufficiently different to be treated separately, they share the objective of allowing individuals to come together for the expression and protection of their common interests. It is not just enough for individuals to freely form associations; they must be allowed to freely gather in order to carry out the objectives of the association. Bearing this in mind, we may proceed by briefly outlining the specific character of each right and the interpretation, if any, given to them by the African Commission.

a. Freedom of Association

The right of freedom of association embraces a complexity of ideas, all of which are yet to be fully worked out in practice under the African Charter. It involves the freedom of individuals to come together for the protection of their interests by forming a collective entity which represents them.[440] These interests may be of a political, economic, religious, social, cultural, professional or labor union nature. Whatever the interest, it must be such that the association is capable of enjoying fundamental rights against the State and will generally have rights against and owe duties to its members. Furthermore, an individual may not have an absolute right to become a member of a particular association so that an association has no obligation to admit or continue the membership of an individual. Equally, an individual cannot be compelled to become a member of an association nor disadvantaged if he or she chooses not to do so.[441]

In guaranteeing the right of freedom of association, Articles 10 and 29(4) of the Charter make it subject to 'abiding by the law' and add an obligation of solidarity, especially national solidarity when it is threatened. These limitations though part of the by now familiar claw back clauses, are supposed to serve the legitimate interest of public order, morality, health and security. There may be the tendency for activists to treat such limitations as avenues, through which the

---

439 Article 29 of the African Charter deals with the duties of the individual, and paragraph 4 specifically provides for the duty to preserve and strengthen social and national solidarity, particularly when national solidarity is threatened.
440 HARRIS et al., supra, note 172, at 421.
441 Id.

State would normally interfere with the exercise of the freedom. This is especially so in the African situation, where it is the order of the day to decree laws that either ban or severely impact the right of freedom of association. In normal circumstances, the limitations are minimum safeguards that ought to be in place to prevent the abuse of the freedom.

The African Commission has been confronted with the importance and interpretation of the Article 10 guarantee of the right of freedom of association. In 1992, the Commission adopted a resolution on the freedom of association to the effect that:

"...1) The competent authorities should not override constitutional provisions or undermine fundamental rights guaranteed by the Constitution and international human rights standards;

2) In regulating the use of this right, the competent authorities should not enact provisions which would limit the exercise of the freedom; and

3) The regulation of the exercise of the right of the freedom of association should be consistent with the states' obligations under the African Charter on Human and Peoples' Rights."[442]

Ankuma has criticized the above resolution as deficient, for the sole reason that its purpose was to strengthen and clarify the corresponding provisions in the Charter; and that it failed to achieve the clarification function.[443] The fact that the Commission thought the right of freedom of association as befitting its resolution goes to show that it attaches great importance to the right as inevitable in a democratic society. Though the resolution may not be seen as dramatic in clarifying the provisions of the Charter on the right of freedom of association, it serves the purpose of emphasis. What is important, however, is that the Commission interprets the right bearing in mind the emphasis it has given to it in the resolution.

In *Civil Liberties Organization (Nigerian Bar Association) v. Nigeria*,[444] the African Commission was called upon to consider the effect of a decree by the Nigerian government establishing a new governing body of the Nigerian Bar Association, the Body of Benchers on the right of freedom of association under Article 10 of the Charter, among other questions. The contentions of the complainant *inter alia*, included the fact that of the 128 members of the Body of Benchers, only 31 were the nominees of the Nigerian Bar Association, while the rest were

---

442 Resolution on the Right to Freedom of Association. *See* RECOMMENDATIONS AND RESOLUTIONS OF THE AFRICAN COMMISSION *supra*, note 420, at 18. *See also* ANKUMA, *supra*, note 363, at 139.
443 *Id.*, ANKUMA, at 139.
444 Communication No. 101/93, ACHPR\LR\A1 (1997), *supra*, note 364, 112 at 113-115.

nominated by the government. The complaint was found admissible and the Commission ruled that the decree violated Article 10 of the Charter, among others, which guarantees the right of freedom of Association; and recommended that it be annulled. Similarly, in *Kenya Human Rights Commission v. Kenya*,[445] the Commission was faced with determining whether a State party violated Article 10 of the Charter. Here, the academic staff of Kenya's public universities decided to form a trade union to represent their interests in negotiations with their respective employers in 1992. The academic staff filed application to register the organization with the Registrar of trade unions, who refused to register it. The organization sought recourse to the African Commission, which ruled the communication inadmissible for non-exhaustion of domestic remedies.

In interpreting the right of freedom of association, there are various issues yet to be dealt with by the African Commission. The Commission has not established a working definition of "association." There is the need for guidance in terms of unequivocal Charter meaning of association; whether it includes professional associations and trade unions. The Charter does not expressly guarantee the right to form and join trade unions. One wonders whether the Commission will be persuaded with the reasoning that the right of freedom to form and join trade unions is a sub-division of freedom of association, and not some special independent right, that should require a special place in the Charter.[446]

The recurring observation in this work regarding the African human rights mechanism is that the system is still evolving in terms of the number of cases that go before the Commission and the development of its jurisprudence. It is therefore hoped that with time the mechanism will grow to adequately address these issues.

b. Freedom of Assembly

As has been observed, the right of freedom of assembly complements the right of freedom of association. Freedom of assembly, however, goes beyond the meeting of formal associations, and includes individuals associating to assemble in their right as individuals. One would think that freedom of assembly envisages holding of public meetings, mounting of demonstrations through marches, picketing and processions. Formal associations may enjoy the right of freedom of assembly because they hold meetings or do assemble. Public meetings and demonstrations

---

445 Communication No. 135/94, *Id*, at 134-136.
446 Perhaps the experience of other regional human rights systems and the UN system will be helpful to the Commission in articulating these issues. These systems, especially the regional ones appear to have answered these questions relative to peculiar circumstances. These circumstances may, however, not be too different since their interpretation is founded on international law.

are, however, also the tools for those outside these associations, whose direct access to the media is limited, but who may be able to gain attention by staging events, which capture the television and newspaper headlines.[447]

The protection of freedom of assembly afforded individuals under Article 11 of the Charter extends to the circumstances raised above. The irony of the situation in the African context is that those actions are more often prohibited and severely punished than not. States rather emphasize the limitations of the rights as set out in the Charter, whether or not the circumstances warrant such limitation, in contravention of Article 11, which prescribes a restrictive interpretation of the limitations. One limitation that is of international acceptance is that the assembly must be peaceful. It follows therefore that for an assembly to be regarded as peaceful it must be without arms. The carrying of arms in an assembly signals an implicit threat of violence, which is likely to make the assembly potentially non peaceful. Other limitations such as national security, the safety, health, ethics and rights and freedom of others, require contextual evaluation. The African Commission is yet to determine the meaning of these limiting concepts as they impact on the freedom of assembly under Article 11 of the Charter, either by way of a complaint before it or via an advisory opinion.

8. Freedom of movement and allied rights

Article 12 of the Charter provides that:

1. Every person shall have the right to move freely and to choose his residence within a State, provided he abides by the law.
2. Every person shall have the right to leave the country in which he resides including his own and has every right to return to his country. This right may be subject to restrictions, enacted in law essential for the protection of national security, law and order, public health or morality (or other peoples' rights and freedoms which are compatible with other rights recognized in the present Charter).
3. Every person shall have the right, when persecuted, to seek and obtain asylum in foreign countries in accordance with the law of these countries and in accordance with international conventions.
4. A non-national legally admitted in a territory of a State Party to the present Charter may only be expelled from it by virtue of a decision taken in accordance with the law.
5. The mass expulsion of non-nationals shall be prohibited. Mass expulsion shall be that which aims at national, racial, ethnic or religious groups.

---

447 HARRIS *et al.*, *supra*, note 172, at 418.

The provisions of Article 12 of the Charter could be divided into three main classes of rights: freedom of movement within and freedom to return to an individual's country of origin or residence, the right to seek and obtain asylum, and the right not to be expelled extrajudicially or en mass.[448] It may be useful to discuss in some detail these classes of rights, which have serious implications in the African context, and more so in a world of increasing international political consequences and economic integration.

a.   Freedom of Movement Within a State, to Leave and Freedom to Return

Freedom of movement and choice of residence within the territory of a State guaranteed under Article 12(1) applies to "every person," which includes aliens and stateless persons. This freedom, as it applies to aliens, is however, subject to the sovereign power of a State to regulate and control the entry of aliens into its territory. This means in effect that an alien does not *per se* have an unqualified right to enter, reside or remain in a particular country; hence the qualification that such a freedom to freely move within a State exists, provided an individual abides by the law. The main issue lies not with the right of an alien to move freely in the territory of a State Party to the African Charter, but the right of nationals or citizens of a State Party. While it is agreeable that every person ought to enjoy this right, it is reasonable to expect that nationals or citizens of a State Party should have a fairly unfettered right to move and choose their residence within the state, unless in exceptional circumstances.

In addition to freedom of movement and choice of residence within the territory of a State, Article 12 guarantees the right of every person to freely leave the country in which he resides and an equal right to return.[449] It is important to note that the right to leave a country is not dependent upon nationality. Thus, anyone has the right to leave any State. States that prevent their nationals or residents from leaving are often criticized. The same could be said of the right of a person to return to his or her country of citizenship or residence. The right of aliens to return to unrelinquished residence is not unqualified. That is why Article 12(2) stipulates that this right may be subject to restrictions, enacted in law essential for the protection of national security, law and order, public health or morality or other peoples' rights and freedoms which are compatible with other rights recognized in the present Charter. Whatever limitations that may be imposed

---

448   Article 12 of the Charter borrows significantly from the provisions of Articles 12 of the International Covenant on Civil and Political Rights, and Article 22 of the American Convention on Human Rights, especially as it relates to the right to seek and be granted asylum. *See also* Articles 2- 4 of the Fourth Protocol to the European Convention on Human Rights on the freedom of movements and allied rights.

449   Article 12(2).

on the freedom to leave and return to one's country of citizenship or nationality, it should be made clear that a person should not be expelled from the territory of a State of which he or she is a national, or deprived of the right to enter it, either expressly or by implication, as has been the case in many African countries.[450] This will go to preclude the use of political exile and other similar punishments for political opponents.

This class of rights has not received any notable attention of the African Commission in the sense that no communication alleging the violation of either the right of freedom of movement and choice of residence within a state or the right to freely leave and return has been recorded. The Commission is yet to establish the contents of these right, and to interpret the circumstances under which the right could be limited. In other words, the proper context of "restrictions enacted in law essential for the protection of national security, law and order, public health or morality or other peoples' rights and freedoms which are compatible with other rights" recognized in the Africa Charter is yet to be determined. It may, however, be instructive for the African system to borrow from the clarification made by the Inter-American system on similar rights, particularly Articles VIII and 22 of the American Declaration and American Convention respectively, dealing with freedom of movement. Under the Inter-American system, refusal to allow a citizen to return home, and denial of the right to leave a State, are violations of freedom of movement.[451] In the same vein, the Inter-American Commission has held that the refusal to grant a national of a State a passport, thereby effectively denying his right to leave, is also a breach of freedom of movement.[452]

b.   Right to Seek and Obtain Asylum

The right of every person to seek and obtain asylum recognized in Article 12(3) is a reflection of Africa's preparedness as a region to recognize and enshrine the protection granted refugees under international law. The situation is also of real practical significance as it is reported that refugee problems are perhaps Africa's

---

450 The African Charter does not expressly make a provision against the expulsion of a person from the territory of a State of which he or she is a citizen or a national.

451 *See Cases 2509 and 2777 (Panama); Case 2719 (Bolivia); Case 2794 (Peru); Case 3411 (Chile); Case 7378 (Guatemala); Case 4288 (Chile)* and *Case 3411 (Chile),* reprinted in DAVIDSON, THE INTER-AMERICAN SYSTEM OF HUMAN RIGHTS, note 229, at 338 (foot notes 345 and 346).

452 *Case 2711 (Uruguay), id.* (foot note 247). Similarly, politically motivated kidnaping and disappearances, resulting in unlawful detention and incarceration of victims have been considered a direct impediment of their freedom of movement and residence. In *Case 10.574 (El Salvador),* the petitioner was kidnaped and tortured by members of the armed forces. He was then told that if he returned home, he be would disappeared. The Inter-American Commission held that this was a violation of Article 22 of the American Convention. *Id.* at 338.

most serious human rights problems.[453] A plain reading of Article 12(3) will tend to suggest that the African Charter guarantees the right not just to seek, but to be granted asylum, provided the person is persecuted, and it can be done in accordance with the law of the State in question and applicable international conventions. It should be observed that while a person may not be prevented from seeking asylum, the grant of asylum is entirely a different matter not attached to the right to seek asylum. Whether or not a person should obtain or be granted asylum rests with the law of the territory in which asylum is sought, and international law.

The Charter gives persecution as a condition for the exercise of the right to seek and obtain asylum, but does not indicate what kind of persecution is necessary for asylum purposes. Generally speaking, a person is afforded refugee status if he or she has been persecuted or has a well founded fear of persecution on account of race, religion, nationality, membership of a particular social group or political opinion.[454] It could be argued that the Charter already identifies the proper standard by referring to the application of the relevant international convention in addition to the domestic law of the State to govern a request for asylum. What is not accounted for under the provision is when the domestic law standard of a State varies from the applicable international law. As was noted in previous discussions, the African Commission is yet to decide on the right to seek and obtain asylum. It will take a determined victim who feels that he or she has been improperly denied the right to seek and obtain asylum in the territory of a State which is a party to the African Charter to present such a communication to the Commission for a proper determination of the content of the right. No such complaint has yet been brought to the Commission.

c. Right Against Extra-Judicial Expulsion or Mass Expulsion

The Charter under Article 12(4) and (5) prohibits two forms of expulsion of persons from the territory of a State Party to the Charter. First, an alien lawfully admitted to any such territory may only be expelled pursuant to a decision reached in accordance with the law. Expulsion occurs when a person is obliged permanently to leave the territory of a State of which he is a resident without being left the possibility of returning later, hence the importance attached to it. The phrase " a decision reached in accordance with law" seems to suggest that an expulsion must have a judicial or quasi-judicial character, where there can be guaranteed some measure of due process. Thus, it would seem that an expulsion based on

---

453 See ANKUMA, supra, note 363, at 139.
454 See Article 1(2) of the Geneva Convention Relating to the Status of Refugees, 1951 and the Protocol Relating to the Status of Refugees, 1967.

either an executive order properly arrived at, or a decision of an appropriate tribunal will be legitimate. In other words, every person legally residing in a member country of the Charter is guaranteed a right against arbitrary expulsion. In the same vein, it could be said that the Charter endorses the expulsion of those not lawfully residing in a member State, but with some qualification. The Charter does not, however, include a right to appeal against such a decision to expel a lawful alien. It could be argued on the other hand, that the right of appeal guaranteed under Article 7(1) of the Charter will be equally applicable to ensure the protection of the alien's rights. The expulsion of alien's lawfully residing in the territories of States Parties to the African Charter has not come before the Commission. One would presume that when it does, the Commission would give a guiding definition on the particularities of the right.

Secondly, the Charter in Article 12(5) prohibits mass expulsion of non-nationals. The Charter goes on to define mass expulsion as one aimed at national, racial, ethnic or religious groups. Unlike the prohibition of the expulsion of lawfully resident non-nationals in Member States, the prohibition of mass expulsion aims to protect groups of persons based on nationality, ethnicity, race and religion, whether or not such groups of persons are lawfully residing in the expelling state. A close reading of this provision would appear to distinguish the risk faced by an individual not lawfully residing in a state, who could be expelled without the effect that en mass expulsion of an identifiable group will have.

Mass expulsion has been an issue of concern in Africa, which the drafters of the Chatter must have had in mind in including the prohibition. A notable example of mass expulsion was the expulsion of Nigerians from Ghana in 1969.[455] It did not, however, stop with that early incident in post-colonial Africa.[456] The African Commission has received communications emanating from Mauritania alleging expulsion of blacks from that country to Senegal and Mali. Because the communication also involved allegations of extra-judicial executions, disappearances and torture, the Commission decided to send an on-the-spot mission.[457]

Freedom of movements and its allied rights under the African Charter remain to be developed. It is not as though there have not been violations of some of these rights by State Parties to the Charter. It is either that the victims are not

---

[455] See ANKUMA, *supra*, note 363, at 140.
[456] Nigeria expelled Ghanaians in 1983, Gabon embarked on collective expulsion of Cameroonians, Nigerians and other Africans in 1994, and very recently Rwandan refugees were expelled from Zaire and other such expulsions were made by Libya and South Africa. *See Ibid.*
[457] *Recontre Africaine pour la Defense Droits de l'Homme v. Mauritania*, Communication No. 96/93. *See* also Communication No. 98/93.

aware of their rights or have slept on their right to seek remedy under the mechanism provided by the Charter.

9. Right to participate in the government of one's country

Article 13 of the African Charter provides:

1. Every citizen shall have the right to freely participate in the government of his country, either directly or through freely chosen representatives according to the rules stipulated by the law.
2. All citizens shall also have the right of access to public services of their country.
3. Every person shall have the right of access to public properties and services in strict equality of all persons before the law.

The provisions of Article 13 of the Charter recognize the importance of representative government in which individuals should have unfettered rights to participate, as well as a reasonably unrestrained right of access to public property and services. There are different manifestations of this right. An individual without any apparent legal disability should be able to stand elections in genuine periodic elections, exercise his or her voting rights, participate in the conduct of public affairs directly or through freely chosen representatives. The same individual should also be able to have access, under general conditions of equality, to the public service and property of his or her country.

The exercise of the rights enshrined in Article 13, is essential for societies to function normally. They are necessary for the development of a civilized and democratic society. African States have only been paying lip service to these rights that are fundamental to nation building. Many a State in Africa has a government of exclusion either as military dictatorship or one-party autocracy. Where there are elements of reasonable democracy, ethnicity is brought into play to defeat the equality that ought to exist. It cannot be said that African governments present an unrestrained opportunity for their citizenry to aspire to the highest political office. This is because by their nature some African governments appear to abhor opposition to such an extent that persons who are not seen to be loyal to the ruling dictator or ruling unpopular party are often denied the right to participate in government.[458] It is understandable that the right to participate in government or have access to public property or services may be subject to some limitations,

---

458 A recent example is the unimaginable exclusion and intimidation that went on in Nigeria for the last fifteen years under the military governments of Generals Ibrahim Babangida and Sani Abacha, which could only be compared to the Mobutu Sese Seko government of Zaire and that of Paul Biya of Cameroon.

which are acceptable in most democratic systems. Such limitations include legal disqualification of leaders for high office, non-reelection to office due to a constitutionally established term of office, and the like.

While the African Commission is yet to precisely describe the characteristics of the right to participation in the government of one's country, it could be guided by the experience of other regional human rights organs,[459] to define the circumstances under which the enjoyment of the class of rights contained in Article 13 of the Charter can be limited. It is worth noting, however that the Commission has engaged in a number of election missions in Africa, which goes to show that it takes a keen interest in seeing the right popularized.

10. The right to property

Article 14 of the Charter provides that "the right to property is guaranteed. It may only be encroached upon in the interest of public need or in the general interest of the community and in accordance with the provisions of appropriate laws." The right to property has gained considerable ground in present day international law, especially as a human right. The recognition of the right under the Charter is followed by the power of a State to encroach upon private property for public or community interest in accordance with appropriate laws. The Charter fails to define what constitutes public or community interests. In addition, the instrument does not contain an express provision for the payment of compensation in situations where such properties are encroached upon by the State. The fact that such acquisition by the State should be in accordance with appropriate laws is not clear enough to determine whether compensation will be paid and what will be the standard for its payment.

Article 14 of the Charter is narrower in context than the corresponding provision under the American Convention,[460] but somewhat more akin to the provisions under the European Convention.[461] The American Convention appears to be more progressive in the recognition of the right to property than any other

---

459 *See* HUMAN RIGHTS, POLITICAL RIGHTS AND REPRESENTATIVE DEMOCRACY IN THE INTER-AMERICAN SYSTEM, ANNUAL REPORT OF THE INTER-AMERICAN COMMISSION ON HUMAN RIGHTS (1990-91) in DAVIDSON, THE INTER-AMERICAN HUMAN RIGHTS SYSTEM, *supra*, note 229, at 342. In this Report the Inter-American Commission, *inter alia*, examined some underlying characteristics of the right to participate in government in the context of the relationship between democracy and human rights.

460 Article 21 of the American Convention.

461 Article 1 of the First Protocol to the European Convention gives unfettered right to a state to interfere with property in a much broader manner. The protocol contains no express reference to a right of compensation at any level in the event of interference with property, except any that might be found in the reference to the general principles of international law.

regional human rights instruments. Even though the American Convention recognizes in Article 21(1) that the right of an individual to own and enjoy property may be subordinated to interest of society, its Article 21(2) specifies that "no one shall be deprived of their property except upon payment of just compensation, for reasons of public utility or social interest..." In reviewing these provisions, the Inter-American Commission has said that the right to own property must be regarded as a fundamental and inalienable right, and that no State, group or person may undertake or conduct activities to suppress the rights upheld in those provisions, including the right to own property.[462] In addition, the Commission maintains that the international instruments protecting the right to property establish universal and regional rules which have become rules of international customary law and as such, are considered obligatory in the doctrine and practice of international law.[463] The African Commission can thus ensure that the power of the State to encroach upon private property for public or community interest is not abused, by requiring States to adhere to the international law principle of payment of just and adequate compensation, even though this might face stiff opposition from State Parties.

Apart from the issue of acquisition of private property and payment of compensation by the state, Article 14 presents a number of questions with regard to property inheritance in Africa, especially as it affects women. In many African cultures, women are not entitled to inherit property, even where they are the survivors of their parents. One wonders, whether Article 14 contemplates this kind of denial of a right to property. There is yet little practice by the African Commission to determine the extent covered by article 14. There is, however, one known case where the Commission has been confronted with the right to property question.[464] In that case the complainant alleged that he had suffered huge financial loss because his property and other possessions were confiscated by the government. Despite the fact that the Commission is said to have sympathized with the victim and sought to settle the case, it failed to state whether or not the right to property had been violated. That case was a missed opportunity for the Commission to set the stage in developing its jurisprudence in that regard. The fact that the Commission may be inclined to pursue settlement, does not prevent it from laying a solid legal foundation upon which a right protected by the Charter can be interpreted.

---

462 DAVIDSON, THE INTER-AMERICAN HUMAN RIGHTS SYSTEM, *supra*, note 229, at 334.
463 *Id.* at 334-335.
464 *John K. Modise v. Botswana*, Communication No. 97/93, *supra*, note 405.

B. Economic, Social and Cultural Rights

The normative character of provisions in human rights instruments on economic, social and cultural rights (ESCR) has been very controversial as against that of civil and political rights (CPR). This controversy greeted the ESCR provisions of the Universal Declaration of Human Rights, as well as those of the International Covenant on Economic, Social and Cultural Rights (ICESCR), culminating in similar controversy on such provisions in regional human rights instruments. Commenting on the situation under the ICESCR, Philip Alston, one of the foremost scholars in this field, identifies as one of the most striking features of the Covenant, the vagueness of the normative implications of the various rights it recognizes. This learned author who is also the Chairman of the UN Committee on Economic, Social and Cultural Rights (ESCR's Committee),[465] reasons that while some of the formulations are not more vague or ill-defined than some of those in the International Covenant on Civil and Political Rights (ICCPR), the difference in the extent of elaboration of their normative content, undertaken both before and after the adoption of the Covenant, is immense.[466]

Some factors have been identified for this lack of agreement on the normative content of ESCRs. First, the content of the ICESCR was not based upon any significant bodies of domestic jurisprudence as was the case with civil and political rights.[467] The example of the phrase, "cruel, inhuman or degrading punishment,"

---

[465] It should be noted that the Economic, Social and Cultural Rights Committee, unlike the Human Rights Committee is not a treaty based body of the UN. It is a creation of the UN Economic and Social Council (ECOSOC) pursuant to ESC Res. 1985/17.

[466] Alston, *The Committee on Economic, Social and Cultural Rights, supra*, note 145, at 490. For further discussions on the development of Economic Social and Cultural Rights, *see* also generally, PAUL HUNT, RECLAIMING SOCIAL RIGHTS: INTERNATIONAL AND COMPARATIVE PERSPECTIVES (Aldershot, England: Dartmouth Publishing Company Limited, 1996); MATTHEW C. R. CRAVEN, THE INTERNATIONAL COVENANT ON ECONOMIC SOCIAL AND CULTURAL RIGHTS: A PERSPECTIVE ON ITS DEVELOPMENT (Oxford: Clarendon Press, 1995); ECONOMIC, SOCIAL AND CULTURAL RIGHTS: A TEXT BOOK (ASBJØRN EIDE, CATARINA KRAUSE & ALLAN ROSAS, eds., Dordrecht: Martinus Nijhoff Publishers, 1995); THE RIGHT TO COMPLAIN ABOUT ECONOMIC, SOCIAL AND CULTURAL RIGHTS: PROCEEDINGS OF THE EXPERT MEETING ON THE ADOPTION OF AN OPTIONAL PROTOCOL TO THE INTERNATIONAL COVENANT ON ECONOMIC, SOCIAL AND CULTURAL RIGHTS HELD FROM 25-28 JANUARY 1995 IN UTRECHT (FONS COOMANS & FRIED VAN HOOF, eds., Utrecht, Netherlands: Netherlands Institute of Human Rights, 1995). (Hereafter; THE RIGHT TO COMPLAIN ABOUT ECONOMIC SOCIAL AND CULTURAL RIGHTS); *Jean-Marie Henckaerts, The Coming of Age of the International Covenant on Economic, Social and Cultural Rights Through the Work of the International Committee on Economic, Social and Cultural Rights* in THE MODERN WORLD OF HUMAN RIGHTS: ESSAYS IN HONOR OF THOMAS BUERGENTHAL 267 (ANTONIO A. CANÇADO TRINADE, ed., San José, Costa Rica: Inter-American Institute of Human Rights, 1996); *Louis B. Sohn, The Contribution of Latin American Lawyers to the Development of the United Nations Concept of Human Rights and Economic and Social Justice* in *id.* 33

[467] Alston, *The Committee on Economic, Social and Cultural Rights,, supra*, note 145, at 490

which is used by Alston in tracing the history of domestication of some aspects of civil and political rights, makes a good reference point, to the effect that the phrase had been the subject of in-depth judicial and academic analysis long before its inclusion in the ICCPR. Thus, unlike economic social and cultural rights, the range of rights recognized in the ICCPR, with the exception of labor-related rights, was considerably in advance of most national legislation.[468] It is therefore still a problem that keeps the international lawyer wondering as to the meaning of rights such as those pertaining to food, education, health care, clothing, shelter, etc., as Alston points out, because there is little direct guidance, if any, in national or domestic law.[469]

Secondly, the international community has failed to develop jurisprudence of any significance on many of the principal economic rights since the adoption in 1966 of the ICESCR, unlike the level of jurisprudential development of civil and political rights. Thus, the meaning and precise policy implications of specific civil and political rights have been the subject of detailed legal analysis and of carefully honed judicial and quasi-judicial interpretation, as well as being spelt out in much greater detail in specialized instruments.[470] The same cannot be said of economic, social and cultural rights. These rights have benefitted from remarkably few of such endeavors and those that have been undertaken have not been revealing.[471] However, some of the relevant UN reports have indicated that in the field of economic and social rights it is easy to generate "a large amount of heat" by detailing the statistics of infant mortality, death by starvation, adult literacy, and general homelessness; but infinitely more difficult are attempts to generate even a small amount of light by identifying the core requirements stemming from recognition of particular rights.[472]

Thirdly, one could add that the political ideologies of Member States of the UN affected the normative characterization of economic, social and cultural rights. While socialist oriented countries tended to emphasize economic and social rights, market oriented States saw political and civil rights as more tangible, and fought more vigorously for their international prescription. The campaign by developed market-oriented States gained an upper hand largely due to the enormous political and economic power of the proponent States over others in international relations,

---

[468] *Id.*
[469] *Id.*
[470] Alston notes, specifically, such instruments as the Standard Minimum Rules for the Treatment of Prisoners and the Convention against Torture. *Id.*
[471] *Id.* at 490.
[472] *Id. citing* GANJI, THE REALIZATION OF ECONOMIC, SOCIAL AND CULTURAL RIGHTS: PROBLEMS, POLICIES, PROGRESS, UN Sales No. E.75.XIV.2 (1975).

particularly in the UN system. The effect that this had on developing countries is that it gave them every reason to avoid serious economic and social obligations.

Finally, one factor in this battle for the normative content of economic, social and cultural rights, is the role of human rights non-governmental organizations (human rights NGOs). Most human rights NGOs were created with very specific mandates, primarily in the area of civil and political rights, and have developed what can only be described as the "traditionalist" approach to human rights.[473] This has created a focus primarily on one aspect of human rights guaranteed by international instruments of supposedly equal status. While this style has its benefits, it also has its downside. Such single-minded pursuit of human rights can be problematic insofar as the wider contextual framework is concerned.[474] There is the tendency for the general reading and understanding both by violators and advocates of human rights, that one aspect of rights is of ultimate importance while the other is not. In this context, economic, social and cultural rights are considered to be, as Oloka-Onyango puts it, "the poor relation of their civil and political counterparts."[475] Similarly, the focus on States as the primary rights-guarantors obviates a critical consideration of the wide variety of extra-State actors, ranging from guerilla groupings to multinational corporations, and from development agencies to arms dealers, who have come to impact upon and influence the range and extent of observation or violation of human rights.[476]

Unlike other international and regional human rights instruments, the African Charter spearheaded the holistic approach to human rights by including civil and political rights and economic, social and cultural rights in one instrument, with a seeming lack of emphasis on the importance of one class of rights over the other. This had led to the African Charter being extolled as a unique conceptualization of human rights, making its mark as the first international instrument enshrining economic, social and cultural rights, as well as other categories of rights ordinarily not considered with much seriousness in the regime of rights. In addition, the preamble to the Charter clearly demonstrates where the emphasis of the document lies, stipulating that it was essential to pay particular attention to the right to development, and that civil and political rights cannot be dissociated from economic, social and cultural rights. In fact, the Charter sees the satisfaction of economic, social and cultural rights as constituting the guarantee of civil and political rights.[477] The emphasis placed by the Charter on economic, social and

---

473 J. Oloka-Onyango, *Beyond the Rhetoric: Reinvigorating the Struggle for Economic and Social Rights in Africa*, 26 CAL. W. INT'L L.J. 1, at 36 (1995).
474 *Id.*
475 *Id.* at 1.
476 *Id.*
477 Paragraph 7 of the preamble to the African Charter.

cultural rights has led some early commentators to believe that in implementing the Charter, the African Commission would grant a State greater latitude if it would promote economic and social rights at the expense of civil and political rights.[478] Unfortunately this assumption appears not to have been realized in the work of the African Commission since its inception.

The basic issue regarding African Charter provisions on economic, social and cultural rights is their implementation in terms of normative content. There is a variety of opinions as to the justiciability or otherwise of these rights. Those who argue that economic, social and cultural rights, as guaranteed by the Charter, are justiciable, appear to be in the minority.[479] The debate on justiciability of the rights should not assume an extreme posture; there is a need to balance whatever position is held. This author tends to agree with Ankuma that economic, social and cultural rights are justiciable under the Charter, but that there is the need for progressive realization of the rights, taking into consideration the circumstances faced by the States Parties.[480]

An examination of the relevant Charter articles on economic, social and cultural rights will reveal what measures, if any, the African Commission has (or should) put in place to ensure the realization of these rights in keeping with the passion exhibited in paragraph 7 of the preamble to the Charter as to their importance.

1. The right to equitable and satisfactory conditions of work

Article 15 of the Charter states that "every person shall have the right to work under equitable and satisfactory conditions, and shall receive equal pay for equal work."[481] On first reading, there may be the tendency to interpret the provisions of Article 15 as guaranteeing the provision of work for every person, irrespective of whether there is work to do or not. This is usually the argument made by passionate opponents of economic, social and cultural rights. Article 15 of the African Charter, as may be said of every similar provision in other international instruments, does not *per se* task State Parties to provide work for every person. It rather presumes a situation where there is or will be work to do, and lays down

---

478 Richard Gittleman, *The African Charter on Human and Peoples' Rights: A Legal Analysis*, 22 VA. J. INT'L L. 667 at 687 (1982).
479 *See* Nana Busia, Jr. & B. Mbaye, *Towards a Framework for the Filing of Communications on Economic, Social and Cultural Rights Under the African Charter, Phase I*, 1 EAST AFRICAN JOURNAL OF PEACE AND HUMAN RIGHTS (1994).
480 ANKUMA, *supra*, note 363, at 144.
481 *See* corresponding provisions of Article 23 of the Universal Declaration of Human Rights (Universal Declaration), and Article 7 of the International Covenant on Economic, Social and Cultural Rights (ICESCR).

obligations of State Parties in such situations. On the other hand, it obligates States to adopt measures and programs that will not only lead to job creation, but also ensure a conducive work environment.

The concept of right to work under equitable and satisfactory conditions, that is enshrined in the Charter, generally implies fair and equal wages, the right to promotion where appropriate, the right to follow one's vocation and to change employment, reasonable work hours, right to paid vacation (leisure and rest) and the likes. The fact that the Charter does not specifically contain each of these provisions, as they are specified in Article 7 of the ICESCR, does not make the Charter provision inadequate. The interpretation of Article 15, would ordinarily lead to elucidating these contents as the necessary equitable and satisfactory conditions of work as laid down in international practice.[482]

However, unlike the Universal Declaration and the ICESCR,[483] the African Charter does not go further to identify trade union rights as relating to the right to work. It may, be argued that trade union rights are covered under the freedom of association and freedom of assembly provisions of the Charter. While this may be so, it is important to point out that trade union rights have gained separate international recognition. Trade unions have become powerful forces to reckon with, in the protection of workers' interests, as against governments and employers. Bringing trade union rights within the freedom of association provision and freedom of assembly of the Charter is relevant only to the extent that a person is guaranteed the right to form or join a trade union. However, despite this lack of direct provision on trade union rights, the Commission has nonetheless elaborated guidelines on trade union rights in its Guidelines for the Submission of State Reports. Under the guidelines, States are obligated to provide information on laws, regulations and court decisions that are designated to promote, regulate, or safeguard trade union rights, which include the right of trade unions to federate and function freely, and the right to strike.[484]

---

482 The International Labor Organization (ILO) has established standards on what equitable and satisfactory conditions of work should be. *See* generally, *Virginia A. Leary, Lesson From the Experience of the International Labour Organization*, supra, note 72, at 587..
483 Article 23 of the Universal Declaration and Article 8 of the ICESCR.
484 PROMOTION, PROTECTION AND RESTORATION OF HUMAN RIGHTS, GUIDELINES FOR NATIONAL PERIODIC REPORTS, ACHPR.Doc.AFR/COM/HRP.5(IV) (Oct. 1988).(Hereafter, OLD GUIDELINES FOR NATIONAL PERIODIC REPORTS), section II (10)-(16), *reprinted* in AFRICAN COMMISSION ON HUMAN AND PEOPLES RIGHTS, SECOND ACTIVITY REPORT OF THE AFRICAN COMMISSION ON HUMAN AND PEOPLES' RIGHTS in AFRICAN COMMISSION ON HUMAN AND PEOPLES' RIGHTS, DOCUMENTATION NO 1: ACTIVITY REPORTS (1988-1990), at 45. While the Guidelines for periodic reports have been revised to make it easier for States Parties to prepare their periodic reports, what is required in elaborating the particular rights provisions of the Charter remains unchanged. The Guidelines are still relevant in elucidating the measures Member States are required to take in applying the

To date, the African Commission is yet to receive or determine any communication alleging the violation of the right to work. In this regard, the situation may not change for a very long time unless there is proper education of the society on the specific aspects of the right to work. In addition, it appears difficult to articulate State responsibility, when most of the violations under Article 15 are done by private actors, such as companies and multinational corporations. Similarly, the requirements of exhaustion of domestic remedies may seriously limit the ability of victims to approach the Commission with communications. The Commission must take some steps, at least in form of resolutions, to define the extent of States' express obligations or imputed obligations to remedy the lack of adequate legal environment for the realization of the prescription of the Charter on the right to work.

2. The right to health

The right to health is covered by Article 16 of the Charter, which states that: (1) every person shall have the right to enjoy the best attainable state of physical and mental health, and (2) States Parties to the present Charter shall take the necessary measures to protect the health of their people and to ensure that they receive medical attention when they are sick. The question may be asked whether the provisions of Article 16 obligate State Parties to provide to every person the best attainable state of physical or mental health. Expecting any State to directly provide for the medical cost of every person within its territory would be unimaginable even if that State enjoys a rich economy. The provisions of Article 16 speak to healthcare rather than to health as a concept of well-being of every individual. A State cannot guarantee the physical and mental well-being of every individual. But a State can and should provide a conducive atmosphere that would enhance the enjoyment of good healthcare rather than undermine it. In the opinion of this author, to realize the provisions of Article 16, States must recognize health as public rather than a private good. Thus, they must adopt measures in the field of primary health care, and arrange for the extension of the benefits of healthcare, in its various categories, to all persons subject to their jurisdiction. Also included should be a comprehensive program of universal immunization against the principal infectious diseases plus the prevention and treatment of endemic, occupational and other diseases. In addition, States have to undertake educational programs for the general population on the prevention and treatment of health problems. There is also the need to identify the highest risk groups and those whose poverty

---

provisions of the Charter domestically. The revision was mainly to reduce the technicality required in States periodic reports. *See* AMENDED GUIDELINES FOR PERIODIC REPORTS, *infra*, note 697.

makes them most vulnerable, to ensure a minimum satisfaction of their health needs. To this end, States should become deeply involved in preventive healthcare, which will at least ensure minimal curative involvement.

More appropriately, the obligation of States under Article 16 is to take necessary measures to protect the health of their people. While this obligation takes into account the above discussion, it goes beyond it to demand appropriate health policies that would advance the health of the citizenry. These policies should in turn ensure appropriate legal standards that empower the people to demand action against the violation of their right to health. One example of this obligation is the need to stop the continuing practice of female genital mutilation (FGM), which has potential health hazards. In many African countries it is continued under the guise of culture, but has not yet attracted enough State sanction against its perpetrators. In the same vein, States must desist from activities that prevent suitable access to healthcare of its citizens. In many cases where the right to life and freedom from torture are violated, States have been known to prevent those under detention from receiving adequate healthcare either from their own physicians or State appointed ones. Where State-appointed physicians are made available most of the times, the treatment is below standard.[485] That should constitute a violation of the right to health enshrined in Article 16. It is not enough for a State to claim financial inability to guarantee the best state of physical and mental health. States must be willing to take measures that advance rather than undermine the realization of access of its citizenry to good healthcare.

The African Commission is yet to fully address the obligations in Article 16 of the Charter, apart from the communication against Zaire, to which government of Zaire refused to respond. There the Commission ruled that the failure of the government to provide basic services such as safe drinking water and electricity, and the shortage of medicines as alleged in the communication, constitutes a violation of Article 16 of the African Charter on the right to health.[486] No other communication on the right to health is yet known to have officially been sent by the Communication Office. Ankuma attributes, in part, this lack of communication on the right to healthcare, to the fact that there are hardly any healthcare

---

485 A glaring example is the untimely death in state detention of Moshood K. O. Abiola of Nigeria, the winner of the June 12 1993 presidential elections in Nigeria. Although he was said to have died of heart attack there is credible evidence that he was denied access to adequate healthcare by the dictatorial regime of the late General Sanni Abacha. This is just an example of many of such occurrences in African countries, which go unpublicized.

486 *Union Inter-africaines des Droits de l'Homme v. Zaire*, Communication No. 100/93. It should, however, be noted that this case was decided on the basis of the unwillingness of Zaire to cooperate with the Commission in providing the necessary information requested by the Commission. This Communication was one of many consolidated communications against Zaire in which the Commission found massive human rights violations.

organizations with observer status at the Commission. She opines that if there were such organizations, they could urge the Commission to place health issues on its agenda. In addition, they could collaborate with the Commission and other NGOs to educate the public on health matters and their connection to human rights. This, according to the author would help in the progressive translation of the right to healthcare into practical reality.[487] One will agree with the opinion of the learned author, which has been stressing the importance of NGOs in the development of human rights. (The impact of NGOs in the African human rights system will be examined in greater details in the latter part of this book). However, the most important point to be made is that the right to health is justiciable in the sense that it can be made an operational right before judicial and quasi-judicial organs.[488]

3. The right to education

Article 17 of the African Charter:

1. Every person shall have the right to education.
2. Every person may freely take part in the cultural life of his community.
3. The promotion and protection of morals and traditional values recognized by the community shall be the duty of the state.

The right to education has become of great importance in international human rights law to proponents of both civil and political rights, and economic, social and cultural rights. Under the European Convention it is treated as a civil and political right,[489] making it for those countries that are parties to the ICESCR, both an economic, social and cultural right, and a civil and political right.[490] Under the Inter-American human rights mechanism, it is one of the economic, social and cultural rights treated as hybrid rights, which are subject to the individual complaint procedure contained in Article 44 of the American Convention.[491]

---

[487] ANKUMA, *supra*, note 363, at 148.
[488] Virginia A. Leary, *The Right to Complain: The Right to Health* in THE RIGHT TO COMPLAIN ABOUT ECONOMIC, SOCIAL AND CULTURAL RIGHTS, *supra*, note 465, 87, at 90.
[489] Article 2, First Protocol to the European Convention. *See* HARRIS, *et al.*, *supra*, note 172, at 540.
[490] It is already provided for under Article 13 of the ICESCR.
[491] The Right to Education is provided for in Article 13 of the Additional Protocol to the American Convention on Human Rights (Protocol of San Salvador). Trade union rights contained in Article 8 are also subject to individual petitions. *See* generally, DAVIDSON, THE INTER-AMERICAN HUMAN RIGHTS SYSTEM, *supra*, note 299, at 33.

The regional instruments mentioned above, as well as the ICESCR contain elaborate provisions on the extent of the right to education. Article 17 of the African Charter lacks specificity on the contents of the right. The African Commission has, however, indicated in its old Guidelines for the Submission of State Reports what constitutes the content of the right to education. The Guidelines[492] show that the right to education comprises the right to primary education, the right to secondary education, the right to post-secondary education, the right to fundamental education, the right to choice of schools, and the principle of free and compulsory education for all. While the Commission is yet to determine the contents of the right to education, it underscored the importance of human rights education in Africa at its 15th Ordinary Session in 1994 by passing a resolution on human rights education.[493] The resolution particularly stressed the importance of educating vulnerable groups such as women, children, internally displaced persons, and victims of armed conflict.

The Commission will have to consider still such broader issues in the right to education as the right to receive education, the right to choice of education and the right to teach. The rights of many sections of the society to receive education have been overlooked on many occasions, without much societal disapproval. A common, but appropriate, example that Ankuma alludes to, is the plight of an unmarried female primary school student, who becomes pregnant, and is dismissed from school for that reason.[494] Apart from infringing on the student's right to receive education, the practice is also discriminatory, as it gives undue advantage to male students, who may have played a part in the pregnancy, over the female students. Similarly, it could be argued that the incessant closing of schools by many African States at the slightest students protests, or indication of protests, is an infringement on their right to education. One would expect that the difference that students' protests make to their right to receive education is where such protests culminate in violence and destruction of property, and where such protests put the life of the generality of society in danger. It is, however, true that the interpretation of what amounts to societal danger is often subject to the interpretation of overzealous State agencies.

The right to choice of education is equally important in elaborating the specific contents of the general right to education as contained in Article 17 of the Charter. This choice may well be that of the particular student but, in most circumstances, it is a right that allows parents to make inputs to the kind of education they think

---

492 OLD GUIDELINES FOR NATIONAL PERIODIC REPORTS, *supra*, note 484, section II(B)(42)-(59).
493 Resolution on Human Rights Education. *See* RECOMMENDATIONS AND RESOLUTIONS OF THE AFRICAN COMMISSION, *supra,* note 420, at 19.
494 ANKUMA, *supra*, note 363, at 149.

is best for their children. It corresponds with the right of parents to have their children educated in conformity with their own religious and philosophical convictions. Thus, it interlinks with the freedom of conscience and religion, and freedom of thought and expression that are equally protected by the Charter as civil and political rights. It may be in this area that the provisions of Article 17(2) and (3) are particularly relevant to ensure that by the choice of an education one may freely take part in the cultural life of his or her community, with a view to promote and protect the moral and traditional values recognized by the community. It should be noted that such moral and traditional values must not negatively impact on the right of one to enjoy the right to education in general or the right to choice of education in particular.

A discussion on the right to education may not be complete without looking into the aspect of the right to teach. Is a teacher limited to a set-out curriculum? To what extent can a teacher go outside the prescribed curriculum to impart knowledge? These questions bring out issues of freedom of expression, freedom of conscience, academic freedom, and to a relative extent, the right to work. Teachers may not go outside or below the prescribed standards, but there should be enough flexibility to allow them to use their expertise to the maximum benefit of the students. It is not uncommon in African States for teachers to be accused of subversive activities as a result of the contents of their teaching materials or based on comments made in the course of teaching the prescribed curriculum. Another aspect of the right to teach is the right of individuals or institutions to provide education outside state-provided education. This also is connected with the right to choice of education. Thus, a State may not stand between a child or a student and an outside provider of education, such as religious bodies or cultural institutions. The right to education under the Charter should be read to include the freedom of individuals and entities to establish and direct educational institutions in accordance with the provisions of national legislation on education that establish minimum curricular requirements and other standards.

While we wait on the African system to elaborate on the broader issues on the right to education, it appears that the Commission will in appropriate circumstances uphold the right to education in accordance with Article 17 of the Charter. In *Union Inter-africaines des Droits de l'Homme v. Zaire*,[495] the African Commission ruled that the closures of universities and secondary schools as alleged in the Communication constituted a violation of Article 17. What is lacking, however, is the required reasoned analysis that will elaborate on these rights. In a case against Nigeria alleging the expulsion of certain students from secondary

---

[495] Communication No. 100/93, *supra*, note 486.

school for improper conduct, the Commission found the Communication inadmissible for lack of exhaustion of domestic remedies.[496]

In arriving at a jurisprudence on the right to education generally, the African system could closely follow the development of the right under the ICESCR, particularly the work of the UN Committee on Economic Social and Cultural Rights. It should be noted that together with a few other rights,[497] the right to education is considered as one of the core economic, social and cultural rights that warrant the adoption of an Optional Protocol to the ICESCR on the right to complain when there is a violation of economic, social and cultural rights.[498]

4. Protection of the family and other rights

Article 18 of the Charter provides that:

1. The family shall be the natural unit and basis of society. It shall be protected by the State which shall take care of its physical health and moral needs.
2. The State shall have the duty to assist the family which is the custodian of moral and traditional values recognized by the community.
3. The State shall ensure the elimination of every discrimination against women and also ensure the protection of the rights of women and the child as stipulated in international declarations and conventions.
4. The aged and the disabled shall have the right to special measures of protection in keeping with their physical and moral needs.

On the surface, one may read Article 18 as a provision primarily on the family, while at the same making provisions for vulnerable groups in the family and the community at large. The truth, however, is that Article 18 contains comprehensive but separate provisions on the family, women's rights, rights of the child, the disabled and the aged. The extent of implementation of the Charter provisions on these rights is a different matter altogether.

a. Protection of the Family

Article 18(1) and (2), while underscoring the importance of the family as the basic unit of the society place obligations on States Parties not only to protect it and take care of its physical and moral health, but also to assist family members in

---

496 *Bamidele Arturu v. Nigeria*, Communication No. 72/92, ACHPR\LR\A\1 (1997), *supra*, note 364, at 83, ¶¶ 8-9.
497 These include the right to adequate housing, the right to health and the right to food.
498 *See* FONS COOMANS & FRED VAN HOFF, THE RIGHT TO COMPLAIN ABOUT ECONOMIC, SOCIAL AND CULTURAL RIGHTS, *supra*, note 465, at vii-viii. *See also* Fons Coomans, *Clarifying the Core Elements of the Right to Education* in *id.*, at 13-15.

fulfilling their duties. In addition to the obligations and duty of State to family, Articles 27(1) and Article 29(1) recognize individual duties to the family. Unlike other human rights instruments, the Charter does not contain any provision on the right of every person to marry or establish a family. It would appear that that is presumed in the recognition of the family as the basic unit of society. The Charter does not specify in what ways a State should protect and assist the family, which means that there is room for a broad interpretation of State obligation in this regard. The African Commission is yet to give insight to the content of State obligations and duties in this regard. In affording protection to the family, the State must not only create a legislative framework which will allow the family to develop to its maximum potential, but must also work actively to create societal conditions in which families might flourish. In addition, the State must take measures to maximize the welfare of the family and of those whom it serves.

Accordingly, there must be particular matters, to which States need to pay attention. The itemized matters in Article 15 of the Additional Protocol to the American Convention on Human Rights (Protocol of San Salvador) are instructive in this regard. First, State Parties need to provide special care and assistance to mothers during a reasonable period before or after child's birth. Second, States are to guarantee adequate nutrition for children at the nursing stage and during the years of school attendance. Third, States Parties need to adopt special measures for the protection of adolescents in order to ensure the full development of their physical, intellectual and moral capacities. Finally, States need to undertake special programs of family training in order to help create a stable and positive environment in which children will receive and develop the values of understanding, respect and responsibility.

Just like many other economic, social and cultural rights, the foregoing obligations and duties of States to the family are progressive and promotional, having a link with the availability of a State Party's resources. This notwithstanding, the obligations and duties provide an insight into the material underpinning of the right to the family, and have much to do with the rights of the child, which therefore, need to be taken into consideration.[499]

b. Rights of the Child

Article 18(3) in its second part ensures the protection of the rights of the child as stipulated in international declarations and conventions. The rights of the child have not received any particular attention under the African Charter. The provision on the rights of the child under the Charter can be said to be a recognition of them

---

[499] DAVIDSON, THE INTER-AMERICAN HUMAN RIGHTS SYSTEM, *supra*, note 229, at 327.

as rights within the Charter, but whose implementation lies elsewhere, hence the express mention of international declarations and conventions. Thus, the Charter envisages an interpretation of the contents of the rights by resorting to such instruments as the Convention on the Rights of the Child[500] and the African Charter on the Rights and Welfare of the Child.[501] The comprehensive African Charter on the Rights and Welfare of the Child sets up a supervisory organ, the African Committee of Experts on the Rights and Welfare of the Child. It follows therefore that a Communication can both be brought before the African Human Rights Commission alleging the violation of the rights of the child under Article 18(3) of the African Charter, but relying on the above specific instruments on the rights of the child, and under Article 44 of the Child's Rights Charter before its Committee of Experts.

One is left to wonder why the OAU deemed it necessary to establish a separate organ to implement the Charter on the Rights and Welfare of the Child. The adoption of the Charter is a good idea. Its implementation should have been brought within the African Charter on Human and Peoples' Rights, at least, as a cost effective measure. In addition, human rights jurisdiction in Africa should reside within the implementation machinery of the Human Rights Charter. Duplicating supervision of different aspects of human rights is likely to be counterproductive.

c. Women's Rights

In addressing women's rights, Article 18(3) obligates States to ensure the elimination of every form of discrimination against women and to also ensure the protection of the rights of women as stipulated in international declarations and conventions. Some African commentators consider the provision on women's rights under the African Charter to be inadequate as it is barely mentioned in one paragraph within the context of the general protection of the family.[502] Such scholars maintain that the foremost concern of Article 18 is the family; that it would be difficult to use Article 18(3) to protect the rights of women, in view of the role of the

---

500 28 I.L.M 1448 (1989). Adopted by the U.N. General Assembly on November 28, 1989. Entered into force on September 2, 1990.
501 Adopted at the 26th Ordinary Session of the ASHG of the OAU, July 1990, OAU Doc.CAB/LEG/ 24.9/49 (1990). *See* also *Africa Legal Materials*, 3 AFRICAN JOURNAL OF INTERNATIONAL AND COMPARATIVE LAW 173-190 (1991). The Charter is now in force, having received the required sixteen instruments of ratification by Member States of the OAU. Current States party to the Charter include, Angola, Benin, Burkina Faso, Cameroon, Cape Verde, Lesotho, Malawi, Mali, Mauritius, Mozambique, Niger, Senegal, Seychelles, Togo, Uganda, and Zimbabwe. *See, Rachel Murray, Human Rights News: Africa*, 18 NETH. Q. HUM. RTS. 282 (2000).
502 ANKUMA, *supra,* note 363, 151-158, at 152.

woman in the traditional African family, and the emphasis in the Charter that the African concept of human rights should be inspired by the virtues of African tradition and the virtues of African civilization.[503]

One will agree with these commentators that the African Charter does not contain elaborate provisions on the rights of women. Thus, the fear expressed by the commentators is understandable. However, it is not absolutely correct that the protection afforded women in Article 18(3) is within the confines of the protection of families, as the paragraph makes a cross-reference to ensuring the protection of the rights of women stipulated in international declarations and conventions. Article 18 as already argued, is a comprehensive, but separate provision dealing with different classes of rights. Just as it was done in other situations where there is lack of clarity in the Charter as to content, the lack of exhaustive provisions can be remedied by innovative interpretation by the implementing organ of the African system. The Charter already prohibits all forms of discrimination against women and that should be the focus of the African system, whether the discrimination is based in the family or outside it. The inherent discrimination against women in African traditional societies could thus be adequately covered by Article 18(3).[504]

On the other hand, the extent of African traditional inhibitions of women, which continue to influence present day laws and practices, may warrant more drastic protective measures of women's rights along the lines argued by women's rights advocates in Africa. In many African customary practices, the right of inheritance in land is completely denied to women. There is every tendency to interpret the status of women to be inferior to that of men. The situation could be captured in Nigeria's initial report to the Committee on the Elimination of Discrimination Against Women (CEDAW), the relevant part of which states:

> The authority in the home is the monopoly of the man... Any attack on discrimination against women must honestly attack cultural and inhibitive factors inherent in the primary unit... In traditional society, a woman is treated as chattel, to be bought and sold, discarded at will, inherited and disposed of with other property upon the death of her husband and without consent... True there are no provisions discriminatory of women in our statute books, but it is equally true that there are no enforceable laws that offer her succor when she is discriminated against by customs, administrative directives and

---

503 *Id.* at 153.

504 Article 18 is complemented by the general nondiscrimination provision in its Article 2 that every person shall be entitled to the enjoyment of the rights and freedoms recognized and guaranteed in the Charter without distinction of any kind such as race, ethnic group, color, sex, language, religion, political or any other opinion, national and social origin, fortune, birth or other status.

discriminative religious practices... There are still no enforceable laws that protect against traditions, attitudes, customs, religion and illiteracy.[505]

This report speaks of the situation in many African States. The tone appears to be that of helplessness. It also gives the impression of a long rooted practice in custom. It, however, points out that no measure has been taken to address the customary shortcomings. Despite how rooted these traditional practices may be, the State must take steps, albeit gradually, and show interest for a change from the status quo. Traditional societies must accept the fact that culture is dynamic. African courts also have a role to play in dismantling such discriminatory practices against women.

The implementing organ(s) of the African system must, however, lead the way in Africa in bringing about a change in the various discriminations against women. The African Human Rights Commission, and the Court, when the Protocol establishing it enters into force, must use every resource within the Charter to realize this. Apart from the provisions of Article 18(3) and Article 2, there is ample interpretative authority under Articles 60 and 61 of the Charter, which allow the drawing of inspiration from international human rights law and general principles of law. Thus, if the implementing organs of the African Charter adopt a progressive and dynamic approach to women's issues, there would be the tendency to enhance the status of women in Africa. There has, been no Communication to the African Commission, which is presently the only implementing organ of the African system, alleging violation of women's rights under Article 18. The Commission has, however, taken a step in its promotive mandate by organizing a seminar on the rights of women in Africa.[506] During the seminar, there were deliberations on the need to adopt an additional Protocol on women's rights, which was preferred to amending the Charter provisions on women's rights, as suggested by some participants.[507] There were contrary views, which considered both suggestions unnecessary since the Charter already provided wide powers which needed to be exploited, and that Article 60 and 61 of the Charter already ensured that other international instruments could be incorporated into the Charter through

---

[505] Claude E. Welch, *Human Rights and African Women: A comparison of Protection Under Two Major Treaties*, 15 No. 3 HUMAN RIGHTS QUARTERLY, 566 (1993), also *reprinted* in ANKUMA, *supra*, note 363, at 153.

[506] The seminar, titled "The African Charter on Human and Peoples' Rights and the Rights of Women in Africa," was held in Lome, Togo from March 8-9, 1995 in collaboration with Women in Law and Development in Africa (WILDAF).

[507] *See* Rachel Murray, *Report on the 1996 Sessions of the African Commission on Human and Peoples' Rights*, 18, No.1-4 HUM. RTS. L. J.16, at 19 (1997). *See* also ANKUMA, *supra*, note 363, at 158.

the interpretation of its provisions.[508] Despite the above arguments, the African Commission, saw the need to expressly address the question of women's rights in Africa. At its 21st ordinary session in Nouakchott, Mauritania, the Commission appointed three Commissioners as a working group to work on a draft Protocol on women's rights.[509] The Commission subsequently appointed one of the Commissioners as Special Rapporteur on the rights of women.[510]

Whatever the persuasions of the various commentators on the situation of women's rights in Africa, the general consensus is that there is the need to promote more vigorously women issues through public education. Such education must be aimed at not only customary practitioners, but also judges and law enforcement officers.

d.   Protection of the Aged and the Disabled

Article 18(4) stipulates that the aged and the disabled shall have the right to special measures of protection in keeping with their physical or moral condition. Like many other aspects of the Charter, this area has not received any attention from the African Commission. This is a very sensitive area of human rights law, especially in Africa where disabled persons for instance, have not been known to be given adequate protection against discrimination, nor opportunities and measures that take their situation into consideration. Often times disabled persons are treated as outcasts. The same could be said of the aged, the only difference being that members of their families assume the responsibility to cater for their welfare in keeping with custom and tradition. The care is usually not adequate since the resources available to them are often very limited.

The protection afforded aged persons under the Charter must not only be interpreted in terms of providing suitable facilities, food and specialized medical care. While these are very essential, they must also be provided with the opportun-

---

508 *Id.*, Rachael Murray.
509 *See* TENTH ANNUAL ACTIVITY REPORT OF THE AFRICAN COMMISSION ON HUMAN AND PEOPLES' RIGHTS, AHG/210(XXXII), 5. The Commissioners appointed were Mrs. Julienne Ondziel-Gnelenga, Dr. Vera Duarte-Martins and Professor E.V.O. Dankwa. The group was later expanded to include the International Commission of Jurists and the African Center for Democracy and Human Rights Studies. *See* also ELEVENTH ANNUAL ACTIVITY REPORT OF THE AFRICAN COMMISSION ON HUMAN AND PEOPLES' RIGHTS, DOC/OS/43(XXIII), 7. *See* REPORT OF THE FIRST MEETING OF THE WORKING GROUP ON THE ADDITIONAL PROTOCOL TO THE AFRICAN CHARTER ON WOMEN'S RIGHTS, DOC/OS/58(XXIV) where the text of the draft Protocol: DOC/OS/58(XXIV) Annex I, is attached, as well as draft terms of reference for the Special Rapporteur on the Rights of Women in Africa, DOC/OS/58(XXIV) Annex II. The draft Protocol was adopted by the African Commission at its 26th session and was forwarded to the Secretary-General of the OAU for by the ASHG.
510 On the recommendation of the study group, Mrs. Julienne Ondziel-Gnelenga was appointed Special Rapporteur on the rights of women at the 23rd Session of the Commission.

ity to engage in productive activities which are suited to their abilities and consistent with their vocations or desires.[511] Old age should not be seen as a discouraging factor for those who are still strong to want to engage in productive activities. The State may thus, be required to foster the establishment of social organizations aimed at improving the quality of life for the elderly.

Similarly, persons who are affected by a diminution of their physical or mental capacities are to be entitled to receive special attention designed to help them achieve the greatest possible development of their personality. To fully achieve this, States must endeavor to engage in the development of programs aimed at providing disabled persons with the resources and environment needed for attaining the development of their personality, including work programs consistent with their possibilities (which could mean their talents and capacities) and freely accepted by them or their legal representatives.[512] In addition, States should consider solutions to specific requirements arising from the needs of disabled persons as a priority component of their urban development. Like in aged persons' circumstances, states should encourage the establishment of social groups in which disabled persons can be helped to enjoy a fuller life.[513]

The larger question on economic, social and cultural rights as guaranteed by the African Charter has always been that of implementation in the face of the weak economies of African states. As has been pointed out, it is reasonable to expect that economic, social and cultural rights be implemented progressively. The progressive implementation must, however, be seen as an obligation by State Parties. If States undertake to adopt legislative and other measures to give effect to the provisions of the Charter, the refusal to adopt such measures, whether as regards, civil and political rights, or economic, social and cultural rights amounts to a violation of the Charter.[514] Thus, for economic, social and cultural rights,

---

511 *See* DAVIDSON, THE INTER-AMERICAN HUMAN RIGHTS SYSTEM, *supra*, note 229, at 358, discussing generally the protection of the elderly and handicapped persons under the San Salvador Protocol to the American Convention on Human Rights. The 1988 Protocol adequately sets out the contents of the rights of the elderly and handicapped persons in the Inter-American system. The African system may well borrow from the contents and the interpretation given to these problems under the Inter-American mechanism.

512 *Id.*

513 *Id.*

514 *See* THE UN COMMITTEE ON ECONOMIC, SOCIAL AND CULTURAL RIGHTS, GENERAL COMMENT NO. 3 which clarifies the obligation of States Parties to the International Covenant on Economic, Social and Cultural Rights as stated in Article 1(1) and (2) of the Covenant. The Committee maintains that the obligation "to take steps" connotes that: "while full realization of the relevant rights might be achieved progressively, steps towards that goal must be taken within a reasonably short time after the Covenant's entry into force for the States concerned. Such steps should be deliberate, concrete and targeted as clearly as possible towards meeting the obligations recognized in the covenant." *Id.*, ¶ 2.

it must be pointed out that what is required of States is some serious political will in that regard. The State need not be a welfare State, but must be willing to provide a conducive environment for the promotion of economic, social and cultural rights. The argument of poverty of African States stands is a sharp contradiction to the incessant looting of the treasury by the majority of their leaders and the corruption in governance that has been elevated to the status of an industry by the ruling class. The Mobutus, Abachas and numerous others in Africa have robbed their masses of the opportunity of minimal economic and social well-being, not just because they did not provide economic and social rights, but because they trampled on the rule of law that would have made them realizable, albeit progressively.

C. Group or Collective Rights

One unique aspect of the African Charter is its inclusion of group, collective or peoples' rights as distinct rights in addition to civil and political rights and economic, social and cultural rights. The notion of peoples' rights seems controversial, and raises a number of questions in the minds of international human rights scholars, depending on the position taken by such scholars.[515] Such questions include: what point is Africa trying to make? What is the definition of "people"? Does it mean that the rights of the individual have become subordinated to peoples' rights? Has the individual person become the object rather than the subject in the concept of the African Charter?

In trying to answer the questions above in the context of African human rights concept, some African scholars have canvassed African traditional way of living in which communal relationship is emphasized. According to one view, "living in Africa means abandoning the right to be an individual, particular, competitive, selfish, aggressive, conquering being... in order to be with others, in peace and harmony with the living and the dead, with the natural environment and the spirits

---

515 *See* for example, PAUL SIEGHART, INTERNATIONAL LAW OF HUMAN RIGHTS 368 (Oxford 1983). The learned author voiced serious criticism and objections of a legal and socio-political nature as to the notion of collective rights and of the rights of peoples in particular. He contends that there is no generally accepted definition of what constitutes peoples, and that it is far from easy to identify the entities that are obliged to respect and secure the rights of peoples. He argues that the worst violations of human rights in history have been perpetrated in the service of inspiring abstractions which have no definite meaning, and thus often were misinterpreted. *See Theo van Boven, The Relations Between Peoples' Rights and Human Rights in the African Charter* 7 No. 2-4 HUM. RTS. L. J. 183, at 191 (1986). On "collective rights", the third generation of rights, *see Louis B. Sohn, The New International Law: Protection of Rights of Individuals Rather than States, supra,* note 344, at 48-64.

that people it or give life to it."[516] The predominant sentiment apparent in the above statement is that in Africa, the individual is totally taken over by the archetype of the totem, the common ancestor or the protective genius, and merges into the group.[517] There is no doubt that the diverse cultures of Africa significantly identify group influence over the individual. The statement of the African Charter, however, goes further than this group identity. By providing for group rights, the Charter does not subordinate individual rights to group rights, neither does it remove the individual from being the subject of the human rights concept. What the Charter tries to do is to establish a link between the inalienable rights of the human person and of peoples in a contextual manner.[518]

The contextual approach to human rights raises the issue of safeguarding, promoting and preserving universal rights and human values in societies with different political, social and cultural backgrounds. It touches upon the question of recognizing the very identity of diverse cultures, civilizations and peoples with due respect for fundamental and universal values of humanity.[519] Similarly, the following preambular paragraph of the African Charter reinforces the relationship between peoples' rights and human rights: "Recognizing, on the one hand, that fundamental human rights stem from the attributes of human beings, which justifies their national and international protection, and on the other hand, that the reality and respect of peoples' rights should necessarily guarantee human rights."[520] This author totally agrees with the interpretation given by van Boven[521] on the significance of the above provision because of the fact that it has two elements to it. First, human rights are the attributes of human beings in that they are inalienable and belong intrinsically to the human person. Second, peoples' or group rights

---

[516] Keba M'Baye, *The Organization of African Unity* (citing Professor Collomb) in INTERNATIONAL DIMENSION OF HUMAN RIGHTS 589 (KAREL VASAK/ALSTON, eds., 1982).
[517] *Id.*
[518] *See van Boven, supra,* note 515, at 186. According to the author, the African Charter reflects faithfully what non-aligned nations sought to express in G. A Res. 32/130, which was adopted on December 19, 1977, though with the abstention of a number of Western Countries. The resolution contained a number of guidelines, concepts and principles, which should be taken into account in the approach to future work within the United Nations system with respect to human rights questions. Two concepts of the relevant part of the resolution are particularly astute:
All human rights and fundamental freedoms of the human person and of peoples are inalienable; and Consequently, human rights questions should be examined globally, taking into account both the over-all context of various societies in which they present themselves, as well as the need for the promotion of the full dignity of the human person and the development and well being of the society.
[519] *Id.*
[520] Preambular paragraph 5 to the African Charter.
[521] *van Boven, supra,* note 515, at 188.

are not in conflict or in competition with human rights, as they are complementary concepts.

Some aspects of the notion of collective rights enshrined in the African Charter are strongly amplified by the U.N. Declaration on the Right to Development.[522] Such endorsement of the principle of collective rights is indicative of their importance rather than their destructive tendencies, contrary to the argument presented by Sieghart. While it may be true that recent experiences and actual practices in different parts of the world have revealed what happens when a misconceived concept is misinterpreted and vehemently enforced, the concept of collective rights cannot be said to be fraught with such dangers as apartheid, or such other concepts that degrade the status of the human person. Van Boven rightly points out that the principle of the right to development, for example, is a notion of peoples' right that is not destructive of individual human rights, but one that places peoples' rights and human rights in mutual relationship as complementary concepts.[523]

One does not contend the fact that there is no generally accepted definition of people, neither does the African Charter offer one. However, there is consensus among jurists that some working characteristics of "peoples" have emerged from studies made under the auspices of UNESCO. Such characteristics, among others, include:

1. An enjoyment by a group of individuals of some or all the following common features:

(i) common historical tradition;
(ii) Ethnic group identity;
(iii) Cultural homogeneity;
(iv) Linguistic unity;
(v) Religious or ideological affinity;
(vi) Territorial connection;
(vii) Common economic life.

2. The group on a whole must have the will to be identified as a people or the consciousness of being a people.[524]

Similarly, as far back as almost two decades ago, valid efforts at describing the meaning of the "peoples"concept had been made by Aurelieu Cristescu, the Special

---

[522] Adopted by G.A. Res. 41/128 of 4 December 1986
[523] *van Boven, supra*, note 515, at 193.
[524] UNESCO Meeting of Experts on International Law, Paris, February, 1990, *reprinted* in ANKUMA, *supra*, note 363, at 161.

Rapporteur of the Sub-Commission on the Prevention of Discrimination and Protection of Minorities in his study on the right to self-determination.[525]

By choosing to create legal obligations out of peoples' rights, the point that Africa is trying to make is that, just like other leading instruments, such as the American Declaration of Independence, the French Declaration of the Rights of Man and of the Citizen, the Universal Declaration of Human Rights, the African Charter is more than a legal instrument. It is also an instrument of liberation; and embodies human aspirations and goals, reflecting constitutive elements of justice.[526] According to van Boven, this is more so, because the struggles for human rights and peoples rights are not only settled in the courts, but also and perhaps more decisively in political fora. Thus, instruments on human rights and peoples rights may function in an extra-legal dimension as a guarantee and as mechanisms to defend freedom. Particularly in the third world, they also serve as tools of the liberation for the deprived, the oppressed, the have-nots and victims of discrimination.[527]

One might agree that the African Charter on Human and Peoples' Rights places itself within the existing governmental and State order of Africa, on the condition, however, of the total liberation of Africa from the yoke of colonialism. At the same time the Charter also points out quite clearly that the existing State order in Africa is not an end in itself, but derives its meaning and legitimacy from the peoples of Africa and from the manner the State structure represents the rights and interests of the peoples of Africa. While States cannot be dispensed with as actors on the national and international scene, the highly innovative element of the African Charter is that it relates to peoples a set of existing or emerging rights which were already identified by inter-governmental fora of the United Nations in connection with States.

The task, however, is on the implementing machinery of the African system to articulate these somewhat challenging, ambitious and innovative provisions on group or collective rights and to interpret them in the letter and spirit of the Charter. The task would not be an easy one in the face of the controversy that

---

[525] AURELIEU CRISTESCU, THE RIGHT TO SELF DETERMINATION: HISTORICAL AND CURRENT DEVELOPMENTS ON THE BASIS OF UNITED NATIONS INSTRUMENTS (United Nations, New York, 1981) Sales No. E80.XIV.3, *cited in* van Boven, *supra*, note 515, at 192. Cristescu lists in paragraph 279 of this study, some elements of a definition of the notion of peoples as follows:
  (a) The term "peoples" denotes a social entity possessing a clear identity and its own characteristics;
  (b) It implies a relationship with a territory, even if the people in question has been wrongly expelled from it and artificially replaced by another population;
  (c) A people should not be confused with ethnic, religious or linguistic minorities, whose existence and rights are recognized in article 27 of the International Covenant on Civil and Political Rights.
[526] *Id.* van Boven, supra note 500, at 192.
[527] *Id.*

surrounds this class of rights. It would take legal dynamism and spirited commitment to achieve this.

Peoples' rights under the Charter span from Article 19 to 24. Article 19 guarantees the equality of all peoples and prohibits the domination of a people by another. Article 20 provides for the right of all peoples to self-determination. Article 21 guarantees the right of all peoples to freely dispose of their wealth and natural resources and to exercise several related rights. Article 22 deals with the right to development, while Article 23 deals with national and international peace and security. Finally article 24 guarantees the rights of all peoples to a satisfactory environment favorable to their development. We will discuss the practice with regards to some of these provisions if any, by the African Commission, and the prospects of such practice, where there is no indication of an existing practice.

1. The right of self-determination

The right of self-determination is conceptually provided for in Article 19 of the Charter, while specifically enumerated in Article 20. Article 19 provides that "All peoples shall be equal; they shall enjoy the same respect and shall have the same rights. Nothing shall justify the domination of a people by another." Article 20 reads as follows:

1. All peoples shall have the right to existence. They shall have the unquestionable and inalienable right to self-determination. They shall freely determine their political status and shall pursue their economic and social development according to the policy they have freely chosen.
2. Colonized or oppressed peoples shall have the right to free themselves from the bonds of domination by resorting to any means recognized by the international community.
3. All peoples shall have the right to the assistance of the State Parties to the present Charter in their liberation struggle against foreign domination, be it political, economic or cultural.

The above Charter provision on the right of self-determination underscores the colonial experience and domination of Africa with a view of eliminating all vestiges of colonialism. The fact, however, that the Charter is a document enacted in post-independent Africa leaves one to wonder on the perceived application of the concept in the future. While Article 20(2) and (3) reinforce opposition to all forms of colonialism, Articles 19 and 20(1) are general guarantees against domination of any kind of peoples. Article 20(2) not only emancipates colonized people, but also "oppressed peoples." As has been rightly observed, the above provisions have left commentators wondering whether the principle of self-determination of "peoples" would apply to groups within sovereign African States who may wish to secede as was the experience in Biafra, Western Sahara and Eritrea.

The African struggle for decolonization was essentially a struggle for the right of self-determination of African people to freely determine their political status and freely pursue their economic, social and cultural development.[528] With the attainment of *de jure* independence of African States the quest for self-determination became reinforced as experiences in the above cited examples have shown. African States have individually, and under the auspices of the OAU, taken the position that self-determination does not apply outside the colonial context, because such post-colonial application of the concept will undermine African unity.[529] The International Court of Justice (ICJ) in a case between Burkina Faso and Mali, has endorsed this theory of African unity as a basis for not applying the principle of self-determination to groups within post-colonial Africa. The ICJ stated that "the maintenance of the territorial status quo in Africa is often seen as the wisest course, to preserve what has been achieved by the peoples who have struggled for their independence, and to avoid a disruption which would deprive the continent of the gains achieved by much sacrifice."[530]

There is no disputing the fact that African unity is indispensable to African development and would be the preferred option of all well meaning Africans. However, events all over Africa have shown that the domination experienced during colonialism, on the basis of which Africa fought for independence, still pervades the continent. Eritrea, Rwanda, Western Sahara, Katanga, Anglophone Cameroon and post-Biafra domination in Nigeria are glaring examples. Some of these cases have shown that there are certain exigent circumstances where the principle of self-determination should be allowed to apply rather than a preference for the human carnage that went on (and still goes on) in most of these examples.

The African Commission is yet to find its bearing on the challenges posed by several of these collective rights. The Commission's position on the right of self-determination is not any different from the views expressed by African States

---

528 S. Kwaw Nyameke Blay, *Changing African Perspectives on the Right to Self-Determination in the Wake of the Banjul Charter on Human and Peoples' Rights*, JOURNAL OF AFRICAN LAW 147 (1985).

529 *Id.* at 153. The late Julius Nyerere, former President of Tanzania was a leading opponent of the Biafra struggle in Nigeria since it was "a set-back for African Unity." In the same vein Emperor Selassie of Ethiopia as head of the Consultative Committee on the Nigeria-Biafra crisis held the view that national unity of individual African States was essential for African unity and therefore the territorial integrity of OAU Member States was non negotiable. *See* OAU Resolution on the Situation in Nigeria, 1967 in IAN BROWNLIE, BASIC DOCUMENTS ON AFRICAN AFFAIRS 364 (Oxford: Clarendon Press, 1971).

530 *Burkina Faso v. Republic of Mali*, I. C. J. REPORT, 554, at 566-567 (1986). *See* also E. Kwakwa, *The Eritrean Question: The Conflict Between the Right to Self-Determination and the interest of States*, 5 Pt. 4 AFR. J.INT'L. & COMP. L. 949 (1993); *cited* in ANKUMA, *supra*, note 363, at 163.

on the issue. The first test case on self-determination that came before the Commission was *Katangese Peoples' Congress v. Zaire*.[531] In that case, the people of Katanga submitted a communication under the auspices of Katangese Peoples' Congress in 1992 requesting the African Commission to recognize the Katangese Peoples' Congress as a liberation movement entitled to support in the achievement of independence for Katanga; recognize the independence of Katanga; and help secure the expulsion of Zaire from Katanga. The complaint alleged that the history of the Kantangese people showed that its territory is separate from Zaire. The communication therefore called on the Commission to find that the people of Katanga were entitled to an independent and separate State.

In its deliberations on the communication, the African Commission identified Article 20(1) of the African Charter as the applicable provision, as there were no allegations of specific breaches of other human rights. The Commission agreed that all peoples have a right to self-determination, but that there may be a controversy as to the definition of the peoples and the content of the right. The Commission identified that the issue in the case was not self-determination for all Zaireans as a people but specifically for the Katangese, but that whether the Katangese consisted of one or more ethnic groups was, for that purpose immaterial, and that no evidence to that effect had been adduced.

The Commission agreed that self-determination may be exercised in a number of ways, such as independence, self-government, local government, federalism, confederalism, unitarism or any other form of relations that accords with the wishes of the people, but that it must be fully cognizant of other recognized principles, such as sovereignty and territorial integrity. The Commission vehemently maintained that it was obliged to uphold the sovereignty and territorial integrity of Zaire as a member of the OAU and a party to the African Charter.[532] It ruled that in the absence of a concrete evidence of violations of human rights to the point that the territorial integrity of Zaire should be called into question, and in the absence of evidence that the people of Katanga were denied the right to participate in government as guaranteed by Article 13(1) of the African Charter, Katanga was obliged to exercise a variant of self-determination that is compatible with the sovereignty and territorial integrity of Zaire.[533] For the above reasons, the Commission declared that the case held no evidence of violations of any rights under the African Charter; and that the request for independence, therefore, had no merit under the African Charter on Human and Peoples Rights.

---

531 Communication No. 75/92, ACHPR\LR\A\1(1997), *supra*, note 364, 90, at 91-92, ¶¶ 21-27.
532 *Id.* ¶ 26.
533 *Id.* ¶ 27.

It is clearly evident from this case that the African Commission does not intend to interpret the right of self-determination as long as there is the right to participate in the government of one's country under Article 13(1) of the Charter. Any other claim would appear to a majority of members of the Commission to be a threat to the territorial and sovereign integrity of an African State.

In view of the above decision, scholars may continue to wonder without end, the actual purport of Article 20 of the Charter. Interpreting the Article to apply only to foreign domination is contradictory of the clear language of the Article. The second and third paragraphs of the Article specifically identify colonized peoples, and to that extent could be said to apply to foreign domination. Paragraph 2 on the other hand, does not only identify colonized people, but also oppressed people. Oppressed people could well be within sovereign African states. In addition, paragraph 1 applies to all peoples, without specific reference to colonized people or foreign domination. In this regard, there is growing consensus that the right of self-determination is not limited to freedom from colonial domination, but extends also to contemporary post-colonial realities.[534]

Be the above as it may, one would agree that there is a need for cautious application of the absolute principle of self-determination in view of the territorial and sovereignty issues at stake. Rather than dismiss every claim of the right to self-determination, the implementing machinery of the African system should adopt strict standards on the right, which would ensure that frivolous claims are not allowed to demean its procedure. The African Human Rights Commission ought to be open-minded enough to consider genuine complaints by genuinely oppressed groups within sovereign African states. Okeke sums it as follows:

> In the final analysis, there seems to be a good case for the qualified exceptional right to secessionist self-determination and it ought not to be rejected outright when a separatist plea is particularly sound. Not to recognize that there can be cases of well founded secessionist pleas is not only to turn a deaf ear to living reality, but also a blind eye to the conceptual deficiency of the old normative framework on the question. It is time to listen with open eyes and minds.[535]

---

[534] See Ifeoma Enemo, *Self-Determination as the Fundamental Basis for the Concept of Legitimate Governance Under the African Charter on Human and Peoples Rights* in LEGITIMATE GOVERNANCE IN AFRICA: INTERNATIONAL AND DOMESTIC LEGAL IMPLICATIONS 403, at 408-418 (EDWARD K. QUASHIGAH AND OBIORA C. OKAFOR, eds., The Hague, London, Boston: Kluwer Law International, 1999); Chinedu Reginald Ezetah, *Legitimate Governance and Statehood in Africa: Beyond the Failed State and Colonial Self-Determination* in *id.*, 419, at 452-459; Christian N. Okeke, *A Note on the Right of Secession as a Human Right*, III ANNUAL SURVEY INT'L. L. & COMP. LAW, 27-35 (1996); Alexandre Kiss, *Peoples' Right to Self-Determination*, 7, No. 2-4 HUM. RTS. L. J., 165, at 170-175 (1986).

[535] Okeke, *supra*, note 534, at 35.

2. Right over wealth and natural resources

Article 21 provides:

1. All peoples shall freely dispose of their wealth and natural resources. This right shall be exercised in the exclusive interest of the people. In no case shall a people be deprived of it.
2. In case of spoliation the dispossessed people shall have the right to the lawful recovery of its property as well as an adequate compensation.
3. The free disposal of wealth and natural resources shall be exercised without prejudice to the obligation of promoting international economic cooperation based on mutual respect, equitable exchange and the principles of international law.
4. States Parties to the present Charter shall individually and collectively exercise the right to free disposal of their wealth and natural resources with a view to strengthening African unity and solidarity.
5. States Parties to the present Charter shall undertake to eliminate all forms of foreign economic exploitation, particularly that practiced by international monopolies, so as to enable their peoples to fully benefit from the advantages derived from national resources.

The right over wealth and natural resources is a component right of self-determination, and has been so regarded since the adoption of the UN Resolution on Permanent Sovereignty Over Natural Resources.[536] One could say that the drafters of the African Charter were inspired by the above resolution.[537] In the 1952 resolution, the General Assembly recognized "that the under-developed countries have the right to determine freely the use of their natural resources ... in order to be in a better position to further the realization of their plans of economic development in accordance with their national interests ..." This principle was one of the early marks of decolonization. During this period, developing countries asserted sovereignty over their natural resources during their struggle for political self-determination and economic development. They argued that sovereignty over natural resources was an essential prerequisite for economic independence and development, and therefore a cardinal component of State

---

536 G.A. res. 1803 (XVII), 17 U.N. GAOR Supp. (No.17) at 15, U.N. Doc. A/5217 (1962).This resolution incorporates the earlier one of 1952. G.A. Res. 523 (VI) (1952).
537 *See* also Articles 1, 2 and 3 in both the International Covenant on Civil and Political Rights and the International Covenant on Economic, Social and Cultural Rights, and Article 47 of the first Covenant, and Article 25 of the second.

sovereignty.[538] Today, the principle has become established as "a fundamental principle of contemporary international law."[539]

A close reading of Article 21 of the Charter reveals that "peoples" and States are guaranteed this right to their wealth and natural resources. While it is the right of all peoples freely to use, exploit, and dispose of their natural wealth and resources,[540] States have the right to exercise control over their natural wealth and resources, and in such a way that will eliminate the excesses of multinational corporations.[541] This interpretation brings back the argument already made in the previous discussion on the right of self determination as to whether "peoples" here could be extended to groups within sovereign African States. It has been observed that the doctrine of permanent sovereignty arose in the context of relations between host States and transnational enterprises engaged in the exploitation of natural resources. As a result, the right of the State to legislate for the public good with respect to the natural resources and economic activities in its territory has become the most common construction given to the doctrine of permanent sovereignty.[542] This construction which is popular in Africa seems misplaced because it tends to ignore the plight of many groups affected by the occurrence of mineral resources in their lands. State legislation in control of such resources often results in serious violations of the rights of such groups, who also often show their dissatisfaction through some not so peaceful means.[543]

---

538 *Franz Xaver Perrez, The Relationship Between "Permanent Sovereignty" and the Obligation Not to Cause Transboundary Environmental Damage*, 26 ENVTL. L. 1187 at 1205 (1996).

539 *Kamal Hossain, Introduction to Permanent Sovereignty over Natural Resources* in INTERNATIONAL LAW ix (KAMAL HOSSAIN & SUBRATA ROY CHOWDHURY eds., 1984). *See also* MILAN BULAJIC, PRINCIPLES OF INTERNATIONAL DEVELOPMENT LAW 283 (2d ed. 1992).

540 The African Charter, Article 21(1)(2)&(3).

541 *Id.*, Article 21(4)&(5).

542 *Ndiva Kofele-Kale, Patrimonicide: The International Economic Crime of Indigenous Spoliation*, 28 VAND. J. TRANSNAT'L L. 45, at 92 (1995).

543 Nigeria is a glaring example of such contentions. The Ogonis and other peoples of the Niger Delta are in constant fights with the government over what they perceive as a violation of their inalienable right to control the wealth and natural resources in their indigenous lands. These struggles have cost many human lives that are either gunned down during demonstrations or in such circumstances as the hanging of the famous Ogoni nine in 1995, the most prominent of whom was Ken Saro Wiwa by the brutal Abacha regime. The government, by legislation, nationalized all mineral resources, oil being the chief one and the major foreign exchange earner. The State therefore perceives as subversive any attempts at questioning its authority over such natural resources without seriously addressing the grievances of the people, which often are totally neglected and lack essential economic and social amenities. The people are not ignorant, they see the enormous wealth derived from the resources taken away from their lands. *See generally, Vincent O. Nmehielle, Oppression of Ethnic Minorities in Nigeria: The Ogoni Case* (Unpublished Seminar Paper on file with Author, 1995). *See also Idowu, A. A., Human Rights, Environmental Degradation and Oil Multinational Companies in Nigeria: The Ogoniland Episode*, 17 NETHERLANDS, O. HUM. RTS. 161 (1999), and *Patrick D. Okonmah, Right to a Clean Environment: The Case for the People of Oil-Producing*

The matter becomes more complicated when States, rather than checking the excesses of multinational corporations, become over-protective of them to the detriment of groups within the State. The present battle between Shell and other oil companies with oil producing communities, in Nigeria, for example, is turning out to be a serious problem for Nigeria, and must not be overlooked. It is, however, ironic that Article 21(5) of the African Charter which requires States "to eliminate all forms of foreign economic exploitation, particularly that practiced by international monopolies," singles out foreign multinationals from all the possible exploiters, which may also include State governments. It appears that the drafters of the African Charter in interpreting the principle of permanent sovereignty over natural resources pinned all the responsibility on foreigners, thus permitting the exploitation of finite Third World natural wealth and resources by indigenous exploiters to continue unabated.[544]

It has been rightly observed that the right of all peoples freely to use, exploit, and dispose of their natural wealth and resources is usually given short shrift in scholarly commentaries.[545] The basic reason for this is the seaming lack of agreement on the fact that "peoples" could mean groups within sovereign States. It has been argued that this neglect is unfortunate because a review of the *travaux préparatoires* on both the Civil and Political Rights Covenant and the Economic, Social and Cultural Rights Covenant reveals that representatives consistently spoke of the rights of peoples and States over their wealth and natural resources.[546] The fact that these and other instruments have incorporated specific provisions on the right of peoples, and these provisions appear in instruments dealing with human rights, suggest that the rights mentioned attach to people qua human beings and not only to the States Parties.[547]

One will agree that these instruments are deliberately silent on the meaning of "peoples," which is critical to appreciating the full import of Article 2(2) of the Civil and Political Rights Covenant, for example, and Article 21 of the African Charter. The interpretation by the African Commission in the *Katangese Peoples' Congress* case[548] on self-determination suggests that "peoples" refers to the State. This author agrees with the view that equating peoples with States makes sense inasmuch as people act through States and State-sponsored agencies.[549] However, and more importantly, "peoples" could also mean all persons within the State.

Communities in the Nigerian Delta, 41 (1) JOURNAL OF AFRICAN LAW, 43-67 (1997).
544 Kofele-Kale, *supra*, note 542, at 93.
545 Id.
546 Id.
547 Id. at 94.
548 Communication 75/92, *supra*, note 531.
549 Kofele-Kale, *supra*, note 542, at 94.

In that case, the power of the State to dispose freely of natural wealth and resources becomes subject to the consent of all persons within the State. This meaning of "peoples" reflects the democratic ideal. In this situation, the citizenry would be entitled to exercise their collective right against the State to benefit from the State's wealth and natural resources.[550]

The African Commission is yet to decide a case that borders directly on Article 21 of the Charter. Some of the cases dealing with violation of personal freedoms may have arisen from circumstances that could be construed as having their root in that provision. It is hoped that, when the Commission or other adjudicative body gets the opportunity, it will take into consideration the reality of the times. The process of economic reforms that will follow in African countries in the next millennium will definitely lead to legal reforms that ought to take into consideration the notion of the rights of peoples (groups within sovereign states) to enjoy the wealth and natural resources on their land, subject to reasonable State control. To be considered also, is the role of multinational corporations in State violation of human rights based on the exploitation of natural resources and similar activities.

3. The right to economic, social and cultural development

Article 22 of the African Charter provides that: "1. All peoples shall have the right to their economic, social and cultural development with due regard to their freedom and identity and in the equal enjoyment of the common heritage of mankind; and 2. States shall have the duty, individually and collectively, to ensure the exercise of the right to development."

The right to development has acquired the status of an internationally recognized right since the early eighties.[551] The right has grown as a branch of international law with related text books, specialized courses and conferences.[552] Keba M'Baye, the first President of the Supreme Court of Senegal and a judge of the International Court of Justice is credited with first formulating the right to development as a human right in the early seventies during the 1972 Strasbourg Inaugural Lecture in which he elaborated upon the economic, legal, moral and

---

550 *Id.*
551 *See* Julia Swanson, *The Emergence of New Rights in the African Charter,* 12 N.Y.L. SCH. J. INT'L & COMP. L. 307 at 317 (1991), citing Marks, *Emerging Human Rights: A New Generation for the 1980s,* 33 RUTGERS L. REV. 441, 442-450 (1981).
552 *Id., Marks,* at 444.

political justifications for the existence of the right to development.[553] The emerging recognition of the right was confirmed by the United Nations General Assembly Declaration on the Right to Development in 1986.[554] This Declaration followed the adoption of the right to development by the General Assembly as a human right in 1979.[555]

As is normal in international law, the right to development has been a controversial subject, provoking lengthy debates as to its legal existence. For proponents of the right like M'Baye, there can be no human rights without development and vice versa.[556] It is further argued that there is higher propensity to violate human rights in underdeveloped countries than in developed ones, thus drawing a correlation between positive protection of human rights to a higher level of economic development.[557] On the other side of the coin, the argument is that the right to development is a mere expression of sentiments devoid of any legal validity.[558] The contention is that the right is "too wooly and does not easily invite the degree of commitment that one expects unequivocally in support of an inescapable conclusion; ... the right to development appears to be more like an idea or ideal couched in a spirit of adventure, a political ideology conceived to be all things to all men in a developing world, especially Africa; it lacks purposeful specificity; it is latent with ambiguity and highly controversial and 'directionless;' it strikes a cord of the advent of the good Samaritan."[559]

This author supports the opinion that rather than engaging in very political and highly polemical debate over the legal character of the right to development, the important emphasis should be on continued dialogue in an attempt to reach a consensus on the content, purpose, and dimensions of the right.[560] The right to development has already come to stay as a human right, and therefore has to be developed, albeit progressively, to serve the general purpose of development. Generally, the right to development consists of the right of individuals to benefit from a development policy based on material and nonmaterial needs and to

---

553 Swanson, supra, note 551, at 444, quoting Keba M'Baye, Le droit au development comme un droit de l'homme, 5 HUM RTS. J. 505 (1972). M'baye was a judge of the International Court of Justice (ICJ), 1982-1991. See also Sohn, supra, note 344, at 52- 56.
554 G.A. Res. 41/128, Annex, 41GAOR Supp. (No.53) at 186, U.N. Doc. A/41/53(1986).
555 G.A. Res. 34//46, para 8, 34 U.N. GAOR Supp. (No. 46) at 171 (1980) reprinted in Sohn, supra, note 344, at 55.
556 See ANKUMA, supra, note 363, at 165.
557 Id.
558 E. Bello, Article 22 of the African Charter on Human and Peoples' Rights, in ESSAYS IN HONOUR OF JUDGE T. O ELIAS, 458 (E. BELLO & B. AJIBOLA, eds., 1992).
559 Id. at 462
560 See Swanson, supra, note 551, at 318. See also Philip Alston, Making Space for New Rights: The Case for the Right to Development, 1 HARV. HUM RTS. Y.B. 3, 22 (1988).

participate in the development policy. It also involves the collective right of a developing country to the establishment of a new international order.[561] The general interpretation to be given to this dimensional approach is that in the end, the human being is viewed as the subject and not the object of the development process.[562] On a practical level, there is a natural translation of the right to development into the right of communities, especially those of indigenous peoples, to develop their culture and maintain possession of their land and cultural resources in the face of economic development policies that threaten their extinction.[563]

Article 22 of the African Charter is an attempt to translate the benefits of the UN Declaration on the Right to Development to Africa. There is no doubt that the concept is quite controversial and its precise definition extremely complex. However, it is clear that the notion of solidarity, or international cooperation and shared responsibility for the welfare and prosperity of all, is the central basis for the realization of this new right.[564] To this end, the Charter implies a progressive obligation of Member States to ensure that while individual freedom is emphasized, economic, social and cultural development will be promoted.

The African Commission has not had a chance to decide any petition on the right to development. According to Ankuma, the only petition in this regard was one against Zimbabwe concerning the legal status of homosexuals in Zimbabwe. The petition alleged that the Zimbabwean legislation criminalizing homosexuality was *inter alia*, a violation of the right to economic, social and cultural development with due regard to the identity of a people and their equal enjoyment of the common heritage of mankind as guaranteed by Article 22. Scholars could not benefit from any decision in this case as the petition was withdrawn.[565] There is therefore no guidance on what the Commission's interpretation of the right is. It is hoped that African realities will guide the Commission in this regard.

4. The right to peace

On the right to peace, Article 23 of the Charter states:

1. All peoples shall have the right to national and international peace and security. The principles of solidarity and friendly relations implicitly affirmed by the Charter

---

561 *Id., Swanson,* at 318.
562 *See Louis B. Sohn, supra,* note 344, at 55-56.
563 *Id.* at 56.
564 *Swanson, supra,* note 551, at 318.
565 *See* ANKUMA, *supra,* note 363, at 166.

of the United Nations and reaffirmed by that of the Organization of African Unity shall govern relations between States.

2. For the purpose of strengthening peace, solidarity and friendly relations, States Parties to the present Charter shall ensure that:

(a) any individual enjoying the right of asylum under Article 12 of the present Charter shall not engage in subversive activities against the country of origin or any other State Party to the present Charter.

(b) their territories shall not be used as bases for subversive or terrorist activities against the people of any other State Party to the present Charter.

Article 23 (1) restates the principle of the preservation of international peace and security, as well as the principle of friendly relations among States, which the UN Charter provides for as some of its main objectives,[566] and which also forms a basic foundation of the OAU.[567] Apart from the restatement of the principle of international peace and security, the paragraph also makes it the right of all peoples. Similarly Article 23 (2) prescribes two specific ways by which States Parties would ensure peace and strengthen solidarity and friendly relations.

The question of peace as a human right, into which some obligations can also be read, is entirely novel, and began with the African Charter. Generally, the law of peace is part of the classical subdivision of the subject matter of international law. Thus, the principle of peaceful coexistence, peaceful change, and prohibition of coercion – all find expression in a variety of national and international legal instruments.[568] Apart from the provisions of Article 1 of the UN Charter, the right to peace has been the subject of debates and study by the UN Commission on Human Rights.[569] These debates culminated in UN General Assembly Res-

---

[566] Article 1(1) &(2) of the UN Charter. 24 U.S.T. 2225, T.I.A.S 7739. The Charter provides as follows: The purpose of the United Nations are:
To maintain international peace and security, and to that end: to take effective collective measures for the prevention and removal of threats to the peace, and for the suppression of acts of aggression or other breaches of the peace and to bring about by peaceful means, and in conformity with the principles of justice and international law, adjustment or settlement of international disputes or situations which might lead to a breach of the peace;
To develop friendly relations among nations based on respect for the principle of equal rights and self-determination of peoples, and to take other appropriate measures to strengthen universal peace...

[567] *See* Article 2(1) (a) & (b) of the Charter of the OAU, which provides that: "The Organization shall have the following purposes: (a) to promote the unity and solidarity of the African States, (b) to co-ordinate and intensify their co-operation and efforts to achieve a better life for the peoples of Africa."

[568] *Swanson, supra*, note 551, at 319.

[569] U.N. Commission on Human Rights Res. 5(XXXII), 60 U.N. ESCOR Supp. (No. 3) at 62, U.N. Doc. E/5768 [E/CN.4/1213] (1976). In this resolution, the Commission pointed out that "every one has the right to live in conditions of international peace and security and fully to enjoy economic, social and cultural rights and civil and political rights." The Commission added that "unqualified respect for and the promotion of human rights and fundamental freedoms require the

olutions, which reaffirmed the right of individuals, States and all mankind to a life in peace.[570]

According to Alston, despite the significance of the above instruments on the right to peace, the elements of the right have never been determined, and that, no effort has yet been undertaken to elevate the term beyond the level of generalities, or to allow it to develop into practical usefulness.[571] While this observation may be correct, in terms of the practical realization of the right to peace, we must recognize the efforts at the UN level to define and develop the contents and elements of the right.[572] For practical purposes, however, it is difficult to see how Article 23(1) of the African Charter can be properly articulated in terms of enforcing the right of all peoples to national and international peace and security. It is true that in Africa, peace and security have become increasingly of grave concern. The Charter does not contain enough contents to aid the enforcement of the right. The two situations in which States are obliged to ensure the achievement of peace, solidarity and friendly relations are not adequate. They limit the whole question of peace to ensuring that an asylee does not engage in subversive activities against his or her own country, or any other State Party to the Charter; and provide a prohibition of the use of the territory of a Member State for subversive or terrorists activities. While these are inherent in the whole agenda of peace, they serve the notion of State sovereignty and non intervention in the internal affairs of a Member State of the OAU, which has been a long standing principle of the regional body, but which has stood in the way of human rights enforcement.

The African Commission has not yet had a chance to consider a communication based on Article 23 of the Charter. The Commission has, however, adopted a number of resolutions on situations in Africa that threatened peace and security in various Member States and the Continent at large.[573] By the nature of Article

---

existence of international peace and security." It must be observed that the Commission's resolution encountered strong opposition from several Western Countries. *See Sohn, supra*, note 334, at 57. For other resolutions of the U.N. Commission on Human Rights, *see* U.N. Commission on Human Rights Res. 4(XXXIII), 62 U.N. ESCOR Supp. (No. 6) at 75, U.N. Doc. E/5927 [E/CN4/1257] (1977); 1979 U.N. ESCOR Supp. (No. 6) at 27, U.N. Doc. E/CN4/1347].

570 Declaration on the Preparation of Societies for Life in Peace, G.A. Res. 33/73, 33 U.N. GAOR Supp. (No. 45) at 55-56, U.N. Doc. A/33/45 (1979). *See also* U.N. Res. 39/11 (1984).
571 *Philip Alston. Peace as Human Right*, 11 BULL. PEACE PROPOSALS. 126, 133 (1981).
572 *See* UNESCO Recommendations of November 19, 1974 (UN Human Rights Compilation) Vol. I(2), at 599. *See also Sohn, supra*, note 344, at 56-59 for detailed discussion on the efforts of the United Nations in defining the elements of the right to peace.
573 Examples include, the Resolution on the Situation in Rwanda, the Resolution on Rwanda, Resolution on South Africa, Resolution on Nigeria, Resolution on the Military, Resolution on Sudan, Resolution on Liberia, Resolution on the Gambia, Resolution on Anti-Personnel Mines, etc. *See*, RECOMMENDATIONS AND RESOLUTIONS OF THE AFRICAN COMMISSION, *supra*, note 420, at 23-41.

23, it would appear that States are in a better position to enforce a violation of the right than individuals, through the inter-state communications procedure.[574] If a State harbors citizens of other States who engage in subversive or terrorist activities against other Member States, those Member States, rather than individuals, will be in a better position to complain under the Charter against the harboring State. The inter-State communications procedure is yet to be used despite accusations by African States in conflicts against other States suspected of aiding opposition groups. The supervisory machinery of the African system must look beyond the two situations provided for in the Article 23(2). The principle that the right to peace, and the right to live in peace, entail more than the obligation of States not to engage in aggressive war, is already firmly established in international law.[575] There are other possible extensions of the right to peace which involve related rights, duties and obligations, many of which are already implied in existing rights and guarantees.[576] For example, the right of all peoples to participate in the decisions of their government regarding war and peace is implicit in recognized rights of political participation. Furthermore, the right of conscientious objection is already contained in the guarantee of freedom of thought and conscience.[577] It has been stressed that this freedom goes beyond refusal purely on grounds of pacifism, but imposes on the individual the obligation of not complying with orders which, if carried out, would violate the right to live in peace.[578]

5. The right to environment

Article 24 of the Charter provides that "all peoples shall have the right to a general satisfactory environment favorable to their development." The first international large scale formulation of concern for the environment in a right-related posture was at Stockholm in 1972.[579] Since then several efforts have been made to

---

574 Article 47 of the Charter.
575 See Bilder, *The Individual and the Right to Peace*, 11 BULL. PEACE PROPOSALS 387 (1982). See also *Alston, Peace as Human Right, supra*, note 556, at 130-131.
576 *Id., Bilder*, at 388.
577 *Id.*
578 Lopatka, *The Right to Live in Peace as a Human Right*, 10 BULL. PEACE PROPOSALS 361, 362 at 366 (1979).
579 Stockholm Declaration of the United Nations Conference on the Human Environment. Adopted by the UN Conference on the Human Environment at Stockholm on June 16, 1972. U.N. Doc. A/CONF.48/14/Rev. 1 at 3. For a detailed commentary on this document, *see* Louis B. Sohn, *The Stockholm Declaration on the Human Environment*, 14 HARV. INT'L. J. 423-515 (1973). *See* also Sohn, *The New International Law: Protection of Rights of Individuals Rather than States, supra*, note 344, at 59-60.

achieve international recognition for a clean and healthy environment. After more than two decades, the Stockholm conference was followed by the Rio Declaration.[580] At the time of the Stockholm Declaration, environmental action was understood to be principally a matter of preventing pollution; and in developing countries was seen as a luxury to be afforded only after industrialization.[581] As environmental issues became increasingly stressed, several national constitutions began to incorporate the right to the environment.[582]

The concept of a healthy environment is therefore, not new. However, the link between a healthy environment and human rights is a recent development.[583] It has been observed that the suggestion to link human rights and the environment was made by René Cassin, who opined that human rights protection should be extended to include "the right to a healthful and decent environment, that is, freedom from pollution, and the corresponding right to pure air and water."[584] It was, however, the African Charter that gave the right to a healthy environment its international codification in a human rights instrument, a provision which Maina suggests to have come about purely by accident, since environmental issues were not of particular importance to African States as developing countries.[585] It may not be correct to say that the right to a healthy environment in the African Charter arose purely by accident. Some African experts participated in the UNESCO's 1980 Mexico City Symposium on Human Rights[586] in which the "right to a healthy

---

580 Rio Declaration on Environment and Development. Adopted by the U.N. Conference on Environment and Development (UNCED) at Rio de Janeiro, Brazil, 13 June, 1992. U.N. Doc. A/CONF.151/26 (vol.1) (1992), 31 I.L.M. 874 (1992).
581 LAKSHMAN D. GURUSWAMY, SIR GEOFFREY W.R. PALMER & BURNS H. WESTON (hereafter GURUSWAMY *et al.*), INTERNATIONAL ENVIRONMENTAL LAW AND WORLD ORDER 229 (West Publishing Company, 1994).
582 Express provisions on the environment exist in the constitutions of Portugal, Spain, Peru and Yugoslavia. Constitutions, which stipulate that the government shall protect the environment, include, Greece, Switzerland, the former Czechoslovakia, the former German Democratic Republic, the Peoples Republic of China, the former USSR, Sri Lanka and Bulgaria. *See Marks, supra*, note 551, at 444. The recent South African Constitution also provides for the right to the environment.
583 *See Chris Maina Peter, Taking the Environment Seriously: The African Charter on Human and Peoples' Rights and the Environment*, 3 Pts. 1 & 2 REVIEW OF THE AFRICAN COMMISSION ON HUMAN AND PEOPLES' RIGHTS 41 (1993) *cited in* ANKUMA, *supra*, note 363, at 168. *See also, Gutto, S., Environmental Rights Litigation, Human Rights and the Role of Non-Governmental and Peoples' Organizations in Africa*, 2 SOUTH AFRICAN JOURNAL OF ENVIRONMENTAL LAW AND POLICY 1-4 (1995), also *cited in* ANKUMA, *supra*, note 363, at 168.
584 ANKUMA, *supra*, note 363, at 168, *citing* René *Cassin, Introduction: The International Law of Human Rights*, 144 RECUEILS DES COURS (1974).
585 *Maina, supra*, note 583, at 41-42.
586 UNESCO, SYMPOSIUM ON NEW HUMAN RIGHTS: THE RIGHTS OF SOLIDARITY, MEXICO CITY, 1980 at 3 UNESCO Doc. 55.81/conf.806/4, *cited in* Sohn, *The New International Law: Protection of Rights of Individuals Rather than States, supra*, note 344, at 60, fn.320.

and ecologically balanced environment" was discussed, which in turn may be traced to the 1972 Stockholm Declaration on the Human Environment.

What exactly does the right to a general satisfactory environment as formulated in Article 24 of the African Charter mean? Ankuma has criticized the provision as vague, and thus subject to divergent interpretations. She, however, notes that the broad formulation of States' obligations leaves room for flexibility, in such a way that it may be possible for States to adhere to their human rights obligations in accordance with their particular situation.[587] There is no doubt that the manner in which the right to environment is formulated in the African Charter does not guarantee a definite interpretation in terms of the contents of the right. This may, however, be a blessing in disguise, if any interpretation to be given to the right takes cognizance of the realities of the situation in accordance with prevailing international law principles. In addition, the right to environment by nature cuts across civil and political rights and economic, social and cultural rights. It is said to have the characteristics of civil and political rights in so far as it requires States to refrain from activities that are harmful to the environment, while on the other hand, it has a feature of economic, social and cultural rights in that it requires States to adopt measures to promote conservation and improvement of the environment.[588] In all, the right to environment has different dimensions. The individual dimension is the right of any victim or potential victim of an environmentally damaging activity to obtain reparation for harm suffered, while the collective dimension involves the duty of the state to assist in cooperating internationally to resolve environmental problems.[589]

The African Commission has not yet been given the opportunity to deal with Article 24 of the Charter as no complaints have been submitted, which allege the violation of satisfactory environment per se, neither has the Commission taken any independent initiative to promote the right. The Commission's initial Guidelines on State Reporting, however, required States to report on measures which they have adopted on the right to a satisfactory environment, especially measures to prohibit pollution and international dumping of toxic wastes.[590] Despite the lack of action on this right at the Commission, it is increasingly becoming important and relevant to Africa, especially after the toxic waste dumping of 1988 in some African countries by international corporations. After the discovery of the toxic waste dumps, the OAU took quick action to forestall future

---

[587] ANKUMA, *supra*, note 363, at 168.
[588] P. Cullet, *Definition of an Environmental Right in a Human Rights Context*, 1 NETHERLANDS Q. HUM. RTS. 28 (1995). The author points out that the different characteristics of the right to environment confirm the view that there is no such thing as a hierarchy of human rights.
[589] Swanson, *supra*, note 551, at 320.
[590] OLD GUIDELINES FOR NATIONAL PERIODIC REPORTS, *supra*, note 484, section III(11) – (13).

occurrences. The same year the OAU Council of Ministers passed a resolution condemning the export of toxic wastes to Africa, and emphasizing that it is a crime against Africa.[591] This resolution was followed by an OAU Convention banning the importation of toxic waste into Africa.[592] In addition, the African Economic Community Treaty concluded in Abuja, Nigeria on 3 June 1998, requires States Parties to improve the environment and take steps against the dumping of toxic wastes.[593]

Apart from the threats posed by toxic wastes exportation and importation into Africa, the threats posed by internal activities carried on by multinational oil and other corporations are real and even more relevant in present day Africa. Efforts by victims of hazardous environmental pollution to protest same, have often met with the infringement of their fundamental human rights. Indigenous communities are in constant battle with such multinational corporations, as well as with States, which are either not bothered, or even aid and abet the violation of the rights of the communities.[594]

It follows, therefore, that in interpreting the obligations enshrined in Article 24 of the African Charter, the primary responsibility lies with States Parties to adopt measures that will effectively address environmental degradation. The right of the individual against the state is contingent upon the existence or otherwise of these measures, and where a demand for such measures results not in assistance but in the violation of other fundamental human rights of the individual. Individuals, in addition, should have the right in domestic law of private action against a direct violator of his or her right to a healthy environment. It is rather unfortunate that many courts in Africa tend to shy away from shaping national environmental laws for the protection of individuals and communities.

This section has been dealing with the various shades of collective rights as enshrined in the African Charter. It must be pointed out that these rights are weak

---

591 OAU Council of Ministers Resolution on Dumping of Nuclear and Industrial Waste in Africa, adopted at Addis Ababa, 23 May 1998. CM/Res. 1153 (XLVIII); 28 I.L.M. 567 (1989).

592 Bamako Convention on the Ban of Importation into Africa and the Control of Transboundary Movement and Management of Hazardous Wastes Within Africa. Concluded at Bamako, 29 January 1991. 30 I.L.M. 775 (1991).

593 Articles 58 & 59 of the Treaty. Article 59 specifically provides that Member States are to take steps individually and collectively to ban the importation of hazardous wastes into their respective countries and are to cooperate in the transboundary movement, management and processing of such wastes. Article 60 envisages the enactment of a protocol on the environment. *See* generally, Akanle, O., *The Legal and Institutional Framework of the African Community* in AFRICAN ECONOMIC COMMUNITY TREATY: ISSUES, PROBLEMS AND PROSPECTS 1 at 26 (M. A. Ajomo & O. Adewale, Eds., 1993).

594 There are several such cases in Nigeria and other parts of Africa, as well as other parts of the developing world. A Latin American example is the ongoing case against Texaco by some indigenous communities in Ecuador.

in the details of their content, but that not withstanding, they have developed an established body of law. The discussions on them are relevant even if only in helping to extract elements that can be used as a basis for their official definition. The African Charter on Human and Peoples' Rights, as has been suggested by van Boven, is a challenging, ambitious and innovative document in the area of group or collective rights. It places individual human rights in the contextual setting of peoples' rights, with due respect for the human person as the central subject of development.[595] It recognizes human rights and peoples' rights in their complementarity to the mutual benefit of all human beings who live in Africa, and of the African peoples.[596] In sum, the African Charter, in making provision for these group, or collective rights, is both a regional response to human rights concerns and a reflection of the realities of Africa.[597] Thus, the document may not be perfect, but it is indeed a positive document. It is true that one test for evaluating the juridical viability of collective rights is their mechanism for enforcement. While making it work may take time, it is achievable if only African States will exude the necessary political will and cooperation.

III OTHER HUMAN RIGHTS INSTRUMENTS

In looking for the normative instruments of the African Human rights mechanism, one need not stop at the African Charter itself. The Charter endorses the notion of "other human rights instruments" to give meaning to the contents of the Charter. In this light, the provisions of Article 60 and 61 of the Charter come handy. Article 60 states that:

> The Commission shall draw inspiration from international law on human and peoples' rights, particularly from the provisions of the various African instruments on human and peoples; rights, the Charter of the United Nations, the Charter of the Organization of African Unity, the Universal Declaration of Human Rights, other instruments adopted by the United Nations and by African countries in the field of human and peoples' rights as well as from the provisions of the various instruments adopted within the specialized agencies of the United Nations of which the Parties to the present Charter are members.

---

[595] van Boven, *The Relations Between Peoples" Rights and Human Rights in the African Charter*, *supra*, note 515, at 194.
[596] *Id.*
[597] *See Motala, Human Rights in Africa: A Cultural, Ideological and Legal Examination*, 12 HASTINGS INT'L. & COMP. L. REV. 373, 408-409 (1989).

Article 61 further provides that:

> The Commission shall also take into consideration, as subsidiary measures to determine the principles of law, other general or special international conventions, laying down rules expressly recognized by Member States of the Organization of African Unity, African practices consistent with international norms on human and peoples' rights, customs generally accepted as law, general principles of law recognized by African States as well as legal precedents and doctrine.

The above provisions can be regarded as the two omnibus articles of the Charter of lasting importance. They bring the African human rights mechanism within the positive influence of the UN and other regional human rights experiences. Article 60 lays out the normative effect of the general international law of human rights, which entails drawing inspiration from the Charter of the United Nations, the Universal Declaration of Human Rights, conventional and treaty instruments of the UN and its specialized agencies, as well as the Charter of the Organization of African Unity and various African human rights instruments. What this means is that the African Commission on Human and Peoples' Rights, or any other organ that will be involved in the implementation of the Charter, must look beyond the Charter in interpreting the norms laid down by the Charter. To this effect, the norms developed by the UN Human Rights Committee, the Economic, Social and Cultural Rights Committee, and other treaty based human rights organs are of somewhat precedential value to the African mechanism at least of a persuasive nature.

Similarly, Article 61 could be read to extend other regional human rights experiences to Africa for proper articulation of the provisions of the African Charter. The principles of human rights law are generally universal and can be found in other regional instruments. The fact that the Article regards whatever inspirations that could be derived here as subsidiary, does defeat the possible positive normative effect from these other sources. What matters is that the "other general or special international conventions" must lay down rules expressly recognized by Member States of the Organization of African Unity. To determine whether an instrument accords with rules and principles recognized by Member States of the OAU, one need not look at the various State practices of these States, but at the regional or international legal instruments to which these States are parties.

The African Commission has not yet determined the purport of Articles 60 and 61 of the Charter in its interpretative mandate under Article 45 of the Charter. Article 45(3) allocates the function of interpreting all the provisions of the Charter to the Commission, at the request of a State Party, an institution of the OAU or an African Organization recognized by the OAU. It could be argued that the

Commission has not exercised this function with regard to Article 60 and 61, because neither a State Party, an institution of the OAU or an African Organization has requested for its opinion on the provisions. The Commission, however, need not wait for a request for advisory opinion on the meaning of Articles 60 and 61, to be able to give meaning to these provisions. It could ordinarily do this in the course of its normal adjudicatory functions, or by adopting a resolution to that effect. Whenever the Commission does apply these omnibus provisions, it could, for instance, borrow from the *Other Treaties* opinion of the Inter-American Court of Human Rights,[598] where the Court interpreted Article 64 of the American Convention, which *inter alia,* allows Member States of the American Convention to consult the Court regarding the interpretation of the Convention or of *other treaties* concerning the protection of human rights in the American States.[599] (Emphasis is author's). The Inter-American Court declared 'other treaties' to mean universal treaties concerning the protection of human right that were applicable also in the American States that ratified them. Thus, the treaties did not need to be those concluded within the Organization of American States (OAS) system.[600] They include, for instance, such treaties as the Convention on the Rights of the Child, which was ratified by most American and African States.

The interpretation of 'other treaties' under the American Convention and the normative prescriptions of Articles 60 and 61 of the African Charter are exactly the same. Thus, a universal treaty that has been accepted by some American States can be interpreted in a parallel case by the Inter-American Court, and also by the African Human Rights Commission. In other words, by these provisions, the African Commission could be persuaded by other international conventions, which though may not have been concluded within the OAU system, but lay down rules recognized by Member States of the OAU, or are customs generally accepted as law or general principles of law recognized by African States. In essence, by a combined effect, Articles 60 and 61 of the Charter make other regional human rights experience persuasively applicable in elucidating the norms contained in the African Charter, where appropriate.

This broad reading of Articles 60 and 61 of the Charter has led to arguments, that there is no need for the amendment of the Charter to bring in new provisions that were either not provided for originally, or not adequately provided for. Two

---

[598] "Other Treaties" Subject to the Consultative Jurisdiction of the Court (Art. 64, American Convention on Human Rights), Advisory Opinion No. OC-1/82 (Inter-Am. Ct. of Human Rights, Sept. 24, 1982). Reprinted in 3 HUM. RTS. L. J. 140 (1982). *See Mary C. Parker, 'Other Treaties': The Inter-American Court of Human Rights Defines Its Advisory Jurisdiction* 33 AM. U. L. REV. 211.
[599] Article 64(1) of the American Convention.
[600] *Parker, supra,* note 598, at 226.

of such areas are the inclusion of an additional protocol on women's rights and the insertion of a provision on non-derogable rights. The reasoning has been that such amendments were unnecessary since the Charter already provides wide powers which need to be exploited, and that Articles 60 and 61 ensured that other international instruments could be incorporated into the Charter through the process of interpretation of its provisions.[601]

There is no doubt that Articles 60 and 61 of the African Charter are wide enough to confer great flexibility in the interpretation of the norms enshrined in the Charter. The Articles would only serve a useful purpose if members of the Commission are brave enough to articulate them to ensure that the rights of potential victims of human violations are not impaired. The Commission must bear in mind that unlike other international agreements, human rights treaties are intended to guarantee the rights of individuals, not to establish reciprocal rights and obligations between States[602] It follows, therefore, that the usefulness of Articles 60 and 61 of the Charter depends on the creative imagination of the Commission, as well increased experience and practice of the African mechanism. Where this is lacking, it would be better to have concrete provisions that prescribe definite obligations.

IV   THE CONCEPT OF DUTY VERSUS RIGHTS UNDER THE AFRICAN CHARTER

The African Charter broke new grounds by enacting duties in a more elaborate and meaningful fashion than any other binding human rights instrument.[603] The duty provisions of the African Charter aimed at the individual are found in Articles 27 to 29. According to Article 27:

1. Every individual shall have duties towards his family and society, the State and other legally recognized communities and the international community.

---

601 *Murray, Report on the 1996 Sessions of the African Commission on Human and Peoples' Rights- 19th and 20th Ordinary Sessions, supra,* note 366, at 18-20.
602 *See Parker,* note 598 at 223.
603 Article 29 (1) of the Universal Declaration of Human Rights provides that "everyone has duties to the community in which alone the free and full development of his personality is possible." The American Declaration on the Rights and Duties of Man, O.A.S. Res. XXX, 9th Conf. (1948), O.A.S. Doc. OEA/Ser. L/V/1.4, Rev. XX (1965), also enumerates duties.

2. The rights and freedoms of each individual shall be exercised with due regard to the rights of others, collective security, morality and common interest.[604]

Article 28 states that: "every individual shall have the duty to respect and consider his fellow beings without discrimination, and to maintain relations aimed at promoting, safeguarding and reinforcing mutual respect and tolerance." Article 29 provides that the individual shall have the duty:

1. To preserve the harmonious development of the family and to work for the cohesion and respect of the family; to respect his parents at all times, to maintain them in case of need;
2. To serve his national community by placing his physical and intellectual abilities at its service;
3. Not to compromise the security of the State whose national or resident he is;
4. To preserve and strengthen social and national solidarity, particularly when the latter is threatened;
5. To preserve and strengthen the national independence and the territorial integrity of his country and to contribute to its defence in accordance with the law;
6. To work to the best of his abilities and competence, and to pay taxes imposed by law in the interest of the society;
7. To preserve and strengthen positive African cultural values in his relations with other members of the society, in the spirit of tolerance, dialogue and consultation and, in general, to contribute to the promotion of the moral well-being of society;
8. To contribute to the best of his abilities, at all times and at all levels, to the promotion and achievement of African unity.

The duty posture of the African Charter as enumerated above has been subjected to criticism. The critics are concerned that it would be a basis for State Parties to the African Charter to perpetrate human rights violations.[605] This view is driven by the gross and persistent violations of human rights in post-colonial African States and the fear that vesting states with more power can only result in more abuses.[606] To dismiss these criticisms as simplistically as Mutua

---

[604] Article 27(2) parallels Article 29(2) of the Universal Declaration, which states: "In the exercise of his rights and freedoms, everyone shall be subject only to such limitations as are determined by law solely for the purpose of securing due recognition and respect for the rights and freedom of others and of meeting the just requirements of morality, public order and the general welfare in a democratic society."

[605] See Makau wa Mutua, *The African Human Rights System in a Comparative Perspective: The Need for Urgent Reformulation*, 5 LEGAL F. 31, 33 (1993); 3 REV. AFR. COM. HUM. & PEOPLES' RTS. 10 (1993).

[606] Makau wa Mutua, *The Banjul Charter and The African Cultural Fingerprint: An Evaluation of the Language of Duties*, 35 VA. J. INT'L L. 339 at 359.

does,[607] in the face of present day African realities would not be proper. It will only amount to a denial of a potently genuine fear. On the other hand, however, the inclusion of duties in the Charter will not per se be an automatic avenue for States to engage in indiscriminate human rights violation. The duties in the Charter, which the individual is charged to observe are not of the nature that could be tied to a particular right, which a State would in turn use as a retaliatory tool. The notion of duties in the Charter is rather another unique dimension of the African Charter in entrenching positive African cultural and traditional values which existed in precolonial Africa, and which complement the notion of rights. If viewed from this angle, critics of the language of duties in the Charter may be persuaded to do a deeper study of the implications of the duties. This author agrees with Mutua that the duty-rights conception of the African Charter could provide a new basis for individual identification with compatriots, the community, and the State. It could forge and instill a national consciousness and act as the glue to reunite individuals and different nations within the modern State, and at the same time set the proper limits of conduct by State officials.[608] The duties enshrined in the Charter could be read as intended to recreate the bonds of the pre-colonial era among individuals and between individuals and States.

Looking at the Charter provisions on duties, one would see that they are meaningful for the smooth working of society. Article 27(1) merely restates the fact that the individual owes a duty to his family, the State, other legally recognized communities and the international community. Article 27(2) places a limitation on the exercise of rights by an individual for the protection of the rights of others, and in the interest of collective security, morality and the interest of others. This is a normal fact of life, which reflects the practical reality that no right is absolute. Individuals are asked to reflect on how the exercise of their rights in certain circumstances might adversely affect the rights of other individuals or the community at large. The duty is based on the presumption that the full development of individual rights is only possible where individuals care about how their actions would impact others. Article 27(2) thus raises the level of care owed to neighbors and the community. The same philosophy is embedded in Article 28. The duty of every person to respect and consider his or her fellow beings without discrimination, and to maintain relations aimed at promoting, safeguarding and reinforcing mutual respect and tolerance, is nothing but a lubricant that oils the wheel of social interaction.

---

607 *Id.* Mutua thinks that such criticisms are simplistic because they are not based on careful assessment of the difficulties experienced by African countries in their miserable attempts to mimic wholesale Western notions of government and the role of the State.
608 *Id.* at 368.

The duties set out in Article 29 stress responsibilities to the family, community and the State. There is nothing wrong for an individual to be reminded that he or she ought to respect his or her parents and to provide them with necessary care and maintenance.[609] This is positive African cultural value, which has been codified for posterity. It is the joy of the African parent to toil and train his or her child, with a great expectation that when that child becomes "somebody" that child would take care of him or her. In the same vein, a person ought to serve his or her community with his or her intellectual and physical capabilities.[610] That is the essence of community service, and it has been a long standing practice in the African past.

The same thing could be said of the duties not to compromise the security of the State, to strengthen social and national solidarity, especially when national solidarity is threatened, and the duty to preserve, strengthen and defend the national independence and territorial integrity of a person's country.[611] This group of duties reminds Africans of the need to preserve their hard-won independence. The duties represent an extension of the principle of self-determination in the external sense, as a shield against foreign domination.[612] The maintenance of social and national solidarity for example, is of utmost importance in present day Africa where many modern States have collapsed or failed.[613] The duty to pay tax[614] is the civic responsibility of every citizen of any country, where the principle of taxation is recognized. The duties to promote positive African culture and African unity[615] are emphases of societal cohesion.

We must also observe that the notion of duty is not just one that is directed against the individual. The Charter prescribes duties to States in addition to the general obligations that apply to them. The State is under a duty to assist the family.[616] Article 25 imposes a duty on states to promote and ensure through teaching, education, publication, the respect of the rights and freedoms contained in the Charter and to see that these freedoms and rights as well as corresponding obligations and duties are understood. Similarly, Article 26 creates a duty for States to guarantee the independence of the courts. The difference between the duties of individuals under the Charter and those of states is that, while those of the

---

[609] Article 29(1).
[610] Article 29(2).
[611] Article 29(3), (4) & (5).
[612] Mutua, *The Banjul Charter and The African Cultural Fingerprint: An Evaluation of the Language of Duties supra*, note 606, at 371.
[613] Liberia, Somalia, Rwanda and Sierra Leone are recent examples where social and national solidarity were not only threatened, but fell apart.
[614] Article 29(6).
[615] Article 29(7) & (8).
[616] Article 18(2).

individuals cannot ordinarily be used to proceed against them under the regional mechanism, those of States amount also to obligations within the Charter, over which they can challenged.

The notion of duties under the African Charter, while not totally without concern as to possible misuse by the political class, whether in military uniform or civilian garb, needs to be evaluated in a different light. It is nothing but an embodiment of the positive dimension of African cultural philosophy, which the Charter tries to codify for the benefit of posterity. Any thinking to the contrary by the ruling class must be resisted by the arguments that we presently make, which are also obvious from the ordinary meaning of the provisions of the Charter.

V   CLAW-BACK CLAUSES UNDER THE CHARTER

The phrase "claw-back clauses" has been used to generally refer to those provisions of the African Charter that tend to limit some of the rights guaranteed under the Charter. They do not qualify as outright derogation clauses that are found in other international human rights instruments. They rather qualify the enjoyment of the right as contingent upon other notions of State prescription. For example, Article 8 grants the freedom of conscience, profession and free practice of religion, "subject to law and order". Under Article 10, an individual has the right to free association "provided that he abides by the law". Similarly freedom of movement of an individual is guaranteed by Article 12 "provided he abides by the law". Citizens have the right to participate freely in their governments "in accordance with the provisions of the law."[617] Article 14 provides for the right to property, but that property may be encroached upon "in accordance with the provisions of appropriate law".

These clauses have been criticized, based on the fact that States are traditionally the most frequent violators of human rights. They also have the power to create and change laws. By inserting clauses that permit rights to be limited by the law, the Charter makes human rights especially vulnerable to the very institution which attacks them most often.[618] The criticism goes further to assert that claw-back clauses in the Charter go further than derogation clauses in that they permit a State, in its almost unbounded discretion, to restrict its treaty obligations or the rights

---

617 Article 13(1).
618 *Flinterman, C. and Henderson. C., The African Charter on Human and Peoples Rights,* in AN INTRODUCTION TO THE INTERNATIONAL PROTECTION OF HUMAN RIGHTS: A TEXT BOOK 315 at 318. (Hanski, R & Suksi, M. Eds., Tarku/Abo: Finland, Abo Akedeni University, 1997).

guaranteed by the Charter.[619] Though derogation clauses, on the other hand, permit suspension of treaty obligations, such suspension is temporary, while that based on claw-back clauses may be permanent. In the same vein, derogations can only be invoked in cases of emergency, unlike claw-back clauses which may be applied in normal circumstances, so long as a national law is passed to that effect.[620] Gittleman opines that while derogation clauses warrant the suspension of only certain obligations and rights, rather than all rights, claw-back clauses have no such limit.[621]

One will agree with the observation that the effect of claw-back clauses as expressed in the African Charter is that it seriously emasculates the effectiveness of the Charter as well as its uniform application by Member States.[622] This is because instead of the Charter having primacy, the various national laws of Member States actually assume a primary place.[623] The effectiveness of the Charter will thus be reduced, since it would appear to be subject to national standards as laid down by domestic law. Such domestic laws could be laws that are made to validate acts of violations deliberately embarked upon by Member States. Various African governments are known for the use of retroactive legislation to achieve their dictatorial tendencies, and will thus find the claw-back clauses a veritable source of inspiration. One must agree that claw-back clauses in the Charter, if not properly construed, will frustrate the enjoyment of some of the rights guaranteed in the Charter. This is because, permitting national law to limit, with a superceding effect, provisions of the Charter, means that the Charter itself permits the perpetration of violations of rights enshrined in it. In other words, the Charter gives rights, but permits them to be taken away, thus not protecting the individuals it is meant to protect.

The African Commission has not categorically construed the claw-back clauses under the Charter. However, the Commission's earlier Guidelines on the submission of State Reports tasked Member States to report on the manner in which Articles 2-13 of the Charter[624] are protected, whether constitutionally or by a Bill of Rights. The Guidelines also required States to indicate whether those

---

619 See Ebow Bondzie-Simpson, *A Critique of the African Charter*, 31 HOWARD L.J. 643, at 660 (1988).
620 *Id.*
621 Richard Gittleman, *The African Charter on Human and Peoples Rights: A Legal Analysis*, 22 VA. J. INT'L L. 667, at 712 (1982).
622 *Id. See* also Rosaline Higgins, *Derogation Under Human Rights Treaties*, 48 BRIT. Y. B. INT'L L. 281; Norris and P. Reiton, *The Suspension of Guarantees: A Comparative Analysis of the American Convention on Human Rights and the Constitutions of the State Parties*, 30 AM. U. L. REV. 189-193 (1981).
623 See Bondzie-Simpson, *supra* note 6 19, at 661.
624 These are generally civil and political rights.

instruments contain derogation clauses and under what circumstances those rights may be derogated from.[625] Ankuma observes that the above requirement of the Guidelines is an indication that the Commission would construe claw-back in a manner that will enhance the protection of human rights rather than to the contrary. She points out that the Commission, in reviewing individual complaints alleging violations of civil and political rights under the Charter, does not concern itself with whether or not there is s State law which limits or prohibits the exercise of the right in question.[626]

This author agrees with the above assertion to the extent that the Commission has on many occasions declared various State actions and legislation that impinge on some of these rights, to be in violation of the Charter, as seen earlier in this chapter with regard to the right to freedom of expression, movement and political participation. This notwithstanding, the Commission needs to make a categorical statement, either by way of a resolution or a finding in the course its adjudicatory function, on the purport of the claw-back clauses scattered all over various articles of the Charter. The common phrases "subject to law", "in accordance with the law", etc., used in claw-back clauses, need interpretation. The Commission could either demand that the law in this case must be a law made by a proper democratic legislature (laws that are not arbitrarily made), which takes public interest into consideration; or a law that does not contravene general principles of international human rights law. General principles of international human rights law must guide the Commission or other supervisory organ in making this categorical statement. There must be the courage to frown at every dictatorial legislation, which most of the time emanates from an individual head of State.

---

[625] OLD GUIDELINES FOR NATIONAL PERIODIC REPORTS, supra, note 484, section I (4)(a)(i)-(iv).
[626] ANKUMA, *supra*, note 363, at 177.

3

INSTITUTIONAL STRUCTURE OF THE AFRICAN SYSTEM

I   THE ORGANIZATION OF AFRICAN UNITY

The place of the Organization of African Unity (OAU) in the institutional framework of the African regional system is well provided for in the African Charter. The Assembly of Heads of State and Government (AHSG), the supreme organ of the OAU is the ultimate source of political authority in the system. The Secretary-General of the OAU also plays a prominent role, especially in the administrative relationship between the African Commission and the OAU.

Under the Charter, members of the African Commission are elected by the AHSG[627] after the Secretary-General would have called for nomination of members of the Commission by the Assembly.[628] In the same vein, the Secretary-General of the OAU appoints the Secretary of the Commission, as well as other necessary complementary staff for the effective discharge of the functions of the Commission.[629] The OAU also provides financial support for the Commission in its regular budget.[630] While there may be nothing wrong on the surface for the AHSG to be involved in the nomination and subsequent election of members of the Commission, some commentators have wondered if it would not be an avenue for making such appointments mere extensions of political largesse.[631] This issue will be more appropriately discussed in the next section where the African Commission will be dealt with more extensively. Apart from the issue of election of the members of the African Commission, the OAU grants to members

---

[627] Article 33
[628] Article 35.
[629] Article 42 of the Charter.
[630] *Id.*
[631] *See* Onje Gye-Wado, *The Effectiveness of the Safeguard Machinery for the Enforcement of Human Rights in Africa*, 2 J. HUM. RTS. LAW &. PRACICE, 142 at 154 (1992).

of the Commission diplomatic privileges and immunities as provided by the General Convention on the Privileges and Immunities of the OAU.[632]

The seemingly most important role of the OAU is its political authority through the AHSG in the ultimate enforcement of the African Charter to provide remedies for violations of the provisions of the Charter. The Commission would have to draw the attention of the AHSG to cases of massive violations of human rights, and then act in accordance with the bidding of the Assembly, which would be aimed at addressing the situation. Similarly, the AHSG has the ultimate authority of deciding whether or not the measures taken within the provisions of the Charter on the procedure of the Commission is to be published for public consumption. More than any other power of the AHSG, this has attracted elaborate commentary from some scholars who see it as a subordination of the Commission to the AHSG, a political body, and thus undermines the effectiveness of the Commission.[633] The specific implication of the place given to the OAU as the supreme political authority in the African system and its impact on the effectiveness or otherwise of the Commission will be discussed in the next segment dealing with the Commission. There is no doubt that the OAU deserves a place in the institutional framework of the African system. What matters is whether that position can be used for a progressive and effective evolution of the system along current international trends in the development of international human rights law. Now that the position of the OAU will be taken over by the African Union, one expects that the seeming progressive provisions of the Constitutive Act of the Union[634] will positively impact the AHSG to properly equip the implementing organs of the African system for the challenges ahead in the new Africa.

II THE AFRICAN COMMISSION ON HUMAN AND PEOPLES RIGHTS

Although it has been rightly pointed out in this study that the OAU did not contemplate a regional human rights mechanism in its Charter, it needs to be observed that Article XX of the OAU Charter[635] empowers the OAU to establish such Special-

---

[632] Article 43 of the Charter.
[633] *See* Wolfgang Benedek, *The African Charter and Commission on Human and Peoples' Rights: How to Make it More Effective*, N. QTLY HUM. RTS. 25 at 29-31 (1993); *Claude E. Welch, The African Commission on Human and Peoples' Rights: A Five Year Assessment*, HUM. RTS. QTLY 43 at 47-49 (1992).
[634] Constitutive Act of the African Union, *supra*, note 328.
[635] Charter of the Organization of African Unity, 479 U.N.T.S. 39/2 (1963). Also I.L.M 766 (1963). *See* Generally, DOCUMENTS OF THE ORGANIZATION OF AFRICAN UNITY 3 (GINO J. NALDI, ed., Mansell Publishing Limited, 1992); BASIC DOCUMENTS OF AFRICAN REGIONAL ORGANIZATIONS

ized Commissions as it may deem necessary. Despite the fact that the Commission on human rights was not one of those Commissions named in the Charter, one can conclude that the power for the establishment of the African Commission may have emanated from the OAU Charter among other persuasive instruments,[636] or exists in the Charter. The African Commission on Human and Peoples' Rights can thus be regarded as a Specialized Commission and organ of the OAU. The Commission is established under Article 30 of the African Charter, within the OAU to promote human rights and ensure their protection in Africa.

A. *Composition of the Commission*

According to the provisions of Article 31 of the African Human Rights Charter, the African Commission is composed of eleven members chosen from among African personalities of the highest reputation, known for their high morality, integrity, impartiality and competence in matters of human and peoples' rights; particular consideration being given to persons having legal experience. The Charter goes further to require that the members of the Commission would serve in their individual capacity,[637] with not more than one national of the same State.[638] The eleven members of the Commission, are elected by secret ballot by the Assembly of Heads of State and Government (AHSG) from a list of persons nominated by States parties to the Charter.[639] The Secretary General of the OAU facilitates the nomination of the members of the Commission by inviting the States Parties four months before the elections to make nominations. He makes a list of the persons nominated available to the Heads of State and Government, at least one month before the elections.[640] The tenure of office for the members of the Commission is six years with an option for reelection. The tenure is, however, staggered in that the tenure of four of the first Commissioners would terminate after two years and that of three others, at the end of four years.[641]

The first eleven Commissioners were elected during the 23rd session of the OAU Summit of July 1987 in Addis Ababa, Ethiopia, and they took a formal oath of allegiance on November 2, 1987 during the first session held in Addis Ababa,

---

VOLUMES 1-4 (LOUIS B. SOHN, ed., Dobbs Ferry, New York: Oceana Publications, 1971-1972).
636 *See* specifically Paragraphs 3 and 4 of the Preamble to the African Charter, which mentions the Charter of the OAU and the Charter of the United Nations, respectively.
637 Article 31(2).
638 Article 32.
639 Article 33.
640 Article 35.
641 Article 36.

Ethiopia.[642] There have been subsequent elections as many of the Commissioners serve out their terms. The Commissioners on their own elect the Chairman and Vice Chairman for a an initial tenure of two years subject to reelection.[643] In carrying out their functions, the Commissioners enjoy diplomatic privileges and immunity under the OAU.[644] Their emoluments and allowances are provided for in the regular budget of the OAU.

A number of issues have been raised regarding the composition of the African Commission, ranging from the mode of election, impartiality of members, gender representation, and equitable geographical and legal culture representation. First, on the mode of election, the fear has been expressed that involvement of the AHSG in the election of members of the Commission raises doubts about the effectiveness of the Commission, as it appears to be a subordination of the Commission to the AHSG.[645] The caution is that, being an election made by politicians as represented in the AHSG, it must be apt, to block the possibility of making such appointments mere extensions of political largesse.[646] It is not in doubt that the above fears may be genuine, especially where States Parties are not committed in ensuring the viability of the human rights mechanism envisaged. However, the fact that the AHSG is involved in the nomination of members of the African Commission does not ordinarily make the Commissioners stooges of their respective home governments. The benefit of the doubt ought to be given to Member States that they will elect people with requisite credibility. After all, there is the moderating factor of political credibility if a country nominates a candidate with doubtful credentials. The totality of Member States may not ordinarily connive to defeat the purpose of the African Charter by electing Commissioners that will fail in their duties.

Secondly, the impartiality of members of the Commission is the corner stone of the mechanism's credibility, as in all other human right systems. The Charter

---

[642] The first members of the Commission, included, Prof. Isaac Nguema of Gabon, who was the first Chairman, Ambassador Ali Badawi El-Sheik of Egypt, Vice Chairman, Mr. Alioune B. Beye of Mali, Mr. Ali M. Buhedma of Libya, Mr. Alexis Gabou of Congo, Mr. Grace S. Ibiingira of Uganda, Mr. S. B. Samega of Gambia, Justice H. R. Kisanga of Tanzania Justice M. D. Mokama of Botswana, Mr. C. L. C Mubanga Chipoya and Mr. Youssoupha Ndiaye of Senegal. *See* specifically THE AFRICAN COMMISSION ON HUMAN AND PEOPLES' RIGHTS, TENTH ANNIVERSARY CELEBRATION, 2 NOVEMBER 1987 – 2 NOVEMBER 1997: ONE DECADE OF CHALLENGE 3 (ACHPR, 1998). (Hereafter, ONE DECADE OF CHALLENGE).

[643] Article 42 of the Charter.

[644] Article 43 of the Charter.

[645] N. S. REMBE, THE SYSTEM OF PROTECTION OF HUMAN RIGHTS UNDER THE AFRICAN CHARTER ON HUMAN AND PEOPLES' RIGHTS: PROBLEMS AND PROSPECTS 25 (Lesotho: Institute of Southern African Studies, National University of Lesotho, 1991).

[646] *See Gye-Wado, supra,* note 631, at 154.

emphasizes that the Commissioners "shall serve in their personal capacity." This means that members of the Commission ought to serve independently without any iota of influence from their home governments, despite the involvement of Member States in their election, or from other sources. One issue that is at stake here is conflict of interest. Apart from being directly influenced by one's home government, conflict of interest can also arise by the nature of a Commissioner's other involvements. This issue has received some attention in terms of the composition of the African Commission. Some observers have criticized the situation that still exists, whereby some members of the African Commission also serve in their home governments either as ministers or ambassadors. The view is that such members can hardly function as independent experts in discharging their functions.[647] Even though some members of the African Commission have tried to refute the challenge of lack of impartiality based on their positions in their home governments, it is a serious matter that ought to be considered by Member States in their process of nominating members of the Commission. There is every possibility that conflict of interest might arise in some of the cases. Apart from that, such members of the Commission are already saddled with enormous tasks in their home States only to be saddled in addition with the enormous work of the Commission. It is not uncommon to notice as many as between four and five members of the Commission being absent from some of the Commission's sessions. This could possibly be as a result of other engagements, which sometimes may be connected with State matters.

The third issue which concerns gender representation, has also attracted some scholarly and activist criticism.[648] From the inception of the Commission, it appeared that the role of women in the Commission was not taken into consideration. One would trace the non-inclusion of women early in the Commission, to the general attitude towards women in Africa. The notion that leadership is a thing for men is widely practiced in Africa. It was not until 1993 that a woman was elected into the Commission after much outcry from many non-governmental organizations (NGOs) and activists.[649] The continuing inclusion of women in

---

647 See ANKUMA, *supra*, note 363. at 18-19. Such example includes two former Commissioners, Mr. Molelekei D. Mokama of Botswana and Alexis Gabou of Congo, who during their term on the Commission also served as Attorney General and Minister of Interior of their respective countries. Presently, Dr. Ali Badawi El-Sheik is Egypt's Ambassador to the Netherlands. Similarly, Mr. Mohammed Hatem Ben Salem is Tunisia's Ambassador to Senegal. There are other members, who are either Presidents of their country's Constitutional Court or members of the Supreme Court.
648 *Id.* at 16.
649 The first woman to be elected to the Commission is Dr. (Mrs.) Vera Valentina De Melo Duarte Martins of Cape Verde, who is presently the Vice Chair of the Commission. Mrs. Duarte was elected during the 1993 Summit of the OAU and commenced her work with the Commission during the 14th Session, the same year. In 1995 Mrs. Julienne Ondziel-Gnelenga of Congo Brazzaville was

the Commission will encourage promotional and protective activities in the areas of human rights that specifically affect women, which before now were hardly in the front burner of the Commission's activities.

Fourthly, maintaining equitable geographical representation at the Commission between the geographical divides of Africa has often been made an issue, and rightly so. The reason for this is the connection between the geographical divides and legal cultures of Africa, and therefore, the need to have these legal cultures represented.[650] The question of legal culture is also tied to language, which like the legal cultures of Africa, is a legacy of colonialism. English, French, Arabic, Portuguese and Spanish are the official languages of various African countries and have been recognized as the working languages of the Commission, with English and French being the major ones in keeping with the OAU Charter.

It follows, therefore, that a representation at the Commission that takes cognizance of the various geographical and legal differences of the component States of Africa will be of immense importance in ensuring human rights protection in all of Africa.[651] It must, however, be observed that the competition for membership of the Commission is, or should be keen, taking into consideration that there are only eleven membership position at the Commission. While attention ought to be given to equitable geographical spread, it should be more important that credible and committed persons are elected into the Commission who will see their duty as one owed to Africa as a continent rather than their particular geographical sub-region.

Finally, the issue of the Secretary General of the OAU appointing the Secretary and staff of the Commission raises the question as to whether the Commission

---

elected to the Commission. During the 23rd Ordinary Session of the Commission, Mrs. Ondziel-Gnelenga was appointed the first Special Rapporteur on the Human Rights of Women in Africa.

650 The generally accepted regional divisions of Africa include, Northern Africa, Central Africa, Southern Africa, Eastern Africa, Western Africa, and the Islands. The two basic legal traditions in Africa are the Common and Civil law traditions, which are based on the legal traditions of Africa's colonial authorities. Those countries who were under British rule imbibed the Common law tradition, while the others are Civil law countries. However, one needs to note the notion of personal law that is growing to be a major legal tradition in Africa. This class includes customary law or what is generally referred to as Native law and Custom. Sharia law is seen as personal law; thus, it is customary law in areas where Common law and Civil law are predominant. On the other hand, there are Islamic States in Africa where Sharia is the main or major legal tradition.

651 In the present composition of the Commission, Northern Africa has three members (Egypt, Tunisia and Algeria); Central Africa has two members (Gabon and Congo Brazzaville); Southern Africa has one member (South Africa); Western Africa has four members. (Senegal, Ghana, Togo and Mali) The seat of the member from Mali is vacant with the untimely death of Mr. Alioune Blondin Beye.; the Islands have one member (Cape Verde). It is easily visible that Eastern Africa is not represented in the Commission. It may arguably be said that Congo Brazzaville is in East Africa.

is actually independent.[652] Administratively speaking, the Commission is an organ of the OAU and thus subject to OAU's financial oversight. Thus, apart from basic parent-organ to organ administrative relationship, which realistically is necessary, the Commission should be independent in appointing its staff. One would think that the provisions of Article 42 are appropriate only transitionally. If it was a transitional provision made to provide for the initial composition of the secretariat of the Commission, there may have been no need to question the role of the Secretary General in appointing the secretariat staff of the Commission. The argument may be made that the fact that the Secretary General of the OAU is involved in the appointment of the secretariat staff does not per se diminish the independence of the Commission. While that may ordinarily be so, there is a need for decentralizing the power of appointment of the Commission's staff for effective working relationship. Other than that, the situation would be one where the secretariat staff would see themselves as responsible only to the Secretary General of the OAU, rather than to the Chairman of the Commission. It may be further argued, however, that the fact that Chairmanship of the Commission is part time, makes it impossible for that working relationship to exist, and therefore, the present trend should be maintained.[653] On the other hand, it would be a serious and novel mark of independence if the Commission is allowed to be responsible in appointing its secretariat staff.

All in all, one would agree that with the right frame of mind aimed at passionately realizing the objective of the Charter, the issue of the person responsible for hiring the staff of the Commission's secretariat may not seriously undermine the independence of the African Commission.

B.   *The commission's Mandate*

The Commission's mandate is covered by chapter II of the African Charter, which comprises Article 45 of the Charter. Article 45 spells out the mandate to consist of promoting human and peoples rights, ensuring the protection of human and

---

652 *See* Article 41 of the African Charter.
653 This same trend cuts across the other regional human rights systems. Under Article 40 of the American Convention on Human Rights, the secretariat services of the Inter-American Commission on Human Rights are furnished by the "appropriate specialized unit of the General Secretariat of the Organization (of American States)..." Similarly old Article 37 of the European Convention on Human Rights provided that "the secretariat of the Commission shall be provided by the Secretary General of the Council of Europe." There is no doubt that drafters of the African Charter were fully persuaded by these other regional instruments in drafting Article 41 of the African Charter.

peoples' rights, interpreting the provisions of the Charter and the performance of any other tasks assigned by the members of the OAU.

1. Promotional mandate

The specifics of the Commission's promotional mandate as spelt out by Article 45 include:

(a) To collect documents, undertake studies and researches on African problems in the field of human and peoples' rights, organize seminars, symposia and conferences, disseminate information, encourage national and local institutions concerned with human and peoples' rights, and should the case arise, give its views or make recommendations to governments.
(b) To formulate and lay down, principles and rules aimed at solving legal problems relating to human and peoples' rights and fundamental freedoms upon which African Governments may base their legislation.
(c) Cooperate with other African and international institutions concerned with the promotion and protection of human and peoples' rights.[654]

There is no denying the fact that for effective protection of human rights, there would be a need for effective promotional activities on a continuing basis. From the foregoing provision of Article 45, it can be seen that the Charter places important emphasis on promotional activities and sees them as fundamental to the whole issue of human rights protection. This has led some critics to see the mandate of the Commission to be more of promotion, rather than protection of human rights.[655] There is no doubt that the mandate of the Commission is heavily slanted toward promotion. The protective mandate of the Commission is, however, equally visible, especially if one looks at the Charter provisions on specific human and peoples' rights, which the Commission is mandated to interpret.

The Commission has over the years made efforts aimed at realizing the areas of its promotional mandate outlined above. The first of this effort was at its second session in Dakar, Senegal in 1998 in which its first Programme of Action was approved, emphasizing research and information dissemination, quasi-legislative,

---

[654] Article 45(1) of the African Charter.
[655] *See Bello, Emmanuel, The Mandate of the African Commission on Human and Peoples Rights*, 1 AFRICAN JOURNAL OF INTERNATIONAL LAW, 55 (1988).

and cooperation activities.[656] Building on this first program of action, the Commission at its eleventh session in March 1992 finalized and adopted another Programme of Action for the Years 1992-1996. The program, as adopted, contained as its main components, the establishment of the information and documentation center; convening seminars, workshops and training courses; promotional activities by Commissioners; translation and distribution of public documents of the Commission, including States Reports and relevant summary records; publication of Annual Reports of the Commission; the Review Bulletin, brochure and other publications; and convening inter-sessional working groups.[657]

There is yet another program of action,[658] which consolidates the proposed activities that have not yet been carried out, which were contained in the initial Programme of Action of 1988 and that of 1996. It goes further to commit the Commission to work towards early adoption and ratification of the Protocol on the proposed African Court on Human and Peoples' Rights.[659]

The African Commission, in recent years, has taken some practical steps towards realizing some aspects of its promotional mandate as contained in the Charter, and as envisioned in the various Plans of Action. One very important step in this direction was the recent establishment of a Documentation Center for

---

[656] Doc. AHG/155(XXIV) ANNEX VIII. On the research and information dissemination activities, the Commission proposed to: *1.* Establish an African Library and documentation Center on Human Rights; *2.* Print and disseminate the African Charter on Human and Peoples' Rights and its Rules of Procedure; *3.* Publish an African Review on Human and Peoples' Rights; *4.* Produce periodical radio broadcasts and television programs on human rights in Africa; *5.* Integrate the teaching of human rights into secondary education sylabi; *6.* Proclaim a Human Rights Day; *7.* Participate in bicentenary activities of the Declaration of the Rights of Man and of the Citizen (1789); *8.* Institute a human rights competition and prize; *9.* Recommend the establishment of national human rights committees; *10.* Recommend the establishment of human rights committees institutes; and *11.* Put together symposia or seminars on apartheid.

The proposed quasi-legislative activities included: *1.* Conducting a Charter ratification campaign within countries which had not yet ratified it; *2.* working on ratification of human rights treaties prepared by international organizations, such as the UN, ILO, etc.; and *3.* Introduction of the Charter provisions into the constitution of states. The Commission outlined its cooperation activities to include: *1.* Cooperation with international inter-state and non-governmental organizations, such as the former European Commission on Human Rights and the Inter-American Commission on Human Rights, the UN Human Rights Commission, the International Commission of Jurists, the International Academy of Human Rights, and Amnesty international; *2.* Cooperation with African organizations, including the Inter-African Union of Lawyers, the Association of African Jurists, and the Association of African International Law; and *3.* Establishing ways of dealing with periodic reports of States.

[657] See Badawi El-Sheikh, I.A., *The African Commission on Human and Peoples' Rights: A Call for Justice* in INTERNATIONAL JUSTICE 283 (KALLIOPI KOUFA, ed., Sakkoulas Publications, 1997).

[658] AFRICAN COMMISSION ON HUMAN AND PEOPLES' RIGHTS, THE MAURITIUS PLAN OF ACTION, 1996-2001. (Hereafter, THE MAURITIUS PLAN OF ACTION, 1996-2001).

[659] *Id.* at 12. Paragraph 46.

human rights studies and research by the Commission in collaboration with NGOs and inter-governmental organizations.[660] There is, however, a need to equip the Center with a basic collection of literature on human rights, international law, African law, general reference, Constitutions of African States, legislation and jurisprudence relating to human rights and major African and international journals dealing with human rights. The Center should be able to list all publications on research and studies on human rights in keeping with the Mauritius Plan of Action. Similarly, the Commission has, with such collaboration as indicated above, organized several seminars, symposia and conferences aimed at promoting various aspects of human and peoples' rights within the African continent.[661] In addition, the Commission has also been cooperating with other human rights institutions in many areas relating to promotion and protection of human rights. Since 1998, in a bid to strengthen cooperation, the Commission as at its 22nd ordinary session in 1997, has granted observer status to more than two hundred NGOs. It is also considering granting special status to national human rights institutions of Member States to enhance the promotion of human rights in the continent.[662] On information dissemination and publication, the Commission records that it has produced and circulated several human rights documents, including the Review of the African Commission on Human and Peoples' Rights, its Annual Activity Reports, the Charter and its Rules of Procedure.[663]

Apart from the organization of conferences, seminars and workshops, aimed at realizing its promotional mandate, the Commission has passed a number of recommendations and resolutions, many of which also serve protective functions.[664] In the same vein, the Commission has developed a procedure by which each Commissioner is assigned a number of Member States for promotional

---

660 This author has made use of the Center. The documentation Center is basically a library manned by a Documentalist/Librarian. The officer- in-charge at the time of the research for this work, Mr. Désiré Ahanhanzo, was generous in allowing this author access to the released documents of the Commission.

661 For a list of such seminars, symposia and conferences, see ONE DECADE OF CHALLENGE, *supra*, note 642, at 9.

662 *See* AFRICAN COMMISSION ON HUMAN AND PEOPLES' RIGHTS, ESTABLISHMENT, (INFORMATION SHEET NO. 1) at 11. (Hereafter INFORMATION SHEET NO. 1).

663 *Id.* at 11.

664 For a list of these recommendations and resolutions, see RECOMMENDATIONS AND RESOLUTIONS OF THE AFRICAN COMMISSION), *supra*, note 420. The recommendations include those to governments to transform their obligations under the Charter into their own legal systems, establish national commissions for human rights, incorporate human rights into teaching curriculum at all levels, using the media to publicize human rights issues. One very important resolution is the recognition of October 21 every year as African Day of Human Rights, passed during the fifth ordinary session of the Commission in April 1989 in Libya. The significance of October 21 is that it was on that day in 1986 that the African Charter entered into force. *See Id.* at 11.

activities. These Commissioners are expected to visit these States and organize lectures, seminars, etc., in collaboration with various institutions aimed at promoting the African human rights mechanism in its entirety. The Commissioners would normally report on their promotional activities at each session of the Commission.[665]

There is no gainsaying the fact that the African Commission appears to have properly organized itself for promotional activities as enshrined in the African Charter. The fact, however, remains that the promotional mandate of the Commission is enormous and the Commission is merely scratching the surface of that mandate. Looking at promotional activities of individual Commissioners as assigned by the Commission, they are only carried out during the inter-sessional period, and the Commissioners concentrate on visiting universities and other institutions of higher learning in the countries assigned to them, giving lectures on the African Charter, African human rights issues and the work of the Commission. While it is good to go to these institutions, the fact is that majority of the people are outside these places. It is no exaggeration to say that an average African is ignorant, not only about his or her rights, but also about the work of the Commission. One would agree with Ankuma that there is the need to extend the Commissioners' promotional activities to rural areas, where the illiteracy rates are quite high. People in rural areas are hardly aware of their rights, which they oftentimes see as a favor from governments.[666]

Similarly, one will endorse the observation of Badawi El-Sheik, a member of the Commission that the Commission needs to do more in connection with the Documentation Center concerning research and publications. It also needs to get feed-backs from governments and NGOs in response to its recommendations.[667] The Commission also has to benefit from, and build on, the relevant experience of the OAU and the UN and other international human rights institutions to avoid duplication and maximize its contributions to the promotion of human rights in the African continent.[668]

---

[665] The distribution of members of the Commission for promotional activities during the inter-sessional period, is based on nationality of members, the language of the Commissioners *vis-a-vis* Member States, in order to improve efficiency, and the distance between Member States to be covered, and the countries of residence of the Commissioners, for financial reasons. *See* AFRICAN COMMISSION ON HUMAN AND PEOPLES RIGHTS, GEOGRAPHICAL DISTRIBUTION OF COUNTRIES AMONG COMMISSIONERS FOR PROMOTIONAL ACTIVITIES. Doc/OS/36e(XXIII). The present (1997-1999).
[666] ANKUMA, *supra,* note, 363 at 21.
[667] *See* Badawi El-Sheikh, *The African Commission on Human and Peoples' Rights: A Call for Justice, supra,* note 657, at 285.
[668] *Id.*

This author shares the opinion that there is need for more human rights promotional work than is presently seen, if the African human rights mechanism is to make any meaningful impact in the resolution of human rights. The Commission must be in the forefront of this task despite the presence of human rights NGOs in the continent. The situation in Africa is a bit different from other regional experiences. Africans, since colonialism have been subjected to intimidation by their successive governments, which the masses even at this age and time, have accepted to be their lot. It will take enormous efforts of reorientation to achieve this. Thus, this author believes that the African Commission will better serve in its promotional mandate, while retaining some aspects of its protective mandate in the new dispensation that the African human rights system is about to enter.[669] One is not ignorant of the limited resources argument, which has been an obstacle in the way of the Commission since its inception from effectively realizing its promotional mandate. While one has to accept the fact that the Commission has over the period of its existence been underfunded, proper prioritization on its part will go a long way in helping to maximize its promotional contributions. One would also expect that increase in the Commission's activities would be convincing enough to attract necessary funding from the OAU and other sources.

2.   Protective mandate

Article 45(2) of the Charter specifies the protective mandate of the African Commission as "ensuring the protection of human and peoples' rights under conditions laid down by the present Charter." Unlike the promotional mandate for which the Charter makes elaborate provision as to contents in Article 45(1), one can assert that Article 45(2) sees the protective work of the Commission as spanning the entire Charter in terms of the specific rights, duties and obligations laid down by the Charter. The Commission has identified two basic areas of its protective work, namely examination of State Reports and examination of complaints or communication, which is further divided into State Communications and other communications (non State complaints). Another emerging aspect of the Commission protective work is the appointment of a Special Rapporteur, on specific human rights themes that the Commission considers as requiring special emphasis.[670]

---

[669] This issue will be dealt with in detail when we consider the relationship between the African Commission and the proposed African Court on Human and Peoples Rights in chapter six.

[670] There are presently three such appointments. At its 16th ordinary session in October 1994, M. Hatem Ben Salem was designated Special Rapporteur on extrajudicial, summary, or arbitrary executions. During the Commission's 20th ordinary session, held in Mauritius from October 21 – 31, 1996, Professor E.V.O. Dankwa, was appointed the Special Rapporteur on Prisons and Conditions in

For the avoidance of unnecessary repetition, detailed analysis of the Commission's protective mandate is reserved for chapter four, which deals with the procedure of the African Commission. The procedure established by the Commission specifically covers examination of State reports and consideration of communications or petitions made by States or individuals. For the present purpose, suffice it to say that the protective mandate requires the Commission to take measures that ensure that individuals enjoy the rights contained in the Charter. This entails ensuring that States do not violate these rights, and if they do, that the victims are reinstated in their rights.[671]

3. Interpretative mandate

The Charter also gives the Commission the power to interpret all the provisions of the Charter at the request of a State Party, an institution of the OAU or an African organization recognized by the OAU.[672] One would read the provision as assigning to the Commission interpretative functions other than the general interpretation of the Charter that the Commission routinely embarks on in its normal promotional and protective function.[673] It appears that this provision envisages the rendering of an advisory opinion to a State Party, an institution of the OAU or an African organization recognized by the OAU.

While a State Party and an institution of the OAU are easily identifiable, the Charter does not define an African organization recognized by the OAU. One wonders whether this will include NGOs, whose presence in the continent may have been recognized by the fact that they have been given observer status by an agency of the OAU. Could it be that they are limited to inter-governmental or national organizations that have in one way or the other been endorsed by the OAU? The point, however, remains that until now neither the OAU nor a State Party has approached the Commission for an interpretation of any of the provisions of the Charter.[674] It has rather been NGOs that have sought and obtained, through draft resolutions, the interpretation of some of the provisions of the Charter, aimed

---

Africa. The third appointment was that of Mrs. Ondziel-Gnelenga as the first Special Rapporteur on the human rights of women in Africa that was made during the 23rd Ordinary Session of the Commission held on April 20 – 29, 1998 in Banjul, The Gambia.

671 See INFORMATION SHEET NO. 1, *supra,* note 662, at 13. The question of whether the victims are actually reinstated in their rights is another matter altogether.
672 Article 45(3) of the African Charter.
673 Under this general interpretation power, the Commission has been able to determine the complaints that come before it, as well as pass numerous resolutions on specific provisions of the Charter. Many of these resolutions serve to clarify some vague and ambiguous provisions of the Charter.
674 INFORMATION SHEET NO. 1, *supra,* note 662, at 16.

at giving clarity to those provisions.[675] These resolutions dealt, for instance, with specific countries, contemporary forms of slavery, human rights education and the military in governance.[676]

The fact that NGOs are allowed to seek an interpretation of some provisions of the Charter from the Commission, as indicated above, appears to have answered our inquiry: whether NGOs are included in "African Organizations recognized by the OAU." The practice of the Commission, in this regard, gives the impression in the affirmative. Thus, through the interpretative mandate of the Commission, NGOs may have contributed towards the development of African human rights jurisprudence.[677] The impact of the NGOs in the African human rights system will be discussed in Chapter 7.

As already alluded to, Article 45(3) envisages an advisory opinion function of the Commission. The principal parties who should make use of this function of the Commission, namely State Parties and organs of the OAU have ignored it. Could it be that these entities have no use for an interpretation of any provision of the Charter, or that they do not see themselves submitting to the authority of the Commission? These institutions must realize that it was expected that they will play a prominent part in ensuring that the Commission fulfils its mandate. State Parties can test the compatibility of their domestic laws with the Charter through this avenue. Similarly, the Commission itself must be bold to embark on a creative interpretation of the Charter in response to the dynamic nature of international human rights principles, knowing that it has the authority to do so. One area where the Commission should do more, is proper interpretation of the Charter provisions on economic, social and cultural rights. This is important because it would help in exhausting the potentials of the Charter as observed by Badawi El-Sheik, and make it a dynamic instrument, which responds to African realities and needs.[678]

---

[675] *Id.*
[676] *See* specifically the SEVENTH AND EIGHT ANNUAL ACTIVITY REPORTS OF THE AFRICAN COMMISSION ON HUMAN AND PEOPLES' RIGHTS adopted in 1994 and 1995 respectively. *See* also the FIFTH ANNUAL ACTIVITY REPORTS OF THE AFRICAN COMMISSION ON HUMAN AND PEOPLES' RIGHTS adopted at the 11th session, 1991-1992, where the Commission elaborated on the right to fair trial and the freedom of association. *See* also RECOMMENDATIONS AND RESOLUTIONS OF THE AFRICAN COMMISSION, *supra*, note 420.
[677] ANKUMA, *supra* note 363, at 26.
[678] *Badawi El-Sheikh, supra,* note 657, at 288.

4. Other tasks

Article 45(4) of the Charter requires that the Commission would perform "any other tasks which may be entrusted to it by the Assembly of Heads of State and Government." This is an omnibus function clause under which the Commission could be assigned additional functions not covered under the African Charter. So far, the Assembly of Heads of State and Government has not entrusted the Commission with any other task outside those authorized in the Charter.[679] One would think that many of the issues of human rights in the continent should fall within the function of this special mechanism provided for under the Charter. Thus, the Commission might be called upon to assume some roles that are presently not assigned to it. One such area is supervising the implementation of the African Convention on the Rights and Welfare of the Child (hereafter, the Child Convention). Maintaining a separate implementation agency for that purpose may have enormous financial implications for the OAU. In addition, the Commission could play additional roles in exceptional circumstances such as the Rwandan crisis and similar cases, other than the adoption of resolutions. Prevention of these conflicts should be the focus, and the Commission may well be suited to undertake such preventive functions.

It, however, needs to be observed that apart from cases where definite legislative instruments rule out the Commission as in the Child Convention, the mandate of the Commission is already wide enough for it to assume any human right related function, even though it is not specifically authorized by the OAU.

III THE SECRETARIAT OF THE AFRICAN COMMISSION

The effective functioning of any human rights system requires an effective secretariat. Thus, the secretariat of the African Commission should play a very important role in the functioning of the Commission and the entire mechanism. Even though the Charter does not specifically assign any particular function to the Secretariat, it has become customary that secretariats of this nature perform administrative and other functions aimed at the day to day working of the system, in line with the mandate of the Commission under the Charter. This is especially so, because Commissions of this nature are composed of part-time members, who by the nature of their appointment cannot easily oversee the day to day running of the secretariat.

---

679 INFORMATION SHEET NO. 1, *supra,* note 662, at 17.

The African Commission through its rules of procedure[680] has identified some pertinent functions of the secretariat under the Secretary of the Commission. The Secretary carries out his or her function under the supervision of the Chairman of the Commission; and these specifically include:

a. Assisting the Commission and its members in the exercise of their functions;
b. Serving as an intermediary for all the communications concerning the Commission;
c. Serving as custodian of the archives of the Commission; and
d. Bringing to the immediate knowledge of the members of the Commission all issues submitted to him or her.[681]

In addition, some functions originally assigned to the Secretary-General of the OAU under the old rules of procedure are now within the competence of the Secretary of the Commission under the new rules.[682] Whether or not these functions were assigned to the Commission's secretariat or to the Secretary-General of the OAU, the practical realities were that the secretariat performed them. It is, however, important that these functions be appropriately assigned to the secretariat as is the practice in similar regional and international institutions.

The manpower and resource implications in carrying out the functions assigned to the secretariat of the African Commission are enormous. This has been one of the areas where the African system has been found wanting, and it has generated a great cause for concern. Under Article 41 of the African Charter, the Secretary-General of the OAU, apart from being charged with the responsibility of appointing the Secretary of the African Commission, is also entrusted with providing the staff and services necessary for the effective discharge of the duties of the Commission. This is necessarily under the budget to be provided by the OAU. Since its inception, the resources made available for the functioning of the secretariat, and to large

---

680 THE AFRICAN COMMISSION FOR HUMAN AND PEOPLES' RIGHTS, RULES OF PROCEDURE OF THE AFRICAN COMMISSION ON HUMAN AND PEOPLES' RIGHTS, revised, and adopted on June 6, 1995. (Hereafter, RULES OF PROCEDURE OF THE AFRICAN COMMISSION OR OF THE COMMISSION). These rules depart greatly from the original rules adopted on February 13, 1988.
681 *Id.* Rule 23.
682 *Id.* Rules 6 and 10 assign to the Secretary of the Commission, in consultation with the Chairman, the function of drawing up the provisional agenda for each ordinary session of the Commission and next session, respectively. This is unlike the old Rules 6 and10, which assigned this function to the Secretary-General of the OAU. *See also* Rules 83, 84(1) and 102(1) of the new rules as against old Rules 83, 84(1) and 101 regarding the appropriate authority, to inform State Parties of the opening date, duration and venue of the Commission's sessions; to inform the Commission of all cases of non-submission of reports or additional information; and to transmit to the Commission the Communications submitted for consideration by the Commission, respectively. These functions were originally those of the Secretary-General of the OAU under the old rules.

extent, the Commission are grossly inadequate.[683] The excuse has always been one of the poor financial position of the OAU, which had not always been able to meet many of its financial obligations. One will agree with the observation that the OAU's failure to meet its obligations to the African human rights system, is a reflection of the importance, or lack thereof, which the Assembly of Heads of State and Government (AHSG) has attached to human rights.[684]

The staffing history of the secretariat has been one of temporary employees and volunteer interns or consultants, many of whom are funded outside the OAU.[685] On the other hand, there has been a quick turnover of secretaries of the Commission. Within ten years of the Commission's existence, it has had three secretaries.[686] The appointment of the present Secretary of the Commission in 1994, was seen as a step in the right direction aimed at professionalizing the secretariat.[687] The appointment of the present personnel in the secretariat is quite commendable. The various Programs or Plans of Action adopted by the Commission, however, require much more in terms of basic staffing of the secretariat.[688] It follows, therefore, that the OAU is quite aware of the personnel needs of the secretariat, but has neglected to address them. It is quite evident that the shortage

---

683 ANKUMA, *supra*, note 363, at 32.
684 *Id.*
685 In 1990-1991 Wolfgang Benedek worked at the Commission as a consultant under outside funding. *See Wolfgang Benedek, supra*, note 618, at 25. In 1991-1992, the UN funded two lawyers to serve as legal officers at the Commission. *See* ANKUMA, *supra*, note 363, at 32. Annually, the African Society of International and Comparative Law sponsors two jurists to work at the Commission. The Danish Human Rights Center and the Raoul Wallenberg Institute have at various times sponsored or seconded staff and interns to the Commission.
686 Mrs. Esther Tchouta-Moussa, 1987-89, who concurrently served as a Legal Adviser at the OAU, Mr. Jean Ngabishema Mutsinzi, 1989-1994, and Mr. Germain Baricako, 1994 – present. *See* specifically, ONE DECADE OF CHALLENGE, *supra*, note 642, at 7.
687 As of December 1998, the secretariat apart from the Secretary of the Commission, is staffed with six (6) lawyers, one (1) Documentalist/Librarian, one (1) Economist/Database Programmer from Denmark, one(1) Press /Information Officer, One (1) Accountant, One (1) Bilingual Secretary, One (1) Receptionist, two (2) Drivers, two (2) Security Guards and one (1) Janitor. *See* NEWS LETTER OF THE AFRICAN COMMISSION ON HUMAN AND PEOPLES RIGHTS vol. 1 Number 1 at 6-7 (October-December, 1998) (Hereafter 1/1, ACHPR NEWS LETTER). What is not known is how many of these staff are on secondment or sponsored by other organizations.
688 For example, the current Plan of Action, THE MAURITIUS PLAN OF ACTION, 1996-2001, *supra*, note 658, at 16, requires the following basic staff composition of the secretariat: In addition to Secretary to the Commission: two people in the Section in charge of promotion, two people in the Section in charge of protection, three people in the Research and Training Department, one person in the Press and Information Department, one person in the Documentation Center, two people as Administrative and Finance support staff, one Registry support staff and four people as Secretariat support staff. The plan however, emphasizes that even if the above proposal as to basic secretariat staffing is implemented in its entirety by the OAU, the Commission would still need additional staff to properly implement the various activities set out in the present Plan of Action.

of personnel at the secretariat has a serious repercussion on the effectiveness of the Commission in realizing its mandate.

One avenue in which the Commission has addressed the lack of adequate staffing of the secretariat, as earlier mentioned, is the acceptance of volunteers, interns and personnel on secondment, and funded by organizations outside Africa. Many of these personnel are non-Africans, and students without much experience. The fact that these personnel are non Africans and without necessary experience, has attracted an elaborate commentary by some African scholars such as Ankuma, to the effect that it could give rise to fundamental problems, which would undermine the legitimacy and credibility of the Commission.[689] Ankuma is of the view that if Western donors and sponsors were genuinely sincere in the human rights of Africans, they should sponsor Africans to work at the Commission, rather than non-Africans.[690] She emphasizes that Africans should have direct input in the work of the Commission, because of the need to develop African human rights jurisprudence, especially as the African Charter provides for the Commission to be inspired by African traditions and values, in addition to international norms, in the resolution of human rights disputes.[691]

There should be a basic agreement with the spirit of the views expressed by this learned author, especially if one has a reminiscence of the realities of colonialism. On the other hand, while it is necessary that foreign donors should give preference to sponsoring Africans, one would think that the time has come for Africa to take its obligations more seriously. Nothing stops African organizations from sponsoring Africans to work at the Commission.[692] Various NGOs receive massive supports, which they spend on non viable projects in the name of justifying the spending of the funds. Some of these funds should be used for staffing the Commission with competent African scholars.

There is no gainsaying the fact that the secretariat of the African Commission needs adequate manpower and infrastructural resources for effective working of the Commission. It needs to be stressed, however, that the primary responsibility in achieving this lies with the OAU or its succeeding African Union. Having established the mechanism, the organization must strive to fulfil its obligations towards it. Africans cannot blame outsiders for its inability to meet its obligations.

---

[689] ANKUMA, *supra*, note 363, at 33.
[690] *Id.* at 36.
[691] *Id.* at 34.
[692] The African Society for International and International Comparative Law must be commended for its continued sponsorship of jurists to work at the Commission, as well as for other contributions that the society makes in enhancing the effective working of the African sytem..

4

PROCEDURES OF THE AFRICAN COMMISSION

The African Charter provides for the procedures of the African Commission in its chapter three.[693] In addition to the procedures set out there, the Commission is empowered to lay down its rules of procedure in carrying out its mandate under the Charter.[694] In this vein, it should be recalled that the Commission is to draw inspiration from general international law on human and peoples' rights.[695] This inspiration, one would agree, is not only in the interpretation of substantive rights provided for under the Charter, but extends to issues of procedure, which though may be specific to particular regional or international human rights instrument, have universal human rights implications.

The objective of this chapter is to examine the procedures of the African Commission in relation to specific areas of its promotional and protective mandates. Bearing the central theme of this study in mind, we will also examine how the procedures of the Commission enhance or otherwise impact the effective resolution of human rights disputes in Africa.

I. STATE REPORTING

The State reporting procedure is of both promotional and protective importance. It is aimed at ensuring that States Parties to the Charter comply with the basic requirements of the Charter in terms of their domestic legislative and other instruments. Under Article 1 of the Charter, Member States undertook to adopt legis-

---

[693] The chapter comprises Article 46 to Article 59 of the Charter.
[694] Article 42(2) of the Charter. As indicated earlier, the first Rules of Procedure of the African Commission on Human and Peoples Rights were adopted in 1988. In 1995, these rules were replaced by new rules adopted at the Commission's 18th Session in Praia, Cape Verde, following an amendment of the 1988 rules. On the State reporting procedure, see RULES OF PROCEDURE OF THE AFRICAN COMMISSION, *supra*, note 680, Rules 81-86.
[695] Articles 60 and 61 of the Charter.

lative and other measures to give effect to the rights contained in the Charter. To ensure that this undertaking is taken seriously, Article 62 of the Charter obligates Member States to submit every two years, from the date that the Charter comes into effect for such members, a report on the legislative or other measures taken with a view to giving effect to the rights and freedoms recognized and guaranteed by the Charter. Although the Charter does not specify the organ to which State reports should be submitted, the Commission rectified this by formally requesting the power to receive the State's reports and accordingly, deal with them, from the Assembly of Heads of State and Government (AHSG), at the Commission's third session held in Libreville, Gabon in 1988.[696]

As a measure of addressing the State reporting procedure, the Commission at is fourth session in Cairo, Egypt, adopted the initial set of Guidelines for Periodic National Reports.[697] The Guidelines were divided into seven parts, each dealing with different aspects of rights and duties contained in the Charter.[698] The objective of the Guidelines according to the Commission, was for the creation of a channel for constructive dialogue between States and itself on the rights contained in the Charter.[699] In addition, while States reported on the measures they had adopted and progress made, as well as any factors and difficulties affecting the degree of the fulfilment of the rights contained in the Charter, the

---

[696] *See* AFRICAN COMMISSION ON HUMAN AND PEOPLES' RIGHTS, STATE REPORTING PROCEDURE, INFORMATION SHEET NO. 4, 2. (Hereafter, INFORMATION SHEET NO. 4).*See* also *Welch, supra,* note 633, at 53; ANKUMA, *supra,* note 363, at 79.

[697] OLD GUIDELINES FOR NATIONAL PERIODIC REPORTS, SUPRA, note 484. As earlier noted these guidelines have been revised and amended. *See* AMENDMENTS OF THE GENERAL GUIDELINES FOR THE PREPARATION OF PERIODIC REPORTS BY STATES PARTIES, DOC./OS/27(XXIII) (Hereafter, AMENDED GUIDELINES FOR THE PREPARATION OF PERIODIC REPORTS BY STATES PARTIES, or AMENDED GUIDELINES), adopted at the 23rd Ordinary Session of the African Commission, April 20-29, 1998 in Banjul, The Gambia.

[698] Part I provided for general guidelines regarding the forms and contents of reports from states on civil and political rights, part II covered economic, social and cultural rights, part III dealt with guidelines on peoples' rights, part IV prescribed guidelines on specific duties under the Charter, part V focused on the elimination of all forms of racial discrimination, part VI dealt with the suppression and punishment of the crime of apartheid, and part VII contained guidelines on forms and contents of reports on the elimination of all forms of discrimination against women.

[699] SECOND ANNUAL ACTIVITY REPORT OF THE AFRICAN COMMISSION ON HUMAN AND PEOPLES' RIGHTS, June 14, 1989, covering the 4th and 5th ordinary sessions (October and April 1989) and the extraordinary session in Banjul in June 1989, as well as intersession activities), *reprinted* in AFRICAN COMMISSION ON HUMAN AND PEOPLES' RIGHTS, DOCUMENTATION No 1: ACTIVITY REPORTS (1988-1990) 45, at 46.. *See* also, INFORMATION SHEET NO. 4, *supra,* note 696, at 5 – 6. Here, the Commission identified three advantages or benefits of the State reporting procedure as follows: 1. Monitoring implementation of the Charter; 2. Identifying difficulties faced by Member States impeding effective implementation of the Charter; and 3. Sharing of information among states in terms of their common experiences, both good and bad, so that States can learn from each other.

Commission on the other hand, would furnish suggestions, advice and other assistance on satisfying the requirements of the Charter.[700] Under the Guidelines, States were to submit initial general reports, followed by detailed periodic reports. Such periodic reports are to contain changes in the States' general legal frameworks.

The old Guidelines on State Reporting were found not to be very useful, as they were too detailed and complex, making it difficult for Member States to follow.[701] While the complexity of the old Guidelines may have impacted the lack of interest of most States Parties in taking the State reporting procedure seriously, one cannot, however, totally ascribe the non-compliance of States in this regard to the Guidelines. The fact remains that there was a general apathy on the part of Member States to comply with their reporting obligations under the Charter.[702]

The Commission, realizing the problems associated with the old Guidelines on state reporting, proceeded to amend them with the aim of simplifying them and making them less cumbersome for States in their submission of initial and periodic reports. A summary of the amended Guidelines, highlighted eleven areas of emphasis and questions covering initial reports, as follows:

1   An initial report (first report) should contain a brief history of the State, its form of government, the legal system and the relationship between the arms of government.
2   The initial report should also include the basic documents: the constitution, the criminal code and procedure and landmark decisions on human rights.
3   The major human rights instruments to which the State is a party and the steps taken to internalize them.

---

700   SECOND ANNUAL ACTIVITY REPORT, *id.* at 46 .
701   *Wolfgang, supra,* note 633, at 32. *See* also *Badawi El-sheik, supra,* note 657, at 284; ANKUMA, *supra,* note 363, at 87.
702   As at early 1998, only 21 Member States of the African Charter had submitted their reports to the Commission and none of the States had been regular in this regard. *See* INFORMATION SHEET NO. 4, *supra,* note 696, at 4. It should be noted that as at October 1998, apart from Morocco, which withdrew its membership of the OAU, Eritrea was the only African country yet to ratify the African Charter, Ethiopia having ratified the Charter in 1998. *See* LIST OF COUNTRIES WHICH HAVE RATIFIED THE AFRICAN CHARTER ON HUMAN AND PEOPLES' RIGHTS, DOC/OS/INF.5(XXIV), 24th Ordinary Session, October 22 – 31, 1998, Banjul, The Gambia. It should be noted, however, that with the ratification of the Charter by Eritrea in May 1999, all Member States of the OAU are now parties to the African Charter. *See* Rachel Murray, *Human Rights News: Africa,* 17 NETH. Q. HUM. RTS. 350 (1999).

4 How the party is implementing the following rights protected by the Charter:
   a Civil and political rights
   b Economic, social and cultural rights
   c Group rights.
5 What the state is doing to improve the condition of the following groups mentioned in the Charter:
   a Women
   b Children
   c The disabled
6 What steps are being taken to protect the family and encourage its cohesion?
7 What is being done to ensure that individual duties are observed?
8 What are the problems encountered in implementing the Charter having regard to the political, economic or social circumstances of the state?
9 How the state is carrying out its obligations under Article 25 of the Charter on human rights education?
10 How the State as an interested party, is using the Charter in its international relations, particularly in ensuring respect for it?
11 Any other information relevant to the implementation and promotion of the Charter.[703]

The areas covered by the amended Guidelines are quite straightforward and simplified enough for States parties to be able to easily meet the requirement of the State reporting obligations under the Charter. Being that the amended Guidelines are quite recent, it may be difficult to really evaluate their effect on the State reporting procedure. Thus, the relationship between the complexity or simplicity of the Guidelines on State reporting and the actual willingness of States Parties may not be apparent for quite some time. It is only fair to continue to judge the State reporting procedure on the practice before the amendment until such a time when the amendment would have gained ground. One hopes that the amendment will serve the purpose of being an incentive to States parties, and that States Parties will have enough will to liberally fulfil this obligation rather than seeing the procedure as a forum to embarrass them. The amendment of the Guidelines does not, however, affect the established procedure of the Commission in this regard.

---

703 *See* AMENDED GUIDELINES, *supra*, note 697. The amendment of the guidelines was preceded by two seminars on the Guidelines organized by the African Commission, one in English, in Harare, Zimbabwe and the other in French, held in Tunis, Tunisia in 1993 and 1994 respectively. The above summary takes account of the conclusion reached at both seminars. It is expected that periodic reports will be updates on the above issues which would have been contained in the initial reports.

A. *Procedure on State Reporting before the Commission*

The procedure of the African Commission in considering State reports can conveniently be divided into three stages – receipt of reports, actual session, and follow up. In addition, the Rules of Procedure make provisions for how to deal with non-submission of reports by States Parties.

1. Receipt of reports

The recommendation requesting the Assembly of Heads of State and Government (AHSG) of the OAU to mandate the Commission to examine State reports requires "the General Secretariat of the OAU to receive the said reports and communicate them to the Commission without delay."[704] In practice, however, most States send their reports directly to the secretariat of the Commission. Where there are reports that are sent to the Secretariat of the OAU, efforts are usually made for them to be sent to the Commission.[705] At the secretariat of the Commission, the reports are studied and communicated to all the Commissioners. In addition to the Commissioners, the secretariat also sends out copies of the reports to institutions or NGOs having observer status with the Commission, and which may have also reported to the Commission on those States.[706] Armed with the information from studying the reports, the secretariat prepares questions that would be addressed to State representatives at the sessions of the Commission. The questions, which may not necessarily be limited to information in the report, are transmitted to the State concerned and to all Commissioners, at least, six weeks before the date of the session at which the report is to be examined.[707] Along with these questions, the Commission sends a letter to the Member State concerned requesting it to send a highly qualified official or delegate to present the report. In addition, the secretariat contacts the Commissioner responsible for promotional activities in the Member State, since the Commissioner would normally be the rapporteur to lead during the discussion of the report.[708]

---

704 *See* INFORMATION SHEET NO. 4, *supra,* note 696, at 8.
705 *Id.*
706 This is in furtherance of Rule 78 of the Rules of Procedure of the Commission, which makes periodic reports and other information submitted by States Parties subject to general distribution in the discretion of the Commission. These institutions or NGOs may in turn be required to submit their observations based on the reports or parts of the reports that were sent to them. *See* RULES OF PROCEDURE OF THE AFRICAN COMMISSION, Rule 82.
707 INFORMATION SHEET NO. 4, *supra,* note 696, at 8.
708 *Id.* at 9.

2. Actual session

The examination of reports of Member States is usually done at the sessions of the Commission. The Commissions meets in ordinary sessions twice a year,[709] except where extraordinary sessions are authorized.[710] The Commission conducts the examination of States' reports in its open sessions, before all participants, including NGOs, national human rights institutions, State representatives and other persons or organizations invited to the session. Despite the presence of these organizations or individuals, only the Commissioners can pose questions to State representatives.[711] The State representative is given the opportunity to present the State's reports, after which the Commission's rapporteur poses questions to him or her. Additional questions are posed to the representative by other Commissioners, and are generally not limited to the line of questions prepared by the secretariat.[712] After the question and answer process, the rapporteur sums up, while the Chairman of the Commission concludes the session.[713]

There may be cases where a State Party may not have sent a State representative to the Commission's session to present its report, even after receiving the Commission's letter to that effect. Under the rule, the State Party is under no obligation to send a representative. It is a matter entirely subject to a State's discretion.[714] Despite this discretionary power of the State Party, the Commission in the past adopted a practice whereby it would not consider a Member State's report if there was no person from the State to present it. The Commission, however, adopted a change in practice at its 23rd ordinary session.[715] The new practice allows two letters of notification to the State concerned to send a representative to present its report, after which if the State does not respond, the Commission goes ahead to examine the State's report and forward its comments to the State concerned.[716]

---

709 *See* RULES OF PROCEDURE OF THE AFRICAN COMMISSION, *supra,* note 680, Rule 2(1).
710 *Id.* Rule 3.
711 INFORMATION SHEET NO. 4, *supra,* note 696, at 9.
712 *Id.*
713 *Id.* at 10. In the past, however, after the question and answer session, the Commission usually went into a close meeting to discuss possible recommendations. This former procedure has been commended as having the advantage of creating a dialogue and at the same time giving the Commission some privacy in making some comments among themselves. *See Id.*
714 *See* RULES OF PROCEDURE OF THE COMMISSION, *supra,* note 680, Rule 83.
715 Held in Banjul, The Gambia from April 20-29, 1998. *See* INFORMATION SHEET NO. 4, *supra,* note 696, at 11.
716 *Id.* at 11.

3. Follow-up procedure

The African Commission adopts a follow-up procedure after the examination of a State Party's periodic report. This comprises a follow-up letter or memorandum to the particular State, summing up the examination process and putting in writing the questions that were not satisfactorily answered during the session.[717] Through this procedure, the Commission then requests the State to submit any additional information that it may require to the secretariat of the Commission. The Commission may if it considers it necessary, fix a time limit for the submission of the comment by the State concerned.[718] In addition, depending on how the Commission perceives the original report of the State concerned, it may decide to exercise the discretion enshrined in Rule 86(2) of the Rules of Procedure by transmitting to the AHSG of the OAU its observations on a State Party's report, the report itself, as well as comments supplied by the State in response to the Commission's follow-up requests.

4. Non-submission of states' reports

The Commission's Rules of Procedure requires the Secretary of the Commission to inform it of all cases of non-submission of reports or additional information by Member States. In such cases, the Commission may authorize the Secretary to send to the State concerned a report or reminder on the submission of the report or additional information.[719] Reminders were initially sent once every six months, but the present practice is once every three months.[720] Where the State concerned does not respond to the reminder by submitting its report or the additional information, the Commission is obligated to point it out in its annual report to the Assembly of Heads of State and Government of the OAU.[721] The mode in which this is done is that the Commission usually attaches a list to its annual activity report showing the status of submission of State periodic reports. The list contains the

---

[717] *See* RULES OF PROCEDURE OF THE COMMISSION, *supra*, note 680, Rule 85(3). The rule provides that "if, following the consideration of the reports, and the information submitted by a State party to the Charter, the Commission decides that the State has not discharged some of its obligations under the Charter, it may address all general observations to the State concerned as it may deem necessary".
[718] *See* RULES OF PROCEDURE OF THE COMMISSION, *supra*, note 680, Rule 86(1).
[719] *Id.* Rule 84(1).
[720] INFORMATION SHEET NO. 4, *supra*, note 696, at 12.
[721] RULES OF PROCEDURE OF THE COMMISSION, *supra*, note 680, Rule 84(2).

names of those States that have submitted their reports, the number of reports submitted, the reports due and those who have not submitted any report.[722]

B.   *Assessment of the State Reporting Mechanism*

The State reporting procedure is a welcome addition to the functions of the African Commission on Human and Peoples' Rights over and above those under the European and American Conventions.[723] It has earlier been observed that the procedure serves both a promotional and protective function. It is promotive of human rights in that it provides a forum for constructive dialogue between the Commission and States Parties. In this vein, it would enable both the Commission and the States Parties as a whole to facilitate the exchange of information among States to develop a better understanding of the common problems faced by States, and a fuller appreciation of the type of measures which might be taken to promote the effective realization of each of the rights contained in the Charter.[724] On the other hand, the protective benefit of the procedure ensures that a comprehensive review is undertaken with respect to national legislation, administrative rules, procedures, and practices, in an effort to ensure the fullest possible conformity with the obligations under the Charter.[725] Similarly, it ensures that the State Party monitors the actual situation with respect to each of the rights on a regular basis and is thus aware of the extent to which the various rights are, or are not being enjoyed by all individuals within its territories or under its jurisdictions.[726]

---

722 INFORMATION SHEET NO. 4, *supra,* note 696, at 12. *See* also the ELEVENTH ANNUAL ACTIVITY REPORT OF THE AFRICAN COMMISSION ON HUMAN AND PEOPLES RIGHTS (hereafter, ELEVENTH ANNUAL ACTIVITY REPORT) 33-35 (1997/1998). The report covers the 22nd and 23rd ordinary sessions of the Commission held in Banjul, The Gambia, from November 2-11, 1997 and from April 20-29, 1998, respectively. As a the 23rd session only 18 State Parties have submitted their reports, most of which were initial reports apart from The Gambia, Senegal, Tunisia, and Zimbabwe, which had submitted their second and third reports respectively. The same number of countries was reflected in the Ninth and Tenth Annual Activity Reports. Compare with 21 countries reported in INFORMATION SHEET NO. 4, *id.*, It appears that there is a conflict on the actual number of countries that have yet submitted their periodic reports. Whatever be the case, even if we take 21 countries to have submitted their reports, that is quite unimpressive.
723 While these systems do have this procedure, the drafters of the African Charter seemed to have been inspired in this regard by the procedure of the UN Human Rights Committee under the Covenant on Civil and Political rights.
724 D. Fisher, *International Reporting Procedures* in GUIDE TO INTERNATIONAL HUMAN RIGHTS PRACTICE 165-185 (HANNUM, HURST, Ed., 1984), *cited* in ANKUMA, *supra,* note 363, at 80, as one of the purposes of the state reporting procedures listed by the UN Committee on Economic, Social and Cultural Rights.
725 ANKUMA, *supra*, note 363, at 80.
726 *Id.*

While the above identified importance of the State reporting procedure cannot be faulted, and there is no doubt that the African Commission has established a framework for the procedure, the effectiveness of the procedure under the African mechanism remains to be seen. The effort towards realizing an effective procedure, it should be observed, is not that of the Commission alone. States Parties are equally obligated to make the procedure effective, as well as non-governmental organizations (NGOs). On the part of the Commission, as has earlier been pointed out, the initial Guidelines on State reporting were very lengthy and too detailed in some areas, and yet lacking specificity in other areas.[727] Similarly, it has been observed that the complexity of the Guidelines made them appear to be more confusing than helpful.[728] The question, however, remains whether the nature of the guidelines would make a State Party not to fulfil its obligation under the Charter, one of which is to submit its initial and periodic reports. It could be argued that, while this will not absolve a State from its reporting obligations, it may induce the State into producing a substandard report. The viability of this argument will in the near future be tested by how the recent amendment to the Guidelines on State reporting would induce the interest of States Parties to honor their reporting obligations, as and when due.

Secondly, the recurring inadequacy of resources at the Commission's secretariat has also hampered the effectiveness of the reporting procedure. The secretariat at a time lacked the capacity to translate State reports. It was suggested that the Commission should seek external support in this regard as a way of remedying this obstacle in the State reporting procedure.[729] The Commission appears to be heeding this advice, as it relates to the publication of examined State reports.[730]

Thirdly, the Commission could do a lot more in its follow up work after a State Party's report may have been considered. The Commission must ensure that additional materials requested from such a State Party must be submitted, as a way of minimizing the present practice whereby States Parties totally neglect to submit the necessary supplementary information to the Commission.[731] In this

---

[727] *Id.* at 87.
[728] *See* Gaer, F. D., *First Fruits: Reporting by States under the African Charter on Human and Peoples' Rights*, NETH. Q. HUM. RTS. 29-42 (1992).
[729] *Wolfgang Benedek, supra* note 633, at 33.
[730] *See* THE AFRICAN COMMISSION ON HUMAN AND PEOPLES' RIGHTS, EXAMINATION OF STATE REPORTS: 13TH ANNUAL SESSION- NIGERIA- TOGO (April 1993). This collection was published with the assistance of the Danish Human Rights Center in the name of the Commission, pursuant to the authority granted to the Center by the Commission at its 16th session in October 1994 to publish the transcripts of the examination of state reports which had so far taken place.
[731] ANKUMA, *supra,* note 363, at 109.

regard, the Commission has been found to have neglected to send reminders to States to provide supplementary information after a report had been examined.[732] The Commission must continue to constantly remind States Parties to submit their supplementary information in much the same way that they are reminded to submit their reports.

Finally, the Commission can enhance the effectiveness of the entire State reporting procedure by adopting the country study approach. This is a dynamic approach inspired by the practice of the Inter-American Commission, under which the African Commission could make use of its powers in Articles 45 and 46 of the Charter to visit countries and investigate the situation and organize hearings.[733]

On the part of States Parties, there appears to be a deliberate attempt to scuttle the State reporting procedures. Less than half of States Parties to the African Charter have submitted their initial reports.[734] For those who did submit, it was done long after their expected dates of submission. In the same vein, submitted reports varied significantly in terms of form and content, and as such, did not conform to the then existing Guidelines. Many of the reports were brief and not sufficiently detailed. In other instances, they were unnecessarily voluminous and not providing adequate and sufficiently accurate information to enable the Commission to effectively examine them.[735]

What States Parties require in ensuring an effective reporting procedure, is a positive attitude and a right frame of mind. There is the tendency to see the reporting procedure and presentation of report as a confrontation that must be defended. It is difficult for most States to see the procedure actually as one that is generally aimed at generating some dialogue on domestic application of the Charter. States must be willing to point out the problems they are facing in actualizing the implementation of the Charter. A rethink of the procedure on the part of States Parties with the above in mind, would make them more cooperative with the Commission. It will make the work of the Commission easier, and at

---

732 *Id.*
733 *See* Wolfgang Benedek, *supra* note 633, at 33.
734 *See* note 722, *supra.*
735 *See* ANKUMA, *supra,* note 363, at 91. Examples of such reports were Ghana's initial report and that of Egypt. While that of Ghana was a mere five pages of insufficient details, that of Egypt was a fifty page volume of unnecessary details, while omitting important aspects of the report on the measures adopted to give effect to the Charter. The initial report of Tanzania on the other hand while commendable, omitted reports on the economic, social and cultural rights and the practical effect of the legislative measures adopted in furtherance of the domestic application of the Charter.

the same time serving the purpose of monitoring the domestic application of the Charter.

NGOs on the other hand have a role to play in the reporting procedure.[736] They are veritable independent sources for the Commission to ascertain the state of human rights in Member States, just like other treaty bodies have benefitted from information supplied by NGOs. This is more so if the NGOs are locally based in such Member States. The information provided by the NGOs will help the Commission in either confirming or contradicting the situation presented by a Member State whose report is under consideration. In this regard, the effectiveness of the reporting procedure, could to a certain extent, be enhanced by NGOs becoming major partners with the Commission in examining annual reports. There are signs of this partnership in the Commission's examination of State reports. Some NGOs have gone as far as preparing alternate reports to those submitted by Member States.[737] These alternate reports most times, go farther than those of States Parties.

Despite this effort made by NGOs in this regard, one would agree with Ankuma that NGOs have not made use of their full potential to exercise influence on the reporting procedure.[738] They need to be involved in advance in knowing what reports would be considered at the sessions of the Commission and be prepared to assist the Commission with necessary information, preferably in writing. Apart from producing alternate reports, NGOs can also lobby members of the African Commission to influence the human rights practice in a given country. This, African NGOs have not done very well.[739] It should be noted that the impact of NGOs on the African human rights system will be discussed in chapter seven of this book.

All said and done, the usefulness of State reporting procedure cannot be quantified. It, however, needs to be done well, if it is to achieve its supposed result. This task belongs to both the Commission and States Parties, as well as the NGOs. By extension, the citizenry also have a role to play. This is because effective promotion and protection of human rights within individual countries

---

[736] *See* O'Flaherty, M., *The Reporting Obligation Under Article 40 of the International Covenant on Civil and Political Rights,* HUM. RTS. Q. 538 (1994).

[737] For example, the alternate report submitted by The Ghana Committee on Human and Peoples' Rights during Ghana's presentation of her initial report at the 14th ordinary session of the Commission was more elaborate and contained more information on the state of human rights in Ghana than the state report. In the same vein NGOs from Nigeria, Algeria, Benin Republic and Tanzania have provided useful information to the Commission in its consideration of reports from those Member States. *See* ANKUMA, *supra,* note 363, at 92.

[738] *Id.* at 94.

[739] *Id.* at 95.

depend not only on government institution. Citizen awareness and participation are vital, and NGOs are central to it.[740]

II THE COMMUNICATIONS PROCEDURE

It is under the communication procedure of the African Commission that cases are brought to the Commission in form of complaints or petitions.[741] The communications that the Commission receives can be either from States against other Member States, or what is referred to as "other communications," depicting individual or non-State communications. The bulk of activities regarding the communications procedure of the Commission has been on "other communications" rather than on those from States Parties. That notwithstanding, we will outline the State Communication procedure and dwell more in our analysis on individual or non-State complaints.[742]

A. *Communication from States*

Communication from States or inter-State communication procedure under the African Charter is not optional unlike the Inter-American system, where the Inter-American Commission may only deal with inter-state complaints if both the complaining State and the accused State, in addition to ratifying the American Convention on Human Rights, have made a further declaration recognizing the inter-state jurisdiction of the Inter-American Commission.[743] The Charter makes provision for two different procedures regarding communications from States. Article 47 of the Charter identifies one of these procedures. Under it,

> If a State Party to the present Charter has good reasons to believe that another State Party to this Charter has violated the provisions of the Charter, it may draw, by written

---

740 Welch, *supra*, note 633, at 54.
741 The Communications procedure spans Articles 47 to 59 of the African Charter. *See* also RULES OF PROCEDURE OF THE AFRICAN COMMISSION, *supra*, note 680, Rules 88 to 101, which deal specifically with inter-state communications.
742 Apart from the fact that tangible activities have not taken place on the inter-state communication procedure, the discussion on individual complaints procedure will involve some issues that are common and equally applicable to the inter-state communication procedure.
743 American Convention on Human Rights, Article 45. The African inter-state complaint procedure is similar to the procedure under the European Convention on Human Rights and Fundamental Freedoms, old Article 25(1), now Article 33, where inter-state complaint is mandatory.

communication, the attention of that State to the matter. This communication shall also be addressed to the Secretary-General of the OAU and to the Chairman of the Commission. Within three months of the receipt of the communication, the State to which the communication is addressed shall give the enquiring State, written explanation or statement elucidating the matter. This should include as much as possible relevant information relating to the laws and rules of procedure applied and applicable, and the redress already given or course of action available.

Article 48 of the Charter prescribes the mode of resolving the dispute giving rise to the above procedure without involving the African Commission if possible.[744] On the other hand, Article 49 allows a State party to bypass the procedure under Articles 47 and 48 and proceed directly with a communication to the Commission through the Chairman, and also to the Secretary-General of the OAU and to the State concerned.[745] While Articles 47 and 48 require three months of exchange of information aimed at the peaceful resolution of the violation complained of before the Commission is seized of the complaint,[746] Article 49 indicates no such period, and the Commission would automatically be seized of the complaint using its normal course of procedure. It appears, however, that despite the clear direct recourse to the Commission prescribed by Article 49, the Commission would still insist on the three months time limit required in Articles 47 and 48 to ensure that the States involved would have sought resolution of their disputes diplomatically.[747]

B.   *Bringing an Inter-State Complaint before the Commission*

Where a State Party to the Charter determines that it would bring a complaint against another State Party under the above procedures, that State must adhere

---

[744] Article 48 provides:
If within three months from the date on which the original communication is received by the State to which it is addressed, the issue is not settled to the satisfaction of the two States involved through bilateral negotiation or by another peaceful procedure, either State shall have the right to submit the matter to the Commission though the Chairman and shall notify the other State involved.

[745] Article 49 reads:
Notwithstanding the provisions of Article 47, if a State Party to the present Charter considers that another State Party has violated the provisions of the Charter, it may refer the matter directly to the Commission by addressing a communication to the Chairman, to the Secretary-General of the Organization of African Unity and the State concerned.

[746] *See also* RULES OF PROCEDURE OF THE AFRICAN COMMISSION, *supra*, note 680, Rules 91-92.

[747] *Id.* Rule 97.

to the Guidelines established for this purpose.[748] Under the Guidelines, the complaining State must:

1. State in writing, *inter alia,* its name, official language, and the year in which it ratified the African Charter;
2. State the name of the accused State, its official language and year it ratified the Charter;
3. State the facts constituting the violation. This must be explained in as much factual detail as possible in terms of what occurred, specifying place, time and dates of the violation if possible;
4. Indicate measures that have been taken to resolve the matter amicably; why the measures if any, failed, or why no measure was used at all. Along this line, the state must also indicate measures taken to exhaust local remedies. All relevant documents in this regard must also be attached;
5. State domestic legal remedies not yet pursued, giving reasons why this has not yet been done;
6. State whether the case has also been referred to other international avenues, such as referral to other international settlement body like the UN or within the OAU system; and
7. Show complaints submitted to the Secretary-General of the OAU and to the accused State, accompanied by any response from these two sources.[749]

The above Guidelines are similar to the requirements in individual complaints in some respects. Under both inter-state communications procedure and individual complaint procedure, the Commission can proceed to consider a communication only after it has ascertained that all domestic legal remedies have been exhausted, unless it is obvious to the Commission that the procedure of achieving these remedies would be unduly prolonged.[750] Similarly, the Commission sees as its primary goal in both procedures, the achievement of friendly settlement.[751] However, unlike the individual compliant procedure, the complaining State is obliged to notify the accused state directly rather than the Commission itself notifying the State.[752] However, the Commission may, if it deems it necessary

---

[748] THE AFRICAN COMMISSION ON HUMAN AND PEOPLES RIGHTS' RIGHTS, GUIDELINES ON THE SUBMISSION OF COMMUNICATIONS: INFORMATION SHEET NO. 2, 14. (Hereafter, INFORMATION SHEET NO. 2).
[749] *Id.*
[750] *See* THE AFRICAN COMMISSION ON HUMAN AND PEOPLES' RIGHTS, COMMUNICATION PROCEDURE: INFORMATION SHEET NO. 3, 18 (1998). (Hereafter, INFORMATION SHEET NO. 3). *See also* RULES OF PROCEDURE OF THE AFRICAN COMMISSION, *supra,* note 680, Rule 97 (c).
[751] *Id. See* also RULES OF PROCEDURE OF THE AFRICAN COMMISSION, *supra,* note 680, Rule 98.
[752] INFORMATION SHEET NO. 3, *supra* note 750, at 18.

ask the States concerned to provide it with additional relevant information.[753] It may also invite the States to make oral or written presentations.[754] The ultimate result of the Commission's consideration of an inter-state communication in the event that it does not secure an amicable settlement of the dispute, is the presentation of a report to the AHSG of the OAU, with sch recommendations as it deems useful.[755]

A closer look at the procedure outlined above, will reveal some underlying concerns. From the provisions of Articles 47, 48 and 49, a State Party which believes that another State Party has violated the provisions of the Charter has the option either to engage in peaceful resolution of the matter or initiate a communication before the Commission, the OAU and the State involved. The point, however, remains that even where the State party proceeds under Article 47, in which case it ought to seek peaceful resolution of the dispute within three months, the State Party should still have a communication pending before the Commission and the Secretary-General of the OAU. One wonders why the drafters of the African Charter inserted these separate provisions. Neither the Charter nor the Rules of Procedure contain any explanation for these procedures. The natural explanation would be that the drafters of the Charter want to stress the principle of peaceful resolution of disputes among Member States in line with the Charter of the OAU.[756] This, as has been seen, and as will be seen later, has been the bedrock of OAU dispute resolution principle to the detriment of human rights dispute resolution in Africa.

Secondly, one would think that the drafters of the African Charter thought that it would be proper to first give opportunity to Member States to address their differences before being subjected to external review. With all due respect, the demarcation of the procedures under Articles 47, 48 and 49, reveals poor drafting, which has affected the Rules of Procedure. There is an attempt to make separate rules for the procedure under Article 47 and the procedures under Articles 48 and

---

753 *Id.*at 19. *See* also, RULES OF PROCEDURE OF THE AFRICAN COMMISSION, *supra*, note 680, Rule 99.
754 INFORMATION SHEET NO. 3, *supra* note 750, at 18. *See* also, RULES OF PROCEDURE OF THE AFRICAN COMMISSION, *supra*, note 680, Rule 100.
755 *Id.* Rule 101(5).
756 *See* Charter of the Organization of African Unity, 479 UNTS 39; I.L.M. (1963), Article XIX, *reprinted* in DOCUMENTS OF THE ORGANIZATION OF AFRICAN UNITY, *supra*, note 635, at 3-10. Under Article XIX of the OAU Charter Member States, among other things, "pledge to settle all dispute among themselves by peaceful means..."

49.[757] At the same time, these rules contain identical provisions, which make cross references to each other. The only difference between the procedures is the three months waiting period in which the complaining State and the accused State need to exchange information or embark on negotiations under Article 47, and at the same time seeking bilateral peaceful resolution of the dispute under Article 48. At this time the communication that may have been filed by the accusing State with the Secretary-General of the OAU and the Chairman of the Commission would remain docile while waiting for the three months time limit under Article 48. The drafters of the Charter should rather have made one provision for inter-state communication in which a time limit for attempts at bilateral peaceful resolution of the dispute should be included, if the complaining State so desires, before the complaining State files a communication with the Commission.

Another question concerning these procedures for which answers are still lacking, is the role of the Secretary-General of the OAU in inter-state communication procedure. States Parties not only address their communications to the Commission but also to the Secretary General of the OAU, both under Article 47 and Article 49. One would think that the Commission should have been the only and proper institution that Communications should be addressed to, while the Commission could use the good offices of the Secretary-General of the OAU in ensuring amicable settlement of disputes between States Parties.

In addition, apart from the fact that the inter-state communication procedure is rarely used,[758] neither the Charter nor the Rules of Procedure indicate the type of disputes or violations of the Charter that is envisaged under Articles 47 and 49. The Complaint by Sudan would have provided an opportunity for Scholars to see how the Commission would have interpreted the obligations of States Parties to each other in this regard. One would, however, think that violation of Article

---

[757] Rules 88 – 92 of the RULES OF PROCEDURE OF THE AFRICAN COMMISSION, *supra*, note 680, deal with the procedure under Article 47, which is concerned with "communications-negotiations," While Rules 93 – 101 deal with the procedure under Articles 48 and 49, which is referred to as procedure for "communication-complaint." Why should a communication be pending under Article 47 before negotiation. It should rather have been that the parties negotiate, failing which a complaint is filed.

[758] To date the African Commission has received only one complaint that is truly an inter-state complaint under the Charter alleging the violation of the Charter by another African State. The complaint was received from Sudan alleging human rights violations by Ethiopian troops in Sudanese territory during the alleged invasion of the Kurmmuk and Gissan regions in Sudan on January 12, 1997. The Commission referred the matter to the OAU Secretariat and advised Sudan to do likewise because Ethiopia was then not a State Party to the Charter and thus, not subject to the Commission's jurisdiction. Another recorded attempted use of this procedure was the complaint filed by Libya against the United States in 1987, after the bombing of Libya by the Reagan Administration. The Commission declared the complaint irreceivable because it was not against an African State, and more so, the United States is not a party to the African Charter. *See* ONE DECADE OF CHALLENGE, *supra,* note 642, at 19.

20 of the Charter dealing with the general question of the right to self determination; and Article 23, which deals with the right to national and international peace and security, would fall within the purview of the procedure. Additionally, the procedure could be used where a State espouses the claims of its Nationals whose rights may have been violated by another State Party to the Charter in terms of the general substantive rights provided under the Charter. What is not clear, however, is whether a State Party can proceed against another State Party for the violation of the rights of citizens of the State proceeded against, rather than those of the citizens of the proceeding State. Generally speaking, that should be another central basis of the inter-state communications procedure framework.

By ratifying the Charter all Member States are obliged to enforce the rights of the citizenry of Africa, irrespective of the nationality of the persons whose rights are violated. Whether African States can take it upon themselves to enforce the violation of human rights against other African States, remains a big question. African States' relations and practice do not give any positive indication of this. Until this happens, the inter-state communications procedure cannot be seen to serve the interest of effective human rights dispute resolution in Africa.

C. Other Communications (non-state or individual complaints)

1. Jurisdiction

In addition to providing for inter-state communications to serve the protective interest of States Parties to the Charter in their demand for remedy to human rights violations, the Charter also empowers the African Commission to receive what it refers to as "other communications." The Charter does not define the term "other communications," neither do the Rules of the Commission. The only clue to this effect can be drawn from Article 55 of the Charter to the effect that "other communications" connote communications that are other than state communications. Article 55 provides:

1. Before each Session, the Secretary of the Commission shall make a list of the communications other than those of States Parties to the present Charter and transmit them to the members of the Commission, who shall indicate which communications shall be considered by the Commission.
2. A communication shall be considered by the Commission if a simple majority of the members so decide.[759]

---

759 See also, RULES OF PROCEDURE OF THE AFRICAN COMMISSION, *supra*, note 680, Rule 102(1).

In effect, the Charter allows the lodging of complaints or petitions by any person, group of persons and any non-governmental organization, containing denunciations or complaints of violation of the Charter by a State Party.[760] It is important to observe that the African Charter is more liberal in allowing individual access than other regional and international systems. The Inter-American system, though similar to the African system in this regard, allows only NGOs legally recognized in one or more Member States of the OAS among the entities that can lodge complaints before the Inter-American Commission.[761] There is no qualification of the entities in the African system. Thus, Human rights NGOs and other NGOs all over the world, whether granted observer status with the African Commission or not, have enjoyed unlimited complaint or petition access on behalf of victims to the Commission. In the same vein, like the American Convention, but unlike the First Optional Protocol to the International Covenant on Civil and Political Rights and the European Convention on Human Rights, the African Charter does not contain any primary requirement that petitioners be the actual victims of the Charter violation;[762] neither is it required that the complainants or petitioners be within the jurisdiction of the respondent State.

Pursuant to the empowerment in Article 55 of the Charter, the African Commission, at its tenth anniversary celebration in October 1997, had received a total of 202 communications or complaints submitted by individuals to the Secretariat of the African Commission.[763] This number of communications may sound to be quite enormous, but if matched against the fact that it spans a period of ten years, one may want to agree with the views of Odinkalu, that the Commission

---

[760] This procedure is similar to the procedure of the Inter-American Commission under Article 44 of the American Convention on Human Rights, where individual access to the Inter-American Commission is mandatory rather than optional. Individual access was optional under the European system before its reform, which began with Protocol 9 to the European Convention. Protocol 9 granted limited individual access to the then existing system, and culminated with the present dispensation of direct individual access to a single European Court of Human Rights, the system having done away with the Commission.

[761] *See* The American Convention on Human Rights, Article 44.

[762] *See* Articles 1 and 2 of the First Optional Protocol to the International Covenant on Civil and Political Rights, and old Article 25 (now Article 34) of the European Convention on Human Rights. It should be observed, however, that both systems in their jurisprudence have enlarged upon their concept of victims.

[763] The Communications or petitions can be summarized as follows:- 46 were against States Parties and declared inadmissible, 16 against non State Parties, 7 against non-African States, 2 against non State entities, 25 considered on the merit, 38 declared admissible but pending decision on the merits, 41 pending seizure by the Commission, 2 pending admissibility decision, 13 closed without a decision, 6 withdrawn before any decision was taken, and 6 settled through amicable settlement. *See* A DECADE OF CHALLENGE, *supra,* note 642, at 19. *See* also DECISIONS OF THE AFRICAN COMMISSION ON HUMAN AND PEOPLES' RIGHTS: 1986 – 1997, *supra,* note 364, for some of these communications published by the Commission.

was not only under-capacitated, but also under-utilized.[764] According to Odinkalu, in 1992, a period of five years after the Commission was constituted, the Commission registered only 76 individual communications, a percentage of 15 communications for each of those years. The Commission was to gain an increase of 69 per cent in 1997 when it hit the 200 mark, which was an indication of positive, if marginal, growth in the confidence and capacity of the Commission.[765] Despite the observed increase in the number of communications in the next five years of the Commission after 1992, the point remains that the number of communications is not representative of the number of ratifications that the Charter has received.[766] One would agree that the under-utilization of the Commission in the above sense is not one that the Commission alone would change. It is a responsibility that must be shared between the Commission and States Parties, victims, their representatives and the NGO community. This is more so because the individual complaint or petition procedure is the most effective avenue for positively transforming the Commission's procedure, in that with it, the Commission is confronted with actual cases.[767]

Under Article 55(2) "a communication shall be considered by the Commission if simple majority of its members so decide." In other words, the Commission may decline jurisdiction in a particular case if a simple majority of members so decide. Apart from the general admissibility requirements contained in the Charter and in the Commission's Rules of Procedure, which must be met before the Commission is seized of a communication, there is nothing either in the Charter or in the Rules that spells out the conditions under which members of the Commission may decide not to hear a particular communication or complaint.[768] One

---

764 Chidi Anselm Odinkalu, *The Individual Complaints Procedure of the African Commission on Human and Peoples Rights: A Preliminary Assessment*, 8 TRANSNAT'L L. & CONTEMP. PROBS. 359 at 403 (1998).
765 *Id.*
766 Eritrea, at this time, was the only African Country that had not ratified the Charter apart from Morocco, which withdrew its membership of the OAU. Thus, there were then fifty-three States Parties to the Charter. Even at fifty-two members, given the fact that Ethiopia only recently ratified the Charter, the best average of communications over the last 5 years is 25 per year, which was an overall approximate average of one communication for every two States Parties. *See Odinkalu, supra*, note 764, at 403.
767 *Id.* at 404.
768 In *Ligue Camerounaise des Droits de l'Homme v. Cameroon*, Communication No. 65/92, the Commission held the power vested on it to consider communications, includes a lesser power of declining to hear them. Under the procedure adopted by the secretariat of the Commission, when the secretariat receives a communication pursuant Article 55 against a State Party to the Charter, the communication is registered and a summary of it is made and it is distributed to all the Commissioners. The secretariat however, has to wait for response from at least seven of the eleven Commissioners to indicate that they approve seizure. Alternatively, if the secretariat does not receive a minimum number of seven responses, the communication would be presented to all the Commis-

is left to wonder whether the provision could be read to the effect that, even where a communication meets all admissibility requirements, the Commission could still choose not hear it, where a simple majority of members so decide. One would think that a power to refuse to hear a communication should depend on the admissibility requirements contained in the Charter and Rules of Procedure, in addition to other such specific provisions. Any thing to the contrary will give the Commission an unfettered discretion to reject cases that need to be addressed, and that would be contrary to the Provisions of Article 56, which deals with admissibility.[769]

The jurisdiction of the Commission is limited to communications or complaints against Sates Parties to the African Charter. While a communication against a non-State Party to the African Charter raises a question of jurisdiction, the practice is to consider whether such a communication is receivable. Rule 102(2) of the Commission's Rules of Procedure, provides that "no communication concerning a State which is not a party to the Charter shall be received by the Commission or placed in a list under Rule 103 of the present Rules."[770] Several of the communications declared irreceivable by the Commission were against States not party to the Charter or non-African States or non-states.[771] There were other cases that the Commission declared irreceivable, either because they did not have merit or based on the perceived mental state of the petitioner, even though they were

---

sioners at the next session. At the session, the Commission decides whether to be seized of the communication by determining whether it alleges any *prima facie* violation of the Charter, or whether it is properly submitted according to the provisions of Article 55 of the Charter. If a simple majority of the Commissioners (6) at the session decide that the Commission be seized of the Communication, the communication will be considered on admissibility in a following session. *See* INFORMATION SHEET NO. 3, *supra,* note 750, at 6. It should be noted that the issue as to whether a communication illustrates a *prima facie* violation of the Charter is an admissibility requirement under Article 56.

769 Article 56 of the Charter compels the hearing of a communication if it satisfies the admissibility requirements. It thus becomes difficult for one to see situations under which the Commission would choose not to hear a communication other than based on admissibility.

770 Under Rule 103(1), the Secretary of the Commission prepares a list of communications submitted to the Commission and attaches a brief summary to them for transmission to members of the Commission.

771 For a list of these communications, *see* DECISIONS OF THE AFRICAN COMMISSION ON HUMAN AND PEOPLES' RIGHTS: 1986 – 1997, *supra,* note 364, at 147. Where the Commission declares a communication irreceivable, the secretariat informs the petitioner or author, who could present the communication again if the defect is remedied. For example, where a non State Party becomes a party to the Charter and subject matter of the communication still exists, the author could re-present the communication.

against States Parties.[772] The Commission has been rightly criticized for basing the receivability or otherwise of a communication against a State Party on the mental state of the petitioner rather than on whether there has been a violation of the Charter.[773] The Commission, however, appears determined to abandon its practice on receivability based on the mental state of the author, as it ruled a year after the *Vitine case* that the mental state of an author of a communication is not sufficient legal basis to declare such communication irreceivable, rather it could be based on the lack of coherence of the communication.[774]

2. Bringing an individual communication before the commission

a. Objective

Despite the lack of a provision to that effect in the Charter and its Rules, the African Commission sees the main objective or goal of the individual complaint procedure as initiating "a positive dialogue, resulting in amicable resolution between the complainant and the State concerned, which remedies the prejudice complained of. A pre-requisite for amicably remedying violations of the Charter is the good faith of the parties concerned, including their willingness to participate in a dialogue."[775] In adopting this position, it has been suggested that the Commission appeared to have been inspired by the somewhat inelegant provision in

---

[772] See *Tanko Bariga v. Nigeria*, Communication No. 57/91, ACHPR\LR\A\1, *supra* note 364, at 49, where the petitioner claimed to be a retired Field Marshall in the Nigerian Army who was made to be retired from the Army without benefits. The Commission declared the communication irreceivable as it lacked merit, noting that the highest rank in the Nigerian Army was General and that the compensation claimed was outrageous. *See* also, *Amuh Joseph Vitine v. Cameroon*, Communication No. 106/93, ACHPR\LR\A\1, *supra* note 364, at 122, where the Commission perceived the author to be insane and declared the communication irreceivable.

[773] ANKUMA, *supra*, note 364, at 57.

[774] *Id.* at 58. The Commission made the ruling during its 15th ordinary session in April 1994, held in Banjul, the Gambia.

[775] *See World Organization Against Torture, Lawyers Committee for Human Rights, Union Interafricaine des Droits de l'Homme, Les Temonis de Jehovah v. Zaire*, Communications 25/89, 47/90, 100/93 (Hereafter, the group of cases against Zaire), ACHPR\LR\A\1, *supra*, note 364, at 23. *See also Comité Culturel pour la Démocratie au Bénin, Badjogounme Hailaire, El Haj Boubacar Diawara v. Benin Republic*, Communication Nos.16/88, 17/88, 18/88, (Hereafter, the Group of Cases against Benin Republic), ACHPR\LR\A\1 *supra*, note 364, 11 at 14 ¶ 35, where the Commission noted that " it is the primary objective of the Commission in the communications procedure to initiate a dialogue between the parties which will result in an amicable resolution to the satisfaction of both and which remedies the prejudice complained of...", also reprinted in *Anselm Odinkalu & Camilla Christensen, The African Commission on Human and Peoples' Rights: Development of its Non-State Communication Procedures*, 20 HUM. RTS. QTLY 235 at 244 (1998). *See* also Makau Mutua, *The African Human Rights Court: A Two-Legged Stool?* 21 HUM. RTS. QTLY. 342 at 349 (1999).

Article 52 of the Charter regarding inter-state communications.[776] That Article in effect, enjoins the Commission to have tried all appropriate means in inter-state communications to reach an amicable solution based on the respect for human and peoples' rights before preparing a report of its findings to be sent to the States involved and the Assembly of Heads of State and Government of the OAU.[777] The question has been raised whether an inter-state procedure, such as that established by Article 52, which aims to remedy inter-state disputes between sovereign parties, usually through political prescriptions, is an appropriate source of inspiration for individual complaints or communications.[778]

This author is of the view that there may be nothing absolutely wrong in the Commission having as one of its objectives, the realization of amicable resolution of human rights disputes presented by individual complaints, even though that objective is inspired by a procedure reserved for inter-state communications. What is wrong, is using the same standard for both inter-state communications and individual complaints in interpreting that objective. While States may use diplomatic means to resolve their disputes, disputes involving violation of individual human rights require much more than dialogue and amicable resolution guided by diplomatic principles, or principles that protect the interests of States over and above those of individuals. The Commission appears not to take into consideration the objective of an individual or an NGO in bringing a complaint to the Commission. Most individuals are not just seeking dialogue, they are seeking justice in accordance with the provisions of the Charter, and also, not a personal vendetta against the violating state.

One will agree with the view that the objective of amicable resolution as enunciated by the Commission is both objective and subjective.[779] It is objective in that the "good faith of the parties concerned, including their willingness to participate in a dialogue is a pre-requisite." Similarly, the amicable resolution must remedy the prejudice complained of. On the other hand, it is subjective in the sense that the amicable settlement must be to the satisfaction of the parties.[780]

---

776 *Odinkalu & Christensen, supra,* note 775, at 423.
777 This principle of amicable resolution of human rights disputes is commonly referred to as friendly settlement in other human rights systems. *See* Article 41(e) of International Covenant on Civil and Political Rights, Article 48 (1)(f) of the American Convention and Article 28(b) (now Article 38(1)(b)) of the European Convention. It should be observed that the American Convention envisages friendly settlement for both individual petition and inter-state communications, while the European Convention limits friendly settlement to petitions submitted by individuals and NGOs. The international covenant like the African Charter appears to specifically provide for it in inter-state complaints.
778 *Odinkalu & Christensen supra,* note 775, at 243.
779 *Id.* at 245.
780 *See* the group of communications against Republic of Benin, *supra,* note 364, at 14 ¶ 35.

It is this criterion upon which the effectiveness of the individual complaints procedure should be based. The question then is, what does the Commission do to ascertain whether the parties are or are not satisfied? Another question that the Commission appears not to have addressed is whether it is in all cases that amicable settlement would be required.[781]

The practice of the Commission on the principle of amicable settlement on some occasions tends to negate the criterion that the parties must be satisfied, as a remedy to the violation of the Charter complained of. There seems to be an undue favor of the States Parties over individuals whose rights have been violated. One of those cases for which the Commission has been criticized in this regard is *Henry Kalenga v. Zambia*.[782] In this case, Henry Kalenga had been held in detention without trial since February 27, 1986. He brought a complaint to the Commission on August 2, 1988 seeking immediate release. Thereafter, the Commission did not receive any further information from him. On March 5, 1991, the Commission received information from the Ministry of Legal Affairs of Zambia that the complainant was released from prison in 1989, and thereafter held that the case had been amicably resolved. According to the Commission:

> When a complainant ceases to correspond with the Commission, this has serious implications for the communications procedure. The Commission must determine if the lack of communication is due to disability, or a desire to cease pursuit of the case. Where the complainant is an individual, the Commission cannot automatically interpret silence as withdrawal of the communication because individuals are highly vulnerable to circumstances that might prevent them from continuing to prosecute a communication.[783] In the instant case, a member of the Commission has had direct contact with the state concerned and is satisfied that the complainant was released last year.[784] Thus, the Commission interprets the complainant's failure to pursue the communication as evidence of satisfaction with the outcome.[785] For these reasons, the Commission *wel-*

---

781 The Commission has not addressed this issue. Its practice however, appears to insinuate that it has to be applied in all cases. The experience of other systems has shown that in exceptional circumstances, where circumstances of the controversy make the option unsuitable or unnecessary, amicable resolution may be skipped, especially if based on the behavior of the state accused of the violation. *See* the decision of the Inter-American Court of Human Rights in *Caballero Delgado and Santana v. Colombia*, Preliminary Objections, Judgment of 21 January, 1994. Series C No. 17, *reprinted* in BUERGENTHAL & SHELTON, PROTECTING HUMAN RIGHTS IN THE AMERICAS: CASES AND MATERIALS, *supra*, note 110, at 124.
782 *Henry Kalenga v. Zambia*, Communication 11/88. *See* ACHPR\LR\A\1, *supra*, note 364, 7 at 8. *See* also *Odinkalu & Camilla Christensen supra*, note 775, at 245. *See* also *Civil Liberties Organization v. Nigeria*, Commuication 67/91, ACHPR\LR\A\1, *supra*, note 364, 71 at 72.
783 *Henry Kalenga v. Zambia*, ACHPR\LR\A\1, *supra* note 364 at 8 ¶ 12.
784 *Id.* ¶ 13.
785 *Id.* ¶ 14.

comes the government's release of the complainant *finds* the case amicably resolved.[786] (Emphasis by the Commission)

In the above decision, the Commission shows that it made contact with the government concerned, but does not show that it made contact with the complainant to ascertain whether indeed the release from prison was an amicable settlement of the complaint, in which the complainant was satisfied. The failure of the Commission to ascertain this appears to be a departure from its own injunction in this case, to the effect that individual complainants "are highly vulnerable to circumstances that might prevent them from continuing to prosecute a communication." The Commission should have attempted making contact with the complainant in the same way it did the State Party, despite the lack of correspondence from the complainant; more so, since the Commission did not know the circumstances surrounding the lack of correspondence. While it is necessary for a complainant to maintain correspondence with the Commission, the mere release of the complainant from prison cannot of itself, and based upon the information supplied by the defending State Party, amount to amicable resolution, which remedies the prejudice complained against, to the satisfaction of the parties without a corroboration from the complainant.

The decision of the Commission in the *Kalenga case* follows its earlier decision in the group of cases against the Republic of Benin, where the Commission found that an amicable resolution had been reached.[787] In these cases the Commission ruled in relevant parts that:

> In these cases there is evidence that the new government has attempted to remedy the injustices committed by the previous administration. It has repealed many of the laws such that detention of individuals on the basis on which the persons in these communications were held would no longer be possible. In addition, the Commission notes the release of political prisoners and of the introduction of amnesty laws. All of the individuals in these particular cases have been released as a result of the new government's actions.[788] In the absence of any dissatisfaction expressed from the complainants, with whom previous correspondence has been regular, the Commission may assume that the actions taken by the government remedy the prejudiced complaint.[789]

---

[786] *Id.* This decision was taken at the 7th session of the Commission in Banjul, the Gambia in April 1990.
[787] *Comité Culturel pour la Démocratie au Bénin, Badjogounme Hailaire, El Haj Boubacar Diawara v. Benin Republic*, Communications 16/88, 17/88, 18/88, ACHPR\LR\A\1, *supra* note 364, at 15.
[788] *Id.* at ¶ 39.
[789] *Id.* ¶ 40.

The finding by the commission also tends to defeat the criterion of good faith dialogue in addition to the requirement of satisfaction of the parties. As has been asserted earlier, the absence of any dissatisfaction expressed from the complainants, is not necessarily a sufficient basis for assuming the presence of satisfaction on their part.[790]

In all these cases, one would be persuaded by the view that it is difficult to maintain that the Commission facilitated or maintained amicable settlement to the satisfaction of the parties.[791] Apart from the issue of contact with the complainants, vis-à-vis the defending State Parties, which is grossly inadequate, the Commission commits the fallacy of generalizing positive actions of State Parties as adequate remedy for the violations complained of, without the input of the victims. Where does the Commission place the issue of damages and compensation? From the ruling of the Commission in these cases, it is doubtful that the views of the complainants were sought regarding terms of settlement of the cases, if any.[792] Most complainants want compensation and damages as a remedy, in addition to a declaration by the Commission that a State's action is a violation of the Charter. The Commission has been reluctant to make such findings and has not been known to have presented the issue of compensation as an integral part of amicable settlement. In other regional human rights systems, the effect of friendly settlement is that the complainants or petitioners and the State Parties reach an agreement facilitated by the Commission, the terms of which are used in declaring amicable settlement, especially where damages are awarded.[793]

b. Admissibility requirements

In addition to the jurisdictional requirements of the Charter in which the Commission determines its competence to receive individual complaints, the Charter lists additional admissibility requirements that such communications must fulfil before they are considered by the Commission on the merits. Article 56 of the Charter outlines seven requirements in this regard, as follows:

---

[790] See Odinkalu & Camilla Christensen supra, note 775, at 246.
[791] Id.
[792] Id.at 247.
[793] See the decision of the Inter-American Commission on Human Rights on cases 10.299, 10.310, 10.496, 10.631 and 19.771 against Argentina, ANNUAL REPORT OF THE INTER-AMERICAN COMMISSION ON HUMAN RIGHTS, 1992-1993, OEA/Ser.L/V/II.83, doc. 14. 1, March 12, 1993, pp. 35-40, reprinted in BUERGENTHAL & SHELTON, PROTECTING HUMAN RIGHTS IN THE AMERICAS: CASES AND MATERIALS, supra, note 110, 125 at 128.

Communications relating to human and peoples' rights referred to in Article 55 received by the Commission, shall be considered if they:

1. Indicate their authors even if the latter request anonymity;
2. Are compatible with the Charter of the Organization of African Unity or with the present Charter'
3. Are not written in disparaging or insulting language against the State concerned and its institutions or to the Organization of African Unity,
4. Are not based exclusively on news disseminated through the mass media,
5. Are sent after exhausting local remedies if any, unless it is obvious that this procedure is unduly prolonged,
6. Are submitted within a reasonable period from the time local remedies are exhausted or from the date the Commission is seized with the matter, and
7. Do not deal with cases which have been settled by these States involved in accordance with the principles of the Charter of the United Nations, or the Charter of the Organization of African Unity or the provisions of the present Charter.[794]

As seen earlier, the secretariat of the Commission must complete the administrative aspects of the communications procedure in accordance with the Charter and the Rules of Procedure of the Commission before the Commissions proceeds to ensure that the admissibility requirements are met.[795] Thus, once the Commission is seized of a communication, a decision has to be taken as to its admissibility: a determination whether the seven conditions outlined by Article 56 have been met. As a matter of principle, all the conditions must be met for a communication to be declared admissible. The decision on admissibility can only be taken after the text of the communication or a brief summary of it has been transmitted to the State Party concerned as an opportunity for it to make its observations.[796] Under its Rules of Procedure, the Commission, generally gives the State Party three

---

[794] African Charter, Article 56. *See* also GUIDELINES ON THE SUBMISSION OF COMMUNICATIONS (INFORMATION SHEET NO. 2) *supra*, note 748, at 10; INFORMATION SHEET NO. 3 *supra*, note 750, at 7-10, and RULES OF PROCEDURE OF THE COMMISSION, *supra*, note 680, Rule 116. Other international and regional human rights instruments contain similar admissibility requirements, with varying differences. *See* Article 5(2) (a) and (b) of the Optional Protocol to the International Covenant on Civil and Political Rights. 999 U.N.T.S 171, I.L.M. 383 (1967), adopted by the U.N. General Assembly at New York on December 16, 1966.G. A. Res. 2200, entered into force on March 23, 1976; Articles 46 & 47 of the American Convention on Human Rights, and old Article 27 (now Article 35) of the European Convention on Human Rights.

[795] *See* INFORMATION SHEET NO. 3, *supra* note 750, at 6.

[796] African Charter, Article 47. *See* also RULES OF PROCEDURE OF THE COMMISSION, *supra*, note 680, Rule 112, and INFORMATION SHEET NO. 3 *supra*, note 750, at 11.

months within which to submit its comments.[797] Because of the incessant delays on the part of States parties in responding to Communications in the past, the Commission has adopted a practice whereby communications are declared admissible if a response is not received from the State Party concerned at the end of three months.[798] The Commission, however, will be willing to review an admissibility decision made in default of response by a State, if there emerge subsequently, new facts that alter the basis of the decision.[799]

When a decision on admissibility is taken on a communication, it is transmitted to both the complainant and the State concerned.[800] Except in circumstances indicated above, generally, a decision on admissibility is final. Thus, if a communication is declared inadmissible, the reason for the inadmissibility would be indicated and this will automatically bring consideration of the communication to a close. To balance up its practice, the Commission allows the reviving of a communication declared inadmissible to be revisited at a later date, if the complainant can provide information to the effect that the grounds for inadmissibility no longer exist.[801] Where, however, a communication is declared admissible, the parties will be informed and requested to send their observations on the merits.

It is pertinent to consider the practice developed by the Commission on the admissibility requirements in the light of how it has enhanced the effectiveness or otherwise, of the mechanism established by the Charter.

---

[797] See RULES OF PROCEDURE OF THE COMMISSION, *supra*, note 680, Rule 117(4). Despite the three months time limit provision of this rule, the Commission has practically allowed States Parties longer time to respond to communications. It is alleged that in some cases it took the Commission up to six years to decide on admissibility. See *Odinkalu & Christensen, supra*, note 775, at 250, referring to the *World Organization against Torture* group of cases against Zaire, *supra*, note 775.

[798] RULES OF PROCEDURE OF THE COMMISSION, *supra*, note 680, Rule 117(2) and (4). This provision was not in the old Rules of Procedure of the Commission. The Commission adopted this procedure as a way of confronting the undue delay on the part of as States Parties in responding to communications. This accords with the principle inherent in international human rights dispute resolution as in other aspects of adjudication.

[799] *Lawyers Committee for Human Rights v. Tanzania*, Communication 66/92, ACHPR\LR\A\1, *supra*, note 364, 69 at 70, ¶¶ 10 -14, also *reprinted* in *Odinkalu & Christensen, supra*, note 775, at 250. In this complaint, the Commission had made an admissibility decision based on non existence or undue prolongation of exhaustion of domestic remedies after waiting for Tanzania's response for over seven months. The Commission however, set aside its admissibility decision after it received information to the contrary.

[800] RULES OF PROCEDURE OF THE COMMISSION, Rule 118(1).

[801] *Id.* Rule 118(2). *See* also, INFORMATION SHEET NO. 3 *supra*, note 750, at 12.

3. Inclusion of author's name

A communication or complaint submitted to the Commission must indicate the name of the author even though the author desires anonymity.[802] The Commission would normally respect the wishes of the author in remaining anonymous, provided anonymity is requested by such author, but for its own purpose, authors of communications must indicate their names.[803] The Commission stretches the requirement of author's name further, by requiring in addition, the address of authors, basically to facilitate correspondence between the Commission's secretariat and complainants. Any communication that did not contain the address of its author was declared inadmissible in part for this reason.[804] The Commission reasoned that for practical reasons, it was necessary that it be able to communicate with, and contact the author, even though the address of the author is not one of the requirements under Article 56 of the Charter.[805]

In requiring the names of authors of communication, the African Commission avoided a mandatory linkage between the authors and victims in the sense of requiring that authors must be alleged victims of rights violations as is provided under the European Convention and Optional Protocol to the Covenant on Civil and Political Rights.[806] The Commission has rather adopted a broad interpretation of Article 55 of the Charter to the effect that "other communications" actually connotes those that are brought by entities other than states. It would therefore, not matter whether complainants are victims themselves or other persons or NGOs on behalf of the victims.[807] The Commission sees this position as "a clear response to practical difficulties faced by individuals in Africa and the often serious or massive violations in Africa that may preclude individual victims from pursuing national or international legal remedies on their own behalf."[808] It is commendable that the Commission recognizes the need to interpret the Charter to enhance effective protection of human rights in Africa. One would expect that this state

---

[802] See the African Charter, Article 56. See also GUIDELINES ON THE SUBMISSION OF COMMUNICATIONS (INFORMATION SHEET NO. 2) supra, note 748, at 10; INFORMATION SHEET NO. 3 supra, note 750, at 7-10, and RULES OF PROCEDURE OF THE COMMISSION, supra, note 680, Rule 116.
[803] See the group of cases against Zaire, supra, note 775.
[804] Tanko Bariga v. Nigeria, Communication 57/91, ACHPR\LR\A\1, supra, note 364, at 49 ¶ 8.
[805] Id.
[806] See supra, note 762.
[807] NGOs routinely petition the Commission on behalf of victims of alleged human rights violations. There is no particular requirement that the NGOs must be based in a State Party to the Charter or African by constitution.
[808] See the group of cases against Zaire, supra, note 775, ¶ 51. On how to submit a communication to the Commission pursuant to Article 55 of the Charter, see generally, INFORMATION SHEET NO. 2, supra, note 748, at 15.

of mind of the Commission will permeate other aspects of the Commission's interpretations.

4. Compatibility with the provisions of the OAU charter or the african charter

The requirement under Article 56(2) of the Charter that a communication must be compatible with the provisions of the OAU Charter or the African Charter before it is admissible, raises some controversy as to the effect of the OAU Charter in this regard. It has been rightly argued that a reading of this provision reveals a possible interpretation that a communication should either be compatible with the Charter of OAU or the African human rights Charter – a suggestion that the OAU Charter itself is a source of rights.[809] It is understandable that a complaint pursuant to the provisions of the African Charter should show a violation under the Charter. On the other hand, the Charter of the OAU does not contain any substantive rights provision. Requiring that a communication under the human rights Charter be compatible with the Charter of the OAU only raises political considerations to which the African Charter will be subjected. Neither the African Charter nor the Rules of the Commission contain any explanation as to the inclusion of the OAU Charter in the above subsection. The inclusion of the OAU Charter, one would think, is to reinforce the principle of non-interference in the so called internal affairs of OAU Member States as the decision of the Commission in the case of *Katangese Peoples' Congress v. Zaire*[810] has shown.

Despite the mention of the OAU Charter, the Commission's practice generally under Article 56(2) of the African Charter is to require that a compliant or communication must show *prima facie* violations of the African Charter to be admissible.[811] Such communications must also not be vague,[812] and must provide sufficient information on which the communication is based.[813] The Commission appears not to have specified tangible indications of *prima facie* violations of the Charter, as some cases that would ordinarily be seen to contain such evidence were ruled inadmissible on that basis.[814] There is thus a need for consistency

---

809 *Odinkalu & Christensen, supra,* note 775, at 253
810 *Supra,* note 531.
811 See *Frederick Korvah v. Liberia,* Communication No. 1/88, ACHPR\LR\A\1, *supra* note 364, at 6 ¶ 6. See also *Ligue Camerounaise des Droits de l'Homme v. Cameroon, supra* note 768.
812 *Seyoun Ayele v. Togo,* Communication No. 35/89, ACHPR\LR\A\1, *supra* note 364, at 35 ¶ 4.
813 *Hadjali Mohaand v. Algeria,* Communication No. 13/88, *Id.,* at 9, ¶ 5.
814 See *Congress for the Second Republic of Malawi v. Malawi,* Communication No. 63/92, *Id.* at 62, ¶ 8. Here the Commission found the communication irreceiveable based on admissibility finding that it was of a general nature and did not allege any specific violation of the Charter in spite of the fact that the communication contained allegations of killing of students taking part in demonstrations, the expulsion of civil servants and teachers of Northern origin, etc. At the same 30th ordinary

to avoid denying individuals or groups the opportunity to challenge the violation of their rights under the Charter. Whether or not a communication raises a *prima facie* violation of the Charter should be based on whether a right contained in the Charter is actually alleged to have been violated, irrespective of whether a particular article of the Charter is cited. This will ensure that the Commission does not overemphasize form at the expense of substance. While form may be important in legal procedures, international protection of human rights is a different breed of such procedures, which may not adhere strictly to the rules on form.

On the issue of compatibility with the Charter of the OAU, the Commission has shown its willingness to subject group and peoples' rights to that test as evidenced in *Katangese Peoples' Congress v. Zaire*,[815] where it decided that the right to self-determination demanded by the Katanga people had no merit under the African Charter because it was not compatible with Article 56(2) as it was in effect, contrary to the principles contained in the Charter of the OAU. According to the Commission, self-determination for the Katanga people is not self-determination for all Zaireans as a people, and as such, the Commission must uphold the sovereignty and territorial integrity of Zaire, a member of the OAU.[816] Subjecting the African Charter to these types of influences by the Charter of the OAU will affect the effectiveness of the Charter in checking the excesses of States Parties to the Charter.

5. Communications not to contain disparaging or insulting language

This provision has been used by the Commission to strike down an otherwise important communication that documented egregious and massive violation of human rights in Cameroon.[817] Unfortunately, the Commission failed to use that opportunity to define what would amount to disparaging and insulting language

---

session of the Commission in which this case was decided, the *Chirwa* group of cases against Malawi, *supra,* note 364, one of which was brought by Amnesty International, were declared admissible because they "gave evidence of a series of serious or massive violations of human rights in Malawi." *See also,* ACHPR\LR\A\1, *supra* note 364, at 63. Some commentators see this disparity in the decision of the Commission to be as a result of the Commission attaching more importance to one author of a communication than the other. *See Odinkalu & Christensen, supra,* note 775, at 254, who assert that the only difference between these cases is that a political party not well known to the Commission submitted one communication, whereas the other communication involved Amnesty International, an NGO whose work the Commission was well acquainted with.

815 *Supra,* note 531. *See also* ACHPR\LR\A\1, *supra,* note 364, at 90, also *reprinted* in *Odinkalu & Christensen supra,* note 775, at 254.
816 *See Odinkalu & Christensen supra,* note 775, at 254.
817 *Ligue Camerounaise des Droits de l'Homme v. Cameroon, supra,* note 768, *reprinted* in *Odinkalu & Christensen supra,* note 775, at 255.

in the context of communications against States Parties. The requirement under Article 56(3) that, to be admissible, communications must not be written in disparaging or insulting language directed against the State, its institutions or the Organization of African Unity, generally lacks clarity. Under the Charter, only States Parties can be petitioned against to the Commission, not their entities or the OAU. Could the drafters of the Charter be outlawing insulting and disparaging languages directed against State entities or the OAU in a communication against a State Party?

In *Ligue Camerounaise des Droits de l'Homme v. Cameroon*, the communication alleged the existence of serious and massive violations of human rights in Cameroon between 1984 and 1989, documenting at least forty-six cases of torture and deprivation of food, repression of free expression, denial of fair hearing, ethnic discrimination, and massacres of civilian populations. The communication contained such statements as "Paul Biya (Cameroon's President) must respond to crimes against humanity," the regime of torturers," and "government barbarisms." While noting that the allegations in the communication constituted a series of serious and massive violations of human rights, the Commission declared the communication inadmissible because of the above phrases, which the Commission held to be "insulting language."

No other international or regional human rights instrument contains this nondisparaging language requirement for purposes of admissibility. One would agree with the observation that the decision of the Commission sets a dangerous precedent in making the provisions of Article 56(3) subjective to the evoked feelings of States Parties.[818] In the opinion of this author, the decision of the Commission amounts to a deprivation of freedom of expression by a human rights implementation organ. It deliberately dismisses the frustrations of victims of human rights abuses and fails to recognize that violations of human rights naturally evoke considerable passion because of the involvement of human life and well being.[819] The so called insulting language of that communication could be the only way a victim of torture could express his or her pain. What is even more disturbing is that the Commission did not find the allegations contained in the communication unsubstantiated. The fact that it based its admissibility decision on a broad interpretation of insulting and disparaging language gives a cause for concern. This is so because from all indications, Article 56(3) will become a basis for the Commission to declare a communication inadmissible even if the veracity of the

---

[818] *Odinkalu & Christensen supra,* note 775, at 255.
[819] *Id.*

allegations contained in it is undoubted or uncontested.[820] The Commission must find a way to remedy this dangerous application of Article 56(3).

6.   Communications not exclusively based on mass media news

Article 56(4) of the Charter stipulates another admissibility requirement to the effect that a communication must not be based exclusively on news disseminated through the mass media. This is another provision on admissibility that is unique to the African Charter, as no other human rights instrument provides for a similar admissibility requirement. Though the Charter does not indicate the reason for this provision, it appears that the provision is aimed at ensuring that authors of communication must be able to investigate and ascertain the truth of the facts before requesting for the Commission's intervention.[821] One would also think that the provision is an indication of dislike for the private mass media by African countries which generally see the mass media not controlled by their governments as oppositions, which in turn, would always distort news items against States. While it is important that allegations contained in communications be verifiable, there would be situations where authors of communications may not gain the requisite investigational access and therefore, must depend on the news disseminated through the mass media, especially where the mass media is credible. Mainstream mass media has been known to be respectable and credible in news reporting. In fact, the mass media ought to play a part in ensuring respect for human rights. The gripe many African leaders have against private mass media is one of fear of being exposed for incessant egregious and gross violations of human rights.

Despite the seeming dislike for the mass media by the drafters of the African Charter, the above requirement has not posed any significant problems in the Commission's admissibility decisions. The Commission is even known to take judicial notice of occurrences in certain Member States, which are generally known through the mass media in consideration of complaints.[822] Thus, the Commission appears to have adopted an approach of totally not discrediting a complaint even though it would have been based on news disseminated through the mass media. In two communications that are yet to be made public by the Commission,[823] despite the allegation by the State Party involved that the communications should

---

[820] *Id.*
[821] *See* INFORMATION SHEET NO. 3, *supra,* note 750, at 9.
[822] ANKUMA, *supra,* note 363, at 64.
[823] Communication Nos. 147/95 and 149/96, *cited* in INFORMATION SHEET NO. 3, *supra* note 750, at 9.

be declared inadmissible because they were exclusively based on news disseminated through the mass media, the Commission declared them admissible.

7. Exhaustion of local remedies

Many, if not all international and regional human rights instruments generally require the exhaustion of domestic legal remedies in human rights disputes against States Parties to those instruments before such disputes are presented before supervisory organs that are created for enforcing the instruments.[824] The requirement for exhaustion of domestic remedies is thus a generally accepted principle of international law to the effect that a State should have the opportunity to provide redress of a wrong under its own legal system before international redress may be invoked against that State.[825]

As in other human rights systems, the African Commission has elaborately deliberated on the exhaustion of domestic remedies, albeit with varying degrees of consistency with generally accepted international standards. Article 56 (5) requires admissibility of communications that "are sent after exhausting local remedies, if any, unless it is obvious that this procedure is unduly prolonged." An interpretation of this subsection would reveal that exhaustion of domestic remedies is required unless such remedies do not exist, or where they exist, they are unduly prolonged to make recourse to them ineffective. Some scholars have rightly argued that the African Charter on its face, is restrictive of the international standards in requiring exhaustion of domestic remedies by excepting the requirement only where the procedures for domestic remedies is unduly prolonged.[826] The argument is that the Charter does not appear to provide relief in situations where domestic remedies, though not unduly prolonged, would be inadequate or where local laws do not ensure due process.[827] This reasoning is informed by the emphasis that the old Rules of Procedure of the Commission placed on the "unduly prolonged" criterion as the only exception to the requirement of exhaustion of domestic remedies under the African system, which influenced early admissibil-

---

824 *See* Article 5(2)(b), First Optional Protocol to the International Covenant on Civil and Political Rights; Article 46(a), American Convention on Human Rights, and old Article 26 (now Article 35(1) of the European Convention on Human Rights.

825 *See* the *Interhandel Case* (Preliminary Objections), ICJ Rep. 7 (1959), *reprinted* in SCOTT DAVIDSON, THE INTER-AMERICAN HUMAN RIGHTS SYSTEM, *supra,* note 229, at 158; *Exceptions to the Exhaustion of Domestic Remedies Case*, Advisory Opinion OC-11/90 of August10, 1990. Series A No. 11. Inter-American Court of Human Rights, OEA/Ser.L/V/III.23/Doc.12, ¶ 34 (1990), *reprinted* in BUERGENTHAL & SHELTON, *supra,* note 110, at 106, and in *Odinkalu and Christensen, supra,* note 775, at 256.

826 ANKUMA, *supra* note 363, at 67.

827 *Id.*

ity decisions of the Commission.[828] This deviates from the generally accepted standard, the requirement of exhaustion of domestic remedies "in accordance with generally recognized principles of international law."[829]

With the adoption of the new Rules of Procedure of the Commission in 1995, it appears that the Commission is willing to follow other systems in subjecting the requirement for exhaustion of domestic remedies to the standard of generally recognized principles of international law. Present Rule 116 of the Rules of Procedure simply provides that "the Commission shall determine questions of admissibility pursuant to Article 56 of the Charter." It would thus appear that the Commission would do this, taking into consideration Articles 60 and 61 of the Charter which requires the Commission to apply principles recognized in international law in carrying out its mandates.

As has earlier been alluded to, the practice of the Commission with regard to exhaustion of domestic remedies has been a mixture of a struggle between an extremely formalistic interpretation of the Charter and the need to be seen as developing the jurisprudence of the individual complaint mechanism of the African system. The Commission has on many occasions ensured that communications complied with the exhaustion of domestic remedies' requirement. Thus, communications based on claims pending in national courts have been declared inadmissible for non-exhaustion of domestic remedies.[830] Similarly, the Commission has held that the requirement to exhaust local remedies in appropriate cases,

---

828 The Old Rule 114(3)provided that "in order to decide on the admissibility of a communication, pursuant to the provisions of the Charter, the Commission shall ensure: (g) that the alleged victim has exhausted all the available local remedies or that the process of such remedies are unduly taking a long time." *See* FIRST ACTIVITY REPORT OF THE AFRICAN COMMISSION ON HUMAN AND PEOPLES RIGHTS, 8 (April 28, 1988) covering the period from November 1987 through April 1988 (1st to 3rd Session).

829 These are the exact words of Article 46 of the American Convention, and substantially that of the old Article 26 (new 35(1)) of the European Convention. The provision of the African Charter is inspired by that of Article 5(2)(b) of the First Protocol to the International Covenant on Civil and Political Rights, which requires exhaustion of "all available" domestic remedies unless "the application of the remedies is unreasonably prolonged." The difference, however, is that while the Human Rights Committee has interpreted the above provision in accordance with generally recognized principles of international law, the African Commission insisted on a rigid interpretation for almost a decade.

830 *See Civil Liberties Organization v. Nigeria*, Communication No. 45/90, ACHPR\LR\A\1, *supra*, note 364, 43, at 44, ¶ 14, also *reprinted* in *Odinkalu and Christensen, supra* note 760, at 256. *See* also *Kenya Human Rights Commission v. Kenya*, Communication No. 135/94, ACHPR\LR\A\1, *supra* note 364, at 134. The Commission has, however, held that where a group of communications dealing with the same fact pattern has been consolidated, the fact that, there are pending domestic proceedings in one or some of the communications will not necessarily affect or prejudice the admissibility of the others, especially where serious and massive violation of human rights are involved. *See* the *Group of Cases against Benin Republic*, *supra*, note 364, 11, at 13, ¶ 26.

includes an obligation to exhaust appellate procedures.[831] The complication here, however, is that the Commission does not seem to see the refusal to allow a complainant the leave to appeal a decision of a lower domestic court as amounting to exhaustion of local remedies. In *Paul Haye v. The Gambia*[832] the fact that the complainant's domestic action was not allowed to go on by the Court of Appeal left him with no further option of remedy. That should have made the Commission to find an exhaustion of domestic remedies. In the same vein, the decision of the Commission in *Kenya Human Rights Commission v. Kenya*[833] did not see an alleged pronouncement by President Arap Moi, the President of Kenya that the remedy sought by the complaints before a domestic court will not be granted, as operating to make any available local remedies ineffective and inadequate. The Commission ought to have found that such pronouncement by the President of a State Party, especially in Africa where rulers are usually powerful beyond the ordinary, would render any available remedy ineffective. It should not have mattered that the dispute giving rise to the communication was still pending in court. There was no guarantee that the presidential pronouncement would not affect the outcome of the matter, nor the length of time it would take to exhaust local remedies in the face of the threat from the President.

In recent times, however, the Commission has tried to embrace the doctrine of adequate and effective exhaustion of local remedies, by attempting to read into the provisions of Article 56(5), the requirement that there must be effective exhaustion of local remedies even though the Charter does not expressly define the threshold of effectiveness that local remedies must meet before they are considered to be required for exhaustion. This has not always been the case, as

---

831 *Paul Haye v. The Gambia*, Communication No. 90/93, ACHPR\LR\A\1, *supra*, note 364, at 105. In this case, the Gambian Supreme Court entered a default judgement on May 28, 1991 in a civil suit against the Communication's author. The trial judge denied the author's application to set aside the judgment. On the same day the same judge also denied the author's application for leave to appeal against the refusal to set aside the judgment. The rules of the Supreme Court applicable to civil proceedings in the Gambia allowed for a further application for leave to appeal. Such an appeal must be made to the Court of Appeal within fourteen days. Under these rules, the Court of Appeal has discretion to allow such an application to be made even after expiration of fourteen days. Here the Court of Appeal refused the communication author's application for review of the Supreme Court's decision denying him an appeal because the application was late for six months. Based on these facts, the Commission declared the communication inadmissible on the ground that national judicial authorities rejected the case as being out of time or for failure to meet other formal requirements. The Commission further observed that if subsequently, the possibility to effectively appeal out of time existed, the author must do so in order to exhaust his domestic remedies. See *Odinkalu and Christensen, supra,* note 775, at 257, where this case is elaborately reprinted.
832 *Paul Haye v. The Gambia*, Id.
833 *Supra*, note 830.

the Commission had been reluctant to do this in earlier complaints.[834] The change of direction by the Commission is commendable, as it will bring the jurisprudence of the African system in line with standards applicable in international law. In the rethinking of its position on this issue, the Commission agrees that a discretionary and extraordinary remedy of a non-judicial nature is both inadequate and ineffective.[835]

Apart from the above set of cases, the Commission has extended the adequate and effective remedy requirement to cases involving serious and massive violation of human and peoples rights. It should be recalled that Article 58 of the Charter attaches some importance to such cases in that they require urgent attention. As in many other cases, the Commission's application of the adequate and effective doctrine in cases revealing serious or massive violation of human rights is inconsistent. In the *group of cases against Zaire*,[836] the Commission innovatively held that:

> The Commission must read Article 56.5 in the light of its duty to ensure the protection of the human and peoples' rights under the conditions laid down by the Charter. The Commission cannot hold the requirement of exhaustion of local remedies to apply literally in cases where it is impractical or undesirable for the complainant to seize the

---

[834] In *Civil Liberties Organization v. Nigeria, supra,* note 830, though the dispute in question was pending before domestic courts, the complainants had secured some interim orders against the government of Nigeria, which orders were not obeyed. Inspite of these orders, the violations continued. The Commission failed to recognize that the local remedy in this case could possibly not have been able to offer protection against the violations complained of. A deliberate disobedience of Court orders by a State Party should have left no doubt in the mind of the Commission that the available local remedies cannot prove to be effective.

[835] See *Constitutional Rights Project (Wahab Akamu et al.) v. Nigeria,* Communication No. 60/91, ACHPR\LR\A\1, *supra* note 364, 55, at 57, also *reprinted* in *Odinkalu and Christensen, supra,* note 775, at 258-259. In this case, the authors of the communication brought it on behalf of, Wahab Akamu, Gbolahan Adeaga, and others sentenced to death under the Robbery and Firearms (Special Provisions) Decree No. 5 of 1984. Under this Decree, special tribunals composed of retired judges, members of the armed forces and the police were set up to try suspected armed robbers. The Decree prohibited any judicial appeals against sentences rendered by the tribunals. The only remedy available to those convicted was either a confirmation or otherwise of the sentences by the governor of a state. The Commission decided that the Decree, which subjected the faith of the convicts to the whims and caprice of a state governor, created a discretionary extraordinary remedy of a non-judicial nature, with the object of the convicts obtaining favor rather than a vindication of right. It further held that it would be improper to insist that the complainants should seek remedies from sources which did not operate impartially and had no obligation to decide according to legal principles. That remedy according to the Commission was "neither adequate nor effective." *See also Recontre Africaine pour la Defense des Droits de l'Homme (RADDHO) v. Zambia,* Communication No. 71/92, ACHPR\LR\A\1, *supra,* note 364,77, at 79, ¶¶ 26-33. In this case the Commission held that local remedies available to West Africans massly deported from Zambia were, in effect, either unavailable or ineffective.

[836] *Supra* note 775.

domestic courts in the case of each individual complaint. This is the case where there are a large number of individual victims. Due to the seriousness of the human rights situation as well as the great number of people involved, such remedies as might theoretically exist in the domestic courts are as a practical matter unavailable or, in the words of the Charter "unduly prolonged.[837]

It appears that the Commission, in addition to the seriousness of the human rights issues involved, also lays emphasis on the number of people involved in the above communication. If that is the case, one wonders why its decision was different in *Union des Scolaires Nigeriens-Union Generale des Etudients Nigeriens au Benin v. Niger.*[838] This case involved a union representing students in Niger Republic, who engaged in a peaceful demonstration after negotiations between them and the government had failed. The demonstration was violently broken up by security agents leaving 14 people dead, 132 people injured with 13 of them seriously injured. A number of teachers and students were arrested and detained. Similar events took place elsewhere in the country with the death of several school children. The situation worsened when a number of other unions became involved.[839] The Commission held that it could not continue with the matter as there was no information from the complainant regarding the exhaustion of local remedies, irrespective of the fact that the government of Niger did not respond to the Commission's request for information on the complaint.[840] The Commission ought not to have dismissed the communication for non exhaustion of local remedies in light of its decision in the *group of cases against Zaire*. This case presented not only a high number of people whose rights were violated, it revealed massive and serious violations of human rights. The fact that the Commission neither heard further from the Complainants nor the government of Niger should have alerted it as to the seriousness of the situation.[841]

The Commission, has however, been forthright in identifying that exhaustion of local remedies is not required where there is apparently no such remedy. This naturally flows from the requirement of Article 56(5) that communications should be accepted *inter alia,* "after exhausting local remedies, if any..." In most of the cases where the Commission has found the non existence of local remedies, it

---

[837] *Id.* at 22, ¶¶ 56-58
[838] *Union des Scolaires Nigeriens-Union Generale des Etudients Nigeriens au Benin v. Niger*, Communication No. 43/90, ACHPR\LR\A\1, *supra* note 364, 36, at 37, ¶¶ 14-15.
[839] *Id.* at 36, ¶ 1.
[840] *Id.* ¶¶ 2-10 & ¶ 15.
[841] For detailed discussion on serious or massive violations, *see* Rachel Murray, *Serious or Massive Violations Under the African Charter on Human and Peoples' Rights: A Comparison with the Inter-American and European Mechanisms,* 17 No. 3 NETH. Q. HUM. RTS., 109 (1999).

is not that there are no judicial organs where remedies should be exhausted, rather the jurisdiction of such judicial organs is usually ousted by persecutive legislation. In *Civil Liberties Organization V. Nigeria*,[842] the Commission ruled that where national legislation or decree ousts the jurisdiction of the court to entertain claims for breaches of fundamental rights under the constitution, such legislation "effectively remove all possible local remedies from national law. As a result the requirement to exhaust local remedies does not apply."[843]

The "unduly prolonged" criterion for making an exception to the provisions of Article 56(5) of the Charter has also received the attention of the Commission. The Commission is, however, yet to arrive at a working definition of unduly prolonged procedure for exhausting local or domestic remedies. In *Louis Emgba Mekongo v. Cameroon*,[844] the Commission decided that the fact that the complainants case had been pending in a Cameroonian court for twelve years was an evidence that procedures for exhaustion of domestic remedies had been unduly prolonged.[845] On the other hand, the Commission withdrew its ruling in one case, where it had earlier decided that the rejection of bail and delay in the appeal procedures, following the rejection for more than two years rendered the remedy unduly prolonged.[846] The reason for this reversal was because the complainant was subsequently released on bail. The Commission ended up holding that the communication was no longer admissible for that reason. This author will agree with Odinkalu and Christensen that the Commission failed to take into account, the two years of fruitless efforts by the complainant in attempting to get bail and to appeal its rejection.[847] Thus, the Commission is yet to define unduly prolonged procedures for exhaustion of domestic remedies under Article 56(5) of the Charter. From all indications, it appears that the Commission will make such a definition based on the circumstances of each case in relation to the length of time involved and the action of the respondent State Party.

---

[842] *Civil Liberties Organization V. Nigeria*, Communication No. 67/91, ACHPR\LR\A\1, *supra*, note 364, at 71.
[843] *Id.* at 72 ¶ 9. *See* also *Civil Liberties Organization (Nigerian Bar Association) v. Nigeria*, Communication No. 101/93, ACHPR\LR\A\1, *supra* note 364, 112, at 113, ¶¶ 13-17.
[844] *Louis Emgba Mekongo v. Cameroon*, Communication No. 59/91, ACHPR\LR\A\1, *supra* note 364, at 51.
[845] *Id.* at 53 ¶¶ 21.
[846] *See Lawyers Committee for Human Rights v. Tanzania*, *supra*, note 799.
[847] Odinkalu and Christensen, *supra*, note 775, at 263.

8. Burden of proving exhaustion of local remedies

From the drafting of Article 56, it appears that the burden of proof to show that local remedies have been exhausted lies with a complainant. This is because the sending of a communication to the Commission and its consideration are dependent on whether local remedies have been exhausted, in addition to other admissibility requirements. This interpretation is emphasized by Rule 104(f) of the Commission's Rules of Procedures to the effect that, the author of a communication may be required to furnish measures taken by him or her to exhaust local remedies, or an explanation why exhaustion of local remedies would be futile. On the other hand, the burden of proof in demonstrating that domestic remedies have not been exhausted lies with the respondent State Party. The latter burden, however, is a defensive one in answer to the assertion by the complainant that local remedies have been exhausted. Thus, the initial burden of proof under the African Charter is somewhat different from the burden under similar situations in other systems. For example, under the American Convention, the initial focus is on the respondent State Party.[848] However, in both systems, where the respondent State contends that local remedies remain to be exhausted, that State has the burden to show that such remedies exist and are both adequate and effective.[849]

It needs to be observed that the practice of the African Commission in demonstrating the burden of proof for the exhaustion of domestic remedies, has also not been a consistent one. In some cases, when the State Party refuses to provide a response to the Commission, the Commission accepts the facts as alleged in the complaints and makes a decision thereon.[850] In other cases, the Commission appears to be more reluctant towards the complainant's allegation. Rather than request for additional information from the complainant in these cases, the Commission declares the communication inadmissible on the grounds that the complain-

---

[848] Under Article 37(3) of the Inter-American Commission's Regulations, the initial burden of proof lies with the respondent State Party, unless it is apparent from the petition itself that the petitioner has failed in this requirement. See SCOTT DAVIDSON, THE INTER-AMERICAN HUMAN RIGHTS SYSTEM, *supra*, note 229, at 165.

[849] *See Recontre Africaine pour la Defense des Droits de l'Homme (RADDHO) v. Zambia, supra*, note 835. Compare the decision of the Inter-American Court of Human Rights in *Velasquez Rodriguez v. Honduras (Preliminary Objections)*, Case 7920, Ser. C, No. 4 INTER-AMERICAN COURT OF HUMAN RIGHTS REPORT 35, OAS Doc. OEA/Ser.L/V/III.17/Doc. 13 (1987), and *Fairben Gabi & Solis Corales v. Honduras, (Preliminary Objections)* Judgement of June 26, 1987, OEA/Ser.L/ VIII.17, Doc. 13 (1987).

[850] *See Odinkalu & Christensen, supra*, note 775, at 265, commenting on the decision of the Commission in *Louis Emgba Mekongo v. Cameroon, supra*, note 844.

ant failed to provide information as to the exhaustion of domestic remedies.[851] It must be noted, however, that the jurisprudence of the Commission is still developing.

The Commission, no doubt, has devoted ample attention to the issue of exhaustion of domestic remedies. One would expect that in developing its jurisprudence the African human rights systems will truly apply general principles of international law applicable in human rights regimes.

9. Submission of communications within a reasonable time

Unlike other regional mechanisms, which limit the submission of complaints to a definite period of time after exhaustion of domestic remedies, the African Charter only requires submission within a reasonable time.[852] The African Commission has not defined what amounts to a reasonable time. Ordinarily, what amounts to a reasonable time is to be determined at the discretion of the Commission having regard to the circumstances of each case. While no reason is given for the adoption of the reasonable time standard by the drafters of the African Charter, one can say that the drafters would have contemplated situations where the likelihood of the exhaustion of domestic remedies would not exist nor be adequate and effective, taking into consideration the nature of administration of justice in Africa.

The case law of the African Commission has not addressed the issue of presentation of communications out of time in relation to Article 56(6) of the Charter. However, some cases dealing with the exhaustion of local remedies have impliedly addressed circumstances that may be used in interpreting what a reasonable time is. For example, in *Louis Emgba Mekongo v. Cameroon*,[853] the Com-

---

851 *Id.* commenting on the decision of the Commission in *International PEN (Senn & Sangare) v. Cote d'Ivoire*, Communication 138/94, ACHPR\LR\A\1, *supra*, note 364, at 139.
852 Article 56 (6) of the African Charter. Compare Articles 46(1)(b) of the American Convention, which imposes a time limit of six months for the presentation of petitions to the Inter-American Commission after the exhaustion of domestic remedies. Article 38(2) of the Inter-American Commission's Regulations, however, enacts a similar provision to Article 56(6) of the African Charter to the effect that where an individual is absolved from the requirement to exhaust local remedies, then the presentation of a petition to the Commission "shall be within a reasonable period of time... as from the time the alleged violation of rights has occurred." The application of the reasonable time standard under the Inter-American system is subject to a waiver of the exhaustion of domestic remedies requirement. In the same vein Article 34 (old Article 26) of the European Convention places also a six month limit for the presentation of petitions within the period that domestic remedies are exhausted. The Optional Protocol to the International Covenant on Civil and Political Rights on the other hand, has no provision on the time limit for the presentation of petitions to the Human Rights Committee. Article 5(b) only exempts the requirement of exhaustion of domestic remedies where they are unduly prolonged.
853 *supra*, note 844.

mission declared the complaint admissible even though the complainant had spent over twelve years pursuing a discretionary presidential remedy after the conclusion of domestic proceedings. Similarly in *John Modise v. Botswana*,[854] the Commission admitted a communication that was submitted nearly after fifteen years had elapsed since judicial proceedings were concluded. The point must be made that, in the above cases, there was evidence before the Commission that during the intervening period, the complainants consistently pursued remedies for the violations about which they complained to no avail.[855] These cases are not the ideal cases for setting the standard as to what amounts to reasonable time. They properly fall into the class of cases where the Commission has either identified lack of the existence of local remedies to exhaust, or where the remedies are inadequate or ineffective. The Commission has rather adopted the position that it is advisable that complaints be submitted as early as possible.[856] Cases that do not have any evidentiary showing of compelling circumstances that would necessitate their being admissible out of reasonable time, would from all indications, not be admissible.

10. Communications settled through other international mechanisms

Article 56(7) of the Charter provides against the admission of communications that "... deal with cases which have been settled by the States involved in accordance with the principles of the Charter of the United Nations, or the Charter of the Organization of African Unity or the provisions of the present Charter." The essence of this provision is to avoid the duplication of procedures for resolving human rights disputes. The emphasis here, it should be noted, is on the settlement of the case by another international or regional mechanism.[857] However, on a first reading of the above provision, there is the tendency to interpret it to mean that the Commission shall not admit a complaint or communication that is pending in an international procedure for settlement, despite the emphasis that the cases would "have been settled" by such procedure. The African Commission fell into this trap in the drafting of its earlier Rules of Procedure. Rule 114(3)(f) of the old Rules of Procedure provided that: "in order to decide on the admissibility of

---

[854] *John Modise v. Botswana*, Communication 97/93, *reprinted* in *Odinkalu and Christensen, supra*, note 775, at 266.
[855] *Odinkalu and Christensen, supra*, note 775, at 266.
[856] INFORMATION SHEET NO. 3, *supra*, note 750, at 10.
[857] See *Mpaka-Nsusu Andre Alphonse v. Zaire*, communication No. 18/88, ACHPR\LR\A\1, *supra*, note 364, at 10 ¶ 7. Here the Commission held that the decision on the merits by the UN Human Rights Committee on the same case with the same parties and on the same issues, and particularly when the decision was in favor of the complainant, fell within Article 56(7).

a communication, pursuant to the provisions of the Charter, the Commission shall ensure: ... that the same issue is not already being considered by another international investigating and settlement body." The effect of this contradictory rule was felt in *Amnesty International v. Tunisia*[858] In that case, Amnesty International instituted a complaint against Tunisia for serious and massive violations of human rights, and later wrote to the United Nations requesting that Resolution 1503 procedure be used in respect of the same case against Tunisia.[859] In its admissibility decision, the Commission relied on old Rule 114(3)(f) to adjudge the communication inadmissible in order to avoid usurpation of the jurisdiction of other bodies who may provide a solution or relevant information, and that it would be futile for the Commission to consider the case at that stage until an outcome was known.[860]

The above case is one where the Commission elevated the provisions of its Rules of Procedure over a provision of the Charter, despite the fact that the intention of the drafters of the Charter is clear on the face of the provision. The Charter outlaws the admissibility of matters "which have been settled" by another international procedure. This case was not only unsettled, but was also brought to the Commission first before the request for the UN 1503 procedure. The Commission also failed to distinguish between the 1503 procedure and the individual complaint mechanism under the Charter, as other international and human rights systems have done. Under the Inter-American system, a Petitioner who has made allegations of human rights violations against a State Party to the UN, and that State Party becomes the subject of the 1503 procedure or one of ECOSOC's special procedures, the petitioner will not be precluded from having his or her complaint admitted by the Inter-American Commission.[861] Similarly, the Human Rights Committee does not consider the examination of a particular human rights situation in a given country under the 1503 procedure to constitute an examination of the "same matter under another procedure of international investigation or settlement," which Article 5(2)(a) of the First Optional Protocol to the International Covenant on Civil and Political Rights makes a bar to admissibility of individual petitions

---

858 *Amnesty International v. Tunisia*, Communication No. 69/92, ACHPR\LR\A\1, *supra* note 364, 73, at 74, ¶¶ 13-15.
859 *Id.* at ¶¶ 1-4.
860 *Id.* at ¶ 15.
861 SCOTT DAVIDSON, THE INTER-AMERICAN HUMAN RIGHTS SYSTEM, *supra,* note 229, at 171. *See also, Case 9748 v. Peru*, Res. No. 30/88 of September 14, 1988 and Case *9786 v. Peru*, Res. No. 33/88 of September 14, 1988, Inter-American Commission on Human Rights, ANNUAL REPORT 1988-89, 30-33, *reprinted in id.*, at 171.

before the Committee.[862] The Human Rights Committee reasoned that the 1503 procedure is designed to consider situations and not individual complaints, and thus could involve the same matter for purposes of Article (5)(2)(a) of the First Optional Protocol.[863]

The African Commission appears to have noticed this sharp contradiction of the Charter by its Rules of Procedure. The Amended Rules of Procedure in Rule 116 provides that "the Commission shall determine the question of admissibility pursuant to Article 56 of the Charter." There is no further reference to the requirements contained in the old Rule 114(3)(f). In other words, the Rules of Procedure would no longer set the requirements for admissibility. In addition, new Rule 104(1)(g) now only requires a communication's author to "furnish clarifications on the applicability of the Charter to his or her communication, and to specify in particular: ... the extent to which the same issue has been "settled" by another international investigation or settlement body." It thus appears that the Commission is ready to apply the actual reading of Article 56(7) of the Charter in determining whether a complaint has been settled by another international procedure. It is hoped that the Commission will utilize this change as liberally as provided by the African Charter, unlike other mechanisms. The irony had been that while on the surface, other mechanisms had stringent requirements as to matters that were pending before other international procedures, their implementing organs nonetheless, were innovative in arriving at liberal interpretations that were inclusive rather than exclusive.[864]

In construing Article 56(7) with regard to such international procedures that are envisaged by the Charter, the Commission has ruled that a complaint to an NGO or to an inter-governmental organization, such as the EEC or Amnesty International does not render a communication inadmissible on the basis of the Article.[865] One would think that this is necessarily obvious.

---

862 *See A et al v. S*, U.N. HUM. RTS. COMM., SELECTED DECISIONS UNDER THE OPTIONAL PROTOCOL at 17, U.N. Doc. CCPR/C/OP/1, U.N. Sales No. E.84.XIV.2(1985).
863 *Id. See* also *Odinkalu and Christensen, supra,* note 775, at 268.
864 Of all the human rights mechanisms, it is only the African Charter that expressly provides that communications should be considered "if they do not deal with cases *which have been settled* by these States involved in accordance with the principles of the Charter of the United Nations, or the Charter of the Organization of African Unity or the provisions of the present Charter."(Emphasis is this author's).
865 *See Louis Emgba Mekongo v. Cameroon, supra,* note 844, 51, at 53 ¶ 22. *See* also INFORMATION SHEET NO.3 *supra,* note 750, at 10.

D. *Post Admissibility Procedure*

1. Consideration of communications on the merits

Following admissibility decisions of the Commission are decisions on the merits, especially where communications are declared admissible. As earlier mentioned, a decision of inadmissibility is final and ends the determination of the communication, unless otherwise reconsidered under the circumstances recognized in the Rules of Procedure.[866] Where, however, a communication is declared admissible, the decision is made known to the State Party as soon as possible by the secretary of the Commission,[867] and sets the stage for consideration of the communication on the merits. The practice of the Commission within the Rules, is to require the State Party concerned to submit in writing within three months to the Commission, its explanations or statements, elucidating the issues under consideration and indicating if possible, measures taken to remedy the situation.[868] It is, however, within the Commission's discretion to extend the period where necessary for the interest of justice. The Commission considers the communication by examining the allegations made by the complainant and the response given by the State concerned with due regard to the provisions of the Charter and other international human rights norms.[869]

There are occasions where a respondent State Party completely ignores or refuses to respond to allegations made by a complainant, or to respond to the request for information by the Commission, thus refusing to cooperate with the Commission. In such situations, the Commission would rely on the facts as presented by the complainant and treat them as given.[870] The Commission is, however, cautious in applying this rule. It has therefore warned that, the fact that the complainant's allegations were not contested, or were partially uncontested by the State does not mean the Commission would accept their veracity without more.[871] The Commission can invoke the power vested in it under Article 46 of the Charter "to resort to any appropriate method of investigation..." to examine such claims. This it could do by getting information from alternative sources and

---

866 *See* RULES OF PROCEDURE OF THE AFRICAN COMMISSION, *supra*, note 680, Rule 118(2).
867 *Id.* Rule 119(1).
868 *Id.* Rule 119(2).
869 *Id.* Rule 120(1). *See* also INFORMATION SHEET NO. 3, *supra*, note 750, at 14.
870 *See Louis Emgba Mekongo v. Cameroon*, *supra*, note 844, 51, at 53 ¶ 26-27. The Commission initiated this practice only in 1994 at its sixteenth ordinary session in an attempt to deal with undue prolongation of the communication procedure due to delays and lack of cooperation from some States Parties in responding to requests aimed at their defending the complaints against them.
871 INFORMATION SHEET NO. 3, *supra*, note 750, at 15.

from third parties.[872] To enhance this, the Commission may well set up a working group of three of its members to whom it would refer the communication, and which would submit final recommendations to it.[873]

After a careful deliberation based on the facts and arguments put forward by the complainant and the respondent State Party, the Commission makes a decision on whether it finds a violation of the Charter or not. Where the Commission finds a violation, it issues recommendations to the State Party concerned.[874] In effect, the Commission's decisions are recommendations. These recommendations are not in themselves legally binding on the States concerned. The avenue that the Commission uses to make them somewhat binding is by including them in its Annual Activity Reports, which it submits to the Assembly of Heads of State and Government of the OAU (AHSG) in conformity with Article 54 of the Charter. The adoption of these reports by the AHSG is presumed to make the decisions contained in them binding on States Parties. The question, however, that begs for an answer, is how a recommendation can become binding. Implementation of recommendations by its nature is subjective in that the State Party to which the recommendations are made, may or may not choose to implement them, based on the State's perception of their consequences on its sovereignty. The bindingness or otherwise of decisions of quasi-judicial organs such as the African Commission becomes a serious problem in human rights dispute resolution, especially in places where respect for human rights is not naturally part of governance objectives or tradition.

2.   Legal representation

The right of legal representation before the African Commission is neither contained in the Charter nor in its Rules of Procedure. The power vested in the Commission under Article 46 to resort to any appropriate means of investigation, and to receive information from any person capable of enlightening it, has been interpreted as forming the basis for representations before the Commission, including legal representation of complainants.[875] Apart from the provisions of Article 46, the practice of the Commission in the consideration of States' periodic Reports is also quite instructive. The Commission normally requires reporting States to send their representatives, who would normally present the reports during the sessions of the Commission in which those reports would be considered. Under the Commission's power in Article 46, the Commission would invite represent-

---

872   *Id.*
873   *See* RULES OF PROCEDURE OF THE AFRICAN COMMISSION, *supra*, note 680, Rule 120(1).
874   *Id.*
875   *See Odinkalu and Christensen, supra,* note 775, at 272. *See* also ANKUMA, note 363, at 71.

atives of States' Parties and complainants alike to refute allegations of complainants and make presentations in proof of their case, respectively. In the case of complainants, their representatives are usually NGOs, which most of the times initiated the communication on their behalf. These representatives are invited to the ordinary sessions of the Commission, where they supply the Commission with additional information regarding the communication, including, where necessary, oral arguments.[876]

The practice of allowing some form of legal representation before the Commission began in 1994 at the Commission's Sixteenth Ordinary Session.[877] It is still not a fully developed practice, but one that is on a case by case basis. Since the initial favorable disposition towards some form of legal representation, the Commission has routinely allowed individuals to be represented by NGOs. In the same vein, States parties routinely send legal representations to argue complaints against them.[878] In cases where individuals do not have legal representation, the Secretariat of the of the Commission has initiated a practice of recommending legal representation in appropriate circumstances.[879]

This encouragement of legal representation is commendable, as it adds to the credibility of the individual complaint mechanism under the African Charter. In addition, it not only accords with the international trend, but it will also help in the development of the jurisprudence of the Commission. It should be noted that one of the short comings of the Commission's mode of making decisions is the lack of legal reasoning. Legal representation will go a long way in changing that, as the procedure would begin to look more like a legal inquiry. The Commission, in light of the legal persuasions of the representatives, would be driven to give opinions that are well reasoned. On the other hand, States Parties will more readily participate in the proceedings as recent events have shown. This is exemplified by the fact that some States are now beginning to send very senior and experienced legal representatives to argue their cases before the Commission.[880]

3. Interim or provisional measures

The Concept of interim or provisional measures serves the purpose of avoiding irreparable damage to victims, or sometimes, complainants, during the course of

---

[876] *Id.* at 273.
[877] The first known case where the Commission allowed for oral presentation of communication was *Louis Emgba Mekongo v. Cameroon, supra,* note 844, upon the request of the author who represented himself.
[878] See Odinkalu and Christensen, *supra,* note 775, at 273.
[879] *Id.*
[880] *Id.* at 274.

the consideration of a communication or petition by a supervisory organ of a human rights mechanism. The utilitarian effect of the concept is usually felt more in places where there is the propensity for serious and massive violation of human rights. In this respect, the Inter-American system unlike the European system, has been more innovative in the development of the concept, and thus has laid a solid foundation on the importance of interim or provisional measures.[881] Just like in the Inter-American system, provisional or interim measures potentially have a significant role to play in the African system due to the character of many of the human rights claims that are brought before the African Commission, and the realities of human rights violations in Africa. One would sometimes agree with the observation that the preventive function of provisional or interim measures, when the lives and physical security of persons are concerned, is far more valuable than the compensatory function of a final decision.[882]

The concept of interim or provisional measures under the African Charter is not specifically provided for. It is rather an issue that is covered by the Rules of Procedure of the Commission. According to Rule 111:

1. Before making its final views known to the Assembly on the Communication, the Commission may inform the State party concerned of its views on the appropriateness of taking provisional measures to avoid irreparable damage being caused to the victim of the alleged violation. In so doing, the Commission shall inform the State party that the expression on its views on the adoption of those provisional measures does not imply a decision on the substance of the communication.
2. The Commission, or when not in session, the Chairman, in consultation with other members of the Commission, may indicate to the parties any interim measure, the adoption of which seems desirable in the interest of the parties or the proper conduct of the proceedings before it.
3. In case urgency [sic] when the Commission is not in session, the Chairman in consultation with other members of the Commission, may take any necessary action on behalf of the Commission. As soon as the Commission is again in session, the Chairman shall report to it any action taken.[883]

The above Rule vests the power to request provisional or interim measures on the Commission as a body, or on the Chairman of the Commission where the

---

[881] *See generally*, Jo. Marie Pasqualucci, *Provisional Measures in the Inter-American Human Rights System: Innovative Development in International Law*, 26 VAND. J. TRANSNAT'L L. 803 (1993).
[882] *Id.* at 820 – 821.
[883] RULES OF PROCEDURE OF THE AFRICAN COMMISSION, *supra*, note 680, Rule 111(1)(2)&(3).

Commission is not in session or in cases of urgency.[884] The request for provisional or interim measures may be made before the Commission makes its recommendation and final report to the AHSG. A question that arises from this practice is, whether the cases which may require a request for provisional or interim measures should have passed the admissibility test, or could cases that have not yet been admitted, warrant the request for interim or provisional measures. The African Commission is yet to give its opinion on this question. However, from the wording of the Rule, it appears that the Rule envisages cases that have been declared admissible, which at the same time show serious and massive violations of human rights, with the tendency to cause irreparable damage to the victims. On the other hand, one would think that the circumstances of the cases, irrespective of admissibility would determine whether or not there should be a request for interim or provisional measures. For example, the Inter-American Commission has maintained that, in a request for provisional measures, the urgent risk of irreparable damage to persons, absolves it from the prior necessity of defining admissibility according to the requirements of the American Convention.[885] In this regard, the Inter-American Commission stated that "such precautionary measures may be requested even when the admissibility of a case has not yet been defined by the Commission pursuant to Article 46 of the Convention, since, by their very nature, provisional measures arise from a reasonable presumption of extreme and urgent risk of irreparable damage to persons.[886]

One will think that in the case of the African Charter, the test should be whether a complaint alleges a *prima facie* violation of the Charter, therefore meriting a seizure of the Commission under Article 55 of the Charter, in addition to a showing of serious and massive violations of human rights, with a reasonable tendency to cause irreparable damage to the victims. It should be noted that in some cases that showed serious and massive violation of human rights, the Com-

---

[884] This is similar to the power vested on the Commission in Article 58 of the Charter dealing with cases of serious and massive violation of human rights, under which the Commission or the Chairman of the Commission, when the Commission is not in session, would draw the attention of the Assembly of Heads of State and Government (AHSG), or its Chairman of the AHSG to those cases. The difference between these powers is that while the Commission has the power to request provisional or interim measures under the Rules, its power to deal with special cases of serious and massive violations of human rights depends on the AHSG or its Chairman requesting the Commission to undertake an in-depth study of the cases. See Murray, *Serious or Massive Violations Under the African Charter on Human and Peoples' Rights: A Comparison with the Inter-American and European Mechanisms, supra,* note 841, at 118-119.

[885] Request for Provisional Measures in *Case 10.548*, INTER-AM. COURT 25, OEA/ser.G/CP, doc.2146 (1991), *reprinted* in *Pasqualucci, supra,* note 881, at 828.

[886] *Id.*

mission had been willing to relax some admissibility requirements.[887] This appears to be the trend of thought of the Commission, though not expressly stated in its application of Rule 111. The Commission has yet applied Rule 111 and requested interim or provisional measures in two cases,[888] one of which has become a beacon of hope on the effect of the African Charter on domestic law in African States. In *Constitutional Rights Project (Zamani Lekwot & 6 Others) v. Nigeria,*[889] a Nigerian NGO submitted a complaint on behalf of Zamani Lekwot, a former army general and six others who were sentenced to death by a military tribunal and awaiting execution. Recognizing that the complaint revealed a case of emergency, the Commission requested the Nigerian government not to execute the victims until the Commission had fully considered the substance of the case. With this request for interim measure the NGO instituted an action in Lagos High Court to stay the execution.[890] The government responded by filing a preliminary objection on the grounds that the court had no jurisdiction to entertain the suit, the same having been ousted by decree. The court, however, avoided a decision on the validity of the decree in question but held that it had jurisdiction to hear the case and issued an injunction against carrying out the execution pending the determination of the complaint before the African Commission. The judgment of the Lagos High Court in relevant part, stated:

> ... The African Charter on Human and Peoples' Rights (Ratification and Enforcement) Act, chapter 10 of the Laws of the Federation of Nigeria, 1990 is a treaty which has been ratified by the Nigeria government and since Nigeria retains its membership of the Organization of African Unity (OAU), chapter 10 is binding on the Federal Military Government. The African Charter on Human and Peoples' Rights (Ratification and Enforcement) Act by virtue of section 1 of Decree 55 of 1992 is also a Decree to enable effect be given in the Federal Republic of Nigeria to the African Charter on Human and Peoples' Rights made in Banjul on January 9, 1983. It is a treaty binding on the federal government of Nigeria. Where a decree, law or edict purports to outs the juris-

---

887 See *The group of cases against Zaire, supra,* note 775.
888 *Constitutional Rights Project (Zamani Lekwot & 6 Others) v.Nigeria,* Communication No. 87/93, ACHPR\LR\A\1, *supra,* note 364,101, at 102, ¶¶ 9-12. See also *Constitutional Rights Project v.Nigeria,* Communication No. 60/91 *Id.* 55, at 56, ¶ 7. These cases deal with execution of death sentences passed by Nigerian military tribunals.
889 Communication No. 87/93, *Id.* 101, at 102, ¶¶ 9-12.
890 *The Registered Trustees of Constitutional Rights Project v. The President of the Federal Republic of Nigeria and 2 others,* (Unreported), Suit No. M/102/93 of May 5, 1993, *reprinted* in 1,2 & 3, JOURNAL OF HUMAN RIGHTS LAW AND PRACTICE 219 (1993). See also ANKUMA, *supra,* note 363, at 72; Precious Beinga Ngabirano, Case Comment: Does Municipal Law Prevail Over International Law? The Registered Trustees of Constitutional Rights Project v. The President of the Federal Republic of Nigeria and Others, 2:1 EAST AFRICAN JOURNAL OF PEACE AND HUM. RTS.102 at 104 (1995).

diction of the court is capable of two meanings, the decree is to be interpreted in the manner which retains or preserves the jurisdiction of the court contrary to Cap. 53 of the Laws of the Federation of Nigeria of 1990 and Decree 55 of 1992, which outs the jurisdiction of the court. Cap. 10, Laws of the Federation of Nigeria preserves and saves the jurisdiction of the court to adjudicate on the interpretation of its provisions. *Thus, any domestic legislation in conflict with the Charter is voi.* The same rule applies even when the contracting state has not ratified the treaty.[891] (Emphasis is this author's)

The effect of the above decision was that the death sentences were later commuted to five years imprisonment. This Nigerian case stands out as one of the successes of the African human rights mechanism regarding the creative use of the Charter by the Commission, human rights NGOs and domestic courts. This case is, however, an isolated one, the gains of which need to be further exploited by the Commission or any other supervisory organ of the African mechanism.

III   REMEDY UNDER THE AFRICAN CHARTER

A question that one may ask regarding the remedial effect of the African Charter, especially in protecting individual human rights, could run thus: even if the commission concludes that there has been a violation of rights, what effective remedy does the African Charter provide? As earlier indicated, the Commission does not make legal decisions, rather it makes recommendations, the legal binding effect of which is doubtful.[892] Looking at the procedures of the Commission, after a communication or complaint has passed the test of admissibility and heard on the merits, the Commission draws up a report of its findings, based on the facts and information received. The report is then communicated to the States Parties concerned, through the Secretary-General of the OAU, and then to the AHSG, together with the recommendations that the Commission deems useful.[893] From this procedure, it is the AHSG that would then determine what remedy will be available to the complainant. This has led to the observation by some early writers on the African system that the Charter in fact, does not offer significant remedies to the generality of the people.[894] This conclusion was reached based on the

---

891 *The Registered Trustees of Constitutional Rights Project v. The President of the Federal Republic of Nigeria and 2 others, supra,* note 890, 224.
892 *See* INFORMATION SHEET NO. 3, *supra,* note 750 at 16.
893 *See* Article 53 of the Charter, and THE RULE OF PROCEDURE OF THE AFRICAN COMMISSION, *supra,* note 665, Rule 120(2).
894 *See* REMBE, THE SYSTEM OF PROTECTION OF HUMAN RIGHTS UNDER THE AFRICAN SYSTEM, *supra,* note 645, at 37-41. *See also Benedek, Supra,* note 633, at 31.

interpretation of Article 58 and the seemingly undue emphasis the Article places on special cases, as well as the power it vests on the AHSG. The Article provides:

1. When it appears after deliberations of the Commission that one or more exceptional situations apparently reveal the existence of a series of serious or massive violations of human and peoples' rights, the Commission shall draw the attention of the Assembly of Heads of State and Government to them.
2. The Assembly of Heads of State and Government may then Request the Commission to undertake an in-depth study of these situations and make a factual report, accompanied by its findings and recommendations.
3. A case of emergency duly noticed by the Commission shall be submitted by the latter to the Chairman of the Assembly of Heads of State and Government who may request in-depth study.

One would tend to agree with Wolfgang Benedek,[895] on his comment about the above provisions. According to him, there is a distinction as to the remedy available in ordinary cases of violations and special cases of violations. He opines that while there appears to be a remedy in the special cases, there is no remedy in the ordinary cases of violation. Special cases are those involving the existence of serious or massive violations of human and peoples' rights. Thus, whether a remedy is available or not is dependent on whether the act complained of is a serious and massive violation of human rights, or requires emergency action, or is an ordinary abuse of human rights.[896] The views of these authors have been criticized by Odinkalu and Christensen as conveying the impression that there is no legal basis under the Charter for the Commission to respond to violations of individual human rights other than Article 58.[897] This author would disagree with this criticism. The views expressed by Benedek and Murray deal with issues of availability of concrete remedies under the Charter for the benefit of all victims of human rights violations, rather than on the competence of the African Commission to implement the individual complaint mechanism. There is no doubt as to the the jurisdiction of the Commission to undertake its protective mandate under the Charter. The issue is that whatever remedy that is available under Article 58 is not conferred by the Commission but the AHSG.

Article 58 makes a mockery of the available remedies under the Charter. The apparent remedy under the Article is in-depth study, which will be requested by

---

895 *Id.*
896 *See* also Rachel Murray, *Decisions of the African Commission on Individual Communications Under the African Charter on Human and Peoples' Rights*, 46 INT'L & COMP. L.Q. 412 at 413 (1997).
897 Odinkalu & Christensen, *supra*, note 775, at 240.

the AHSG after the deliberations of the Commission would have revealed special cases, which in turn reveal a series of serious or massive violations of human and peoples rights; or cases to which the Commission draws the AHSG's attention. What remedy if any, does in-depth study or recommendations provide? The Assembly of Heads of States and Governments is not a body that is in session all year round, nor does the Commission have the power to summon such assembly. The AHSG has not been known to order such in-depth study as suggested by Article 58.[898] Indeed, the AHSG has rather been known to be strongly guided by the objective of the OAU of non intervention in member countries' internal affairs, which has been the organization's attitude towards human rights violations by its members. A former Chairman of the Commission summed up the situation thus:

> The enforcement procedure is unsatisfactory. In the absence of a court and effective measures to a breach, the Charter may well be a paper tiger except for public opinion that may be whipped up against the offender. The Commission may investigate, discuss and make recommendations to the states concerned. Do these include the award of damages, restoration or reparation? The Assembly can only ask the commission to make in-depth studies. The Charter does not state that it can condemn an offending state.[899]

The issue of remedy in law cannot be over emphasized. An aggrieved State or individual, whose rights have been violated has recourse to a higher tribunal or court for further redress. Redress may take the form of an apology, reparations or damages for alleged wrong doing, condemnation of the acts of the violator, injunction in the case of continuing a wrong, or the removal of the sources of wrong, for example, the repeal of a legislation or the enactment of a new one.[900] The African Commission, unlike other human rights supervisory and enforcement organs, has been very reluctant to award damages or reparations even in cases that it determines that there have been violations of the Charter. In *Louis Emgba Mekongo v. Cameroon*, the Commission found that the complainant was entitled to reparations for the prejudice he had suffered, but that the valuation of the amount of such reparation should be determined in accordance with the legal system of Cameroon.[901] The Commission abandoned its responsibility in this

---

[898] See Murray, *Serious or Massive Violations Under the African Charter on Human and Peoples' Rights: A Comparison with the Inter-American and European Mechanisms, supra,* note 841, at 118-119.
[899] UMOZURIKE, U. O., THE AFRICAN CHARTER ON HUMAN AND PEOPLES' RIGHTS 25 (Nigerian Institute of Advanced Legal Studies, 1992).
[900] REMBE,, *supra,* note 645, at 37.
[901] *Louis Emgba Mekongo v. Cameroon,* Communication No. 59/91 *supra,* note 844, 51 at 54.

case, which was based on a judicial appeal that had been pending for twelve years.[902] How could the Commission expect the complainant to get justice from the same courts that denied him the same justice for twelve years. The Complainant came to the Commission to seek the justice that had been elusive under the Cameroonian legal system, only to be turned back to it.

Even if it is argued that the recommendations the Commission makes in the individual complaint mechanism under the African Charter, are some form of remedy, their enforcement is lacking. There is no mechanism that can compel State Parties to abide by these recommendations, neither has the Commission laid down procedures to supervise their implementation.[903] Much depends on the good will of the States concerned.[904] The obvious inherent lack of effective remedy in the African human rights mechanism over the years has definitely impacted on the effectiveness of the entire mechanism as far as protection against violations of individuals' rights is concerned. It is in this regard among others, that the current initiative, amending the African Charter to provide for a court, and in turn reforming the African system, is commendable. It is hoped that the emerging court will be one without the limitations suffered by the Commission; and would serve to align the new roles to be performed by the Commission with those to be performed by the court

An issue that is related to the remedy question is the element of publicity of the Commission's procedures relating to the communications or complaints before it. The effect of publicity in the field of human rights protection cannot be quantified. Publicity brings about a resultant shame, which serves as a deterrence to future violations.[905] In this regard, Article 59(1) of the Charter, provides that "all measures taken within the provisions of the present Charter shall remain confidential until such a time as the Assembly of Heads of State and Government [AHSG] shall otherwise declare." In the first seven years of the Commission's existence, the Commission interpreted this Article to mean that it could neither mention the cases, the countries complained against, nor the stage reached in

---

902 *Id.* at 53 ¶ 20.
903 INFORMATION SHEET NO. 3, *supra*, note 750, at 17.
904 *Id.* The only thing that the Commission does in this regard is that its secretariat sends letters of reminders to states that have been found to have violated provisions of the Charter, calling upon them to honor their obligations under Article 1 of the Charter "... to recognize the rights, duties and freedoms enshrined in this Charter and ... adopt legislative and other measures to give effect to them.." The first letters are usually sent immediately after the adoption of the Commission's Annual Activity Report by the AHSG, and subsequent letters are sent "as often as necessary." *See Id.*
905 E.V.O Dankwa, *Commentary on the Rules of Procedure of the African Commission on Human and Peoples' Rights*, in PROCEEDINGS OF THE SECOND ANNUAL CONFERENCE OF THE AFRICAN SOCIETY OF INTERNATIONAL AND COMPARATIVE LAW 30 (1990).

individual cases.[906] The Commission thus disclosed nothing about the communications considered under its individual communications procedure.[907] What effect will a human rights mechanism have if the freedom to make its activities public is taken away? Other international procedures encourage the publication of reports and other activities of the systems under which they are set up. The success of the Inter-American and European systems were largely achieved by the freedom they enjoyed to publicize their activities and decisions. Reports of the European Commission, when the Commission was in existence, were published in nearly all cases by the Committee of Ministers,[908] while the Inter American Commission on its own, by virtue of article 51(3) of the American Convention on Human Rights, decides whether to publish its report or not.

Inspired by the practice of other systems, and based largely on incessant criticisms of the Commission's lack of innovative interpretation of Article 59 of the Charter, the African Commission lifted the veil that shrouded its consideration of communications in its Seventh Annual Activity Report in 1994. For the first time, this report made information available on the first fifty-two communications decided by the Commission. The information included were a summary of the parties to the communication, the factual background, and the Commission's summary decisions.[909] This was improved upon by the Eight and Ninth Activity Reports which contained full texts of the Commission's final decisions, and subsequent annual reports that now routinely publicize both decisions on the merits and those that declare communications inadmissible.[910] These reports are, however, published after the AHSG adopts them and approves of their publication.

Ankuma cautions that despite the important development with respect to publicity, the concept of confidentiality remains problematic. She points out that the Commission could further enhance the development of its jurisprudence by publishing how it reaches its decisions on admissibility and the substantive rights in the Charter,[911] as well as supporting its decisions with clear and persuasive

---

906 *Benedek, supra,* note 633, at 29, *See* also *Odinkalu & Christensen, supra,* note 775, at 277.
907 *Odinkalu & Christensen, Id.* The publicity practice of the Commission was limited to issuing documents to the public concerning its activities in the forms of final commuiqués, which are usually issued at the end of each ordinary session, press releases, and its Annual Activity Reports, which become a public document only after adoption by the AHSG. Included among the publications of the Commission is the Review of the African Commission on Human and Peoples' Rights, which is a journal containing articles and information on the African mechanism. The information contained in these documents in their totality, never sufficiently reflected the deliberations and decisions of the Commission. *See* ANKUMA, *supra,* note 363, at 75.
908 European Convention on Human Rights, old Article 32(3).
909 *Odinkalu & Christensen, supra,* note 760, at 277. *See* also ANKUMA, *supra,* note 348, at 75.
910 *Odinkalu & Christensen, Id..*
911 ANKUMA, *supra,* note 363, at 77.

legal reasoning.[912] In this regard, the Commission needs to make use of the vast body of international law on human rights to develop its jurisprudence if the African mechanism is to make any meaningful impact on the domestic laws of State Parties.

---

912 *Id.* at 75.

5

REFORMING THE AFRICAN HUMAN RIGHTS SYSTEM

I   BASES FOR REFORM

Despite the international acclaim that heralded the adoption of the African Charter by the OAU Heads of State and Government in 1981, and its subsequent entry into force in 1986, the demand for the reform of the African Human rights mechanism began within five years of its existence. This demand is basically on two fronts: the alleged inadequacy or inherent normative flaws of some contents of the Charter, and the lack of adequate or effective enforcement institutions, which should necessitate a reformulation or an amendment of the Charter. On the normative front, such issues as the prevalence of "clawback" clauses come under attack. As we have earlier noted in chapter two of this work, the argument is strong that clawback clauses essentially confine the Charter's protection of rights to the definitions in national laws.[913] Thus, States are permitted to restrict basic human rights to the extent allowed by domestic law.[914] In the same vein, scholars agree that what the African Charter needs is an excision of the clawback clauses in favor of a derogation provision, which will specify non-derogable rights, and which rights States can derogate from, when, and under what circumstances, in keeping with the generally accepted principles of international law.[915]

Secondly, ample attention has been drawn to the Charter provision on women's rights. The fear has been expressed that the Charter would not adequately protect the rights of women, and hence, should be revised to specifically address issues

---

[913] *See* Welch, *The African Commission on Human and Peoples' Rights: A Five Year Assessment, supra,* note 633, at 46. *See* also, Mutua, *The African Human Rights System in a Comparative Perspective: The Need for Urgent Reformulation, supra,* note 605, at 32-33.

[914] Mutua, *The African Human Rights Court: A Two Legged Stool, supra,* note 775, at 358; Benedek, *The African Charter and Commission on Human and Peoples' Rights: How to Make it More Effective, supra,* note 633, at 26-27; ANKUMA, *supra,* note 363, at 176-177; and *Bondzie-Simpson, A Critique of the African Charter on Human and Peoples" Rights, supra,* note 619, at 660-661.

[915] Mutua, *supra,* note 775, at 358. *See* also *Benedek, supra,* note 633, at 27.

that pertain to women rather than lumping women's rights with provisions on the family, the child and the disabled, under Article 18.[916] According to Mutua, this fear stems from the concern that the family provisions under the Charter are thought to condone and support repressive and retrogressive structures and practices of social and political ordering.[917] Accordingly, these provisions, which place duties to the family on the State and individuals, have been interpreted as entrenching oppressive family structures that marginalize and exclude women from participation in most spheres outside the home.[918] In the same manner, there is also the feeling that the provision supports the discriminatory treatment of women on the basis of gender, in marriage, property ownership, and inheritance, and impose on them unconscionable labor and reproductive burdens.[919] Despite the spirited defense that scholars, including this author in the early part of this book, have made of the transparency of the Charter in the totality of its provisions pertaining to women, such as outlawing all forms of discrimination against women, and in its gender equality provisions, among others, the agitation for a different instrument that defines the rights of women in accordance with the trend in international law, keeps mounting, and genuinely so. The contention is that the Charter does not, for example, explicitly guarantee such rights as the right of consent to marriage and the equality of spouses during marriage, and such other specific contemporary issues that border on women's rights. In addition, the argument maintains that the Charter, as a document that is inspired by the virtues and the values of African civilization, cannot *per se* be an effective tool to protect the rights of women in view of the role of women in the traditional African family.[920]

Thirdly, the Charter has been criticized for not containing some fair hearing guarantees such as public hearing of cases, the provision of legal assistance, the right to an interpreter, the right against self-incrimination, the right to cross-examine witnesses and the right to compensation, which other international and regional human rights instruments are known to guarantee.[921]

As we noted earlier, there were mixed reactions to the various proposals for the amendment of the Charter with regard to the above issues. During its 19th ordinary session,[922] the African Commission deliberated at length on this issue.

---

916 *See* ANKUMA, *supra,* note 363, at 151-152.
917 *Mutua, supra,* note 775, at 359.
918 *Id.*
919 *Id.*
920 On the argument for a separate document on the rights of women, *see* generally, ANKUMA, *supra,* note 363, at 151-158.
921 *Id.* at 123-132.
922 Held at Ouagadougou, Burkina Faso on March 26 to April 4, 1996.

In response to the general dissatisfaction that had been expressed with the Charter, the debate centered around the creation of additional protocols, under Article 66, or an amendment of the Charter as a whole under Article 68.[923] Several arguments were made against amending the Charter. Firstly, it was felt that there was a need for a stable document that would not be subject to frequent change. Secondly, amendment was seen as unnecessary, since the Charter already provided wide powers which needed to be exploited, and that Articles 60 and 61 ensured that other international instruments could be incorporated into the Charter through the interpretation of its provisions.[924] The contention was therefore, that greater experience was needed. Furthermore, there were other members who cautioned that there was a great danger with the amendment procedure, in that states would not support alterations that would make the Charter more, rather than less restrictive.[925] NGO representatives in their contribution to the issue of amending the Charter, highlighted the need to first pinpoint the weaknesses in the Charter in order to see how best to tackle them. To this end, the African Commission decided to establish a working group under Commissioner Ndiaye to collaborate with those experts working on the Additional Protocol on an African Court of Human Rights.[926]

There is no doubt, that there are various areas where the African Charter does not totally follow other international human rights instruments as already indicated, which may require a rethinking of the Charter, either by express amendment or by informed interpretation of the provisions under the powers provided in the Charter. It must be realized, however, that not all aspects of the Charter can be applied by interpreting an implication of general principles of international law on human rights. There must be areas where concrete steps of amendment should be taken. What determines whether or not an amendment should be carried out is the adequacy, or lack of effective application of the Charter in its present form. It should not be because of a desire for a "stable document that would not be subjected to frequent change," nor should it be because States would not support the amendment if it makes the Charter more, rather than less restrictive. After all, the European Convention has gone through various revisions and amendments in the form of additional protocols. That has not destroyed its stability. Thus, the view of NGOs, that it was proper to first identify the weaknesses of the Charter, is instructive. It is only then, that the areas proposed for amendment will be placed

---

923 *See Muray, Report on the 1996 Sessions of the African Commission on Human and Peoples Rights- 19th and 20th Sessions, supra,* note 507, at 19.
924 *Id.*
925 *Id.*
926 *Id.*

on the scale of importance, practicality and desirability in terms of effectiveness and lending credibility to the Charter. This author believes that it was in this vein that the African Commission at its 21st[927] ordinary session in Nouakchott, Mauritania appointed three Commissioners to work on a draft Protocol on women's rights. The draft Protocol contains twenty-one Articles on various issues of women's rights not provided for under the Charter.[928] There must have been a thoughtful consideration of the arguments made by proponents of the need to emphasize women's rights in the African mechanism more expressly than through just innovative interpretation of the Charter.

Another issue in the discourse on the reformulation of the African human rights system, is the institutional framework of the African mechanism. The African Commission which is charged with implementing and enforcing the Charter, has over the years been seen in different lights, albeit, without significant praise. To some, with respect to the performance of the Commission in general, the Commission is a disappointment,[929] and lacks an effective tool to ensure compliance with the norms enshrined in the Charter.[930] To others, the situation with the Commission, though unsatisfactory could be remedied,[931] with the necessary revision of the Charter.[932] The argument is that the Charter does not equip the Commission with sufficient protective powers, but rather, an elaborate promotional mandate, which the Commission had failed to aggressively take advantage of.[933] Similarly, it is argued that in articulating the protective mandate of the Commission, neither the Charter nor the Commission provides for enforceable remedies, or a mechanism for encouraging and tracking State compliance with decisions

---

[927] Held on April 15-24, 1997. *See* TENTH ANNUAL ACTIVITY REPORT OF THE AFRICAN COMMISSION ON HUMAN AND PEOPLES' RIGHTS, *supra*, note 509.

[928] *See* REPORT OF THE FIRST MEETING OF THE WORKING GROUP ON THE ADDITIONAL PROTOCOL TO THE AFRICAN CHARTER ON WOMEN'S RIGHTS, *supra*, note 509, where the text of the draft Protocol: DOC/OS/58(XXIV) Annex I, is attached, as well as draft terms of reference for the Special Rapporteur on the Rights of Women in Africa, DOC/OS/58(XXIV) Annex II.

[929] *Mutua, The African Human Rights Court: A Two Legged Stool, supra*, note 775, at 345. *See also Mutua, The African Human Rights System in a Comparative Perspective: The Need for Urgent Reformulation, supra*, note 605, at 32-33.

[930] *Bondzie-Simpson, supra*, note 619, at 662.

[931] *Welch, The African Commission on Human and Peoples' Rights: A Five Year Assessment, supra*, note 633, at 53.

[932] *Benedek, The African Charter and Commission on Human and Peoples' Rights: How to Make it More Effective, supra* note 633, at 26.

[933] *Mutua, supra*, note 605, at 33.

that the Commission makes.[934] In this respect, to many victims, the Commission's findings are said to be "too remote, if not virtually meaningless."[935]

One will agree with the critics of the Commission, to the extent that earlier members of the Commission did not demonstrate a resolve to realize the spirit of the Charter in ensuring the protection of human rights in Africa. The reason for this lack of resolve has been attributed to the closeness of many of those Commissioners with State Parties. Most of the Commissioners were prominent officials in their States of origin and would not want to rock the boat, in effect.[936] It could be argued that these Commissioners needed to kowtow to their States of origin for their own safety, since many African States at that time were constantly engaged in gross violations of human rights. As noted in chapter three, this raises a lot of questions on the independence and impartiality of the members of the Commission. Lamenting this situation of the early Commission in a call for a reformulation of the Charter, Mutua wrote in 1992:

> Due to these deficiencies, after more than four years in operation, the African Commission has had little or no effect on the human rights discourse on the continent. Its institutional structures for implementation need a major restructuring. In addition to revising the Charter's substantive provisions, the Commission's powers should be clarified. The Commission should be given precise, identifiable powers expressly limited to: the examination of periodic state reports; the authority to carry out investigative human rights missions to member states, with a mandate to prepare publicly available reports and recommendations; the exercise of all the promotional functions outlined in Article 45(1)(a) and (c). All judicial and quasi-judicial functions should vest in a new institution, the African Human Rights Court to be created by the revised Charter.[937]

The African Commission has, however, come a long way since its early beginnings. It must be acknowledged that the Commission has had its fair share of financial difficulties and neglect by the OAU, which has greatly contributed in hampering the effectiveness of the Commission. However, as has earlier been noted, the Commission has recently begun to command some respect with regard to its functions. In its promotional functions, the Commission has, over the years, increased the organization of conferences, seminars, workshops and symposia to

---

934 *Mutua, supra,* note 775, at 349.
935 *See* THE AFRICAN SOCIETY OF INTERNATIONAL AND COMPARATIVE LAW, REPORT ON THE 16TH SESSION OF THE AFRICAN COMMISSION ON HUMAN AND PEOPLES' RIGHTS, 62-83 (1996), *reprinted* in *Mutua, supra,* note 775, at 349.
936 *Mutua, supra,* note 605, at 34.
937 *Id.*

provide a forum for open discussions on human rights in Africa.[938] Similarly, the Commission has taken some bold steps in asserting its protective mandate. It has revised its Rules of Procedure[939] in order to make its procedures more effective, as well as its Guidelines on States reporting.[940] More significantly, the Commission now routinely publishes its decisions with regard to the individual complaint mechanism, removing the confidentiality that shrouded that procedure. In addition, the Commission has also taken some steps that have the potential to increase its impact on States. Its appointment of Special Rapporteur on Summary and Extra-Judicial Execution, on Prisons and Conditions of Detention, and on Women's Rights, is potentially significant, if the offices are used to investigate, report, and facilitate dialogue with states.[941] Furthermore, the Commission's country-specific and thematic resolutions raise its visibility and engage States directly.[942]

Finally, the Commission has progressively taken steps to shorten the duration of its individual complaint procedure, especially with regard to its admissibility decisions.[943] In its initial years of existence, covering the period up until the sixteenth ordinary session, it often took between two years and six and half years, or more for the Commission to render a decision on admissibility.[944] Now, the Commission routinely renders admissibility decisions within six months, or on average, between six months and one year and a half.[945] These improvements in the workings of the Commission could be attributed to the growing confidence that members of the Commission seem to be having in themselves. This confidence could in turn be linked to the growing wind of change blowing across the continent: the preference for democratic government. The fall of apartheid and the institution of democracy in South Africa, tend to be the greatest challenge to other African countries in this direction.

While commending the successes recorded by the African Commission, there remains the larger question as to the effectiveness of the African human rights mechanism in its totality. The issue of enforcement of the Charter and the remedies available to users of the mechanism, as well as a streamlining of the Commission's functions, is very central. Despite the signs of progress in the Commission's

---

938 ANKUMA, *supra*, note 363, at 22.
939 RULES OF PROCEDURE OF THE AFRICAN COMMISSION ON HUMAN AND PEOPLES' RIGHTS, *supra*, note 680.
940 *See* AMENDED GUIDELINES, *supra*, note 697.
941 *Mutua, supra*, note 775, at 350.
942 *Id.*
943 *Odinkalu and Christensen, supra*, note 775, at 274.
944 *Id.* at 274-275.
945 *Id.*

individual complaint mechanism, the decisions it renders have been argued to be somewhat formulaic. "They do not always reinforce jurisprudence from national and international tribunals, nor do they fire the imagination. They are non-binding and attract little, if any, attention from governments of Member States."[946] It is in this regard that the OAU seeks to enhance the effectiveness of the Charter by reforming the mechanism and supplementing the African Commission with an African Court on Human and Peoples' Rights.

II   THE DEBATE ON AN AFRICAN COURT OF HUMAN RIGHTS

The debate for the establishment of an African Court of Human Rights predates the founding of the OAU. As earlier indicated, this debate began in 1961 in Lagos during the African Conference on the Rule of Law, organized by the International Commission of Jurists.[947] One of the recommendations and resolutions of that conference was the creation of a court of appropriate jurisdiction to which recourse would be available to all persons under the jurisdiction of the signatory States. This was to be done via a proposed African Convention on Human Rights, which was to lay down the basis for future efforts for the establishment of rules and mechanisms for the regional promotion and protection of human rights, and to give effect to the Universal Declaration of Human Rights.[948] It was, however, troubling that about twenty years later when Africa adopted a human rights instrument, the idea of the court earlier mooted was not to be, but rather a Commission as the implementing institution of the mechanism. Some scholars of African human rights were of the view that a weak enforcement machinery as seen in the African Commission was all that was feasible at the time of the adoption of the African Charter, which would have made the establishment of a court premature at that time. Thus, subsequent establishment of a court would therefore, depend on how the initial organ functioned.[949] In the same vein, Keba Mbaye, one of the founding fathers of the African Charter opined that the Charter constituted what African States were wiling to accept in 1981 and was therefore,

---

946 *Mutua, supra,* note 775, at 348.
947 The famous Law of Lagos, 1961.
948 *See* EZE, *supra* note 1, at 195. *See* also REGIONAL PROTECTION AND PROMOTION OF HUMAN RIGHTS IN AFRICA, TWENTY-NINTH REPORT OF THE COMMISSION TO STUDY THE ORGANIZATION OF PEACE 4 (1980); ANKUMA, *supra,* note 363, at 193. *See* also generally, REGIONAL PROMOTION AND PROTECTION OF HUMAN RIGHTS, TWENTY-EIGHT REPORT OF THE COMMISSION TO STUDY THE ORGANIZATION OF PEACE (1980). This Commission was Chaired by Louis B. Sohn.
949 EZE, *supra,* note 1, at 226.

only a stage which could be improved upon at a later date.[950] Such improvement according to the learned scholar would be the basis for the amendment and revision of the provisions of the Charter.[951]

Early reactions to the idea of an African Court of Human Rights were varied. Critics of the proposition often argued that the idea of a court was not in keeping with African traditional ways of dispute resolution. They maintained that mediation and conciliation were the proper avenues to go, being mechanisms rooted in African tradition.[952] Thus, the establishment of the African Commission was enough an avenue to deal with issues of human rights dispute resolution in Africa. The tenability of that argument today remains to be judged against the realities of the present day Africa in light of the ineffectiveness of the present mechanism under the Charter. One may ask why it should it be in the area of human rights that African traditional considerations should prevail. Domestic legal institutions have been modeled far from African traditional ways of dispute resolution; they rather duplicate the various legal systems of Africa's colonial past. According to Dieng, "the delights of traditional anthropology should not lull us to the point of obscuring reality. Today, the time has come to accede to the demands of Africans who feel it indispensable for the victims of human rights violations, or their representatives, to have recourse to judicial process on demand."[953]

There is also the objection based on infringement on national sovereignty of Member States.[954] This objection has always been an issue in international law. Scholars have argued that one of the ways to remove this fear from Member States to any international mechanism, like a court of human rights, is to provide for an optional clause similar to article 36 of the Statute of the International Court of Justice (ICJ).[955] Alternatively, there has often been the suggestion of two bases of jurisdiction, compulsory jurisdiction and advisory jurisdiction, solely for attracting the generality of the membership of the mechanism sought to be achieved. While it is desirable to attract many state members to an international or regional mechanism, it should be noted that human rights law should supersede the notion of national sovereignty.[956] Individuals are the beneficiaries of international human

---

950 ANKUMA, *supra*, note 348, at 193.
951 *Id.*
952 *See* the Address by Adama Dieng, Secretary General of the International Commission of Jurists at the meeting of Government Experts on the question of the creation of an African Court on Human and Peoples' Rights held in Cape Town, South Africa 3-4 (September 6 - 12, 1995), in which he commented on the African traditional mode of dispute resolution.
953 *Id.*
954 *Dumas, Nanette, Enforcement of Human Rights Standards: An International Human Rights Court and Other Proposals*, 13 HASTINGS INT'L & COMP. L. Rev. 593 (1990).
955 *Id.*
956 *Id.*

rights law and thus must be shielded from the sovereignty argument. States must accept that human rights law is inherently a limit on the scope of State action. For example, a State cannot torture people as a matter of State policy any more than it can wage aggressive war. In modern international law, sovereignty does not confer the right to do either. The opinion of the Inter-American Court of Human Rights in one of its advisory opinions[957] on the real nature of human rights instruments is persuasive. According to the Court:

> [M]odern human rights treaties in general, and the American Convention in particular, are not multilateral treaties of the traditional type concluded to accomplish the reciprocal exchange of rights for the mutual benefit of the contracting states. Their object and purpose is the protection of the basic rights of individual human beings, irrespective of their nationality, both against the state of their nationality and all other contracting States. In concluding these human rights treaties, the States can be deemed to submit themselves to a legal order within which they, for the common good, assume various obligations, not in relation to other states, but toward all individuals within their jurisdiction...

The above quote indicates the importance of the individual in human rights jurisprudence even though individuals are not *per se* subjects of international law. It is even arguable that human rights treaties make them subjects of international law.

Apart from the earlier arguments against the establishment of a human rights court which reigned after the Law of Lagos and during the preparation of the African Charter, the whole debate for the establishment of a human rights court in Africa has over the years been narrowed down to two possible polar view points. One view holds that a human rights court must be established as soon as possible to salvage the entire African system from near total "irrelevance and obscurity."[958] According to this view, "the deficiencies of the African system, both normative and institutional, are so crippling that only an effective human rights court can jump-start the process of its redemption."[959] The establishment of the court here is seen as a way of putting some teeth and bite into the system in order to effectively restrain States.[960] The other view is the gradualist school, which though is not totally opposed to the establishment of a court of human

---

[957] Advisory Opinion OC-2/82, Ser.A, No.2, 29 (1982). This opinion is based on the effect of Reservations on entry into force of the American Convention.
[958] *See Mutua, supra,* note 775, at 351.
[959] *Id.*
[960] *Id.*

rights, calls for a gradual approach towards the establishment of the court.[961] This school sees the work of the African system as primarily promotional and not adjudicative.[962] The school sees the major problem in Africa to be the lack of awareness by the general populace of its rights and the process of vindicating those rights.[963] To this school, the regional system must therefore first educate the public by promoting human rights. The task of protection, which would include a court is thus less urgent.[964] In this direction, according to Mutua, critics argue that a court might be paralyzed by the same problems that have beset the African Commission. They therefore urge that the African Commission be strengthened instead of dissipating scarce resources to create another, possibly impotent institution.[965]

The concerns by the gradualist school for resources and the strengthening of the Commission, as well as the need to improve promotion of human rights in Africa is a credible one. They cannot, however, take away the importance of a human rights court in a regime for regional protection of human rights. What is needed is a realignment of the roles of the Commission vis-a-vis the Court. One would agree with Mutua that the gradualist school has in the past several years given way to the proponents of a human rights court, as it had become clear by the mid 1990s even to pro-establishment figures, that the African system needed some overhauling.[966] The argument whether or not a human rights court is necessary in Africa has thus become moribund. The readiness of African States is expressed in the resolution of the Assembly of Heads of State and Government[967] during the Summit of the OAU in Tunis in June 1994, in which the Secretary General of the organization was called upon to summon experts to meet on the establishment of an African Court of Human Rights, to enhance the efficiency of the African Commission on Human and Peoples' Rights. That resolution has today materialized into a Protocol on the African Charter for the creation of a court.[968]

---

961 See ANKUMA, *supra* note 363, at 194.
962 Mutua, *supra* note 775, at 351, *citing* ANKUMA, *supra*, note 363.
963 *Id*, Mutua, at 351.
964 *Id.* at 352.
965 *Id.*
966 *Id.*
967 Resolution AHG/230(XXX), *supra*, note 321, during the 30th ordinary session of the Assembly of Heads of State and Government, Tunis, Tunisia, June 1994.
968 PROTOCOL TO THE AFRICAN CHARTER ON HUMAN AND PEOPLES' RIGHTS ON THE ESTABLISHMENT OF AN AFRICAN COURT ON HUMAN AND PEOPLES' RIGHTS, OAU DOC.CAB/LEG/66.5 (1998) (Hereafter, PROTOCOL ON THE AFRICAN COURT ON HUMAN AND PEOPLES' RIGHTS), adopted and signed at the OAU Summit in Ouagadougou, Burkina Faso in June 1998.

It is necessary here to emphasize the rationale for the establishment of a court of human rights in Africa in the face of present realities, as follows: First, the African Commission as presently structured and mandated is merely a committee making recommendations to the Assembly of Heads of State and Government of the Organization of African Unity, which holds the ultimate word. This procedure appears to subject the resolution of human rights dispute in Africa to subjective political considerations. Accordingly, it inevitably weakens the position of the Commission in its protective functions.[969] A sincere effort at eradicating the short comings of the present mechanism will necessarily entail the setting up of a court. A question that may arise in this regard is, whether solving the problem necessarily requires a court; whether a stronger Commission would not solve the problem. The basic issue here is enforcement, a power which may not easily be given to a commission by Member States. Also, practice has shown that even within the UN system, a commission does not possess the authority to issue a binding and enforceable decision.

Second, experience of other regional counterparts of the African system has shown that a court is necessary for the articulation of international legal principles at the regional level. There needs to be an authoritative statement of these principles by a judicial organ. This could be either through the court's exercise of compulsory jurisdiction, or a jurisdiction of an advisory nature.[970] This will necessarily lead to uniformity in the definition of international human rights obligations assumed by States Parties, which in turn will lead to development of standards in the region concerning other issues that will come before the court. Uniformity would create a system fair to both the defending States Parties and the victims, rather than permit human rights violators to go unpunished, as in the present mechanism. Both the European and the Inter-American human rights systems show that a human rights court is an essential, if not an indispensable component of an effective regime for the protection of human rights. Norms prescribing State conduct are not meaningful unless they are anchored in functioning and effective institutions.

Third, human rights enforcement is likely to be more easily realized with the establishment of a court than in the present situation. A case coming before the court will entail publicity rather than the confidentiality and secrecy that is still

---

[969] *See*, REMBE, *supra*, note 645, at 43-45.
[970] It could be said that the Inter American Court achieved it major success in the human rights situations of Central and Southern American countries from the articulation of international legal principles under the appropriate instruments as applicable, primarily by way of advisory opinions. The same can be said of the International Court of Justice (ICJ) and the European Court of Human Rights. It has to take a court in the traditional sense for a legal principle to be properly articulated and followed, especially in international law; and particularly, human rights law.

noticeable in the present system, despite the efforts by the Commission to let the public in into its procedures. Even where a decision of a court is not binding, because it is an advisory opinion, it usually attracts far reaching publicity and promotes compliance. States are known to have complied with advisory decisions, either in ending violations of human rights or adopting laws that follow the opinion of the court.[971] In human rights law, adverse publicity serves as a form of sanction.[972] The condemnation of a State action by a regional court attaches a serious obligation on the State Party, and therefore, more effective in commanding the respect of that State. In addition, domestic courts, especially courts in Common Law traditions in Africa will look to the court for direction and precedents in their application of human rights instruments at the domestic level.[973] One example of this is the avowed impact of the European Court of Human Rights on Zimbabwean domestic law in the absence of any such African equivalent.[974]

Fourth and finally, the court as a regional human rights organ, can be an important instrument in sustaining constitutional democracies and facilitating the fulfilment of human rights which are now universally recognized.[975] The domestic systems that ought to be in place are such that will be created in commitment to the basic values of the modern international movement in the form of democracy, humane government; and the fulfilment of the basic human rights established by the international system[976] and oftentimes guaranteed by domestic constitutions, without assurance of protection. A court therefore, would definitely be an external check to make sure that democracies follow the rules.

---

971 This has been particularly so in the Case of the Inter-American system where the exercise of the Advisory jurisdiction of the court set the ground for enunciating doctrinal principles in international human rights law as it affects the Americas. For more detail on the Advisory jurisdiction of the Inter-American Court, *see* Buergenthal, Thomas, *The Advisory Practice of the Inter-American Human Rights Court,* 79 AM. J. OF INT'L LAW 1 (1985).

972 *See* REMBE, *supra,* note 645, at 39.

973 *See Registered Trustees of the Constitutional Rights Projects v. The President of the Federal Republic of Nigeria and 2 Others, supra,* note 890.

974 *See* generally, Lovemore Madhuku, *The Impact of the European Court of Human Rights in Africa: The Zimbabwean Experience,* 8 AFRICAN J. INT'L & COMP. L., 932- 943 (1996).

975 *See* Reisman, W. Michael, *Practical Matters For Consideration In The Establishment of a Regional Human Rights Mechanism: Lessons From The Inter-American Experience,* ST. LOUIS-WARSAW TRANSATLANTIC L. J. 89, at 100 (1995).

976 *Id.*

III THE MAKING OF THE AFRICAN COURT ON HUMAN AND PEOPLES RIGHTS[977]

The adoption of Resolution 230/30 of June 1994[978] by the OAU requesting the Secretary-General of the organization to convene a meeting of Government experts to ponder in conjunction with the African Commission over the means to enhance the efficiency of the Commission, particularly, the establishment of an African Court on Human and Peoples' Rights, led to a series of events in fashioning out an additional Protocol to African Charter on Human and Peoples' Rights on the establishment of the court. Responding to the above resolution, the Secretary-General of the OAU in collaboration with the government of South Africa convened a meeting of government legal experts in Cape Town, South Africa, from September 6 to 12, 1995.[979] The meeting of the experts was facilitated by a draft prepared by African experts, which were assembled by the OAU secretariat in collaboration with the African Commission on Human and Peoples' Rights and the International Commission of Jurists (ICJ) in a meeting earlier held in Cape Town on 4-5 September, 1995.[980] The outcome of the Cape Town Meeting was the first Draft Protocol to the African Charter on Human Rights on the court.[981]

The Cape Town draft Protocol was to be considered at the 64th ordinary session of the Council of Ministers of the OAU in Yaounde from July 1-5 July 1996. The Council, however, deferred the consideration of the draft protocol because the comments and observations received from Member States of the OAU before the

---

[977] The drafting history of the African Protocol on the establishment of an African Court of Human Rights centers around the Cape Town, Nouakchott and Addis Ababa draft Protocols. These drafts were arrived at various meetings of legal experts and representatives of Member States of the OAU in the cities from which they derived their names.

[978] OAU Res. AHG/230(XXX), *supra*, note 321.

[979] *See* REPORT OF THE GOVERNMENT EXPERTS MEETING ON THE ESTABLISHMENT OF AN AFRICAN COURT ON HUMAN AND PEOPLES' RIGHTS, 6-12 September, 1995, Cape Town, South Africa, OAU/LEG/EXP/AFCHR/RPT.(I)Rev.1. (Hereafter, the CAPE TOWN LEGAL EXPERTS' REPORT) *reprinted* in *Ibrahim Ali Badawi El-Sheikh, Draft Protocol to the African Charter on Human and Peoples' Rights on the Establishment of an African Court on Human and Peoples' Rights: Introductory Note*, 9 AFRICAN J. INT'L. & COMP. L. 943-952 (1997), which gives a brief and pointed history of the Protocol on the African Court. *See* also, REPORT OF THE SECRETARY-GENERAL ON THE CONFERENCE OF MINISTERS OF JUSTICE/ATTORNEYS-GENERAL ON THE DRAFT PROTOCOL ON THE ESTABLISHMENT OF THE AFRICAN COURT ON HUMAN AND PEOPLES' RIGHTS, DOC.CM/2051(LXVII). (Hereafter, THE SECRETARY-GENERAL'S REPORT ON THE CONFERENCE OF MINISTERS OF JUSTICE/ATTORNEYS-GENERAL ON THE DRAFT PROTOCOL).

[980] THE CAPE TOWN LEGAL EXPERTS' REPORT, *supra*, note 979.

[981] DRAFT PROTOCOL TO THE AFRICAN CHARTER ON HUMAN AND PEOPLES' RIGHTS ON THE ESTABLISHMENT OF THE AFRICAN COURT ON HUMAN AND PEOPLES' RIGHTS, OAU/LEG/EXP/AFCHPR/PROT.(I)Rev.1 (Hereafter, THE CAPE TOWN DRAFT PROTOCOL).

conference were insufficient.[982] By the time the 65th session was held in February 1997 in Tripoli, Libya, the General Secretariat of the OAU had received comments and observations from ten countries including the initial three, and the Cape Town draft Protocol was considered.[983] The Council of Ministers *inter alia*, decided that another governmental experts meeting be held in April 1997 to finalize the draft Protocol, taking into consideration the comments and observations received from Member States.[984] Pursuant to the above decision, and at the invitation of the government of Republic of Mauritania, the General Secretariat convened a meeting of Government Experts in Nouakchott from 11-14 April, 1997 at which Member States were invited, and members of the African Commission were also in attendance.

The second Government Experts Meeting considered the Draft Protocol article by article taking into account the comments and observations received by about twenty countries.[985] The meeting amended the Cape Town draft and adopted a new draft,[986] to be presented for consideration and adoption by the Council of Ministers at its Sixty-sixth ordinary session.[987] At that session, while the Council of Ministers took note of the draft as amended by the Second Conference of Government Experts in Nouakchott, it requested all Member States to submit their further comments and observations to the General Secretariat of the OAU on or

---

[982] Only three Member States submitted their comments and reactions, namely, Mauritius, Lesotho and Burkina Faso.

[983] In all, comments and observations were received from the following countries: Mauritius, Lesotho, Burkina-Faso, Senegal, Tunisia, Sierra Leone, Benin, Cote d'Ivoire, Madagascar and Ethiopia. *See* THE SECRETARY-GENERAL'S REPORT ON THE CONFERENCE OF MINISTERS OF JUSTICE/ATTORNEYS-GENERAL ON THE DRAFT PROTOCOL, *supra*, note 979, ¶ 9. What was interesting here in the case of Ethiopia was that at this time Ethiopia was not a State Party to the African Charter, but was participating in activities for an amendment of the Charter to establish a human rights court. As already indicated, Ethiopia ratified the Charter on June 15, 1998.

[984] *Id.* at ¶ 10.

[985] Mauritius, Lesotho, Burkina-Faso, Senegal, Tunisia, Sierra Leone, Benin, Cote d'Ivoire, Madagascar, Ethiopia, Namibia, South Africa, Egypt, Swaziland, The Gambia, Tanzania, Algeria, Burundi, Niger and Togo. *See Id*, ¶¶ 11-12.

[986] DRAFT PROTOCOL TO THE AFRICAN CHARTER ON HUMAN AND PEOPLES' RIGHTS ON THE ESTABLISHMENT OF THE AFRICAN COURT ON HUMAN AND PEOPLES' RIGHTS, OAU/LEG/EXP/AFCHPR/PROT(2), (Hereafter, THE NOUAKCHOTT DRAFT PROTOCOL). *See also* REPORT OF THE SECOND GOVERNMENT LEGAL EXPERTS MEETING ON THE ESTABLISHMENT OF AN AFRICAN COURT ON HUMAN AND PEOPLES' RIGHTS, OAU/LEG/EXP/AFCHPR/RPT(2) (Hereafter, The NOUAKCHOTT LEGAL EXPERTS' REPORT).

[987] *See* REPORT OF THE SECRETARY-GENERAL ON THE CONFERENCE OF MINISTERS OF JUSTICE/ATTORNEYS-GENERAL ON THE DRAFT PROTOCOL ON THE ESTABLISHMENT OF THE AFRICAN COURT ON HUMAN AND PEOPLES' RIGHTS TO THE COUNCIL OF MINISTERS, SIXTY-SIXTH ORDINARY SESSION, 26-30 May, 1997, Harare, Zimbabwe, Doc.CM/2020(LXVI). (Hereafter, REPORT TO THE COUNCIL OF MINISTERS' SIXTY-SIXTH ORDINARY SESSION), *reprinted* in *Badawi El-Sheikh*, *supra* note 979, at 944.

before 31 August, 1997. Further, the Council requested the General Secretariat to convene in Addis Ababa, a third Government Legal Experts Meeting enlarged to include diplomats to examine and finalize the draft Protocol to be submitted to the Conference of Minsters of Justice/Attorneys-General for consideration and adoption, which will further be submitted to the Council of Ministers of the OAU.[988] The third Legal Experts Meeting including diplomats was convened in Addis Ababa, Ethiopia from 8 to 11 December, 1997. The meeting considered the Nouakchott draft Protocol along with the comments from Member States.[989] After intense deliberations, the meeting adopted another amended text of the draft Protocol.[990] Following the third government legal experts' meeting was the Conference of Ministers of Justice/Attorneys-General which held in Addis Ababa on 12 December, 1997. The Conference which was scheduled for two days was able to complete its work in one day and adopted the draft Protocol after very minor amendments by consensus.[991] The OAU Council of Ministers approved

---

[988] Res. CM/Dec.348(LXVII). *See also* REPORT TO THE COUNCIL OF MINISTERS' SIXTY-SIXTH ORDINARY SESSION, Doc. CM/2020(LXVI), *supra*, note 987, and THE SECRETARY-GENERAL'S REPORT ON THE CONFERENCE OF MINISTERS OF JUSTICE/ATTORNEYS-GENERAL ON THE DRAFT PROTOCOL, *supra*, note 979, ¶ 10.

[989] *See* COMMENTS AND OBSERVATIONS RECEIVED FROM MEMBER STATES ON THE DRAFT PROTOCOL ON THE ESTABLISHMENT OF AN AFRICAN COURT ON HUMAN AND PEOPLES" RIGHTS, OAU/LEG/EXP/AFCHPR/Comm.(3) and addendum 1, (hereafter COMMENTS AND OBSERVATIONS ON THE DRAFT PROTOCOL), *reprinted* in *Badawi El-Sheikh*, *supra*, note 979, at 944. In addition to the comments from Member States, additional amendments were submitted and circulated during the meeting. The comments were from Namibia, South Africa, Egypt, Senegal, Burkina Faso, Swaziland, The Gambia, Tanzania, Algeria, Burundi, Niger and Togo. The meeting was attended by 113 delegates from 45 Member States. *See also* THE SECRETARY-GENERAL'S REPORT ON THE CONFERENCE OF MINISTERS OF JUSTICE/ATTORNEYS-GENERAL ON THE DRAFT PROTOCOL, *supra* note 979, ¶ 17.

[990] DRAFT PROTOCOL TO THE AFRICAN CHARTER ON HUMAN AND PEOPLES' RIGHTS ON THE ESTABLISHMENT OF THE AFRICAN CHARTER ON HUMAN AND PEOPLES' RIGHTS, OAU/LEG/AFCHPR/PROT.(III) Rev.1 (Hereafter, THE ADDIS ABABA DRAFT PROTOCOL). *See also* REPORT OF THE THIRD GOVERNMENT LEGAL EXPERTS MEETING, ADDIS ABABA, ETHIOPIA, OAU/LEG/EXP/AFCHPR/RPT(III) Rev.1 (Hereafter, THE ADDIS ABABA LEGAL EXPERTS' REPORT).

[991] The Conference was attended by 19 Ministers of Justice/Attorneys-General as well as Vice Ministers, Solicitors-General, Judges, Ambassadors, Public Prosecutors and other senior government officials from 45 Member States. The Conference issued a communique (CM/2051(LXVII) Annex 1) at the end of its deliberations recommending the Draft Protocol for adoption by the Council of Ministers and the Assembly of Heads of State and Government. *See* THE SECRETARY-GENERAL'S REPORT ON THE CONFERENCE OF MINISTERS OF JUSTICE/ATTORNEYS-GENERAL ON THE DRAFT PROTOCOL, *supra* note 979, ¶ 19-23. *See* also, *Gihon Hagos, African Human Rights Court on the Cards*, AFR. NEWS, 11 Dec. 1997, available in LEXIS, News Library, CURNWS File; *Gihon Hagos, Africa at Large*; *Conference Adopts Protocol on African Human Rights Court*, AFR. NEWS, 13 Dec. 1997, available in LEXIS, News Library, CURNWS File;

the Draft Protocol in February 1998,[992] while the Assembly of Heads of State and Government adopted the Protocol in June 1998.[993] Thus, the movement that began at Lagos in 1961 became a reality. Apart from the reasons given for the need for the creation of a human rights Court, Member States of the OAU eventually realized that the attainment of the objectives of the African Charter requires the establishment of a human rights Court to complement and reinforce the mission of the African Commission.[994]

The analysis, however, of the salient provisions of the Protocol will be done in chapter 6 when we examine the new African Court in light of the Protocol and other regional and international experiences. That section will reveal the legislative history of the Protocol in terms of how its provisions were arrived at, following the revision of the Cape Town draft by the Nouakchott draft, and the subsequent revision of the Nouakchott draft by the Addis Ababa Draft, which in turn became the present Protocol after minor formal amendments by the Conference of Ministers of Justice/Attorneys-General which held in Addis Ababa on 12 December, 1997.

---

[992] *International Conference on Human Rights Commission Opens in Addis*, XINHUA NEWS AGENCY, 18 May, 1998, available in LEXIS, News Library, CURNWS File.

[993] *See Pursuit for Peace Remains Major Task of Africa: Salim*, XINHUA NEWS AGENCY, 8 June, 1998, available in LEXIS, News Library, CURNWS File; *Gino J. Naldi & Konstantinos Magliveras, Reinforcing the African System of Human Rights: The Protocol on the Establishment of a Regional Court of Human and Peoples' Rights*, 16 NETHERLANDS Q. HUM. RTS. 431 (1998), and *African Foreign Ministers Discuss Human Rights,* PAN AFRICAN NEWS AGENCY, April 15, 1999.

[994] *See* the Preamble to the Protocol on the Establishment of an African Court on Human and Peoples Rights, ¶ 7.

6

THE PROTOCOL ON THE ESTABLISHMENT OF THE AFRICAN COURT ON HUMAN AND PEOPLES' RIGHTS

The adoption of the Protocol on the African Court of Human and Peoples' Rights[995] at the Summit of the Organization of African Unity Summit in Ouagadougou, Burkina Faso in June 1998 breaks further grounds in African human Rights discourse. It is yet an advancement of the emerging idea, within the modern African State, that its conduct towards its citizens is no longer an internal, domestic matter.[996] It is also an acknowledgment of the general ineffectiveness of the African human rights mechanism as presently constituted, taking into consideration what prevails in other regions.[997] Drafters of the Protocol agree that they were inspired by existing regional instruments which established the European and Inter-American Human Rights Courts, the Statute of the International Court of Justice, as well as the Report of the International Law Commission on the International Criminal Tribunal.[998] Similarly, in drafting the Protocol, paramount consideration was given to the need of the African continent, in view of the human rights situation in African countries, recent political developments in many of these countries and the best manner in which the greatest protection of human rights could be achieved.[999] The hope therefore, is that the Court will strengthen the regional system and aid it in realizing its promise. The African Court, no doubt, is a potentially significant development in the protection of human rights at the

---

[995] PROTOCOL TO THE AFRICAN CHARTER ON HUMAN AND PEOPLES' RIGHTS ON THE ESTABLISHMENT OF AN AFRICAN COURT ON HUMAN AND PEOPLES' RIGHTS, supra, note 953. The Protocol is not yet in force. It is expected to come into force after fifteen instruments of ratification or accession have been deposited with the Secretary-General of the OAU by virtue of Article 34. As at present only two States, namely, Senegal and Burkina Faso have ratified the Protocol. See *African Foreign Ministers Discuss Human Rights, supra* note 993; *Murray, Human Rights News: Africa, supra,* note 687,350-351.

[996] *Mutua, supra,* note 775, at 353.

[997] *Id.*

[998] See EXPLANATORY NOTES TO THE PROTOCOL TO THE AFRICAN CHARTER ON THE ESTABLISHMENT OF AN AFRICAN COURT ON HUMAN AND PEOPLES' RIGHTS 1 (6-12 September, 1995), Cape Town South Africa. (Hereafter EXPLANATORY NOTES TO THE CAPE TOWN DRAFT).

[999] *Id.*

continental level in view of the continent's history of serious human rights violations. It is also an avenue for effectively addressing the normative and institutional shortcomings of the African human rights mechanism in general. However, one would agree with Mutua that for the hope expressed above to be realized, the court must avoid the pitfall that trapped the African Commission.[1000] This must be done from the outset to enable the Court to occupy its rightful place in the new African dispensation.

This chapter will examine the Protocol on the African Court on Human and Peoples Rights in the light of Court's potential to effectively deal with human rights dispute resolution in Africa. The experiences of other regional systems will be instructive and persuasive in this regard.

I   ESTABLISHING THE COURT

The underlying philosophy or rationale for the creation of the Human Rights Court is hinged on the conviction expressed in the preamble of the Protocol, that the attainment of the objectives of the African Charter requires the establishment of an African Court of Human Rights to complement and reinforce the mission of the African Commission on Human and Peoples' Rights.[1001] This is in addition to other preambular reaffirmations and emphases on the principles and objectives recognized in the Charter of the OAU, the African Charter on Human and Peoples' Rights, and the work of the African Commission.[1002] Generally, the Preamble seeks to place the Protocol in the wider context of a natural progression in the achievement of the legitimate aspirations of the African peoples and draws a causal link between the objectives of the OAU, including freedom, equality and justice, and the establishment of the Court.[1003]

Article 1 of the Protocol establishes the Court, with an inherent emphasis that it is established "within the Organization of African Unity."[1004] This emphasis was not contained in both the Cape Town and the Nouakchott Draft Proto-

---

1000 *Mutua, supra,* note 775, at 353.
1001 See the last paragraph of the Preamble to the Protocol.
1002 *See* other Preambular Paragraphs to the Protocol.
1003 *Gino J. Naldi & Konstantinos Magliveras, Reinforcing the African System of Human Rights: The Protocol on the Establishment of a Regional Court of Human and Peoples' Rights, supra* note 993, at 433.
1004 PROTOCOL ON THE AFRICAN COURT ON HUMAN AND PEOPLES' RIGHTS, *supra,* note 968, Article 1.

cols.[1005] Perhaps it was taken for granted, and rightly so, in these earlier versions of the Protocol, that the Court is being established "within the OAU," as was the case in both the European and Inter-American Courts as organs of the Council of Europe and the Organization of American States, respectively. There is nothing in the drafting history of the Protocol that explains the inclusion of the above phrase in the final version of the Protocol. One would only say that drafters of the Protocol want to maintain uniformity with the African Charter on the establishment of the Commission in Article 30 of the Charter, which provides that the Commission is established "within the Organization of African Unity." It could also be presumed that there is the need to emphasize that the Court is an Organ of the OAU, for the avoidance of doubt, to ward off the possible challenges of opposing Member States of the OAU.

II   RELATIONSHIP BETWEEN THE COURT AND THE COMMISSION

There is no doubt that the establishment of an African Court of Human Rights would definitely impact the work of the African Commission. Against this background, earlier suggestions had been that the Commission should be abolished and replaced by a court, since the Commission had proved ineffective. The prevailing view, however, was that the Court should reinforce the role of the Commission,[1006] and that view became the main thrust of the Protocol on the Court. In the opinion of this author, the coexistence of the Court and the Commission would therefore warrant the need for a proper clarification of the functions to be performed by each of these bodies in the new dispensation. While the mandate of the African Commission is clearly set out in Article 45 of the African Charter, entailing promotive, protective and other functions, Article 2 of the Protocol in dealing with the relationship between the Commission and the Court does not make any specific provision on that relationship, as regards particular functions. It rather generally provides that "[t]he Court shall, bearing in mind the provisions of this Protocol, complement the protective mandate of the African Commission on Human and Peoples' Rights hereinafter referred to as 'the Commission,' conferred upon it by the African Charter on Human and Peoples' Rights, hereinafter referred to as the Charter." An inference that can be drawn from this

---

1005 Article 1 of these drafts merely provided that "there shall be established an African Court on Human and Peoples' Rights 'hereinafter referred to as the Court,' the organization, the jurisdiction and functioning of which shall be governed by the present Protocol."

1006 *Naldi & Magliveras,, supra,* note 993, at 433. *See also Gino J. Naldi & Konstantinos Magliveras, The Proposed African Court of Human and Peoples' Rights: Evaluation and Comparison,* 8 AFRICAN J. INT'L & COMP. L. 994, at 946 (1996).

provision is that the function of the Court is clearly limited to the protective provisions of the African Charter. According to the drafters of the Protocol, it was necessary to state clearly the relationship between the Commission and the Court at the beginning of the Protocol to prevent confusion as to certain clauses which may seem as a duplication of the mandate of the Commission.[1007] It was emphasized that the Court would not replace the Commission, but was being established to strengthen the protective mandate of the Commission. On the other hand, the Commission would retain its protective and promotional mandate as established in the African Charter, but would find it desirable to refer greater majority of the cases to the Court after it had first considered them.[1008] As will be pointed out later, this author is of the opinion that this would have been an opportunity to assign different roles to the Court and the Commission.

Despite the explanation given by the drafters of the Protocol, one would agree with the suggestion by Naldi & Magiliveras that the potential for duplication of effort by the Commission and the Court exists.[1009] The authors identify one of such areas to include the Commission's quasi-judicial function under Article 45(3) of the Charter, which vests the Commission with the power to interpret all provisions of the Charter at the request of a State Party, an institution of the OAU or an African Organization recognized by the OAU. From all indications, despite the creation of the Court, the Commission retains this power of interpretation. What may not be clear is the extent to which the Commission will exercise this function, along-side the Court, and which body would defer to the other. It appears, however, that the interpretative mandate of the Commission is narrower than that of the Court, as it is limited to interpreting only the provisions of the African Charter. On the other hand, Article 3 of the Protocol extends the jurisdiction of the Court to the interpretation and application of the Charter, the Protocol and any other relevant human rights instruments ratified by the State concerned. This is further explained by drafters of the Cape Town draft to the effect that Article 3 takes note of the fact that the Commission has jurisdiction under Article 45 of the Charter to interpret the provisions of the Charter. Thus, a dispute relating to any interpretation made by the Commission can therefore, be submitted to the Court.[1010] There is thus no doubt that the Court would occupy a primary place

---

1007 *See* EXPLANATORY NOTES TO THE CAPE TOWN DRAFT, *supra,* note 998, at 2, specifically dealing with Article 2.
1008 *Id.*
1009 *Naldi & Magliveras, Reinforcing the African System of Human Rights: The Protocol on the Establishment of a Regional Court of Human and Peoples' Rights, supra,* note 993, at 434.
1010 *See* EXPLANATORY NOTES TO THE CAPE TOWN DRAFT, *supra,* note 998, at 2, specifically dealing with Article 3. The drafters maintain that as the Charter and the Protocol constitute one regime, the sharing of the interpretation role brings out the complementary nature of the two institutions.

in the interpretation of not only the provisions of the Charter but other human rights documents that are applicable in cases before it. Other areas of concern in the relationship between the Court and the Commission boarder mainly on jurisdiction. These issues, more appropriately, will be highlighted in succeeding segments, with an emphasis on the structural relationship between the Court and the Commission.

III JURISDICTION AND ACCESS TO THE COURT

It is true that the effectiveness of a judicial organ especially in the international plane will be largely dependent on the jurisdiction conferred upon, and assumed, by the organ.[1011] In the case of the African Court on Human and Peoples' Rights, the Protocol contains various shades of jurisdiction and access to the Court, ranging from adjudicatory or contentious jurisdiction to advisory jurisdiction. The contentious jurisdiction of a Court of this nature is either compulsory or optional, and dependent on how access to the court is prescribed.

A. Adjudicatory or Contentious Jurisdiction

This is usually referred to as the ordinary jurisdiction of a human rights court or other international tribunal in determining contentious disputes that come before it on the merit. According to Judge Piza Escalante of the Inter-American Court of Human Rights, it is this form of jurisdiction that is likely to be relied upon most frequently in guaranteeing the rights protected by a human rights instrument.[1012] The main object of a court's contentious jurisdiction is to rule on whether a State has violated any rights contained in a particular human rights instrument for which the victim seeks redress,[1013] in this case, rights contained in the African Charter on Human and Peoples' Rights. The exercise of this jurisdiction by the Court will enable it to apply the instruments and issue a decision on the merit which may include the award of reparations or other remedies where the Court finds a violation.

Additionally, the Rules of Procedure of the Commission and the Court would ensure that an issue for interpretation is not submitted by the same parties at the same time to both institutions.

1011 See Naldi & Magliveras, *supra* note 993, at 434.

1012 Judge Escalante's explanation to his dissenting vote in the decision of the Inter-American Court of Human Rights in *Viviana Gallardo et al, v. Costa*, No. G. 101/81, judgment of November 13, 1981, 20 I.L.M. 1424 (1981); 9 Hum. Rts. L.J. 328 (1981).

1013 DAVIDSON, SCOTT, THE INTER-AMERICAN COURT OF HUMAN RIGHTS, *supra*, note 229, at 62.

The Protocol, in Article 3(1) extends the jurisdiction of the Court to "all cases and disputes submitted to it concerning the interpretation and application of the Charter, this Protocol and any other relevant Human Rights instrument ratified by the States concerned."[1014] This provision, while not only important, is quite innovative. While it is initially similar in wording to new Article 32 (1) of the European Convention and Article 62(3) of the American Convention, it is broader in scope than the similar provisions of these instruments, which limit the jurisdiction of their various Courts to the application of the Conventions and their Protocols. It has been argued that this provision has the potential of extending the jurisdiction of the Court over any treaty dealing with issues of human rights applicable in Africa, such as the OAU Convention on Refugees, the African Charter on the Rights and Welfare of the Child, UN human rights instruments, and even other African regional and sub-regional instruments, such as the African Economic Community (AEC) treaty, the treaty of the Economic Community of West African States (ECOWAS) and other such treaties which in one way or the other, mention human rights issues.[1015]

The intention of the drafters of the Protocol appears to be to endow the Court with as wide a jurisdiction as possible in human rights issues in Africa. They insist that the Court should have the jurisdiction to interpret and apply all African human rights treaties, including those which are to come into effect in the future, for example, an African Convention against Torture.[1016] Despite the fact that Article 3(1) requires that the treaties in question must have been ratified by the States concerned, the provision is a bold and radical step in the right direction, which has the potential of ultimately shaping African human rights jurisprudence, even at the domestic level. Naldi and Magliveras, however, point out that this wide-ranging power of the Court is not without problems, especially regarding their application and enforcement.[1017] The authors particularly contemplate the possibility of overlapping jurisdiction with other regional and sub-regional judicial organs such as the AEC Court and the ECOWAS Court. According to the authors, it does not appear that the Protocol provides for the exclusivity of the Court's competence in the face of possible exclusion of other courts by the instruments creating these regional and sub-regional Courts.[1018]

1014 The Cape Town and Nouakchott Drafts limited the application of other human rights instruments to "other applicable African Human Rights instrument."
1015 *Naldi & Magliveras, supra,* note 993, at 435.
1016 *See* EXPLANATORY NOTES TO THE CAPE TOWN DRAFT, *supra,* note 998, at 2.
1017 *Naldi & Magliveras, supra,* note 998, at 435. The authors particularly cite Article 22(1) of the Protocol on the ECOWAS Court of Justice which excludes any other mode of dispute settlement than that prescribed by the ECOWAS treaty or its particular Protocol.
1018 *Id.* at 435-436.

While this concern may not be easily waved off, the point must be made that a combined reading of the object and purpose of the African Charter and the Protocol, gives a strong indication that the Court will have primary jurisdiction on human rights issues in the continent. It therefore follows that the human rights Court will be able to have jurisdiction to interpret other African regional and sub-regional instruments which deal with human rights issues. The responsibility of effectively utilizing the opportunity presented by the Protocol in this regard, lies with the Judges elected to the Court. Their willingness to interpret the Protocol for the general benefit of meaningfully resolving human rights disputes in the continent would determine how far the Protocol will go in this regard.

Article 3(2) of the Protocol preserves the Court's power to rule or decide a dispute as to its jurisdiction. There is no indication in the drafting history of the Protocol about the meaning of this provision. What is clear is that the drafters of the Protocol chose to conform to similar provisions in other regional human rights instruments.[1019] Some observers would, however, think that this is also in conformity with the general principle of international law as suggested by Lauterpatch in the *Norwegian Loans case*,[1020] that there is an inherent power of a tribunal to interpret the text establishing its jurisdiction. The suggestion has also been made that the power of the Court to determine preliminary objections, which may be within the ambit of the Court's Rules of Procedure, could derive from the above provision despite the fact that the Protocol does not make any express provision to that effect.[1021]

B. Jurisdictional Access to the Court in Contentious Cases

Under Article 5(1) of the Protocol, the entities with the right of direct access to the Court include: (a) the Commission; (b) the State Party which has lodged a complaint to the Commission; (c) the State Party against which a complaint has been lodged at the Commission; (d) the State Party whose citizen is a victim of human rights violation; and (e) African Intergovernmental Organizations. Article 5(2) allows a State that has an interest in a case to request permission from the Court to join in the proceedings. Under Article 5(3), Non-governmental Organizations (NGOs) with observer status before the Commission and individuals may

---

[1019] For instance, Article 32 (2) of the European Convention as amended by Protocol 11 makes similar provision in exactly the same words.
[1020] *Norwegian Loans Case*, ICJ Reports, 9 at 34 (1957), *reprinted* in *Naldi & Magliveras, supra* note 998, at 437.
[1021] *Naldi & Magliveras, Id.*

institute cases directly before the Court in accordance with the provisions of Article 34(6) of the Protocol. Article 34(6) stipulates the condition precedent for NGO and individual submission of cases directly to the Court: a declaration by a State Party accepting such NGO and individual submission of cases, without which the Court would not, under any circumstance receive any petition from an NGO or individuals. In Article 5, there is a demarcation in the right of access to the Court between the Commission and the State Parties on the one hand, and individuals and NGOs on the other. While the Commission and State Parties are privileged to approach the Court without any declaration to that effect by States Parties, NGOs and individuals are not so privileged. The States Parties against which NGOs and individuals want to proceed, must have accepted the jurisdiction of the Court to entertain such complaints.

The drafting history of the Protocol is replete with variety of views on the right of access to the Court to be accorded individuals or entities other than States and the Commission. There was in effect, a struggle to adopt either the position under the Inter-American system, the old European system, or the UN system, under the First Optional Protocol to International Covenant on Civil and Political Rights, or a variation of these systems.[1022] The Cape Town Draft provided that "... the Court may, on exceptional grounds allow individuals, non-governmental organizations and groups of individuals to bring cases before the Court, without first proceeding under Article 55 of the Charter."[1023] The Cape Town Draft did not require separate acceptance by the State Parties of the Court's competence

---

1022 It should be recalled that under Article 61 of the American Convention only States Parties and the Inter-American Commission have the right to submit cases to the Inter-American Court. Thus, individuals do not have access to the Court, even though individual access to the Inter-American Commission is automatic under Article 44. In the same vein, the European Convention before subsequent amendments via Protocols 9 and 11, limited access to the European Court of Human Rights to the High Contracting Parties and the European Human Rights Commission under Article 44, but recognized individual access to the former European Commission on Human Rights only after a declaration by a State party to that effect. Protocol 9, however, introduced individual access to the Court after the consideration of a case by the Commission, where the respondent State has ratified the Protocol. The European Convention has been amended since by Protocol 11, which makes provision for the Court as the only institutional organ of the European system, and providing for direct individual access to the Court. As stated earlier in this work, the Protocol entered into force on November 1, 1998. The Optional Protocol to the International Covenant on Civil and Political Rights is primarily an instrument that recognizes the competence of the UN Human Rights Committee to receive cases from individuals, when ratified by the particular State Party concerned. The inter-play of these various instruments and their effect on human rights dispute resolution in these systems, as well as their application to the African situation, were strongly in the minds of the drafters of the Protocol on the establishment of the African Court.

1023 CAPE TOWN DRAFT, supra, note 981, Article 7. See also Badawi El-Sheikh, Draft Protocol to the African Charter on Human and Peoples' Rights on the Establishment of an African Court on Human and Peoples' Rights: Introductory Note, supra, note 979, at 947.

to receive such cases.[1024] The Nouakchott draft modified the access of non-State entities limiting it to "urgent cases or serious, systematic or massive violations of human rights," but subject to a declaration by States Parties accepting the competence of the Court to receive such cases.[1025] The Legal experts at the Nouakchott meeting, arrived at this compromise after a very controversial and prolonged debate, apparently succumbing to reservations by some delegates, notably from Nigeria and Sudan, who preferred an optional clause for submission by Member States to the contentious jurisdiction of the Court.[1026] The Addis Ababa draft tried to modify, both in form and substance, the various provisions relating to individual access to the Court that were contained in the earlier drafts. In form, instead of having separate articles on the access of the Commission and States Parties on the one hand, and that of NGOs and individuals on the other, it consolidated them in the same Article. In substance, the optional character of the competence of the Court to receive individual and NGO complaints arrived at the Nouakchott Legal Experts' meeting was retained, but without the qualification of cases in terms of urgency or seriousness or situations of massive violations of human rights.[1027] Thus, the current Article 5 of the Protocol was arrived at.

In arriving at Article 5, the drafters of the Protocol also borrowed from earlier human rights instruments. It is a normal practice in international protection of human rights to grant States Parties a seemingly unfettered right of access to a human rights Court or other such institutional organ. Thus, making the African Commission and States Parties to the African Charter as the primary entities entitled to submit cases to the Court is not *per se* an innovation. That has been the practice under the former European and Inter-American systems. The Protocol, however, appears to have borrowed more from the European system based on

---

1024 The drafters of that document contended that there may be instances where it may be necessary for victims of human rights abuse or their representatives and NGOs to file complaints directly in Court without first approaching the Commission, especially where irreparable harm may be caused by the delay in consideration of the matter. Such persons do not have the right for their complaints to be heard and therefore a preliminary hearing has to establish whether the Court will hear the matter. They argue that this provision which gives the Court original jurisdiction, once domestic remedies have been exhausted, being unique, is in keeping with the unique provisions of the Charter which allowed the Commission, in Article 55 of the Charter to receive "other communications," and as such, was moving in the right direction. *See* EXPLANATORY NOTES TO THE CAPE TOWN DRAFT, *supra*, note 998, at 4.
1025 NOUAKCHOTT DRAFT PROTOCOL, *supra*, note 986, Article 6(1) & (5).
1026 *See* NOUAKCHOTT LEGAL EXPERTS' REPORT, *supra* note 986, at 6. Most delegates were actually of the view that the Court should be accessible to individuals and non-governmental organizations just like the Commission and States Parties. It was even pointed out that instruments of other regional human rights systems were being amended to allow individuals and NGOs to have access to the their Courts without let or hindrance. *Id.*
1027 *Badawi El-Sheikh, supra,* note 979, at 947.

the old Convention. Article 5 (b), (c) and (d) of the Protocol are similar to the provisions of Article 48 of the European Convention before the Convention's amendment by Protocol 11.[1028] This provision is absent in the American Convention. What, however, appears to be an innovation in jurisdictional access to the Court is the provision of Article 5(e), which allows African Intergovernmental Organizations to submit cases to the Court. The fact that this access is with regard to contentious cases rather than in the Court's advisory opinion provision makes it more interesting.[1029] Article 64 of the American Convention allows the organs of the Organization of American States (OAS) that are listed in chapter X of the OAS Charter to consult the Court regarding the interpretation of the Convention, or of other treaties concerning the protection of human rights in American States. As far as the interpretation of the above provision goes, it refers to the ability of the OAS organs to make use of the advisory jurisdiction of the Inter-American Court.[1030]

The Protocol does not identify the circumstances under which those intergovernmental agencies may proceed before the Court. Is it as victims of human rights violations or as violators? There is nothing in the drafting history of the Protocol that gives an indication of what gave rise to this provision. While it is the Court that can answer this question when it is constituted, it appears reasonable that African Inter-governmental Organizations would fare better having access to the Court pursuant to the advisory jurisdiction of the Court. If not, there should be a balance whereby such inter-governmental organizations could also be proceeded against by the Commission, States Parties and non-state entities within the competencies allowed by the Protocol.[1031] It, however, becomes more com-

---

1028 Compare new Article 36 of the European Convention, as amended by Protocol 11, which now only requires that: "In all cases before a Chamber or the Grand Chamber, a High Contracting Party, one whose national is an applicant, shall have the right to submit written comments and to take part in the hearings."

1029 Such intergovernmental organizations already fall into the class of the entities that may request advisory opinion of the Court under Article 4 of the Protocol.

1030 Similarly, there is no direct provision in the European Convention allowing European intergovernmental organizations access to the contentious jurisdiction of the Court. It may, however, be argued that since access is now open to even individuals under the European Convention as amended by Protocol 11, such intergovernmental organizations, where they exist, may be accommodated. The reading of Article 34 of the new European Convention does not read this interpretation as it already lists "any person, non-governmental organization or group of individuals" claiming to be victims of human rights violations, as those from which the European Court may receive applications.

1031 The scenario here would anticipate African intergovernmental organizations such as the Economic Community of West African States (ECOWAS), African Economic Community (AEC), Southern Africa Development Community (SADC) and the like organizations, submitting cases before the Court. Against whom would these organizations be proceeding? Could they be petitioned against by the Commission, States Parties and individuals who are aggrieved in one way or other regarding the violation of the African Charter?

plicated, knowing that these organizations are not States Parties, and thus cannot be parties to the African Charter nor the Protocol, and therefore, not subject to be petitioned against, either to the African Commission, or to the Court.

There is no doubt that Article 5 gives States Parties greater advantage in terms of access to the Court over individuals. One would, however, agree with the opinion that the Protocol does not seem to endow States Parties with a generally direct access to the Court without any condition.[1032] From the wording of Article 5, it appears that a prior Communication to the Commission, either by a State, or against a State, is generally a condition precedent for instituting proceedings before the Court by States,[1033] the only possible exception being the scenario envisaged by Article 5(d), where a State Party whose citizen is a victim of human rights violation is entitled to submit the case to the Court.[1034] Even under this provision it is not definitely clear that the State espousing the claim of its citizen should not have proceeded first to the Commission. Thus, only the Commission can be said to have been given unlimited access to the Court. The Commission could use this unlimited access not only in referring cases to the Court, but also to initiate new cases before the Court, especially cases which reveal the existence of a series of serious or massive violations of human and peoples' rights as envisaged by Article 58 of the Charter.[1035] This would, however, require a reformulation of Article 58 to give direct power to the Commission in this regard, and remove the interference by the Assembly of Heads of State and Government of the OAU (AHSG), which has been criticized as the obstacle to the effective realization of this provision.[1036]

The idea of allowing States, whose citizens are victims of human rights violations to submit cases before the Court under Article 5(d) of the Protocol, as earlier mentioned, is an African codification of the provisions of old Article 48(b) of the European Convention.[1037] It allows a State to espouse the claims of its citizens. This is a provision which presupposes that African States would be so concerned as to be interested in the vindication of the rights of their citizens against other States Parties. The provision may be said to be ambitious owing

---

1032 *Naldi & Magliveras, supra,* note 993, at 437.
1033 It appears, however, that Article 5(b) and (c) of the Protocol suggest that there needs not be an outcome of the complaint lodged by a State or against a State before the State proceeds to the Court. One would agree that not only would the interest of justice not be served if this is the case, it would be an imprudent procedure that will ridicule the object of the Protocol. If the involvement of the Commission is envisaged, the Commission should be given the opportunity to determine the case before it goes to the Court unless the exigencies of the circumstances warrant otherwise.
1034 *Naldi & Magliveras, supra,* note 993, at 437.
1035 *Id.*
1036 *See Benedek, supra,* note 633, at 31; *Murray, supra,* note 841, at 118-119.
1037 Compare Article 36 of the European Convention as amended by Protocol 11.

to the fact that African practice does not support the above conclusion. Even though practice of African States in this regard gives room for little hope, the provision may be an avenue to bring alive inter-state petitions, since it appears that only a State can be the respondent under the provision. The provision should not, however, be used to deny individuals' ability to seek a vindication of their rights, especially where the respondent State has accepted the jurisdiction of the Court to receive cases from individuals and NGOs.

One other feature of the Protocol regarding access to the Court is the provision under Article 5(2) which allows a State Party that has an interest in a case to submit a request to the Court to be permitted to join.[1038] Though the Protocol does define what "interest" here means,[1039] the provision could be said to encompass the provisions of Article 5(c), but with broader implications. It is broader in the sense that a State Party may not only espouse a claim by its citizen whose rights have been violated, but may seek to join a case brought by an individual, its citizen, or an NGO, where the State perceives an interest. Whatever the term "interest" might mean, the Court must be guided by its own interest for the proper administration of justice. Caution must, however, be exercised by States Parties since real danger exits in that States could exercise their rights to intervene too readily in an attempt to subvert the administration of justice.[1040]

The access given to individuals and NGOs in the Protocol is a welcome development in African human rights practice and jurisprudence, despite its limitation to prior declaration by States Parties accepting the Court's jurisdiction to allow such access. This provision is, no doubt, a compromise between the view that individuals should be given unrestricted access to the Court on the one hand, especially in" exceptional circumstances" as emphasized in the Cape Town draft, or in cases of "serious, systematic or massive violations of human rights," as espoused by the Nouakchott draft; and the view on the other hand, that in all the above cases, there was the need for individual access to be optional.[1041] The

---

1038 Under new Article 36(1) of the European Convention, a variation of this provision is that in all cases before the European Court, a State Party one of whose national is an applicant shall have the right to submit written comment and to take part in the hearing.
1039 Cape Town and Nouakchott Drafts required that States have a "legal interest." See Articles 5(2) of both drafts. The final version eliminated the qualification of the interest to be shown by States parties as a legal one.
1040 *Naldi & Magliveras, supra*, note 993, at 438.
1041 The proponents of unrestricted individual access argued that no complaints had ever been filed before the African Commission by any State Party against another State Party, but that Individuals, NGOs and groups make the Commission function. Similarly, it was contended that individuals and NGOs would be the ones to make the Court function, and more so, if they are allowed to have unrestricted access to the Court. *See* THE NOUAKCHOTT LEGAL EXPERTS' REPORT, *supra*, note 972, at 6 ¶¶ 21-24. Despite this plausible argument, the narrower point of view prevailed.

compromise which represents the final position is that, rather than limit individual access to exceptional circumstances or cases of serious, systematic and massive violations of human rights, let access be given to individuals and NGOs without qualifying the violation, but that such access should be made optional to States Parties. This allows both violations of a serious nature and those of less serious nature to be brought before the Court, even though a declaration of a State Party accepting individual access is required.[1042] Even at this, the Protocol goes further than the American Convention, which does not give individual access to the Inter-American Court of Human Rights,[1043] and the European Convention in its original form before its various amendments via Protocol 9 and the more exhaustive Protocol 11.[1044]

Despite the compromise on jurisdictional access of individuals and NGOs to the Court, Naldi and Magliveras argue that there is a fear that the Court might not become fully operational when the Protocol enters into force.[1045] This fear is a result of the fact that some avid perpetrators of human rights violations like Nigeria and Sudan would not be brought to account, since it is improbable that they would accept the jurisdiction of the Court over individual complaints, if at all they would even ratify the Protocol.[1046] This fear is a genuine one, but we

---

1042 *See Naldi & Magliveras, supra,* note 993, at 438-439.
1043 Under the American Convention, individuals are allowed to participate only at the level of the Inter-American Commission. Once the Commission decides to refer a case to the Court, the petitioner loses his or her status and is technically barred from participating in the proceedings. Only the Commission and the defendant State are considered parties to the case before the Court. This has given rise to what has been described as inequality of arms in the Inter-American system. For a detailed discussion on this, *see José Miguel & Lisa I. Bhansali, Procedural Shortcomings in the Defense of Human Rights: An Inequality of Arms, supra,* note 286, 421-440, at 435. However, as was indicated in chapter 1, the recent revised Rules of Procedure of the Inter-American Court changes the status of victims before the Court, as Rule 23 of the Rules gives *locus standi* to petitioners, victims, their families and their accredited representatives from the stage when the Inter-American Commission refers a case to the Court. They can now present pleadings, proffer evidence and arguments directly to the court.
1044 Before the original text of the European Convention was adopted, a serious difference of opinion arose as to the question whether a European Court of Human Rights should be created at all. Since the proposal to create a Court with compulsory jurisdiction did not receive the support of the majority of the States, it was contemplated that it should not be included in the draft Convention. A compromise solution was reached, reflected in old Articles 46 and 48 of the Convention, which provided that the Court had compulsory jurisdiction only if the State concerned had recognized its jurisdiction by a declaration to that effect, or had otherwise consented to it. Even at that, individual access was not recognized. A declaration recognizing the jurisdiction of the Court was to allow the Commission or States Parties to proceed before the Commission in contentious cases, and not individuals. For more on this, *See* JACOBS & WHITE, THE EUROPEAN CONVENTION ON HUMAN RIGHTS, *supra,* note 172, at 280-392.
1045 *Naldi & Magliveras, supra,* note 993, at 439.
1046 *Id.*

must be optimistic, especially in the face of the wind of change that is blowing across Africa. While it is true that many African States have had, and continue to have a sorry human rights record, recent events give an indication of a desire to embrace international obligation in this area by some of these countries. No one could have imagined or believed the sudden change of events in Nigeria. Nigeria now has a democratic government, which is making concerted efforts to address human rights violations.[1047]

It must, however, be pointed out that the access granted to NGOs qualifies the NGOs to be those with observer status with the Commission, invariably excluding NGOs, which though may want to proceed before the Court, do not have observer status with the Commission. This departs from the position under Article 55 of the African Charter, which allows "communications other than those of States Parties" to be submitted to the African Commission on Human and Peoples' Rights. In the application of this provision, the practice of the Commission has been to receive communications generally from NGOs, irrespective of whether such NGOs have observer status with the Commission or not. One would have thought that the drafters of the Protocol would have been consistent with the African Charter in allowing NGO access to the Court, especially as the drafting history of the Protocol does not contain any pertinent reason why the NGOs must be ones with observer status with the Commission. Accordingly, one would only hope that when constituted, the Court would use its Rules of Procedure to rectify this seeming contradiction of the spirit of the African Charter.

C.   Advisory Jurisdiction

The advisory jurisdiction of any international or regional tribunal involves a formal rendering of legal opinions on issues presented before it, even though those opinions have no binding legal effect in the form of requiring positive or negative action from the parties. Notwithstanding that advisory opinions are not legally binding, the practice of the Inter-American Court shows that it can go a long way to affect the conduct of States with respect to human rights. The use of advisory

---

[1047] The new Government of Nigeria under President Olusegun Obasanjo came to power on May 29, 1999 after a general election, following the sudden death of the military dictator, General Sani Abacha on June 8, 1998. Since coming into office the new government has taken substantial steps aimed at instilling respect for human rights, which was non-existent under the military dictatorships that overran Nigeria from 1983 to May 28, 1999. The government constituted an inquiry into human rights violations and abuses during this period, and retired military officers who held political positions within this period. There is now a continuing effort to subject the military to civilian governance and authority.

opinion is particularly important in the sense that it may be the only way that a court can have the benefit of looking into an issue that involves a State that is not a party to the instrument vesting jurisdiction on the merits in the court.

Article 4 of the Protocol endows the African Court with advisory jurisdiction. Article4(1) provides that "at the request of a Member State of the OAU, the OAU, any of its organs, or any African organization recognized by the OAU, the Court may provide an opinion on any legal matter relating to the Charter or any other relevant human rights instruments, provided that the subject matter of the opinion is not related to a matter being examined by the Commission." This provision is similar to the mandate of the African Commission under Article 45(3) of the African Charter.[1048] This is seen as having a potential for duplication of functions between the Court and the Commission.[1049] While this is true, one would expect that the Court should gain primary place in issuing advisory opinions, especially if the Charter is fine-tuned to accommodate the reform envisaged in the Protocol. In addition, States Parties will be more willing to request the opinion of the Court than that of the Commission. As was noted earlier in this book, the advisory function of the Commission has never been utilized by States Parties to the African Charter.

Comparatively, the advisory jurisdiction of the African Court is broader in scope than that of the European Court under Article 45 of the European Convention, but similar to that of the Inter-American Court in Article 64(1) of the American Convention, except that the Protocol extends *locus standi* to other African organizations recognized by the OAU.[1050] On the other hand, while the Article 64(2) of the American Convention allows the Inter-American Court to render opinion, regarding the compatibility of a State's domestic law with human rights instruments at the request of Member States of the OAS, the Protocol does not contain any express provision to that effect.[1051] There is no doubt that Afri-

---

[1048] Article 45(3) lists one of the functions of the Court as interpreting "all the provisions of the present Charter at the request of a State Party, an institution of the OAU or an African Organization recognized by the OAU."

[1049] *Naldi & Magliveras, supra,* note 993, at 439.

[1050] *Id.* Under Article 47(1) of the new European Convention, only the Committee of Ministers of the Council of Europe may request advisory opinion from the European Court on legal questions concerning the interpretation of the Convention and its protocols. Under Article 47(2), such opinions, however, would not deal with any question relating the content or scope of the rights or freedoms defined in Section 1 of the Convention and its Protocols, or with any other question which the Court or the Committee of Ministers might have to consider in consequence of any such proceedings as could be instituted in accordance with the Convention. Article 47(3) requires that a decision of the Council of Ministers to request an advisory opinion of the Court should require a majority vote of the representatives entitled to sit on the Committee.

[1051] *Naldi & Magliveras, supra,* note 993, at 439-440.

can States may be reluctant to test the compatibility of their domestic laws with the African Charter through the Court's advisory jurisdiction, especially in response to the OAU principle of non-interference in internal affairs of States. This can, however, be overcome through the contentious jurisdiction of the Court, where a law of the State Party concerned is challenged by individuals or NGOs, and the State Party has accepted the jurisdiction of the Court to hear individual and NGO complaints.

One inference that can be drawn from the provisions of Article 4(1) of the Protocol is that African States which are not parties to the Protocol may request advisory opinion. What is important is that the States are Member States of the Organization of African Unity.[1052] It follows therefore, that African States which are parties to the African Charter, but have not ratified the Protocol are qualified to request advisory opinion.[1053] This accords with the particular practice of the Inter-American system whereby the Inter-American Court is regarded as, not just a Convention organ, but also as an institution of the Organization of American States (OAS) in matters relating to human rights.[1054] The exercise of advisory jurisdiction in this regard will be highly relevant in those areas of the Charter where the question of justiciability as a result of the nature of the subject matter, may be doubtful. The court may be able to articulate principles aimed at progressive development of the questions.[1055]

Naldi & Magliveras point out that the power of the Court to render advisory opinion under Article 4(1) is discretionary with the use of the word "may" by the Protocol, to the effect that the Court may decline to exercise its advisory jurisdiction.[1056] One would expect that discretion here is more that of the Member States of the OAU, or other entities allowed to make use of the Court's advisory jurisdiction. The Court would not exercise its advisory jurisdiction if OAU Member States and these entities do not choose to request the Court's advisory opinion. The authors, however, admit that one cannot conceive the circumstances under which the Court would decline to exercise its advisory jurisdiction, other than

---

[1052] The only obvious case in point where an African State may not be able to request an advisory opinion of the Court is that of Morocco, which withdrew its membership in the OAU in 1985, apparently in protest of the organization's handling of its dispute with the Saharawi Arab Republic (Western Sahara).
[1053] *See Naldi & Magliveras, supra* note 993, at 439-440.
[1054] For a detailed reading, Thomas Buergenthal, *The Advisory Practice of the Inter-American Human Rights Court, supra,* note 229, at 1.
[1055] It would be in the interest of many States Parties to the African Charter to ascertain their obligations under the Charter regarding economic, social and cultural rights in the light of the argument of the binding nature of provisions of the Charter dealing with these rights, vis-a-vis the principle of progressive development.
[1056] *Naldi & Magliveras, supra* note 993, at 439-440.

the prohibition from rendering an opinion on a matter related to an issue being examined by the Commission.[1057]

To enhance the development of the Court's advisory jurisdiction, Article 4(2) compels the Court to give reasons for its opinion, allowing judges of the Court to deliver separate or dissenting opinions. This accords with the provisions of other regional instruments.[1058]

D. Subject Matter Jurisdiction

A probing question arises regarding the substantive rights that the African Court will apply in cases that come before it on the merit in the light of the fact that the African Charter contains and guarantees a plethora of rights in the domain of the traditional civil and political rights,[1059] economic, social and cultural rights,[1060] and its innovation of peoples' and other group rights.[1061] Also, the duty aspect comes to mind. Will States have the right to petition the Court to ask for individuals or group of individuals to perform their duties under the Charter? From all indications, the drafters of the Protocol did not think of a particular subject matter over which the Court should exercise jurisdiction, but the entire provisions of the African Charter. This is evident from the provision of Article 3(1) of the Protocol, which extends the jurisdiction of the Court to all disputes concerning the interpretation of the Charter, the Protocol and other relevant human rights instruments ratified by the States concerned. In other words, the subject matter over which the Court would exercise jurisdiction is the subject matter provided for in the African Charter, the Protocol and relevant human rights instruments.

To many, the argument may be that for practical purposes, it would be expedient that the Court inquires into the traditional civil and political and civil rights and those aspects of economic, social and cultural rights that could be said to be tangibly enforceable.[1062] Such other rights as falling under the category of not being tangibly enforceable could then form a substantial aspect of the Court's advisory jurisdiction. One would agree that it will take some of these questions coming to the court before an appropriate interpretation of the obligations

---

1057 *Id.*
1058 *See* Article 66 of the American Convention and new Article 49(1) & (2) of the European Convention.
1059 AFRICAN CHARTER ON HUMAN AND PEOPLES' RIGHTS, Articles. 3-13.
1060 *Id.* Article. 14-18.
1061 *Id.* Article 20-24.
1062 Such rights as property rights guaranteed under Article 14 and such other hybrid rights.

imposed by the Charter regarding them can be reached, since they appear somewhat controversial. The court will indeed be very equipped to give the legal direction in this regard, and thus could set a standard for other regional and international systems.[1063] As mentioned earlier, this could be an area where the African Commission and other entities permitted by the Protocol will be effective, especially in seeking advisory opinion of the Court on the actual meaning and principles governing the realization of the economic, social, cultural and peoples' rights aspects of the Charter.

It needs to be stated, however, that this author does not believe that social and economic rights are totally not realizable. They go a long way to complement Civil and Political rights, especially in developing countries, where the need to have a conducive atmosphere for realizing basic necessities of life should be balanced with the need to realize civil liberty. The point, however, that should be made is that economic, social and cultural rights generally require progressive development based on a progressive commitment on the part of States. The irony unfortunately, is that the rampant corruption of the ruling class, whether military or civilians, especially in Africa in the face of needed economic, social and cultural developments, makes the issue complicated. Even though developed countries may not readily accept economic, social and cultural rights as rights, these countries, nevertheless, go to great lengths to provide the conducive atmosphere for these rights to thrive in the various forms they take in their domestic settings.

IV   APPLICABLE LAW AND CONSIDERATION OF CASES

A.   *Sources of Law*

Article 7 of the Protocol empowers the Court to apply the provisions of the African Charter and any other relevant human rights instruments ratified by the States concerned. This provision is reminiscent of Articles 60 and 61 of the African Charter, which requires the Commission to draw inspiration from principles of international law. It is, however, broader than Articles 60 and 61 in that it does not specify with particularity, these other relevant human rights instruments. Thus, it would be true that the Court will be free to adopt whatever source that it deems most appropriate in the circumstances, including general and particular international

---

[1063] The Court could build on the practice of the UN Economic, Social and Cultural Rights Committee in defining the obligations of States Parties to the African Charter on economic, social and cultural rights. In this vein, the Court will find the General Comments of the Committee as a veritable source for making its interpretations.

law, as suggested by Naldi and Magiliveras.[1064] An innovative application of this provision will no doubt give rise to a distinctive jurisprudence that unifies African human rights practice with general principles of international law, including customary international law.

One question that may arise in this regard is, whether it matters that the relevant human rights instruments would have been ratified by the States concerned as required by the provision. Could the States Concerned be those that are primarily involved in a proceeding before the Court, or generally, States Parties to the Protocol, or Member States of the OAU? It would appear that the better interpretation would be States in proceedings before the Court. What if the principle in question has acquired the status of customary international law or the status of *jus cogens,* which is not subject to ratification by States, despite being codified in the Charter? It would appear that it does not matter whether or not the States concerned have ratified these other relevant human rights instruments in the situation mentioned above, especially, as most human rights principles, in the areas of civil and political rights, have acquired the status of customary international law, and possibly, *jus cogens.* One would agree that the status of economic, social, cultural and other group rights as customary international law is still doubtful. It will therefore, be interesting to see if the Court builds a distinctive jurisprudence emphasizing the economic, social and cultural rights, even though they are still a matter of controversy within conservative Western circles.[1065]

B. *Consideration of Cases*

The Protocol under Article 8 specifies that the Rules of Procedure of the Court shall lay down the detailed conditions under which the Court shall consider cases brought before it, bearing in mind the complementarity between the Commission and the Court. The Cape Town and Nouakchott drafts variously made provisions, detailing the conditions for considering cases. These provisions were, however, considered to be inadequate.[1066] It should be recalled that the Charter makes

---

[1064] *Naldi & Magliveras, supra,* note 993, at 442-443.
[1065] *Id.* at 443.
[1066] Article 8 of the Nouakchott draft, for example, reads:
   1. The Court shall not consider a matter before it originating under the provisions of Article 49 of the Charter until such time as the Commission has prepared a report in terms of Article 52 of the Charter.
   2. The Court shall not consider a case originating under the provisions of Article 55 of the Charter until the Commission has considered the matter and prepared a report or taken a decision.

detailed provisions on the conditions for considering inter-State communications by the Commission under Articles 49 and 52, and other communications under Articles 55 and 56. These details were omitted in Article 8 of the Protocol, probably to give the Court flexibility to formulate in its Rules of Procedure, other conditions not contained in the Charter.

Despite the reluctance of the drafters of the Protocol in the above regard, Article 6 makes provisions on admissibility of cases submitted by individuals and NGOs to the Court, to the effect that the Court may request the opinion of the Commission on the admissibility of such cases when deciding on their admissibility.[1067] Further, the Court is required to rule on the admissibility of the cases taking into account the provisions of Article 56 of the Charter.[1068] It therefore, follows, that the admissibility requirements before the consideration of "other communications" under the Charter, would be applicable in the Court's consideration of individual and NGO cases. Thus, there is the likelihood that the Rules of Procedure of the Court would contain similar requirements as in the Charter. It is not clear why the drafters of the Protocol were reluctant in providing for the conditions in the Protocol. Could it be that the Court's Rules of Procedure will emphasize the conditions for considering inter-state cases, those filed by the Commission and African inter-governmental organizations, or are there going to be additional admissibility requirements for individual and NGO cases other than those provided for in Article 56 of the Charter? One is also left to wonder to what extent the Court would make exceptions to the strict interpretation of the admissibility requirements contained in the Charter. Would the Court be innovative and overlook technical or minor procedural irregularities in the interest of justice? It has been rightly observed that a narrow, formalistic approach is inappropriate to human rights instruments.[1069] In other words, the Court could review the admissibil-

---

3. The Court may deal with the case only if the matter is brought before it, within three months of the decision of the Commission.

4. Having accepted a case as stipulated in the provisions of Article 55 of the Charter, the Court may decide to reject it if, after due consideration, the Court establishes the existence of one of the grounds of inadmissibility in Article 56 of the Charter.

Drafters of the final version of Protocol rejected the formulation of Article 8 in the earlier drafts. It was generally observed that the Article as formulated in these drafts had not catered for all cases envisaged to be brought before the Court. Accordingly, it was decided that the heading and body of the article should be amended. It was proposed that a new and single paragraph should replace the previous four paragraphs of the article. *See* THE SECRETARY-GENERAL'S REPORT ON THE CONFERENCE OF MINISTERS OF JUSTICE/ATTORNEYS-GENERAL ON THE DRAFT PROTOCOL, *supra,* note 979, at 5 ¶ 18.

[1067] PROTOCOL ON THE AFRICAN COURT ON HUMAN AND PEOPLES' RIGHTS, Article 6(1).

[1068] *Id.* Article 6(2). Article 6(3) of the Protocol, however, gives the Court an option to either consider the cases or transfer them to the Commission.

[1069] *Naldi & Magliveras, supra,* note 993, at 441.

ity decision of the Commission in keeping with the trend among human rights control machineries.[1070]

Article 9 of the Protocol enjoins the Court to try to reach amicable settlement in a case pending before it in accordance with the provisions of the Charter. Article 52 of the Charter specifically requests the African Commission to pursue amicable resolution in inter-state communications, with all appropriate means before preparing a report of its findings and recommendations. Strictly speaking therefore, the requirement of the Charter regarding amicable settlement is with regard to inter-state communications before the Commission. As noted earlier, the Commission has, however, extended it to individual communications, and held that the primary objective of the Communications procedure is to initiate a positive dialogue, resulting in an amicable resolution between the complainant and the State concerned, which remedies the prejudice complained of.[1071] It may thus not matter that the Court may elect to try amicable settlement in either individual cases or cases initiated by States against each other. What actually matters here is whether it is more appropriate for the Court rather than the Commission to be involved in facilitating amicable settlement. While there is no doubt that settlement may arise at any stage of the proceeding, the Commission is more suited to carry out that function than the Court. From the provisions of the Protocol, most of the cases that will go before the Court would have passed through the Commission, in which case, they are mostly cases that are not resolved that will proceed to the Court. Could it be that the Protocol envisages settlement that would have arisen after the Commission has failed to achieve one, or would the Court have an original duty to try to achieve amicable settlement in all cases where the Commission failed, or in cases that are filed directly before the Court, without passing through the Commission?[1072] In this author's view, it is inconceivable that the Court

---

1070 Rule 118(2) of the Rules of Procedure of the African Commission allows the Commission to reconsider its decision on admissibility if a request for reconsideration is made to it. Similarly, both the Inter-American Court and the old European Court are empowered to review admissibility decisions made by their respective Commissions. See generally, HARRIS, et al, supra, note 172, at 651-666; and DAVIDSON, THE INTER-AMERICAN HUMAN RIGHTS SYSTEM, supra, note 229, at 81-82.

1071 See Odinkalu and Christensen, supra, note 775, at 245, citing the decision of the Commission in the group of communications against Zaire. See also RULES PROCEDURE OF THE AFRICAN COMMISSION, supra, note 680, Rule 98.

1072 This provision on amicable settlement was initially absent in the Cape Town draft. It was introduced in the Nouakchott draft by the Tunisian delegation. Despite the criticism that the function properly belongs to the Commission as mandated by the Charter, it was adopted at Addis Ababa and at the Conference of Attorneys General and Misters of Justice. See specifically, THE NOUAKCHOTT LEGAL EXPERTS REPORT, note 921, at 7. See also, THE SECRETARY-GENERAL'S REPORT ON THE CONFERENCE OF MINISTERS OF JUSTICE/ATTORNEYS-GENERAL ON THE DRAFT PROTOCOL, supra, note 979, at 9 ¶ 20. The drafters of the Protocol appear to have been influenced by the European

could do that, except in circumstances where it is unequivocally clear that settlement could still be achieved despite the fact that the Commission failed, or where a case is filed with the Court directly. Even in the latter situations, the Court may be justified in referring the cases to the Commission to pursue amicable settlement.

In considering cases, the Court is required to conduct its proceedings in public under Article 10(1), except, as may be provided for in its Rules of Procedure. Because the Court is yet to be functional, one does not know what circumstances to be included in the Rules of Procedure that would permit the Court to hold in camera proceedings. It, however, readily comes to mind that cases involving children or other very sensitive issues may require the exclusion of the public.[1073]

Article 10(2) introduces the choice of legal representative by a party before the Court. It further recommends free legal representation in the interest of justice. The African Charter and the Rules of Procedure of the Commission scarcely contain express provisions on legal representation.[1074] The Commission has rather recently begun to develop rules and practice, on a case by case basis, concerning representation, presumably with a view of aiding its ability to adopt informed decisions.[1075] The lack of provision for free legal representation for indigent parties has been an issue on which the African Charter has been criticized, given the abject poverty in many regions of Africa.[1076] Including free legal representation in the Protocol is a significant attempt to ensure the realization of the right of fair trial. One would, however, agree with the reasoning that this gesture will prove effective only if the necessary funds exist.[1077] It is, however,

---

Convention as amended by Protocol 11. Article 38 (1) (b) of the Convention requires the European Court to place itself at the disposal of the parties concerned with securing a friendly settlement of the matter on the basis of respect for human rights as defined in the Convention and its protocols. On the other hand, the American Convention in Article 48(1)(f), which is similar in wording with the European provision, vests this function on the Inter-American Commission. The difference here, however, which could be extended to the African system, is that the European system, having abolished the Commission leaves the Court to carry out a combined function of the former Commission and the Court. In the Inter-American and African systems where Commissions are retained, the Commissions rather than the Court should primarily carry out the function of amicable settlement, except in cases where there is direct access to the Courts without passing through the Commissions.

1073 Compare new Article 40(1) of the European Convention, which requires the European Court's hearing to be in public unless the Court in exceptional circumstances, decides otherwise. The Court has found the protection of the interest of children to require a restriction on public hearing in *O, H, W, B and R v. United Kingdom*, 1987, Series A, Vols. 120 and 121, *reprinted* in *Naldi and Magliveras, supra,* note 993, at 441.

1074 *Odinkalu and Christensen, supra,* note 775, at 273.

1075 *Id.*

1076 ANKUMA, *supra,* note 363, at 126-127.

1077 *Naldi and Magliveras, supra,* note 993, at 442.

not clear from the Protocol who may provide the legal representation recommended in Article 10(2). The Cape Town draft noted that while legal aid was important to ensure the interest of justice, the Court would not be able to afford the cost of providing legal assistance to every complainant. It is stated that the second part of Article 10(2) will allow NGOs to provide such assistance.[1078] The reports of subsequent drafts do not contain anything contrary to the above view expressed in the Cape Town draft. It becomes a bit troubling that the burden of providing legal assistance could be shifted to NGOs in the Protocol. It is acceptable that the Court may not be in a position to provide legal assistance to every complainant, but the responsibility is primarily that of States Parties. It is expected that NGOs would voluntarily come in to help the Court in view of the enormity of the problems that the Court may face in this regard. What is not right is the anticipation of NGO legal assistance in a treaty as an answer to the obligation of States Parties to provide legal assistance to those who come before the Court, and may require it.

Article 10(3) provides for the protection of any person, witnesses or representative of the parties, who appear before the Court, and their enjoyment of all facilities in accordance with international law, necessary for discharging their functions, tasks and duties in relation to the Court. This extension of immunity to parties, witnesses and representatives of parties who come before the Court is a standard practice aimed at ensuring the protection of human rights.[1079] It should enable individuals or groups of persons to appear before the Court without fear of retribution.[1080] Apart from the fact that the protection of witnesses is a standard practice, its relevance in the African human rights mechanism cannot be overemphasized. In many parts of Africa, State harassment and intimidation of parties and witnesses against the State is not uncommon. This provision should enable the Court, if properly and creatively utilized to develop its provisional measures practice.

1078 *See* EXPLANATORY NOTES TO THE CAPE TOWN DRAFT, *supra*, note 998, at 4.
1079 The provisional measure practice of the Inter-American system under Article 63(2) of the American Convention covers all persons who appear before the Inter-American. Court. Thus, States are prohibited from either instituting proceedings against witnesses or expert witnesses nor bring illicit pressure to bear on them or their families on account of declarations or opinions they have delivered before the Court. *See* HARRIS and LIVINGSTONE, *supra*, note 229, at 545.
1080 *Naldi and Magliveras*, *supra*, note 993, at 442.

V   ORGANIZATION OF THE COURT

A.   *Structure*

The structure of the African Court is unlike the European model, but more akin to the Inter-American model. The court has a single court structure without division into chambers or grand chambers as in the European system.[1081] As a single court, Article 28(2) of the Protocol provides that "the judgment of the Court decided by majority shall be final and not subject to appeal."[1082] In the Cape Town draft, the idea of a court with chambers was considered. Article 20 of the draft also provided that the Court may establish, if the need arose, two chambers consisting of five judges each. The part of this provision regarding the possible creation of chambers was not contained in subsequent drafts, nor in the Protocol as adopted. Article 23 of the Protocol simply provides that the Court shall examine cases brought before it, if it has a quorum of at least seven judges.

Article 24 of the Protocol provides for a registry of the Court, enabling the Court to appoint its own Registrar and other staff of the registry from among nationals of Member States of the OAU, according to the Rules of Procedure.[1083] The power given to the Court to appoint its own staff is a welcome development. This is a departure from the provisions of Article 41 of the African Charter regarding the Registry of the African Commission. As mentioned in Chapter three, under Article 41 of the Charter, the Secretary General of the OAU is responsible for appointing the Secretary and staff of the Commission. This has continually raised the question, whether the Commission is actually independent. With the power to hire its staff, the Court is in position to attract utmost loyalty from such staff.

As head of the Court's Registry, the Registrar of the Court would have his office and residence at the place where the Court has its seat.[1084] Article 25 of the Protocol leaves the determination of the seat of the Court to the Assembly of the OAU, but with input from the Court where a change of the seat of the Court is necessary. Furthermore, the Court could convene in the territory of any Member State of the OAU where majority of members of the Court consider it desirable,

---

1081 *See* Articles 27-31 of the European Convention as amended by Protocol 11. Article 67 of the American Convention makes the judgment of the Inter-American Court final and not subject to appeal.
1082 Compare Article 67 of the American Convention.
1083 It is interesting to note that the staff of the Court's Registry are to be drawn from Member States of the OAU, rather than from the States that have ratified the African Charter, or the Protocol.
1084 PROTOCOL ON THE AFRICAN COURT ON HUMAN AND PEOPLES' RIGHTS, Article 24(2).

subject to the consent of the State concerned.[1085] This provision on the seat of the Court is a direct influence of the provisions of Article 58 of the American Convention, which contains an almost exact wording.

In considering the seat of the Court, the emphasis should not be on a particular geographic region, but where the facilities necessary for an effective functioning of the Court can easily be obtained or expanded, taking into consideration relative proximity to Member States of the OAU. The tendency has been to identify a particular African State with relative democratic stability as a basis for determining the seat of an Organ of the OAU, as was the case in siting the seat of the African Commission in Banjul, The Gambia. At that time, the Gambia was adjudged to be an "unstained democratic State." On the other hand, the facilities for effective operation of the Commission were lacking, and still remains lacking. The Gambia does not have a university or other appropriate research centers that could enhance the work of the Commission.

B. *Composition*

Article 11 of the Protocols provides for eleven judges, nationals of Member States of the OAU to compose the Court, who are elected in their individual capacity, from among jurists of high moral character and of recognized practical, judicial or academic competence and experience in the field of human and peoples' rights. The African model follows the Inter-American model, where the number of judges is only a fraction of actual membership of the Organization of American States, (OAS).[1086] This is in contrast to the situation under the European system where the Court consists of the number of judges equal to that of the High Contracting Parties.[1087] An interesting aspect of the Court's composition is that, like the situation under Inter-American Court,[1088] the judges need only be nationals of

---

[1085] *Id.* Article 25(1) & (2).
[1086] *Naldi and Magliveras, supra*, note 993, at 443. Under Article 52(1) of the Inter-American Convention, which appears to have influenced Article 11 of the African Protocol in its phrasing, the Inter-American Court consists of seven judges, nationals of Member States of the OAS. *See also,* DAVIDSON, THE INTER-AMERICAN HUMAN RIGHTS SYSTEM, *supra,* note 229, at 123.
[1087] *See* Article 20 of the European Convention as amended by Protocol 11. The position under the European system while inclusive of all Member States of the Council of Europe, would be unrealistic for Africa, taking into consideration the number of parties and the fiscal implications. It would be impracticable, at least for now to have all the 53 members of the OAU represented in the Court. One would think that in addition to fiscal considerations, the drafters of the Protocol wanted to be consistent with the provisions of the African Charter on the number of members of the African Commission. Article 31 of the Charter provides that the Commission shall consist of eleven members.
[1088] *See* Article 52(1) of the American Convention.

Member States of the OAU rather than just Member States that have ratified the African Charter or the Protocol itself. This would allow competent judges to be elected to the Court even though they are nationals of Member States of the OAU, that have not ratified the African Charter.[1089]

The Protocol also stresses the fact that the judges would be elected in their individual capacity. The implication is that the judges must not follow instructions from the State of their nationality or other external influences.[1090] Linked to the requirement that the judges be elected in their individual capacity is the further requirement that the judges be elected among jurists of high moral character and recognized practical, judicial or academic competence and experience in the field of human rights. In other word, the judges could be attorneys at law, judges or academics with proven competence and experience in the field of human rights.[1091] This is one area where the Protocol differs sharply with the practice of the European and Inter-American systems, and for which its drafters are commended. The European and American Conventions are criticized for being unduly restrictive on the qualification of the judges to their Courts.[1092] Under the European Convention, the judges in addition to possessing high moral character, must possess qualifications required for appointment to high judicial office or be juriconsults of recognized competence.[1093] Similarly, the American Convention stipulates in addition, that the judges possess the qualification required for the exercise of the highest judicial functions in the State of which they are nationals or in the State that proposes them as candidates.[1094] The contention is that the above requirements unduly restrict the number of qualified persons to membership of the Court.[1095]

Membership of the African Court is by election. The election is, however, preceded by nomination of the judges by States Parties to the Protocol. Each State Party may propose up to three candidates, two of whom should be nationals of

---

1089 Two common examples that are usually given in this regard are the nomination of Professor Thomas Buergenthal, a citizen of the United States of America, who later became the President of the Inter-American Court, as a judge of the Inter-American Court by Costa Rica even though the United States had not ratified the American Convention, and the election of R. St. John MacDonald, a national of Canada as a judge of the European Court of Human Rights in the early 1990s. *See Naldi and Magliveras, supra,* note 993, at 444. The European example even stretched the situation further by allowing the election of a non national of Member States of the Council of Europe. In professor Burgenthal's case, even though the United States had not ratified the American Convention, it is a Member State of the OAS.
1090 *Id.*
1091 *Id.*
1092 *Id.*
1093 *See* Article 21(1) as modified by Protocol 11.
1094 Article 52(1).
1095 *Naldi and Magliveras, supra,* note 993, at 444.

the nominating State.[1096] But in actual composition of the court, however, no two judges may be nationals of the same State.[1097] Under Article 13(1) the Secretary-General of the OAU is mandated upon entry into force of the Protocol, to request each State Party to present within ninety (90) days of such request, its nominees for the office of judge of the Court. After receiving the nominations from Member States of the OAU, the Secretary-General is required to prepare a list in an alphabetical order of the candidates nominated and transmit it to Member States at least thirty days before the next session of the Assembly of Heads of State and Government of the OAU (AHSG).[1098] It is important to note that under Article 13, nomination of judges is done by only parties to the Protocol, while the list of nominated candidates is transmitted to Member States of the OAU in general. Naldi and Magliveras correctly give two probable reasons for the inclusion of non State Parties to the Protocol in the process. First, the possibility that nationals of non State Parties may be nominated, thus, the need for those Member States of the OAU to comment on the suitability of candidates who are their nationals. Second, because judges are elected by the whole OAU Assembly rather than by only States Parties to the Protocol.[1099]

In electing the judges of the Court the AHSG conducts a secret ballot from the list prepared by the Secretary-General of the OAU.[1100] The Protocol does not indicate the level of majority required for electing judges to the Court. Under Article 13(1) of the Cape Town draft , there was the requirement that judges be elected by two-thirds majority of votes of the members present and voting. This requirement was, however, deleted during the Nouakchott amendment and has remained the same in the Protocol. It has been argued that, despite the amendment, the effect of the two-thirds majority contained in the Cape Town draft remains unchanged.[1101] This is because the Rules of Procedure of the AHSG stipulates a two-thirds majority for decision making by the Assembly.[1102] The argument

---

1096 PROTOCOL ON THE ESTABLISHMENT OF AN AFRICAN COURT OF HUMAN RIGHTS, Article 12 (1). Article 12(2) enjoins that due consideration be given to adequate gender representation in the nomination process.
1097 *Id*, Article 11(2).
1098 *Id.* Article 13(2).
1099 *Naldi and Magliveras, supra,* note 993, at 444-445. The authors point out that this is unlike the position under Article 53(1) of the American Convention to the effect that even though the election of judges of the Inter-American Court of Human Rights takes place in the OAS Assembly, only States Parties to the American Convention are allowed to vote.
1100 PROTOCOL ON THE ESTABLISHMENT OF AN AFRICAN COURT OF HUMAN RIGHTS, Article 14 (1).
1101 *See Naldi and Magliveras, supra,* note 993, at 445.
1102 This was the basis for deleting the two-thirds majority requirement contained in Article 13(1) of the Cape Town Draft during the Nouakchott meeting. It was as a result of the explanation given by the OAU Legal Adviser at the meeting, that AHSG has its own Rules of Procedure which are followed in conducting all elections including those of members of the African Commission. He

goes further that the requirement for two-thirds majority of the AHSG is stringent compared to other similar provisions in the European and American Conventions, which require majority of votes cast and an absolute majority vote, respectively.[1103] Thus, the opinion is that, apart from the fact that the two-thirds majority requirement might prove problematic if no general consensus can be reached on the candidates to be elected at the first election, insisting on such stringent voting requirement because of an existing provision in the Rules of Procedure of the AHSG appears to be too formalistic an approach, and raises the suspicion that the AHSG may exert undue influence on the African Court.[1104] While the above concerns are genuine, one would expect that the AHSG would not frustrate any particular election, especially since the same procedure is used in electing members of the African Commission.[1105]

The Protocol considers it necessary that adequate gender representation be taken into consideration both in nominating and electing members of the Court.[1106] This requirement became necessary due to the glaring absence of similar provisions in the African Charter on the composition of members of the Commission. Thus, there was no conscious effort to include women in the Commission until it attracted much criticism from scholars and activists alike.[1107] It is hoped that States Parties and Member States of the OAU would rise above the seeming prevailing prejudice against female leadership in Africa, and respectively nominate and elect equally qualified women to the Court.

In a somewhat similar provision, Article 14(2) of the Protocol calls on the AHSG to ensure that there is a representation of the main regions of Africa and of their principal legal traditions in the Court as a whole. An express provision in this regard was also not contained in the African Charter, but it became an issue in the composition and functioning of the African Commission. As mentioned in chapter three with regard to the Commission, such provision is aimed at accom-

---

thus clarified that the said rule stipulates for a two-thirds majority for decision making by the AHSG. See the NOUAKCHOTT LEGAL EXPERTS' REPORT, *supra*, note 971, at 7, ¶ 31.

1103 *Naldi and Magliveras, supra* note 993, at 445, referring to Articles 22(1) of the European Convention, and 53(1) of the American Convention.

1104 *Id.*

1105 Note that Article 33 of the African Charter provides that the members of the African Commission shall be elected by secret ballot by the Assembly of Heads of State and Government from the list of persons nominated by the States Parties to the Charter. While it may be an easier mode of election to adopt a simple majority rule in electing members of the Court, it must be observed that till date, there had not been any known case where by the use of the two-thirds majority rule in the Rules of Procedure of the AHSG, had resulted in an impasse in the election of members of the African Commission.

1106 *See* PROTOCOL ON THE ESTABLISHMENT OF AN AFRICAN COURT OF HUMAN RIGHTS, Articles 12 (2) and 14(3).

1107 *See* ANKUMA, *supra*, note 363, at 16.

modating the various African geographical divides and principal legal traditions, in order to maintain equitable representation in both the Commission and the Court. Customary law or Native law and custom, Islamic law, Common law and Civil law as legal traditions, are prominent in various African legal systems, and would definitely come before the Court in one way or the other in its proceedings. The question has, however, been raised whether this provision could be observed in the same way as the gender representation requirement in Article 14(3), since it is not required in the nomination process (as is the case with adequate gender representation) that the nominating States take into consideration Africa's geographical regions and legal traditions.[1108] This author would think that, the fact that the consideration of geographic regions and legal traditions are not made requirements in the nomination process would not in itself defeat the intention of the drafters of the Protocol to achieve equitable geographic representation and legal traditions. There is the presumption that the nomination process would be Africa-wide in these terms, while the election process would harmonize the requirements in Article 14(2). In addition, the experience with the Commission would be instructive. The express requirement of taking gender representation into consideration both in the nomination process and during the election is, to this author, an attempt to emphasize the need to involve women in African leadership, which has not been the case.

Under Article 15(1) judges of the African Court are to be elected for a period of six years with re-election for only one term. The drafters of the Protocol appear to have followed the European and Inter-American systems by adopting a six-year term.[1109] However, the Protocol like the American Convention prescribes re-election for only one time. The European system on the other hand, does not require any specific number of permissible re-elections, thus adopting the practice under the Statute of the International Court of Justice's (ICJ).[1110] The Protocol requires that the term of four judges elected at the first election would expire at the end of two years, and the term of four more judges expiring at the end of four years.[1111] Those judges whose terms would expire at the end of the initial

---

1108 *Naldi and Magliveras, supra,* note 993, at 445-446.
1109 *See* Article 23(1) of the European Convention as amended by Protocol 11, and Article 54(1) of the American Convention.
1110 *Naldi and Magliveras, supra,* note 978, at 446. It must, however, be noted that Article 23(6) and (7) of the European Convention provides that the term of office of judges shall expire when they reach the age of 70 years, or until replaced.
1111 PROTOCOL ON THE ESTABLISHMENT OF AN AFRICAN COURT OF HUMAN RIGHTS, Article15(1). This provision mirrors Article 36 of the African Charter on the term of members of the African Commission. It should be noted that Article 36 of the Charter does not indicate a definite period for which members of the Commission may be re-elected. It means that while members of the Commission may be re-elected as often as necessary, the judges of the Court can be re-elected only once.

periods of two years and four years are to be chosen by lot by the Secretary-General of the OAU immediately after the first election of the judges.[1112] A judge elected to replace another judge whose term of office has not expired is required to hold office only for the remainder of the predecessor's term.[1113]

Article 20 of the Protocol prescribes the modality for filling vacancies in the Court, incase of death, or the resignation of a judge of the Court. Under Article 20(1), the President of the Court is required to immediately inform the Secretary-General of the OAU, who in turn would declare the seat vacant from the date of the death, or from the date the resignation took effect. A judge whose seat becomes vacant must be replaced unless the remaining period of the term of the judge is less than one hundred and eighty (180) days.[1114] The filling of a vacancy in the Court follows the same procedure earlier discussed on the composition of the Court.[1115]

C. Functioning of the Court

Article 16 of the Protocol prescribes an oath of office for judges of the Court after their election. The oath consists in the judges making a solemn declaration that they would discharge their duties impartially and faithfully. This provision was not contained in the Cape Town draft. It was introduced in the Nouakchott draft and retained in the Protocol. At its introduction, the provision was adopted unanimously without any objection, and adopted at Addis Ababa without any amendments,[1116] presumably, due the fact that an oath of office as a requirement is a standard practice in all national and international courts, and is mainly of a symbolic nature.[1117]

For effective functioning of the Court, Article 21 of the Protocol establishes the offices of the President and the Vice President, to be elected from among the

---

1112 *Id.* Article 15(2). Similar practice exists in the European and the Inter-American systems. *See* Article 23(2) of the European Convention and Article 54(1) of the American Convention. While under the European Convention, the choice by lot is made by the Secretary-General of the Council of Europe, the choice under the American Convention is determined in the General Assembly of the OAS after the election.

1113 PROTOCOL ON THE ESTABLISHMENT OF AN AFRICAN COURT OF HUMAN RIGHTS, Article15(3).

1114 *Id.* Article 20(2).

1115 *See Id.* Article 20(3). This meas that the processes of nomination by States Parties, the request of list of nominees from States Parties and transmission of same to Member States of the OAU by the Secretary-General, and election by the AHSG will be observed.

1116 *See* the NOUAKCHOTT LEGAL EXPERTS' REPORT, *supra*, note 986, at 8 ¶ 33. *See also* the ADDIS ABABA LEGAL EXPERTS' REPORT, *supra*, note 990, at 6 ¶ 24.

1117 *Naldi and Magliveras*, *supra*, note 993, at 446.

judges for a term of two years. The President and the Vice President may be re-elected only once. Under this provision, the President is to perform his or her judicial function on a full time basis with a further requirement that he or she should reside at the seat of the Court.[1118] The provision of Article 21(2) seems to emphasize Article 15(4), to the effect that all the judges, except the President would perform their functions on a part time basis.[1119] This provision generated a lot of debate and attracted serious objections by some of the delegates to the Ministers of Justice Conference at Addis Ababa. The objections were based on the fear that judges acting on a part-time basis may occupy positions or engage in professions that might be incompatible with their responsibilities as judges.[1120] There was also the fear that a part-time Court will cast doubts on the image of the Court as a Court of law.[1121] The insistence on a full time court led to the suggestion to either reduce the number of judges to seven and make them full time, or have a number of judges from the eleven judges to act next to the president on full time basis.[1122] These objections were countered by arguments of the heavy financial implications if all the judges would work on a full time basis. In the same vein, it was argued that the Court's initial volume of work might not justify the appointment of full time judges.[1123] A consideration of the various arguments led to a compromise whereby the second part of Article 15(4) was adopted to the effect that the AHSG may change the arrangement of part-time judges as it deems appropriate.[1124]

There is no doubt that for effectiveness, the judges ought to serve full time to enable them to devote their utmost attention to their judicial functions at the regional Court. The desire for effectiveness should, however, be balanced with availability of resources, at least in the early period of the Court's operation. This is especially so because it is not envisaged that Court will be inundated with very many cases in its early years. On the other hand, the AHSG should be sensitive to the situation as time progresses, by ensuring the appointment of full time judges if the work load of the Court increases in such a manner that manifests a need for such appointment. It is only hoped that the frequent precarious financial

---

1118 PROTOCOL ON THE ESTABLISHMENT OF AN AFRICAN COURT OF HUMAN RIGHTS, Article21(2). Article 21(3) provides that the functions of the President and the Vice President would be set out in the Rules of Procedure of the Court.
1119 The provision however gives the AHSG the discretion to change this arrangement as it deems appropriate.
1120 *Badawi El-Sheikh, supra,* note 979, at 948. *See* also *Naldi and Magiliveras, supra* note 993, at 448-449.
1121 *Badawi El-Sheikh, Id..*
1122 *Id.*
1123 *Id. See* also *Naldi and Magliveras, supra,* note 993, at 449.
1124 *Id., Badawi El-Sheikh; Naldi and Magiliveras.*

situation of the OAU will not be used as an excuse to prevent the realization of a full-time Court.

The quorum of the Court is set at seven judges by Article 23 of the Protocol. As already discussed this provision was a revision of Article 20 of the Cape Town draft, which apart from providing for a quorum of seven judges went further to recommend the establishment of two chambers consisting of five judges each if the need arises. One would think that the drafters of the Cape Town draft envisaged the possibility of an increased work load that would necessitate the creation of additional chambers akin to the new European Court. By deleting this provision, the Protocol intends the Court to operate as a single chamber, insinuating that the Court's workload will be rather light.[1125]

Under Article 22 of the Protocol, a judge who is the national of any State which is a party to a case submitted to the Court is excluded from hearing the case. This provision runs counter to its original formulation in Article 19 of the Cape Town draft. The drafters of the Cape Town draft felt that judges from such States should retain the right to hear such cases. The reasoning at the Cape Town proceedings was that the decision to continue to participate in a case, or otherwise, should be left to the judge and not the subject of a predetermined rule.[1126] It was emphasized that the principle should be that, as persons of integrity and independence, the judges should be free to participate in all cases, including those involving their States of origin.[1127] The present provision first appeared in the Nouakchott draft where there was a change of mind from the position under the Cape Town draft. At the Nouakchott proceedings, this change arose principally to avoid having *ad hoc* judges in the Court.[1128] No wonder that at the Third Legal Experts' Meeting in Addis Ababa, the proposal of including the notion of *ad hoc* judges was unanimously rejected, preventing an amendment of the provision.[1129]

Eliminating the right of judges to hear cases involving their States of origin and the absence of a provision for *ad hoc* judges in the Protocol, have been termed surprising. The contention is that, the right of judges to hear such cases and provisions for *ad hoc* judges are considered to be relevant procedural rules accepted by international tribunals.[1130] It appears that there is a desire on the

---

1125 *Naldi and Magliveras, supra,* note 993, at 449.
1126 *See* EXPLANATORY NOTES TO THE CAPE TOWN DRAFT, *supra,* note 998, at 6
1127 *Id.*
1128 *See* the NOUAKCHOTT LEGAL EXPERTS' REPORT, *supra,* note 986, at 8 ¶ 39.
1129 *See* the ADDIS ABABA LEGAL EXPERTS' REPORT, *supra,* note 990, at 7 ¶ 28.
1130 *See Naldi and Magliveras, supra,* note 993, at 449. The learned authors refer to the provisions of Articles 27(2) of the European Convention, 55(1) & (2) of the American Convention, 10(2) & (3) of the Statute of the Inter-American Court, 31(1) of the ICJ Statute and Article 16(4) of the

part of the drafters of the Protocol to depart from this practice. There is nothing in the Protocol indicating the reasons for the seeming distaste for judges to hear cases in which their Sates of origin are parties, or for not allowing *ad hoc* judges in the Court. One would rather assume that the drafters of the Protocol were determined to guard against nationalistic interests interfering with administration of justice in the Court. In the practice of allowing *ad hoc* judges in international tribunals, despite its perceived advantages, the tendency is that those judges are primarily appointed to represent the interest of their States of origin, which are parties to the cases; and not necessarily to ensure the administration of justice. If the intention is therefore to eliminate unnecessary over protection of national interest, then the African system would have removed one of the obstacles against the administration of justice in international tribunals, especially those involving accountability for human rights violations.[1131]

VI   JUDICIAL AND SUNDRY EMPOWERMENT OF THE COURT

A.   *Independence*

Article 17(1) of the Protocol provides that the independence of the Judges of the Court shall be fully ensured in accordance with international law. This provision, initiated in the Nouakchott draft, is a revision of Article 15(1) of the Cape Town Draft.[1132] The Cape Town provision was amended because it was considered to be overburdened with biased language.[1133] The implication may have been that the Cape Town provision over assumed that there was the tendency for the independence of the Court to be compromised by States Parties. While this may be true, looking at the provision critically, it should be conceded that the Cape

---

Statute of the European Court of Justice.

[1131] This author is not totally against the appointment of *ad hoc* judges in international tribunals, nor is the integrity or impartiality of *ad hoc* judges under question. There may be situations in which *ad hoc* judges may be useful in the resolution of international disputes. The emphasis here is that there should not be an unwholesome desire by States Parties to use the position of *ad hoc* judges to interfere with administration of justice in the resolution of human rights disputes. The insistence by States Parties to a case to have *ad hoc* judges to represent their interests, impacts the impartiality question. It presupposes that unless such States Parties are represented by *ad hoc* judges, the regular judges in the case would not be impartial.

[1132] Article 15(1) of the Cape Town draft provides:
Judges shall be independent in the exercise of their functions. The Court shall decide matters before it impartially, on the basis of fact and in accordance with law, without restriction, undue influence, inducement, pressure, threat or interference, direct or indirect, from any quarter or for any reason.

[1133] *See* the NOUAKCHOTT LEGAL EXPERTS' REPORT, *supra*, note 986, at 8 ¶ 34.

Town draft's emphasis was against a practice which is common in African domestic administration of justice.

In ensuring independence of the judges, Article 17(2) makes provision against conflict of interests by restraining judges from hearing cases in which they may have previously taken part as agents, counsel, advocates for one of the parties, or as a member of a national or international court, or a commission of inquiry, or in any other capacity. This provision has been observed to be a judicial guarantee granted to litigant parties before the Court for the protection of their own legitimate interests.[1134] The same provision gives the Court jurisdiction to determine any dispute or doubt arising from this conflict of interest provision, especially as there might be instances of disputed conflict of interest, given the blanket provision and scope of possible areas of conflict indicated by the Protocol.[1135] In the same vein, the Protocol protects judges as a way of assisting them in the performance of their duties. Article 17(3) confers on judges of the Court all immunities which are extended to diplomatic agents in international law from the moment of their election and throughout their term of office.[1136] Furthermore, under Article 17(4), judges would not be liable for any decision or opinion issued in exercise of their function.[1137]

Article 18 of the Protocol appears to consolidate the independence of judges of the Court by providing that the position of the judge of the Court is incompatible with any activity that might interfere with the independence or impartiality of such a judge, or the demands of the office as determined in the Rules of Procedure of the Court.[1138] In the original formulation of this provision, Article 16 of the Cape Town draft provided in addition, that any doubt on what amounted to incompatible activities would be settled by the Court. This part of the provision was deleted during the Nouakchott revision and remains so in the Protocol. No reason was given for deleting that part of the provision. The observation is that such issues would be dealt with in the Court's Rules of Procedure.[1139]

[1134] *Naldi and Magliveras, supra,* note 993, at 447. The authors observe that there is no directly similar provision under the European or American Convention.

[1135] *See Id.*

[1136] *See* similar provision in the American Convention, Article 70(1).

[1137] *Id.* Article 70(2). The Cape Town draft emphasized that the independence provision of the Protocol is crucial for the functioning of the Court, and therefore, derives from Article 10 of the 1985 UN Basic Principles on the Independence of the Judiciary. Thus, in order to ensure that the judges perform their functions without fear or favor and with the diligence required of them, it is necessary to provide the maximum immunity permissible under international law. *See* EXPLANATORY NOTES TO THE CAPE TOWN DRAFT PROTOCOL, *supra,* note 998, at 5.

[1138] *See* similar provisions in Article 71 of the American Convention and Article 21(3) of the European Convention as amended by Protocol 11.

[1139] *Naldi and Magliveras, supra,* note 993, at 447.

The provision of the Protocol on the incompatibility of activities of judges of the Court is a welcome development, which will ensure that the judges of the Court are not engaged in activities that conflict with their role as judges. The absence of a similar provision in the African Charter with regard to members of the African Commission, has resulted in a fluid situation in terms of what constitutes an incompatible activity of members of the Commission. It has often been a common criticism against the Commission that some members of the Commission also serve in their home governments, either as ministers, ambassadors or other State officers, thus casting doubt on their ability to function as totally independent experts in discharging their functions.[1140]

Article 19(1) of the Protocol ensures that a judge would not be suspended or removed from office unless, by the unanimous decision of the other judges of the Court, where the judge concerned has been found to be no longer fulfilling the requirements for the judgeship of the Court. Article 19(2) requires that such a decision of the Court would become final unless it is set aside by the OAU Assembly at its next session. Article 19(2) is an amendment of a similar provision in Article 17(2) of the Cape Town draft, which simply stipulated that the decision of the Court would be final, taking effect immediately. During the Nouakchott proceedings in which the Cape Town provision was amended, there was prolonged debate as to which body should be endowed with the power to suspend and remove judges of the Court.[1141] The view of the delegates who felt that the AHSG should have a hand in the suspension and removal of the judges eventually prevailed, thus leading to the present provision, which makes the decision of the Court subject to being set aside by the AHSG.

One would have expected that the situation under the Cape Town draft should have been allowed to remain as that provision ensures the security of tenure of the judges more than the present provision.[1142] In the same vein, the position under the Cape Town draft accords more with the practice of other regional human rights system. Under Article 24 of the new European Convention, no judge of the European Court of Human Rights may be dismissed from his office unless

---

1140 *See* generally, ANKUMA, *supra*, note 363, at 18-19.
1141 Some delegates, of which Nigeria and Tunisia played a prominent part, were of the view that since it is the Assembly of Heads of State and Government (AHSG) of the OAU that elects, the judges, that should be the body that should be involved in their removal. Some other delegates, however, strongly felt that the formulation allowing the AHSG to play a part in the suspension and removal of the judges was unnecessary as the Court should be given the power to suspend and remove any judge without any outside interference, in conformity with the provisions of most human rights instruments and the practices prevailing in Member States. *See* the NOUAKCHOTT LEGAL EXPERTS' REPORT, *supra*, note 986, at 8 ¶¶ 36-37.
1142 *See* EXPLANATORY NOTES TO THE CAPE TOWN DRAFT PROTOCOL, *supra*, note 998, at 6.

the other judges decide by a majority of two-thirds that he has ceased to fulfil the required conditions. The American Convention gives the OAS Assembly the power to determine the sanction to be applied against members of the Inter-American Commission or judges of the Inter-American Court only at the request of the Commission or the Court.[1143] Naldi and Magliveras rightly argue that, apart from practical issues that may arise from the application of Article 19(2), the provision somewhat subordinates the Court to the OAU Assembly, thus jeopardizing its independence,[1144] and that it negates the principle of *competence-competence* that appears to apply throughout the Protocol.[1145]

Another aspect of independence of the African Court envisaged in the Protocol is the funding of the Court. Article 32 provides that "expenses of the Court, emoluments and allowances for judges and the budget of its registry, shall be determined and borne by the OAU, in accordance with the criteria laid down by the OAU in consultation with the Court. This provision improves on the Article 44 of the African Charter regarding the funding of the African Commission. Article 44 of the Charter merely states that "provision shall be made for the emoluments and allowances of the members of the Commission in the regular budget of the Organization of African Unity." The practical effect of this provision is that, while the funding of the Commission may not have been of primary importance, the case of the Court appears to be somewhat different. The drafters of the Protocol envisaged a situation in which the independence of the Court would be taken into consideration in its funding and in the drawing up of its budget. Both the Cape Town and the Nouakchott drafts contained the phrase "...and bearing in mind the independence of the Court" in their respective provisions for the budget of the Court.[1146] This phrase was, however, deleted from the final version of the Protocol without necessarily undermining the independence of the Court.

The notion of emphasizing the independence of the Court with regards to its budget is not that the Court is expected to be financially independent of the OAU. As an organ of the OAU, it necessarily follows that it should be funded by that

---

1143 *See* Article 73 of the American Convention. It means therefore, that the power to discipline a judge of the Inter-American Court resides with the Court rather with the States Parties to the American Convention. Even though States Parties appear to play a part, it is at the invitation of the Court after the Court has found justifiable grounds for such action as set forth in the statute of the Court. The part played by the States parties is, however, limited to determining the sanction to be applied.
1144 *Naldi and Magliveras, supra,* note 993, at 447.
1145 *Id.* at 448.
1146 *See* Article 30 of the Cape Town draft and Article 31 of the Nouakchott draft. The reason for this according to the drafters, is that the Court should draw up its own budget to ensure its independence and effective function. In addition, in setting the emoluments and allowances of the judges, due consideration will have to be given to the importance and independence of the office of the Judges. *See* EXPLANATORY NOTES TO THE CAPE TOWN DRAFT PROTOCOL, *supra,* note 998, at 9.

organization, but in such a manner that will not undermine its independence as a regional judicial organ. In other words, the Court should not be neglected financially or made to be beggarly, if it is expected to function effectively. Again, it is the Court that should determine its financial needs.

There is no doubt that financing international and regional institutions is a big issue, more so for African institutions. The problem in the case of Africa is that many Member States of the OAU are not known to respect their financial obligations under the guise of poor financial state. As a result, many of them oppose the establishment of human rights institutions for lack of resources to maintain such institutions. There is no disputing the fact that the work of the human rights Court in Africa will require enormous financial resources.[1147] While lack of adequate financial resources can be a reasonable argument, it takes more of a political will to make an effort to establish, finance and sustain the Court. If all African States determine to meet their financial obligations to the OAU, there is no doubt that the Court will be firmly established and gradually sustained in a fairly independent manner. One can venture to insinuate that it costs more to violate human rights than to protect them.

B. Evidence and Rules of Procedure

Article 26 of the Protocol makes provision for the kind of evidence the Court is empowered to request in cases that come before it. Article 26(1) provides that "the Court shall hear submissions by all parties and if deemed necessary, hold an enquiry. The States concerned shall assist by providing relevant facilities for the efficient handling of the case." This final rendering of the provision is slightly different in wording from the provision originally made in the Cape Town Draft.[1148] The observation is that the present provision is an undisputed amelioration of the corresponding provisions of the Cape Town draft, which gave the Court a considerable degree of discretion to hear submissions.[1149] The inference from this is that the needed considerable discretion for the Court to carry out as many inquiries as possible appears to be absent in the final formulation of the provision, which should not have been the case, given the abysmal African human rights record, the ability of recalcitrant States to destroy or withhold crucial evidence,

---

[1147] Staff lawyers need to be hired to process and assist the Court with basic legal analysis of cases, judges have to be paid, the needed infrastructure will have to be in place, etc.

[1148] Under the Cape Town draft, Article 24(1) provided that: "as far as possible, after due consideration, the Court will hear the submissions by all parties and if deemed necessary hold an inquiry. The States concerned shall assist by providing relevant facilities to the efficient handling of the case."

[1149] *Naldi and Magliveras, supra,* note 993, at 449.

and the apparent inability of the African Commission to properly exercise its functions.[1150] There is no doubt that the human rights record of African States is not enviable, and that the African Commission has not lived up to expectations. This author, however, does not share the view that this part of Article 26(1) is a watered-down version of the Cape Town draft provision in terms of the effective functioning of the Court on evidentiary issues. The power of the Court here rather appears to be more mandatory than under the Cape Town draft. This position is reinforced by the second part of Article 26(1), which categorically makes it mandatory for the States concerned to provide relevant facilities for efficient handling of cases before the Court. The Court, by these provisions, has unreserved authority to apply the Protocol. The fact that the provision does not prescribe sanctions for noncompliance does not make it unenforceable.[1151] Moreover, it is doubtful that the Court will stand by while a provision of the Protocol is disregarded with levity by a State Party.

Under Article 26(2), the Court is empowered in its discretion to receive written and oral evidence including expert testimony, on the basis of which it is required to make its decision. This provision, though broadly drafted is a welcome supplement to Article 26(1). The provision ensures that the Court will not only hear submissions by the parties before it, but from third parties that may not be directly involved in the case. The general nature of the provision leaves the Court with a wide discretion to decide what entities are allowed to present evidence and the types of evidence it would allow, and on the basis of which it would make its decisions.[1152]

The importance of this provision is not only that it widens the pool of persons that the Court can receive evidence from, or the type of evidence that the Court can allow, it will also enrich the jurisprudence of the Court. This is especially so if the Court interprets the provision as allowing it to receive representations from individuals and NGOs where a *prima facie* interest in the outcome of a case brought by a privileged applicant can be shown.[1153] In addition, the advisory jurisdiction of the Court would be greatly enhanced by NGO participation, as the Inter-American experience has shown. It has been a feature of the proceedings of the Inter-American Court of Human Rights that a number of NGOs have pro-

---

[1150] *Id.*
[1151] While admitting that the second part of Article 26(1) of the Protocol is undoubtably an important provision which will enhance the jurisdiction of the Court, Naldi and Magliveras fear that if the provision were not to be accompanied by the imposition of sanction in cases of compliance, unscrupulous States may find no difficulty in disregarding it. *Id*, at 450.
[1152] *Naldi and Magliveras, supra,* note 993, at 450.
[1153] *Id.*

vided the Court with *amicus curiae* briefs.[1154] While there is no provision which deals explicitly with the issue of whether the Court is entitled to take notice of such briefs under the American Convention, it has been suggested that Article 34(2) of the Court's Rules would appear to provide an adequate constitutional basis for it to receive such briefs.[1155] Thus, by means of *amici curiae*, the Inter-American Court has secured considerable amount of participation by academic institutions, NGOs and individuals in its advisory proceedings.[1156] The participation of these entities has further enriched the jurisprudence of the Court even though advisory opinions *per se* are not binding.[1157]

Article 33 of the Protocol empowers the Court to determine its own procedures and to draw up its Rules of Procedures, with a further requirement that the Court consults the African Commission as appropriate. Giving the Court the power to determine its procedural rules is consistent with international practice.[1158] The further requirement that the Court should consult the African Commission where appropriate, is an obvious provision that would ensure that the Rules of the Court and those of the Commission do not conflict.

[1154] DAVIDSON, THE INTER-AMERICAN HUMAN RIGHTS SYSTEM, *supra*, note 229, at 147.
[1155] *Id.* The Rule states that:
the Court may, in consultation with the parties, entrust any body, office, commission or authority of its choice with the task of obtaining information expressing an opinion, or making a report upon any specific point.
[1156] *Antônio Augusto Cançado Trindade, The Operation of the Inter American Court of Human Rights* in HARRIS & LIVINGSTONE, *supra*, note 229, 133 at 142
[1157] It should be observed, however, that a provision similar to Article 46 of the African Charter would have been more appropriate in vesting the African Court with express power to receive representations and opinions from NGOs, individuals and other entities capable of enlightening it. Under Article 46 of the Charter, the African "Commission may resort to any appropriate method of investigation; it may hear from the Secretary-General of the Organization of African Unity or any other person capable of enlightening it" Article 24(2) of the Cape Town draft envisaged the possibility of the Court allowing *amicus curiae* briefs by NGOs which have an interest in a particular matter, by providing: "the Court may receive written and oral evidence and *other representations* including ..." (Emphasis not in the draft). *See* EXPLANATORY NOTES TO THE CAPE TOWN DRAFT PROTOCOL, *supra*, note 998, at 7. The Nouakchott meeting felt the need to delete "other representation"as reflected in Article 25(2) of the Nouakchott draft and Article 26(2) of the Protocol for the reason that the phrase was unnecessary. *See* the NOUAKCHOTT LEGAL EXPERTS' REPORT, *supra*, note 986, at 9 ¶ 42. *See* also the ADDIS ABABA LEGAL EXPERTS' REPORT, *supra*, note 990, at 7 ¶ 30. Could it then be that the drafters of the Protocol actually intended the Court to receive other representations, since the consensus appears to be that the present provision already covers them?
[1158] *See* Articles 26(d) and 60 of the European and American Conventions, respectively. Similarly, Article 42(2) of the African Charter empowers the African Commission to lay down its Rules of Procedure.

C. Remedial Powers of the Court

1. Findings

Under Article 27 of the Protocol, the Court is empowered to make findings and order appropriate remedies when there is a violation of any rights, unlike the African Commission under the African Charter.[1159] According to Article 27(1), if the Court finds that there has been a violation of a human and peoples' right, it is required to make appropriate orders to remedy the violation, including the payment of fair compensation. The original version of this provision in Article 25 of the Cape Town draft read as follows:

1. If the Court finds that there has been a violation of a human and peoples' right, it shall order an appropriate measure to remedy the situation.
2. The Court may also order, that the consequences of the measure or situation that constituted the breach of such right be remedied and that fair compensation or reparation be paid or made to the injured party.

The Cape Town version was heavily amended, at the Nouakchott meeting. This resulted in not only the merger of paragraphs 1 and 2, but a deletion of some important words in the provision as reflected in the final version of the Protocol.[1160] The amendment was as a result of the reservations raised by Sudan and Egypt on the formulation of the article.[1161] Apart from the reservations raised by the delegates of these countries, there appears to be no other reason for deleting the original formulation of the provision. The suggestion is that the provision in the Cape Town draft is preferable to Article 27(1) of the Protocol due to its

---

[1159] It should be recalled that under Article 58(1) & (2) of the African Charter the Commission should only draw to the attention of the AHSG, those exceptional situations that reveal the existence of a series or serious or massive violations of human and peoples' rights after its deliberations. The ASHG may then request the Commission to undertake an in-depth study of the situations and make a factual report, accompanied by its findings and recommendations.

[1160] Compare Article 63(1) of the American Convention, which reads:
If the Court finds that there has been a violation of a right or freedom protected by this Convention, the Court shall rule that the injured party be ensured the enjoyment of his right or freedom that was violated. It shall also rule, if appropriate, that the consequences of measure or situation that constituted the breach of such right or freedom be remedied and that fair compensation be paid to the injured party.
While Article 27(1) of the Protocol borrowed the style in the American Convention, it chose to leave out certain aspects that emphasize that the practices which led to the violation are not repeated in the future, and restitution. It is however commendable that the Protocol goes further than the American Convention by including reparation and not only fair compensation as one of the available remedies.

[1161] *See* the NOUAKCHOTT LEGAL EXPERTS' REPORT, *supra*, note 986, at 9 ¶ 42.

expansion of the scope of restitution to "fair compensation or reparation to be paid or made to the injured party," thereby introducing the possibility of restitution in kind.[1162]

In effect, the amendment of the Cape Town draft leaves Article 27(1) of the Protocol to be drafted in very broad terms. This may, however, be a blessing in disguise, if the judges are poised to take a progressive outlook in the interpretation of the provision. It is the uncertainty of the position that the judges would take that attracts the view that it is important that the Court be granted express powers to order recalcitrant States to revoke practices or domestic legislation which have led to human rights violations.[1163] It is hopeful that the Court will be persuaded by the experience of other systems to achieve the larger purpose of the African Charter, by not being overly restrictive in its interpretation of the provisions of the Protocol. The Inter-American Court, for example, in the *Aloeboete Case* (Reparations), avoided a restrictive interpretation of Article 63(1) of the American Convention, which only refers to "fair compensation to be paid to the injured party" without expressly providing for reparation. The Court not only ordered the respondent State to pay a sum of money to the beneficiaries of the victims, but also as reparation, the reopening of a school and a medical dispensary in the village where the majority of the bereaved families resided.[1164]

2. Provisional measures

The power of the Court to order provisional measures is conferred by Article 27(2) of the Protocol, which provides that "in cases of extreme gravity and urgency, and when necessary to avoid irreparable harm to persons, the Court shall adopt such provisional measures as it deems necessary."[1165] The Protocol departs from the African Charter, which does not contain any provision that empowers the Commission to order provisional measure. As mentioned earlier in chapter four, the African Commission's power to request provisional measure is covered by

---

1162 *Naldi and Magliveras, supra,* note 993, at 450.
1163 *Id.*
1164 *Aloeboete et al v. Suriname, (Reparations),* Judgment of 10 September, 1993, ¶ 116; 15 INTER-AM. CT. H.R. (Ser. C); 14 HUM. RTS. L. J. 425 (1993), also *reprinted* in *Naldi and Magliveras, supra,* note 993, at 451. On reparations in the Inter-American system, *See* specifically, *Dinah Shelton, Reparations in the Inter-American System* in THE INTER-AMERICAN SYSTEM OF HUMAN RIGHTS, *supra,* note 229, at 151.
1165 *See* Article 63(2) of the American Convention. Article 27(2) of the Protocol is a verbatim rendition of the American Convention. *See also* Rule 36 of the Rules of Procedure of the European Court of Human Rights.

its Rules of Procedure.[1166] It should be re-emphasized that States are not bound to adopt provisional measures ordered by the Commission.[1167]

The importance of the Court's ability to order provisional measures cannot be over stressed. By their nature, provisional measures arise from a reasonable presumption of extreme and urgent risk of irreparable damage to persons.[1168] The example of the Inter-American system has shown the importance of the use of provisional measures in human rights protection.[1169] Under that system, the granting of provisional measures has become an increasing important aspect of contemporary case law of the Inter-American Court, given the emergency relief it has secured, and indeed the lives it has saved, thus demonstrating clearly the preventive function of international protection of human rights.[1170]

The African Court could thus be inspired by the Inter-American experience, even regarding the question as to how the Court would treat orders for provisional measures by the Commission, in terms of whether such provisional measures will continue in force, or whether the Court would adopt them.[1171] Under the Inter-American practice, the Inter-American Commission does not have the capacity to order provisional measures, but could request provisional measures from the Inter-American Court.[1172] Once the Court orders the measures based on the request of the Commission, it necessarily follows that such orders have the legal value of the judgment of the Court.[1173] Similarly, under Rule 36(2) of the Rules of Procedure of the European Court of Human Rights, any interim measures

---

1166 RULES OF PROCEDURE OF THE AFRICAN COMMISSION, Rule 111.

1167 This is because under Rule 111, the Commission merely recommends its views to the State Party concerned on the appropriateness of taking provisional measures. In addition, the Commission is required to inform the State Party that the expression of its views on the adoption of those provisional measures do not imply a decision on the substance of the case.

1168 *See* the decision of the Inter-American Court on the request for Provisional measures in *Case 10.548*, *supra*, note 870. *See* also *Trindade, supra,* note 1156, at 146

1169 *See* Pasqualucci, *Provisional Measures in the Inter-American System: Innovative Development in International Law, supra,* note 881, at 803.

1170 *Trindade, supra*, note 1156, at 146. Some of the cases in which the Court has ordered provision measures to protect the rights to life and to humane treatment of witnesses *suo motu*, or on the request of the Inter-American Commission include: *Velásquez Rodríguez, Godínez Cruz, Fairé Garbi and Solis Corrales v. Honduras* (1988), 9 HUM. RTS. L. J 104 at 105; *Cabellro Delgado and Santana v.Colombia* (1994), *Blake v. Guatemala*(1995), 3 IHRR 539 (1996); *Bistíos-Rojas v. Peru* (1990-1991), 11 HUM. RTS. L.J. 275; *Chunimá v. Guatemala* (1991-1992), *Reggiardo Tolosa v. Argentina* (1993-1994), 2 IHRR 411 (1995) *Colotenago v. Guatamala* (1994-1996), 2 IHRR 414, 421 (1995); *Carpio Nicolle v. Guatemala* (1995-1996), 3 IHRR 529 (1996), *reprinted Id.* at 145-146.

1171 *Naldi and Magliveras, supra,* note 993, at 452.

1172 *Id. See* also *Trindade, supra,* note 1156, at 145 for the cases in which the Inter-American Commission requested provisional measures from the Inter-American Court.

1173 *Naldi and Magliveras, supra,* note 993, at 452.

ordered by the former European Commission remained recommended after the case had been brought before the Court, unless and until the Court decided differently or ordered its own provisional measures.[1174] In the same vein, it is expected that whatever provisional or interim measures ordered by the African Commission under Rule 111 of its Rules of Procedure should remain in force or be adopted by the African Court, especially where the State to whom the measure is addressed, has accepted the jurisdiction of the Court to receive individual or non-state complaints.

3. Judgement and enforcement

In making provisions for the Judgment of the African Court and its execution, the drafters of the African Protocol adopted some of the provisions of the American and the European Conventions, while at the same time maintaining some provisions that are unique to the Protocol. Article 28(1) of the Protocol requires the Court to render its judgment within ninety (90) days of having completed its deliberations. It was thought necessary in the Nouakchott draft to include a time limit within which judgments of the Court will be delivered.[1175] This is entirely a novel idea not contained in either the American Convention or the European Convention. There was, however, no reason given for this requirement. One would assume that the purpose of the time limit is to prevent undue delay by the Court in rendering its opinions.

The judgment of the Court decided by majority would be final and not subject to appeal.[1176] Even though there would be no appeal against the judgement of the Court, the Court is empowered to review its decisions in the light of new evidence under the conditions that would be set out in its Rules of Procedure.[1177] In the same vein, the Court enjoys the power to interpret its decisions.[1178] Article 28(5) requires that the judgment of the Court be read in open Court, due notice having been given to the parties. The Protocol further requires the judgment of

---

1174 *Id.*
1175 *See* the NOUAKCHOTT LEGAL EXPERTS' REPORT, *supra*, note 986, at 9 ¶ 43.
1176 PROTOCOL ON THE ESTABLISHMENT OF AN AFRICAN COURT OF HUMAN AND PEOPLES' RIGHTS, Article 28(2). *See* similar provisions in Article 67 of the American Convention and Article 44(1) of the European Convention.
1177 PROTOCOL ON THE ESTABLISHMENT OF AN AFRICAN COURT OF HUMAN AND PEOPLES' RIGHTS, Article 28(3). This provision is consistent with Rule 118 of the Rules of Procedure of the African Commission, which confers the Commission with the power to reconsider a Communication declared inadmissible.
1178 *Id.* Article 28(4). Compare Article 67 of the American Convention.

the Court to be reasoned,[1179] a requirement not contained in the African Charter regarding the Commission's decisions. In cases where the judgment of the Court is not unanimous, either in whole or in part, any judge would be entitled to deliver a separate or dissenting opinion.[1180]

Execution of the judgment of the Court is covered by Article 30 of the Protocol, which requires that, by being parties to the Protocol, it is an undertaking by the States to comply with the judgement of the Court in any case to which they are parties, and within the time limit stipulated by the Court, as well as guarantee its execution.[1181] The execution process, however, begins with a notification of the Court's judgment to the parties and to Member States of the OAU and the African Commission.[1182] Similarly, the Council of Ministers of the OAU would also be notified, and shall have the responsibility of monitoring the execution of the judgment on behalf of the Assembly of Heads of State and Government of the OAU.[1183]

A number of issues can be raised with regard to the execution or enforcement of the Court's judgement. First, how will judgments awarding compensatory damages or reparations be enforced against recalcitrant States? Second, what will be the scope of monitoring the execution of the judgment of the Court by the Council of Ministers of the OAU on behalf of the AHSG? Third, what will the Court do, and to a larger extent, the AHSG, if the judgment of the Court is not complied with by a party? These issues have not been resolved on the face of the Protocol. On the first issue, the precedent left by the American Convention, albeit, persuasively, is unsatisfactory. Article 68(2) of the American Convention states that execution of the judgement of the Inter-American Court may be executed in the country concerned in accordance with domestic procedure governing the execution of judgment against the State.[1184] This position appears to have influenced the decision of the African Commission in the case of *Louis Emgba Mekongo v.*

1179 PROTOCOL ON THE ESTABLISHMENT OF AN AFRICAN COURT OF HUMAN AND PEOPLES' RIGHTS, Article 28(6). *See* similarly, Article 66(1) of the American Convention, and Article 45(1) of the European Convention.

1180 PROTOCOL ON THE ESTABLISHMENT OF AN AFRICAN COURT OF HUMAN AND PEOPLES' RIGHTS, Article 28(7). *See* Article 66(2) of the American Convention and Article 45(2) of the European Convention.

1181 Compare Article 46(1) of the European Convention and Article 68(1) of the American Convention. These conventions do not require their Courts to stipulate a time limit for State to comply with their judgments.

1182 PROTOCOL ON THE ESTABLISHMENT OF AN AFRICAN COURT OF HUMAN AND PEOPLES' RIGHTS, Article 29(1).

1183 *Id.* Article 29(2).

1184 *Naldi and Magliveras supra,* note 993, at 452.

Cameroon[1185] in which the Commission found, *inter alia*, that the complainant was entitled to reparation for the prejudice he had suffered, but that the valuation of the amount of such reparation should be determined in accordance with the legal system of Cameroon. One would agree with the argument that this type of solution is not satisfactory to the extent that national procedural law may significantly restrict or even prohibit the execution of judgement against a State.[1186]

On the second issue, it is reasonable to expect that the scope of monitoring the judgment of the Court by the Council of Ministers of the OAU should not be limited to mere keeping of a record of compliance with orders made in the judgment, as insinuated by Naldi and Magliveras.[1187] It should rather be one that puts the Council of Ministers in a position of equal partners in the effective functioning of the African system. The experience of the European system should be persuasive in this regard. New Article 46(2) of the European Convention provides that the final judgment of the European Court of Human Rights shall be transmitted to the Committee of Ministers, which shall supervise its execution.[1188] In carrying out this mandate, the Committee of Ministers has developed rules for supervising the execution of the judgments of the European Court of Human Rights.[1189] Whenever the Court decides that there has been a violation, the Committee invites the respondent State to advise it of the measures it has taken in pursuance of the judgement. The Committee would then take note of the information supplied by the State and satisfies itself of compliance with the judgment of the Court. Even though the Committee may not have any sanction available to it, it can bring to bear on a recalcitrant State, considerable political pressure to ensure compliance.[1190] In the same vein, the OAU Council of Ministers can be innovative in monitoring the execution of the judgment of the African Court on behalf of the AHSG.

To answer the third question raised above, the African Court has not been granted any express power to ensure that its judgments are adhered to, and thus

---

1185 *Louis Emgba Mekongo v. Cameroon supra*, note 844, 51 at 54.
1186 *Naldi and Magliveras supra*, note 993, at 452.
1187 *Id.*
1188 It needs to be observed that just like the OAU Council of Ministers, the Committee of Ministers under the European Convention is a Political organ of the Council of Europe not established in connection with the adoption of the European Convention on Human Rights. *See* JACOBS & WHITE, THE EUROPEAN CONVENTION ON HUMAN RIGHTS, *supra*, note 72, at 393.
1189 JACOBS & WHITE, THE EUROPEAN CONVENTION ON HUMAN RIGHTS, *supra*, note 172, at 393, *citing Batsch, The Supervisory Functions of the Committee of Ministers Under Article 54- a Postcript to Luedicke-Belkacem-Koç* in F. MATSCHER & H. PETZOLD, PROTECTING HUMAN RIGHTS: THE EUROPEAN DIMENSION 47-54 (Köln, 1990).
1190 JACOBS & WHITE, *supra*, note 172, at 398.

appears powerless to react when its decisions are ignored.[1191] The Court is rather required under Article 31 of the Protocol to submit to each regular session of the OAU Assembly, a report on its work during the previous year. The report is required to specify in particular, the cases in which a State has not complied with the Court's judgment.[1192] Apart from this report, there is nothing else that the Court is required to do, and rightly so in the opinion of this author. Similarly, it is not obvious what the OAU Assembly would do about those cases that the States have not complied with the judgment of the Court. It is, however, actually up to the OAU Assembly to protect the integrity of the system after the Court has fulfilled its role, by adopting whatever political measures that are necessary to secure compliance with the Court's judgement. This is, however, unknown in the history of the OAU, especially as the Charter of the OAU does not contain any provision that suggests that a member of the organization can be suspended or expelled, unlike the situation under the European mechanism.[1193] One only hopes that the current idea of rethinking the Charter of the OAU and regional governance, will make the regional organization more progressive in dealing with human rights issues in Africa.[1194]

[1191] *Naldi and Magliveras, supra,* note 993, at 453.

[1192] Compare Article 65 of American Convention. Note that unlike Article 31 of the African Protocol, Article 65 of the American Convention requires the Inter-American Court to make pertinent recommendation in its report to the OAS General Assembly specifying the cases in which a State has not complied with its judgments.

[1193] Under Article 8 of the Statute of the Council of Europe, a serious breach of its Article 3 by a Member State may result in the suspension or expulsion of the State. By the terms of Article 3 of the Statute, every Member State of the Council of Europe must accept the principles of the rule of law and the enjoyment of all persons within its jurisdiction of human rights and fundamental freedoms. Thus, a pronouncement of the European Court of Human Rights that a Member State has violated the European Convention, amounts to a breach of Article 3, and could result in the withdrawal of the State from the Council of Europe or expulsion of the State. *See* JACOBS & WHITE, *supra,* note 172, at 398. The enforcement power of the European Committee of Ministers was exercised in *Stran Greek Refineries and Stratis Andreadis v. Greece, supra,* note 293, *reprinted* in *Naldi and Magliveras, supra,* note 993, at 453-454, where Greece was pressured to pay the just satisfaction awarded by the European Court of Human Rights against her which she refused to pay within the allotted time.

[1194] At the Summit of the OAU in Algeria in July 1999, the organization resolved that it was no longer going to be business as usual in the continent. The Assembly of Heads of State and Government agreed, for example, that the seizure of power in Member States through military coups will no longer be recognized in the continent. This resolution was translated into a firm principle of the regional body in Article 31 of the Constitutive Act of the new African Union, which deals with suspension of members of the Union. The article provides that "governments which shall come to power through unconstitutional means shall not be allowed to participate in the activities of the Union."

VII   RATIFICATION, ENTRY INTO FORCE AND AMENDMENT OF THE PROTOCOL

Article 34(1) provides that the Protocol shall be open for signature and ratification or accession by any State Party to the Charter. This means that a Member State of the OAU that is not a party to the African Charter cannot sign the Protocol unless such State first becomes a party to the Charter. The instrument of ratification or accession to the Protocol would normally be deposited with the Secretary-General of the OAU.[1195] According to Article 34(3), the entry into force of the Protocol would take place thirty days after fifteen instruments of ratification or accession have been deposited.[1196] Before fifteen instruments of ratification was accepted as the number necessary for the Protocol to come into force, there was a prolonged debate by the delegates on the need to have a higher number in order to make the Court more credible.[1197] With fifteen ratifications, the expectation is that it may not prove very troublesome in obtaining the necessary ratification needed for the Protocol to enter into force in view of the fact that there are 52 signatories to the African Charter.[1198] For any State ratifying or acceding to the Protocol after its entry into force, the Protocol would come into force on the date that the State deposits its instrument of ratification or accession.[1199]

Article 35 of the Protocol provides two modes of amending the Protocol, namely through the request of a State Party[1200] and a proposal of the Court itself.[1201] Under the former method, a State Party makes a written request to the Secretary-General of the OAU, who is required to present the request to the OAU Assembly, which may adopt the amendment by simple majority[1202] after

---

1195 PROTOCOL ON THE ESTABLISHMENT OF AN AFRICAN COURT OF HUMAN AND PEOPLES' RIGHTS, Article 34(2). Under Article 34(5), it is also the responsibility of the Secretary-General to inform all member States of the entry into force of the Protocol. It should be observed that all Member States of the OAU have now ratified the African Charter, and thus eligible to sign the Protocol.
1196 The Protocol is yet to enter into force as the required fifteen ratifications (15) are yet to be realized. It should be noted that all Member States of the OAU have ratified the African Charter, with the ratification by Ethiopia in 1998, and the recent ratification of the Charter by Eritrea. *See* Murray, *Human Rights News: Africa, supra,* note 702, at 350-351.
1197 *See* the NOUAKCHOTT LEGAL EXPERTS' REPORT, *supra,* note 986, at 9 ¶¶ 48-50. *See* also the ADDIS ABABA LEGAL EXPERTS' REPORT, *supra,* note 990, at 9 ¶ 34. The Cape Town draft had earlier provided for eleven instruments of ratification in Article 31(3).
1198 *See Naldi and Magliveras, supra,* note 993, at 453-454.
1199 PROTOCOL ON THE ESTABLISHMENT OF AN AFRICAN COURT OF HUMAN AND PEOPLES' RIGHTS, Article 34(4).
1200 *Id.* Article 35(1).
1201 *Id.* Article 35(2).
1202 The Cape Town draft in Article 32(1) required two-thirds majority. It was thought appropriate in the Nouakchott and Addis Ababa meetings to amend the provision to read "simple majority" in line with Article 68 of the Charter on the amendment of the Charter itself. *See* the NOUAKCHOTT LEGAL EXPERTS' REPORT, *supra,* note 986, at 10 ¶ 52.

all State Parties may have been duly informed of it, and the Court has given its opinion on the amendment. It is not clear who will request the opinion of the Court on the proposed amendment. One would assume that the OAU Assembly through the office of the Secretary-General, would be the appropriate body to request the opinion of the Court here. The latter method would involve the Court proposing amendments to the Protocol as it may deem necessary through the Secretary-General of the OAU. One would expect that, since the Secretary-General is not in a position to approve amendments to the Protocol, the Court's proposal for amendment will be subject to the same rule as the former method.

Article 35(3) provides that an amendment shall come into force for each State Party which has accepted it thirty days after the Secretary-General of the OAU has received notice of the acceptance.[1203] Just like under the African Charter, it has been argued that the effect of this provision is that the amendments approved by the OAU Assembly will not enter into force for all States Parties simultaneously, but only to those who are prepared to accept them.[1204] In other words, the Court would be obliged to apply both the amended and unamended Protocols depending on whether the respondent State Party has or has not accepted the amendments.[1205] The contention is that it is absurd for an amendment to be valid and not valid at the same time; amendments should have general validity and applicability as the instrument amended.[1206]

Like the African Charter, the Protocol is silent about the withdrawal of a State Party from being a party to the Protocol. It is argued that despite the silence of the Charter, it does not appear that a denunciation of the Charter is prohibited.[1207] Whether or not denunciation is possible under the African Charter, one would agree that the bigger question is the effect of the withdrawal of a member of the OAU from the organization in relation to the withdrawing State's obligation as a party to the African Charter and the Protocol.[1208] The withdrawal of Morocco from the OAU in 1985 is an example. The difference, however, is

---

[1203] This provision mirrors Article 68 of the African Charter. A difference that is noticeable is the absence of the requirement that the accepting State would do so within its constitutional procedure as in the Charter. One would assume that this is readily obvious.

[1204] *Naldi and Magliveras, supra,* note 993, at 455.

[1205] *Id.*

[1206] *See Bondzie-Simpson, supra,* note 619, at 664.

[1207] *Naldi and Magliveras, supra,* note 993, at 455. The authors argue that it was the clear intention of the of the parties during the defining stage of the Charter that the possibility of withdrawal should exist, *citing* G. J. NALDI, THE ORGANIZATION OF AFRICAN UNITY: AN ANALYSIS OF ITS ROLE 114 (Mansell, London, 1989).

[1208] *Naldi and Magliveras, supra,* note 993, at 455, noting that under Article 32 of the OAU Charter, at the end of one year from the date a Member State announced its withdrawal, the Charter shall cease to apply to that Member and its membership will be terminated.

that Morocco was not a party to African Charter. Thus, it would follow that since under Article 63(1) of the African Charter only members of the OAU can be parties to the African Charter, the effect of withdrawal from the OAU would not only mean the termination of membership of the organization, but also from being a party to the Charter.[1209] It is, however, doubtful that a State Party which withdraws its membership of a regional body, can absolutely absolve itself from the human rights obligations assumed during its membership of the body. While allowing for a denunciation by a State Party, the American and European Conventions do not exonerate their State Parties from obligations assumed under their respective Conventions with respect to acts which may constitute a violation of those obligations and which were taken before the denunciation became effective.[1210] The same principle can be emulated in the African mechanism in interpreting the obligation of African States that may eventually choose to opt out of the regional arrangement.

The Protocol on the establishment of the African Court no doubt breaks new grounds, and is a welcome development in African Human rights discourse, and in terms of African human rights dispute resolution. The Protocol measures up to other international and regional instruments of its kind, as it especially fills the lacunae in the African Charter by providing for a workable institutional framework in the African system. Apart from the questions of prompt ratification of the Protocol and the provision of the necessary material and moral support for the effective functioning of the Court, there are still areas of concern such as the relationship between the Court and the African Commission regarding their various mandates. This author shares the view expressed by Dr. Makau Mutua, that the African Charter needs to be revised to address these concerns.[1211] The protective functions of the African Commission should be exclusively vested in the Court. On the other hand, the Commission should be charged with promotional functions, including the consideration of State reports and facilitating dialogue with NGOs and government institutions in Member States, to encourage the incorporation of human rights norms in to State policies and domestic legislation.[1212] Similarly, the Commission will be effective in aiding the Court in initiating and conducting friendly settlement or amicable resolutions of the cases that come before the Court. It is true that the unambiguous demarcation of areas of competence between the Court and the Commission should alleviate the problem of hierarchy and competi-

---

[1209] Compare new Article 58(3) of the European Convention, which allows for withdrawal from membership of the Council of Europe and therefore a termination of being a Party to the Convention.
[1210] *See* Article 78(1) of the American Convention and Article 58(2) of the European Convention. *See* also *Naldi and Magliveras, supra,* note 993, at 456.
[1211] *Mutua, The African Human Rights Court: A Two-Legged Stool?, supra,* note 775, at 360-361.
[1212] *Id.*

tion between the two institutions, and might enhance cooperation and mutual reinforcement, thereby bringing about a division of labor that should prevent, in the words of Mutua, "tainting one body with the baggage of the other."[1213] The effect of this would be that, while the Commission clearly becomes a regional body involved in promoting human rights, with quasi-protective functions, as appropriately as are clearly necessary, the Court becomes the judicial organ of the African human rights system.[1214] Generally, the scenario envisaged is one that adopts the object of the European reform under Protocol 11 to the European Convention: a single Court with exclusive protective mandate. On the other hand, an African modification of the European model will retain the African Commission based on the peculiar needs of Africa. The peculiarity of the African situation requires an equally important emphasis on promotion and human rights education of a largely unschooled majority of people, on the notion of rights.[1215] This author does not expect that Member States of the OAU will in present the circumstances, easily accommodate this view. It should, however, be the basis for a further reform of the African human rights system in the not too distant future, to ensure full realization of the objectives contained in the African Charter and its additional Protocol. Any thing to the contrary will definitely bring about an unhealthy duplication of procedures, which will encompass both the Commission and the Court. The tendency is that this duplication of procedures will result in a pattern of time wasting and lengthy procedures, which in turn will operate to defeat the objectives of the reform.

[1213] *Id.* at 361.

[1214] See *Id.* There is no doubt that there maybe some aspects of protective work that will be appropriate for the Commission to carry on. Such areas include the facilitation of friendly settlement in situations mentioned earlier in this chapter, receiving and considering state reports, fact-finding missions, engaging in country studies and issuing reports, etc.

[1215] While under the European reform, the European Commission was abolished and the system replaced by a single Court, the African system should maintain the two organs as is presently the case, but with clearly distinct roles as indicated above. See Nmehielle, *Towards an African Court of Human Rights: Structuring and Empowering the Court, supra,* note 4, at 23-29.

7

NON-GOVERNMENTAL HUMAN RIGHTS ORGANIZATIONS AND THE AFRICAN HUMAN RIGHTS SYSTEM

Non-governmental organizations (NGOs) have played significant roles in human rights discourse as far back as before 1945 when the UN Charter was adopted. According to Korey, it was, however, not until many years after the adoption of the Universal Declaration that there would "be created the prominent international human rights NGOs with which the contemporary world is familiar."[1216] In any case, it was these NGOs, both the early pioneers of the forties and the later groups

---

[1216] WILLIAM KOREY, NGOS AND THE UNIVERSAL DECLARATION OF HUMAN RIGHTS: A CURIOUS GRAPEVINE 1, at 2-3 (New York: St. Martin's Press, 1998). On NGOs generally, *See* also, THE CONSCIENCE OF THE WORLD: THE INFLUENCE OF NON-GOVERNMENTAL ORGANIZATIONS IN THE U.N. SYSTEM (PETER WILLETTS, ed.,Washington, D.C.: The Brookings Institution,1996); HENRY J. STEINER, DIVERS PARTNERS: NON-GOVERNMENTAL ORGANIZATIONS IN THE HUMAN RIGHTS MOVEMENT (Cambridge, Massachusetts: Harvard Law School Human Rights Program and Human Rights Internet, 1991); THOOLEN, HANS & BERTH VERSTAPPEN, HUMAN RIGHTS MISSIONS: A STUDY OF THE FACT-FINDING PRACTICE OF NON-GOVERNMENTAL ORGANIZATIONS (Dordrecht: Martinus Nijhoff Publishers, 1986); MONITORING HUMAN RIGHTS IN EUROPE, (ARIE BOLD, LISELOTTE, MANFRED NOVAK & ALLAN ROSAS, eds., Dordrecht: Martinus Nijhoff Publishers, 1994); *Rachel Brett, The Contribution of NGOs to the Monitoring and Protection of Human Rights in Europe* in MONITORING HUMAN RIGHTS IN EUROPE 121-144 (ARIE BOLD, LISELOTTE, MANFRED NOVAK & ALLAN ROSAS, eds., Dordrecht: Martinus Nijhoff Publishers, 1994); *Rachel Brett, The Role and Limits of Human Rights NGOs at the United Nations*, 43 POLITICAL STUDIES, SPECIAL ISSUE, 96-110 (1995); *Cynthia Price Cohen, The Role of Non-governmental Organizations in the Drafting of the Convention on the Rights of the Child*, 12 HUM. RTS. QTLY., 137-147 (1990); Nigel S. Rodley, *The Work of Non-Governmental Organizations in the World-wide Promotion and Protection of Human Rights*, 90/1 BULLETIN OF HUMAN RIGHTS, 84-93 (1991); *David Weissbrodt, The Contribution of International Non-governmental Organizations to the Protection of Human Rights* in HUMAN RIGHTS IN INTERNATIONAL LAW: LEGAL AND POLICY ISSUES 403-438 (THEODOR MERON, ed., Oxford: Clarendon Press,1984); *Laurie S. Wiseberg, Protecting Human Rights Activists and NGOs: What More can be Done?*13 HUM. RTS. QTLY., 525-544 (1990); *Michael H. Posner & Candy Whittome, The Status of Human Rights NGOs*, 25 COLUM. HUM. RTS. L. REV. 269 (1994); *Steve Charnovitz, Two Centuries of Participation: NGOs and International Governance,* 18 MICH. J. INT'L. L. 183 (1997); and *Karsten Nowrot, Legal Consequences of Globalization: The Status of Non-Governmental Organizations under International Law,* 6 IND. J. GLOBAL L. STUD. 579 (1999).

that put human rights on the journalistic and academic map of the world.[1217] The desire to prevent future horrors reminiscent of the atrocities of World War II, evoked the slogan "Never Again," leading to the birth of the Universal Declaration. As rightly suggested, the answer to the difficult questions that resulted in the above phrase, was not to be found in States, but in non-state actors, in NGOs.[1218] To Korey, the NGOs would take on the challenge of transforming the words of the Declaration from a standard into reality; and would assume the function of implementing the demands of international morality, to the extent that the Universal Declaration itself, in the course of time, would be transformed from a mere moral manifesto or a common standard into customary international law that carried a veritable obligatory character.[1219] Thus, out of the foundation laid in the Universal Declaration have grown other international human rights instruments and mechanisms in which NGOs have continued to play a prominent part.

Apart from the participation of NGOs at the universal level of the United Nations, they continue also to be involved at the various regional bodies that are active in the field of human rights, which have established and developed regional human rights mechanisms. The Council of Europe, the Organization of American States (OAS), the Organization of African Unity (OAU) and other sub-regional entities have developed mechanisms that recognize the participation of NGOs.[1220]

This chapter is devoted to considering the impact of human rights NGOs on the African human system. The focus here will be on the roles they have played and their impact so far in relation to the work of the African Commission on Human and Peoples rights under the mandate given to it in the African Charter. Additionally, the impact the NGOs will have on the new dispensation of the establishment of the African Court on Human and Peoples Rights under the Protocol to the African Charter, will be inquired into. The chapter will conclude with a consideration of the role NGOs will play in the future of human Rights in Africa.

1217 KOREY, *supra*, note 1216, at 3.
1218 *Id.* at 2.
1219 *Id.*
1220 Rachel Brett, *Non-Governmental Actors in the Field of Human Rights* in AN INTRODUCTION TO THE INTERNATIONAL PROTECTION OF HUMAN RIGHTS: A TEXT BOOK 327, at 331 (RAIJA HASK & MARKKU SUKSI, eds., Turku Abo, Finland: Institute for Human Rights, Abo Akademi University, 1997). *See* also Martin A. Olz, *Non-Governmental Organizations in Regional Human Rights Systems*, 28 COLUM. HUM. RTS. L. REV. 307, at 326-369 (1997).

I   STATUS OF NGOS UNDER THE AFRICAN CHARTER

No where does the African Charter on Human and Peoples' Rights expressly define the status of non-governmental organizations in the regional framework for human rights protection. However, the Charter envisages the importance of NGOs in the effective functioning of the African human rights system. In defining the promotional mandate of the African Commission, Article 45(1)(a) enjoins the Commission to "encourage national and local institutions concerned with human and peoples' rights...", in addition to collecting documents, undertaking studies and researches on African problems in the field of human rights and organizing seminars, conferences and such other tasks. Similarly, the Commission is mandated to "co-operate with other African and international institutions concerned with the promotion and protection of human and peoples' rights.[1221] Again, Article 45(3), which governs the interpretative mandate of the Commission confers the power on the Commission to "interpret all the provisions of the present Charter at the request of a State Party, an institution of the OAU or an African organization recognized by the OAU. It has been pointed out in chapter three that neither a State Party nor an institution of the OAU has sought an opinion of the Commission in the exercise of this interpretative mandate. The observation was also made that it has rather been NGOs that have sought and obtained through draft resolutions, the interpretation of some provisions of the Charter, aimed at giving clarity to the meaning of those provisions. Finally, under Article 55 of the Charter NGOs are among the entities that can submit communications other than those of State Parties to the Charter.

One must agree that the above provisions say nothing particularly on the status accorded NGOs under the Charter, other than the fact that they are entities that could possibly play a role in the African human rights mechanism. However, the Rules of Procedure of the Commission concerning NGOs, go further than the provisions of the Charter to recognize NGOS as deserving consultative and observer statuses at the Commission. Rule 75 of the Commission's Rules of Procedure makes provision for NGO observer status. According to the Rule, "non-governmental organizations, granted observer status by the Commission, may appoint authorized observers to participate in the public sessions of the Commission and of its subsidiary bodies." Similarly, Rule 76 provides for consultation with NGOs such that the "Commission may consult the non-governmental organizations either directly or through one or several committees set up for this purpose. These

---

[1221] AFRICAN CHARTER ON HUMAN AND PEOPLES RIGHTS, Article 45(1)(c).

consultations may be held at the invitation of the Commission or at the request of the organization.

The only reasonable conclusion to be drawn from the application of the above Rules is that NGOs are an integral part of the human rights mechanism set up under the African Charter. This is particularly so because there in nothing in the Charter that expressly restricts the participation of any type of organization in the African human rights system.

II NGOs AND THE AFRICAN COMMISSION

The relationship between NGOs and the African Commission is a unique one, which has been developed by the practice of the Commission. In fact, no other regional human rights system has developed the kind of relationship that the African system has with NGOs.[1222] The practice of the Commission in developing the kind of relationship it has with NGOs is largely derived from the role that the Charter envisages that NGOs would play in the African system, on the basis of which the Commission made express provisions on the status of NGOs in its Rules of Procedure. It has been suggested that one of the reasons for the recognition of NGO participation in the African system might be because NGOs were strongly involved in the drafting process of the African Charter, in addition to the fact that the practice of other human rights system clearly showed the benefit of NGO contributions.[1223] The relationship between the Commission and NGOs has resulted in cooperation of diverse kinds, culminating in NGO participation in the promotive and protective mandates of the Commission. It must, however, be observed that the cooperation between the Commission and NGOs cannot realistically be fitted into the categories of promotion and protection. It is often the case that these areas of cooperation overlap. The separation below is only intended to demarcate the provisions of Article 45 of the African Charter on the promotional and protective mandates of the Commission in relation to the cooperative activities between the Commission and NGOs.

[1222] Benedek, *The African Charter and Commission on Human and Peoples' Rights: How to Make it Work, supra,* note 633, at 34-35. *See also Olz, supra,* note 1220, at 372; ANKUMA, *supra,* note 363, at 186.
[1223] *Olz, supra,* note 1220, at 364.

A. Promotion-based Cooperation

To actualize the provisions of Article 45(1) (a) (b) and (c) of the African Charter as far promotion of human rights is concerned, the Commission at its second session in Dakar in 1988, included cooperation with both inter-governmental organizations and international NGOs, as well as Africa-based NGOs in its first Program of Action.[1224] Since the adoption of the first Plan of Action and its subsequent reviews, the Commission has been willing to engage in cooperative activities with NGOs in various ways.[1225] In this regard, scholars and even the Commission agree that the most fruitful and successful joint venture, or cooperation between the Commission and NGOs relate to the organization of a series of workshops and seminars prior to the Ordinary Sessions of the Commission.[1226] Notable among these workshops are those organized by the International Commission of Jurists (ICJ) in collaboration with the Commission and other human rights NGOs. These workshops have been held since 1991, with the attendance of African and international NGOs, as well as representatives of inter-governmental organizations and academic institutions.[1227] The importance of these workshops is that they serve as fora for mutual exchange of ideas between the Commission and NGOs, which identify ways of contributing to the work of the Commission. The workshops discuss various topics that touch on the effective functioning of the African system to enhance the Commission's promotional and protective mandates under the African Charter. These workshops would usually result in the adoption of resolutions on thematic issues or on the human rights situations in particular countries, as well as reports which are presented at the Commission's Ordinary Sessions.[1228] An example of the effective cooperation between the

---

[1224] Calude E. Welch, Jr., *The African Commission on Human and Peoples" Rights: A Five-Year Report and Assessment*, supra, note 633, at 14-15. The Commission's current Plan of Action still emphasizes cooperation with NGOs in the promotion of human rights based on the experience gained in the past ten years of the Commission's existence. See THE MAURITIUS PLAN OF ACTION (1996-2001), *supra*, note 658, at 12-15.

[1225] *Olz, supra*, note 1220, at 365.

[1226] ANKUMA, *supra*, note 363, at 187. See also, *Olz, supra*, note 1220, at 365; THE MAURITIUS PLAN OF ACTION (1996-2001), *supra*, note 658, at 2.

[1227] *Olz, Id*. See also, CLAUDE, E. R. WELCH, JR., PROTECTING HUMAN RIGHTS IN AFRICA: ROLES AND STRATEGIES OF NON-GOVERNMENTAL ORGANIZATIONS 167 (Philadelphia: University of Pennsylvania Press,1995); ONE DECADE OF CHALLENGE, *supra*, note 642, at 10.

[1228] *Olz, supra*, note 1220, at 365. For basic documentation on conclusions and recommendations made by the first ten workshops on the participation of NGOs on the work of the African Commission on Human and Peoples' Rights, *see* PARTICIPATION OF NON-GOVERNMENTAL ORGANIZATIONS IN THE WORK OF THE AFRICAN COMMISSION ON HUMAN AND PEOPLES' RIGHTS: A COMPILATION OF BASIC DOCUMENTS 15-75 (INTERNATIONAL COMMISSION OF JURISTS, ed., 1996).

Commission and NGOs is the joint drafting of the revised Rules of Procedure of the African Commission.[1229]

B. Protective Cooperation

Apart from engaging in promotive activities with NGOs, which have popularized the African Commission among NGOs, the Commission has also made NGOs partners in its protective work. The first of such steps is the granting of observer and consultative statuses to NGOs under the Rules of Procedure of the Commission, in furtherance of the enjoinment of the Charter in Article 45 (1)(c) to "cooperate with other African and international institutions concerned with the promotion and protection of human and peoples' rights." Thus, by virtue of Rules 75 and 76 of the Commission's Rules of Procedure, NGOs may be granted observer and consultative statuses respectively. While there is no formal indication of how application for observer status is made, the Commission has developed some guidelines to that effect.[1230] It is the practice to appoint a particular member of the Commission as Rapporteur for each application for observer status. The Rapporteur Commissioner will have to review the organization's constitution, sources of funding, its annual report and plan of action, and if satisfied, the Commission formally grants observer status to the organizations at one of its sessions.[1231] As at 1998, the Commission which started granting observer status to NGOs at its third session in Libreville, Gabon in 1988, had granted observer status to 205 organizations, 150 of which are Africa-based organizations.[1232] The Commission, since 1998 was, however, directed by the AHSG of the OAU at the thirty-fourth Ordinary Session of the OAU to review its criteria for granting

---

1229 Olz, Id.
1230 See Rachel Murray, Report on the 1996 Sessions of the African Commission on Human and Peoples Rights, supra, note 507, at 17.
1231 Id. See also Olz, supra, note 1220, at 367. According to Muray, at the Commission's 20th Session, observer status was denied some organizations for a number of reasons, one of which was the source of funds. As one of the organizations obtained the majority of its funding from the United States government rather than from members' contributions, some members of the Commission were anxious of the potential influence of a non-African State in the work of the Commission.
1232 See ONE DECADE OF CHALLENGE, supra, note 642, at 20. For a list of Organizations granted Observer Status with the African Commission on Human and Peoples' Rights as at 1997, see U. OJI UMOZURIKE, THE AFRICAN CHARTER ON HUMAN AND PEOPLES RIGHTS, Appendix C 194-228 (The Hague: Martinus Nijhoff Publishers, 1997).

observer status for reasons of efficiency, and to suspend further granting of observer status until the adoption of the new criteria.[1233]

Granting observer status to an NGO, enables that NGO to delegate its representatives to participate in the Commission's deliberations which are not closed to the public, and allows it time at sessions for interventions to be made. NGO representatives are constantly reminded that they have no right under the Charter or the Commission's Rules of Procedure to be given the floor, but rather a privilege accorded to them by the Commission, apparently in recognition of the partnership between the Commission and the NGOs, which requires positive cooperation and assistance from the NGOs.[1234]

The benefits of observer status to NGOs in terms of their contributing to human rights protection in the African system are quite interesting. These NGOs are entitled to receive information on the time, location and agenda of the ordinary sessions of the Commission. They can request the Commission to include a particular issue on the agenda, as well as present oral statements, though for a limited time during the sessions of the Commission. Besides participating in the sessions of the Commission, the observers can obtain the official records, documents and publications of the Commission. In addition, they can request States' periodic reports submitted to the Commission by States Parties to the Charter, and in turn submit their own reports on human rights situation in particular countries.[1235] The only obligation of NGOs is to reciprocate their participation in the sessions of the Commission, by submitting reports on their activities every two years in order to maintain their observer status, as well as to continue to participate in the Commission's sessions. The Commission has at various times, however, noted that a considerable number of NGOs with observer status did not maintain contact with the Commission.[1236]

The opportunities given to NGOs by the African Commission places them in a position to substantially contribute to the protection of human rights under the Charter. This is particularly important for the State reporting mechanism, which is yet to be effective due to the failure of States Parties to comply with their obligation to submit periodic reports under the Charter. One would agree with the observation that NGOs have the potential to exercise remarkable influence on

---

[1233] Declaration and Decisions adopted by the Thirty-Fourth Ordinary Session of the Assembly of Heads of State and Government, AHG/Dec. 126 (XXXIV) (1998).
[1234] *Rachel Murray, supra,* note 507, at 18.
[1235] *See Astrid Danielsen & Gerd Oberleitner, Human Rights News: Africa,* 13 NETH. Q. HUM. RTS. 80, at 82 (1995).
[1236] *Rachel Murray, supra,* note 507, at 18. The Commission maintains that out of the 205 organizations that have so far been granted observer status, only about 30% have submitted their activity reports as required by the Commission. *See* DECADE OF CHALLENGE, *supra* note 642, at 20.

the States' reporting procedure.[1237] This is because NGO activities make them more accessible to alternative information that supervisory human rights organs may not have in the examination of States' periodic reports. By providing credible independent reports, the Commission will be in a better position to see the whole picture that would enhance the effectiveness of the process. In other words, the importance to treaty bodies of independent information supplied by NGOs, which either verify or contradict the information supplied by States, cannot be over-emphasized.[1238]

In the experience of the African system, while generally, NGOs are yet to make full use of their potential to exercise influence on the State reporting procedure, some have seized the opportunity to make their impact felt by providing alternative country report, which the African Commission relied on in its examination of some State reports.[1239] Despite the fact that NGOs are yet to fully manifest their impact in the State reporting procedure, the participation of NGOs in the sessions of the Commission has yielded fruits in other areas of cooperation. The establishment of the position of a Special Rapporteur on Extra-judicial and Summary Executions in 1994, is credited to Amnesty International, which made the recommendation to the Commission for that position.[1240] Similarly, NGOs have provided technical support to the Commission, as well as personnel (interns) on secondment to the Secretariat of the Commission.[1241] By far the most important impact of NGOs on the protection of human rights in the African system is in the non-state or individual complaint mechanism. Most of the 202 non-state communications that have been submitted to the African Commission as at 1998, were filed by NGOs on behalf of individuals,[1242] a phenomenon made possible by a generous interpretation of article 55 of the Charter to allow individuals and NGOs to file com-

---

[1237] D. Fischer, *International Reporting Procedures*, in GUIDE TO INTERNATIONAL HUMAN RIGHTS PRACTICE 168 (HURST HANNUM, ed., 1984).

[1238] See M. O'Flaherty, *The Reporting Obligations Under Article 40 of the International Covenant on Civil and Political Rights: Lessons to be Learned from Consideration by the Human Rights Committee on Ireland's First Report*, HUM. RTS. Q. 538 (1994), *reprinted* in ANKUMA, *supra*, note 363, at 93.

[1239] ANKUMA, *Id. citing* the example of the first report of Ghana which was presented during the 14th session of the Commission in 1993. During the presentation of the report, a representative of the Ghana Committee for Human and Peoples' Rights presented an alternate report, which gave information on the human rights situation in Ghana, as well as particular aspects of human rights violations. Other NGO representatives in Algeria, Benin Republic, Nigeria and Tanzania are known to have provided useful information to the Commission in its examination of State reports, just as some international NGOs like the ICJ and its Center for the Independence of Judges (CJIL) have regularly informed the Commission of human rights breaches in African countries. *Id*, at 94.

[1240] *Id*, at 187.

[1241] *Id.*, at 188.

[1242] *See* ONE DECADE OF CHALLENGE, *supra*, note 642, at 19.

munications or petitions before the Commission. There is no gainsaying the fact that NGO involvement in the individual complaint procedure of the African mechanism has spearheaded the development of the jurisprudence of the African Commission, which promises to get better as NGO participation increases. In the same vein, NGOs can do more, besides bringing individual complaints in furtherance of the protective mandate of the Commission.[1243]

III   THE PLACE OF NGOs UNDER THE PROTOCOL ON THE AFRICAN COURT

The Protocol on the establishment of the African Court on Human and Peoples' Rights, like the African Charter envisages the role of NGOs in the activities of the African Court. Clearly, NGOs are allowed direct access in bringing cases to the Court, but with the limitation that such access is dependent on the respondent State making a declaration accepting the competence of the Court to receive such cases.[1244] Furthermore, this right of access is limited to NGOs with observer status before the African Commission. While it may not be worthwhile revisiting the controversies and the compromises surrounding the adoption of the position limiting individual and NGO access to the Court, there is nothing in the drafting history of the Protocol indicating why such NGOs must have observer status with the Commission.[1245] Under the African Charter on Human and Peoples' Rights, NGOs generally are allowed access to the Commission in the submission of non-state communications. One would have expected that to be the case here. Since the Protocol would be part of the Charter, the Court would do well to interpret it to complement the intention of the Charter of not restricting NGO participation in the regional mechanism.

One would agree that the place of NGOs under the Protocol to institute cases before the African Court will only be meaningful if States Parties readily accept the competence of the Court to allow NGO access. It becomes important therefore, that NGOs engage in lobbying Member States of the OAU, not only to ratify the

---

1243 NGOs can further enhance the protective functions of the Commission by assisting the Commission in its fact-finding missions, either as a body or through individual Commissioners. This they can do by arranging meetings with Commissioners on and provide them with alternate credible information, especially where the countries visited by the Commission refuse to cooperate. *See Olz, supra,* note 1220, at 366.

1244 *See* PROTOCOL ON THE ESTABLISHMENT OF AN AFRICAN COURT ON HUMAN AND PEOPLES' RIGHTS, Article 3 & Article 34(6).

1245 The requirement first appeared in the Nouakchott draft, Article 6, without any explanation. *See* The NOUAKCHOTT LEGAL EXPERTS' REPORT, *supra,* note 986, at 6 ¶ 21. The Cape Town draft did not Contain that requirement.

Protocol, but also to make further declarations accepting the competence of the Court to receive individual and NGO petitions. It is not expected that this will be an easy task, as it is less likely that NGOs will get the maximum cooperation from most Member States in this regard. Until this is realized, NGOs may not do much in participating in the contentious jurisdiction of the African Court.

Unlike the issue of access to the Court in Contentious cases, other NGOs roles under the Protocol are not expressly stated. These roles can, however, be asserted if NGOs are inclined to do so, and the Court itself is willing to be innovative in its Rules of Procedure and practice. For example, representatives of NGOs can play the role of legal advisers to the Commission in cases brought by the Commission to the Court, a practice that is well established in the Inter-American system,[1246] especially where direct NGO access to the Court is not possible. The basis for this NGO assistance to the Commission will be under the cooperation and consultation envisaged under Article 45 of the African Charter between them. Like under the Inter-American experience, NGO representatives, acting as legal advisers to the Commission, can draft memoranda to the Court, introduce and examine witnesses and participate in oral arguments as a way of helping the Commission.[1247] This analysis is without prejudice to this author's earlier opinion emphasizing the need for distinct functions between the Commission and the Court in the African system. The above suggestion is appropriate under the present circumstances of the African system in which the Commission and the Court are required to undertake protective functions.

Another aspect of NGO roles that can be asserted with the cooperation of the Court, is the situation envisaged under Article 26(2) of the Protocol in which the Court is endowed with the discretion to "receive written and oral evidence including expert testimony..." The history behind this provision points to the fact that the intention of drafters of the Protocol is to bring within this provision the possibility of allowing *amicus curiae* briefs by NGOs which have an interest in a particular matter.[1248] The Court can enhance the importance of NGOs in this regard by adopting Rules of Procedure that achieve this intention of the drafters

---

1246 On this practice in the Inter-American System, *see* generally, *Claudia Grossman, Disappearances in Honduras: The Need for Direct Victim Representation in Human Rights Litigation*, 15 HASTINGS INT'L. & COMP. L. REV. 363 (1992); *Juan Mendez & Joe Miguel Vivanco, Disappearance in the Inter-American Cour: Reflections on a Litigation Experience*, 13 HAMLINE L. REV. 507 (1990), also *reprinted* in *Olz, supra*, note 1220, at 358.

1247 *See* David Padilla, *The Inter-American Commission on Human Rights of the Organization of American States: A Case Study*, 9 AM. U. J. INT'L. & POL'Y 95, at 109 (1995), *reprinted* also in *Olz, supra* note 1220, at 359.

1248 *See* EXPLANATORY NOTES TO THE CAPE TOWN DRAFT PROTOCOL, *supra*, note 983, at 7 dealing with Article 22 of that draft, the original formulation of Article 26(2) of the Protocol.

of the Protocol in a fairly more express manner, which in turn will ensure an easier interpretation of the provision. The experience of the Inter-American Court is an indication of the importance of *amicus curiae* practice. Since the Inter-American Court was established, it has received over 100 *amicus* briefs from various NGOs and institutions.[1249] NGOs must, thus be determined to assist the Court in ensuring the emergence of a jurisprudence that all actors within the African system can be proud of, both in the Court's contentious and advisory jurisdictions.. Even where NGO access to the Court in contentious cases have not been recognized, the Court can be impressed upon to allow amicus briefs that would enlighten it in arriving at its decision. It therefore goes without saying that NGOs defintely have a prominent role to play under the Protocol.

IV   NGOS AND THE FUTURE OF HUMAN RIGHTS IN AFRICA

Apart from their role under the African Charter and under the Protocol establishing the Court, NGOs must play a significant part in the general human rights struggle in Africa. The expectation in this regard, is that Africa-based NGOs must take the lead. It is heartening that, NGO activities in furtherance of human rights causes in the continent have dramatically increased in recent times, as it has not always been the case. According to Welch, "organized human rights groups can now be found in most African countries unlike a decade ago.[1250] The author further maintains that:

> In the late 1980s, more than a third of the human rights NGOs based in Africa were located in South Africa; in nearly twenty countries, the assiduous researchers of Human Rights Internet could not identify a single organization working directly for human rights or social justice, while in another dozen countries they could find only one or two somewhat peripheral organizations. Specifically, no nationally-based and focused NGO [apart from branches of entities like Amnesty International or the Inter-African Committee] could be found in Angola, Burundi, Central African Republic, Chad, Comoros, Congo, Djibouti, Eritrea, Ethiopia, Gabon, Guinea, Guinea-Bissau, Liberia, Libya, Madagascar, Malawi, Mozambique, Rwanda, Seychelles, Somalia, and Western Sahara...[1251]

In the same direction, Kiwanuka attributes the paucity of human rights NGOs in Africa, *inter alia*, to the lack of resources, intimidation and high handedness of

---

1249 *Olz, supra*, note 1220, at 359-360.
1250 WELCH, *supra*, note 1227, at 3, writing in 1995.
1251 *Id.* at 34 (fn 1).

African dictators, resulting in flight of potential activists, and general unfavorable political and social circumstances, which had their origin in colonialism.[1252] These reasons for the obvious lack of many NGO involvement in human rights activities before now, have further been articulated as follows:

> human rights, as a concept around which people are prepared and permitted to organize, has not yet gained adequate legitimacy or the potency in many parts of the continent, despite the history of egregious violations Africans have suffered both in the colonial and post-independent period.... In many countries, the political space necessary to organize human rights groups does not exist. Organizations which attempt to monitor government behavior and hold officials accountable to international human rights standards are considered subversive. ... those courageous enough to speak out for human rights, or to defend those whose rights are violated, may be severely sanctioned: isolated, and lacking sufficient popular support in societies, they may be imprisoned, tortured, killed or forced into exile.[1253]

The dramatic increase in the activities of NGOs in the present dispensation is not because these obstacles identified in the above quote have been removed; in fact, they continue to abound. The only explanation to it therefore, is, the need and determination to respond to the challenges posed by the persistent gross human rights violations in Africa based on inspiration from the experiences of other regions of the world. Africans have realized that despite the invaluable support given by NGOs based abroad, the implementation of the strategies of the fight must be made at home by those conversant with the landmarks. This realization must be pursued to its logical conclusion in terms of objectives, strategies and reaffirmation of roles. The role an NGO plays is determined by its objectives. The implementation of the objectives is by roles, which is further impacted by the strategies that the NGO adopts.[1254]

1252 Richard Kiwanuaka, *On the Paucity of Human Rights NGOs in Africa,*.HUM. RTS. INTERNET REP. Vol. 11, No. 4 (Nov. 1986), 10-12.
1253 WELCH, *supra,* note 1227, at 34 (fn 1).
1254 For various strategies adopted by NGOs in the promotion and protection of human rights *see, Laurie S. Wiseberg, The Role of Non-Governmental Organizations* IN HUMAN RIGHTS IN THE WORLD COMMUNITY: ISSUES AND ACTION 373 -382. (RICHARD PIERRE CALUDE AND BURNS H. WESTON, eds., Philadelphia: University of Pennsylvania Press, 1992), also *reprinted* in WELCH, *supra* note 1157, at 69. See also *Gauis Ezejiofor, The Role of NGOs in the Securement of Legitimate Governance in Africa: The Lessons of the Nigerian Experience* in LEGITIMATE GOVERNANCE IN AFRICA: INTERNATIONAL AND DOMESTIC LEGAL PERSPECTIVES (Hereafter, LEGITIMATE GOVERNANCE IN AFRICA) 331 at 332 (EDWARD K. QUASHIGAH & OBIORA C. OKAFOR, eds., The Hague: Kluwer Law International, 1999) ; *Kwadwo Appiayegi-Atua, The Role of Human Rights NGOs in the Current Democratic Dispensation in Africa: The Lessons of the Ghanian Experience* in *Id.* 311, at 312.

The general objectives of many African human rights NGOs are the promotion and protection of human rights, while playing different roles and adopting different strategies to achieve these objectives. We must agree that human rights NGOs in Africa are still relatively new and lack the necessary expertise and resources to fully realize their objectives in the face of the stiff opposition and suspicion they face from their home governments. In view of this, Africa-based NGOs must adopt clear-cut strategies or approaches that will make a lasting mark in the continent's perception of the concept of human rights. The present contribution of Africa-based NGOs to the mechanism set up under the African Charter while commendable, is only a minute part of the job in the continent. There must be more investments in the education and empowerment of the various societies in Africa. The average African is uninformed on the notion of rights, or generally, Africans have been desensitized from the notion of rights because of long-spanning violations that have grown to be the norm rather than the exception. There is therefore the need for NGOs to adopt the education strategy. Knowledge it is said, is power and at the same time, is emancipating. Not many African NGOs have adopted the education strategy, despite the undisputed need for it.[1255] In the same vein, the educated masses must be empowered in terms of being politically mobilized, especially the disadvantaged groups, to fight for their rights. There is no doubt that getting to mobilize the masses can attract governmental repression, which may make this approach unattractive to some NGOs. Still, it is important that societies must be mobilized.

Similarly, African NGOs must adopt the enforcement approach by seeking redress in domestic courts, while at the same time pursuing every available international recourse. It should, however, be emphasized that domestic enforcement of human rights or advocacy is the foundation for enjoying human rights protection among members of the society. It will make no sense if the doctrines of international human rights cannot be translated into domestic legal application. Along this line, NGOs must be ready to provide legal assistance to victims of human rights violation, train paralegal personnel to provide basic legal services, or mobilize network of lawyers to provide *pro bono* legal services. These services would ensure that if domestic law guarantees a right, its violation would lead to seeking available remedies.

Another approach that NGOs can adopt, or develop further in achieving the objectives is the gathering and dissemination of information. This will involve a properly evaluated documentation in an accurate manner, of the abuses they seek to correct. As Scoble remarks, "without accurate and timely information,

---

[1255] WELCH, *supra,* note 1227, at 50.

there can be no rational and effective NGO policies on human rights."[1256] Documentation of human rights abuses is of great importance in affording the society and the international community an alternative view to issues that would otherwise be seen from the information provided by governments, and as such, must be a serious affair. According to Brett, "the accuracy of an NGO documentation is its most basic currency, since the act of most governments accused of human rights violations is to challenge the facts stated or the interpretation of them."[1257] The information obtained by NGOs can be used in various ways, depending on the assessment of the particular NGO of the most likely course to produce the desired result. It can be used in regional or international procedures to which NGOs have access.[1258] Similarly, it can be used as a bargaining chip with the government on the areas that the documentation deals with, in such a way that a threat of publication may also encourage the government to respond. The publication itself coupled with adequate media coverage can produce a desired effect, depending on the country under scrutiny.[1259]

NGOs can also play a prominent part in standard-setting, both locally, regionally and internationally. NGO involvement in the negotiation of new standards has become necessary because, their role "in standard-setting, as with their involvement in implementation procedures, arises from their grounding in the realities of human rights violations in practice. This means that often they are more aware than governments of weaknesses and gaps, thus leading them to push for new standards, or the strengthening of existing ones."[1260] African NGOs particularly, need to begin to exploit the benefits of this approach in the protection of human rights locally and in the region.They must ensure that where laws are redrafted, there is a reflection of international norms, the result of which in most African States would be a higher threshold for protecting human rights.[1261] They must make use of the wind of democratic change that started blowing across Africa in the form of constitutional reforms in the 1990s by continuing to press for new treaties, urging implementation of existing ones, and using major political transitions to incorporate human rights norms into national laws and constitutions.[1262]

1256 Harry M. Scoble, *Human Rights Non-Governmental Organizations in Black Africa: Their Problems and Prospects in the Wake of the Banjul Charter* in HUMAN RIGHTS AND DEVELOPMENT IN AFRICA 117, AT 118 (CLAUDE E. WELCH, JR.& RONALD I. MELTZER, eds., Albany: State University of New York Press, 1984), also *reprint*ed in WELCH, *supra*, note 1227, at 70.
1257 *Rachel Brett, Non-Governmental Actors in the Field of Human Rights, supra*, note 1220, at 337.
1258 *Id.*
1259 *Id.*
1260 *Id.* at 336.
1261 WELCH, *supra*, note 1227, at 72.
1262 *Id.*

This author is by no means giving the impression that Africa-based NGOs are hardly involved in educating African societies on the notion of rights, enforcement of rights, empowering disadvantaged groups, documentation, or in standard-setting. While there are some NGOs that employ a variety of these strategies, they have done so in a relatively limited manner. Despite their handicap, some of the NGOs have, however, recorded some commendable successes.[1263] The limitations are not entirely of the making of the NGOs *per se*, but the result of the circumstances that they have come to face as they evolve, which appear apparent given African political and social situations. Some of these limitations include severe financial constraints, lack of adequate member-network, leadership issues, among others.

On the financial front, Africa-based human rights NGOs are affected by budget constraints, which makes them dependent on foreign foundations and foreign governments or governmental institutions.[1264] Most times, this results in NGO activities that must fit into the mandate of the funding organizations, without much consideration to whether proposed projects are relevant to societies' needs.[1265] Apart from this, the reaction of many African governments is to see these NGOs as "irresponsible and unpatriotic elements working for imperialists and neo-colonialists," and the donors as "meddlesome and mischievous busybodies who employ human rights activists as agents of destabilization."[1266] Similarly, NGOs lack the necessary member-network that would have ensured some form of funding that is based on membership commitment. African societies are yet to appreciate their own involvement as partners with NGOs in the struggle to achieve a culture of rights. This is further complicated by unfavorable economic environment in African societies. Majority of the masses in Africa are poor, and thus lack the fiscal power to support NGOs.

[1263] For example, two prominent Nigeria-based NGOs that have proved successful in adopting a mix of the strategies discussed above include, Civil Liberties organization (CLO) and Constitutional Rights Project (CRP). Others have emerged in response to the adverse human rights situation that engulfed Nigeria in the last 15 years under military governance.

[1264] WELCH, *supra* note, 1227, at 75-76, 293-313.

[1265] *Id.* at 297. *See* also, *Ezejiofor, supra* note 1254, at 334. Commenting on the foreign source of funding of Nigerian human rights NGOs, Ezejiofor asserts that:

"this phenomenon has created its own problems. According to one commentator, it fosters a dependent attitude on part of the organizations. It undermines initiative, superimposes a donor perspective in the definition of goals and objectives and disorients civil organizations by pre-occupying them with tasks of aid administration, thus vitiating the empowerment project. It has also given rise to the proliferation of national human rights NGOs and this seems to have affected their effectiveness. The desire to control the disbursement of such funds seems irresistible and has induced most foundation members of the first and foremost human right NGO in Nigeria to withdraw from it to found other organizations in which they occupy controlling positions."

[1266] *Ezejiofor*, at 335.

Leadership issues also, greatly affect the effectiveness of Africa-based NGOs. As aptly put by Welch,

> most African NGOs have yet to make the crucial transition from leadership by the "founding father" or "founding mother" to selection of new heads and directions without organizational collapse. The first generation of chairs/presidents remains in control. To a substantial extent, the organizations are personalized: "Phill" or "Clement" or "Tokunbo" or "Professor Mesfin" remains at the center and sets the agenda. When they leave for international conferences, the pace of activity slows. Their staffs rarely number as many as eight. Yes, decisions may be made relatively rapidly with a small cadre, but all the necessary skills (especially in budget control and documentation) cannot be carried by an individual. Broadening and deepening of leadership are essential.[1267]

The individualized nature of many Africa-based NGOs no doubt, has not helped the image or credibility of some of the organizations. There is the tendency to regard the leaders of such NGOs as empire builders interested in enriching themselves with foundation funds, despite the obvious contributions that some of these organizations make. Africa-based NGOs need to recognize the need for diversity of skills and bring in professionalism in human rights promotion and protection. The spate of splits into different NGO initiatives tends to confirm the misgivings that detractors of human rights NGOs have. What is needed is a coordinated effort of professionals who are determined to make a lasting impact on the yet emerging concept of human rights promotion and protection in the continent. This will result in organizations that permeate rural Africa rather than just being active only in one or two major cities, as is presently the case with most African NGOs.

The above observations notwithstanding, it must be acknowledged that organized human rights groups now abound in Africa in response to the awareness of human rights issues that have faced the continent. Just like international human rights NGOs played a prominent part in shaping the universal system under the United Nations, NGOs generally, and Africa-based NGOs in particular, must play a central role in shaping the human rights discourse in Africa. Increased NGO participation in the regional human rights initiative is anticipated in view of recent developments in OAU human rights Agenda. The adoption of the Protocol on the establishment of the African Court on Human and Peoples' presents a new opportunity for NGO participation in the development of not only a virile jurisprudence of the African human rights mechanism, but also sensitizing African societies on the notion of rights.

[1267] *Id.* at 293.

CONCLUSIONS

A discussion on human rights in Africa, must necessarily resolve the question: whether law was a feature of African pre-colonial governance, and whether human rights, as a concept was ever present in pre-colonial African legal thought. While this study is not an investigation of pre-colonial African legal philosophy, it amply restates the consensus that the existence of law in pre-colonial Africa was a result of the development of African societies in that era. As a rule of conduct, law existed in pre-colonial Africa to govern the relations within these societies. In the same vein, human rights as a universal concept was part of pre-colonial African governance, despite the fact that it may not have been exactly in the formal sense, as developed in Western legal thought. Similarly, the place of colonialism in shaping respect for, or the exertion of negative influence in the development of modern human rights notions in Africa is another preliminary question that this study tried to answer. Colonialism in Africa was not only founded on racism, it denied and inhibited fundamental human rights, and was essentially against the promotion and protection of human rights in Africa. There is also no arguing the fundamental negative effect of colonialism on independent Africa, the consequences of which can be seen in the high-handedness and authoritative nature of many post-colonial African regimes, which have adopted the oppressive mechanisms of the colonial masters against their own people. Despite international and regional efforts to achieve respect for human rights, the situation remains a serious issue that deserves serious attention in Africa.

Thus, for more than ten years since the African Charter on Human and Peoples Rights came into force, the question has been: how effective is the Charter, in the resolution of human rights dispute in Africa? Answers to this question have varied from one commentator to the other. To some, referring to the African system under the supervision of the African Commission on Human and Peoples' Rights, the following view has been advanced: "We cannot and should not continue to delude ourselves that we have a human rights system. What we have is a facade, a yoke that African leaders have put around our [Africans'] necks." As a result, advocates needed to "cast it off and reconstruct a system that we can proudly proclaim as ours."[1268] To others, however, the evolution of the African system has been "steady, but unremarkable,"[1269] while yet, to OAU entities, such as its Council of Ministers, the work of the Commission has been "excellent."[1270]

The views expressed by each of the above observers represent their perception of the African system, within a particular period of time. This book has, however, revealed that the growth of the African system has been steady, but not remarkable, as pointed out by Dr. Oloko-Onyango. It is far from excellent, unlike the Council of Minsters of the OAU would want us to believe. We must observe, however, that the African system has come a long way in the attempt to entrench itself as a regional human rights mechanism. The system has grown from the initial Commission that was too weak to even mention the communications submitted to it under the individual complaint mechanism, or the States Parties against which such communications were submitted, in its interpretation of the confidentiality principle in Article 59 of the Charter, to one that in 1994 was brave enough to begin to publicize the outcome of its consideration of individual complaints, including its views and recommendations of such considerations. Additionally, the Commission has revised its Rules of Procedure and Guidelines for National Periodic Reports in an effort to address the deficiencies in those documents. It has appointed some of its members as special rapporteurs on extra-judicial executions in Africa, prison and conditions of detention in Africa and on the rights of women in Africa. In the same vein, the Commission has made some considerable progress in its individual complaint mechanism. A review of the Commission's decisions over the years, reveals that while room remains for considerable improvement, the quality of its reasoning in decision making has continued to positively evolve. In interpreting its procedures, the Commission has been pragmatic in applying the requirements for admissibility of communications,[1271] an example of which is, the non rigid requirement of exhaustion of domestic remedies in communications that reveal the existence of serious and massive violations of human rights, even though at various times, the Commission appeared inconsistent, unclear and confusing in applying these principles.[1272] On the other

---

1268 See Mutua, *The African Human Rights System in Comparative Perspective: The Need for Urgent Reformulation, supra,* note 605, at 35.
1269 See Oloko-Onyango, *Beyond the Rhetoric: Reinvigorating the Struggle for Economic and Social Rights in Africa, supra,* note 473, at 52.
1270 Decision CM/Draft/Dec.26(LXVII) of the Sixty-Seventh Session of the Council of Ministers of the OAU, CM/DRAFT/DECISIONS (LVII) REV. 1 (1998) ¶ 1.
1271 Odinkalu & Christensen, *The African Commission on Human and Peoples' Rights: The Development of its Non-State Communication Procedures, supra,* note 775, at 279.
1272 *Id.*

hand, the enthusiastic readiness of the Commission to conclude that an amicable settlement has been reached in many cases, without confirmation from the complainant, is a source for concern. This concern is further reinforced by the fact that the Commission fails to record any terms of such settlement, or institute any mechanism to monitor the compliance of States Parties with the presumed settlement.[1273]

Despite the improvement of the African system over the years, the overall effectiveness of the system is of paramount importance. Apart from the African Commission, as the supervisory organ, States Parties play a prominent part, either in their taking the system seriously, or in ignoring it. Many States Parties have neglected their obligation to submit periodic reports to the Commission on the steps they have taken to implement the Charter in their domestic legislation. Additionally, the system has suffered neglect in terms of lack of adequate resources for the operation of the African Commission and its secretariat. Member States of the OAU, the parent body of the system have not always complied with their financial obligations, which in turn has hampered the resources available to the Commission. This has resulted in under-staffing at the Commission's secretariat, especially with regard to professional staff.

By far the most important avenue for the African system to achieve its overall effectiveness is through ensuring normative and remedial effectiveness of the African Charter. Normatively, certain substantive provisions of the Charter contradict the notion of rights, by permitting States to restrict rights to the maximum extent allowed by domestic laws, which in the context of Africa have been highly draconian. Here, "clawback" clauses come to mind. They permeate the provisions dealing with fundamental freedoms, making it easy for recalcitrant States to effortlessly engage in human rights violation under the guise of subjecting such rights to "law and order," thus permitting *de facto* suspension of any of the rights guaranteed by the Charter, through the enactment of legislation. The Charter should rather specify a general derogation clause in accordance with international practice, in which case there will also be a list of non-derogable rights.

Similarly, the remedial effectiveness of the Charter should ensure that the rights guaranteed under the Charter can be translated into effective remedies, which are aimed at addressing violations of those rights. Under the present system in which the African Commission is the sole supervisory organ, there is no effective remedy. Thus, even if the Commission reaches a conclusion that there has been a violation of the Charter, the Charter does not provide for any effective remedies, except that the Commission will make its recommendation to the Assembly of Heads

---

[1273] *Id.*

of State and Government (AHSG). Moreover, this is with regard to cases that reveal "a series of serious and massive violations of human rights," to which the Commission is required to draw the attention of the AHSG, which in turn would authorize the Commission to engage in in-depth studies and make recommendations. Thus, in all other situations under the Charter, the Commission is not expected to do anything. While the Commission has assumed the power of making recommendations to the States concerned in these other situations, its recommendations are advisory and not binding on those States; they attract little attention from the States, if any.

It is as a result of this lack of effective remedy under the African Charter that steps were taken to reform the African system. They resulted in the establishment of the African Court on Human and Peoples' Rights under the Protocol on the Establishment of an African Court on Human and Peoples' Rights, to *inter alia,* complement and reinforce the protective functions of the African Commission. This reform, no doubt, has long been overdue. There is also no doubt that the Court would make a difference in the resolution of human rights disputes in the African system, as a court is more likely to ameliorate the general remedial ineffectiveness of the Commission under the African Charter. The hope, therefore, is that the Court will strengthen the regional system and aid it in realizing its promise. Thus, the adoption of the Protocol on the establishment of the Court by the Assembly of Heads of States and Government of the OAU in 1998, is yet another advancement of the African human rights system. By its provisions, the Protocol generally accords with the standard of other regional instruments for the protection of human rights.

There are, however, shortcomings in the Protocol, two of which are fundamental to achieving a meaningful reform of the African system: the limitation of access of individuals and NGOs to the Court, and the lack of provisions for separate institutional roles for the Commission and the Court. Concerning access to the Court, the African Commission, States and inter-governmental organizations have automatic access to the Court, while individual and NGO accesses to the Court are optional to States. Upon ratification, States would make declarations whether they accept individual access to the Court. Unless a State makes a declaration accepting individual and NGO access, individuals and NGOs would not have standing before the Court, no matter the grievance they may have under the Charter. This is a serious shortcoming that needs rethinking. It may have been convenient to limit individual access to encourage States to ratify the Protocol, it is, however, disappointing that, while the European system is leading the way on direct individual access to human rights Courts, the African system is interested in curtailing such access. After all, it is individuals and NGOs, rather than the Commission, States Parties, or regional inter-governmental organizations, that will be primary beneficiaries of the Court, as the Court is not meant to be an institution for the protection of rights of States or OAU organs. A human rights court is primarily a forum for protecting citizens against States and State agencies. A further amendment of the African Charter must address this issue.

Secondly, the institutional role relationship between the Court and the African Commission is far from what is expected in the reform of the African system. Unlike the new European system, the Court does not replace the African Commission, but the Commission is still allowed to carry on its protective function in addition to the broad promotional mandate it has under the Charter. While the two organs are technically independent, the Court may request the Commission's opinion with regard to the admissibility of a case brought by individuals and NGOs. In determining the admissibility of a complaint, the Court, like the Commission, is required to take into account the requirements of admissibility under the Charter, in which case the Court may consider the cases or transfer them to the Commission.

While it is good that the Protocol retained the African Commission, the drafters of the Protocol should have assigned different institutional roles to the Commission and the Court. A court was not contemplated by the drafters of the African Charter, and as a result, the Commission was vested with both promotional and protective functions, such as the individual complaint procedure, which make the Commission to look like a court because of the quasi-judicial character of such functions. Now, however, the Commission should better operate as a human rights promotional organ of the African system, while retaining the function of monitoring States reporting obligations, and facilitating dialogue with NGOs and government institutions in Member States to encourage the incorporation of human rights norms into State policies and domestic legislation, and undertaking country studies. In addition, the Commission could assist the protective function of the Court in the area of helping to facilitate friendly or amicable settlement. As indicated in this book, the rational for advocating a solely promotional role for the Commission is because, in the peculiarity of Africa, human rights promotion is equally as important as their protection. While it is desirous to achieve a higher level of human rights protection in the continent, such protection cannot be achieved where promotion is woefully lacking. It needs reiterating that the average African is not informed about his or her rights, and there must be a serious investment of resources and manpower to realize this, for a smooth operation of the protective dimension of the African Charter. Promotion will therefore require the full attention of the Commission, and thus it is not necessary to add to the Commission's work or duplicate the protective functions of the Court.

With the Court fully responsible for the protective mandate of the African system, it becomes the sole adjudicatory organ of the system. In this role, the Court will be focused on "vindicating the rule of law by providing justice in individual cases," as well as in inter-state cases; "protecting rights through deterrence and behavior modification; and expounding legal instruments and making law through elucidation and interpretation," as has been suggested regarding the UN Human Rights Committee[1274] Under this kind of institutional framework, the Court would directly receive individual and inter-state complaints, make decisions with regard to admissibility of complaints and award damages and reparations. In the same vein, the Court would be able to develop a respectable advisory jurisdiction in which it could elucidate principles of law in the controversial aspects of economic, social and cultural or group rights, and make a name for itself among other regional mechanisms.

While the suggestion of different institutional roles for the African Court and the Commission may be termed ambitious, it must be observed that it appears to be the most efficient way of fully achieving the mandates enshrined in the African Charter: the effective realization of human rights protection and promotion in the continent, and in the most economic manner. By the time the Protocol comes into force, the position envisaged under it will only duplicate the process, and would require more than twice the resources that are needed. The experience of the European system has shown that the performance of the same functions by a Commission and a Court, would not only result in waste of resources, but in an overcharged system of which lengthy procedures and time wasting are the hallmarks.

Whether or not the suggestions in this book are accepted, one thing is clear: the African Human Rights Court has come to stay by the will of Member States of the OAU, and the many years of NGO lobbying and advocacy. The ultimate success of the Court in achieving effective human rights dispute resolution in Africa will depend on the attitude of all relevant parties. Going by the record of the Commission, there may be the tendency to say that there is not enough ground for optimism, especially because the Commission had always been hampered by resource constraints. There is no gainsaying the fact that the Court will not be able to meet the expectation of Africans, and indeed, the international community, if the African Union does not provide it with material and moral support to allow it to function as an independent and significant institution that it ought to be. We should, however, be optimistic that the Court will receive the necessary support that it deserves. This optimism can be built on the prompt ratification of the Charter. With the yet few ratifications of the Protocol establishing the Court, the

---

1274 *See Henry J. Steiner, Individual Claims in a World of Massive Violations: What Role for the Human Rights Committee* in THE FUTURE OF THE UN HUMAN RIGHTS TREATY MONITORING. 12, at 31(PHILIP ALSTON & JAMES CRAWFORD, eds., New York: Cambridge University Press, 2000).

human rights community, especially NGOs, have a duty to perform towards realizing this era in the African system for the protection of human rights. This they can do by mounting vigorous lobbying of Member States of the OAU, and undertaking campaigns on the ratification of the Protocol, and the further declaration of the States accepting individual and NGO accesses to the Court.

SELECT BIBLIOGRAPHY

BOOKS

AFRICAN COMMISSION ON HUMAN AND PEOPLES' RIGHTS, ESTABLISHMENT, (Information Sheet No. 1).

AJAYI, F & ESPIE, I., eds., A THOUSAND YEARS OF WEST AFRICAN HISTORY (Ibadan: Ibadan University Press, 1965)

AJOMO, M.A., & ADEWALE, O., eds., AFRICAN ECONOMIC COMMUNITY TREATY: ISSUES, PROBLEMS AND PROSPECTS (Lagos, Nigeria: Nigerian Institute for Advanced Legal Studies, 1993).

AKINDELE, R.A., ed., THE ORGANIZATION OF AFRICAN UNITY, 1963-1988: A ROLE ANALYSIS AND PERFORMANCE REVIEW (Ibadan, Nigeria: Vantage Publishers 1988).

ALEXANDROV, S.A., SELF-DEFENSE AGAINST THE USE OF FORCE IN INTERNATIONAL LAW (The Hague/London/Boston: Kluwer Law International, 1996).

ALSTON, P. ed., The UNITED NATIONS AND HUMAN RIGHTS: A CRITICAL APPRAISAL (Oxford: Clarendon Press, 1992).

ALSTON, P. & CRAWFORD, J., eds., THE FUTURE OF THE UN HUMAN RIGHTS TREATY MONITORING (New York: Cambridge University Press, 2000).

ALSTON, P., ed., THE EUROPEAN UNION AND HUMAN RIGHTS (Oxford/New York: Oxford University Press, 1999).

ALSTON, P., ed., PROMOTING HUMAN RIGHTS THROUGH BILL OF RIGHTS: COMPARATIVE PERSPECTIVES (Oxford University Press, 1995).

ALSTON, P., ed., THE INTERNATIONAL DIMENSIONS OF HUMAN RIGHTS (Second Edition, Vol. 2, Westport, Connecticut: Greenwood Press; Paris, France UNESCO, 1982, Originally edited by Karel Vasak).

ALSTON, P. & PARKER, S., eds., CHILDREN, RIGHTS AND THE LAW (Oxford, England: Clarendon Press, 1992).

ALTERNATIVE HISTORIES AND NON-WRITTEN SOURCES: NEW PERSPECTIVE FROM THE SOUTH (Proposal for an International Seminar organized by the South-South Exchange Programme for Research on History of Development (SEPHIS), Amsterdam, at La Paz, 12-15 May 1999).

ANKUMA, E.A., THE AFRICAN COMMISSION ON HUMAN AND PEOPLES' RIGHTS, PRACTICE AND PROCEDURES (The Hague/London/Boston: Martinus Nijhoff Publishers, 1996).
AN-NA'IM, A. & DENG, F, eds., Human Rights In Africa: Cross- Cultural Perspectives (1990).
ANIKPO, M., & SHEPHERD, JR. G.W., eds., EMERGING HUMAN RIGHTS: THE AFRICAN POLITICAL ECONOMY CONTEXT, STUDIES IN HUMAN RIGHTS NUMBER 8 (New York: Greenwood Press, 1990).
ARIE, B., LISELOTTE, NOVAK, M., & ROSAS, A., eds., MONITORING HUMAN RIGHTS IN EUROPE (Dordrecht: Martinus Nijhoff Publishers, 1994).
AYITTEY, G., AFRICA BETRAYED (New York: Transnational Publishers Inc., 1992).

BASSIOUNI, M.C. & MOTALA, Z., eds., THE PROTECTION OF HUMAN RIGHTS IN AFRICAN CRIMINAL PROCEEDINGS (Martinus Nijhoff Publishers, 1995).
BENTWICH, N. & MARTIN, A., A COMMENTARY ON THE CHARTER OF THE UNITED NATIONS (London: Routledge and Kegan Paul Ltd., 1950).
BOAHEN, A.A., & WEBSTER, J.B., HISTORY OF WEST AFRICA (New York: Praeger, 1970).
BOLD, A., LISELOTTE, NOVAK, M., & ROSAS, A., eds., MONITORING HUMAN RIGHTS IN EUROPE 121-144 (Dordrecht: Martinus Nijhoff Publishers, 1994).
BRIERLY, J.L., THE LAW OF NATIONS: AN INTRODUCTION TO THE INTERNATIONAL LAW OF PEACE (Sixth Edition, Oxford: Clarendon Press, 1963).
BROWNLIE, I, BASIC DOCUMENTS ON AFRICAN AFFAIRS (Oxford: Clarendon Press, 1971).
BROWNLIE, I, PRINCIPLES OF PUBLIC INTERNATIONAL LAW (5th Edition, Oxford: Clarendon Press, 1998).
BUERGENTHAL, T. & SHELTON, D., PROTECTING HUMAN RIGHTS IN THE AMERICAS: CASES AND MATERIALS (International Institute of Human Rights, Strasbourg/N.P. Engel, Fourth Revised Edition, 1995).
BUERGENTHAL, T, INTERNATIONAL HUMAN RIGHTS IN A NUTSHELL (2nd Edition, St. Paul, Minnesota: West Publishing Company, 1995).
BULAJIC, M., PRINCIPLES OF INTERNATIONAL DEVELOPMENT LAW 283 (2d ed. 1992).
BUSTELO, M.R. & ALSTON, P., eds., WHOSE NEW WORLD ORDER: WHAT ROLE FOR THE UNITED NATIONS (Sydney, Australia: Federation Press, 1991).

CARTER, B.E., & TRIMBLE, P.R., INTERNATIONAL LAW (2nd Edition, Boston/New York/Toronto/London, 1995).
CARTER, B.E., & TRIMBLE, P.R., INTERNATIONAL LAW: SELECTED DOCUMENTS (Edition, Boston/New York/Toronto/London, 1995).
CERVENKA, Z., THE ORGANIZATION OF AFRICAN UNITY AND ITS CHARTER 102 (New York: Frederick A. Praeger, Publishers, 1968).
CLAUDE, R.P. & WESTON, P.H, eds., HUMAN RIGHTS IN THE WORLD COMMUNITY: ISSUES AND ACTION (Philadelphia: University of Pennsylvania Press, 1992).
COHEN, R. *et al*, eds., HUMAN RIGHTS AND GOVERNANCE IN AFRICA (Florida: University Press of Florida, 1993).

COOMANS, F. & VAN HOOF, F. eds., THE RIGHT TO COMPLAIN ABOUT ECONOMIC, SOCIAL AND CULTURAL RIGHTS: PROCEEDINGS OF THE EXPERT MEETING ON THE ADOPTION OF AN OPTIONAL PROTOCOL TO THE INTERNATIONAL COVENANT ON ECONOMIC, SOCIAL AND CULTURAL RIGHTS HELD FROM 25-28 JANUARY 1995 IN UTRECHT (Utrecht, Netherlands: Netherlands Institute of Human Rights, 1995).

CRAVEN, M.C.R., THE INTERNATIONAL COVENANT ON ECONOMIC, SOCIAL, AND CULTURAL RIGHTS: A PERSPECTIVE ON ITS DEVELOPMENT (Oxford: Clarendon Press, 1995).

CRISTESCU, A., THE RIGHT TO SELF DETERMINATION: HISTORICAL AND CURRENT DEVELOPMENTS ON THE BASIS OF UNITED NATIONS INSTRUMENTS (United Nations, New York, 1981)

CROWTHER, M., WEST AFRICA UNDER COLONIAL RULE (London: Hutchinson, 1968).

DAVIDSON, B., OLD AFRICA REDISCOVERED (London, Longman Group Ltd., 1970).

DE SALVIA, M. & VILLIGER, M., eds., THE BIRTH OF THE EUROPEAN HUMAN RIGHTS LAW: STUDIES IN HONOR OF CARL AAGE NØRGAARD (Nomos Verlagsgesellschaft, Baden-Baden, 1998).

DE LA CRUZ, H.B., VON POTOBSKY, G & SWEPSTON, L, THE INTERNATIONAL LABOR ORGANIZATION: THE INTERNATIONAL SYSTEM AND BASIC HUMAN RIGHTS (West View Press, 1996).

DIXON, M., TEXT BOOK ON INTERNATIONAL LAW (Second Edition, London: Blackstone Press Limited, 1993).

DONNELLY, J., UNIVERSAL HUMAN RIGHTS IN THEORY AND PRACTICE (1989).

EIDE, A., KRAUSE, C., & ROSAS, A., eds., ECONOMIC, SOCIAL AND CULTURAL RIGHTS: A TEXT BOOK (Dordrecht: Martinus Nijhoff Publishers, 1995).

EIDE, A., et al. eds., THE UNIVERSAL DECLARATION OF HUMAN RIGHTS: A COMMENTARY (Oslo: Scandinavian University Press, 1992).

EL-AYOUTY, Y., ed., THE ORGANIZATION OF AFRICAN UNITY AFTER THIRTY YEARS (Westport, Connecticut: Praeger Publishers / Greenwood Publishing Group 1994).

ELIAS, T.O., THE NATURE OF AFRICAN CUSTOMARY LAW (Manchester University Press, 2nd Impression, 1962).

ELIAS, T.O, AFRICA AND DEVELOPMENT OF INTERNATIONAL LAW (Martinus Nijfoff, 1988).

ELIAS, T.O, NWABARA, S.N., & AKPAMGBO, C.O., AFRICAN INDIGENOUS LAWS (Enugu, Nigeria: Government Printer, 1975).

EZE, O.C., HUMAN RIGHTS IN AFRICA: SOME SELECTED PROBLEMS (The Nigerian Institute of International Affairs/Macmillian Nigeria Publishers Ltd, 1984).

GANJI, THE REALIZATION OF ECONOMIC, SOCIAL AND CULTURAL RIGHTS: PROBLEMS , POLICIES, PROGRESS, UN Sales No. E.75.XIV.2 (1975).

GHAI, J.P & MCAUSLAN, W.B., PUBLIC LAW AND POLITICAL CHANGE IN KENYA (Nairobi: Oxford University Press, (1970).

GHANDHI, P.R., THE HUMAN RIGHTS COMMITTEE AND THE RIGHT OF INDIVIDUAL COMMUNICATION: LAW AND PRACTICE, (Aldershot: Ashgate Publishing, Ltd., 1998).

GHEBALI, V., THE INTERNATIONAL LABOUR ORGANISATION :A CASE STUDY ON THE EVOLUTION OF U.N. SPECIALIZED AGENCIES (The Hague: Martinus Nijhoff Publishers, 1989).
GLUCKMAN, H., THE IDEA IN BARTOSE JURISPRUDENCE (New Haven: Yale University Press, 1962).
GLUCKMAN, M., THE JUDICIAL PROCESS AMONG THE BARTOSE OF NORTHERN RHODESIA (Manchester: Manchester University Press, 2nd edition, 1967).
GOODRICH, L. & HAMBRO, E., CHARTER OF THE UNITED NATIONS: COMMENTARY AND DOCUMENTS (Boston: World Peace Foundation, 1949).
GOODRICH, L., THE UNITED NATIONS (New York: Thomas Crowell Company, 1959).
GURUSWAMY, L.D., PALMER, G.W.R., & WESTON, B.H., INTERNATIONAL ENVIRONMENTAL LAW AND WORLD ORDER (St. Paul, Minnesota: West Publishing Company, 1994)
GURUSWAMY, L.D., PALMER, G.W.R., & WESTON, B.H., SUPPLEMENT OF BASIC DOCUMENTS TO INTERNATIONAL ENVIRONMENTAL LAW AND WORLD ORDER (St. Paul, Minnesota: West Publishing Company, 1994)

HANSKI, R. & SUKSI, M., eds., AN INTRODUCTION TO THE INTERNATIONAL PROTECTION OF HUMAN RIGHTS: A TEXT BOOK (Tarku/Abo, Finland: Institute for Human Rights, Abo Akademi University, 1997).
HARRIS, D.J., O'BOYLE, M. & WARBRICK, C., LAW OF THE EUROPEAN CONVENTION ON HUMAN RIGHTS (London: Butterworths, 1995).
HARRIS, D.J. & LIVINGSTONE, S., eds., THE INTER-AMERICAN SYSTEM OF HUMAN RIGHTS (Oxford: Clarendon Press, 1998).
    HENKIN, L., NEUMAN, G.L., ORENTLICHER, D.F., & LEEBRON, D.W., HUMAN RIGHTS (New York: Foundation Press, 1999).
HENRY J. STEINER, DIVERS PARTNERS: NON-GOVERNMENTAL ORGANIZATIONS IN THE HUMAN RIGHTS MOVEMENT (Cambridge, Massachusetts: Harvard Law School Human Rights Program and Human Rights Internet, 1991).
HIGGINS, R., PROBLEMS AND PROSPECTS: INTERNATIONAL LAW AND HOW WE USE IT (Oxford: Oxford University Press, 1994).
HOOKER, M.B., LEGAL PLURALISM: AN INTRODUCTION TO COLONIAL AND NEO-COLONIAL LAWS (Oxford: Clarendon Press, 1975).
HOSSAIN, K. & CHOWDHURY, S.R., eds., INTERNATIONAL LAW (1984).
HUMPHREY, J., HUMAN RIGHTS AND THE UNITED NATIONS: A GREAT ADVENTURE (1984)
HUDSON, M., INTERNATIONAL LEGISLATION (New York: Oceana Publications, 1970).
HUMPHREY, J., HUMAN RIGHTS AND THE UNITED NATIONS: A GREAT ADVENTURE (1984).
HUNT, P., RECCLAIMING SOCIAL RIGHTS: INTERNATIONAL AND COMPARATIVE PERSPECTIVES (Aldershot, England: Dartmouth Publishing Company Limited, 1996)
HURST, H., GUIDE TO INTERNATIONAL HUMAN RIGHTS PRACTICE (2nd ed., 1992).
HURST, H., ED. GUIDE TO INTERNATIONAL HUMAN RIGHTS PRACTICE (1984).
INTERNATIONAL COMMISSION OF JURISTS, ed., PARTICIPATION OF NON-GOVERNMENTAL ORGANIZATIONS IN THE WORK OF THE AFRICAN COMMISSION ON HUMAN AND PEOPLES' RIGHTS: A COMPILATION OF BASIC DOCUMENTS (Geneva, 1996).

JACOBS, F.G. & WHITE, R.C.A., THE EUROPEAN CONVENTION ON HUMAN RIGHTS (2nd Edition, Oxford, Clarendon Press, 1996).
JANIS, M., KAY, R.S., & BRADLEY, A., EUROPEAN HUMAN RIGHTS LAW: TEXT AND MATERIALS (Oxford Clarendon Press, 1995).

KALU, A.U., & OSINBAJO, Y, eds., Perspective On Human Rights (Nigeria: Federal Ministry of Justice, 1992).
KIRGIS, JR. F.L., INTERNATIONAL ORGANIZATIONS IN THEIR LEGAL SETTING (St. Paul, Minnesota: West Publishing Company, Second Edition 1993).
KOUFA, K., ed., INTERNATIONAL JUSTICE (Sakkoulas Publications, 1997).

LANDY, E.A., THE EFFECTIVENESS OF INTERNATIONAL SUPERVISION: THIRTY YEARS OF ILO EXPERIENCE (1966).
LAWSON, R. & DE BLOIS, M., eds., THE DYNAMICS OF THE PROTECTION OF HUMAN RIGHTS IN EUROPE (The Hague, Martinus Nijhoff Publishers, 1994).
LUGARD, L., THE DUAL MANDATE IN BRITISH TROPICAL AFRICA (Hamden, Conn.: Archon Books, (1965).
LESCURE, K. & TRINTIGNAC, F., INTERNATIONAL JUSTICE FOR FORMER YUGOSLAVIA: THE WORK OF THE INTERNATIONAL CRIMINAL TRIBUNAL OF THE HAGUE (The Hague, The Netherlands: Kluwer Law International 1996).

MACDONALD, R. ST. J, MATSCHER, F., & PETZOLD, H. eds., THE EUROPEAN SYSTEM FOR THE PROTECTION OF HUMAN RIGHTS (Dordrecht: Martinus Nijhoff Publishers, 1993).
MAKARCZYK, J., ed., THEORY OF INTERNATIONAL LAW AT THE THRESHHOLD OF THE 21ST CENTURY: ESSAYS IN HONOR OF KRYSZTOF SUKBISZEWSKI (The Hague/London/Boston: Kluwer Law International, 1996).
MALUWA, T., INTERNATIONAL LAW IN POST-COLONIAL AFRICA (The Hague/London/ Boston: Kluwer Law International, 1999).
MANN, K. & ROBERTS, R., SOCIAL HISTORY OF AFRICA: LAW IN COLONIAL AFRICA (Portsmouth, New Hampshire: Heinemann/ London: James Currey, 1991).
MCCARTHY-ARNOLDS, E., et al., eds. AFRICA, HUMAN RIGHTS AND THE GLOBAL SYSTEM (Westport, Connecticut: Greenwood Press, 1994).
MCGOLDRICK, D., THE HUMAN RIGHTS COMMITTEE: ITS ROLE IN THE DEVELOPMENT OF THE INTERNATIONAL COVENANT ON CIVIL AND POLITICAL RIGHTS (1991).
MEEK, C.K., LAW AND AUTHORITY IN A NIGERIAN TRIBE (London: Oxford University Press, 1937).
MERILLS, J.G., THE DEVELOPMENT OF INTERNATIONAL LAW BY THE EUROPEAN COURT OF HUMAN RIGHTS (2nd Edition, Manchester: Manchester University Press, 1993).
MERON, T, ed., HUMAN RIGHTS IN INTERNATIONAL LAW: LEGAL AND POLICY ISSUES (Oxford: Clarendon Press, 1984).

NALDI, G.J., ed., DOCUMENTS OF THE ORGANIZATION OF AFRICAN UNITY (Mansell Publishing Limited, 1992).

NALDI, G.J., THE ORGANIZATION OF AFRICAN UNITY: AN ANALYSIS OF ITS ROLE (Mansell, London, 1989).
NELSON, J.L., & GREEN, V.M., eds, INTERNATIONAL HUMAN RIGHTS: CONTEMPORARY ISSUES (New York: Human Rights Publishing Group, 1980).
NMEHIELLE, V.O., THE AFRICAN CHARTER ON HUMAN AND PEOPLES' RIGHTS AND THE HUMAN RIGHTS QUESTION IN NIGERIA (LL.M Thesis, University of Notre Dame Law School, Notre Dame, Indiana, 1996).
NOVAK, M., & SWINEHART, T., eds., HUMAN RIGHTS IN DEVELOPING COUNTRIES: YEARBOOK (Kehl: N.P. Engel Publishers, 1989).
NOVAK, M., UN Covenant on Civil and Political Rights: Commentary (N.P. Engel, 1993)
NYERERE, J., UJAMA: ESSAYS IN SOCIALISM (London: Oxford University Press, 1968).

PROCEEDINGS OF THE SECOND ANNUAL CONFERENCE OF THE AFRICAN SOCIETY OF INTERNATIONAL AND COMPARATIVE LAW (1990).

QUASHIGAH, E.K., & OKAFOR, O.C., eds., LEGITIMATE GOVERNANCE IN AFRICA: INTERNATIONAL AND DOMESTIC LEGAL IMPLICATIONS (The Hague/London/Boston: Kluwer Law International, 1999).
QUIROGA, C.M., THE BATTLE OF HUMAN RIGHTS: GROSS SYSTEMATIC VIOLATIONS AND THE INTER-AMERICAN SYSTEM (Dordrecht: Martinus Nijhoff Publishers, 1988).

REGIONAL PROTECTION AND PROMOTION OF HUMAN RIGHTS IN AFRICA, TWENTY-NINTH REPORT OF THE COMMISSION TO STUDY THE ORGANIZATION OF PEACE (1980).
REGIONAL PROMOTION AND PROTECTION OF HUMAN RIGHTS, TWENTY-EIGHT REPORT OF THE COMMISSION TO STUDY THE ORGANIZATION OF PEACE (1980).
REMBE, N.S., THE SYSTEM OF PROTECTION OF HUMAN RIGHTS UNDER THE AFRICAN CHARTER ON HUMAN AND PEOPLES' RIGHTS (Lesotho: Institute of African Studies, National University of Lesotho, 1991).
ROBERTSON, A.H., THE COUNCIL OF EUROPE (2nd Edition, Manchester:Manchester University Press, 1961).
ROBERTSON, A. & MERRILS, J., HUMAN RIGHTS IN THE WORLD: AN INTRODUCTION TO THE STUDY OF THE INTERNATIONAL PROTECTION OF HUMAN RIGHTS (Third Edition, Manchester: Manchester University Press, 1992).
ROBERTSON, A.H., HUMAN RIGHTS IN EUROPE (3rd Edition, Manchester:Manchester University Press, 1993).
RODNEY, W., HOW EUROPE UNDERDEVELOPED AFRICA (London, Bogle-L'Ouverture, 1972),

SCHWEBEL, S., ed., THE EFFECTIVENESS OF INTERNATIONAL DECISIONS (1971).
SELASSIE, B.H., THE EXECUTIVE IN AFRICAN GOVERNMENTS (London Heinemann, 1974).
SHIHATA, I., THE WORLD BANK IN A CHANGING WORLD (Dordrecht: Martinus Nijhoff Publishers, 1991).
SIEGHART, P., INTERNATIONAL LAW OF HUMAN RIGHTS 368 (Oxford 1983)
SIVJI, I.G., THE CONCEPT OF HUMAN RIGHTS IN AFRICA (CORDESIA, 1989)

SLOMENSON, W.R., FUNDAMENTAL PERSPECTIVES OF INTERNATIONAL LAW (2nd Edition, St. Paul, Minnesota: West Publishing Company, 1995).
SOHN, L.B., RIGHTS IN CONFLICT, THE UNITED NATIONS AND SOUTH AFRICA (Irvington, New York: Transnational Publishers, 1994).
SOHN, L.B., ed., BASIC DOCUMENTS OF AFRICAN REGIONAL ORGANIZATIONS VOLUMES 1-4 (Dobbs Ferry, New York: Oceana Publications, 1971-1972).
SOHN, L.B., ed., BASIC DOCUMENTS OF THE UNITED NATIONS (Brooklyn, New York: Foundation Press, 1968).
SOHN, L.B., BROADENING THE ROLE OF THE UNITED NATIONS IN PREVENTING, MITIGATING OR ENDING INTERNATIONAL OR INTERNAL CONFLICTS THAT THREATEN INTERNATIONAL PEACE AND SECURITY (Washington, D.C.: International Rule of Law Center, George Washington University Law School, 1997).
STEINER, H.J. & ALSTON, P., INTERNATIONAL HUMAN RIGHTS IN CONTEXT: LAW, POLITICS AND MORALS (Oxford: Clarendon Press, 1996).

TARDOFF, W., GOVERNMENTS AND POLITICS IN AFRICA (Indiana University Press, 1984).
THE AFRICAN COMMISSION ON HUMAN AND PEOPLES' RIGHTS, TENTH ANNIVERSARY CELEBRATION 2 NOVEMBER 1987 - 2 NOVEMBER: ONE DECADE OF CHALLENGE 1997, (ACHPR, 1998)
THE AFRICAN COMMISSION ON HUMAN AND PEOPLES' RIGHTS, COMMUNICATION PROCEDURE, INFORMATION SHEET NO. 3, 18 (1998).
THE AFRICAN COMMISSION ON HUMAN AND PEOPLES' RIGHTS, DECISIONS OF THE AFRICAN COMMISSION ON HUMAN AND PEOPLES' RIGHTS 1986-1997 (ACHPR\LR\A\1, 1997).
THE AFRICAN COMMISSION ON HUMAN AND PEOPLES RIGHTS' RIGHTS, GUIDELINES ON THE SUBMISSION OF COMMUNICATIONS, INFORMATION SHEET NO. 2
THE AFRICAN COMMISSION ON HUMAN AND PEOPLES RIGHTS' RIGHTS, REPORT OF THE SPECIAL RAPPORTEUR ON PRISONS AND CONDITIONS OF DETENTION (1997).
THE AFRICAN SOCIETY OF INTERNATIONAL AND COMPARATIVE LAW, REPORT ON THE 16TH SESSION OF THE AFRICAN COMMISSION ON HUMAN AND PEOPLES' RIGHTS (1996).
THOMPSON, K.W. ed., THE MORAL IMPERATIVES OF HUMAN RIGHTS: A WORLD SURVEY (Washington, D.C.: University Press of America, 1980).
THOOLEN, HANS & BERTH VERSTAPPEN, HUMAN RIGHTS MISSIONS: A STUDY OF THE FACT-FINDING PRACTICE OF NON-GOVERNMENTAL ORGANIZATIONS (Dordrecht: Martinus Nijhoff Publishers, 1986).
TOMASEVSKI, K, DEVELOPMENT AID AND HUMAN RIGHTS Revisited (London: Pinter Publishers, 1993).
TRINDADE, A.A.C., ed., THE MODERN WORLD OF HUMAN RIGHTS; ESSAYS IN HONOR OF THOMAS BURGENTHAL (San José: Inter-American Institute of Human Rights, 1996).

UMOZURIKE, U.O., THE AFRICAN CHARTER ON HUMAN AND PEOPLES RIGHTS (The Hague: Martinus Nijhoff Publishers, 1997).
UMOZURIKE, U.O, INTERNATIONAL LAW AND COLONIALISM IN AFRICA, (Nwamaife, 1979).
UMOZURIKE, U.O., THE AFRICAN CHARTER ON HUMAN AND PEOPLES' RIGHTS (Nigerian Institute of Advanced Legal Studies, 1992).

UNITED NATIONS HUMAN RIGHTS CENTER, HUMAN RIGHTS: A COMPILATION OF DOCUMENTS, UN Doc.ST/HR 1/HR Rev. 5, parts 1 & 2 (1994).
UNITED NATIONS, UNITED NATIONS IN THE FIELD OF HUMAN RIGHTS (New York: United Nations, 1994).

VALITICOS, N., INTERNATIONAL LABOR LAW (Boston: Kluwer Law & Taxation Publishers, 1995).
VAN DEVORT, T.R., INTERNATIONAL LAW AND ORGANIZATION (Sage Publications, 1994).
VAN DIKE, P. & VAN HOOF, G.J.F, THEORY AND PRACTICE OF THE EUROPEAN CONVENTION ON HUMAN RIGHTS (2nd Edition, Deventer: Kluwer, 1990).
VINCENT, R.J. HUMAN RIGHTS AND INTERNATIONAL RELATIONS (Cambridge: Cambridge University Press, 1986).

WELCH, JR., C.E.R., PROTECTING HUMAN RIGHTS IN AFRICA: ROLES AND STRATEGIES OF NON-GOVERNMENTAL ORGANIZATIONS (Philadelphia: University of Pennsylvania Press, 1995).
WELCH, JR., C.E. & MELTZER, R.I., eds., HUMAN RIGHTS AND DEVELOPMENT IN AFRICA , at (Albany: State University of New York Press, 1984).
WILLETTS, P., ed, THE CONSCIENCE OF THE WORLD: THE INFLUENCE OF NON-GOVERNMENTAL ORGANIZATIONS IN THE U.N. SYSTEM (Washington, D.C.: The Brookings Institution, 1996).
WILLIAM KOREY, NGOS AND THE UNIVERSAL DECLARATION OF HUMAN RIGHTS: A CURIOUS GRAPEVINE (New York: St. Martin's Press, 1998).

ARTICLES

Acheampong, K.A., Our Common Morality Under Siege: The Rwanda Genocide and the Concept of Universality of Human Rights, 4 REV. AFR. COM. HUM. & PEOPLES' RTS. 20 (1994).
Adoo, A., Africa: Democracy Without Human Rights, 15 HUM. RTS. Q. 703 (1993).
African Foreign Ministers Discuss Human Rights, PAN AFRICAN NEWS AGENCY, April 15, 1999.
Aginam, O., Legitimate Governance Under the African Charter on Human and Peoples' Rights in LEGITIMATE GOVERNANCE IN AFRICA: INTERNATIONAL AND DOMESTIC LEGAL PERSPECTIVES 12 (QUASHIGAH, E.K. & OKAFOR, O.C., eds., The Hague, Kluwer Law International, 1999).
Akanle, O., The Legal and Institutional Framework of the African Community in AFRICAN ECONOMIC COMMUNITY TREATY: ISSUES, PROBLEMS AND PROSPECTS 1 at 26 (M.A. AJOMO & O. ADEWALE, eds., 1993).
Alexandre, K., The Role of the Universal Declaration of Human Rights in the Development of International Law in UNITED NATIONS, BULLETIN OF HUMAN RIGHTS: SPECIAL ISSUE: FORTIETH ANNIVERSARY OF THE UNIVERSAL DECLARATION OF HUMAN RIGHTS 47-52 (New York: United Nations, 1988).

Alston, P., Peace as Human Right, 11 BULL. PEACE PROPOSALS. 126 (1981).
Alston, P., UNESCO Procedure For Dealing With Human Rights Violations 20 SANTA CLARA L. REV. 665 (1980).
Alston, P., The Committee on Economic, Social and Cultural Rights in THE UNITED NATIONS AND HUMAN RIGHTS: A CRITICAL APPRAISAL 473 (PHILIP ALSTON, ed. Oxford: Clarendon Press, 1992).
Alston, P., Making Space for New Rights: The Case for the Right to Development, 1 HARV. HUM. RTS. Y.B. 3, 22 (1988).
Amoa, P., The African Charter on Human and Peoples' Rights- An Effective Weapon for Human Rights? 4 AFR. J. INT'L & COMP. L. 226 91992).
Andrews, J.A., The European Jurisprudence of Human Rights, 43 MD. L. REV. 463 (1984).
Ankuma, E, The "Emergency" Provision of the African Charter on Human and Peoples' Rights, 4 REV. AFR. COM. HUM. & PEOPLES' RTS. 47 (1994).
Anthony, A.E., Beyond the Paper Tiger: The Challenge of a Human Rights Court in Africa, 32 TEX. INT'L. L.J. 511 (1997).
Appiayegi-Atua, K., The Role of Human Rights NGOs in the Current Democratic Dispensation in Africa: The Lessons of the Ghanian Experience in LEGITIMATE GOVERNANCE IN AFRICA: INTERNATIONAL AND DOMESTIC LEGAL PERSPECTIVES 311 at 312. (EDWARD K. QUASHIGAH & OBIORA C. OKAFOR, eds., The Hague: Kluwer Law International, 1999).
Ayangwe, C., Obligations of States Parties to the African Charter on Human and Peoples' Rights, 10 AFR. J INT'L & COMP. L. 625 (1998).
Ayine, D.M., Ballots as Bullets?: Compliance with Rules and Norms Providing for the Right to Democratic Governance, African Perspective, 10 AFR. J INT'L & COMP. L. 709 (1998).

Badawi El-Sheikh, I.A., The African Commission on Human and Peoples' Rights: A Call for Justice in INTERNATIONAL JUSTICE 283 (KALLIOPI KOUFA, ed., Sakkoulas Publications, 1997).
Badawi El-Sheikh, I.A., Draft Protocol to the African Charter on Human and Peoples' Rights on the Establishment of An African Court on Human and Peoples' Rights: An Introductory Note, 9 AFR. J. INT'L. L. 943 (1997).
Badawi El-Sheikh, I.A., The African Commission on Human and Peoples' Rights: Prospects and Problems, 7 NETHERLANDS Q. HUM RTS. 272 (1989).
Batsch, The Supervisory Functions of the Committee of Ministers Under Article 54- a Postcript to Luedicke-Belkacem-Koç in F. MATSCHER & H. PETZOLD, PROTECTING HUMAN RIGHTS: THE EUROPEAN DIMENSION 47-54 (Köln, 1990).
Bello, E., The Mandate of the African Commission on Human and Peoples Rights, 1 AFRICAN JOURNAL OF INTERNATIONAL LAW, 55 (1988).
Bello, E., Article 22 of the African Charter on Human and Peoples' Rights, in ESSAYS IN HONOUR OF JUDGE T. O ELIAS, 458 (E. BELLO & B. AJIBOLA, eds., 1992).
Benedek, W., The African Charter and Commission on Human and Peoples' Rights: How to Make it More Effective, NETHERLANDS. Q. HUM. RTS. 25 at 29-31 (1993).

Bernhardt, R., Reform of the Control Machinery Under The European Convention on Human Rights: Protocol No. 11, 89 AM. J. INT'L L. 145 (1995).
Bilder, The Individual and the Right to Peace, 11 BULL. PEACE PROPOSALS 387 (1982).
Blay, S.K.N., Changing African Perspectives on the Right to Self-Determination in the Wake of the Banjul Charter on Human and Peoples' Rights, JOURNAL OF AFRICAN LAW 147 (1985).
Bondzie-Simpson, E., A Critique of the African Charter on Human and Peoples Rights, 31 HOWARD LAW JOURNAL 643, (1988).
Bowen, J.S., Power and Authority in the African Context: Why Somalia did not have to Starve -the Organization of African Unity (OAU) as an Example of the Constitutive Process, 14 NAT'L BLACK L. J. 92 (1995).
Boukrif, H., La Cour afriaine des droits de l'homme et des peuples: un organe judiciaire au service des droits de l'homme et des peuples Afrique 10 RADIC 60 (1998).
Bratza, N., & O'Boyle, M., The Legacy of the Commission to the New Court Under The Eleventh Protocol in THE BIRTH OF THE EUROPEAN HUMAN RIGHTS LAW: STUDIES IN HONOR OF CARL AAGE NØRGAARD 377(MICHELLE DE SALVIA & MARK VILLIGER, eds., 1998*)*.
Brett, R., The Contribution of NGOs to the Monitoring and Protection of Human Rights in Europe in MONITORING HUMAN RIGHTS IN EUROPE 121-144 (ARIE BOLD, LISE-LOTTE, MANFRED NOVAK & ALLAN ROSAS, eds., Dordrecht: Martinus Nijhoff Publishers, 1994).
Brett, R., Non-Governmental Actors in the Field of Human Rights in AN INTRODUCTION TO THE INTERNATIONAL PROTECTION OF HUMAN RIGHTS: A TEXT BOOK 327, at 331 (RAIJA HASK & MARKKU SUKSI, eds., Turku Abo, Finland: Institute for Human Rights, Abo Akademi University, 1997).
Brett, R., The Role and Limits of Human Rights NGOs at the United Nations, 43 POLITICAL STUDIES, SPECIAL ISSUE, 96-110 (1995).
Buergenthal, T., The Advisory Practice of the Inter-American Human Rights Court, 79 AM. J. OF INT'L LAW 1 (1985).
Buergenthal, T., Self-Executing and Non-Self-Executing Treaties in National and International Law, IV RECUEIL DES COURS, 305 (1992)
Buergenthal, T., The Evolution of International Human Rights (Paper on File with Author, 1997)
Busia, Jr. N., & Mbaye, B., Towards a Framework for the Filing of Communications on Economic, Social and Cultural Rights Under the African Charter, Phase I, 1 EAST AFRICAN JOURNAL OF PEACE AND HUMAN RIGHTS (1994).

Carver, R., How African Governments Investigate Human Rights, THIRD WORLD LEG. STUDS.161 (1988).
Cassin, R., Introduction: The International Law of Human Rights, 144 RECUEILS DES COURS (1974).

Cerna, C., The Inter-American Commission on Human Rights: Its Organization and Examination of Petitions, in THE INTER-AMERICAN SYSTEM OF HUMAN RIGHTS 65 (DAVID J. HARRIS & STEPHEN LIVINGSTONE, eds., Oxford: Clarendon Press, 1998).

Charnovitz, S., Two Centuries of Participation: NGOs and International Governance, 18 MICH. J. INT'L. L. 183 (1997).

Chemillier-Gendreau, M. L'Afrique et les générales de realisation des droits de l'homme, 11 RADIC 1 (1999).

Claudia Grossman, Disappearances in Honduras: The Need for Direct Victim Representation in Human Rights Litigation, 15 HASTINGS INT'L. & COMP. L. REV. 363 (1992).

Charney, J.I., Compromissory Clauses and the Jurisdiction of the International Court of Justice, 81 AM. J. INT'L L. 855 (1987).

Cohen, C.P., The Role of Non-governmental Organizations in the Drafting of the Convention on the Rights of the Child, 12 HUM. RTS. Q. 137-147 (1990).

Coomans, F., UNESCO and Human Rights in AN INTRODUCTION TO THE INTERNATIONAL PROTECTION OF HUMAN RIGHS: A TEXT BOOK 181 ((RAIJA HANSKI & MARKU SUKSI, eds., Tarku/Abo, Finland: Institute for Human Rights, Abo Akademi University, 1997).

Coomans, F., Clarifying the Core Elements of the Right to Education in THE RIGHT TO COMPLAIN ABOUT ECONOMIC, SOCIAL AND CULTURAL RIGHTS: PROCEEDINGS OF THE EXPERT MEETING ON THE ADOPTION OF AN OPTIONAL PROTOCOL TO THE INTERNATIONAL COVENANT ON ECONOMIC, SOCIAL AND CULTURAL RIGHTS HELD FROM 25-28 JANUARY 1995 IN UTRECHT 13 (FONS COOMANS & FRIED VAN HOOF, eds., Utrecht, Netherlands: Netherlands Institute of Human Rights, 1995).

Dakas, A.D., Right to Development: Has it a Significance of its own?, 4 REV. AFR. COM. HUM. & PEOPLES' RTS. 68 (1994).

Cullet, P., Definition of an Environmental Right in a Human Rights Context, 1 NETHERLANDS Q. HUM. RTS. 28 (1995).

Danielsen, A., & Oberleitner, G., Human Rights News: Africa, 13 NETHERLANDS Q. HUM. RTS. 80, at 82 (1995).

Dankwa, E.V.O., Commentary on the Rules of Procedure of the African Commission on Human and Peoples' Rights, in PROCEEDINGS OF THE SECOND ANNUAL CONFERENCE OF THE AFRICAN SOCIETY OF INTERNATIONAL AND COMPARATIVE LAW 30 (1990).

Dankwa, V., Flinterman, C., & Leckie, S., Commentary to the Maastricht Guidelines on Violations of Economic, Social and Cultural Rights, 20 HUM. RTS. Q. 705 (1998).

de Vey Mestdagh, K., Reform of the European Convention on Human Rights in a Changing Europe in THE DYNAMICS OF THE PROTECTION OF HUMAN RIGHTS IN EUROPE 337 (RICK LAWSON & MATTHIJS DE BLOIS eds., 1994)

Deng, F., Cultural Approach to Human Rights among the Dinka, in HUMAN RIGHTS IN AFRICA: CROSS- CULTURAL PERSPECTIVES 243 (ABDULAHI AN-NA'IM and FRANCIS DENG, eds., 1990).

Donnelly, J., Human Rights and Western Liberalism, in HUMAN RIGHTS IN AFRICA: CROSS-CULTURAL PERSPECTIVES (ABDULAHI AN-NA'IM and FRANCIS DENG, eds., 1990).

Drzemczewski, A., The European Human Rights Convention: A New Court of Human Rights in Strasbourg as of November 1, 1998, 55 WASH. & LEE. L. REV. 697 (1998).
Andrew Drzemczewski, A Major Overhaul of the European Human Rights Convention Control Mechanism: Protocol No. 11 in COLLECTED COURSES OF THE ACADEMY OF EUROPEAN LAW 121 (Academy of European Law, ed., 1995)
Drzemczewski, A. & Meyer-Ladewig, J., Principal Characteristics of The New EHCR Control Mechanism As Established By Protocol No. 11 Signed on May 11, 1994, 15 HUM RTS. L. J. 81(1994).
Drzewicki, K., The United Nations Charter and the Universal Declaration of Human Rights in AN INTRODUCTION TO THE INTERNATIONAL PROTECTION OF HUMAN RIGHTS: A TEXT BOOK 65 (RAIJA HANSKI & MARKU SUKSI, eds., Tarku/Abo, Finland: Institute for Human Rights, Abo Akademi University, 1997).
Dumas, Nanette, Enforcement of Human Rights Standards: An International Human Rights Court and Other Proposals, 13 HASTINGS INT'L & COMP. L. REV. 593 (1990).

Enemo, I., Self-Determination as the Fundamental Basis for the Concept of Legitimate Governance Under the African Charter on Human and Peoples Rights in LEGITIMATE GOVERNANCE IN AFRICA: INTERNATIONAL AND DOMESTIC LEGAL IMPLICATIONS 403, AT 408-418 (EDWARD K. QUASHIGAH & OBIORA C. OKAFOR, *eds.*, The Hague/ London/ Boston: Kluwer Law International, 1999).
Ezejiofor, G., The Role of NGOs in the Securement of Legitimate Governance in Africa: The Lessons of the Nigerian Experience in LEGITIMATE GOVERNANCE IN AFRICA: INTERNATIONAL AND DOMESTIC LEGAL PERSPECTIVES 331, AT 332 (EDWARD K. QUASHIGAH & OBIORA C. OKAFOR, EDS., The Hague: Kluwer Law International, 1999).
Ezetah, C.R., Legitimate Governance and Statehood in Africa: Beyond the Failed State and Colonial Self-Determination in LEGITIMATE GOVERNANCE IN AFRICA: INTERNATIONAL AND DOMESTIC LEGAL IMPLICATIONS 419 (EDWARD K. QUASHIGAH AND OBIORA C. OKAFOR, eds., The Hague, London, Boston: Kluwer Law International, 1999).

Fall, I., Les Méchanismes de Protection et de Promotion des droits de l'homme développé au sien du système de Nations Unies, 4 REV. AFR. COM. HUM. & PEOPLES' RTS. 11 (1994).
Farer, T., The Rise of the Inter-American Human Rights Regime: No Longer a Unicorn, not yet an Ox in THE INTER-AMERICAN SYSTEM OF HUMAN RIGHTS 31-64 (DAVID J. HARRIS & STEPHEN LIVINGSTONE, eds., Oxford: Clarendon Press, 1998).
Fernyhough, T, Human Rights and Precolonial Africa, in HUMAN RIGHTS AND GOVERNANCE IN AFRICA 39 (RONALD COHEN *et al,* eds., Florida: University Press of Florida, 1993).
Fischer, D., International Reporting Procedures, in GUIDE TO INTERNATIONAL HUMAN RIGHTS PRACTICE 168 (HURST HANNUM, ed., 1984).

Flinterman, C. and Henderson. C., *The African Charter on Human and Peoples Rights*, in AN INTRODUCTION TO THE INTERNATIONAL PROTECTION OF HUMAN RIGHTS: A TEXT BOOK 315 AT 318. (HANSKI, R & SUKSI, M. eds., Tarku/Abo: Finland, Abo Akedeni University, 1997).

Gaer, F.D., *First Fruits: Reporting by States under the African Charter on Human and Peoples' Rights*, NETHERLANDS Q. HUM. RTS. 29-42 (1992).

Gittleman, R., *The African Charter on Human and Peoples' Rights: A Legal Analysis*, 22 VA. J. INT'L L. 667 AT 687 (1982).

Gonide, P.F., *The Relationship of International Law and National Law in Africa*, 10 AFR. J. INT'L & COMP. L. 244 (1998).

Gómez, V., *The Interaction Between the Political Actors of OAS, the Commission and the Court* in THE INTER-AMERICAN SYSTEM OF HUMAN RIGHTS 172 (DAVID J. HARRIS & STEPHEN LIVINGSTONE, eds., Oxford: Clarendon Press, 1998).

Gutto, S., *Environmental Rights Litigation, Human Rights and the Role of Non-Governmental and Peoples' Organizations in Africa*, 2 SOUTH AFRICAN JOURNAL OF ENVIRONMENTAL LAW AND POLICY 1-4 (1995).

Gye-Wado, O., *The Effectiveness of the Safeguard Machinery for the Enforcement of Human Rights in Africa*, 2 J. HUM. RTS. LAW &. PRACICE, 142 AT 154 (1992).

Hagos, G., *African Human Rights Court on the Cards*, AFR. NEWS, 11 Dec. 1997.

Hagos, G., *Africa at Large; Conference Adopts Protocol on African Human Rights Court*, AFR. NEWS, 13 Dec. 1997

Harris, D.J., *Regional Protection of Human Rights: The Inter-American Achievement* in THE INTER-AMERICAN SYSTEM OF HUMAN RIGHTS (DAVID J. HARRIS & STEPHEN LIVINGSTONE, eds., Oxford: Clarendon Press, 1998).

Henckaerts, J., *The Coming of Age of the International Covenant on Economic, Social and Cultural Rights Through the Work of the International Committee on Economic, Social and Cultural Rights* in THE MODERN WORLD OF HUMAN RIGHTS: ESSAYS IN HONOR OF THOMAS BURGENTHAL 267 (ANTONIO A. CANÇADO TRINADE, ed., San José, Costa Rica: Inter-American Institute of Human Rights, 1996).

Higgins, R., *Derogation Under Human Rights Treaties*, 48 BRIT. Y. B. INT'L L. 281.

Higgins, R., *Africa and the Covenant on Civil and Political Rights During the First Five Years of the Journal: Some Facts and Some Thoughts*, 5 AFR. J. INT'L & COMP. L. 55 (1992).

Hossain, K., *Introduction to Permanent Sovereignty over Natural Resources* in INTERNATIONAL LAW IX (KAMAL HOSSAIN & SUBRATA ROY CHOWDHURY eds., 1984).

Howard, R., *Evaluating Human Rights in Africa: Some Problems of Implicit* Comparisons, 6 HUM. RTS. Q. 160 (1984).

Howard, R., *Group Versus Individual Identity in the African Debate on Human Rights*, in HUMAN RIGHTS IN AFRICA: CROSS- CULTURAL PERSPECTIVES (ABDULAHI AN-NA'IM AND FRANCIS DENG, eds., 1990).

Idowu, A.A., Human Rights, Environmental Degradation and Oil Multinational Companies in Nigeria: The Ogoniland Episode, 17 NETHERLANDS Q. HUM. RTS. 161 (1999).
International Conference on Human Rights Commission Opens in Addis, XINHUA NEWS AGENCY, 18 May, 1998.

Kwakwa, E., The Eritrean Question: The Conflict Between the Right to Self-Determination and the interest of States, 5 Pt. 4 AFR. J.INT'L & COMP. L. 949 (1993).
Kiss, A., Peoples' Right to Self-Determination, 7, No. 2-4 HUM. RTS. L. J., 165 (1986).
Kiss A., The Role of the Universal Declaration of Human Rights in the Development of International Law in UNITED NATIONS, BULLETIN OF HUMAN RIGHTS: SPECIAL ISSUE: FORTIETH ANNIVERSARY OF THE UNIVERSAL DECLARATION OF HUMAN RIGHTS 47-52 (New York: United Nations, 1988).
Kiwanuaka, R.N., On the Paucity of Human Rights NGOs in Africa, Hum. Rts. Internet Rep. Vol. 11, No. 4 (Nov. 1986), 10-12.
Kiwanuaka, R.N., The Meaning of "People" in the African Charter on Human and Peoples' Rights, 82 AM. J. INT'L. L. 80 (1988).
Klerk, Y., Protocol No. 11 to the European Convention for Human Rights: A Drastic Revision of the Supervisory Mechanism under the ECHR, NETHERLANDS Q. HUM. RTS. 35 (1996).
Kofele-Kale, N., Patrimonicide: The International Economic Crime of Indigenous Spoliation, 28 VAND. J. TRANSNAT'L L. 45, AT 92 (1995).

Leary, V., Lessons from the Experience of the International Labor Organization in THE UNITED NATIONS AND HUMAN RIGHTS: A CRITICAL ANALYSIS (PHILIP ALSTON, ed., Oxford: Clarendon Press, 1992).
Leary, V., Human Rights at the ILO: Reflections on Making the ILO User Friendly in THE MODERN WORLD OF HUMAN RIGHTS; ESSAYS IN HONOR OF THOMAS BURGENTHAL 375 (ANTONIO A. CANÇADO TRINDADE, ed., San José: Inter-American Institute of Human Rights, 1996).
Leary, V.A., The Right to Complain: The Right to Health in THE RIGHT TO COMPLAIN ABOUT ECONOMIC, SOCIAL AND CULTURAL RIGHTS: PROCEEDINGS OF THE EXPERT MEETING ON THE ADOPTION OF AN OPTIONAL PROTOCOL TO THE INTERNATIONAL COVENANT ON ECONOMIC, SOCIAL AND CULTURAL RIGHTS HELD FROM 25-28 JANUARY 1995 IN UTRECHT 87 (FONS COOMANS & FRIED VAN HOOF, eds., Utrecht, Netherlands: Netherlands Institute of Human Rights, 1995).
Legesse, A., Human Rights in African Political Culture, in THE MORAL IMPERATIVES OF HUMAN RIGHTS: A WORLD SURVEY (K.W. THOMPSON *ed.;* Washington, D.C.: University Press of America, 1980).
Lopatka, The Right to Live in Peace as a Human Right, 10 BULL. PEACE PROPOSALS 361, 362 at 366 (1979).

Madhuku, L., The Impact of the European Court of Human Rights in Africa: The Zimbabwean Experience, 8 AFRICAN J. INT'L & COMP. L., 932- 943 (1996).

Magnarella, P.J., Preventing Inter-Ethnic Conflict and Promoting Human Rights Through More Effective Legal, Political, and Aid Srtuctures: Focus on Africa, 23 GA. J. INT'L. L. 327 (1993).

M'Baye, K., Human Rights in Africa in THE INTERNATIONAL DIMENSIONS OF HUMAN RIGHTS 583 (KAREl VASAK/ PHILIP ALSTON, eds; Greenwood Press, 1982).

Marks, S., The Complaint Procedure of the United Nations Educational, Scientific and Cultural Organization in H. HANUM, GUIDE TO INTERNATIONAL HUMAN RIGHTS PRACTICE 86 (2nd ed., 1992).

McCaueley, K.M., Women on the European Commission and the Court of Human Rights: Would Equal Representation Provide More Effective Remedies? DICK J. INT'L L. 151 (1994).

Medina, C., The Role of Country Reports in the Inter-American System of Human Rights in THE INTER-AMERICAN SYSTEM OF HUMAN RIGHTS 115 (DAVID J. HARRIS & STEPHEN LIVINGSTONE, eds., Oxford: Clarendon Press, 1998).

Medina., C., The Inter-American Commission on Human Rights and the Inter-American Court of Human Rights: Reflections on a Joint Venture, 12 HUM. RTS. Q. 439 (1990).

Mendez, J., & Vivanco, J.M., Disappearance in the Inter-American Cour: Reflections on a Litigation Experience, 13 HAMLINE L. REV. 507 (1990).

Merrils, J.G., The Council of Europe (I): The European Convention on Human Rights in AN INTRODUCTION TO THE INTERNATIONAL PROTECTION OF HUMAN RIGHTS: A TEXT BOOK 221 (RAIJA HANSKI & MARKU SUKSI eds., 1997).

Meron, T., Norm Making and Supervision in International Human Rights: Reflections on Institutional Order, 76 AM. J. INT'L L. 754 (1982).

Miguel, J. & Bhansali, L.L., Procedural Shortcomings in the Defense of Human Rights: An Inequality of Arms in the Inter-American System of Human Rights in THE INTER-AMERICAN SYSTEM OF HUMAN RIGHTS 421 (DAVID J. HARRIS & STEPHEN LIVINGSTONE, eds., Oxford: Clarendon Press, 1998).

Mojekwu, C.C., International Human Rights: The African Perspective in INTERNATIONAL HUMAN RIGHTS: CONTEMPORARY ISSUES 85-95 (J. L. NELSON & V.M. GREEN, eds., New York: Human Rights Publishing Group, 1980).

Moller, J., The Universal Declaration of Human Rights: How the Process Started in THE UNIVERSAL DECLARATION OF HUMAN RIGHTS: A COMMENTARY (ASBJORN EIDE, *et al* eds., Oslo: Scandinavian University Press, 1992).

Murray, R., Serious or Massive Violations Under the African Charter on Human and Peoples' Rights: A Comparison with the Inter-American and European Mechanisms, 17 NO. 3 NETHERLANDS O. HUM. RTS., 109 (1999).

Murray, R., Report on the 1996 Sessions of the African Commission on Human and Peoples' Rights - 19th and 20th Ordinary Sessions: 26 March - 4 April, and 21-31 October 1996, 18 HUM. RTS. J., 16 (1997).

Mutua, M., The Banjul Charter and the African Cultural Fingerprint: An Evaluation of Language of Duties, 35 VA. J. INT'L L. 339 (1995).

Mutua, M. The African Human Rights Court: A Two-Legged Stool? 21 HUM. RTS. Q. 342-363 (1999).

Mutua, M., *The African Human Rights System in a Comparative Perspective: The Need for Urgent Reformulation,* 5 LEGAL F. 31, 33 (1993).

Nagan, W.P., *African Human Rights Process: A Contextual Policy-Oriented Approach,* 21 Sw. U. L. Rev. 63 (1992).

Naldi, G.J., & Magiliveras, K., *Reinforcing the African System of Human Rights: The Protocol on the Establishment of a Regional Court of Human and Peoples' Rights,* 16 NETHERLANDS Q. HUM. RTS. 431 (1998).

Naldi, G.J., & Magiliveras, K, *The Proposed African Court on Human and Peoples' Rights: Evaluation and Comparison,* 8 AFR. J. INT'L. & COMP. L. 944 (1996).

News Letter of the African Commission on Human and Peoples Rights Vol. 1 Number 1 (October-December, 1998).

Ngabirano, P.B., *Case Comment: Does Municipal Law Prevail Over International Law? The Registered Trustees of Constitutional Rights Project v. The President of the Federal Republic of Nigeria and Others,* 2:1 EAST AFRICAN JOURNAL OF PEACE AND HUM. RTS.102 (1995).

Nguema, I., *Violence, droits de l'homme et Dévelopment en Afrique,* 4 REV. AFR. COM. HUM. & PEOPLES' RTS. 56 (1994).

Nguema, I., *Africa, Human Rights and Development* in UNITED NATIONS, DISARMAMENT 75 (New York: United Nations, 1991).

Nmehielle, V.O., *Towards an African Court of Human Rights: Structuring and Empowering the Court,* VI ANNUAL SURVEY INT'L. & COMP. L. (2000).

Nmehielle, V.O., *Oppression of Ethnic Minorities in Nigeria: The Ogoni Case* (Unpublished Seminar Paper on file with Author, 1995).

Norris and Reiton, P., *The Suspension of Guarantees: A Comparative Analysis of the American Convention on Human Rights and the Constitutions of the State Parties,* 30 AM. U. L. REV. 189-193 (1981).

Nowrot, K., *Legal Consequences of Globalization: The Status of Non-Governmental Organizations under International Law,* 6 IND. J. GLOBAL L. STUD. 579 (1999).

O'Flaherty, M., *The Reporting Obligation Under Article 40 of the International Covenant on Civil and Political Rights,* HUM. RTS. Q. 538 (1994).

Odinkalu, C.A., *The Individual Complaints Procedure of the African Commission on Human and Peoples Rights: A Preliminary Assessment,* 8 TRANSNAT'L L. & CONTEMP. PROBS. 359 (1998).

Odinkalu, A. & Christensen, C., *The African Commission on Human and Peoples' Rights: The Development of its Non-State Communication Procedures,* 20 HUM. RTS. Q. 235 (1998).

O'Flaherty, M., *The Reporting Obligations Under Article 40 of the International Covenant on Civil and Political Rights: Lessons to be Learned from Consideration by the Human Rights Committee on Ireland's First Report,* HUM. RTS. Q. 538 (1994).

Okeke, C.N., *A Note on the Right of Secession as a Human Right,* 3 ANNUAL SURVEY INT'L. L., 27-35 (1996).

Okeke, C.N., Intrenational Law in The Nigerian Legal System, 27 CAL. WESTERN INT'L. L. J 311 (1997).

Okere, B.O., The Protection of Human Rights in Africa and the African Charter on Human and Peoples' Rights: A Comparative Analysis with the European and the American Systems, 6 HUM. RTS. Q.141 (1984).

Okoth-Ogendo, H.W.O., Human and Peoples Rights: What Point is Africa Trying to Make in HUMAN RIGHTS AND GOVERNANCE IN AFRICA 74 (RONALD COHEN et al, eds., Florida: University Press of Florida, 1993).

Oloka-Onyango, J., Beyond the Rhetoric: Reinvigorating the Struggle for Economic and Social Rights in Africa, 26 CAL. W. INT'L L.J. 1, AT 36 (1995).

Olz, M.A., Non-Governmental Organizations in Regional Human Rights Systems, 28 COLUM. HUM. RTS. L. REV. 307 (1997).

Opsahl, T, The Human Rights Committee in THE UNITED NATIONS AND HUMAN RIGHTS: A CRITICAL APPRAISAL 369-443 (PHILIP ALSTON ED. Oxford: Clarendon Press, 1992).

Oputa, C.A., Crime and the Nigerian Society in ELIAS, T.O., NWABARA, S.N., & AKPAMGBO, C.O., AFRICAN INDIGENOUS LAWS 12 (Enugu, Nigeria: Government Printer, 1975).

Otto, D., Non-governmental Organizations in the United Nations System: The Emerging Role of International Civil Society, 18 HUM. RTS Q. 107 (1996).

Onyekpere, E., Democracy, Human Rights, Dictatorships and the Nigerian Judiciary, 3 J. HUM. RTS. L. & PRACTICE 51 (1993).

Padilla, D., The Inter-American Commission on Human Rights of the Organization of American States: A Case Study, 9 AM. U. J. INT'L. & POL'Y 95 (1995).

Parker, M.C., 'Other Treaties': The Inter-American Court of Human Rights Defines Its Advisory Jurisdiction, 33 AM. U. L. REV. 211 (1983)

Pasqualucci, J.M., Provisional Measures in the Inter-American Human Rights System: Innovative Development in International Law, 26 VAND. J. TRANSNAT'L L. 803 (1993).

Pasqualucci, J.M., The Inter-American Human Rights System: Establishing Precedents and Procedure in Human Rights Law, 26 U. MIAMI INTER-AM. L. REV. 297 1995).

Perrez, F.X., The Relationship Between "Permanent Sovereignty" and the Obligation Not to Cause Transboundary Environmental Damage, 26 ENVTL. L. 1187 (1996).

Peter, C.M., Taking the Environment Seriously: The African Charter on Human and Peoples' Rights and the Environment, 3 REV. AFR. COMM. HUM. & PEOPLES' RTS. 41 (1993).

Posner, M.H., & Whittome, C., The Status of Human Rights NGOs, 25 COLUM. HUM. RTS. L. REV. 269 (1994).

Pursuit for Peace Remains Major Task of Africa: Salim, XINHUA NEWS AGENCY, 8 June, 1998.

Quashiga, E.K, Legitimate Governance: The Pre-Colonial African Perspective in LEGITIMATE GOVERNANCE IN AFRICA: INTERNATIONAL AND DOMESTIC LEGAL PERSPECTIVES 43 (EDWARD K. QUASHIGA & OBIORA C. OKAFOR, eds., The Hague: Kluwer Law International, 1999).

Quashiga, E.K., Religious Freedom and Vestal Virgins: The Trokosi Practice in Ghana, 10 AFR. J. INT'L & COMP. L. 193 (1998).

Ramcharan, B.G., The Travaux Préparatoires of the African Commission on Human Rights 13 HUM. RTS. J. 307 (1992).

Reisman, W.M., Practical Matters For Consideration In The Establishment of a Regional Human Rights Mechanism: Lessons From The Inter-American Experience, ST. LOUIS-WARSAW TRANSATLANTIC L. J. 89, AT 100 (1995).

Rieter, E., Interim Measures by the World Court to Suspend the Execution of Individuals: The Breard Case, NETHERLANDS Q. HUM. RTS. 475 (1998).

Robertson, A.H., The European Convention for the Protection of Human Rights, 27 BRITISH YR. BOOK INT'L L 145 (1950).

Rodley, N.S., The Work of Non-Governmental Organizations in the World-wide Promotion and Protection of Human Rights, 90/1 BULLETIN OF HUMAN RIGHTS, 84-93 (1991).

Salcedo, J.A.C., The Place of the European Convention in International Law in THE EUROPEAN SYSTEM FOR THE PROTECTION OF HUMAN RIGHTS (MACDONALD et al, eds., Dordrecht: Martinus Nijhoff Publishers, 1993).

Samson, K., The Standard-Setting and Supervisory System of the International Labour Organization in AN INTRODUCTION TO THE INTERNATIONAL PROTECTION OF HUMAN RIGHS: A TEXT BOOK (RAIJA HANSKI & MARKU SUKSI, eds., Tarku/Abo, Finland: Institute for Human Rights, Abo Akademi University, 1997).

Scheinin, M. International Human Rights in National Law in AN INTRODUCTION TO THE INTERNATIONAL PROTECTION OF HUMAN RIGHTS: A TEXT BOOK 343 (Raija Hanski & MarkKu Suksi, eds., Turku/Abo, Finland: Institute of Human Rights, Abo Akedemi University, 1997).

Schermers, H.G., Adaptation of the 11 the Protocol to the European Convention on Human Rights, 20 EUROPEAN LAW REV. 559 (1995).

Schermers, H.G., The Eleventh Protocol to the European Convention on Human Rights, 19 EUROPEAN LAW REV. 367 (1994).

Scoble, H.M., Human Rights Non-Governmental Organizations in Black Africa: Their Problems and Prospects in the Wake of the Banjul Charter in HUMAN RIGHTS AND DEVELOPMENT IN AFRICA 117, (CLAUDE E. WELCH, JR.& RONALD I. MELTZER, eds., Albany: State University of New York Press, 1984).

Shelton, D., Reparations in the Inter-American System in The Inter-American System of Human Rights, 151 (DAVID J. HARRIS & STEPHEN LIVINGSTONE, eds., 1998).

Shelton, D., The Jurisprudence of the Inter-American Court of Human Rights, 10 AM. U. J. INT'L L. & POL'Y, 333 (1994).

Skogly, S.I., The Position of the World Bank and the International Monetary Fund in the Human Rights Field in AN INTRODUCTION TO THE INTERNATIONAL PROTECTION OF HUMAN RIGHS: A TEXT BOOK 193-205 AT 195. (RAIJA HANSKI & MARKU SUKSI, eds., Tarku/Abo, Finland: Institute for Human Rights, Abo Akademi University, 1997).

Sohn, L.B., The Stockholm Declaration on the Human Environment, 14 HARV. INT'L. J. 423-515 (1973).

Sohn, L.B., The New International Law: Protection of the Rights of Individuals Rather than States, 32 AM. U. L. REV. 1 (1982).
Sohn, L.B., Enhancing the Role of the General Assembly of the United Nations in Crystalizing International Law in THEORY OF INTERNATIONAL LAW AT THE THRESHHOLD OF THE 21ST CENTURY: ESSAYS IN HONOR OF KRYSZTOF SUKBISZEKI 550 (MAKARCZYK, J., ed., The Hague/London/Boston: Kluwer Law International, 1996).
Sohn, L.B., The Contribution of Latin American Lawyers to the Development of the United Nations Concept of Human Rights and Economic and Social Justice in THE MODERN WORLD OF HUMAN RIGHTS: ESSAYS IN HONOR OF THOMAS BURGENTHAL 33 (ANTONIO A. CANÇADO TRINADE, ed., San José, Costa Rica: Inter-American Institute of Human Rights, 1996).
Steiner, H.J., Individual Claims in a World of Massive Violations: What Role for the Human Rights Committee in THE FUTURE OF THE UN HUMAN RIGHTS TREATY MONITORING 15, at 31.(PHILIP ALSTON & JAMES CRAWFORD, eds., Cambridge University Press, 2000).
Swanson J., The Emergence of New Rights in the African Charter, 12 N. Y. SCH. J. INT'L & COMP. L. 307 (1991).

Tejan-Cole, A., Human Rights Under the Armed Forces Revolutionary Council (AFRC) in Sierra Leon, 10 AFR. J. INT'L & COMP. L. 481(1998).
Tomasevski, K., The World Bank and Human Rights in HUMAN RIGHTS IN DEVELOPING COUNTRIES: YEARBOOK 75-102 (MANFRED NOVAK & THERESA SWINEHART, eds., Kehl: N.P. Engel Publishers, 1989).
Trindade, A.A.C., The Inter-American Human Rights System at the Dawn of the New Century: Recommendations for Improvement of its Mechanism of Protection in THE INTER-AMERICAN SYSTEM OF HUMAN RIGHTS 397 (DAVID J. HARRIS & STEPHEN LIVINGSTONE, eds., Oxford: Clarendon Press, 1998).
Trindade, A.A.C., The Operation of the Inter-American Court of Human Rights, in THE INTER-AMERICAN SYSTEM OF HUMAN RIGHTS 133 (DAVID J. HARRIS & STEPHEN LIVINGSTONE, eds., Oxford: Clarendon Press, 1998).

Umozurike, U.O., International Law and the African Slave Trade 16(2) HOWARD L.J. 334-349 (1971).
Umozurike, U.O, The Significance of the African Charter on Human and Peoples' Rights in PERSPECTIVE ON HUMAN RIGHTS 45 (AWA U. KALU & YEMI OSINBAJO, eds., Nigeria: Federal Ministry of Justice, 1992).

Valticos, N., The International Labour Organization in THE EFFECTIVENESS OF INTERNATIONAL DECISIONS 134 (S. SCHWEBEL, ed., 1971).
vander Wilt, H., The OAS System for the Protection of Human Rights in AN INTRODUCTION TO THE INTERNATIONAL PROTECTION OF HUMAN RIGHTS: A TEXT BOOK 305 (RAIJA HANSKI & MARKU SUKSI eds., Tarku/Abo, Finland: Institute for Human Rights, Abo Akademi University, 1997).

van Boven, T., *The Relationship Between Peoples' Rights and Human Rights in the African Charter* 7 HUM. RTS. Q. 183 (1986).

Warbrick, C., *Coherence and the European Court of Human Rights: The Adjudicative Background of the Soering Case* 11 MICH. J. INT'L L. 1073 (1990).

Weibe, V., *The Prevention of War Through the Use of the Human Rights System*, 27 N.Y.U J. INT'L L & POL. 409 (1995).

Wembou, M.D., *Les mormes internationales relatives aux droits de l'homme et leur application dans la léislation interne des etats africains: problèmes et perspectives*, 11 RADIC 51 (1999).

Wiseberg, L.S., *The Role of Non-Governmental Organizations* IN HUMAN RIGHTS IN THE WORLD COMMUNITY: ISSUES AND ACTION 373-382. (RICHARD PIERRE CALUDE AND BURNS H. WESTON, eds., Philadelphia: University of Pennsylvania Press, 1992)

Weissbrodt, D., *The Contribution of International Non-governmental Organizations to the Protection of Human Rights* in HUMAN RIGHTS IN INTERNATIONAL LAW: LEGAL AND POLICY ISSUES 403-438 (THEODOR MERON, ed., Oxford: Clarendon Press, 1984).

Weissbrodt, D. & Farley, R., *The UNESCO Human Rights Procedure: An Evaluation*, 16 HUM. RTS. Q. 391-415 (1994).

Welch, C.E., *The African Commission on Human and Peoples' Rights: A Five Year Assessment*, HUM. RTS. QTLY 43 (1992).

Welch, C.E., *The African Charter and Freedom of Expression in Africa*, 4 BUFF. HUM. RTS. L. REV.103 (1998).

Welch, C., *The O.A.U. and Human Rights: Towards a New Definition*, 19 JOURNAL OF MODERN AFRICAN STUDIES 401 (1981).

Welch, C., *The Organization of African Unity and the Promotion of Human Rights*, 29 JOURNAL OF MODERN AFRICAN STUDIES 535 (1991).

Welch, C.E., *Human Rights and African Women: A comparison of Protection Under Two Major Treaties*, 15 No. 3 HUMAN RTS. Q. 566 (1993)

Wiredu, K., *An Arkan Perspective on Human Rights*, in HUMAN RIGHTS IN AFRICA: CROSS-CULTURAL PERSPECTIVES 243 (ABDULAHI AN-NA'IM AND FRANCIS DENG, eds., 1990).

Wiseberg, L.S., *The Role of Non-Governmental Organizations* in HUMAN RIGHTS IN THE WORLD COMMUNITY: ISSUES AND ACTION 373-382. (RICHARD PIERRE CALUDE AND BURNS H. WESTON, eds., Philadelphia: University of Pennsylvania Press, 1992)

Wiseberg, L.S., *Protecting Human Rights Activists and NGOs: What More can be Done?*13 HUM. RTS. Q. 525-544 (1990).

APPENDICES

THE CHARTER OF THE ORGANIZATION OF AFRICAN UNITY
(49 U.N.T.S. 39/2, I.L.M. 766 (1963))

We, the Heads of African States and Governments assembled in the City of Addis Ababa, Ethiopia;

CONVINCED that it is the inalienable right of all people to control their own destiny;

CONSCIOUS of the fact that freedom, equality, justice and dignity are essential objectives for the achievement of the legitimate aspirations of African Peoples;

CONSCIOUS of our responsibility to harness the natural and human resources of our continent for the total advancement of our peoples in all spheres of human endeavor;

INSPIRED by a common determination to promote understanding among our peoples and cooperation among our States in response to the aspiration of our peoples for brotherhood and solidarity, in a larger unity transcending ethnic and national differences;

CONVINCED that, in order to translate this determination into dynamic force in the cause of human progress, conditions for peace and security must be established and maintained;

DETERMINED to safeguard and consolidate the hard-won independence as well as the sovereignty and territorial integrity of our States, and to fight against neo-colonialism in all its forms;

DEDICATED to the general progress of Africa;

Persuaded that the Charter of the United Nations and the Universal Declaration of Human Rights, to the Principles of which we reaffirm our adherence, provide a solid foundation for peaceful and positive co-operation among S;
states;

DESIROUS that all African States should henceforth unite so that the welfare and well-being of their peoples can be assured;

RESOLVED to reinforce the links between our States by establishing and strengthening common institutions;

HAVE agreed to the present Charter.

ESTABLISHMENT
Article I

The High Contracting Parties do by the present Charter establish an organization to be known as the ORGANIZATION OF AFRICAN UNITY.

The Organization shall include the Continental African States, Madagascar and other Islands surrounding Africa.

PURPOSES
Article II

1. The Organization shall have the following purposes:
a. to promote the unity and solidarity of African States;
b. to co-ordinate and intensify the their cooperation and efforts to achieve a better life for the Peoples of Africa
c. to defend their sovereignty, their territorial integrity and independence;
d. to eradicate all forms of colonialism from Africa; and
e. to promote international cooperation, having due regard to the Charter of the United Nations and the Universal Declaration of Human Rights.
2. To these ends, the Member States shall co-ordinate and harmonize their general policies, especially in the following fields:
a. political and Diplomatic co-operation;
b. economic co-operation, including transport and communications;
c. educational and cultural co-operation;
d. health, sanitation, and nutritional co-operation;
e. Scientific and technical co-operation; and
f. co-operation for defense and security.

PRINCIPLES
Article III

The Member States, in pursuit of the purposes stated in Article II, solemnly affirm and declare their adherence to the following principles:

1.1. the sovereign equality of all Member States;
2.2. non-interference in the internal affairs of States;
3.3. Respect for the sovereignty and territorial integrity of each State and for its inalienable right to independent existence;
4.4. peaceful settlement of disputes by negotiation, mediation, conciliation or arbitration;
5.5. unreserved condemnation, in all its forms, of political assassination as well as subversive activities on the part of neighboring States or any States;
6.6. absolute dedication to the total emancipation of the African territories which are still independent;
7.7. affirmation of a policy of non-alignment with regard to all blocks.

MEMBERSHIP
Article IV

Each independent sovereign African State shall be entitled to become Member of the Organization.

RIGHTS AND DUTIES OF MEMBER STATES
Article V

All Member States shall enjoy equal rights and have equal duties.

Article VI

The Member States Pledge themselves to observe scrupulously the principles enumerated in Article III of the present Charter.

INSTITUTIONS
Article VII

The Organization shall accomplish its purposes through the following principal institutions:
1. the Assembly of Heads of State and Government;
2. the Council of Minsters;
3. the General Secretariat;
4. the Commission of Mediation, Conciliation and Arbitration.

THE ASSEMBLY OF HEADS OF STATE AND GOVERNMENT
Article VIII

The Assembly of Heads of State and Government shall be the supreme organ of the Organization. It shall, subject to the provisions of the Charter, discuss matters of common concern to Africa with a view to co-ordinating and harmonizing the general policy of the Organization. It may in addition review the structure, functions and acts of all the organs and specialized agencies which may be created in accordance with the present Charter.

Article IX

The Assembly shall be composed of the Heads of State and Government or their duly accredited representatives and it shall meet at least once a year. At the request of any Member State and on approval by a two-thirds majority of Member States, the Assembly shall meet in extraordinary session.

Article X

1. Each Member State shall have one vote.
2. All resolutions shall be determined by a two-thirds majority of Member of the Organization.
3. Questions of procedure shall require a simple majority. Whether or not a question is one of procedure shall be determined by a simple majority of all Members States of the Organization.
4. Two-thirds of the total membership of the organization shall form a quorum at any meeting of the Assembly.

Article XI

The Assembly shall have the power to determine its own rules of procedure.

COUNCIL OF MINISTERS
Article XII

1. The Council of Ministers shall consist of Foreign Ministers or such other Ministers as are delegated by the Government of Member States.
2. The Council of Ministers shall meet at least twice a year. When requested by any Member State and approved by two-thirds majority of all Member States, it shall meet in extraordinary session.

Article XIII

1. The Council of Ministers shall be responsible to the Assembly of Heads of State and Government. It shall be entrusted with the responsibility of preparing conferences of the Assembly.
2. It shall take cognizance of any matter referred to it by the Assembly. It shall be entrusted with the implementation of the decision of the Assembly of Heads of State and Government. It shall co-ordinate inter-African co-operation in accordance with the instructions of the Assembly and in conformity with Article II(2) of the present Charter.

Article XIV

1. Each Member State Shall have one vote.
2. All resolutions shall be determined by a simple majority of the Council of Ministers.
3. Two-thirds of the total membership of the Council of Ministers Shall form a quorum for amy meeting of the Council.

Article XV

The Council shall have the power to determine its own rules of procedure.

GENERAL SECRETARIAT
Article XVI

There shall be a Secretary-General of the Organization, who shall be appointed by the Assembly of Heads of State and Government. The Secretary-General shall direct the affairs of the Secretariat.

Article XVII

There shall be one or more Assistant Secretaries-General of the Organization, who shall be appointed by the Assembly of Heads of State and Government.

Article XVIII

The functions and conditions of service of the Secretary-General, of the Assistant Secretaries-General and other employees of the Secretariat shall be governed by the provisions of this Charter and the regulations approved by the Assembly of Heads of State and Government.

1. In the performance of their duties the Secretary-general and the staff shall not seek or receive instruction from any government or from any other authority external to the Organization.
2. Each member of the Organization undertakes to respect the exclusive character of the responsibilities of the Secretary-General and the staff and not to seek to influence them in the discharge of their responsibilities.

COMMISSION OF MEDIATION, CONCILIATION AND ARBITRATION
Article XIX

Member States pledge to settle all disputes among themselves by peaceful means and, to this end decide to establish a Commission of Mediation, Conciliation and Arbitration, the composition of which and conditions of service shall be defined by a separate Protocol to be approved by the Assembly of Heads of State and Government. Said Protocol shall be regarded as forming an integral part of the present Charter.

SPECIALIZED COMMISSIONS
Article XX

The Assembly shall establish such specialized Commission as it may deem necessary, including the following:

1. Economic and Social Commission;
2. Educational, Scientific, Cultural and Health Commission;
3. Defense Commission.

Article XXI

Each Specialized Commission referred to in Article XX shall be composed of the Ministers concerned or other Ministers or Plenipotentiaries designated by the Governments of the Member States.

Article XXII

The functions of the specialized Commissions shall be carried out in accordance with the provisions of the present Charter and of the regulations approved by the Council of Ministers.

THE BUDGET
Article XXIII

The budget of the Organization prepared by the Secretary-General shall be approved by the Council of Minsters. The budget shall be provided by contributions from Member States in accordance with the scale of assessment of the United Nations; provided, however, that no Member State shall be assessed an amount exceeding twenty per cent of the yearly regular budget of the Organization. The Member States agree to pay their respective contributions regularly.

SIGNATURE AND RATIFICATION OF CHARTER
Article XXIV

1. This Charter shall be open to all independent sovereign African States and shall be ratified by the signatory States in accordance with their constitutional processes.
2. The original instrument, done, if possible in African languages, in English and French, all texts being equally authentic, shall be deposited with the government of Ethiopia which shall transmit certified copies thereof to all independent sovereign African States.
3. The instruments of ratification shall be deposited with the Government of Ethiopia, which shall notify all signatories of each such deposit.

ENTRY INTO FORCE
Article XXV

This Charter shall enter into force immediately upon receipt by the Government of Ehiopia of the instrument of ratification from two-thirds of the signatory States.

REGISTRATION OF THE CHARTER
Article XXVI

This Charter shall, after due ratification, be registered with the Secretariat of the United Nations through the Government of Ethiopia in conformity with Article 102 of the Charter of the United Nations.

INTERPRETATION OF THE CHARTER
Article XXVII

Any question which may arise concerning the interpretation of this Charter shall be decided by a vote of two-thirds of the Assembly of Heads of State and Government of the Organization.

ADHESION AND ACCESSION
Article XXVIII

1. Any independent sovereign African State may at any time notify the Secretary-General of its intention to adhere or accede to this Charter.
2. The Secretary-General shall, on receipt of such notification, communicate a copy of it to all the Member States. Admission shall be decided by a simple majority of the Member States. The decision of each Member State shall be transmitted to the Secretary-General, who shall, upon receipt of the required number of votes, communicate the decision to the State concerned.

MISCELLANEOUS
Article XXIX

The working languages of the Organization and all its institutions shall be, if possible, African languages, Arabic, English, French and Portugese.

Article XXX

The Secretary-General may accept, on behalf of the Organization, gifts, bequests and other donations made to the Organization, provided that this is approved by the Council of Ministers.

Article XXXI

The Council of Ministers shall decide on the privileges and immunities to be accorded to the personnel of the Secretariat in the respective territories of the Member States.

CESSATION OF MEMBERSHIP
Article XXXII

Any State which desires to renounce its membership shall forward a written notification to the Secretary-General. At the end of one year from the date of such notification, if not withdrawn, the Charter shall cease to apply with respect to the renouncing State, which shall thereby cease to belong to the Organization.

AMENDMENT OF THE CHARTER
Article XXXIII

This Charter may be amended or revised if any Member State makes a written request to the Secretary-General to that effect; provided, however, that the proposed amendment is not submitted to the Assembly for consideration until all Member States have been duly notified of it and a period of one year has elapsed. Such an amendment shall not be effective unless approved by at least two-thirds of all Member States.
IN FAITH WHEREOF, WE, the Heads of State and Government have signed this Charter.

Done in the City of Addis-Ababa, Ethiopia, this 25th day of May, 1963.

II

APPENDIX V
CONSTITUTIVE ACT OF THE AFRICAN UNION

(Adopted by the Thirty-Sixth Ordinary Session of the Assembly of Heads of State and Government of the Organization of African Unity on 11 July, 2000, Lome, Togo)

We, Heads of State and Government of the Member States of the Organization of African Unity (OAU):

1. The President of the Peoples Democratic Republic of Algeria

2. The President of the Republic of Angola

3. The President of the Republic of Benin

4. The President of the Republic of Botswana

5. The President of Burkina Faso

6. The President of the Republic of Burundi

7. The President of the Republic of Cameroon

8. The President of the Republic of Cape Verde

9. The President of the Central African Republic

10. The President of the Republic of Chad

11. The President of the Islamic Federal Republic of the Comoros

12. The President of the Republic of the Congo

13. The President of the Republic of Côte d'Ivoire

14. The President of the Democratic Republic of Congo

15. The President of the Republic of Djibouti

16. The President of the Arab Republic of Egypt

17. The President of the State of Eritrea

18. The Prime Minister of the Federal Democratic Republic of Ethiopia

19. The President of the Republic of Equatorial Guinea

20. The President of the Gabonese Republic

21. The President of the Republic of The Gambia

22. The President of the Republic of Ghana

23. The President of the Republic of Guinea

24. The President of the Republic of Guinea Bissau

25. The President of the Republic of Kenya

26. The Prime Minister of Lesotho

27. The President of the Republic of Liberia

28. The Leader of the 1st of September Revolution of the Great Socialist Peoples Libyan Arab Jamahiriya

29. The President of the Republic of Madagascar

30. The President of the Republic of Malawi

31. The President of the Republic of Mali

32. The President of the Islamic Republic of Mauritania

33. The Prime Minister of the Republic of Mauritius

34. The President of the Republic of Mozambique

35. The President of the Republic of Namibia

APPENDIX II

36. The President of the Republic of Niger

37. The President of the Federal Republic of Nigeria

38. The President of the Republic of Rwanda

39. The President of the Sahrawi Arab Democratic Republic

40. The President of the Republic of Sao Tome and Principe

41. The President of the Republic of Senegal

42. The President of the Republic of Seychelles

43. The President of the Republic of Sierra Leone

44. The President of the Republic of Somalia

45. The President of the Republic of South Africa

46. The President of the Republic of Sudan

47. The King of Swaziland

48. The President of the United Republic of Tanzania

49. The President of the Togolese Republic

50. The President of the Republic of Tunisia

51. The President of the Republic of Uganda

52. The President of the Republic of Zambia

53. The President of the Republic of Zimbabwe

INSPIRED by the noble ideals, which guided the founding fathers of our Continental Organization and generations of Pan-Africanists in their determination to promote unity, solidarity, cohesion and cooperation among the peoples of Africa and African States;

CONSIDERING the principles and objectives stated in the Charter of the Organization of African Unity and the Treaty establishing the African Economic Community;

RECALLING the heroic struggles waged by our peoples and our countries for political independence, human dignity and economic emancipation;

CONSIDERING that since its inception, the Organization of African Unity has played a determining and invaluable role in the liberation of the continent, the affirmation of a common identity and the process of attainment of the unity of our continent and has provided a unique framework for our collective action in Africa and in our relations with the rest of the world.

DETERMINED to take up the multifaceted challenges that confront our continent and peoples in the light of the social, economic and political changes taking place in the world;

CONVINCED of the need to accelerate the process of implementing the Treaty establishing the African Economic Community in order to promote the socio-economic development of Africa and to face more effectively the challenges posed by globalization;

GUIDED by our common vision of a united and strong Africa and by the need to build a partnership between governments and all segments of civil society, in particular women, youth and the private sector, in order to strengthen solidarity and cohesion among our peoples;

CONSCIOUS of the fact that the scourge of conflicts in Africa constitutes a major impediment to the socio-economic development of the continent and of the need to promote peace, security and stability as a prerequisite for the implementation of our development and integration agenda;

DETERMINED to promote and protect human and peoples' rights, consolidate democratic institutions and culture, and to ensure good governance and the rule of law;

FURTHER DETERMINED to take all necessary measures to strengthen our common institutions and provide them with the necessary powers and resources to enable them discharge their respective mandates effectively;

RECALLING the Declaration which we adopted at the Fourth Extraordinary Session of our Assembly in Sirte, the Great Socialist Peoples Libyan Arab Jamahiriya, on 9.9.99, in which we decided to establish an African Union, in conformity with the ultimate objectives of the Charter of our Continental Organization and the Treaty establishing the African Economic Community;

HAVE AGREED AS FOLLOWS:

Article 1
Definitions

In this Constitutive Act:

"Act" means the present Constitutive Act;

"AEC" means the African Economic Community;

"Assembly" means the Assembly of Heads of State and Government of the Union;

"Charter" means the Charter of the OAU;

"Commission" means the Secretariat of the Union;

"Committee" means a Specialized Technical Committee of the Union;

"Council" means the Economic, Social and Cultural Council of the Union;

"Court" means the Court of Justice of the Union;

"Executive Council" means the Executive Council of Ministers of the Union;

"Member States" means a Member State of the Union;

"OAU" means the Organization of African Unity;

"Parliament" means the Pan-African Parliament of the Union;

"Union" means the African Union established by the present Constitutive Act.

Article 2
Establishment

The African Union is hereby established in accordance with the provisions of this Act.

Article 3
Objectives

The objectives of the Union shall be to:

(a) achieve greater unity and solidarity between the African countries and the peoples of Africa;

(b) defend the sovereignty, territorial integrity and independence of its Member States;

(c) accelerate the political and socio-economic integration of the continent;

(d) promote and defend African common positions on issues of interest to the continent and its peoples;

(e) encourage international cooperation, taking due account of the Charter of the United Nations and the Universal Declaration of Human Rights;

(f) promote peace, security, and stability on the continent;

(g) promote democratic principles and institutions, popular participation and good governance;

(h) promote and protect human and peoples' rights in accordance with the African Charter on Human and Peoples' Rights and other relevant human rights instruments;

(i) establish the necessary conditions which enable the continent to play its rightful role in the global economy and in international negotiations;

(j) promote sustainable development at the economic, social and cultural levels as well as the integration of African economies;

(k) promote co-operation in all fields of human activity to raise the living standards of African peoples;

(l) coordinate and harmonize the policies between the existing and future Regional Economic Communities for the gradual attainment of the objectives of the Union;

(m) advance the development of the continent by promoting research in all fields, in particular in science and technology;

(o) work with relevant international partners in the eradication of preventable diseases and the promotion of good health on the continent.

Article 4
Principles

The Union shall function in accordance with the following principles:

(a) sovereign equality and interdependence among Member States of the Union;

(b) respect of borders existing on achievement of independence;

(c) participation of the African peoples in the activities of the Union;

(d) establishment of a common defence policy for the African Continent;

(e) peaceful resolution of conflicts among Member States of the Union through such appropriate means as may be decided upon by the Assembly;

(f) prohibition of the use of force or threat to use force among Member States of the Union;

(g) non-interference by any Member State in the internal affairs of another;

(h) the right of the Union to intervene in a Member State pursuant to a decision of the Assembly in respect of grave circumstances, namely: war crimes, genocide and crimes against humanity;

(i) peaceful co-existence of Member States and their right to live in peace and security;

(j) the right of Member States to request intervention from the Union in order to restore peace and security;

(k) promotion of self-reliance within the framework of the Union;

(l) promotion of gender equality;

(m) respect for democratic principles, human rights, the rule of law and good governance;

(n) promotion of social justice to ensure balanced economic development;

(o) respect for the sanctity of human life, condemnation and rejection of impunity and political assassination, acts of terrorism and subversive activities;

(p) condemnation and rejection of unconstitutional changes of governments.

Article 5
Organs of the Union

1. The organs of the Union shall be:

(a) The Assembly of the Union;
(b) The Executive Council;
(c) The Pan-African Parliament;
(d) The Court of Justice;
(e) The Commission;

(f) The Permanent Representatives Committee;
(g) The Specialized Technical Committees;
(h) The Economic, Social and Cultural Council;
(i) The Financial Institutions;

2. Other organs that the Assembly may decide to establish.

Article 6
The Assembly

1. The Assembly shall be the supreme organ of the Union.

2. The Assembly shall meet at least once a year in ordinary session. At the request of any Member State and on approval by a two-thirds majority of the Member States, the Assembly shall meet in extraordinary session.

3. The Office of the Chairman of the Assembly shall be held for a period of one year by a Head of State or Government elected after consultations among the Member States.

Article 7
Decisions of the Assembly

1. The Assembly shall take its decisions by consensus or, failing which, by a two-thirds majority of the Member States of the Union. However, procedural matters, including the question of whether a matter is one of procedure or not, shall be decided by a simple majority.

2. Two-thirds of the total membership of the Union shall form a quorum at any meeting of the Assembly.

Article 8
Rules of Procedure of the Assembly

1. The Assembly shall adopt its own Rules of Procedure.

Article 9
Powers and Functions of the Assembly

1. The functions of the Assembly shall be to:

    (a) determine the common policies of the Union;

(b) receive, consider and take decisions on reports and recommendations from the other organs of the Union;

(c) consider requests for Membership of the Union;

(d) establish any organ of the Union;

(e) monitor the implementation of policies and decisions of the Union as well ensure compliance by all Member States;

(f) adopt the budget of the Union;

(g) give directives to the Executive Council on the management of conflicts, war and other emergency situations and the restoration of peace;

(h) appoint and terminate the appointment of the judges of the Court of Justice;

(i) appoint the Chairman of the Commission and his or her deputy or deputies and Commissioners of the Commission and determine their functions and terms of office.

2. The Assembly may delegate any of its powers and functions to any organ of the Union.

Article 10
The Executive Council

1. The Executive Council shall be composed of the Ministers of Foreign Affairs or such other Ministers or Authorities as are designated by the Governments of Member States.

2. The Executive Council shall meet at least twice a year in ordinary session. It shall also meet in an extra-ordinary session at the request of any Member State and upon approval by two-thirds of all Member States.

Article 11
Decisions of the Executive Council

1. The Executive Council shall take its decisions by consensus or, failing which, by a two-thirds majority of the Member States. However, procedural matters, including the question of whether a matter is one of procedure or not, shall be decided by a simple majority.

2. Two-thirds of the total membership of the Union shall form a quorum at any meeting of the Executive Council.

Article 12
Rules of Procedure of the Executive Council

The Executive Council shall adopt its own Rules of Procedure.

Article 13
Functions of the Executive Council

1. The Executive Council shall coordinate and take decisions on policies in areas of common interest to the Member States, including the following:

   (a) foreign trade;

   (b) energy, industry and mineral resources;

   (c) food, agricultural and animal resources, livestock production and forestry;

   (d) water resources and irrigation;

   (e) environmental protection, humanitarian action and disaster response and relief;

   (f) transport and communications;

   (g) insurance;

   (h) education, culture, health and human resources development;

   (i) science and technology;

   (j) nationality, residency and immigration matters;

   (k) social security, including the formulation of mother and child care policies, as well as policies relating to the disabled and the handicapped;

   (l) establishment of a system of African awards, medals and prizes.

2. The Executive Council shall be responsible to the Assembly. It shall consider issues referred to it and monitor the implementation of policies formulated by the Assembly.

3. The Executive Council may delegate any of its powers and functions mentioned in paragraph 1 of this Article to the Specialized Technical Committees established under Article 14 of this Act.

Article 14
The Specialized Technical Committees
Establishment and Composition

1. There is hereby established the following Specialized Technical Committees, which shall be responsible to the Executive Council:

   (a) The Committee on Rural Economy and Agricultural Matters;

   (b) The Committee on Monetary and Financial Affairs;

   (c) The Committee on Trade, Customs and Immigration Matters;

   (d) The Committee on Industry, Science and Technology, Energy, Natural Resources and Environment;

   (e) The Committee on Transport, Communications and Tourism;

   (f) The Committee on Health, Labour and Social Affairs; and

   (g) The Committee on Education, Culture and Human Resources.

2. The Assembly shall, whenever it deems appropriate, restructure the existing Committees or establish other Committees.

3. The Specialized Technical Committees shall be composed of Ministers or senior officials responsible for sectors falling within their respective areas of competence.

Article 15
Functions of the Specialized Technical Committees

Each Committee shall within its field of competence:

(a) prepare projects and programmes of the Union and submit it to the Executive Council;

(b) ensure the supervision, follow-up and the evaluation of the implementation of decisions taken by the organs of the Union;

(c) ensure the coordination and harmonization of projects and programmes of the Union;

(d) submit to the Executive Council either on its own initiative or at the request of the Executive Council, reports and recommendations on the implementation of the provisions of this Act; and

(e) carry out any other functions assigned to it for the purpose of ensuring the implementation of the provisions of this Act.

Article 16
Meetings

Subject to any directives given by the Executive Council, each Committee shall meet as often as necessary and shall prepare its Rules of Procedure and submit them to the Executive Council for approval.

Article 17
The Pan-African Parliament

1. In order to ensure the full participation of African peoples in the development and economic integration of the continent, a Pan-African Parliament shall be established.

2. The composition, powers, functions and organization of the Pan-African Parliament shall be defined in a protocol relating thereto.

Article 18
The Court of Justice

1. A Court of Justice of the Union shall be established;

2. The statute, composition and functions of the Court of Justice shall be defined in a protocol relating thereto.

Article 19
The Financial Institutions

The Union shall have the following financial institutions whose rules and regulations shall be defined in protocols relating thereto:

(a) The African Central Bank;
(b) The African Monetary Fund;
(c) The African Investment Bank.

Article 20
The Commission

1. There shall be established a Commission of the Union, which shall be the Secretariat of the Union.

2. The Commission shall be composed of the Chairman, his or her deputy or deputies and the Commissioners. They shall be assisted by the necessary staff for the smooth functioning of the Commission.

3. The structure, functions and regulations of the Commission shall be determined by the Assembly.

Article 21
The Permanent Representatives Committee

1. There shall be established a Permanent Representatives Committee. It shall be composed of Permanent Representatives to the Union and other Plenipotentiaries of Member States.

2. The Permanent Representatives Committee shall be charged with the responsibility of preparing the work of the Executive Council and acting on the Executive Councils instructions. It may set up such sub-committees or working groups as it may deem necessary.

Article 22
The Economic, Social and Cultural Council

1. The Economic, Social and Cultural Council shall be an advisory organ composed of different social and professional groups of the Member States of the Union.

2. The functions, powers, composition and organization of the Economic, Social and Cultural Council shall be determined by the Assembly.

Article 23
Imposition of Sanctions

1. The Assembly shall determine the appropriate sanctions to be imposed on any Member State that defaults in the payment of its contributions to the budget of the Union in the following manner: denial of the right to speak at meetings, to vote, to present candidates for any position or post within the Union or to benefit from any activity or commitments, therefrom;

2. Furthermore, any Member State that fails to comply with the decisions and policies of the Union may be subjected to other sanctions, such as the denial of transport and communications links with other Member States, and other measures of a political and economic nature to be determined by the Assembly.

Article 24
The Headquarters of the Union

1. The Headquarters of the Union shall be in Addis Ababa in the Federal Democratic Republic of Ethiopia.

2. There may be established such other offices of the Union as the Assembly may, on the recommendation of the Executive Council, determine.

Article 25
Working Languages

The working languages of the Union and all its institutions shall be, if possible, African languages, Arabic, English, French and Portuguese.

Article 26
Interpretation

The Court shall be seized with matters of interpretation arising from the application or implementation of this Act. Pending its establishment, such matters shall be submitted to the Assembly of the Union, which shall decide by a two-thirds majority.

Article 27
Signature, Ratification and Accession

1. This Act shall be open to signature, ratification and accession by the Member States of the OAU in accordance with their respective constitutional procedures.

2. The instruments of ratification shall be deposited with the Secretary-General of the OAU

3. Any Member State of the OAU acceding to this Act after its entry into force shall deposit the instrument of accession with the Chairman of the Commission.

Article 28
Entry into Force

This Act shall enter into force thirty (30) days after the deposit of the instruments of ratification by two-thirds of the Member States of the OAU.

Article 29
Admission to Membership

1. Any African State may, at any time after the entry into force of this Act, notify the Chairman of the Commission of its intention to accede to this Act and to be admitted as a member of the Union.

2. The Chairman of the Commission shall, upon receipt of such notification, transmit copies thereof to all Member States. Admission shall be decided by a simple majority of the Member States. The decision of each Member State shall be transmitted to the Chairman of the Commission who shall, upon receipt of the required number of votes, communicate the decision to the State concerned.

Article 30
Suspension

Governments which shall come to power through unconstitutional means shall not be allowed to participate in the activities of the Union.

Article 31
Cessation of Membership

1. Any State which desires to renounce its membership shall forward a written notification to the Chairman of the Commission, who shall inform Member States thereof. At the end of one year from the date of such notification, if not withdrawn, the Act shall cease to apply with respect to the renouncing State, which shall thereby cease to belong to the Union.

2. During the period of one year referred to in paragraph 1 of this Article, any Member State wishing to withdraw from the Union shall comply with the provisions of this Act and shall be bound to discharge its obligations under this Act up to the date of its withdrawal.

Article 32
Amendment and Revision

1. Any Member State may submit proposals for the amendment or revision of this Act.

2. Proposals for amendment or revision shall be submitted to the Chairman of the Commission who shall transmit same to Member States within thirty (30) days of receipt thereof.

3. The Assembly, upon the advice of the Executive Council, shall examine these proposals within a period of one year following notification of Member States, in accordance with the provisions of paragraph 2 of this Article;

4. Amendments or revisions shall be adopted by the Assembly by consensus or, failing which, by a two-thirds majority and submitted for ratification by all Member States in accordance with their respective constitutional procedures. They shall enter into force thirty (30) days after the deposit of the instruments of ratification with the Chairman of the Commission by a two-thirds majority of the Member States.

Article 33
Transitional Arrangements and Final Provisions

1. This Act shall replace the Charter of the Organization of African Unity. However, the Charter shall remain operative for a transitional period of one year or such further period as may be determined by the Assembly, following the entry into force of the Act, for the purpose of enabling the OAU/AEC to undertake the necessary measures regarding the devolution of its assets and liabilities to the Union and all matters relating thereto.

2. The provisions of this Act shall take precedence over and supersede any inconsistent or contrary provisions of the Treaty establishing the African Economic Community.

3. Upon the entry into force of this Act, all necessary measures shall be undertaken to implement its provisions and to ensure the establishment of the organs provided for under the Act in accordance with any directives or decisions which may be adopted in this regard by the Parties thereto within the transitional period stipulated above.

4. Pending the establishment of the Commission, the OAU General Secretariat shall be the interim Secretariat of the Union.

5. This Act, drawn up in four (4) original texts in the Arabic, English, French and Portuguese languages, all four (4) being equally authentic, shall be deposited with the Secretary-General of the OAU and, after its entry into force, with the Chairman of the Commission who shall transmit a certified true copy of the Act to the Government of each signatory State. The Secretary-General of the OAU and the Chairman of the Commission shall notify all signatory States of the dates of the deposit of the instruments of ratification or accession and shall upon entry into force of this Act register the same with the Secretariat of the United Nations.

IN WITNESS WHEREOF, WE have adopted this Act.

Done at Lome, Togo, this 11th day of July, 2000.

III

THE AFRICAN CHARTER ON HUMAN AND PEOPLES' RIGHTS

(*OAU.Doc.CAB/LEG/67/3, Rev.5; 59 I.L.M. (1981) Adopted by the 18th Assembly of the Heads of State and Government of the Organization of African Unity on June 26, 1981 at Nairobi, Kenya; entered into force on October 21, 1986).*

PREAMBLE

The African States members of the Organization of African, parties to the present convention entitled 'African Charter on Human and Peoples' Rights'

RECALLING Decision 115(XVI) of the Assembly of Heads of State and Government at its Sixteenth Ordinary Session held in Monrovia, Liberia, from 17 to 20 July 1979 on the preparation of 'a preliminary draft on an African Charter on Human and Peoples' Rights providing *inter alia* for the establishment of bodies to promote and protect human and peoples' rights';

CONSIDERING the Charter of the Organization of African Unity, which stipulates that 'freedom, equality, justice and dignity are essential objectives for the achievement of the legitimate aspirations of the African peoples';

REAFFIRMING the pledge they solemnly made in Article 2 of the said Charter to eradicate all forms of colonialism from Africa, to coordinate and intensify their cooperation and efforts to achieve a better life for the peoples of Africa and to promote international cooperation having due regard to the Charter of the United Nations and the Universal Declaration for Human Rights;

TAKING INTO CONSIDERATION the virtues of their historical tradition and the values of African civilization which should inspire and characterize their reflection on the concept of human and peoples' rights;

RECOGNIZING on the one hand, that fundamental human rights stems from the attributes of human beings, which justifies their international protection and on the other hand that the reality and respect of peoples' rights should necessarily guarantee human rights;

CONSIDERING that the enjoyment of rights and freedoms also implies the performance of duties on the part of everyone;

CONVINCED that it is henceforth essential to pay a particular attention to the right to development and that civil and political rights cannot be dissociated from economic, social and cultural rights in their conception as well as universality and that the satisfaction of economic, social and cultural rights is a guarantee for the enjoyment of civil and political rights;

CONSCIOUS of their duty to achieve the total liberation of Africa, the peoples of which are still struggling for their identity and genuine independence, and undertaking to eliminate colonialism, neo-colonialism, apartheid, Zionism and to dismantle aggressive foreign military bases and all forms of discrimination, particularly those based on race, ethnic group, color, sex, language, religion or political opinions;

REAFFIRMING their adherence to the principles of human and peoples; rights and freedom contained in the declarations, conventions and other instruments adopted by the Organization of African Unity, the Movement of Non-Aligned Nations Countries and the United Nations;

FIRMLY CONVINCED of their duty to promote and protect human and peoples' rights and freedoms taking into account the importance traditionally attached to these rights and freedoms in Africa;

HAVE AGREED AS FOLLOWS:

PART I: RIGHTS AND DUTIES
CHAPTER I
HUMAN AND PEOPLES' RIGHTS

Article 1

The Member States of the Organization of African Unity parties to the present Charter shall recognize the rights, duties and freedoms enshrined in this Charter and shall undertake to adopt legislative or other measures to give effect to them.

Article 2

Every individual shall be entitled to the enjoyment of the rights and freedoms recognized and guaranteed in the present Charter without distinction of any kind such as race, ethnic group, color, sex, language, religion, political or any other opinion, national and social origin, fortune, birth or other status.

Article 3

1. Every individual shall be equal before the law.

2. Every individual shall be entitled to equal protection of the law.

Article 4

Human beings are inviolable. Every human being shall be entitled to respect for his life and the integrity of his person. No one may be arbitrarily deprived of his life.

Article 5

Every individual shall have the right to the respect of the dignity inherent in a human being and to the recognition of his legal status. All forms of exploitation and degradation of man particularly slavery, slave trade, torture, cruel, inhuman or degrading punishment and treatment shall be prohibited.

Article 6

Every individual shall have the right to liberty and to the security of his person. No one may be deprived of his freedom except for reasons and conditions previously laid down by the law. In particular, no one may be arbitrarily arrested or detained.

Article 7

1. Every individual shall have the right to have his cause heard. This comprises:
   a) the right to an appeal to competent national organs against acts of violating his fundamental rights as recognized and guaranteed by conventions, laws, regulations and customs in force;
   b) the right to be presumed innocent until proved guilty by a competent court or tribunal;
   c) the right to defense, including the right to be defended by counsel of his choice;
   d) the right to be tried within a reasonable time by an impartial court or tribunal.

2. No one may be condemned for an act or omission which did not constitute a legally punishable offence at the time it was committed. No penalty may be inflicted for an offence for which no provision was made at the time it was committed. Punishment is personal and can be imposed only on the offender.

Article 8

Freedom of conscience, the profession and free practice of religion shall be guaranteed. No one may, subject to law and order, be submitted to measures restricting the exercise of these freedoms.

Article 9

1. Every individual shall have the right to receive information.

2. Every individual shall have the right to express and disseminate his opinion within the law.

Article 10

1. Every individual shall have the right to free association provided that he abides by the law.

2. Subject to the obligation of solidarity provided for in Article 29 no one may be compelled to join an association.

Article 11

Every individual shall have the right to assemble freely with others. The exercise of this right shall be subject only to necessary restrictions provided for by the law in particular those enacted in the interest of national security, the safety, health ethics and rights and freedom of others.

Article 12

1. Every individual shall have the right to freedom of movement and residence within the borders of a State provided he abides by the law.

2. Every individual shall have the right to leave any country including his own, and to return to his country. This right may only be subject to restrictions, provided for by law for the protection of national security, law and order, public health or morality.

3. Every individual shall have the right, when persecuted. To seek and obtain asylum in other countries in accordance with the law of those countries and international conventions.

4. A non-national legally admitted in a territory of a State Party to the present Charter, may only be expelled from it by virtue of a decision taken in accordance with law.

5. The mass expulsion of non-nationals shall be prohibited. Mass expulsion shall be that which is aimed at national, racial, ethnic or religious groups.

Article 13

1. Every citizen shall have the right to participate freely in the government of his country, either directly or through freely chosen representatives in accordance with the provisions of the law.

2. Every citizen shall have the right to equal access to the public services of his country. Every individual shall have the right of access to public property and services in strict equality of all persons before the law.

Article 14

The right to property shall be guaranteed. It may only be encroached upon in the interest of public need or in the general interest of the community and in accordance with the provisions of appropriate laws.

Article 15

Every individual shall have the right to work under equitable and satisfactory conditions, and shall receive equal pay for equal work.

Article 16

1. Every individual shall have the right to enjoy the best attainable state of physical and mental health.

2. States Parties to the present Charter shall take necessary measures to protect the health of their people and to ensure that they receive medical attention when they are sick.

Article 17

1. Every individual shall have the right to education.

2. Every individual may freely take part in the cultural life of his community.

3. The promotion and protection of morals and traditional values recognized by the community shall be the duty of the State.

Article 18

1. The family shall be the natural unit and the basis of society. Ti shall be protected by the State which shall take care of its physical health and morals.

2. The State shall have the duty to assist he family which is the custodian of morals and traditional values recognized by the community.

3. The State shall ensure the elimination of every discrimination against women and also ensure the protection of the rights of women and the child as stipulated in international declarations and convention.

4. The aged and the disabled shall also have the right to special measures of protection in keeping with their physical or moral needs.

Article 19

All peoples's shall be equal; they shall enjoy the same respect and shall have the same rights. Nothing shall justify the domination of a people by another.

Article 20

1. All peoples shall have the right to existence. They shall have the unquestionable and inalienable right to self-determination. They shall freely determine their political status and shall pursue their economic and social development according to the policy they have freely chosen.

2. Colonized or oppressed peoples shall have the right to free themselves from the bonds of domination by resorting to any means recognized by the international community.

3. All peoples shall have the right to assistance of the States Parties to the present Carter in their liberation struggle against foreign domination, be it political, economic or cultural.

Article 21

1. All peoples shall freely dispose of their wealth and natural resources. This right shall be exercised in the exclusive interest of the people. In no case shall a people be deprived of it.

2. In case of spoilation the dispossessed peoples shall have the right to the lawful recovery of its property as well as an adequate compensation.

3. The free disposal of wealth and natural resources shall be exercised without prejudice to the obligation of promoting international economic cooperation based on mutual respect, equitable exchange and the principles of international law.

4. States Parties to the present Charter shall individually and collectively exercise the right to free disposal of their wealth and natural resources with a view to strengthening African unity and solidarity.

5. States parties to the present Charter shall undertake to eliminate all forms of foreign economic exploitation particularly that practised by international monopolies so as to enable their peoples to fully benefit from the advantages derived from their national resources.

Article 22

1. All peoples shall have the right to their economic, social and cultural development with due regard to their freedom and identity and in the equal enjoyment of the common heritage of mankind.

2. States shall have the duty, individually or collectively, to ensure the exercise of their right to development.

Article 23

1. All peoples shall have the right to national and international peace and security. The principles of solidarity and friendly relations implicitly affirmed by the Charter of the United Nations and reaffirmed by that of the Organization of African Unity shall govern relationships between States.

2. For the purpose of strengthening peace, solidarity and friendly relations, States Parties to the present Charter shall ensure that:
    a) any individual enjoying the right of asylum under Article 12 of the present Charter shall not engage in subversive activities against his country of origin or any other country State Party to the present Charter.
    b) their territories shall not be used as bases for subversive or terrorist activities against the people of any other State Party to the present Charter.

Article 24

all peoples shall have the right to a general satisfactory environment favorable to their development.

Article 25

states Parties shall have the duty to promote and ensure through teaching, education and publication, the respect of rights and freedoms contained in the present Charter and to see it that these freedoms abd rights as well as corresponding obligations and duties are understood.

Article 26

States Parties to the present Charter shall have the duty to guarantee the independence of the Courts and shall allow the establishment and improvement of appropriate national institutions entrusted with the promotion and protection of the rights and freedoms guaranteed by the present Charter.

CHAPTER II
DUTIES

Article 27

1. Every individual shall have duties towards his family and society, the State and other legally recognized communities and the international community.

2. The rights and freedoms of each individual shall be exercised with due regard to the rights of others, collective security, morality and common interest.

Article 28

Every individual shall have the duty to respect and consider his fellow beings without discrimination, and to maintain relations aimed at promoting, safeguarding and reinforcing mutual respect and tolerance.

Article 29

The individual shall also have the duty:

1. To preserve the harmonious development of the family and to work for the cohesion and respect of the family; to respect his parents at all times, to maintain them incase of need;
2. To serve his national community by placing his physical and intellectual abilities at its service;

3. Not to compromise the security of the State whose national or resident he is;
   To preserve and strengthen social and national solidarity, particularly when the later is threatened;

4. To preserve and strengthen the national independence and the territorial integrity of his country and to contribute to its defense in accordance with the law;

5. To work to the best of his abilities and competence, and to pay taxes imposed by law in the interest of the society;

6. To preserve and strengthen positive African cultural values in his relations with other members of the society, in the spirit of tolerance, dialogue and consultation, and in general, to contribute to the promotion of the moral well being of society;

7. To contribute to the best of his abilities, at all times and at all levels, to the promotion and achievement of African Unity.

PART II: MEASURES AND SAFEGUARDS
CHAPTER I
ESTABLISHMENT AND ORGANIZATION OF THE AFRICAN COMMISSION ON HUMAN AND PEOPLES' RIGHTS

Article 30

An African Commission on Human and Peoples' Rights, hereinafter called 'the Commission', shall be established within the Organization of African Unity to promote human and peoples' rights and ensure their protection in Africa.

Article 31

1. The Commission shall consist of eleven members chosen from amongst African personlities of the highest reputation, known for their high morality, integrity, impartiality and competence in matters of human and peoples' rights, particular consideration being given to persons having legal experience.

2. The members of the Commission shall serve in their personal capacity.

Article 32

The Commission shall not include more than one national of the same State

Article 33

The members of the Commission shall be elected by secret ballot by the Assembly of Heads of State and Government, from a list of persons nominated by the States Parties to the present Charter.

Article 34

Each State Party to the present Charter may not nominate more than two candidates. The candidates must have the nationality of one of the States to the present Charter. When two candidates are nominated by a State, one of them may not be a national of that State.

Article 35

1. The Secretary-General of the Organization of African Unity shall invite States Parties to the present Charter at least four months before the election to nominate candidates.

2. The Secretary-General of the Organization of African Unity shall make an alphabetical list of the persons nominated and communicate it to the Heads of State and Government at least one month before the elections.

Article 36

The Members of the Commission shall be elected for a six year period and shall be eligible for re-election, however, the term of office of four of the members elected at the first election shall terminate after two years and the term of office of three others at the end of four years.

Article 37

Immediately after the first election, the Chairman of the Assembly of Heads of State and Government of the Organization of African Unity shall draw lots to decide the names of those members referred to in Article 36.

Article 38

After their election, the members of the Commission shall make a solemn declaration to discharge their duties impartially and faithfully.

Article 39

1. In case of death or resignation of a member of the Commission the Chairman of the Commission shall immediately inform the Secretary-General of the Organization of African Unity, who shall declare the seat vacant from the date of death or from the date the resignation takes effect.

2. If, in the unanimous opinion of other members of the Commission, a member has stopped discharging his duties for any reason other than a temporary absence, the Chairman of the Commission shall inform the Secretary-General of the Organization of African Unity, who shall declare the seat vacant.

3. In each of the cases anticipated above, the Assembly of Heads of State and Government shall replace the member whose seat became vacant for the remaining period of his term unless the period is less than six months.

Article 40

Every member of the Commission shall be in office until the date his successor assumes office.

Article 41

The Secretary-General of the Organization of African Unity shall appoint the Secretary of the Commission. He shall provide the staff and services necessary for the effective discharge of the duties of the Commission. The Organization of African Unity shall bear the cost of the staff and services.

Article 42

1. The Commission shall elect the Chairman and Vice for a two-year period. They shall be eligible for re-election.

2. The Commission shall lay down its rules of procedure.

3. Seven members shall form the quorum.

4. In case of equality of votes, the Chairman shall have a casting vote.

5. The Secretary-General may attend the meeting of the Commission. He shall neither participate in deliberations nor shall he be entitled to vote. The Chairman of the Commission may, however, invite him to speak.

Article 43

In discharging their duties, members of the Commission shall enjoy diplomatic privileges and immunities provided for in the General Convention on the Privileges and Immunities of the Organization of African Unity.

Article 44

Provision shall be made for the emoluments and allowances of the members of the Commission in the Regular Budget of the Organization of African Unity.

CHAPTER II
MANDATE OF THE COMMISSION

Article 45

1. The functions of the Commission shall be:
    1. To promote Human and Peoples' Rights and in particular:
        a) To collect documents, undertake studies and researches on African problems in the field of human and peoples' rights, organize seminars symposia and conferences, disseminate information, encourage national and local institutions concerned with human and peoples' rights, and should the case arise, give its views or make recommendations to Governments.
        b) To formulate and lay down, principles and rules aimed at solving legal problems relating to human and peoples' rights and fundamental freedoms upon which African Governments may base their legislation.
        c) Co-operate with other African and international institutions concerned with the promotion and protection of human and peoples' rights.

2. Ensure the protection of human and peoples' rights under conditions laid down by the present Charter.

3. Interpret all provisions of the present Charter at the request of a State Party, an institution of the Organization of African Unity or an African Organization recognized by the OAU.

4. Perform any other tasks which may be entrusted to it by the Assembly of Heads of State and Government.

CHAPTER III
PROCEDURE OF THE COMMISSION

Article 46

The Commission may resort to any appropriate method of investigation; it may hear from the Secretary-General of the Organization of African Unity or any other person capable of enlightening it.

COMMUNICATION FROM STATES

Article 47

If a State Party to the present Charter has good reasons to believe that another State Party to this Charter has violated the provisions of the Charter, it may draw by written communication the attention of that State to the Matter. This communication shall also be addressed to the Secretary-General of the OAU and to the Chairman of the Commission. Within three months of the receipt of the communication, the State to which the communication is addressed shall give the enquiring State, written explanation or statement elucidating the matter. This should include as much as possible relevant information relating to the laws and rules of procedure applied and applicable and the redress already given or course of action available.

Article 48

If within three months from the date on which the original communication is received by the State to which it is addressed, the issue is not settled to the satisfaction of the two States involved through bilateral negotiation or by other peaceful procedure, either State shall have the right to submit the matter to the Commission through the Chairman and shall notify the other State involved.

Article 49

Notwithstanding the provisions of Article 47, if a State Party to the present Charter considers that another State Party has violated the provisions of the Charter, it may refer the matter directly to the Commission by addressing a communication to the Chairman, the Secretary-General of the Organization of African Unity and the State concerned.

Article 50

The Commission can only deal with a matter submitted to it after making sure that all local remedies, if they exist, have been exhausted, unless it is obvious to the Commission that the procedure of achieving these remedies would be unduly prolonged.

Article 51

1. The Commission may ask the States concerned to provide it with all relevant information.

2. When the Commission is considering the matter, States concerned may be represented before it and submit written or oral representation.

Article 52

After having obtained from the States concerned and from other sources all the information it deems necessary and after having tried all appropriate means to reach an amicable solution based on the respect for Human and Peoples' Rights, the Commission shall prepare within a reasonable period of time from the notification referred to in Article 48, a report stating the facts and its findings. This report shall be sent to States concerned and communicated to the Assembly of Heads of State and Government.

Article 53

While transmitting its report, the Commission may make to the Assembly of Heads of State and Government such recommendation as it deems useful.

Article 54

The Commission shall submit to each ordinary Session of the Assembly of Heads of State and Government a report of its activities.

OTHER COMMUNICATIONS

Article 55

1. Before each Session, the Secretary of the Commission shall make a list of the Communications other than those of States Parties to the present Charter and transmit them to the members of the Commission, who shall indicate which communications should be considered by the Commission.

2. A communication shall be considered by the Commission if a simple majority of its members so decide.

Article 56

Communications relating to human and peoples' rights referred to in Article 55 received by the Commission, shall be considered if they:

1. Indicate their authors even if the latter requests anonymity'

2. Are compatible with the Charter of the Organization of African Unity or with the present Charter,

3. Are not written in disparaging or insulting language directed against the State concerned and its institutions or to the Organization of African Unity,

4. Are not based exclusively on news disseminated through the mass media,

5. Are sent after exhausting local remedies, if any, unless it is obvious tht this procedure is unduly prolonged,

6. Are submitted within a reasonable period from the time local remedies are exhausted or from the date the Commission is seized with the matter, and

7. Do not deal with cases which have been settled by these States involved in accordance with the principles of the Charter of the United Nations, or the Charter of the Organization of African Unity or the provisions of the present Charter.

Article 57

Prior to any substantive consideration, all communications shall be brought to the knowledge of the State concerned by the Chairman of the Commission.

Article 58

1. When it appears after deliberations of the Commission that one or more communications apparently relate to special cases which reveal the existence of a series of serious or massive violations of human and peoples' rights, the Commission shall draw the attention of the Assembly of Heads of State and Government to these special cases.

2. The Assembly of Heads of State and Government may then request the Commission to undertake an in-depth study of these cases and make a factual report, accompanied by its findings and recommendations.

3. A case of emergency duly noticed by the Commission shall be submitted by the latter to the Chairman of the Assembly of Heads of State and Government who may request and in-depth study.

Article 59

1. All measures taken within the provisions of the present Charter shall remain confidential until such a time as the Assembly of Heads of State and Government shall otherwise declare.

2. However, the report shall be published by the Chairman of the Commission upon the decision of the Assembly of Heads of State and Government.

3. The report on the activities of the Commission shall be published by its chairman after it has been considered by the Assembly of Heads of State and Government.

CHAPTER IV
APPLICABLE PRINCIPLES

Article 60

The Commission shall draw inspiration from international law on human and peoples' rights, particularly from the provisions of various African instruments on human and peoples' rights, the Charter of the United Nations, the Charter of the Organization of

African Unity, the Universal Declaration of Human Rights, other instruments adopted by the Nations and by African Countries in the field of human and peoples' rights as well as from provisions of various instruments adopted within the specialized agencies of the United Nations of which the parties to the present Charter are members.

Article 61

The Commission shall also take into consideration, as subsidiary measures to determine the principles of law, other general special international conventions, laying down rules expressly recognized by member States of the Organization of African Unity, African practices consistent with international norms on human and peoples' rights, customs generally accepted as law, general principles of law recognized by African States as well as legal precedents and doctrines.

Article 62

Each State Party shall undertake to submit every two years, from the date the present Charter comes into force, a report on the legislative or other measures taken with a view to giving effect to the rights and freedoms recognized and guaranteed by the present Charter.

Article 63

1. The present Charter shall be open for signature, ratification or adherence of the member States of the Organization of African Unity.

2. The instruments of ratification or adherence to the present Charter shall be deposited with the Secretary-General of the Organization of African Unity.

3. The present Charter shall come into force three months after the reception by the Secretary-General of the instruments of ratification or adherence of a simple majority of the member States of the Organization of African Unity.

PART III: GENERAL PROVISIONS

Article 64

1. After the coming into force of the present Charter, members of the Commission shall be elected in accordance with the relevant Articles of the present Charter.

2. The Secretary-General of the Organization of African Unity shall convene the first meeting of the Commission at the Headquarters of the Organization within three months of constitution of the Commission. Thereafter, the Commission shall be convened by its Chairman whenever necessary but at least once a year.

Article 65

For each of the States that will ratify or adhere to the present Charter after its coming into force, the Charter shall take effect three months after the date of the deposit by the State of its instrument of ratification.

Article 66

Special protocols or agreements may, if necessary, supplement the provisions of this present Charter.

Article 67

The Secretary-General of the Organization of African Unity shall inform member States of the Organization of the deposit of each instrument of ratification or adherence.

Article 68

The present Charter may be amended if a State Party makes a written request to that effect to the Secretary-General of the Organization of African Unity. The Assembly of Heads of State and Government may also consider the draft amendment after all the States Parties have been duly informed of it and the Commission has given its opinion on it at the request of the sponsoring State. The amendment shall be approved by a simple majority of the States Parties. It shall also come to force for each State which has accepted it in accordance with its constitutional procedure three months after the Secretary-General has received notice of the acceptance.

ADOPTED BY THE EIGHTEENTH ASSEMBLY OF HEADS OF STATE AND GOVERNMENT, JUNE 1981, NAIROBI, KENYA.

RULES OF PROCEDURE OF THE AFRICAN COMMISSION ON HUMAN AND PEOPLES' RIGHTS

(Adopted on 6 October 1995 as a revision of the initial Rules of 13 February 1988)

The African Commission on Human and Peoples' Rights,
Having Considered the African Charter on Human and Peoples' Rights,
Acting in accordance with Article 42 of the Charter,
Has adopted the present revised Rules of Procedure.

GENERAL PROVISIONS
ORGANIZATION OF THE COMMISSION
CHAPTER I - SESSIONS

Rule 1 - Number of Sessions

The African Commission on Human and Peoples' Rights (hereinafter referred to as "the Commission") shall hold sessions which may be necessary to enable it carry out satisfactorily its functions in conformity with the African Charter on Human and Peoples' Rights (hereinafter referred to as " the Charter").

Rule 2 - Opening Date

1. The Commission shall normally hold two ordinary Sessions a year each lasting for about two weeks.

2. The ordinary Sessions of the Commission shall be convened a a date fixed by the Commission on the proposal of its Chairman and in consultation with the Secretary General of the Organization of African Unity (OAU) (hereinafter referred to as "The Secretary-General").

3. The Secretary-General may change under exceptional circumstances, the opening date of a session in consultation with the Chairman of the Commission.

Rule 3 - Extraordinary Sessions

1. The Commission may decide to hold extraordinary sessions. When the Commission is not in session, the Chairman may convene extraordinary session in consultation with the members of the Commission.

The Chairman of the Commission shall also convene extraordinary sessions:

a. At the request of the majority of the members of the Commission or

b. At the request of the current Chairman of the Organization of African Unity.

2. Extraordinary sessions shall be convened as soon as possible on a date fixed by the chairman, in consultation with the Secretary-General and the other members of the Commission.

Rule 4 - Place of Meetings

The sessions shall normally be held at the Headquarters of the Commission. The Commission, in consideration with the Secretary-General may decide to hold a Session elsewhere.

Rule 5 - Notification of the Opening Date of the Sessions

The Secretary of the Commission (hereinafter refereed to as the Secretary), shall inform members of the Commission of the date and venue of the first meeting of each session. This notification shall be sent, in the case of an Ordinary Session, at least eight weeks, if possible, before the Session.

CHAPTER II - AGENDA

Rule 6 - Drawing up the Provisional Agenda

1. The Provisional Agenda for each Ordinary Session shall be drawn up by the Secretary in consultation with the Chairman of the Commission in accordance with the provisions of the Charter and these Rules.

2. The Provisional Agenda shall include if necessary, items on: "Communications from States," and "Other Communications" in conformity with the provisions of Article 55 of the Charter. It should not contain any information relating to such communications

3. Except as specified on the communications, the Provisional Agenda shall include all the items listed by the present Rules of Procedure as well as items proposed by:
a) The Commission at a previous Session;

APPENDIX IV

    b   The Chairman of the Commission or another member of the Commission;
    c)   A State Party to the Charter;
    d) The Assembly of Heads of State and Government or the Council of Ministers of the Organization of African Unity;
    e)   The Secretary-General of the Organization of African Unity on any issue relating to the functions assigned to him by the Charter.
    f)   A national liberation movement recognized by the Organization of African Unity or by a non-governmental organization;
    g) A specialized institution of which the States Parties to the Charter are members

4. The items to be included in the provisional agenda under sub paragraph b, c, f and g of paragraph 3 must be communicated to the Secretary, accompanied by essential documents, not later than eight (8) weeks before the opening of the Session.

5. a) All national liberation movements, specialized institutions, intergovernmental or non-governmental organizations wishing to propose the inclusion of an item in the Provisional Agenda must inform the Secretary at least ten (10) weeks before the opening of the meeting. Before formally proposing the inclusion of an item in the Provisional Agenda, the observations likely to be made by the Secretary must duly be taken into account.
   b) All proposals made under the provisions of the present paragraph shall be included only in the Provisional Agenda of the Commission, if at least two thirds (2/3) of member present and voting so decide.

6. The Provisional Agenda of the Extraordinary Session of the Commission shall include only the item proposed to be considered at that Extraordinary Session.

Rule 7 - Transmission and Distribution of the Provisional Agenda

1. The Provisional Agenda and the essential documents relating to each item shall be distributed to the members of the Commission by the Secretary who shall endeavor to transmit them to members at least six (6) weeks before the opening of the Session.

2. The Secretary shall communicate the Provisional Agenda of that session and have the essential documents relating to each Agenda item distributed at least six weeks before the opening of the session of the Commission to the members of the Commission, member States Parties to the Charter, to the current Chairman of the Organization of African Unity and observers.

3. The draft agenda shall also be sent to the specialized agencies, to non-governmental organizations and to the national liberation movements concerned with the agenda.

4. In exceptional cases the Secretary may, while giving his reasons in writing, have the essential documents relating to some items of the Provisional Agenda distributed at least four (4) weeks prior to the opening of the Session.

Rule 8 - Adoption of Agenda

At the beginning of each session, the Commission shall if necessary, after the election of officers in conformity with Rule 17, adopt the agenda of the Session on the basis of the Provisional Agenda referred to in Rule 6.

Rule 9 - Revision of the Agenda

The Commission may, during the Session, revise the Agenda if need be, adjourn, cancel or amend items. During the Session, only urgent and important issues may be added to the agenda.

Rule 10 - Draft Provisional Agenda for Next Session

The Secretary shall, at each session of the Commission, submit a Draft Provisional Agenda for the next session of the Commission indicating with respect to each item, the documents to be submitted on that item and the decisions of the deliberative organ which authorized their preparation so as to enable the Commission to consider these documents as regards the contribution they make to its proceedings, as well as their urgency and relevance to the prevailing situation.

CHAPTER III - MEMBERS OF THE COMMISSION

Rule 11 - Composition of the Commission

The Commission shall be composed of eleven (11) members elected by the Assembly of Heads of State and Government hereinafter referred to as "the Assembly," in conformity with the relevant provisions of the Charter.

Rule 12 - Status of the Member

1. The members of the Commission shall be eleven (11) personalities appointed in conformity with the provisions of Article 31 of the Charter.

2. Each member of the Commission shall sit on the Commission in a personal capacity. No member may be represented by another person.

Rule 13 - Term of Office of the Members

1. The term of office of the members of the Commission elected on 29 July 1987 shall begin from that date. The term of office of members of the Commission elected at subsequent elections shall take effect from the day following the expiry date of the term of office of the members of the Commission they shall replace.

2. However, if a member is re-elected at the expiry of his or her term of office, or elected to replace a member whose term of office has expired or will expire, the term of office shall begin from that expiry date.

3. In conformity with Article 39(3) of the Charter, the member elected to replace a member whose term of office has not expired shall complete the term of office of his or her predecessor, unless the remaining term of office is less than six (6) months. In the latter case there shall be no replacement.

Rule 14 - Cessation of Functions

1. If in the unanimous opinion of the other members of the Commission, a member has stopped discharging his duties for any reason other than a temporary absence, the Chairman of the Commission shall inform the Secretary-General of the Organization of African Unity, who shall then declare the seat vacant.

2. In case of death or resignation of a member of the Commission, the Chairman shall immediately inform the Secretary-General who shall declare the seat vacant from the date of the death or from the date on which the resignation took effect. The member of the Commission who resigns shall address a written notification of his or her resignation directly to the Chairman or to the Secretary-General and steps to declare his or her seat vacant shall only be taken after receiving the said notification. The resignation shall make the seat vacant.

Rule 15 - Vacant Seat

Every seat declared vacant in conformity with Rule 14 of the present Rules of Procedure shall be filled on the basis of Article 39 of the Charter.

Rule 16 - Oath

Before coming into office, every member of the Commission shall make the following solemn commitment at a public hearing. "I swear to carry out my duties well and faithfully in all impartiality."

CHAPTER IV - OFFICERS

Rule 17 - Election of Officers

1. The Commission shall elect among its members a Chairman and Vice Chairman.

2. The elections referred to in the present Rule shall be held by secret ballot. Only the members present shall vote, the member who shall obtain the two-thirds majority of the vote of the members present and voting shall be elected.

3. If no member obtains this two-thirds majority in a second, third and fourth ballot, the member having the highest number of votes at the fifth ballot shall be elected.

4. The officers of the Commission shall be elected for a period of two (2) years. They shall be eligible for re-election. None of them, may, however, exercise his or her functions if he or she ceases to be a member of the Commission.

Rule 18 - Power of the Chairman

The Chairman shall carry out the functions assigned to him by the Charter, the Rules of Procedure and the decisions of the Commission. In the exercise of his functions, the Chairman shall be under the authority of the Commission.

Rule 19 - Absence of the Chairman

1. The Vice Chairman shall replace the Chairman during a session if the latter is unable to attend a whole or part of a session.

2. In the absence of both the Chairman and Vice Chairman, members shall elect an acting Chairman.

Rule 20 - Functions of the Vice Chairman

The Vice Chairman, acting in the capacity of the Chairman, shall have the same rights and the same duties as the Chairman.

Rule 21 - Cessation of Functions of an Officer

If any of the officers ceases to carry out his or her functions or declares that he or she is no longer able to serve as an officer or exercise the functions of a member of the Commission, a new officer shall be elected for the remaining term of office of his or her predecessor.

CHAPTER V - SECRETARIAT

Rule 22 - Functions of the Secretary-General

1. The Secretary-General or his representative may attend the meeting of the Commission. He shall neither participate in the deliberations, nor in the voting. He may, however, be called upon by the Chairman of the Commission to make written or oral statements at the sittins of the Commission.

2. He shall appoint, in consultation with the Chairman of the Commission, a Secretary of the Commission.

3. He shall, in consultation with the Chairman provide the Commission with the necessary staff, means and services for it to carry out effectively the functions and mission assigned to it under the Charter.

4. The Secretary-General acting through the Secretary shall take all the necessary steps for the meetings of the Commission.

Rule 23 - Functions of the Secretary to the Commission

The Secretary of the Commission shall be responsible for the activities of the Secretariat under the general supervision of the Chairman, and particularly:
a) He/She shall assist the Commission and its members in the exercise of their functions;
b) He/She shall serve as an intermediary for all communications concerning the Commission;
c) He/She shall be the custodian of the archives of the Commission;
d) The Secretary shall bring immediately to the knowledge of the members of the Commission all the issues that will be submitted to him/her.

Rule 24 - Estimates

Before the Commission approves a proposal entailing expenses, the Secretary shall prepare and distribute, as soon as possible, to the members of the Commission, the financial implications to the proposal. It is incumbent on the Chairman to draw the attention of the members of the Commission to those implications so that they discuss them when the proposal is considered by the Commission.

Rule 25 - Financial Rules

The financial rules adopted pursuant to the provisions of Article 41 and 44 of the Charter, shall be appended to the present Rules of Procedure.

Rule 26 - Financial Responsibility

The Organization of African Unity shall bear the expenses of the staff and the facilities and services placed at the disposal of the Commission to carry out its functions.

Rule 27 - Record of Cases

A special record, with a reference number and initialed, in which shall be entered the date of registration of each petition and communication and that of the closure of the procedure relating to them before the Commission, shall be kept at the Secretariat.

CHAPTER VI - SUBSIDIARY BODIES

Rule 28 - Establishment of Committees and Working Groups

1. The Commission may during a session, taking into account the provisions of the Charter establish if it deems it necessary for the exercise of its functions, committees or working groups, composed of the members of the Commission and send them any agenda item for consideration and report.

2. These committees or working group may, in consultation with the Secretary-General, be authorized to sit when the Commission is not in session.

3. The members of the Committees or working groups shall be appointed by the Chairman subject to the approval of the absolute majority of the other members of the Commission.

Rule 29 - Establishment of Sub-Commissions

1. The Commission may establish sub-Commissions of experts after prior approval of the Assembly.

2. Unless the Assembly decides otherwise, the Commission shall determine the functions and composition of each sub-Commission.

Rule 30 - Offices of the Subsidiary Bodies

Unless the Commission decides otherwise, the subsidiary bodies of the Commission shall elect their own officers.

Rule 31 - Rules of Procedure

The Rules of Procedure of the Commission shall apply, as far as possible to the proceedings of its subsidiary bodies.

CHAPTER VII - PUBLIC SESSIONS AND PRIVATE SESSIONS

Rule 32 - General Principle

The sittings of the Commission and of its subsidiary bodies shall be held in public unless the Commission decides otherwise or it appears from the relevant provisions of the Charter that the meeting shall be held in private.

Rule 33 - Publication of Proceedings

At the end of each private or public sitting, the Commission or its subsidiary bodies may issue a communiqué.

CHAPTER VIII - LANGUAGES

Rule 34 - Working Languages

The Working languages of the Commission and of all its institutions shall be those of the Organization of African Unity.

Rule 35 - Interpretation

1. The address delivered in one of the working languages shall be interpreted in the other working languages.

2. Any person addressing the Commission in a language other than one of the working languages, shall, in principle, ensure the interpretation in one of the working languages. The interpreters of the Secretariat may take the interpretation of the original language as a source language for their interpretation in other working languages.

Rule 36 - Languages to be used for Minutes of Proceedings

The summary of the minutes of the sittings of the Commission shall be drafted in the working languages.

*Rule 37 - Languages to be used for Resolutions
and other Official decisions*

All official decisions and documents of the Commission will be rendered in the working languages.

Rule 38 - Tape Recordings of the Session

The Secretariat shall record and preserve the tapes of the sessions of the Commission. It may also record and conserve the tapes of the sessions of the committees, working groups and sub-commissions if the Commission so decides.

Rule 39 - Summary Minutes of the Sessions

The Secretariat shall draft the summary minutes of the public and private sessions of the Commission and of its subsidiary bodies. It shall distribute them as soon as possible in a draft form to the members of the Commission and to all other participants in the session. All those participants may, in thirty (30) days following the receipt of the draft minutes of the session, submit corrections to the secretariat. The Chairman may, under special circumstances, in consultation with the Secretary-General, extend the time for the submission of the corrections. In case the corrections are contested, the Chairman of the Commission or the Chairman of the subsidiary body whose minutes they are, shall resolve the disagreement after having listened to, if necessary, the tape recordings of the discussions. If the disagreement persists, the Commission or the subsidiary body shall decide. The corrections shall be published in a distinct volume after the closure of the session.

*Rule 40 - Distribution of the Minutes of the Private
Sessions and Public Sessions*

1. The final summary minutes of the public and private sessions shall be the document intended for general distribution unless, the Commission decides otherwise.

2. The minutes of the private sessions of the Commission shall be distributed forthwith to all members of the Commission.

Rule 41 - Reports to be Submitted After each Session

The Commission shall submit to the current Chairman of the Organization of African Unity, a report on the deliberations of each session. This report shall contain a brief summary of the recommendations and statements on issues to which the Commission would like to draw the attention of the current Chairman and member States of the Organization of African Unity.

Rule 42 - Submission of Official Decisions and Reports

The Text of the decisions and reports officially adopted by the Commission shall be distributed to all members of the Commission as soon as possible.

CHAPTER X - CONDUCT OF THE DEBATES

Rule 43 - Quorum

The quorum shall be constituted by seven (7) Members of the Commission, as specified in Article 42(3) of the Charter.

Rule 44 - Additional Powers of the Chairman

1. In addition to the powers entrusted to him/her under the provisions of the present Rules of Procedure, the Chairman shall have the responsibility to open and close each session; he/she shall direct the debates, ensure the application of the present rules of Procedure, grant the use of floor, submit to a vote matters under discussion and announce the result of the vote taken.

2. Subject to the provisions of the present Rules of Procedure, the Chairman shall direct the discussions of the Commission and ensure order during meeting. The Chairman may during the discussion of an agenda item, propose to the Commission to limit the time allotted to speakers, as well as the number of interventions of each speaker on the same issue and close the list of speakers.

3. He/She shall rule on the points of order. He/She shall also have the power to propose the adjournment and the closure of debates as well as the adjournment and suspension of a sitting. The debate shall deal solely with the issues submitted to the Commission and the Chairman may call a speaker, whose remarks are irrelevant to the matter under discussion, to order.

Rule 45 - Points of Order

1. During the debate of any matter a member may, at any time, raise a point of order and the point of order shall be immediately decided by the Chairman, in accordance with the Rules of Procedure. If a member appeals against the decision, the appeal shall immediately be put to the vote and if the Chairman's ruling is not overruled by the majority of the members present, it shall be maintained.

2. A member raising a point of order cannot, in his or her comments deal with the substance of the matter under discussion.

Rule 46 - Adjournment of Debates

During the discussion on any matter, a member may move the adjournment of the debate on the matter under discussion. In addition to the proposer of the motion one member may speak in favour of and one against the motion after which the motion shall immediately be put to the vote.

Rule 47 - Limit the Time Accorded Speakers

The Commission may limit the time accorded to each speaker on any matter, when the time allotted for debates is limited and a speaker spends more time than the time accorded, the Chairman shall call him to order.

Rule 48 - Closing the List of Speakers

The Chairman, may during a debate, read out the list of speakers and with the approval of the Commission, declare the list closed. Where there are no more speakers, the Chairman shall, with the approval of the Commission, declare the debate closed.

Rule 49 - Closure of Debate

A member, may during at any time move for the closure of the debate on the matter under discussion, even if the other members or representatives expressed the desire to take the floor. The authorization to take the floor on the closure of debate shall be given only to two speakers before the closure, after which the motion shall immediately be put to the vote.

Rule 50 - Suspension or Adjournment of the Meeting

During the discussion of any matter, a member may move for the suspension or adjournment of the meeting. No discussion on any such motion shall be permitted and it shall be immediately be put to the vote.

Rule 51 - Order of Motions

Subject to the provisions of Rule 45 of the present Rules of Procedure the following motions shall have precedence in the following order over all the other proposals or motions before the meeting.
a) To suspend the meeting
b) To adjourn the Meeting
c) To adjourn the debate on the item under discussion
d) For the closure of the debate of the item under discussion

Rule 52 - Submission of Proposals and Amendment of substance

Unless the Commission decides otherwise, the proposals, amendments or motions of substance made by members shall be submitted in writing to the secretariat; they shall be considered at the first siting following their submission.

Rule 53 - Decision on Competence

Subject to the provisions of Rule 45 of the Rules of Procedure, any motion tabled by a member for a decision on the competence of the Commission to adopt a proposal submitted to it shall immediately be put to the vote.

Rule 54 - Withdrawal of a Proposal or a Motion

The sponsor of a motion or a proposal may still withdraw it before it is put to the vote, provided that it has not been amended. A motion or a proposal thus withdrawn may be submitted again by another member.

Rule 55 - New Consideration of a Motion

When a proposal is adopted or rejected, it shall not be considered again at the same session, unless the Commission decides otherwise. When a member moves the new consideration of a proposal, only one member may speak in favor of and one against the motion, after which it shall immediately be put to the vote.

Rule 56 - Interventions

1. No member may take the floor at a meeting of the Commission without prior authorization of the Chairman. Subject to Rules 45, 48, 49 and 50 the Chairman shall grant the use of the floor to speakers in the order in which it has been requested.

2. The debates shall deal solely with the matter submitted to the Commission and the Chairman may call to order a speaker whose remarks are irrelevant to the matter under discussion.

3. The Chairman may limit the time accorded to speakers and the number of interventions which each member may make on the same issue, in accordance with Rule 44 of the present Rules.

4. Only two members in favour and two against the motion fixing such time limits shall be granted the use of the floor after which the motion shall be put to the vote. For questions of procedure the time allotted to each speaker shall not exceed five minutes,

unless the Chairman decides otherwise. When the time allotted to discussions is limited and a speaker exceeds the time the Chairman shall immediately call him to order.

Rule 57 - Right of Reply

The right of reply shall be granted by the Chairman to any member requesting it. The member must, while exercising this right be brief as possible and take the floor preferably at the end of the sitting at which this right has been requested.

Rule 58 - Congratulations

The congratulations addressed to the newly elected members to the Commission shall only be presented by the Chairman or a member designated by the latter. Those addressed to the newly elected officers shall only be presented by the outgoing Chairman or a member designated by him.

Rule 59 - Condolences

Condolences shall be exclusively presented by the Chairman on behalf of all the members. The Chairman may, with the consent of the Commission, send a message of condolence.

CHAPTER XI - VOTE AND ELECTIONS

Rule 60 - Right to Vote

Each member of the Commission shall have one vote. In the case of equal number of votes the Chairman shall have a casting vote.

Rule 61 - Asking for a Vote

A proposal or a motion submitted for the decision of the Commission shall be put to the vote if a member so requests. If no member asks for a vote, the Commission may adopt a proposal or a motion without a vote.

Rule 62 - Required Majority

1. Except as otherwise provided by the Charter or other rules of the present Rules of Procedure, decisions of the Commission shall be taken by a simple majority of members present and voting.

2. For the purposes of the present Rules of Procedure, the expression "members present and voting" shall mean members voting for or against. The members who shall abstain from voting shall be considered as non-voting members.

3. Decisions may be taken by consensus, failing which, the Commission shall resort to voting.

Rule 63 - Method of Voting

1. Subject to the provisions of Rule 68, the Commission, unless it otherwise decides, shall normally vote by show of hands, but any member may request the roll-call vote, which shall be taken in the alphabetical order of the names of the members of the Commission beginning with the member whose name is drawn by lot by the Chairman. In all the votes by roll-call each member shall reply "yes", "no" or "abstention." The Commission may decide to hold a secret ballot.

2. In case of vote by roll-call, the vote of each member participating in the ballot shall be recorded in the minutes.

Rule 64 - Explanation Vote

Members may make brief statements for the only purpose of explaining their vote, before the beginning of the vote or once the vote has been taken. The member who is the sponsor of a proposal or a motion cannot explain his vote on that proposal or motion except if it has been amended.

Rule 65 - Rules to be Observed While Voting

A ballot shall not be interrupted except if a member raised a point of order relating to manner in which the ballot is held. The Chairman may allow members to intervene briefly, whether before the ballot beginning or when it is closed, but solely to explain their vote.

Rule 66 - Division of Proposals and Amendments

Proposals and amendments may be separated if requested. The parts of the proposals or of the amendments which have been adopted shall later be put to the vote as a whole; if all the operative parts of a proposal have been rejected , the proposal shall be considered to have been rejected as whole.

Rule 67 - Amendment

An amendment to a proposal is an addition to, deletion from or revision of part of that proposal.

Rule 68 - Order of Vote on Amendments

When an amendment is moved to a proposal, the amendment shall be voted on first. When two or more amendments are moved to a proposal, the Commission shall first vote on the amendment furthest removed in substance from the original proposal and then on the amendment next furthest removed therefrom and so until all the amendments have been put to the vote. Nevertheless when the adoption of an amendment implies the rejection of another amendment, the latter shall not be put to the vote. If one or several amendments are adopted, the amended proposal shall then be put to the vote.

Rule 69 - Order of Vote on the Proposal

1. If two or more proposals are made on the same matter, the Commission, unless it decides otherwise, shall vote on these proposals in the order in which they were submitted.

2. After each vote the Commission may decide whether it shall put the next proposal to the vote.

3. However, the motions which are not on the substance of the proposal shall be voted upon before the said proposals.

Rule 70 - Elections

Elections shall be held by secret ballot unless the election is for a post for which only one candidate has been proposed and that candidate has been agreed by the members of the Commission.

CHAPTER XII - PARTICIPATION OF NON-MEMBERS OF THE COMMISSION

Rule 71 - Participation of States in the Deliberations

1. The Commission or its subsidiary bodies may invite any State to participate in the discussion of any issue that shall be of particular interest to that State.

2. A State thus invited shall have no voting right, but may submit proposals which may be put to the vote at the request of any member of the Commission or of the subsidiary body concerned.

Rule 72 - Participation of Persons or Organizations

The Commission may invite any organization or persons capable of enlightening it to participate in its deliberations without voting rights.

Rule 73 - Participation of Specialized Institutions and Consultation with the Latter

1. Pursuant to the agreements concluded between the Organization of African Unity and the Specialized Institutions, the latter shall have the right to:
   a) Be represented in the public sessions of the Commission and its subsidiary bodies;
   b) Participate, without voting rights, through their representatives in deliberation on issues which shall be of interest to them and to submit, on these issues, proposals which may be put to vote at the request of any member of the Commission or the interested subsidiary body.

2. Before placing on the provisional agenda an issue submitted by a Specialized Institution, the Secretary-General should initiate such preliminary consultations as may be necessary, with this institution.

3. When an issue proposed for inclusion in the provisional agenda of a session, or which has been added to the agenda of a session pursuant to Rule 5 of the present Rules of Procedure contains a proposal requesting the Organization of African Unity to undertake additional activities relating issues concerning directly one or more specialized institutions, the Secretary-General should enter into consultation with the institutions concerned and inform the Commission of the ways and means of ensuring coordinated utilization of the resources of the various institutions.

4. When at a meeting of the Commission, a proposal calling upon the Organization of African Unity to undertake additional activities relating to issues directly concerning one or several specialized institutions, the Secretary-General, after consulting as far as possible, the representatives of the interested institutions, should draw the attention of the Commission to the effects of that proposal.

5. Before taking a decision on the proposals mentioned above, the Commission shall make sure that the institutions concerned have been duly consulted.

Rule 74 - Participation of Other Inter-Governmental Organizations

1. The Secretary shall inform, not later than 4 weeks before a session, non-governmental organizations with observer status of the days and agenda of a forthcoming session.

2. Representatives of Inter-Governmental Organizations to which the Organization of African Unity has granted permanent observer status and other organizations recognized by the Commission, may participate, without voting rights, in the deliberations of the Commission on issues falling within the framework of the activities of these organizations.

CHAPTER XIII - RELATIONS WITH AND REPRESENTATION OF NON-GOVERNMENTAL ORGANIZATIONS

Rule 75 - Representation

Non-governmental organizations, granted observer status by the Commission, may appoint authorized observers to participate in the public sessions of the Commission and of its subsidiary bodies.

Rule 76 - Consultation

The Commission may consult the non-governmental organization either directly or through one or several committees set up for this purpose. These consultations may be held at the invitation of the Commission or at the request of the organization.

CHAPTER XIV - PUBLICATION AND DISTRIBUTION OF THE REPORT AND OTHER OFFICIAL DOCUMENTS OF THE COMMISSION

Rule 77 - Report of the Commission

Within the framework of the procedure of the communication among States Parties to the Charter, refereed to in Articles 47 and 49 of the Charter, the Commission shall submit to the Assembly a report containing, where possible, recommendations it shall deem necessary. The report shall be confidential. However, it shall be published by the Chairman of the Commission after reporting unless the Assembly directs otherwise.

Rule 78 - Periodical Reports of Member States

Periodical Reports and other information submitted by States Parties to the Charter as requested under Article 62 of the Charter, shall be documents for general distribution. The same thing shall apply to other information supplied by a State Party to the Charter, unless the Commission decides otherwise.

Rule 79 - Reports on Activities of the Commission

1. As stipulated in Article 54 of the Charter, the Commission shall each year submit to the Assembly, a report on its deliberations, in which it shall include a summary of the activities.

2. The report shall be published by the Chairman after the Assembly has considered it.

Rule 80 - Translation of Reports and other Documents

The Secretary shall endeavor to translate all reports and other documents of the Commission into the working languages.

PART TWO
PROVISIONS RELATING TO THE FUNCTIONS OF THE COMMISSION

CHAPTER XV - PROMOTIONAL ACTIVITIES

REPORT SUBMITTED BY STATES PARTIES TO THE CHARTER UNDER ARTICLE 62 OF THE CHARTER

Rule 81 - Contents of Report

1. States Parties to the Charter shall submit reports in the form required by the Commission on measures they have taken to give effect to the rights recognized by the Charter and on the progress made with regard to the enjoyment of these rights. The report should indicate, where possible, the factors and difficulties impeding the implementation of the provisions of the Charter.

2. If a State Party fails to comply with Article 62 of the Charter, the Commission shall fix the date for the submission of that State Party's report.

3. The Commission may, through the Secretary-General, inform States Parties to the Charter of its wishes regarding form and contents of the reports to be submitted under Article 62 of the Charter.

Rule 82 - Transmission of Reports

1. The Secretary may, after consultation with the Commission, communicate to the specialized institutions concerned, copies of all parts of the reports which may relate to their areas of competence, produced by Member States of these institutions.

2. The Commission may invite the specialized institutions to which the Secretary has communicated parts of the report, to submit observations relating to these parts within a time limit that it may specify.

Rule 83 - Submission of Reports

The Commission shall inform, as early as possible, Member States parties to the Charter, through the Secretary, of the opening date, duration and venue of the Session at which their respective reports shall be considered. Representatives of the States Parties to the Charter may participate in the session of the Commission at which their reports shall be considered. The Commission may also inform a State Party to the Charter from which it wanted complementary information, that it may authorize its representative to participate in a specific session. This representative should be able to reply to questions put to him/her by the Commission and make statements on reports already submitted by this State. He may also furnish additional information from his State.

Rule 84 - Non-submission of Reports

1. The Secretary shall, at each session, inform the Commission of all cases of non-submission of reports or of additional information requested pursuant to Rules 81 and 85 of the Rules of Procedure. In such cases, the Commission may send, through the Secretary, to the State Party to the Charter concerned, a report or reminder relating to the submission of the report or additional information.

2. If, after the reminder referred to in paragraph 1 of this Rule, a State Party to the Charter does not submit the report or the additional information requested pursuant to Rules 81 and 85 of the Rules of Procedure, the Commission shall point it out in its yearly report to the Assembly.

Rule 85 - Examination of Information Contained in Reports

1. When considering a report submitted by a State Party to the Charter under Article 62 of the Charter, the Commission should first make sure that the report provides all necessary information including relevant legislation pursuant the provisions of Rule 81 of the Rules of Procedure.

2. If in the opinion of the Commission, a report submitted by a State Party to the Charter, does not contain adequate information, the Commission may request this State to furnish the additional information required, by indicating the date on which the information needed should be submitted.

3. If, following the consideration of the reports, and the information submitted by a State Party to the Charter, the Commission decides that the State has not discharged some of its obligations under the Charter, it may address all general observations to the State concerned as it may deem necessary.

Rule 86 - Adjournment and Transmission of Reports

1. The Commission shall, though the Secretary, communicate to States Parties to the Charter for comments, its general observations made following the consideration of the reports and the information submitted by States Parties to the Charter. The Commission may, when necessary fix a time limit for the submission of the comments by the States Parties to the Charter.

2. The Commission may also transmit to the Assembly, the observations mentioned in paragraph 1 of this Rule, accompanied by copies of the reports it has received from the States Parties to the Charter as well as the comments suppled by the latter if possible.

Rule 87 - Promotional Activities

1. The Commission shall adopt and carry out a program of action which gives effect to its obligations under the Charter, particularly Article 45(1).

2. The Commission shall carry out other promotional activities in member states and elsewhere on a continuing basis.

3. Each member of the Commission shall file a written report on his/her activities at each session including countries visited and organizations contacted.

CHAPTER XVI - PROTECTION ACTIVITIES
COMMUNICATIONS FROM THE STATES PARTIES
TO THE CHARTER

SECTION I - PROCEDURE FOR
THE CONSIDERATION OF COMMUNICATIONS
RECEIVED IN CONFORMITY WITH ARTICLE 4
OF THE CHARTER:
PROCEDURE FOR COMMUNICATIONS-NEGOTIATIONS

Rule 88 - Procedure

1. A communication under Article 47 of the Charter should be submitted to the Secretary-General, the Chairman of the Commission and the State Party concerned.

2. The Communication referred to above should be in writing and contain detailed and comprehensive statement on the actions denounced as well a the provisions of the Charter alleged to have been violated.

3. The notification of the Communication to the State Party to the Charter, the Secretary-General and the Chairman of the Commission shall be done through the most practical and reliable means.

Rule 89 - Register of Communications

The Secretary shall keep a permanent register for all communications received and under Article 47 of the Charter.

Rule 90 - Reply and Time Limit

1. The reply of the State Party to the Charter to which a communication is addressed should reach the requesting State Party to the Charter within 3 months following the receipt of the notification of the communication.

2. It shall be accompanied particularly by:
   a) Written explanations, declarations or statements relating to the issues raised;
   b) Possible indications and measures taken to end the situation denounced;
   c) Indications on the law and rules of procedure applicable or applicable;
   d) Indications on the local procedures for appeal already used, in process or still open.

Rule 91 - Non-Settlement of the Issue

1. If within three (3) months from the date of the notification of the original communication is received by the addressee State, the issue has not been settled to the satisfaction of the two interested parties, through the selected channel of negotiation or through any other peaceful procedure selected by the common consent of the parties, the issue shall be referred to the Commission, in accordance with the provisions of Article 48 of the Charter.

2. The issue shall also be referred to the Commission if the addressee State Party to the Charter fails to react to the request made under Article 47 of the Charter, within the same 3 months period of time.

Rule 92 - Seizing of the Commission

At the expiration of the 3 months' time limit referred to in Article 47 of the Charter, and in the absence of a satisfactory reply or in case the addressee State Party may submit the communication to the Commission through a notification addressed to its Chairman, the other interested State Party and the Secretary-General.

SECTION II - PROCEDURE FOR THE CONSIDERATION OF THE COMMUNICATION RECEIVED IN CONFORMITY WITH ARTICLES 48 AND 49 OF THE CHARTER PROCEDURE FOR COMMUNICATION-COMPLAINT

Rule 93 - Seizing of the Commission

1. Any communication submitted under Articles 48 and 49 of the Charter may be submitted to the Commission by any one of the interested States Parties through notification addressed to the Chairman of the Commission, the Secretary-General and the State Party concerned.

2. The notification referred to in paragraph 1 of the present Rule shall contain information on the following elements accompanied particularly by:
   a) Measures taken to try resolve the issues pursuant to Article 47 of the Charter including the text of the initial communications and any future written explanation from the interested States Parties to the Charter relating to the issue;
   b) Measures taken to exhaust local procedure for appeal;
   c) Any other procedure for the international investigation or international settlement to which the interested States Parties have resorted.

Rule 94 - Permanent Register of Communications

The Secretary shall keep a permanent register for all communications received by the Commission
under Articles 48 and 49 of the Charter.

Rule 95 - Seizing of the Members of the Commission

The Secretary shall immediately inform members of the Commission of any notification received pursuant to Rule 91 of the Rules of Procedure and shall send to them, as early as possible, a copy of the notification as well as relevant information.

Rule 96 - Private Session and Press Release

1. The Commission shall consider the communications referred ti in Articles 48 and 49 of the Charter in closed session.

2. After consulting the interested States Parties, the Commission may issue though the Secretary, release on its private sessions for the attention of the media and the public.

Rule 97 - Consideration of the Communication

The Commission shall consider a communication only when:

a) The procedure offered to the States Parties by Article 47 of the Charter has been exhausted;
b) The time limit set in Article 48 of the Charter has expired;
c) The Commission is certain that all the available local remedies have been utilized and exhausted, in accordance with the generally recognized principles of international law, or that the application of these remedies is unreasonably prolonged or that there are no effective remedies.

Rule 98 - Amicable Settlement

Except as the provisions of the present Rules of Procedure, the Commission shall place its good offices at the disposal of the interested States Parties to the Charter so as to reach an amicable solution on the issue based on the respect of human rights and fundamental liberties, as recognized by the Charter.

Rule 99 - Additional Information

The Commission may through the Secretary, request the States Parties or one of them to communicate additional information or observations orally or in writing. The Commission shall fix a time limit for the submission of the written information or observations.

Rule 100 - Representation of States Parties

1. The States Parties to the Charter concerned shall have the right to be represented during the consideration of the issue by the Commission and to submit observations orally or in writing or in ether form.

2. The Commission shall notify, as soon as possible, the States Parties concerned, thugh the Secretary of the opening day, the duration and venue of the session at which the issue will be examined.

3. The procedure to be followed for the presentation of oral or written observations shall be determined by the Commission.

Rule 101 - Report of the Commission

1. The Commission shall adopt a report pursuant to Article 52 of the Charter within 12 months following the notification referred to in Article 48 of the Charter and Rule 90 of the present Rules of Procedure.

2. The provisions of paragraph 1 of Rule 99 of these Rules of Procedure shall not apply to the deliberations of the Commission relating the adoption of the report.

3. The report referred to above shall concern the decisions and conclusions that the Commission will reach.

4. The report of the Commission shall be communicated to the States Parties concerned though the Secretary.

5. The report of the Commission shall be sent to the Assembly though the Secretary-general together with the recommendations that it shall deem useful.

CHAPTER XVII - OTHER COMMUNICATIONS
PROCEDURE FOR THE CONSIDERATION OF THE COMMUNICATIONS RECEIVED IN CONFORMITY WITH ARTICLE 55 OF THE CHARTER

SECTION I - TRANSMISSION OF COMMUNICATIONS TO THE COMMISSION

Rule 102 - Seizing of the Commission

1. Pursuant to these Rules of Procedure, the Secretary shall transmit to the Commission the Communications submitted to him for consideration by the Commission in accordance with the Charter.

2. No communications concerning a State which is not a party to the Charter shall be received by the Commission or placed in a list under Rule 103 of the present Rules.

Rule 103 - List of Communications

1. The Secretary of the Commission shall prepare lists of communications submitted to the Commission pursuant to Rule 101 above, to which he/she shall attach a brief summary to their contents and regularly cause the lists to be distributed to members of the Commission. Besides, the Secretary shall keep a permanent register of all these communications which shall be made public.

2. Full text of each communication referred to the Commission shall be communicated to each member of the Commission on request.

Rule 104 - Request for Clarification

1. The Commission, through the Secretary, may request the author of a communication to furnish clarifications on the applicability of the Charter to his/her communication, and to specify in particular:
   a) His name, address, age and profession by justifying his very identity, if ever/she is requesting the Commission to be kept anonymous;
   b) Name of the State Party referred to in the Communication;
   c) Purpose of the Communication;
   d) Provisions of the Charter allegedly violated;
   e) The facts of the claim;
   f) Measures taken by the author to exhaust local remedies, or explanation why local remedies will be futile;
   g) The extent to which the same issue has been settled by another international investigation or settlement body.

2. When asking for clarification or information, the Commission shall fix an appropriate time limit for the author to submit the communication so as to avoid undue delay in the procedure provided for by the Charter.

3. The Commission may adopt a questionnaire for the use by the author of the communication in providing the above-mentioned information.

4. The request of the clarification referred to in paragraph 1 of this rule shall not prevent the inclusion of the communication on the lists mentioned in paragraph 1 of Rule 102 above.

Rule 105 - Distribution of Communications

For each communication recorded, the Secretary shall prepare as soon as possible, a summary of the relevant information received, which shall be distributed to the members of the Commission.

SECTION II - GENERAL PROVISIONS GOVERNING THE CONSIDERATION OF THE COMMUNICATIONS BY THE COMMISSION OR ITS SUBSIDIARY BODIES

Rule 106 - Private Sessions

The Sessions of the Commission or its subsidiary bodies during which the communications are examined as provided for in the Charter shall be private.

Rule 107 - Public Sessions

The sessions during which the Commission may consider other general issues, such as the application procedure of the Charter, shall be public.

Rule 108 - Press Release

The Commission may issue, through the Secretary and for the attention of the media and the public, releases on the activities on the activities of the Commission on its private session.

Rule 109 - Incompatibility

1. No member shall take part in the consideration of a communication by the Commission:
   a) If he/she has any personal interest in the case, or

b) If he/she has participated, in any capacity, in the adoption of any decision relating to the case which is the subject of the communication, or

2. Any issue relating to the application of paragraph 1 above shall be resolved by the Commission.

Rule 110 - Withdrawal of a Member

If, for any reason, a member considers that he/she should not take part or continue to take part in the consideration of a communication, he/she shall inform the Chairman of his/her decision to withdraw.

Rule 111 - Provisional Measures

1. Before making its final views known to the Assembly of on the communications, the Commission may inform the State Party concerned of its views on the appropriateness of taking provisional measures to avoid irreparable damage being caused to the victim of the alleged violation. In so doing the Commission shall inform the State Party that the expression of its views on the adoption of those provisional measures does not imply a decision on the substance of the communication.

2. The Commission, or when it is not in session, the Chairman, in consultation with other members of the Commission, may indicate to the parties any interim measure, the adoption of which seems desirable in the interest of the parties or the proper conduct of the proceedings before it.
In case [of] urgency when the Commission is not in session, the Chairman in consultation with other members of the Commission, may take necessary action on behalf of the Commission. As soon as the Commission is again in session, the Chairman shall report to it any action taken.

Rule 112

Prior to any substantive consideration, every communication should be made known to the State concerned through the Chairman of the Commission, pursuant to Article 57 of the Charter.

SECTION III - PROCEDURES TO DETERMINE ADMISSIBILITY

Rule 113 - Time Limits for Consideration of the Admissibility

The Commission shall decide, as early as possible and pursuant to the following provisions whether or not the communication shall be admissible under the Charter.

Rule 114 - Order of Consideration of the Communication

1. Unless otherwise decided, the Commission shall consider the communications in the order they have been received by the secretariat.

2. The Commission may decide, if it deems it good, to consider jointly two or more communications.

Rule 115 - Working Groups

The Commission may set up one or more working groups, each composed of three members at most, to submit recommendations on admissibility as stipulated in Article 56 of the Charter.

Rule 116 - Admissibility of the Communications

The Commission shall determine questions of admissibility pursuant to Article 56 of the Charter.

Rule 117 - Additional Information

1. The Commission or working group set up under Rule 113, [may] request the State Party concerned or the author of the communication to submit in writing additional information or observation relating to the issue of admissibility of the communication. The Commission or the working group shall fix a time limit for the submission of the information or observation to avoid the issue dragging on too long.

2. A communication may be declared admissible if the State Party concerned has been given the opportunity to submit the information and observations pursuant to paragraph 1 of this Rule.

3. A request under paragraph 1 of this Rule should indicate clearly that the request does not mean any decision any decision whatsoever has been taken on the issue of admissibility.

4. However, the Commission shall decide in [on] the issue of admissibility if the State Party fails to send a written response within three (3) months from the date of notification of the text of the communication.

Rule 118 - Decision of the Commission on Admissibility

1. If the Commission decides that a communication is inadmissible under the Charter, it shall make its decision known as early as possible, through the Secretary to the

author of the communication and, if the communication has been transmitted to a State Party concerned, to that State.

2. If the Commission has declared a communication inadmissible under the Charter, it may reconsider this decision at a later date if it receives a request for reconsideration.

SECTION IV - PROCEDURES FOR THE CONSIDERATION OF COMMUNICATIONS

Rule 119 - Proceedings

1. If the Commission decides that a communication is inadmissible under the Charter, its decision and text of the relevant documents shall as soon as possible, be submitted to the State Party concerned through the Secretary. The author of the communication shall also be informed of the Commission's decision through the Secretary.

2. The State Party to the Charter concerned shall, within the 3 ensuing moths, submit in writing to the Commission, explanations or statements elucidating the issue under consideration and indicating, if possible, measures it was able to take to remedy the situation.

3. All explanation or statements submitted by a State Party pursuant to the present Rule shall be communicated, through the Secretary, to the author of the communication who may submit in writing additional information and observations within a time limit fixed by the Commission.

4. States Parties from whom explanations or statements are sought within specified times shall be informed that if they fail to comply within those times the Commission will act on the evidence before it.

Rule 120 - Final Decision of the Communication

1. If the communication is admissible, the Commission shall consider it in the light of all the information that the individual and the State Party concerned has [have] submitted in writing; it shall make known its observations on this issue. To this end, the Commission may refer the communication to a working group, composed of 3 of its members at most, which shall submit recommendations to it.

2. The observations of the Commission shall be communicated to the Assembly through the Secretary-General and to the State Party concerned.

3. The Assembly or its Chairman may request the Commission to conduct an ind-depth study on these cases and to submit a factual report accompanied by its findings and

recommendations, in accordance with the provisions of the Charter. The Commission may entrust this function to a Special Rapporteur or a working group.

FINAL CHAPTER - AMENDMENT OF THE RULES OF PROCEDURE

Rule 121 - Method of Amendment

Only the Commission may modify the present Rules of Procedure.

Rule 122 - Method of Suspension

The Commission may suspend temporarily, the application of any Rule of the present Rules of Procedure, on condition that such a suspension shall not be incompatible with any applicable decision of the Commission or Assembly or with any relevant provision of the Charter and that the proposal shall have been submitted 24 hours in advance. This condition may be set aside if no member opposes it. Such a suspension may take place only with a specific and precise object in view and should be limited to the duration necessary to achieve that aim.

DELIBERATED AND ADOPTED BY THE COMMISSION AT ITS 18TH SESSION HELD IN PRAIA, CAPE VERDE

V

PROTOCOL TO THE AFRICAN CHARTER ON HUMAN AND PEOPLES' RIGHTS ON THE ESTABLISHMENT OF AN AFRICAN COURT ON HUMAN AND PEOPLES' RIGHTS

(OAU.DOC.CAB/LEG/66.5 (1998), adopted and signed at the OAU Summit in Ouagadougou, Burkina Faso in June 1998. The Protocol is not yet in force. It is expected to come into effect after 15 ratifications. As at present only Senegal and Burkina Faso have rarified the Protocol).

The Member States of the Organization of African Unity hereinafter referred to as the OAU, States Parties to the African Charter on Human and Peoples' Rights:

Considering that the Charter of the Organization of African Unity recognizes that freedom, equality, justice, peace and dignity are essential objectives for the achievement of the legitimate aspirations of the African Peoples;

Noting that the African Charter on Human and Peoples' Rights reaffirms adherence to the principles of human and peoples' rights, freedoms and duties contained in the declarations, conventions and other instruments adopted by the Organization of African Unity, and other international Organizations;

Recognizing that the twofold objectives of the African Charter on Human and Peoples' Rights is to ensure on the one hand promotion and on the other protection of human and peoples' rights, freedoms and duties;

Recognizing further, the efforts of the African Commission on Human and Peoples' Rights in the promotion and protection of human and peoples' rights since its inception in 1987;

Recalling resolution AHG/Res.230 (XXX) adopted by the Assembly of Heads of State and Government in June 1994 in Tunis, Tunisia, requesting the Secretary-General to convene a Government experts' meeting to ponder, in conjunction with the African Commission, over the means to enhance the efficiency of the African Commission and to consider in particular the establishment of an African Court on Human and Peoples' Rights;

Noting the first and second Government legal experts' meeting held respectively in Cape Town , South Africa (September 1995) and Nouakchott, Mauritania (April 1997), and the third Government Legal Experts meeting held in Addis Ababa, Ethiopia (December 1997), which was enlarged to include diplomats;

Firmly convinced that the attainment of the objectives of the African Charter on Human and Peoples' Rights requires the establishment of an African Court on Human and Peoples' Rights to complement and reinforce the functions of the African Commission on Human and Peoples' Rights.

HAVE AGREED AS FOLLOWS:

Article 1 ESTABLISHMENT OF THE COURT

There shall be established within the Organization of African Unity an African Court on Human and Peoples' Rights hereinafter referred to as "the Court, " the organization, jurisdiction and functioning of which shall be governed by the present Protocol.

Article 2 RELATIONSHIP BETWEEN THE COURT AND THE COMMISSION

The Court shall, bearing in mind the provisions of this Protocol, complement the protective mandate of the African Commission on Human and Peoples' Rights hereinafter referred to as " the Commission," conferred upon it by the African Charter on Human and Peoples' Rights, hereinafter to as "the Charter."

Article 3 JURISDICTION

1. The jurisdiction of the Court shall extend to all cases and disputes submitted to it concerning the interpretation and application of the Charter, this Protocol and any other relevant Human Rights instruments ratified by the States concerned.

2. In the event of a dispute as to whether the Court has jurisdiction, the Court shall decide.

Article 4 ADVISORY OPINIONS

1. At the request of a Member State of the OAU, the OAU, any of its organs, or any African organization recognized by the OAU, the Court may provide an opinion on any legal matter relating to the Charter of any other relevant human rights instruments, provided that the subject matter of the opinion is not related to a matter being examined by the Commission.

2. The Court shall give reasons for its advisory opinions provided that every judge shall be entitled to deliver a separate or dissenting decision.

Article 5 ACCESS TO THE COURT

1. The following are entitled to submit cases to the Court.
   a. The Commission;
   b. The State Party which has lodged a complaint to the Commission;
   c. The State Party against which the complaint has been lodged at the Commission;
   d. The State Party whose citizen is a victim of human rights violations;
   e. African Intergovernmental Organizations.

2. When a State Party has an interest in a case, it may submit a request to the Court to be permitted to join.

3. The Court may entitle relevant Non-Governmental Organizations (NGOs) with observer status before the Commission, and individuals to institute cases directly before it, in accordance with article 34 of this Protocol.

Article 6 ADMISSIBILITY OF CASES

1. The Court, when deciding on the admissibility of a case instituted under article 5(3) of this Protocol, may request the opinion of the Commission which shall give it as soon as possible.

2. The Court shall rule on the admissibility of cases taking into account the provisions of Article 56 of the Charter.

3. The Court may consider cases or transfer them to the Commission.

Article 7 SOURCES OF LAW

The Court shall apply the provisions of the Charter and any other relevant human rights instruments ratified by the States concerned.

Article 8 CONSIDERATION OF CASES

The Rules of Procedure of the Court shall lay down the detailed conditions under which the Court shall consider cases brought before it, bearing in mind the complementarity between the Commission and the Court.

Article 9 AMICABLE SETTLEMENT

The Court may try to reach an amicable settlement in a case pending before it in accordance with the provisions of the Charter.

Article 10 HEARINGS AND REPRESENTATION

1. The Court shall conduct its proceedings in public. The Court may, however, conduct proceedings in camera as may be provided for in the Rules of Procedure.

2. Any party to a case shall be entitled to be represented by a legal representative of the party's choice. Free legal representation may be provided where the interest of justice so require.

3. Any person, witness or representative of the parties, who appears before the Court, shall enjoy protection and all facilities, in accordance with international law, necessary for the discharging of their functions, tasks and duties in relation to the Court.

Article 11 COMPOSITION

1. The Court shall consist of eleven judges, nationals of Member States of the OAU, elected in an individual capacity from among jurists of high moral character and of recognized practical, judicial or academic competence and experience in the field of human and peoples' rights.

2. No two judges shall be nationals of the same State.

Article 12 NOMINATIONS

1. States parties to the Protocol may each propose up to three candidates, at least two of whom shall be nationals of that State.

2. Due consideration shall be given to adequate gender representation in the nomination process.

Article 13 LIST OF CANDIDATES

1. Upon entry into force of this Protocol, the Secretary-General of the OAU shall request each State Party to the Protocol to present, within ninety (90) days of such a request, it nominees for the office of judge of the Court.

2. The Secretary-General of the OAU shall prepare a list in alphabetical order of the candidates nominated and transmit it to the Member States of the OAU at least thirty days prior to the next session of the Assembly of Heads of State and Government of the OAU hereinafter referred to as "the Assembly."

Article 14 ELECTIONS

1. The judges of the Court shall be elected by secret ballot by the Assembly from the list referred to in Article 13(2) of the present Protocol.

2. The Assembly shall ensure that in the Court as a whole there is representation of the main regions of Africa and of their principal legal traditions.

3. In the election of the judges, the Assembly shall ensure that there is adequate gender representation.

Article 15 TERM OF OFFICE

1. The judges of the Court shall be elected for a period of six years and may be re-elected only once. The term of office of four judges elected at the first election shall expire at the end of two years, and the terms of four more judges shall expire at the end of four years.

2. The judges whose terms at to expire at the end of the initial periods of two and four years shall be chosen by lot to be drawn by the Secretary-General of the OAU immediately after the first election has been completed.

3. A judge elected to replace a judge whose term of office has not expired shall hold office for the remainder of the predecessor's term.

4. All judges except the president shall perform their functions on a part-time basis. However, the Assembly may change this arrangement as it deems appropriate.

Article 16 OATH OF OFFICE

After their election, the judges of the Court shall make a solemn declaration to discharge their duties impartially and faithfully.

Article 17 INDEPENDENCE

1. The independence of the judges shall be fully ensured in accordance with international law.

2. No judge may hear any case in which the same judge has previously taken part as agent, counsel or advocate for one of the parties or as a member of a national or international court or a commission of inquiry or in any other capacity. Any doubt on this point shall be settled by decision of the Court.

3. The judges of the Court shall enjoy, from the moment of their election and throughout their term of office, the immunities extended to diplomatic agents in accordance with international law.

4. At no time shall the judges of the Court be held liable for any decision or opinion issued in the exercise of their functions.

Article 18 INCOMPATIBILITY

The position of a judge of the Court is incompatible with any activity that might interfere with the independence or impartiality of such a judge or the demands of the office as determined in the Rules of Procedure.

Article 19 CESSATION OF OFFICE

1. A judge shall nor be suspended or removed from office unless, by the unanimous decision of the other judges of the Court, the judge concerned has been found to be no longer fulfilling the required conditions to be a judge of the Court.
2. Such decision of the Court shall become final unless it is set aside by the Assembly at its next session.

Article 20 VACANCIES

1. In case of death or resignation of a judge of the Court, the President of the Court shall immediately inform the Secretary-General of the Organization of African Unity, who shall declare the seat vacant from the date of the death or from the date on which the resignation takes effect.

2. The Assembly shall replace the judge whose office became vacant unless the remaining period of the term is less than one hundred and eighty (180) days.

3. The same procedure and considerations as set out in Articles 12, 13 and 14 shall be followed in the filling of vacancies.

Article 21 PRESIDENCY OF THE COURT

1. The Court shall elect its President and one Vice-President for a period of two years. They may be re-elected only once.

2. The President shall perform judicial functions on a full-time basis and shall reside at the seat of the Court.

3. The functions of the President and the Vice-President shall be se out in the Rules of Procedure of the Court.

Article 22 EXCLUSION

If a judge is a national of any State which is a party to a case submitted to the Court, that judge shall not hear the case.

Article 23 QUORUM

The Court shall examine cases brought before it, if it has a quorum of at least seven judges.

Article 24 REGISTRY OF THE COURT

1. The Court shall appoint its own Registrar and other staff of the registry from among nationals of Member States of the OAU according to the Rules of Procedure.
2. The office and residence of the Registrar shall be at the place where the Court has its seat.

Article 25 SEAT OF THE COURT

1. The Court shall have its seat at the place determined by the Assembly from among States Parties to this Protocol. However, it may convene in the territory of any Member State of the OAU when the majority of the Court considers it desirable, and with the prior consent of the State concerned.

2. The seat of the Court may be changed by the Assembly after due consultation with the Court.

Article 26 EVIDENCE

1. The Court shall hear admissions by all parties and if deemed necessary, hold an enquiry. The States concerned shall assist by providing relevant facilities for the efficient handling of the case.

2. The Court may receive written notice and oral evidence including expert testimony and shall make its decision on the basis of such evidence.

Article 27 FINDINGS

1. If the Court finds that there has been a violation of a human or peoples' right, it shall make appropriate orders to remedy the violation, including the payment of fair compensation or reparation.

2. In cases of extreme gravity and urgency, and when necessary to avoid irreparable harm to persons, the Court shall adopt such provisional measures as it deems necessary.

Article 28 JUDGMENT

1. The Court shall render its judgment within ninety (90) days of having completed its deliberations.

2. The judgement of the Court decided by majority shall be final and not subject to appael.

3. Without prejudice to sub-article 2 above, the Court may review its decision in the light of new evidence under conditions to be set out in the Rules of Procedure.

4. The Court may interpret its own decision.

5. The judgment of the Court shall be read in open Court, due notice having been given to the parties.

6. Reasons shall be given for the judgment of the Court.

7. If the judgment of the Court does not represent, in whole or in part, the unanimous decision of the judges, any judge shall be entitled to deliver a separate or dissenting opinion.

Article 29 NOTIFICATION OF JUDGEMENT

1. The parties to the case shall be notified of the judgment of the Court and it shall be transmitted to the Member States of the OAU and the Commission.

2. The Council of Ministers shall also be notified of the judgment and shall monitor its execution on behalf of the Assembly.

Article 30 EXECUTION OF JUDGMENT

The States Parties to the present Protocol undertake to comply with the judgment in any case to which they are parties within the time stipulated by the Court and to guarantee its execution.

Article 31 REPORT

The Court shall submit to each regular session of the Assembly, a report on its work during the previous year. The report shall specify, in particular, the cases in which a State has not complied with the Court's judgment.

Article 32 BUDGET

Expenses of the Court, emoluments and allowances for judges and the budget of its registry, shall be determined and borne by the OAU, in accordance with criteria laid down by the OAU in consultation with the Court.

Article 33 RULES OF PROCEDURE

The Court shall draw up its Rules and determine its own procedures. The Court shall consult the Commission as appropriate.

Article 34 RATIFICATION

1. This Protocol shall be open for signature and ratification or accession by any State Party to the Charter.

2. The instrument of ratification or accession to the present Protocol shall be deposited with the Secretary-General of the OAU.

3. The Protocol shall come into force thirty days after fifteen instruments of ratification or accession have been deposited.

4. For any State Party ratifying or acceding subsequently, the present Protocol shall come into force in respect of that State on the date of the deposit of its instrument of ratification or accession.

5. The Secretary-general of the OAU shall inform all Member States of the entry into force of the present Protocol.

6. At the time of ratification of this Protocol or any time thereafter, the State shall make a declaration accepting the competence of the Court to receive any petition under Article 5(3) of this Protocol. The Court shall not receive any petition under Article 5(3) involving a State Party which has not made such a declaration.

7. Declarations made under sub-article (6) above shall be deposited with the Secretary-General, who shall transmit copies thereof to the States Parties.

Article 35 AMENDMENTS

1. The present Protocols may be amended if a State Party to the Protocol makes a written request to that effect to the Secretary-General of the OAU. The Assembly may adopt, by simple majority, the draft amendment after all the States Parties to the present Protocol have been duly informed of it and the Court has given its opinion on the amendment.

2. The Court shall also be entitled to propose such amendments to the present Protocol as it may deem necessary, though the Secretary-General of the OAU.

3. The amendment shall come into force for each State Party which has accepted it thirty days after the Secretary-General of the OAU has received notice of the acceptance.

INDEX

A

Abolition of Forced Labor Convention 19
Access, right of - 265, 317
· individuals 265, 270
· non-State entities 267
· States Parties 269, 270
Access to justice 103
Adamant governments 62
Admissibility requirements 205, 278, 326, 329
Advisory capacity 63, 65
Advisory jurisdiction 250, 253
Advisory opinion 181, 272
AEC Court 264
African Charter on Human Rights 2, 71, 215, 306
African Charter on the Rights and Welfare of the Child 133
· interpretation 311
African civilization 244
African Commission on Human and Peoples' Rights 71, 82, 170, 231
· effectiveness 247
· gender representation 173
· geographical representation 174
· impartiality 172
· independence 175
· jurisprudence 84
· mode of election 172
· procedures 236
· promotion of human rights 176
· publicity practice 239
· recommendations 231, 239
African Conference on the Rule of Law 249
African Convention on the Rights and Welfare of the Child 183
African Court on Human and Peoples' Rights 72, 249, 253
· access 328
· Additional Protocol 245, 259
· funding 294
· judges 282, 289, 292
  - ad hoc - 290
· jurisprudence 296
· mandate 261, 262
· Registrar 282
· Rules of procedure 278, 278
· seat 282
African Economic Community Treaty 157
African Intergovernmental Organizations 268
African languages, indigenous - 102
African leaders 16
African legal philosophy 83
African needs 83
African organizations 186
African scholars 186
African societies 7, 10, traditional - 25
African tradition 250
African states, principle of - 81

African Union, Constitutive Act - 72, 81, 170
African unity, theory of - 143
Almadu 89
American Declaration on the Rights and Duties of Man 55
Amicable settlement 93, 208, 279, 327; see also friendly settlement
Amicus curiae briefs 297, 318
Amnesty 108
Amnesty International 228, 316
Anonymity 214
Annual activity report 193, 231
Apartheid 24, 34
Appeal, right to - 97
Assistance by interpreter, right of - 102

B
Basic services 127
Benin 210
Biafra 143
Binding obligations 38
Botswana 99, 227

C
Cameroon 143, 216, 224, 226, 238, 303
Capital punishment 88
Child labor 89
Civil and political rights 35, 58
Clawback clause(s) 92, 105, 165, 243
Collective rights 138, 157
Collective security 163
Colonialism 17, 32, 67, 81, 325
 · assimilation policy 20
 · association policy 21
 · double standards 32
 · indirect rule 21, 23
 · paternalism 22
 · repugnancy clause 26
 · similation policy 20
Commercial hegemony 17
Committee on Economic, Social and Cultural Rights 39
Committee on the Elimination of Discrimination Against Women 134
Communalism 8
Compensation 94, 119, 211, 298
 · right to 103, 244
Competent court 97
Complaints, individual - 203, 228, 316
 · admissibility 211
 · effectiveness 209
 · mandatory linkage 214
 · victims 214
Compulsory jurisdiction 250, 253
Concept of Human Rights 11, 13,
Concept of Law 10
Conciliation 250
Confidentiality, concept of - 240
Conflict of interests 173, 292
Congress of African Jurists 68
Conscientious objection, right of - 154
Consultative status 311, 314
Convention Against Torture and Other Cruel, Inhuman and Degrading Treatment or Punishment 40
Convention on the Elimination of All Forms of Discrimination Against Women 40
Convention on the Prevention and Punishment of the Crime of Genocide 40
Convention on the Rights of the Child 40, 133, 160
Correspondence 210
Corruption 138
Cote D'Ivoire 108
Covenant of the League of Nations 31
Council of Europe 44, 78
 · Committee of Ministers 47, 51-52
Country study approach 196
Crimes against humanity 82
Criminal procedure 95
Cultural domination 102
Cultural values 164

Custom 7, 11,
Customary behavior 7
Customary international law 36, 56, 120, 277
Customary law 18, 25

D
Damages 211
Decolonization 146
Defence, right to - 97
Definition of rights 33
Dehumanizing practices 89
Democratic governance 59
Democratization process 72
Deprivation of life
 · arbitrary 85
 · definition 86
Derogation clauses 165, 327
Development, right to - 123, 140, 149
Dictatorship 45
Discrimination 244
Dispute resolution 250
Dissenting opinion 302
Documentation of human rights 322
Domestic jurisdiction 34
Domestic jurisprudence 121
Domestic legal remedies 200
Domestic remedies 61, 219, 326
 · exhaustion of 90/91
 · 'unduly prolonged' 224
Domestic servitude 89
Donors 186
Double jeopardy, freedom from - 103
Due process of law 94
Duplication of procedures 227
Duty rights, conception of - 163

E
Economic, social and cultural rights 35, 276
ECOWAS Court 264
Effective appeal 95
Effective remedy 236, 239, 327
Emergency, state of - 93

Empires 8
Enforcement 264
Enforcement approach 321
Enforcement institutions 243
Enforcement of judgment 65
Enforcement procedures 41
Equality of arms 98
Eritrea 143
European Commission of Human Rights 47
European Convention on Human Rights 44
 · civil and political rights 45
 · individual petitions 50
 · inter-state cases 50
 · protocols 46, 47
European Court of Human Rights 47, 273, 303
 · judges 49
European liberalism 13
Exceptional circumstances 270
Execution of judgment 302
Executory force 65
Expert testimony 318
Exploitation, foreign economic - 148
Ex-post facto laws 101
Expulsion 115, 116, 304
Extra-judicial execution 87

F
Fair hearing, right of - 95, 244
Fair wages 125
Fair trial, right of - 280
Family provisions 244
Female genital mutilation 127
Feudalism 8
Food and Agricultural Organization (FAO) 41
Forced Labor Convention 19
Forced Labor 28, 89,
Forced marriages 89
Foreign domination 145
Friendly settlement 61, 200

G

Gambia 221
Gender equality 82, 244, 287
Gender representation 286
General principles of law 160
Genocide 82
Geographical identity 9
Good faith 211
Group rights 139
Guidelines for the Submission of State Reports 129

H

Health care 126
Historical practices 13
Holistic approach 123
Homosexuals 151
Human person, integrity of - 88
Human Rights Committee 38/39
Human Rights education 129

I

Ideologies 122
Immunity 281
Impartial court 99
Impartiality 247
Independence of State Party 59
Individual access 204
Individual rights 139
Indoctrination 104
Information, right to receive - 106
Inherent powers 265
Inter-American Commission on Human Rights 56, 60, 115, 198
Inter-American Convention on Human Rights
 · civil and political rights 58
 · individual petitions 60
 · inter-state complaints 60
Inter-American Convention for the Prevention and Punishment Torture 59
Inter-American Court of Human Rights 62, 160, 296
 · advisory jurisdiction 63, 65
 · contentious jurisdiction 63
 · individual access 64
Interim measures 233, 300
International Commission of Jurists 255, 313
International cooperation 32
International Convention on the Elimination of All Forms of Racial Discrimination 40
International cooperation 77
International Court of Justice 143
International Covenant on Civil and Political Rights 37, 38
International Covenant on Economic, Social and Cultural Rights 38, 121
International Criminal Court 80
International Labor Organization (ILO) 19, 28, 41,
International Monetary Fund (IMF) 41
International peace and security, principle of - 152
International standards 103
Interpretation, power of - 262
Interpretation of rights 84
Inter-State communications procedure 154, 198, 287
 · peaceful solution 201
 · types of disputes 202
Irreparable damage 91, 234

J

Jehova's Witnesses 106
Journalists 107
Judicial remedy 96
Jurisdiction 203, 263
Jurisprudence 182
Jurisprudential development 122
Jus cogens 277

K

Katanga 143, 144
Kenya 112, 221
Kinship, principle of 14

L

Law and order 105
League of Nations 29
· Covenant 31
Legal aid 103, 281
Legal aid programmes 98
Legal assistance 98
Legal cultures of Africa 174
Legal principle 77
Legal representation, right of - 98
Legal system 7
traditional - 10; see also African societies
Legal traditions 287
Limitations prescribed by law 105
Locus standi 273

M

Malawi 86
Margin of discretion 105
Marital servitude 89
Marriage, right to consent to - 244
Mass media 218
Mauritania 117
Mediation 250
Military dictatorships 96
Misrule 18
Morality 163
Morocco 306
Multinational corporations 147, 157

N

National consciousness 163
National security 59
National sovereignty 250
Natural law 11
Niger Republic 223
Nigeria 91, 100, 109, 111, 134, 148, 235
Nigerian Armed Robbery and Firearms Act 96
Nigerian Civil Disturbances Act 95
Nigerian Robbery and Firearms Tribunal 100

Non-compliance 65, 189
Non-derogable rights 59, 161, 243, 327
Non-Governmental Organizations 123, 181, 195, 197, 204, 232, 265, 272, 309
Non-interference, principle of - 215, 274
Non-intervention 69, 81
Non-justiciability, doctrine of - 93
Non-State complaints 180
Normative instruments 158
Normative reference system 37

O

Observer status 311, 314
Ogoni people, Movement for the Survival of - 91
Oil companies 148
Omnibus provisions 159
Opinio juris 36
Oppressed people 145
Optional clause 250
Oral arguments 232
Organization of African Unity (OAU) 43, 67, 75, 169
· Assembly of heads of State and Government 71, 169, 231
· Charter 75, 215
  - Article II 77
  - Article III 80
  - normative value 80
  - obligations 79
  - preamble 76
  - purposes 78
· Convention on Refugees 70
· General Convention on the Privileges and Immunities 170
· Secretary-General 169, 171
Organization of American States (OAS) 54

P

Pan Africanism 68
Peaceful coexistence, principle of - 152

Peoples' rights 139, 140, 148
Permanent sovereignty, doctrine of - 147
Persecution 116
Petitions 204
Political exclusion 65
Political prisoners 210
Political systems 9
Pollution 155
Positive obligation 59
Poverty 138
Precautionary measures 234
Pre-colonial Africa 7, 163, 325
Presumption of innocence 96
Principles of international law 220, 276
Professionalism 324
Promotion of human rights 252, 311, 329
Property inheritance 120
Protective powers 246, 262
Protocol of Buenos Aires 57
Protocol of San Salvador 132
Protocol of Washington 59
Provisional measures 62, 299
Public hearing, right to - 102, 280
Public interests 119
Publicity 91

Q
Quasi-judicial function 262

R
Racial discrimination 75
Racism 67, 325
Ratification 330
Reasonable time
· concept of - 99
· standard of - 226
Redress 238
Refugees 70
Refugee status 116
Religion 11
Remedies 298
· adequate and effective - 222

Reparations 238, 263, 299
Representation, free legal - 280
Resolution 1503 procedure 228
Resolutions 181
Resources, inadequate - 184
Responsibilities 164
Restitution in kind 299
Retroactive legislation 166
Retroactive punishment 101
Review decisions 301
Rio Delcaration on Environment and Development 155
Rules of procedure 184
Rwanda 87, 143

S
San Francisco Conference of 1945 32
Satisfaction, requirement of - 209
Security of State Party 59
Self determination, principle of - 67, 75, 143
Self incrimination, right against - 103, 244
Self-rule 28
Sirte Declaration 71
Slave-owning societies 8
Slave trade 17
Slavery, contemporary - 88
Solidarity
· national - 110, 164
· obligation of - 110
Sources of law 10, 11,
Sovereignty, principle of - 144
Special Rapporteur 180
Special Rapporteur on Summary and Extra-Judicial Executions 87, 316
Staffing 185
State communications 180, 198
· guidelines for the Submission of - 200
State reports 187, 316
· effectiveness of - 195
· examination of - 180, 192

INDEX

- guidelines for the Submission of - 129, 188
- reminders 193

Stockholm Declaration on the Human Environment 154
Strike, right to - 125
Substantive rights 35, 275
Sudan 106
Supervisory mechanism 38/39,

T

Teach, right to - 130
Tenure of office 171
Territorial integrity, principle of - 144
Territorial states 9
Thought, freedom of - 104
Time limit 301
Torture 217
Toxic wastes, dumping of - 156
Trade unions 112, 125,
Traditional cultures 89
Traditional practices 135
Transferred punishment 101
Treaty of Berlin (1885) 17
Trokosi 89
Tunisia 228

U

United Nations Charter 30, 31,
United Nations Declaration on the Right to Development 140, 151
United Nations Economic and Social Council (ECOSOC) 31
United Nations Educational, Scientific and Cultural Organization (UNESCO) 41
United Nations High Commissioner for Refugees (UNHCR) 41, 42,
United Nations Human Rights Commission 34
United Nations Human Rights Committee 159, 228

United Nations Resolution on Permanent Sovereignty over Natural Resources 146
United Nations specialized agencies 41
United Nations trusteeship system 31
Universal Declaration of Human Rights 29, 34, 38, 75,
- legal status 36

V

Vacation, right to paid - 125
Victimization of relatives 101
Violation of human rights 34
Volunteers 186

W

War crimes 82
Western Sahara 143
Women 133, 173
- discrimination against - 134

Women's rights 161, 243, 246
World Bank 41
World Health Organization (WHO) 41

Z

Zaire 106, 127, 130, 144, 216, 222
Zambia 93, 209
Zimbabwe 151

International Studies in Human Rights

1. B. G. Ramcharan (ed.): *International Law and Fact-finding in the Field of Human Rights.* 1982   ISBN 90-247-3042-2
2. B. G. Ramcharan: *Humanitarian Good Offices in International Law.* The Good Offices of the United Nations Secretary-General in the Field of Human Rights. 1983   ISBN 90-247-2805-3
3. B. G. Ramcharan (ed.): *The Right to Life in International Law.* 1985   ISBN 90-247-3074-0
4. P. Alston and K. Tomaševski (eds.): *The Right to Food.* 1984   ISBN 90-247-3087-2
5. A. Bloed and P. van Dijk (eds.): *Essays on Human Rights in the Helsinki Process.* 1985   ISBN 90-247-3211-5
6. K. Törnudd: *Finland and the International Norms of Human Rights.* 1986   ISBN 90-247-3257-3
7. H. Thoolen and B. Verstappen: *Human Rights Missions.* A Study of the Fact-finding Practice of Non-governmental Organizations. 1986   ISBN 90-247-3364-2
8. H. Hannum: *The Right to Leave and Return in International Law and Practice.* 1987   ISBN 90-247-3445-2
9. J. H. Burgers and H. Danelius: *The United Nations Convention against Torture.* A Handbook on the Convention against Torture and Other Cruel, Inhuman or Degrading Treatment or Punishment. 1988   ISBN 90-247-3609-9
10. D. A. Martin (ed.): *The New Asylum Seekers: Refugee Law in the 1980s.* The Ninth Sokol Colloquium on International Law. 1988   ISBN 90-247-3730-3
11. C. M. Quiroga: *The Battle of Human Rights.* Gross, Systematic Violations and the Inter-American System. 1988   ISBN 90-247-3687-0
12. L. A. Rehof and C. Gulmann (eds.): *Human Rights in Domestic Law and Development Assistance Policies of the Nordic Countries.* 1989   ISBN 90-247-3743-5
13. B. G. Ramcharan: *The Concept and Present Status of International Protection of Human Rights.* Forty Years After the Universal Declaration. 1989   ISBN 90-247-3759-1
14. A. D. Byre and B. Y. Byfield (eds.): *International Human Rights Law in the Commonwealth Caribbean.* 1991   ISBN 90-247-3785-0
15. N. Lerner: *Groups Rights and Discrimination in International Law.* 1991   ISBN 0-7923-0853-0
16. S. Shetreet (ed.): *Free Speech and National Security.* 1991   ISBN 0-7923-1030-6
17. G. Gilbert: *Aspects of Extradition Law.* 1991   ISBN 0-7923-1162-0
18. P.E. Veerman: *The Rights of the Child and the Changing Image of Childhood.* 1991   ISBN 0-7923-1250-3
19. M. Delmas-Marty (ed.): *The European Convention for the Protection of Human Rights.* International Protection versus National Restrictions. 1991   ISBN 0-7923-1283-X

International Studies in Human Rights

20. A. Bloed and P. van Dijk (eds.): *The Human Dimension of the Helsinki Process.* The Vienna Follow-up Meeting and its Aftermath. 1991 ISBN 0-7923-1337-2

21. L.S. Sunga: *Individual Responsibility in International Law for Serious Human Rights Violations.* 1992 ISBN 0-7923-1453-0

22. S. Frankowski and D. Shelton (eds.): *Preventive Detention.* A Comparative and International Law Perspective. 1992 ISBN 0-7923-1465-4

23. M. Freeman and P. Veerman (eds.): *The Ideologies of Children's Rights.* 1992
ISBN 0-7923-1800-5

24. S. Stavros: *The Guarantees for Accused Persons Under Article 6 of the European Convention on Human Rights.* An Analysis of the Application of the Convention and a Comparison with Other Instruments. 1993 ISBN 0-7923-1897-8

25. A. Rosas and J. Helgesen (eds.): *The Strength of Diversity.* Human Rights and Pluralist Democracy. 1992 ISBN 0-7923-1987-7

26. K. Waaldijk and A. Clapham (eds.): *Homosexuality: A European Community Issue.* Essays on Lesbian and Gay Rights in European Law and Policy. 1993
ISBN 0-7923-2038-7; Pb: 0-7923-2240-1

27. Y.K. Tyagi: *The Law and Practice of the UN Human Rights Committee.* 1993
ISBN 0-7923-2040-9

28. H.Ch. Yourow: *The Margin of Appreciation Doctrine in the Dynamics of European Human Rights Jurisprudence.* 1996 ISBN 0-7923-3338-1

29. L.A. Rehof: *Guide to the* Travaux Préparatoires *of the United Nations Convention on the Elimination of All Forms of Discrimination against Women.* 1993 ISBN 0-7923-2222-3

30. A. Bloed, L. Leicht, M. Novak and A. Rosas (eds.): *Monitoring Human Rights in Europe.* Comparing International Procedures and Mechanisms. 1993 ISBN 0-7923-2383-1

31. A. Harding and J. Hatchard (eds.): *Preventive Detention and Security Law.* A Comparative Survey. 1993 ISBN 0-7923-2432-3

32. Y. Beigbeder: *International Monitoring of Plebiscites, Referenda and National Elections.* Self-determination and Transition to Democracy. 1994 ISBN 0-7923-2563-X

33. T.D. Jones: *Human Rights: Group Defamation, Freedom of Expression and the Law of Nations.* 1997 ISBN 90-411-0265-5

34. D.M. Beatty (ed.): *Human Rights and Judicial Review.* A Comparative Perspective. 1994 ISBN 0-7923-2968-6

35. G. Van Bueren, *The International Law on the Rights of the Child.* 1995
ISBN 0-7923-2687-3

36. T. Zwart: *The Admissibility of Human Rights Petitions.* The Case Law of the European Commission of Human Rights and the Human Rights Committee. 1994
ISBN 0-7923-3146-X; Pb: 0-7923-3147-8

37. H. Lambert: *Seeking Asylum.* Comparative Law and Practice in Selected European Countries. 1995 ISBN 0-7923-3152-4

International Studies in Human Rights

38. E. Lijnzaad: *Reservations to UN-Human Rights Treaties.* Ratify and Ruin? 1994
    ISBN 0-7923-3256-3
39. L.G. Loucaides: *Essays on the Developing Law of Human Rights.* 1995
    ISBN 0-7923-3276-8
40. T. Degener and Y. Koster-Dreese (eds.): *Human Rights and Disabled Persons.* Essays and Relevant Human Rights Instruments. 1995   ISBN 0-7923-3298-9
41. J.-M. Henckaerts: *Mass Expulsion in Modern International Law and Practice.* 1995
    ISBN 90-411-0072-5
42. N.A. Neuwahl and A. Rosas (eds.): *The European Union and Human Rights.* 1995
    ISBN 90-411-0124-1
43. H. Hey: *Gross Human Rights Violations: A Search for Causes.* A Study of Guatemala and Costa Rica. 1995   ISBN 90-411-0146-2
44. B.G. Tahzib: *Freedom of Religion or Belief.* Ensuring Effective International Legal Protection. 1996   ISBN 90-411-0159-4
45. F. de Varennes: *Language, Minorities and Human Rights.* 1996   ISBN 90-411-0206-X
46. J. Räikkä (ed.): *Do We Need Minority Rights?* Conceptual Issues. 1996
    ISBN 90-411-0309-0
47. J. Bröhmer: *State Immunity and the Violation of Human Rights.* 1997
    ISBN 90-411-0322-8
48. C.A. Gearty (ed.): *European Civil Liberties and the European Convention on Human Rights.* A Comparative Study. 1997   ISBN 90-411-0253-1
49. B. Conforti and F. Francioni (eds.): *Enforcing International Human Rights in Domestic Courts.* 1997   ISBN 90-411-0393-7
50. A. Spiliopoulou Åkermark: *Justifications of Minority Protection in International Law.* 1997   ISBN 90-411-0424-0
51. A. Boulesbaa: *The U.N. Convention on Torture and the Prospects for Enforcement.* 1997
    ISBN 90-411-0457-7
52. S. Bowen (ed.): *Human Rights, Self-Determination and Political Change in the Occupied Palestinian Territories.* 1997   ISBN 90-411-0502-6
53. M. O'Flaherty and G. Gisvold (eds.): *Post-War Protection of Human Rights in Bosnia and Herzegovina.* 1998   ISBN 90-411-1020-8
54. A.-L. Svensson-McCarthy: *The International Law of Human Rights and States of Exception.* With Special Reference to the *Travaux Préparatoires* and Case-Law of the International Monitoring Organs. 1998   ISBN 90-411-1021-6
55. G. Gilbert: *Transnational Fugitive Offenders in International Law.* Extradition and Other Mechanisms. 1998   ISBN 90-411-1040-2

International Studies in Human Rights

56. M. Jones and L.A. Basser Marks (eds.): *Disability, Divers-ability and Legal Change.* 1998   ISBN 90-411-1086-0

57. T. Barkhuysen, M.L. van Emmerik and P.H.P.H.M.C. van Kempen (eds.): *The Execution of Strasbourg and Geneva Human Rights Decisions in the National Legal Order.* 1999   ISBN 90-411-1152-2

58. S. Coliver, P. Hoffman, J. Fitzpatrick and S. Bowen (eds.): *Secrecy and Liberty: National Security, Freedom of Expression and Access to Information.* 1999   ISBN 90-411-1191-3

59. W.S. Heinz and H. Frühling: *Determinants of Gross Human Rights Violations by State and State-Sponsored Actors in Brazil, Uruguay, Chile, and Argentina.* 1960-1990. 1999   ISBN 90-411-1202-2

60. M. Kirilova Eriksson: *Reproductive Freedom.* In the Context of International Human Rights and Humanitarian Law. 1999   ISBN 90-411-1249-9

61. M.B. Eryilmaz: *Arrest and Detention Powers in English and Turkish Law and Practice in the Light of the European Convention on Human Rights.* 1999   ISBN 90-411-1269-3

62. K. Henrard: *Devising an Adequate System of Minority Protection.* Individual Human Rights, Minority Rights and the Right to Self-Determination. 2000   ISBN 90-411-1359-2

63. K. Tomaševski: *Responding to Human Rights Violations.* 1946–1999. 2000.   ISBN 90-411-1368-1

64. L.-V.N. Tran: *Human Rights and Federalism.* A Comparative Study on Freedom, Democracy and Cultural Diversity. 2000.   ISBN 90-411-1492-0

65. C. Tiburcio: *The Human Rights of Aliens under International and Comparative Law.* 2001   ISBN 90-411-1550-1

66. E. Brems: *Human Rights: Universality and Diversity.* 2001   ISBN 90-411-1618-4

67. L.-A. Sicilianos and C. Bourloyannis-Vrailas (eds.): *The Prevention of Human Rights Violations.* 2001   ISBN 90-411-1672-9

68. K. Hastrup and G. Ulrich (eds.): *Discrimination and Toleration:* New Perspectives. 2001   ISBN 90-411-1711-3

69. V.O.O. Nmehielle: *The African Human Rights System: Its Laws, Practice and Institutions.* 2001   ISBN 90-411-1731-8

This series is designed to shed light on current legal and political aspects of process and organization in the field of human rights.

MARTINUS NIJHOFF PUBLISHERS – THE HAGUE / BOSTON / LONDON